10.50

JAPAN AND CHINA

JAPAN and CHINA:
from War to Peace, 1894-1972

Marius B. Jansen
Princeton University

Rand McNally College Publishing Company / Chicago

Rand McNally History Series
Fred Harvey Harrington, *Advisory Editor*

Cover: Five-clawed imperial dragon, symbol of the Emperor of China, the Son of Heaven. Courtesy of the Minneapolis Institute of Arts.

The maps on pages 8, 409, and 421 are from *The Rise of Modern China* by Immanuel C. Y. Hsu. Copyright © 1970 by Oxford University Press, Inc. Reprinted by permission.

Current printing (last digit)
15 14 13 12 11 10 9 8 7 6 5 4 3 2 1

for Marya

Contents

List
of Maps

List
of Illustrations

Introduction

TWICE IN RECENT YEARS an extended period of convalescence, during which it was impossible to continue with normal work, led me to experiment with a summation of the twentieth-century histories of China and Japan. At one level, this represents the fulfillment of a request for a general history I first accepted almost two decades ago, when the century was also that much younger. It is interesting to speculate how different this volume might have been if I had undertaken it then, for the scholarly terrain has changed in many ways. As the acknowledgments at the end of this book will show, my specific obligations are very largely to work that has appeared during the last twenty years. An effort to draw on all of what is now available would have required a much longer and more comprehensive account, and I have chosen to focus this particularly upon the interplay between China and Japan in the course of their responses to the modern world.

The contemporary scene has, if anything, changed even more dramatically. Twenty years ago prevailing wisdom spoke of Japan's economic crisis as endemic; the Chinese alliance with the Soviet Union seemed to promise intermittent danger for what was optimistically called the free world, and Japan, so recently dependent upon American assistance and approval, seemed isolated in Asia. Today Japan's economic problems have been transformed by a period of spectacular industrial growth that has made the country the third most productive in the world. The Chinese-Soviet tie has given way to bitter hostility in which each has welcomed accommodation with America, as protection against the other, and Japan, which plays an increasingly important role in the economies of all its neighbors in East and Southeast Asia, has resumed direct relations with China.

Throughout the twentieth century American awareness of East Asia has grown in depth, but never sufficiently to prepare for what lay ahead. On the eve of his administration President McKinley told an eager office seeker that there was still a consulate open but that it was in Manila, which he described as a place "away around on the other wide of the world"; he apologized that he "did not know exactly where," as he had not had time to look it up. Since then three of America's four twentieth-century wars have had their origin in East Asia, and the headlines of our time have familiarized us with place names a good deal more obscure than Manila.

East Asia will remain the sharpest test for American understanding and wisdom in the last quarter of this century. The appearance of China and Japan, autonomous and equal, as central actors in international affairs marks a new stage in the history of our time. From 1895 to 1945 the course of East Asia was largely channeled by their inability to reach a working relationship together, and their success or failure to do this in the decades ahead will set the contours of this period. Postwar Japan has become a full member of the "advanced," "developed" or "modernized" world, but despite a century of striving the Japanese are still experimenting with their world role. Their success in working this out will be of critical importance, for Japan's new economic power makes its opportunity to affect the international environment scarcely less important than its ability to affect its own domestic environment. The China which it faces has once again attained full autonomy and national consciousness, also after a long period of effort, and is now embarked upon a very different path of modernization. Sino-Japanese relations have always had a dimension of larger world rivalries as well, and this will continue to be so. The response of the United States to these mighty changes will say a good deal about the way the rest of the century will be lived on both sides of the Pacific. Certainly a first requirement is to try to see these changes in their proper context, and that is what I have tried to do in this survey of the recent past.

What follow are twelve interpretive essays that center around the development of the relations between China and Japan within the setting of the responses both societies made to the challenge of modern times. In organization and content these essays reveal my belief that the dimension of Sino-Japanese relations provides a central focus for following the dynamics of that response. Thus I begin with Shimonoseki and the treaty that ended the Sino-Japanese War of 1894–95 and end with the agreement reached in Peking by Premier Chou En-lai and Prime Minister Tanaka Kakuei in 1972. Most of what lies between these events transcends the theme of diplomatic relations narrowly construed. The deeper currents were those of cultural influence, revolution and reconstruction, and the students and their books counted for as much as the soldiers and their guns. Consequently the account is not a summary of diplomatic happenings, nor are the chapters divided into national divisions. Each essay takes the story a step farther than the last, although it is often necessary to retrace a step in search of different tracks. I have at any rate found it helpful to follow this pattern of development and hope that others, too, will find it useful.

Today it is the chief requirement of a book that it lead its readers on to other work, for it cannot hope to contain them very long. In scholarship, as in international affairs, East Asia has achieved autonomy. It is imperfectly understood in terms of generalizations developed for the Western world, it requires the definition of its own cultural context, and it demands the use of its own sources and languages as media for understanding the modern world. During the last two decades scholarship on twentieth-century East Asia has multiplied many times, and these essays cross the boundaries of numerous areas of specialization. For the most part I have relied on Japanese and Western scholarship. Footnotes have been avoided, and acknowledgments made at the end of the book. Of course there is much more that could be cited, and even more to come, for our understanding of this era is only beginning to come into focus. Several colleagues—Professors John D. Langlois, Jr., of Bowdoin, Leo Ou-fan Lee and Lynn T. White, III of Princeton—have helped by reading all or part of the manuscript. Dante Yip provided invaluable assistance in the course of proofing and preparing the index, and saved me from many slips. My patient editors at Rand McNally could not have been more helpful. I retain full responsibility for the errors that remain, of course, and hope that other students will add their criticism and suggestions. I shall be well rewarded if these essays suggest some of the discovery and reward of working toward the goal of an integrated view of twentieth-century East Asia.

Princeton, 1975   Marius B. Jansen

JAPAN AND CHINA

CHAPTER 1

The Problem

*The history of East Asia in the twentieth century has been domi-*nated by the struggle of China and Japan to modernize their institutions and societies. Their success in doing this has been determined by two factors: the degree to which traditional social institutions and attitudes prepared for necessary changes and the way external forces operated to help or hinder this process. As the century opened, China and Japan were almost the only examples of attempted modernization in the non-Western world. It was crucial to their histories, and to the history of the modern world, that each of them had to carry out this effort in close competition with the other. Their mutual relations provide a central focus for examining the history of East Asia in the twentieth century because the influence of each country constitutes a major element in the intellectual and institutional development of the other. These concerns are too often neglected in accounts focused upon their mutual confrontation with the West, but they will receive primary emphasis in this book.

In East Asia the twentieth century arrived before the nineteenth had closed, with the victory of Japan over China in 1895. All Japanese, and most Chinese, saw that victory as evidence of Japanese success in modernization through the application of Western technology and organization. If Japan's reforms had made Shimonoseki possible, it was Shimonoseki that convinced most Chinese of the need for reforms. The war seemed to bring into sharp relief the requirements for effective competition in the contemporary world. Three-quarters of a century later, historians do not always agree on the definition and requirements of modernization, but its principal elements have become reasonably clear during an age of development and nation building.

Basic to the modernity that the Meiji Japanese saw as "civilization" was the willingness to make changes. There needed to be a spirit of enterprise, individual and collective, which would try to appropriate the tools useful to self and community. An intellectual awareness of the need to experiment with changes, therefore, was a first requirement for national regeneration.

Most obvious in the contrast between modern and nonmodern societies, in the eyes of East Asian leaders, was the use of machinery and inanimate energy in the Western world. Railroads carried more goods, carried them farther and more cheaply than did backs and carts. They carried rural produce to the growing cities, where labor congregated. They bound together the parts of what had been loosely centralized and organized communities, carried workers and students to cities and marshaled conscripts from villages to garrison towns. In the process the country became a unit. As early as 1873 the Japanese traveler Kume Kunitake, an official scribe, found in statistics of railroad trackage a scale of modernity on which countries could be compared. Arsenals and shipyards, the source of strength in the modern world, were needed no less surely. To pay for these it was necessary to expand trade, and to establish national independence it seemed necessary to free domestic production from dependence upon the manufactured goods imported from the West. In nineteenth-century East Asia this required a bootstraps effort. There were no aid programs, no international banks and no cold war rivalries for nineteenth-century modernizers to exploit. They had to pay their way.

None of these things could be realized without the cooperation and willingness to sacrifice on the part of the populace. The commoners would have to be reached and told of the issues that were at stake. Education for modernity and national values was, therefore, a major goal. If people could read they could be reached, and in being taught to read they could be persuaded about the things that mattered. Much of the activity of the second half of the nineteenth century in Japan had the quality of an uninterrupted lesson. Teachers on all levels, whether in lower schools, government bureaus, newspaper columns, army barracks, machine shops or popular novels, preached the same sermon. The future belonged to the active, the ambitious, the independent, the frugal and the patriotic. These were the facts of life. They were proved in the science of Herbert Spencer, whose social Darwinism flooded the bookstores of East Asia in the 1880s and 1890s. It could be shown that there were orders and stages of human development, that competition and ability determined progress within them and that victory went to the modern, who were the civilized. The publicist Fukuzawa Yukichi could see as a "kind of religious war" a struggle between a more modernized Japan and a less modernized China.

Although these assumptions of modernity through technology and organization often seem superficial today, the nineteenth-century leaders who held them cannot be blamed for their ignorance of what the twentieth century would bring. They were right in believing that nationalism and popular participation were essential to survival in the world they knew. They had no idea that nationalism and activation, armed with technology, would send almost ten million Europeans marching to their death a few years later. They were right in emphasizing the urgency of mass education and a more effective system of communication. The destructive powers of nationalism and of technological barbarism were not yet in sight. The ambiguities of modernity, and the dilemmas of growth in China and Japan, still lay in the future. Most contemporary Westerners were, if anything, more sweeping in their confidence, less tolerant of deflection from a universal panacea, and more smug about the blessings that "progress" must bring. The English traveler Isabella Bird Bishop was one of many who deplored the Korea of her times in language as strong as any Fukuzawa could have used; she called attention to "this archaic condition of things, this unspeakable grooviness, this irredeemable, unreformed Orientalism." The American educator Griffis, returning from Fukui to Kyoto through some of the most beautiful country in the world, found his heart beat faster at the sight of "telegraph poles; their bare, grim, silent majesty . . . as eloquent as pulses of light." The assumption that universal laws of historical progression required that every country change convinced even so romantic an antimaterialist as Lafcadio Hearn, who moderated his despair over the "beastly modernization" of which he was witness with affirmation of the truth of Herbert Spencer's laws of human development.

In both China and Japan, however, modernization had to be carried out under the shadow of the economic and military power of the West, and this produced distinctive elements in the drive for change. In both cases the basic motives were defensive in nature. Modernization came to East Asia at the points of guns. It was military defeat by the West that first roused the Chinese in the 1840s, and the balance of the nineteenth century had seen Imperial China decline in power during an unbroken series of Western military and political advances. In Japan it was the appearance of Commodore Perry's squadron in 1853 and the knowledge of what Western military and naval power could do and what it had done to China that triggered the political and social reforms of the Meiji period. Similar ships and weapons forced the Koreans to open their doors to international relations in the 1870s. This outside challenge meant that an emphasis on national survival would take first place in all efforts to modernize. There was not a free choice, for the alternative to modernization was extinction. This problem was common to all East Asian countries, and as a result their leaders saw themselves in ways not always realized in the West. The conflicts between them were too public to escape narration, but the common concerns and cultural bonds, though no less important, were more elusive and difficult to discern.

For all East Asian countries this element of compulsion and reaction brought with it distinctive psychological and intellectual tensions. The Western world had experienced changes of attitudes and institutions as great as those East Asia was to know. But these had matured over a longer period of time, and their intellectual and technological sources were indigenous. The social and moral strains of modernization in Europe were no less severe—indeed, the violence that accompanied modernization was as great as any Asia would know—but it could not be seen as caused by the outside world. Moral and philosophical conflicts in the modernizing West were no less basic than those experienced in East Asia, but they were tensions that had developed within a continuous historical framework. In East Asia, however, the entire range of dilemmas associated with modernization was complicated by dimensions of the internal and the external conflict and a sharper sense of discontinuity. Chinese and Japanese intellectuals had to face the problem of combining cultural individuality with "Western" modernity and often asked themselves whether they could be, for instance, Japanese *and* modern, Japanese *and* Christian, Chinese *and* nationalist. As the philosopher Inoue Enryō put it in the 1880s, "How can Japan be made Japan?" He lamented that "our people are no longer Japanese, and our country is no longer Japan." The changes of values individuals faced were frequently more obvious, and they seemed more difficult, than those their Western counterparts had known. As a result the process of modernization, however inevitable, could never be entirely separated from problems of identity, intrusion and humiliation.

The twentieth century, however, did bring to an end much of the simplistic and undifferentiated imagery that had characterized the initial confrontations of East and West. When the Japanese scholar-statesman Fujita Tōko saw Hollanders in the 1820s, he concluded from the similarity of their dress to pictures he had seen of Russians that the professed national divisions of Europe were a sham designed to camouflage a single plot against Japan. Early Japanese modernizers also regarded Western civilization as a single package, in which each part was essential to the other. Bullets and bibles, steam engines and beef eating, all seemed part of the whole. But familiarity with the West brought with it knowledge of its variety. The twentieth century also brought dramatic experience of great change in the structure of Western presence and power. The European empires that seemed so invincible to nineteenth-century statesmen proved fragile in the face of twentieth-century pressures, and the system of international relations that Japanese leaders spent a generation struggling to join virtually collapsed at the moment of their success. Modernization could no longer be seen as adherence to a fixed standard and system; instead it became participation in a universe of flux.

This participation was the more perplexing because the experience of East Asian statesmen had so little precedent for a world of equal nation-states. This was particularly the case with China. The Chinese had long been accustomed to a radically different world view, one in which their country was by definition "the

Middle Country," the center of a universe of civilization and morality. The Chinese emperor presided over an ecumenical world order that was given meaning by the values of the Chinese tradition. It was inclusive rather than exclusive and open to all who aspired to mastery of the language and customs of civilization. There could be no competing centers, for China's truth and morality were true in all places. To deal with other countries on a basis of equality would have meant granting equal value to radically different institutions and standards, thereby denying the primacy of a tradition that had been real and vital for millennia. No other civilization in the world could claim so unbroken and majestic a continuity. No other world order approached the majesty of China's scheme of international relations. Imperial China was not merely a great power, for even that term implies the possibility of comparison; it was, instead, the cultural colossus of the world it knew. Except for Japan, which had official relations with China for only brief periods, other near neighbors in Central and Southeast Asia accepted a role in the tributary system and sent at regular intervals envoys who were rewarded by the greater magnanimity of the court at Peking. In the eighteenth century, arrangements had been made to permit a limited number of Western traders to participate on the fringes of Chinese life and trade through Macao and Canton. But this activity was directed and exploited locally; the relationships worked out were between traders, not officials, and there was no thought of equality for the foreigners involved. When the English sent an ambassador in 1793 with proposals for formal diplomatic and commercial relations, their proposal provoked a sublime expression of indifference from the Ch'ien-lung emperor. He dismissed the idea with scorn. The English could not possibly play a role at court, he judged. Their "language will be unintelligible"; how could they be expected to "wear Chinese court costumes,...be placed in a certain residence," and "never be allowed to return to their own countries"? "This is indeed a useless undertaking," the emperor concluded. Although he had been gracious enough to accept King George's gifts, "There is nothing we lack, as your principal envoy and others have themselves observed. We have never set much store on strange or ingenious objects, nor do we need any of your country's manufactures."

This definition of China as the center of a universal order died hard precisely because it had been so correct. Indeed, as Bertrand Russell wrote of Ch'ien-lung's response to the English, "No one has begun to understand China until this document has ceased to seem absurd." One result was a tendency for similar attitudes to crop up in settings divorced from the original context of Confucian culture. Thus in the 1850s Englishmen heard with delight of a Christian revolution in central China establishing the Heavenly Kingdom of Great Peace, founded by a convert who had received visions in which he saw himself as a younger brother of Jesus. When a British party moved to Nanking to greet what they thought would be brothers in the faith, their welcome was an edict strikingly similar in tone to that of 1793, with greetings "to the brethren from afar that they may all understand the rules of ceremony. Whereas God the Heavenly Father has sent our

Sovereign down on earth, as the true Sovereign of all nations in the world, all people in the world who wish to appear at his Court must yield obedience to the rules of ceremony." And those rules, as the sometime spiritual counselor of the Taiping ruler, the Reverend Issachar Roberts of Tennessee discovered, involved his own conversion to the rebels' brand of Christianity and instructions to proselytize for them in the West. However different, the claims of Mao Tse-tung a century later to primacy in the world communist movement are not unrelated to this lofty assumption of a Chinese world order.

Japan's premodern experience of international society was less structured than that of China, and its beliefs of world order were less reciprocated by others than were those of its powerful neighbor. Nevertheless Japan too was imperfectly prepared for participation in a multistate system. With the exception of sporadic contacts with China and very limited relations with Korea, and despite sixteenth-century experimentation with maritime activity, Japan's experience was overwhelmingly parochial and insular. It was sufficiently so to encourage and reinforce the insistence of the native cult on the special, in fact the divine, origin and nature of Japan and to underscore the contrast with all outsiders. The outside world itself was differentiated between "near" outsiders—the Chinese and Koreans who formed the culture zone in which Japan participated—and the more distant and outer beings. But its perception was complicated by hierarchical assumptions that were reflected throughout Japanese mythology and society, assumptions that contained little tolerance for equality of treatment or status.

The Chinese were at the apex of Japan's awareness for many centuries, so much so that an early Meiji edict warned that Westerners were not to be considered as animals, but that they should be treated with the same respect as Chinese. "China" was a land of culture, the home of sages who peopled mountain scenes in classical Japanese painting. The wars of 1894 and 1904 gave hundreds of thousands of Japanese a substantial, firsthand experience of a "China" for the first time and changed this idyllic image forever. The thousands of Chinese students who came to Tokyo thereafter had to struggle against an image much less favorable. As Japan turned to the West for technological and organizational inspiration, Western countries rose to replace the Chinese at the top of these standings, until identification with "China" or "Asia" was something to be avoided. During the same period, new teachings about the superiority of Japan's polity were being diffused in village, school and conscript organizations. The twentieth-century development of Japanese strength found Japanese parochialism posing new and formidable challenges to the international order.

The course of relations between China and Japan was also affected by the Western powers. To a degree the competition between China and Japan created a situation in which outside powers' image of either country was in part a function of their image of the other. Imperial England favored China until it was convinced of Japan's greater importance as an ally. Twentieth-century America began with respect and approval for the Japanese underdog and then changed to a more romantic and emotional commitment to China that grew stronger as difficulties with Imperial Japan multiplied. As the tables turned in the 1950s, Japan profited from fears of Chinese communism, but when the Japanese position changed from patronized ward to competitor in the 1960s, the way was prepared for new departures in China policy that quickly brought to the surface earlier and more romantic views of the mainland.

These external considerations complicated the problems the countries of East Asia encountered in their need for mutual adjustment. However different their preparations for response to the challenge of the modern world had been, at midpoint in the nineteenth century, China, Korea and Japan were governed by men who wanted to be left alone. They desired no change in the international system they knew, and they had little desire for closer contact with their near neighbors. There were no formal relationships between the governments of Japan and Korea or China; Chinese merchants came to Nagasaki, and Japanese merchants to Korea, but neither group carried the status of national representatives. Korean missions came annually to China, but their infrequent visits to Japan had been given up.

Almost immediately after contact with the West was initiated, the problems of adjustment to the new world of nation-states first came to focus on the border areas that seemed to affect the stability and security of each country. The modern world had little tolerance for the ambiguities of boundary and sovereignty that characterized the traditional order in East Asia, and new concerns of security emphasized the importance of what had long seemed marginal to countries that looked inward. Japan and China first quarreled over Okinawa and the Ryukyus and then over Taiwan; disagreement over their role in Korea brought them close to war in the 1880s. In 1894 challenges aroused by their mutual responses to the West resulted in a destructive East Asian war. Japanese and Chinese armies destroyed the Korean city of Pyongyang in the course of fighting each other, and Japanese warships sent the Chinese navy, which had been built in the same European shipyards, to the bottom of the Yellow Sea in a struggle that opened Chinese waters further to European penetration.

Identical challenges had produced mutual rivalry instead of a common response, and "modernization" brought to East Asia the same disruptive by-products of the state system that Europe had experienced earlier. The result was large-scale contact between Chinese, Japanese and Koreans for the first time in the history of East Asia.

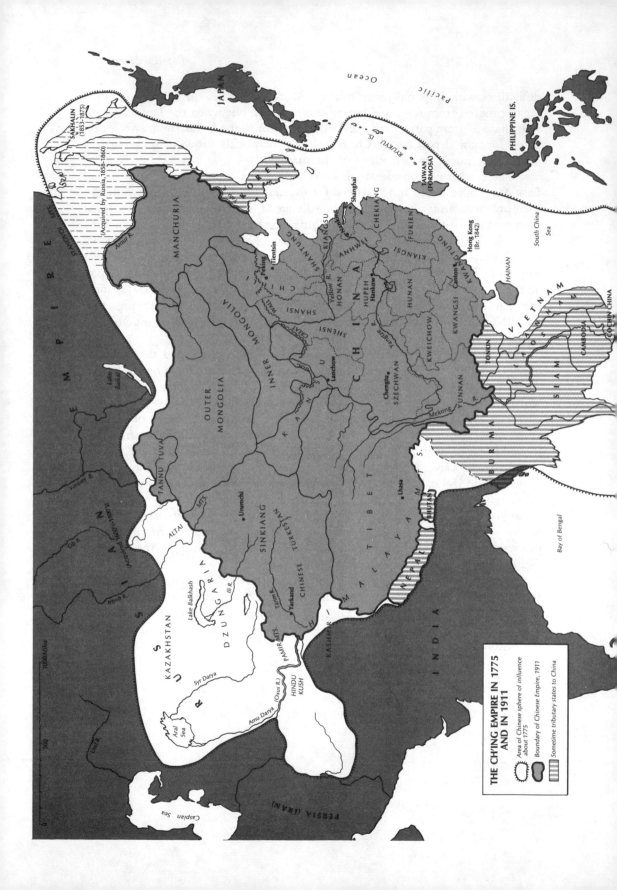

THE CH'ING EMPIRE IN 1775 AND IN 1911

Area of Chinese sphere of influence about 1775

Boundary of Chinese Empire, 1911

Sometime tributary states to China

Pacific Ocean

PHILIPPINE IS.

JAPAN

SAKHALIN (1853–1875)

(Acquired by Russia, 1858–1860)

STANOVOI MTS.

MANCHURIA

KOREA

RYUKYU IS.

TAIWAN (FORMOSA)

South China Sea

HAINAN

Hong Kong (Br. 1842)

Canton

KWANGTUNG

FUKIEN

CHEKIANG

KIANGSI

KIANGSU

Shanghai

Nanking

ANHWEI

HUPEH

Hankow

HUNAN

KWEICHOW

KWANGSI

YUNNAN

Yangtze R.

HONAN

Yellow R.

SHANTUNG

CHIHLI

Peking

Tientsin

SHANSI

SHENSI

Great Wall

KANSU

Lanchow

SZECHWAN

Chengtu

Mekong R.

C H I N A

VIETNAM

TONKIN

COCHIN CHINA

CAMBODIA

S I A M

L A O S

BURMA

Bay of Bengal

INDIA

NEPAL

BHUTAN

Lhasa

T I B E T

H I M A L A Y A S   M T S.

KASHMIR

HINDU KUSH

PAMIR MTS.

CHINESE TURKESTAN

Yarkand

Tarim R.

SINKIANG

Urumchi

TIEN SHAN MTS.

DZUNGARIA

Lake Balkhash

Ili R.

ALTAI MTS.

TANNU TUVA

OUTER MONGOLIA

INNER MONGOLIA

Lake Baikal

Yenisey R.

Ob R.

Irtish R.

(Acquired 1600–1900's)

U S S R

KAZAKHSTAN

Syr Darya

Aral Sea

Amu Darya (Oxus R.)

Ural R.

Caspian Sea

PERSIA (IRAN)

E M P I R E

0   500   1000 Miles

CHAPTER 2

Imperial China

After the Japanese capture of the hills overlooking the Shantung anchorage of Weihaiwei forced the capitulation of the Chinese fleet in February 1895, the Japanese commander, Admiral Itō, addressed this consolation to Admiral Ting of the Chinese forces: "No doubt," he wrote,

> there are various reasons for the defeats of your army and navy, but there is one primary cause, which no one who considers the matter impartially will find difficult to perceive. It cannot have escaped the notice of a man of your clear-sightedness. The present condition of your country is not due to the fault of a few persons in power, but it is really the result of the system of government. You are well aware how the Japanese Empire had to throw away the old system and adopt the new. Your country, also, must adopt this new way of living. If your country does this, all will be well, but if it rejects it, it cannot help but fall sooner or later.

Admiral Itō went on to urge his adversary to wait for the time "when your country will require your services for its reformation," and he encouraged him to come to Japan instead of returning home to accept responsibility for the Chinese defeat. But Admiral Ting proved the better samurai. He turned his face toward Peking and committed suicide. Itō showed his respect by providing a warship and guard to return the body to the Chinese capital. The journalist Tokutomi eulogized him in a lead article on 21 February: "Although Ting Ju-ch'ang was our enemy, I cannot help but respect and admire him. Enmity is temporary, but respect endures forever."

1. *China and Modernization*

IT SEEMS CLEAR that Admiral Itō was correct in attributing China's problems to institutional rather than to personal shortcomings, and any analysis of twentieth-century China must begin with consideration of the way the governmental patterns of Imperial China affected or impeded its development as a nation-state. These institutions had matured over two millennia, and they represented a set of politically sophisticated and tested devices for ruling the world's largest and most populous country. China's central government reached from the emperor, who ruled at Peking with the advice of his Six Boards, through provincial governors and circuit intendants to the district magistrate. This last official ruled one of the fifteen-hundred–odd *hsien,* usually an area of several hundred square miles and several hundred thousand inhabitants. Officialdom numbered about forty thousand bureaucrats, arranged in nine major ranks and selected through the civil service examinations regularly held at *hsien,* provincial and national capitals. Of the million men who might have achieved some sort of standing through the examination system (sometimes by purchase of degree), more than one-tenth held high rank and degree, and were aspirant, active or retired officials. High officials were servants of the emperor; they were moved regularly (on the average of three years) to prevent their forming local interest groups, and they could not serve in their own locality for the same reason. The vast repository of official records which their reports and regulations constitute testifies to the bureaucratic complexity and maturity of the imperial system.

Below the central officials, and within the *hsien,* was a different world. This one was firmly based on the local level and administered by official underlings like yamen runners, clerks and functionaries of many sorts. This was a world related to the other by the presence of local elite usually designated as "gentry," or "sash wearers." Success in the examination system brought with it privileges of dress and audience with the magistrate, immunity from corporal punishment and the responsibilities of personifying the code of virtue and morality. These responsibilities often took the form of public readings of imperial injunctions to morality. The local gentry were in some sense subject to the magistrate and dependent on his favor. But they also lived alongside a deeply rooted local bureaucracy to whom most local government functions were delegated. Gentry support and prestige were important for local morale and education. The local bureaucracy was essential to the day-to-day aspects of the imperial government.

Gentry served as bearers of the cultural tradition. A village had no prouder distinction than the production of a promising youth who went through the examination system to high office. His feat would usually be solemnized by a plaque hung inside the gates of the walls that divided the village from its fields. Success in the examinations was the entrance for both official and local eminence. That success, in turn, depended upon mastery of the written tradition. Schooling in the difficulties and beauties of the classics, ability to write with a handsome hand and in the rigorous canons of grace and balance that examination essays required and character traits reflecting the code that was taught and examined were expected of the elite. Loyalty, filiality, wisdom, humanity, decorum and learning all reinforced each other. Whatever their status and duty, the elite had a special stake in the existing cultural and institutional configuration of their society and its traditions. It provided for them, and they sustained it. Threats to it were simultaneously threats to them and, through them, to the values which made China great. The areas of flexibility were limited, for the bearers of the tradition could not seek change that would risk that tradition itself. The elite was deeply involved in the perpetuation of the system. Although China's administrative system was, in one sense, relatively "modern," with its provision for the opening of bureaucratic opportunity to talent, this meritocracy also made it more difficult to introduce modernizing innovations without extensive destruction and alteration of the existing order. Foreigners often misunderstood this and assumed that because China had official mobility, a powerful central government and a working emperor it should be able to modernize more rapidly than a country less united and less "rational" in its organization.

In 1904 General Yamagata, the builder of the Japanese armies and a leading commander in the Sino-Japanese War, put it this way:

> Granted a strong Emperor, it would be more easy to change China than it was to change Japan.... In China the system of laws is similar all over the country.... The Emperor is supreme, and has direct authority over everything in his empire.... the currency is also centralized to a greater or less degree; the military system lends itself to conscription and is centralized, as are also the taxes. Thus, theoretically, everything is along the line of the described changes....

China lacked a strong emperor during much of the nineteenth century, but in fact no emperor, however strong, would have found it easy to make drastic changes. The emperor's authority was unlimited by law, but it was defined by the cultural and institutional order at whose apex he stood. With a stake in the ideological purity of the tradition, one he exercised through the examinations, he could not easily justify sweeping changes based on outside example. More important still was the fact that the elite of his society, the gentry, had strong roots in the social order and a personal stake in the status quo. However flexible an emperor might have proven, most of the gentry were less so and deeply resistant to increasing the real power of the central government in the areas they controlled.

There was a congruence of moral, intellectual, institutional, political and familial authority patterns which resisted change.

These general considerations hampered modernization in China, but there were additional and specific contingencies in the nineteenth century. One was that modern Imperial China, a multinational conglomerate with its "five races" of Chinese, Mongols, Manchus, Tibetans and Moslems, had been ruled since the seventeenth century by the non-Chinese Manchus. The dynasty had exercised care in the prevention of total absorption by the ethnic Chinese through the preservation of Manchuria as a racially pure hinterland, hunting ground and military preserve. It forced the subject Chinese to wear their hair in a queue, it regulated and restricted intermarriage between Chinese and Manchus and Mongols, and it placed ethnically distinct army components at key garrisons throughout the country. Thus nineteenth-century China was ruled by a foreign dynasty. By then many of the earlier restrictions had been weakened and the Manchus had become substantially Chinese in cultural respects, but they remained sensitive to the need for special distinctions and to the danger that national feeling among Chinese could focus against them.

The foreign dynasty was likely to be the first target of national consciousness. The Taiping rebels of the 1850s were quick to seize upon their rulers' foreign origin. "China has a Chinese dress and Chinese customs," their charges went; why should it adopt those of the Manchus? On the other hand the Taiping challenge to traditional civilization was so basic that most Chinese conservatives had felt it more important to defend their civilization in Manchu service than to espouse an antiforeign nationalism. The early years of the twentieth century, when revolutionary nationalists denounced the foreign rulers, confronted conservatives with the same difficult decision. The foreign dynasty which defended and attained legitimacy within the traditional institutional pattern thus had the result of retarding and deflecting the emergent sense of national differentiation.

Nineteenth-century Chinese civilization also posed philosophical and moral problems for early modernizers. Conventional interpretations of the classics emphasized moral abstractions rather than practical statecraft, and this knowledge was accepted as criterion of public service by the government and thus articulated by every aspirant to office and status. A tradition that sought sanction and wisdom in the past found nineteenth-century beliefs in the certainty of progress uncongenial. It was possible to advocate the use of Western technology and weapons, but to accept nineteenth-century science intact would have required for some a willingness to jettison the whole complex of values that made civilized life possible. Some nineteenth-century reformers tried to argue that Confucius had been misunderstood and that, properly interpreted, he provided for many of the political outlooks necessary to their day. But the main current of the tradition was more loyal to the classical spirit and less attuned to the needs of the present. In 1873 Kume Kunitake, official scribe for the Iwakura mission, noted that the recent achievements of the West had been made possible by development of what was "foolishness" to Japanese, the practical application of science. In the years that followed Chinese leaders repeatedly asked Japanese guests how they could justify abandoning the wisdom of tradition and the sages for the practicality of the West. The only possible response to this had to be posed in terms of practical advantage and future results, but it was an answer that was not very congenial to conservatives in either country.

In addition to these general considerations there were more specific and immediate reasons for the difficulties China experienced in responding to the West in the nineteenth century. The West came at a time when the Manchus were without effective leadership. The great emperors of earlier centuries had been replaced by lesser men so hemmed in by court and family ritual and routine as to be almost powerless. The memoirs of the last ruler, known to the West as "Henry" Pu-yi (P'u-i), paint a striking picture of a fledgling son of heaven whose responsibilities to heaven through his parents and especially mothers—real mother, adoptive father's consorts, dowager empress—counted for far more than did power and force.

Political weakness had been accompanied by economic crisis. A great population increase in recent centuries was putting ever greater pressure on food production and administrative efficiency. It was a setting in which government setbacks could quickly be reflected in rebellion. Throughout his career as a revolutionary leader Sun Yat-sen operated on the assumption that it required only a spark to ignite the distress and discontent of his countrymen. The turbulent social history of nineteenth- and early twentieth-century China showed that he was right. For over a century governments had to be fully as concerned with domestic order as with outside dangers.

The process through which Chinese defenses were first breached began with an issue on which no Chinese government could compromise. This was the import of opium. The larger issues of equal relations between states might well have eventually brought England and China to a confrontation, but it was English insistence upon satisfaction for contraband opium that had been seized and destroyed that precipitated the first encounter in 1839. Later confrontations forced Peking to legalize import of the drug, and by mid-century the existence of treaty ports and trade channels made it impossible to control or stop the narcotics trade for many decades. Discussions of reforms and modernizing invariably ran afoul of reminders that such measures represented surrender to the purveyors of filth and crime, fit representatives of countries ignorant of the languages and customs of civilization. Such talk was not mere rhetoric. A civilization based upon status and familial relationships was shocked by egalitarianism, one based upon patriarchal family rule was horrified by feminism, and one concentrated upon respect for forebears was incredulous that rules of monogamy could prevent the production of heirs. Consequently, for many Chinese conservatives it was fitting that opium should have been the issue that proved the point.

After 1839 China suffered an unbroken series of humiliations and setbacks. Two rounds of wars with the Western powers ended in seizure of Peking and the burning of the Summer Palace. China's principal port cities became Western footholds in a new order of international relations that had evolved. It was transitional and not yet modern, and China's relations were less with the "family of nations" than with a league of jealous partners who successively demanded new and greater privileges. The most-favored–nation clause, first secured by American delegate Caleb Cushing in 1844, prevented any single power from dominating the Chinese coast at the same time that it prevented China from choosing between its foreign claimants in order to manipulate their jealousy. Treaty ports contained areas set aside for foreign commerce, usually sold to foreign firms at auction by foreign consulates. Some foreign concessions, as at Shanghai, were sectors entirely removed from Chinese jurisdiction. Western law followed Western merchants, for under the provisions of extraterritoriality all cases involving Westerners were subject to Western courts. And tariffs fixed by treaty made it impossible for China to utilize the trade for income or to protect its own nascent factory system.

Treaty ports became enclaves of Western influence. There missionaries set up schools and printed their materials, newspapers brought word of the outside world, and young Chinese learned about the West at first hand in a hybrid cultural setting. In the ports property was secure from the demands of officialdom, so that Chinese as well as foreign entrepreneurs found it attractive to invest there. Modern China began in these islands of Western influence, oriented toward the Atlantic world by every ship that sailed, and it gradually became conscious of the conservatism that seemed to dominate the hinterland. Inevitably the treaty ports also sheltered those in flight from Chinese law. Revolutionaries, bandits and criminals gathered there. As Chiang Kai-shek later put it, the ports were a "refuge for lawlessness, immorality, and evil"; however, they also provided refuge for Chiang as a young revolutionary. The treaty-port order was neither Western nor Chinese, traditional nor modern. It depended for its maintenance on cooperation between the top of the Manchu-Chinese bureaucracy and the representatives of the Western powers. The Westerners were interested in profit, which depended upon enforcement of the commercial regulations of the treaties they had forced upon the Chinese. The most important of these, the imposition of a regularized tariff, ended up as the responsibility of a uniquely hybrid agency. The Imperial Maritime Customs developed during the emergency of danger to Shanghai during the Taiping Rebellion, and it survived until the eve of World War II as a Chinese-Western bureaucracy whose efficiency and incorruptibility made it a major source of Chinese government funds after the local taxes were lost to local governments.

China's nineteenth-century efforts for reform were played out in a confusion of domestic and international politics. Damaging as foreign humiliation was, however, the harm it did was less concrete than damage done by domestic insurrection and disorder. The Taiping Rebellion, which, between 1850 and 1864, laid the central and most productive provinces waste, was the central disaster. The rebellion was sparked by a discontented and unsuccessful examination candidate whose fevered mind found in Christian pamphlets an explanation for the evils of his time. Convinced he was a younger brother of Jesus, he led a rebellion that fed on ethnic, economic and political discontent. Its capital was established at Nanking, and it nearly toppled the dynasty. In fourteen years of almost unbroken war the Heavenly Kingdom of Great Peace evolved a crude doctrine that combined traditional values with Christian belief and practice and a primitive communism. Religious fervor made it impossible for the Taipings to ally with other dissidents, however, and their cultural radicalism spurred the Confucian gentry to take the lead in their suppression. For the ineffectual Manchu military, the gentry substituted their own local corps, drilled in Confucian doctrine and loyal to themselves. The Taiping threat to Chinese civilization thus brought the bearers of the Chinese tradition to the full support of the non-Chinese monarchy. Taiping threats to Western trade also helped persuade Western powers to help through the organization of the Maritime Customs, the provision of ships and arms and the organization of a volunteer corps commanded initially by an American, Frederick Townsend Ward, and later by an Englishman, General Charles Gordon.

The danger posed by the Taipings seemed greater than that posed by the Westerners, and it helped persuade the Manchus of the importance of reaching an accommodation with the latter. The rebellion devastated central China, killed an estimated twenty million people and caused incalculable economic and cultural destruction. The second round of treaty-port wars, between 1856 and 1860, came during the years in which the Manchus were most hard-pressed in the Yangtze Valley and limited in their capacity to resist. Nor was the Taiping Rebellion the only domestic insurrection; others in north and northwest China overlapped with and followed the Taiping disorder and helped maintain a setting of almost unbroken military crisis for the Manchus.

Internal rebellion and external pressure made it inevitable that China would lose control over its border dependencies. In the modern world boundaries are clearly drawn, and there is no tolerance for divided or partial allegiance. This is a fairly recent development, the product of mass communication, education and centralized administration. In Western Europe most borders became clear during the nineteenth century; in Eastern Europe the process began in the early twentieth century, and in South and Southeast Asia it is still in progress. In East Asia the process affected China first, for the empire was surrounded by a circle of dependencies within the traditional tribute order. When these dependencies became the objects of imperialist ambition and rivalry, the Manchu court, beset with foreign threats and domestic rebellion, was in a very poor position to do much about it. Alienation of Chinese territory in addition to the treaty ports began with the cession of Hong Kong to Britain in 1842. The second round of wars resulted in grants to England of the New Territories at Hong Kong and the Maritime Provinces to Russia, which almost succeeded in appropriating a large part of Chinese Turkestan shortly afterward. To the south, Britain added Burma to its Indian possessions after wars in 1826, 1852 and 1885. The French moved in on Saigon and, later, Hanoi; by 1887 they had added Cambodia, Annam and

Tong-King to the French empire. Chinese successes on land distinguished the Sino-French War, 1883-85, but French naval power proved decisive.

This series of disasters made political change in China more urgent and also more difficult. Economic development was virtually impossible under conditions of war and rebellion, and it was difficult to maintain even the previous state of production. Domestic conditions became steadily worse. The Chinese regime lost access to much of its revenue from land as rebellions blocked transport even from areas not in rebellion. A locally imposed tax on all goods in transit became a principal source of revenue. *Likin,* as it was called, began as an emergency measure, and it remained an effective brake on economic rationality. Much of the time the central government could control neither the land tax nor the local transport tax. Local administration and revenue came increasingly into the hands of leaders who had organized regional forces during the course of the Taiping suppression.

The last half-century of Manchu rule was remarkable for the power and influence of the great governors general. These men were loyal to the dynasty, but they were also conscious of the way policies and decisions affected their own interests. Since they were Chinese and not Manchus, their emergence altered the balance of political power in important ways. Regional political control was consolidated by their local corps, units commanded by men whose close ties with their regional associates produced a new sort of cohesion. These units were equipped with modern arms, drilled by modern techniques, indoctrinated with traditional ideology and commanded by local leaders; they proved far superior to both the Manchu units and the traditional conscript units which were plagued by inefficiency and corruption.

Although the court at Peking worked with considerable success to maintain control over such units through the manipulation of their organizers, in many respects these developments represented localism at a time when an effective national response would have called for more centralization. In the hands of a major figure like Li Hung-chang, however, such units represented much of the modern military potential of Manchu China.

Li Hung-chang, who won fame and authority during his role in suppression of the Taipings, came to dominate China's internal politics and foreign relations during his tenure as viceroy at Tientsin in the 1880s and 1890s. Under his leadership the Peiyang fleet grew to impressive proportions; roughly comparable to Japan's emerging battle fleet in size, its ships were built in the yards of Stettin and Elswick, as were the Japanese. The Chinese flagships, armed with ten-inch steel, were far heavier than the Japanese, but the Japanese placed their trust in speed and rapid-firing guns that could sweep the superstructure of the Chinese ships. The tactics of both adversaries in 1894 were the subject of intense interest for Western naval experts, who had not seen a substantial naval battle since the Italian-Austrian exchange at Lissa in 1866.

Japanese military leaders watched the growth of Chinese military power with care and apprehension. The results of the Sino-Japanese War nevertheless showed that their concern was unfounded. General Yamagata later described the localism that characterized Chinese land forces as an important weakness.

> I discovered a great weakness in the army of Li Hung-chang, and one which I could appreciate from its resemblance to a weakness which had been encountered at the time of the Restoration in Japan, which consisted of the feudal retainers under different feudal lords. This weakness was that Li Hung-chang, besides drawing a considerable portion of his soldiers from his own native place, also obtained his officers there. Thus, when anything happened to an officer in his army, he could not be replaced from among the troops under the command of the other generals. Thus it was necessary to send to Li Hung-chang's native province for all new officers.

Nor was the Peiyang fleet prepared for the needs of modern war. Procurement officials had seen little sense in spending good money for shells in time of peace, and the Chinese flagships were seriously short of steel shells though adequately supplied with duds. The war was seen as a northern effort only, and largely Li Hung-chang's responsibility; when Admiral Ting's fleet surrendered at Weihai-wei, one captain, requesting permission to rejoin his unit in the southern fleet, explained that "Kwangtung has nothing to do with the present war." The war, indeed, was China's first modern naval encounter and perhaps her last, for until recent years China has had no naval capability of any significance.

2. *The Road to Shimonoseki*

LI HUNG-CHANG'S TRIP to Shimonoseki to sue for peace in 1895 marked the end of several decades of hopes and misgivings over Sino-Japanese relations. At mid-century Li had made a natural assumption of Chinese leadership in reform and resistance to the West; like his colleagues, he spoke of "controlling" China's Eastern as well as Western foreigners by "prestige and virtue." As Li put it in 1863, "If we have some weapons with which to stand on our own feet, they will attach themselves to us, and watch the short-comings or strength of the Westerners." Then, as Japan's program of institutional change got underway in the 1860s, Chinese condescension turned to grudging admiration. By 1870, when he was appointed governor general of the capital district (Chihli), Li felt that particular efforts should be made to befriend Japan, and even suggested the possibility of sending officials to reside there, with a view to preventing Japan from siding with the West.

By that time formal governmental relations had been inaugurated between the two countries. In 1868 the new Meiji government of Japan had sent emissaries to China to announce its succession and request modern treaty relations. Because of China's preoccupation with crises, it was 1870 before a Japanese ambassador could be received. The request for a modern treaty roused some misgivings in China, but it resulted in a treaty, signed in 1871, that incorporated modern diplomatic representation and included language of cooperation against the West through provisions for good offices in case either country came into conflict with a third power. The treaty provided for extraterritoriality for citizens of both countries but ruled out the most-favored–nation clause and merchant consuls. Within the year, however, the Japanese, instead of ratifying the agreement, asked for changes in the provisions for good offices. Although the effort failed, it gave evidence of the importance the Meiji leaders would attach to steps to separate themselves from China in Western evaluation.

The upshot of this negotiation was a treaty endorsed in 1873 by the Japanese foreign minister in Peking. At Peking ceremonies for the reception of foreign representatives, Foreign Minister Soejima, the highest ranking representative then in China, was also the first to be received in audience by the Chinese emperor. There was at this time a considerable aura of friendship between Japan and China, one augmented by a Japanese decision to return Chinese coolies that had been liberated from a Peruvian ship that had taken shelter in Japanese waters.

Soejima's stay in Peking also prepared the way for the first direct confrontation between Japan and China. Taiwanese aborigines had murdered Okinawan fishermen, and the Meiji government, under great pressure from members who desired a more active foreign policy, had decided to utilize this incident to strengthen its claim to Okinawa and experiment with a claim on Taiwan. Thus Soejima sounded out Chinese officials about the nature of China's control over Taiwan and, by extension, other tributaries. He accepted their disavowal of direct control—without explaining that this would lay the groundwork for justification of Japanese intervention. After his return to Tokyo, Japan launched a punitive expedition against Taiwan that startled the Peking government and nearly led to war. The mediation of the English minister to Peking made possible a settlement with the Japanese leader Ōkubo; its terms provided for Chinese compensation for the Okinawans killed, payment for "improvements" left behind by the Japanese military in Taiwan and expressions of Chinese intent to restrain Taiwanese in the future.

Li Hung-chang and his colleagues now began to view Japan as a source of danger. The Japanese changes began to seem too completely emulative of the West, and in an exchange with the new Japanese minister to Peking, Li expressed his surprise and shock at Japan's willingness to cut itself off from the cultural traditions of East Asia. He warned the Peking government that Japan's "power is daily expanding, and her ambition is not small." Again, he noted that "Although the various European powers are strong, they are still seventy thousand *li* away, whereas Japan is as near as in the courtyard, or on the threshold. . . . Undoubtedly she will become China's permanent and great anxiety."

As viceroy of Chihli it fell to Li Hung-chang to bear responsibility for the maintenance of Korea, China's nearest, most strategic and most important tributary. Western contenders for influence were present in the British and Russian empires, but the Japanese interest was more intense and closer at hand. The problem began with a scornful Korean response to the embassy with which the Meiji government announced its accession and requested formal treaty relationships.

The response so stung Japan's samurai leaders, already straining under numerous frustrations, that the issue of a possible punitive expedition against Korea produced the first substantial split in the new Japanese government, and Korean policy remained an explosive and divisive issue throughout the next three decades of Japanese politics.

Partly to lessen these sources of irritation in Japan, the Chinese advised the Koreans to return a favorable response to Japanese efforts to "open" Korea to Western-style treaty relations in 1876. Again the tribute system served all parties poorly, for the treaty spoke of the "independence" of Korea, a term that meant quite different things to the Japanese than to the Chinese. The Koreans next worked out treaties with other powers, beginning with the United States in 1882, and gradually found themselves part of the treaty-port maritime world of East Asia.

Korean politics now became embroiled with issues of independence and reform. The Chinese were determined to maintain their close tributary, and within Korea conservatives stressed the traditional world order and the Chinese tie. Koreans anxious for reforms argued for independence from China and, almost inevitably, cultivated Japanese ties. In so doing they helped to stimulate Japanese activists and nationalists who were impatient with their government's cautious, pro-Western course. The Korean monarch sent three different missions to Japan between 1876 and 1882; he opened the ports of Inchon, Pusan and Wonsan to Japanese trade, and he began a reorganization of a new, modern-armed palace guard. Student groups were sent to both Japan and China. A Japanese minister took up residence in Seoul in 1880 and achieved a considerable ascendancy among reform-minded Koreans.

Japanese-Korean politics were inextricably associated with the career of Kim Ok-kyun, a well-born young aristocrat who first visited Japan in 1882. While he was there, the Japanese-trained palace guard in Seoul was attacked by units of the old army, which went on to sack the Japanese legation and put its staff to flight. Chinese troops were rushed in to pacify the disorder and prevent worse violence, and thereafter Li Hung-chang installed a representative, Yüan Shih-k'ai, in Seoul to oversee Chinese interests. The Korean customs service became a virtual branch of the Chinese Imperial Maritime Customs, and Koreans and Japanese began to think of direct action to challenge the Chinese dominance. Late in 1884 the dissidents chose the occasion of the dedication of a new post office to strike against their conservative opponents. With the help of the Japanese legation guard in Seoul and the Japanese-trained palace guard, they surrounded the palace, assassinated several opponents and tried to execute a coup d'etat. But Yüan Shih-k'ai was soon on the scene with one thousand five hundred Chinese troops, and this show of force, together with the anger of the anti-Japanese mobs of Seoul, forced a quick recognition of defeat and retreat to the ships at Inchon.

The Japanese government, preoccupied with internal reforms, and the Chinese, newly defeated by France, were both anxious to avoid a frontal conflict. Out of a meeting between Li Hung-chang and the Japanese statesman Itō

Hirobumi came a Tientsin agreement of 1885, which called for mutual abstention from interference in Korea, consultation in the event either found it necessary to dispatch troops and agreement upon selection of advisers from other
countries to assist in Korean reforms. In the months that followed, first Russian
and then American influence rose in Korea. The Russians, however, were distrusted by all other powers because of the imperialist interest they were
presumed to represent, while the Americans had little support from their own
government and were limited to the exercise of personal influence. The real competition remained between the Japanese and Chinese, and after 1885 the Chinese
were clearly ahead.

Kim Ok-kyun and other reformers were in exile in Japan for the decade
after 1884. Rumors of Japanese filibustering attempts terrified many conservatives in Korea, and in 1885 the revelation of a bizarre plot to invade Korea
seemed to confirm these fears. Within Korea Yüan Shih-k'ai took advantage of
many of his opportunities to increase Chinese power and influence. In 1894 a request from the Korean government to assist in the suppression of a sectarian
revolt seemed to make it possible to transform Korea into a real Chinese satellite.
By then the Japanese government, however, its program of institutional reforms
completed and its house in order, was ready to take a stronger line abroad.

As the Korean government was struggling with the Tonghak movement, its
unfortunate handling of its enemies of the 1880s provided a popular issue for advocates of war in Japan. The Korean government had remained in fear of Kim
Ok-kyun, Pak Yŏng-hyo and other radicals of the 1884 movement who remained in exile in Japan. In 1894, a small band of well-subsidized Koreans came
to Japan to gain the radicals' confidence and kill them. The setting was promising. The Korean reformers had lost most of their visibility and popularity in
Japan. Kim Ok-kyun had lived under police surveillance on the Bonins and in
Hokkaido, and he was weary of Japan and ready to try his luck elsewhere. His
new Korean friends persuaded him that a warmer welcome might await him in
Shanghai, and one accompanied him there on a Japanese vessel. On 28 March, as
Kim Ok-kyun was resting in his upstairs room in a Japanese inn in the International Settlement, he was murdered by this man. Kim was not Japanese, so the
rules of extraterritoriality did not seem to cover his corpse; after some hesitation
the British consul permitted the transfer of the corpse and the murderer, who
had been apprehended, to Chinese authorities. These in turn yielded to Korean
importunity and turned both over to the Korean government—delivered them,
in fact, on a Chinese warship. The Korean government proceeded to shower
honors on the assassin and dishonor on the corpse. It was cut up and its parts sent
to all sectors of the country as a graphic warning of the fate that awaited "traitors." At the same time a branch of the plot, aimed at Pak Yŏng-hyo in Tokyo,
failed. The band of Korean assassins there was tracked down, and several of them
were dislodged from the Korean Mission in Tokyo.

The Japanese consul in Shanghai and the foreign office in Tokyo belatedly
saw that this disposition of the matter would provide prime material for political

agitation at home, and they did what they could, none of it sufficient or in time, to dissuade the Korean government from its conduct in the matter. Diet speakers characterized the incident as an insult to the Japanese flag, under whose protection the Korean exiles had been, and popular agitators were quick to link it to Li Hung-chang and Yüan Shih-k'ai. What began as the murder of one Korean by another Korean thus came to seem a trial of Japan's stature and dignity. Kim's former friends and associates in Japan quickly resumed the cause they had abandoned while Kim was with them to eulogize their martyred guest and friend. (In 1973 the kidnapping of opposition leader Kim Dae Jung from Tokyo to Seoul, allegedly by agents of the Korean Embassy, produced a comparable storm of complaint in the Japanese press.)

In this setting the Japanese government, in late May of 1894, began to hear of requests from Korea to Yüan Shih-k'ai for military assistance to put down a rebellion. By the time definite word of the Chinese landings on 5 June arrived in Tokyo, the decision had been made for a strong response. Japanese troops, originally a mixed brigade, began arriving on 12 June. Five days earlier an Imperial Military Headquarters (Dai Hon'ei) had been set up. Clearly, the Tokyo government was preparing for action.

By the time the Japanese troops arrived, the Korean rebels were no longer a danger. The real problem now was the confrontation of Japanese with Chinese military strength. Prompt withdrawal of both forces, as urged by outside powers, would clearly have been a great disappointment for the Japanese public, which was expecting some kind of long-awaited "solution" to the "Korean problem." It would also have left the Chinese in a state to reap benefits from their intervention. These issues were argued out by Meiji leaders in long meetings. Finally the decision was reached to make a move for basic changes in the Korean situation in the direction of modern reforms. The Chinese would be asked to cooperate and cosponsor. If they refused, as the Japanese expected them to, Japan would be prepared to force the issue. At the end of June the Japanese decided to demand that Korea make a set of reforms comparable to those announced at the beginning of the Meiji period in Japan: respect for foreign representatives, a modern system of governmental accounting and expenditure, army reforms, Western-style education, a modern currency system, improved transportation, amnesty for political prisoners, Koreans to be sent abroad for study, equal status for Japanese and Chinese officials and residents in Korea and improvements in the harbor at Inchon. By 12 July the Tokyo government had decided on war, and instructed its minister in Seoul to "use any pretext available" to justify direct action.

The Koreans hesitated, and they were encouraged by the Chinese, who refused to cosponsor these sweeping changes with their Japanese rivals. Japanese troops seized the Seoul royal palace and forced the king to announce the end of Korean dependence upon China and to request Japanese assistance against China. On 25 July a Chinese troop transport was sunk, and war was formally declared on 1 August. "War has begun between Japan and China," the Tokyo publicist Fukuzawa Yukichi editorialized. "But if we trace its origins it is a war between a

BATTLE OF THE YELLOW SEA, re-created by a Meiji artist.

country which is trying to develop civilization and a country which disturbs the development of civilization." A practical decision to force a military solution had now been translated into a duty forced upon Japan by the dictates of civilization and the higher law of history.

In formal terms the difference between the Chinese and Japanese armies was not marked, but most observers expected a Chinese victory. Kozaki Hiromichi, who was in London when war broke out, describes a visit to the office of the journalist W. T. Stead:

> He stood up abruptly and tapping me on the shoulder said, "Your country has committed a serious blunder. For a little, weak country like Japan to fight a big, strong country like China is suicidal. Japan will be obliterated like a fly in the flame."

But there were many things that favored the Japanese cause. One was position; the opening engagements found the Japanese troops at Seoul, in better positions and strength than their Chinese opponents who were in the provinces where they had been suppressing rebels. Another was preparation; the Japanese were uniformly armed, while the Chinese had a variety of guns (although many were Mauser and Krupp and of excellent quality) that would have complicated a more efficient supply service than theirs. The dash and willingness of the Japanese commanders to take risks also counted for much. They quickly outran the capacity of their supply service to keep up with them from the docks at Inchon and Pusan, and at the pivotal battle at Pyongyang, they had only three days' supplies of food and ammunition. Had the battle been an extended one, they would have been forced to yield the day. But instead the Japanese seized the forts that commanded the Pyongyang valley to rain down a punishing volley on the larger Chinese army that held it. The real sufferers, of course, were the Koreans, who fled the city to leave it to the looters. The redoubtable Mrs. Bishop remarked sadly that "both the Chinese who fled and the Japanese who occupied posed as the friends of Korea, and all this wreck and ruin was brought about not by enemies, but by those who professed to be fighting to give her independence and reform."

The Pyongyang battle defeated China's best land forces. Thereafter other Japanese armies commanded by General Yamagata landed in Korea and crossed the Yalu into Manchuria. Still other units landed in south Manchuria, on the Liaotung Peninsula, to seize Dairen and Port Arthur, where the Germans had begun construction of a naval base for the Chinese. Meanwhile the Chinese naval forces fared no better. At the crucial battle of the Yellow Sea in September the Chinese ships fared badly and retired, first to Port Arthur and, after it was endangered, to Weihaiwei. The fall of that anchorage and the surrender of the Chinese fleet of Admiral Ting led to the exchange between Admiral Itō and Admiral Ting with which this chapter opened.

Early in 1895 the Chinese made their first efforts to negotiate peace, but the Japanese rejected their envoys because their credentials were not in order. As a result the Peking court restored Li Hung-chang to the honors and titles of which he had been stripped because of the Chinese defeats and sent him to Shimonoseki in March. The change of estate that had befallen Li Hung-chang was symbolic of his country's decline. In the spring of the previous year, before the outbreak of hostilities, he had made a triumphant inspection trip of China's military forces and bases in the Yellow Sea and returned to the congratulations of Chinese and foreign observers. When he met now with Itō Hirobumi to work out the arrangements for an end to the war, he reminded him of their meeting in Tientsin a decade earlier. "In Asia," said Li Hung-chang, "our two countries, China and Japan, are the closest neighbors, and moreover have the same language [i.e., transcription system]. How could we be enemies? Now for the time being we are fighting each other, but eventually we should work for permanent friendship.... we ought vigorously to maintain the general stability of Asia, and establish perpetual peace and harmony between ourselves, so that our Asiatic yellow race will not be encroached upon by the white race of Europe." Itō professed his pleasure with this idea, but then went on that "Ten years ago when I was at Tientsin, I talked about reform with you. Why is it that up to now not a single thing has been changed or reformed? This I deeply regret." Alas, replied Li with elaborate compliments for Itō's achievements, "Affairs in my country have been so confined by tradition that I could not accomplish what I desired."

Nor could the aged statesman have his will with Itō. His first request, for a cease-fire, was countered with a demand for Japanese army control over the rail connections between Shanhaikuan, Tientsin, and Taku and Chinese provision of all Japanese military expenditures during the period of the cease-fire. Observers reported that Li Hung-chang changed color at this realization of Japanese confidence and muttered "Cruel!"

Japanese chauvinism came to his aid in unexpected fashion. A self-appointed patriot, sure that the crafty statesman was somehow outwitting his countrymen, shot Li as he was leaving the meeting place. The Japanese government, its eyes on foreign sympathy, reversed itself and granted the cease-fire. Fortunately, Li was not killed, and the negotiators were soon able to continue with their work.

But the outcome was predictable from the fact that the war had been quick, cheap and popular and that it had roused an extraordinary amount of Japanese chauvinism. One newspaper announced a competition for war songs to arouse feelings of hatred for the "national enemy," and schoolchildren all over the country sang lyrics like this, from "On to Peking":[1]

> China long ago was the land of the teachings of the sages,
> But as dynasties changed and the years passed
> She gradually has fallen behind in progress,
> She prides herself on being Middle Flowery Land,
> In reverse proportion to the barbarity of her heart;
> Unless we destroy her ignorance,
> The night of the East will never dawn.

Woodblock prints showing war scenes sold in enormous quantities. They showed Japanese in heroic poses, models of discipline and order, soldiers whose modern and Western appearance contrasted with the confused masses of quaintly dressed Chinese soldiers who milled about in confusion or scurried out of danger. Stage plays reinforced this with lampoons of Li Hung-chang, who was portrayed as a corrupt, vacillating and crafty old rascal. And popular politicians vied with each other in calling for drives to Peking and the cession of China's coastal provinces.

In this climate of opinion the military, who knew exactly what they wanted of China, were sure to have their will over the few voices that called for moderation. The imperial navy had its eyes on Taiwan, with a view to future activity to the south; the imperial army, on the other hand, advocated retention of the Liaotung Peninsula in south Manchuria, where Port Arthur had fallen to Japan. This, its spokesmen argued, was necessary to support the strategic boundaries of Korea and to control the approaches to Peking. The vainglory of the masses, the bellicosity of the politicians and the self-confidence of the military forced the

---

[1]Donald Keene, trans., "The Sino-Japanese War of 1894–95 and Its Cultural Effect on Japan," in *Tradition and Modernization in Japanese Culture,* ed. D. H. Shively (Princeton: Princeton University Press, 1971), pp. 142–43.

civilian Japanese leaders to raise the cost of peace for China and led them to risk Western displeasure and intervention.

The Treaty of Shimonoseki was signed on 17 April. By its terms the Chinese: (1) recognized the independence of Korea; (2) ceded to Japan the Liaotung Peninsula, Taiwan and the Pescadores; (3) agreed to pay an indemnity of 200 million *taels* within a seven-year period; and (4) extended to Japan the full range of privileges earlier given Western countries under the unequal treaties. In addition four more treaty ports (one of them Chungking) were to be opened to all nations, the Japanese were granted navigation rights on the Yangtze and the right to develop manufacturing on Chinese soil.

One aspect of this treaty stirred the jealousy of Japan's European competitors, who showed that Japan's membership status in the concert of powers was still not first-class. On 23 April representatives of Russia, Germany and France advised the Tokyo government to return the Liaotung Peninsula "for the sake of the peace of Asia." With little ability to withstand a coalition of three major powers, the Japanese government reluctantly substituted an additional indemnity of 30 million *taels* for its foothold in Manchuria.

The Sino-Japanese War closed the treaty-port era of nineteenth-century imperialism and ushered in a new stage of territorial imperialism. Japan was no longer subject to imperialism; it became a participant. This development intensified discussion of reform and change within China at the same time that it triggered imperialist competition. In 1890 General Yamagata had written that only China and Japan could maintain their autonomy in the face of European greed and power. By 1895 there was room for doubt about China, and authors began to write ominously about the impending breakup of that country. China was no longer a contender for mastery in Korea, and the contest there now lay between Japan and Russia. Great Britain now began to look upon Japan as helpful in containing Russian imperialism, while Japan was being drawn increasingly into the discordant concert of European ambitions in East Asia.

3. After Shimonoseki

IT WAS TO BE EXPECTED that the disasters experienced in the war against Japan would have particularly far-reaching effects in China. Earlier defeats had been administered by the advanced countries of the West, but this final humiliation had been dealt by a small, hitherto insignificant, neighbor, itself most recently the object of Western imperialism. Shimonoseki brought the first sizable surrender of Chinese territory and the loss of China's most important tributary. Under provisions of Article 6 of the Shimonoseki treaty, moreover, Japanese subjects were declared free to engage in manufacturing in all open ports and cities in China, they could import machinery into China at nominal duties, and the goods manufactured by them enjoyed the same limited duties and taxation as Japanese

SHIMONOSEKI PEACE CONFER-
ENCE. In this recreated painting by a
Meiji artist, Itō, right, and Mutsu,
center, sit facing Li Hung-chang.

exports. The most-favored–nation clause immediately made the same privileges available to all other countries that benefited from the unequal treaties. Soon a network of port-city–based industries, foreign owned and controlled, treaty protected and virtually untaxed, created further problems for Chinese regimes. The post-Shimonoseki scene was also darker because of the heavy indemnity which the Chinese had to pay the Japanese. Unable to strengthen their premodern taxation system to raise such staggering sums, the Chinese had to resort to foreign loans predicated upon future customs revenue, the only predictable source of national income.

    Within months of the Treaty of Shimonoseki, in July 1895, Russia and France secured for their own interests a loan to China of 400 million gold francs, guaranteed against the customs receipts. Additional promises were made to Russia guaranteeing that she would receive rights equal to those given any other power in supervising or administering Chinese revenues. The following year Li Hung-chang, in St. Petersburg (as was General Yamagata) for the coronation of the czar, granted the Russians a secret treaty of alliance and permission to extend the Trans-Siberian Railroad across Manchuria directly to Vladivostok. This extension became the Chinese Eastern Railway.

France's reward for its part in the Triple Intervention came equally soon. In July 1895 the Chinese border with Annam was defined in accordance with French wishes; China opened three new treaty ports on the border and reduced transit dues, granted the French permission to extend the Annamese railway into Chinese territory and gave the French priority in mining exploration and development in the southern provinces of Yunnan, Kwangsi and Kwangtung. (Thus the rail network over which Chinese supplies would later enter North Vietnam was laid.) The British, concerned about their position, secured changes in the Burmese border in February 1897, opened new riverports in Kwangtung and Kwangsi and received permits to connect Burmese railway lines with those in Yunnan when they were completed. (The Yunnan lines were not completed, however, and it required a tortuous overland highway (the "Burma Road") to bring British supplies into China in the 1930s.) Chinese dissatisfaction with these border decisions was resolved only by the pacts between Burma and the People's Republic of China in 1960.

Thus the partition of China (indeed of all Asia except for Japan) by Western imperialist powers seemed imminent. The United States entered the race with the decisions to annex Hawaii and the Philippines. Thoughts of improving communications and bases for the China fleet led to inquiries about the acquisition of a naval base at Samsah Bay in Fukien. These American attempts proved abortive, for the area was adjacent to Taiwan and therefore within the Japanese sphere.

In the same years growing missionary activity in all areas of China provided new sources of dispute. The last decades of the nineteenth century saw the emergence of new and enthusiastic mission groups that abandoned the security of treaty-port mission compounds to travel throughout the countryside, where they established isolated posts and worked for individual conversion through popular preaching. The China Inland Mission, for example, had 784 workers in China by 1900, and was particularly direct in its assaults on what it considered pagan customs in rural China. Estimates of the mission movement varied widely. Few could dispute the positive gains in education and medicine and the pressure for reforms in social customs like foot binding and concubinage that missions brought. But it was also clear that hundreds of enthusiasts, modestly educated in their own culture and grossly ignorant of China's, contributed greatly to the instability and tensions of relations between Chinese and foreigners. The missionaries were not always as insensitive as charged by twentieth-century historians, and the Chinese were certainly not as crudely antiforeign as many missionaries charged. Many of the missionary organizations fought clear of governmental assistance because they were suspicious of all forms of temporal authority. Others, and especially branches of the Catholic movement which had French government backing, found it necessary to invoke frequent assistance for converts they felt were receiving unfair treatment from local authorities. Western diplomats were usually not eager to take up the missionary cause; they considered them pushy and unwise and tried to dissuade them from traveling alone in the countryside. But no representative could ignore violence and murder, and when these broke out, it was often the treaty-port merchants who stood to gain and were the most vociferous in demanding strong diplomatic action to defend the representatives of Western civilization. Diplomatic demands for satisfaction usually took the form of indemnities or additional privileges on grounds that Chinese officials had not done anything to stop the outrages. In fact, however, the officials concerned were usually weak and content to protect lives at the cost of missionary installations, which could always be rebuilt. They tried to soothe their people by vaguely worded proclamations which were seized upon as evidence of bad faith by the aggrieved foreigners, whose demands for satisfaction ended by further weakening the position of the officials.

As the prestige of officialdom declined, it came under attack from below as well. Secret societies, local officials and local gentry resentful of central government orders to leave missionaries and converts alone, all stood to gain from the increasing disorder into which China was falling. Thus, riots at the Szechwan city of Chengtu in 1895 led to French acquisition of the railway rights to Yunnan from Annam, in addition to heavy indemnities that were grossly in excess of the physical damage to mission stations in Chengtu and, finally, American and British insistence on the permanent dismissal of the provincial viceroy. As a recent judgment has it, "The ambassador of a Western power, unable or unwilling to control the passions of his own people, had forced the public humiliation of a Chinese governor-general for the same failure."

But all this was only preliminary to demands that China make territorial concessions. Germany, one of the powers that took part in the Triple Intervention, had sought a port on the China coast as a coaling station and base since 1895. By the spring of 1897 it had settled on Kiaochow Bay in Shantung, but the Russians claimed prior rights in the area. Then, in November of that year, word reached Berlin of the murder of two German missionaries in southern Shantung. The kaiser telegraphed the czar that "I am under obligation to the Catholic party in Germany to show that I am in a position to come to the defense of their missionaries. Punishment is necessary and it will bring advantages to all Christians," and sent German ships to occupy the bay. After prolonged negotiation during which the Chinese tried to persuade the Germans to accept less elsewhere, Kiaochow was leased to Germany for ninety-nine years, together with extensive mining rights and concessions for two railways.

The principal barrier to this had not been the powerless Manchu government but Germany's jealous competitors. The English first opposed this grab and then decided against resisting it because of a fear that the Germans would try for something farther south and closer to British interests on the Yangtze. The Russians, who first tried to block the German occupation of Kiaochow, decided that it provided an appropriate occasion for them to move into Port Arthur and the Liaotung Peninsula city of Dairen from which they, together with the Germans and French, had dislodged the Japanese by the Triple Intervention. In March 1898 Russia obtained a twenty-five–year lease to that area. It became the focus for

naval development and for a southern ice-free port connection to the Chinese
Eastern and the Trans-Siberian Railroad.

The English now decided to balance things by leasing Weihaiwei, the northern Shantung anchorage in which the Japanese had trapped the Chinese fleet two
years earlier, for as long as the Russians held Port Arthur. Shortly afterwards the
French claimed as their territorial concessions the Kwangchow Bay in
Kwangtung. Again the English felt it necessary to balance things, this time by
adding the New Territories to their Kowloon holdings opposite Hong Kong.

The balanced privileges of the treaty-port system had now been supplemented by a series of zones or spheres, in which Western powers completely controlled a port which served as center of an area in which they had exclusive or
prior opportunity for development of extractive industry and modern communications. France and Russia were based on their territorial holdings to the
south and north of China. In Manchuria the Russians had the most promising of
all the territorial bases: a naval base at Port Arthur, a good commercial port at
Talienwan (Dairen), the rail rights of the Chinese Eastern Railway (later the
South Manchuria Railway) and the large and underdeveloped racial homeland of
the Manchus. Japan had urged China not to alienate any part of the province of
Fukien, which lay off its new colony in Taiwan. Japanese policies of development
on Taiwan worked to exploit ties between the islanders and their neighbors on
the mainland. But the largest stakes of all were in the hands of the maritime
powers of Germany and, especially, England. The English sphere of influence
comprehended the entire Yangtze Valley. The armies of commerce and Christianity were predominantly English-speaking. The English had some four-fifths
of China's foreign trade, they received concessions to build about half of the total
mileage of rail development allotted to outsiders, and as the largest trading nation, they secured for England the office of Inspector General of the Imperial
Maritime Customs.

It is not surprising that most foreign observers spoke of an impending
breakup of China. It seemed entirely possible that the spheres of influence might
grow until they met, that foreign control would be intensified and that China
would become a series of colonies of the Western powers. In 1903 Russian Count
Witte summed up the matter by saying that "the problem of each country concerned is to obtain as large a share as possible of the outlived Oriental states,
especially of the Chinese Colossus." On the other hand, it was important to all
contestants that the final division take place under conditions of good order, lest
they be caught at a disadvantage in the final scramble. None wanted a general
war over China, and most saw matters proceeding so satisfactorily that they
should not be disturbed.

4. The Hundred Days

ULTIMATELY IT WAS NOT so much the jealousy of the powers that saved
China's territorial integrity as it was the rise of a national concern and aware-

ness on the part of Chinese. This was a development that moved through three principal stages. The first was the awakening and alarm of reform intellectuals. The scholars K'ang Yu-wei and Liang Ch'i-ch'ao, the leaders of this group, serve as its symbols, and their brief day of leadership opportunity came during the summer months of 1898. A second, less studied but possibly more important stage, came with the tactics and concern of high officials who showed a new awareness of Chinese sovereignty in their dealings with foreign representatives and held to the minimum or negated the practical effects of diplomatic concessions. The third phase came with the development of highly emotional and intense nationalistic consciousness on the part of the vast body of the literate who were reached and moved by the outpouring of lament and alarm over the humiliations China had to endure. Chinese students were the conscience and provided the voice for this host, but its influence went far beyond their numbers. Furthermore, all three stages developed under the impact and pressure of the tumultuous and frequently xenophobic resentment of Western encroachments and privileges that pervaded the world of rural China. The disastrous outcome of the battles of the Sino-Japanese War and the contents of the Treaty of Shimonoseki combined to make a national disgrace out of what had seemed a sectional problem. It was one thing to be bested by European states but quite another for Chinese to realize that a small and insignificant neighbor had in a few decades increased its strength enough to defeat the Middle Country.

It was inevitable for indignation to flare first among the elite. No group could be more disposed toward involvement than aspiring examination candidates, and no arrangements for rousing such interest could improve on the gatherings at provincial capitals and at Peking. The national examinations might draw as many as eight thousand men, most of them young and all of them aspiring to state service, all educated and trained to think of themselves as a natural elite. Moreover, the interval between examinations and announcement of the results provided a tense and nervous period of waiting; in ordinary times there were complaints of the frivolity and self-indulgence shown by the candidates. The Ch'ing emperors often warned against organizations of scholars. But the national disasters in China in the 1890s made it justifiable for them to join in patriotic protest. Some of the earliest voluntary political associations, and the germ of future student nationalism and political participation, all flowed naturally from the prolonged presence in capital cities of large numbers of ambitious, educated and self-confident young men. In later decades, when education for national service became oriented increasingly toward the West, the location of such groups was to shift to cities on the fringe of China where modern education became centered. Age levels lowered. After 1900 thousands gathered in Tokyo. Boxer indemnity remissions, which went for education, made it possible for other groups to assemble in Paris and other Western centers. Modernization finally brought the student concentration back to the new universities established in China's great cities. As the wheel came full circle the thousands, augmented manyfold, could be found again in Peking.

The response to the Treaty of Shimonoseki was nationwide. Many leading officials, including Chang Chih-tung and Liu K'un-i, memorialized the court to urge that the treaty be rejected and the war continued. More important, and more difficult for the court to persuade, were the thousands of literati who signed over 130 petitions of protests. One authority estimates that over 2,500 men endorsed the petitions opposing the treaty. Most of the arguments were similar. The indemnity would require a foreign loan and increase China's bondage to the West. Taiwan was the key to south China's defense; to give it up would be unfilial in view of the K'ang-hsi emperor's achievement in wresting it from the hands of Ming partisans. To contemplate the cession of Liaotung was to prejudice the security of the dynasty's imperial tombs in Manchuria. The Shimonoseki treaty's commercial provisions would give Japanese merchants control of interior trade in China. Even England, a much stronger power than Japan, had not received the privileges the Shimonoseki treaty proposed to grant the Japanese. The treaty would permanently weaken China. There were grounds to suspect that it incorporated private gains for Li Hung-chang and his followers. China, the memorialists argued, could still win if it resumed the war. The most famous memorial was that of K'ang Yu-wei, a brilliant young scholar who secured the backing of 603 middle-ranking candidates from sixteen provinces for a memorial he submitted in May of 1895. He called for rejection of the treaty, for moving the court inland to get it out of the reach of Japanese armies, and for instituting a series of sweeping reforms.

K'ang and the other protesters were not heeded. But their sensitivity to further foreign insults provided the slogans and program for the most ambitious program of changes to be produced in nineteenth-century China. Under slogans of *tzu ch'iang* (strengthen ourselves), *pien fa* (change the laws) and *fu kuo ch'iang ping* (enrich the country, strengthen its armies), these men called for sweeping institutional changes.

Earlier reform programs of viceroys like Li Hung-chang had attempted to utilize the machinery and weapons of the West, but it was only now that Chinese turned to face the true dimensions of the intellectual and institutional problems that faced their country. At this distance it is difficult to realize how profoundly Chinese thinkers had to alter the system of values they held. Slogans calling for wealth and power ("enrich the country, strengthen its armies"), for instance, had a dubious background, for they were associated with the tactics of the first, legalist emperor of Ch'in at the beginning of Imperial China (tactics long deplored, but finally praised publicly by Mao Tse-tung in the 1970s). While Japanese leaders, accustomed to rule by their military and the exercise of force, could grasp the slogan without hesitation (and had, in fact, heard it used in feudal domains from their youth), Chinese thinkers had to square it with a value orientation in which "wealth and power" were unworthy goals. Thus a frank search for the elements of state strength required a restructuring of moral priorities. One step toward this was the increasing identification of that moral order with the country and society that had given it birth. China became less the center of the cultural order, and it began to be conceived of as a beleaguered country, surrounded by the "ravenous wolves" of imperialism, and forced to change its values, institutions and technology in self-defense. Western powers were dangerous precisely because they placed such emphasis on wealth and strength, and they could be resisted only if China did the same thing. The translator Yen Fu could write in 1898 that "There can be no Way without a state and a people to sustain it," and the increasing identification of a Chinese state with ultimate moral values meant a gradual shift of emphasis from the strength of values to the strength of the state. What good was the millenial splendor of Chinese civilization unless it was represented by a living Chinese state? Or the teachings of the sages unless they could be realized in action? "China" was becoming more country and less civilization.

After the Sino-Japanese War, reformers were also brought to reevaluate the Western countries and thinkers whose institutions and ideas had created the contemporary world. The sweep of Herbert Spencer's synthesis, which had earlier affected Meiji Japan powerfully, now made its impact on China also. China's discomfiture could be fitted into a larger theory of evolution and development, and Western theorists could be permitted to share some of the credit for working this out. Specialists in Western learning reflect this view most clearly. Benjamin Schwartz's study shows this progression in the thought of the translator Yen Fu. Family difficulties forced Yen Fu to turn from traditional learning to Western writings in order to qualify for service in the schools attached to the Foochow shipyard. He won placement there with a prize-winning essay on "Life-long filial devotion to One's Parents" and was then assigned to study English. In 1877 he was sent to study in England. Here he sought at firsthand the secrets of Western wealth and power. Upon his return to China he tried without success to enter official service by the main examination gate and thereafter became a translator-technician of Western learning. After China's defeat by Japan he threw himself into the task of writing and translating and served up to his countrymen the works of Spencer, Mill, Montesquieu and Adam Smith. As his choice of authors shows, Yen Fu believed in the necessity of an intellectual commitment before wealth and strength could be built. The Chinese sages, he argued, "knew the direction of the course of destiny and were able to regulate it, complete it, cooperate with it, and lead the world to a state of peace." Similarly, he argued, Western sages had understood the course of evolution, and learned to cooperate with it for modern social and technological development. His essays, "On the Speed of World Change," "On Strength," "On our Salvation," and others, all written in 1895, showed that he sought in his Western sages the material for national salvation. As with early Japanese students of Western thought and institutions, the political economists' concern with general welfare came for him to mean the wealth and power of the state. The overwhelming urgency of national strength seldom brought him to concern himself with individual well-being.

The need to justify utilization of Western ideas and institutions found new arguments in the apparent success of nineteenth-century Japan in combining modern with traditional institutions. Thus, shortly after the war with Japan, Chang Chih-tung, who had been a leading advocate of war, wrote that "Confucianism is in danger, and to rescue the truth we must turn to Japan for the present." A grudging tolerance and then admiration of Meiji Japan began to characterize reformers in China. But it was even more important for those reformers to harmonize the changes they desired with the Chinese tradition, so that they could be seen as the fruition and not the rejection of that tradition. Professor K.C. Hsiao has shown that this was the particular contribution of K'ang Yu-wei, whose career produced the last creative efflorescence of Confucian thought.

K'ang (1858-1927) was born in south China. His family, which had produced a notable line of gentry scholars, launched him on a thorough program of traditional education aimed at the examination system. But he was too independent, and his interests were too broad, for him to be content with this safe course. Instead he read widely in Confucian, Buddhist and, after he entered his twenties, Western learning. In 1882 he visited Shanghai, and there and in Hong Kong he developed a lively respect for the vigor of Western civilization and organization. His first memorial urging reforms was written in 1888, but he did not become known as a leader of reform until 1895, when he composed his famous denunciation of the Shimonoseki treaty for his fellow examination candidates in Peking. K'ang came out of that examination with the coveted *chin shih* degree. The national crisis and his personal achievements now guaranteed him an audience for his views.

K'ang worked out an intellectual and philosophical position of great power and appeal. His study of the classics had convinced him that the currently accepted versions of those works were forgeries dating from the time of Christ and that an alternate series of disputed texts represented the true learning of antiquity. In a startling and revolutionary book published in 1891 he attacked the orthodox "Sung" learning as in reality "Hsin" learning, so named for the interregnum during which a heterodox minister had fabricated it. K'ang's reconstruction of Confucius showed him as a system builder and reformer, a man who had been totally misunderstood and misinterpreted by the special pleaders who had dominated Confucian studies. "I realized," he wrote of his studies of Sung learning, "that Confucius could not have been so bigoted and narrow as that"; of earlier formulations, he contended that "it could not be so fragmentary and confused as that. For if it stopped only there, Confucius would be a sage but not a divine being." K'ang concluded that Confucius conceived of time as moving through three ages, one of disorder, a second of ascending peace and a concluding era of universal peace. As the world approached integration and peace, the institutions of representative democracy became appropriate and necessary. K'ang believed in universal values of equality, which brought him into conflict with the traditional institutions of family government as well as political organization, and believed it was his personal mission to spread this doctrine of enlightenment to all. Elements of a messianic Mahayana Buddhism and of a reinterpreted and dynamic Confucianism combined with a grasp of what the modern world required of China to produce in K'ang writings a synthesis of tradition with the present and added to it the vision of a universal future. K'ang possessed great self-confidence and a sense of mission. "My appearance in this world," he wrote, "is solely for the purpose of saving all living beings.... I begin with the land that gave me birth, with the people I chance to meet, the many for whom I have close affection." His conclusions from his study of Western science were expressed in four "principles of truth" that recall the Buddha's four postulates: every man, he said, is part of "the primordial stuff of heaven and earth"; he has soul and intelligence, though each intelligence differs; he is born with a "disposition both to love and to hate," but love is "more beneficial"; and he is "born with good faith, while deceit is acquired through his contact with evil customs." Here Buddhism, Mencius, and Mo Tzu found echo, while the conclusions from the whole carried revolutionary assertions of man's right to equality and democracy.

From these philosophical bases K'ang moved into politics to attack what seemed the most pressing ills of his time and country. Tradition had now provided legitimation for reforms made urgent by the contemporary world, and he could work to help to implement them. Evolution, so clearly the dominant strand of nineteenth-century Western thought, need no longer be approached as something purely foreign. It was possible to find in the Chinese tradition bases for much that had seemed new. Yet K'ang was also profoundly revolutionary. His utopian ideas had developed by the time he entered the national political scene, but he had not expressed them fully. He was well known for his denunciation of conventional Confucian wisdom, but for most of his admirers he represented intellectual brilliance rather than specific recommendations for change. His most revolutionary work, a utopian forecast entitled *The Great Commonwealth*, was written in 1902, but he published the first part only in 1919 and the more controversial sections were not published until after K'ang's death in 1927. Thus he was a good deal more radical than his contemporaries realized.

After his memorial of 1895 became known, K'ang rapidly gained a following. His interpretation of the classics, and especially his popular *Confucius as a Reformer*, excited many young scholars. Liang Ch'i-ch'ao, his most important disciple, took the lead in organizing a Protect the Country Association. Its program spoke of protecting the national territory, population and faith, by which was meant the worship of Confucius. K'ang apparently saw in a proposed cult of Confucius an institution that would have provided for Chinese loyalties some of the dynamics the imperial cult provided in Japan. Conservatives, however, were quick to disapprove; "If this view of Confucius is taught," one memorialized, "every scholar would entertain the idea of altering the institutions.... schools which are established to educate talented men would instead confuse and poison the minds of the people. That would lead the empire into disorder."

But the empire was already in disorder resulting from the defeat by Japan and the imperialist advances that followed. There was also movement at court. The empress dowager, Tz'u-hsi was beginning to retire, and Kuang-hsü, the

DOWAGER EMPRESS TZ'U-HSI (1835-1908). Tz'u-hsi entered the palace in 1851 as a concubine, and dominated it from 1860-1908, ruling directly for 37 years and indirectly for 11. She personally directed the succession of the last two Manchu emperors, thwarted the Hundred Days, favored the Boxers, and presided over the institutional reforms of the last years of the dynasty.

young emperor, beginning to take over. Li Hung-chang had lost ground to new candidates for imperial favor, Liu K'un-i and Chang Chih-tung. A number of officials, including the imperial tutor Weng T'ung-ho, spoke to the emperor about K'ang Yu-wei, who was received in audience in June and began presenting the court with proposals for reform. The summer of 1898 saw K'ang in his prime of intellectual and personal vigor and able to influence imperial decisions directly.

The "Hundred Days," as the interval of reform became known, lasted from June to September. A flood of edicts issued from the palace. They bore on the bureaucratic system, finance, a constitution, the army and navy, the development of Chinese Turkestan, the integration of Manchus with Chinese, education for women as well as men, revision of the calendar and dating systems, removal of the capital, agriculture, industry, commerce and mining. Some of this was ostensibly inspired by Japanese example, drawn from a history of Japan which K'ang wrote for the emperor. "As soon as I had completed one chapter," K'ang wrote, "it was immediately presented to the emperor, who would then press me to send in another. The emperor was delighted to read of the success of all the measures taken by the Japanese." Unlike the Japanese changes, however, the Chinese were not preceded by an overthrow of the previous government.

And they were a great deal more precipitate. "As for the old officials," K'ang told the emperor, "let them stay on for the time being. But they are conservative in every way, and so I request that Your Majesty issue more decrees to make them aware of your real intention. All reform matters should be proclaimed by special decrees and then they will have no way to refute or criticize them." K'ang also struck directly at the examination system. "Since Your Majesty is already aware of the harm of the eight-legged essay, could we abolish it?" The emperor said, "We could." K'ang continued: "Since Your Majesty already considers that it can be abolished, may I request that Your Majesty immediately issue a clear decree, which should not be sent down for discussion by the ministries. If it is sent down to be discussed by the ministries, the ministers would refuse to put it into effect." The emperor's reply again, we are told, was "Yes."

Edicts thus ended the stereotyped examinations for public office, ordered that a modern school system be set up, ordered officials to travel abroad, ordered the restructuring of the central government, abolished sinecures of many kinds and replaced the archaic but profitable military establishment with modern units. Every sector of the Chinese elite felt its privileges threatened. Soon K'ang and his young disciples felt that conservatives were working with the empress dowager to stop the reforms and began to fear a coup by units of the army under Jung-lu. K'ang now made a major miscalculation. He decided to rely on Yüan Shih-k'ai as his ally within the military. Yüan was called to court, appointed to high office and then asked to anticipate a coup by Jung-lu by moving against him first. Instead Yüan, who was close to Jung-lu, confided in him. Jung-lu sped to the palace to tell the empress dowager, who confined the emperor and then sent soldiers to arrest the reformers. K'ang and Liang managed to escape. Six of the reformers, including K'ang's brother, were executed, and K'ang himself was under the ban with a price on his head.

The fate of the reform of 1898 was affected by personality as much as it was by ideology. It was not just a matter of enlightened reformers versus obscurantist opponents. The problem was rather in the way K'ang's crash program seemed to threaten vested interests in and around the court and throughout Chinese society. As officials saw the dissolution of their bureaus and scholars faced the loss of the credentials on which they had expended a lifetime of study, it was natural for them to seek and find in K'ang's writings evidence of rashness and madness. K'ang and his disciples had gained a hearing because of what seemed an imminent partition of China. One of the first documents K'ang prepared for his emperor, in fact, described the partitions of Poland. But legitimacy through Confucian example was not enough to sway the loyalties of the contemporary elite, which was deeply involved in the congruence of livelihood, ideology and power. Although K'ang won the support of a young and enthusiastic emperor, even that meant little when the empress dowager took over from her unfortunate nephew to thwart the reformers' threat to herself and her favorites.

For K'ang Yu-wei the overthrow of the reform movement did not threaten his loyalty to the Ch'ing house. During the ten years of life that remained to Kuang-hsü, K'ang busied himself with propaganda in his behalf and with societies calling for a form of constitutional government for China. He refused to accept the Manchu abdication of 1911 as permanent, and continuing to work vainly for a restoration, he appeared briefly as a minister in a short-lived attempt staged by a warlord in 1917. K'ang's faith in Confucianism as a religion grew rather than weakened, and his attitude toward the Western example underwent a subtle change as a faint distaste crept in where there earlier had been chiefly admiration of order and progress. K'ang's writings in the first decade of the twentieth century emphasized caution as well as reform. His essays emphasized the dangers of catchword slogans of republicanism, and in a "Discourse on China's Perilous Situation Caused by the Error of Completely Following Europe and America and Abandoning the National Heritage Completely," (1913) he came down on the side of the Chinese tradition and "National Soul."

In the same years K'ang turned his thoughts to the ideal society of the future. In 1902 he completed his utopian *The Great Commonwealth.* Now, in the words of Professor K. C. Hsiao, he "de-sinified Confucius" by deifying him, and he came to universalization as an alternative to Westernization. The great commonwealth was to know neither states, nor classes, nor differences of rank or sex. K'ang worked for goals of "hedonism, humanitarianism, and egalitarianism" and saw them realized through the ends of democracy, socialism and science. His utopian world was frankly communistic, one in which the abolition of institutions like property, family and state that made for selfishness and corruption would end all need for controls or restraints. Family institutions would not only be unnecessary but illegal, with "mating agreements" made for up to one year and renewable if desired. Science, sanitation, health and industry would make life comfortable, leisure abundant and culture universal. Ironically, then, this last creative Confucian, whose desire for the monarchy made him almost a laughing stock of republican intellectuals by the time of his death in 1927, was simultaneously a critic of the most tenacious institutions of traditional society. K'ang himself believed firmly in freedom, individuality and self-expression, and the institutions he projected for his utopia trusted only to human nature to guard against excesses of formalization and regimentation. The "great community" was to leave its doors permanently open for individuals to move on to "immortality and buddhahood" and, finally, in K'ang's words, "to roam in the heavens" in a state of "transcendental freedom."

The exodus of the followers of K'ang Yu-wei from court did not mean that all reform influence was at an end. Viceroys such as Chang Chih-tung and Liu K'un-i sponsored reforms of their own, although they were more concerned with the possible results of a premature abandonment of traditional values than K'ang had been. The best expression of their views was a small book Chang Chih-tung presented to the Kuang-hsü emperor in July 1898. It was immediately ordered distributed to leading officials. *An Exhortation to Learn* was designed to counter the radicalism of K'ang Yu-wei, but it struck some of the same notes. Chang wrote that the object of his book was to make people know the shame of not being like Japan, Turkey, Siam and Cuba and to know the fear that China was headed for the fate of India, Annam, Burma, Korea, Egypt and Poland unless it changed its customs and learned that Western governmental methods were more important than Western implements. From these premises Chang went on to discuss the salvation of China by maintaining the dynasty, by conserving Confucianism and by protecting the Chinese race. He spoke next of the importance of education and urged the conversion of existing educational institutions into a modern system of state-supported education. He favored abolition of the eight-legged essay in the examinations. On the other hand, he argued, it was essential to keep the problem in perspective: "if we do not use Chinese knowledge to consolidate the foundation first and get straight in our own minds what our interests and purposes are, then the strong will become rebellious leaders and the weak will become slaves [of the foreigners]. ..." For Chang the classics remained essential. China could change its laws but not its principles and human relationships, its methods but not the Way of the Sages, its technology but not its principles. The court at Peking also continued to make moves toward reform after the empress dowager resumed her regency. But they were cautious moves. An edict of late September assured officials that reforms were to be made not for the sake of novelty but to strengthen the empire, and it went on to stress the particular importance of the abolition of official sinecures. Universities and higher schools already established were to be allowed to stand, but the establishment of lower schools should be left to the "convenience of the local inhabitants. Local officials are ordered to exercise discretion with due consideration for local conditions." A November decree, however, made it clear that institutions had to undergo change: "Laws and institutions are not bad when they are first established, but as time goes on defects accumulate making it necessary to change them in order to meet the requirements of the time. But if no attention is paid to the actual situation, a set of new defects would then be produced as new laws are enacted."

The Empress Dowager Tz'u-hsi was a woman of great shrewdness and character, Kuang-hsü, who was her nephew, had long been under her strict control. (Liang Ch'i-ch'ao wrote that in youth the emperor had been called to order by reprimands and whipping.) As a dowager, Tz'u-hsi was still the apex of the dynasty, able to command the loyalties of many of her former officials. It was not without precedent for her to assert the precedence that imperial Confucianism accorded her. "The emperor being ill," the court announcement stated, "the empress-dowager has resumed the regency." The emperor never recovered his freedom and lived a prisoner until his death in 1908. A few months after the empress dowager's coup, she selected as heir to the throne a son of Prince Tuan, one of her favorites. This choice became impolitic after the Boxer Rebellion, at which time she selected a son of Prince Chun, for whom she had earlier selected as bride a daughter of Jung-lu. Her choices were decisive at every turn. The choice for the succession did not fall on Prince Chun's son until 1908, the year in which both dowager and Kuang-hsü died.

Pu-yi, the child who then succeeded, became known to the world by the name of Henry, one he selected from a list of English royalty prepared for him by his English tutor. His rule ended while he was still in infancy, but the palace institutions went on unchanged for years thereafter. Decades later Pu-yi served the Japanese as puppet emperor of Manchuokuo and the Chinese communists as reformed pentitent. His autobiography, which appeared in the 1960s, provides a striking picture of the life of a powerless Manchu emperor, and a minor, in the twilight of the dynasty, and it sheds some light on the setting in which Kuang-hsü ended his years. Pu-yi writes that

> Whenever I think of my childhood my head fills with a yellow mist. The glazed tiles were yellow, my sedan-chair was yellow, my chair cushions were yellow, the linings of my hats and clothes were yellow, the girdle round my waist was yellow, the dishes and bowls from which I ate and drank, the padded cover of the rice-gruel saucepan, the material in which my books were wrapped, the window curtains, the bridle of my horse.... everything was yellow. This imperial colour, the so-called brilliant yellow, was used exclusively by the imperial household and made me feel from my earliest years that I was unique and had a heavenly nature different from that of everybody else.... From my infancy I was accustomed to having people kotow to me. They included old officials of the Ch'ing Dynasty and the elders of my own clan, men in the court robes of the Ch'ing Dynasty and officials of the Republic in Western dress.... Whenever I went for a stroll in the garden a procession had to be organized. In front went a eunuch from the Administrative Bureau whose function was roughly that of a motor horn: he walked twenty or thirty yards ahead of the rest of the party.... Next came two chief eunuchs advancing crabwise on either side of the path; ten paces behind them came the centre of the procession—the Empress Dowager [i.e., now, Kuang-hsü's empress, Lung Yu] or myself. If I was being carried in a chair there would be two junior eunuchs walking beside me to attend to my wants at any moment; if I was walking they would be supporting me. Next came a eunuch with a large silk canopy followed by a large group of eunuchs of whom some were empty-handed and others were holding all sorts of things: a seat, changes of clothing, umbrellas and parasols ... boxes of various kinds of cakes ... jugs of hot water and a tea service ... cases of medicine and first-aid equipment.... At the end of the procession came the eunuchs who carried commodes and chamber pots.... This motley procession of several dozen people would proceed in perfect silence and order.

Despite this panoply of royalty, the demands of filiality had precedence. Pu-yi entered the palace as the adopted son of the emperors T'ung-chih and Kuang-hsü, with the result that "all their wives became my mothers.... I addressed all of them as 'August Mother.'.... Every morning I would go to pay them my respects. A eunuch would put down a hassock covered with yellow silk for me to kneel on, and after kneeling to them for a moment I would get up and stand to one side waiting for them to make their usual remarks.... It was always the same—a few dry and stereotyped remarks; sometimes they would give me a few clay toys or something of the kind." Thus the complexities of Manchu clan relationships combined with the demands of Confucian propriety to create a setting in which the "Lord of Ten Thousand Years," as the eunuchs called the emperor, was scarcely the master of one. When the princes were weak and the matriarchal council contained a person of ability, experience, and outside contacts, especially in the army, like Tz'u-hsi, the "Lord of Ten Thousand Years" could be a virtual prisoner.

5. The Boxers

IN 1900 the concern Chinese intellectuals and officials were beginning to show for their country's ability to withstand the pressures of the West were dwarfed by a sudden outburst of xenophobic antiforeignism on the part of the masses in north China. The Manchu leaders, ready to seize upon any popular movement that seemed to hold out some hope for freedom of maneuver, decided to try to utilize the outburst by turning it against the foreigners. The movement began as resistance to the dynasty and ended in support of it, as Peking first tolerated and finally authorized its actions. The dynasty was saved by the loyalty and clear-headed action of three great statesmen who refused to heed its commands, with the result that it could return to power under the convenient fiction that the Boxers had been rebels. After the fall of Peking, the dynasty was saddled with large foreign indemnities that went, in considerable measure, to subsidize modern education. And this brought with it a modern revolution.

Secret societies combining sorcery with political opposition were as old as popular Taoism, and their suppression had always been a test of government vigilance and strength. Behind the formal, Confucian rationality and decorum of China there lay a world of popular belief, practice and association, a sphere whose tumult and color always fascinated Chinese novelists and alienated official annalists. North China was ripe for such movements at the end of the decade. It had not been laid waste in the Taiping wars, but it had felt at first hand the effects of the war against Japan and the series of imperialist grabs that followed. In 1898 and 1899 it had known floods, drought and famine. The area was the chief focus of foreign and Chinese pressure for railroad and telegraph development. Peasants saw rails replacing the traditional tracking of barges along the rivers and canals, and the hardships of livelihood seemed worse because they were associated with foreign pressure and influence.

Moreover, new tests for tolerance were at hand in the imperial court's decision, in 1899, to allow Catholic clergy magistral status. Similar opportunities extended to the Protestant British were declined. The origin of this decision was to be found in a series of antimissionary incidents that had made it possible for

Western powers to demand additional privileges or territory in settlement. Peking now sought to avoid such developments by setting up machinery for local settlement that incorporated the clergy into the local power structure. Therefore, it ordered that "In the different degrees of the ecclesiastical hierarchy, the Bishops being, in rank and dignity, the equals of Viceroys and Governors, it is expedient that they be authorized to demand to see the Viceroy and the Governor. . . . Vicar General and Archpriest are authorized to demand to see the Treasurers, Provincial Judges, and Taotais. . . . to avoid numerous diplomatic proceedings, however, the Bishop and the missionaries may equally address themselves at once to the local authorities, with whom they may negotiate and conclude the affair." But the move did not work. Protestant missionaries refused the arrangement, and so their difficulties continued to require redress at high levels. And for the Catholics, who did use the new status, temptations to overplay the role often proved irresistible.

The Boxers were distantly related to the salvationist White Lotus Society of eighteenth-century Buddhism. Their ritual included sorcery, calisthenics and invocation of supernatural powers that granted them immunity from harm or wound. There was nothing uniquely anti-Christian, or even antiforeign, about this, except the setting and combination of elements. Movements of protest in mid-twentieth–century Africa have often included most of the elements that came together in the Boxer movement. What was unusual about the movement was its timing and its appeal for the conservatives in power in Peking. The Boxers came just at a juncture of defensive nationalism in which the government felt inclined to heed popular resistance to further grants to outsiders. In 1899 an Italian request for a bay and base had been flatly turned down, and after this success the court encouraged its viceroys to resist further demands. Its language became very firm and was often reminiscent of the orders telling feudal lords in Tokugawa Japan to fire "without thinking twice." Thus one edict warned, "Never should the word 'peace' fall from the mouths of our high officials, nor should they harbor it for a moment in their breasts. With such a country as ours, with her vast area, stretching out for several tens of thousands of *li,* her immense natural resources and her hundreds of millions of inhabitants, if all would prove their loyalty to their Emperor and love of their country, what indeed is there to fear from any strong invader? Let us not think of making peace, nor rely solely upon diplomatic maneuvers." These brave words were accompanied by efforts to rebuild some of the military strength that had been lost in the war with Japan.

Like most secret society movements, the Boxers began as an antidynastic group. They focused on hatred of the foreigners and overthrow of the Manchus. Authorities naturally saw them as dangerous, and for a time the movement was carefully watched. There is no doubt that it would have been well within the power of the authorities to repress the movement. In Shantung, where German leases for railroad and ore development had alarmed many people, the Boxers first scored some successes, but they were crushed when Yü-hsien was replaced by Yüan Shih-k'ai as governor in December 1899. Yüan instituted a vigorous program of mutual responsibility in local control that made it impossible for the Boxers to operate under his rule. Yü-hsien, on the other hand, had encouraged the Boxer attacks on missions and Christians, and in his next post, that of governor of Shansi, his tolerance of Boxer activities changed to approval and direction of the execution of forty-six missionaries. More generally, it seems clear that many officials interpreted the empress dowager's resumption of the regency to mean opposition against all steps toward modernization. This, coupled with her endorsement of the stern line against the outside powers, may well have helped to produce official favor for Boxer activities in ways she did not immediately realize or approve. One additional element concerned the parochial, Manchu interests of the Peking government. The reformers of 1898 had been overwhelmingly Chinese, and the victims of their plans for administrative rationalization would have included a disproportionately large number of nonproductive Manchus. The defeat of the reformers had given the Manchus another chance, and the empress dowager's regime was dominated by imperial princes and other high-ranking Manchus. Jung Lu and Yü-hsien were Manchus. Thus the historian Fang Chao-ying discerns "two movements, both aiming at the expulsion of the foreigners and foreign influence"; one was the Boxers, and the other "arose among the nobles in Peking." The latter, centered "among the uneducated nobles and superstitious courtiers," he concludes, is properly described as "led by the Empress Dowager." There is no question that her ultimate approval was crucial to the court's appraisal of the Boxers.

There were a number of steps toward official utilization and approval. One was a decision late in 1898 to set up local militia units for the maintenance of order. It was a simple measure to propose, or overlook, the merging of these with Boxer units, thereby lending the dignity of a semiofficial body to the dissemination of Boxer diatribes against Christians and foreigners. Undoubtedly the court's stand was also affected by the behavior and tone adopted by the foreign representatives in Peking, who had become convinced of the importance of maintaining a "high posture" when dealing with China and felt that any weakening of their stand would encourage antiforeign outrages. For several years after 1895, antiforeign activity tended to be small in scale, usually confined to agitation rather than violence. Frequently local gentry and officials encouraged or at least permitted the distribution of tracts calling down heaven's punishment on native Christians and their foreign mentors. Then, during 1898 and 1899, the incidents became a movement. Boxer organizations began to recruit followers with the specific goal of fighting Christian converts. In the spring of 1899, with the appointment of Yü-hsien as governor of Shantung, the movement changed its slogans to "Uphold the Ch'ing, exterminate the foreigners." As the Boxers became supporters of the dynasty and the foreign powers more insistent in their demands, the dynasty's choice between them became more difficult.

The court vacillated. Officials were told to control the Boxers but not to hurt them. A "pacification mission" was sent to the Boxers early in June 1900 led by Kang-i, a man who encouraged the Boxers and became their strongest sponsor in court discussions. Then on 10 June the foreign representatives, alarmed by the progress of the movement and indignant because of their inability to secure protection for Christians and obtain satisfaction for earlier murders, called in the allied troops that were available on the China coast. The court now ordered the expedition resisted. It was a session in which it was safer to be quiet than to resist and in which the zealots and the ignorant spoke. One participant has written,

> Suddenly at noon of the sixteenth [of June 1900], the princes, high officials and heads of the six ministries and the nine bureaus were summoned by the empress to a meeting in the eastern chamber of the I-lüan Palace. There more than a hundred officials participated and the room was filled with kneelers while the latecomers knelt outside the door.... The emperor was very serious, and he first blamed the officials for their failure in suppressing the rioters. A reader of the Hanlin Academy ... moved forward on his knees and said, "Your servant has just seen Tung Fu-hsiang, who wishes to receive orders to drive away the [Boxer] rioters." He had not finished his sentence before Prince Tuan raised his big thumb and interrupted in a sharp voice, "Well! This is the best way to disappoint the people!" Liu ... was so frightened that he could not finish his speech.... The director of the court of sacrificial worship, Yüan Ch'ang, said loudly, "The minister Yüan Ch'ang also has something to report." The emperor ordered him to come to the front. He then reported in detail that the Boxers were really rebellious and unreliable people and that even if they possessed magic power, this power had never been able to achieve a success from ancient to modern times. The empress dowager interrupted, "Magic power may be unreliable; but are the patriotic minds of the people also undependable?"

Here we have in brief outline the makings of a perfectly believable situation: honest but timorous officials, loud-mouthed braggarts, and an empress who finds it convenient to let the voice of the mob become, in Confucian parlance, the voice of the people and consequently that of heaven.

Whatever doubt remained was eliminated by mid-June. The European forces took the Taku forts, but they were too few to force their way to Peking. Court conservatives persuaded the empress that the foreigners had demanded she step down in favor of the Kuang-hsü emperor. Three days later the siege of the Peking legations began, not to be broken until new and larger foreign armies broke into Peking on 14 August. The following day the court fled to Sian. It did not return to Peking until 7 January 1902. The Boxer Rebellion had been confined to a few provinces. It received the support of only some officials and the positive opposition of many. Within Peking Jung-lu himself, chairman of the Board of War, held back on the use of artillery and other force against which the legations could not have hoped to stand. Clearly he hoped that the ministers would accept his safe-conduct for a march to the sea and thereafter realized that the foreigners would soon be calling the tune. But whether or not he could have made his safe-conduct good for the ministers, their departure would have meant the slaughter of at least six thousand Chinese Christians who had taken refuge in the embassies.

The conduct of the most powerful of the governors and governors general was particularly striking. Yüan Shih-k'ai turned a deaf ear to orders for support for the war against the foreigners, and although he never approached open insubordination, he used every delaying tactic available to him, while he kept firm control of events within Shantung. Li Hung-chang, whose warnings from Canton went unheeded in Peking, joined with the great Yangtze viceroys Chang Chih-tung and Liu K'un-i to assure the foreigners that the entire matter represented a loss of control by the empress and not an expression of her will, so that then and later the rising could be considered a rebellion instead of an antiforeign war. Chang Chih-tung himself engaged in informal diplomacy with highly placed Japanese and did his best to see that Japan might in some measure balance the other powers' insistence on punishment for China. These statesmen provided the bridge over which Western powers could retreat to renew their dealings with the Manchu dynasty. It had in fact become essential to them, for no other form of organization was in sight and the alternative of division was unpalatable and unworkable. By their position and performance Liu, Chang and Yüan guaranteed themselves an important role in the determination of policy in the years after the Boxer movement came to an end. Li Hung-chang, who negotiated the final protocol with the powers, died in 1901.

The protocol that was signed 7 September 1901 in Peking contained the following provisions: China would apologize for the victims of Boxer outbreaks with monuments in international cemeteries and visits to Japan and Germany by high officials to atone for the murders of Japanese Legation Chancellor Sugiyama and the German minister, Baron von Ketteler. China accepted restrictions on its import of arms; it agreed to raze the forts at Taku in order not to impede communications between Peking and the sea; it agreed that the legation quarters would be under foreign control and without rights of residence for Chinese; and it agreed to maintain key connection points between Tientsin and Peking in foreign hands, to publish edicts forbidding membership in antiforeign societies, and to ban civil service examinations in cities where foreigners had been killed. China agreed to punishments for ten high officials and over one hundred others, and it promised to pay in gold an indemnity of 450 million *taels* over a period of forty years. This constituted a heavy, almost a crushing, burden of debt and humiliation for the Middle Country. At the capital there was soon new evidence of foreign superiority in the form of expiatory statues and an enlarged and fortified legations quarter. (It was in these quarters that foreign military officers— George Marshall, Joseph Stilwell, Ishiwara Kanji and Itagaki Seishirō among others—gained their familiarity with China. These same statues and barracks were among the first objects of Chinese attention after the capital fell to Mao Tse-tung's armies in 1949.) The new indemnities were set by the powers in accordance with claims submited by their nationals ("Representatives shall make an approximate estimate of their amount after examination of the claims preferred by persons under their protection, and shall claim the total sum, without giving either details or explanation," as the protocol put it), and they added up to a heavy burden. Throughout Chinese society a new awareness of the desperate need for modernization of intellect and institutions now grew rapidly. And the frequent allocation of the indemnity funds to educational purposes contributed importantly to the diffusion of this awareness.

6. Conclusion

AS AN ALLIED ARMY of twenty thousand troops neared Peking in August 1900, there were many who speculated on the imminent abolition of the Manchu dynasty and the breakup of Imperial China. Closer examination of the difficulties involved in the assembling of that small army and of the jealousies it aroused, however, suggests some important factors in the survival of the dynasty and the country. No agreement was possible among the competing powers. Few were fully satisfied with what they had gained, but most were agreed that division might create greater dangers than a return to the pre-Boxer situation. Even Count Witte, Russia's leading Asian planner, noted that "premature division of China by the Powers concerned would deprive Russia of China's most desirable provinces." In the event, the Russians came closest to choosing and holding their share in Manchuria, but the negotiations that followed proved Count Witte right. There was no real alternative to the dynasty.

A second reason, and perhaps a more important one, lay with the new agility and awareness of Chinese officials. A recent study of their response to the German presence in Shantung shows them much more sensitive to issues of sovereignty, much more adept at using the arguments and provisions of international law against those who had introduced those techniques to China and, consequently, able to hold European gains to the minimum. The Chinese diplomats of that era now seem agile and resourceful losers, skillful in the use of the few weapons that were available to them to balance, prod, worry and reassure the Western diplomats with whom they had to work. The new weapons of boycott skillfully hurt the trading nations in the areas ostensibly most important to them. Also, as will be seen, the position of Chinese diplomats was immeasurably strengthened by the rise of an intense and emotional nationalism along the China coast.

There were also major trading powers that worked hard to maintain the existing state of affairs in China and strove to ward off a partition. Great Britain and the United States had comparable aims and cooperated in measures it was hoped would slow the process of division. As the allied armies neared Peking the United States made known its hopes for an "Open Door." The phrase had first been used in notes sent to the powers in September 1899 by Secretary of State John Hay. Hay acted after consultation with the British, who shared his preference for the commercial equality built into the treaty-port system (through the most-favored–nation clause), and who knew that they could survive any commercial challenge but feared political controls that could shut a market. Hay's notes asked the powers not to interfere with treaty ports or vested interests within their spheres, to agree that duties should continue to be collected by the Chinese government as theretofore and to refrain from claiming preferential shipping or freight charges within their zones. Although the response to the first notes was not uniformly encouraging, Hay announced unanimous acceptance. Then, in July 1900, as the army neared Peking, Hay sent a second note, adding the American hope that the settlement would preserve China's territorial and administrative entity, "protect all rights guaranteed to friendly powers by treaty and international law, and safeguard for the world the principle of equal and impartial trade with all parts of the Chinese Empire."

The Open Door notes did not prevent the breakup of China, but they helped illustrate some forces that operated against that breakup. Within less than two decades they had also assumed a substantive importance as a basic tenet of American policy and belief and, thus, came to take on a meaning and life of their own.

CHAPTER 3

Imperial Japan

At the time of the Sino-Japanese War, most Japanese saw their struggle with China as a confrontation of civilization with backwardness, and they found the results convincing proof of their superior institutions and morality. When war broke out, the publisher and educator Fukuzawa Yukichi announced in a lead editorial that "We intend only to develop world civilization and to defeat those who obstruct it . . . this is not a war between people and people and country and country, but a kind of religious war." The Christian leader Uchimura Kanzō agreed, arguing that since Japan's purposes were unselfish and pure, it was reasonable to describe Japan's as a "righteous" war. As he put it, "Japan's victory shall mean free government, free religion, free education, and free commerce for 600,000,000 souls that live on this side of the globe." And for the journalist Tokutomi Sohō, restless after a quarter century of Japanese weakness before the West, the war meant that "the true nature of our country, our national character, will emerge like the sun breaking through a dense fog." The success of Japan's modern institutions had caused a euphoric confidence. The historian's first problem is the analysis of possible reasons for the success of the institutions.

1. Tokugawa Japan and Modernization

MANY NINETEENTH-CENTURY OBSERVERS assumed that Japan would find it much more difficult to modernize than China. The country seemed less united than Imperial China. Its society was more stratified and less mobile. Its bureaucratic system and experience were less apparent, and they seemed less modern. Given a Western threat comparable to that experienced by China, there seemed reason to expect Japan to come apart instead of growing in strength and unity. Yet the Sino-Japanese War proved that Japan, and not China, had made the more successful transition.

Tokugawa Japan was at first glance a series of garrison states under the arbitrary rule of an hereditary class of sword-carrying samurai who permitted the lower orders no rights and little hope. The country was divided into petty principalities, and it bore little resemblance to a modern nation-state. And yet, as recent studies have shown, the adjustment to the changes consequent to urbanization and central administration made Japanese society capable of rapid response to new challenges and stimuli.

The disunity inherent in Tokugawa institutions was real enough. The shogun, who occupied the apex of a hierarchy of military rulers, held lands producing about one-quarter of the total agricultural production. His domains were concentrated in the strategic Tokyo and Osaka plains and included the communication routes between them to facilitate his domination of the national economy. Much of his land was parceled out to family retainers. Those who held lands producing more than ten thousand units (*koku,* about five bushels) of rice annually were rated as lords, or daimyo, and these again were divided and arranged by order of relationship, loyalty and size. In all there were about 275 daimyo realms. Only the largest of these were natural units, often provincewide in size; many were further subdivided among lesser vassals and often substantially autonomous in administration.

But local autonomy was weakened by military and ceremonial arrangements that made for shogunal security. All feudal lords were required to take up residence at Edo, as modern Tokyo was called, in alternate years. The lords' families and heirs were required to remain at Edo as hostages during their absences in their fiefs. As a result the top ranks of the feudal class became largely separated from the domains and almost entirely Edo-centered. The shogun's capital, already the seat of councils for the administration of his own lands, became the focus of the politics and ambition of every fief in Japan. It also became the economic and cultural center of Japan. A second urban center at Osaka emerged as an economic entrepot at which daimyo marketed their agricultural surplus in order to obtain the money they required for travel, residence and support during their residence at Edo. Edo was able to dominate its vassals. In the seventeenth century the earlier shoguns rearranged their vassals' territories at will, though they left them considerable autonomy in administration. In the eighteenth century the shogunate felt able to issue directives on how to handle peasant rebellions to all daimyo, and by the end of the century it was prepared with instructions for educational orthodoxy as well. Its reasons for doing so were clear; communications and commerce had knit the fiefs into a country, so that disorder in any part affected the whole.

These national trends had been preceded by regional integration in all parts of Japan. The castle towns that dotted the coastal communication lines had become collecting points for the lower ranking feudality in each fief. Subfiefs had gradually been replaced by larger units of administration. The samurai changed from land owners to professional administrators. Everywhere in Japan local economies came to center on the towns and their needs. Initially focused upon the ruling class's needs for goods, services and luxuries, the castle towns now became the regional centers of agricultural and artisan production and distribution. The development of urban centers in Tokugawa Japan had few parallels in the premodern world up to that time, and recent studies by Gilbert Rozman stress the importance of this for later changes in Japanese society.

There was also a sense in which local autonomy of administration permitted useful preparation for the multistate world of the nineteenth century. Feudal lords anxious to increase their income in order to meet their expenses tried many measures: they encouraged the development of new strains of seeds and new agricultural technology, and they encouraged and often forced the cultivation of cash crops. They also did their best to develop the exploitation of raw materials, whether mineral or forest products. There were systems of sustained-yield forestry, encouragement of local specialities like paper-making, cane and cotton production. These measures operated to limit and sometimes challenge the Tokugawa control of market activities, and they also operated to prepare many for the future through commercial transactions of considerable complexity. In many domains regulations controlled "foreign" (extraprovince) traders and activities, in order to protect and increase the "national" (provincial) revenue. In the nineteenth century comparable measures would be instituted on a national scale. By then Japanese producers and traders were accustomed to exhortation and direction from their political leaders and prepared for arguments which cited the well-being of the political unit as justification for whatever sacrifice had to be made. The Japanese terms for province and country were the same, and late nineteenth-century campaigns for economic growth could use unchanged the slogans used by daimyo a few decades earlier.

To nineteenth-century observers, the social structure of Japan seemed as unsuited to the needs of a modern state as its fragmented political structure. The nationally administered civil service examinations of Imperial China, with their mystique of upward mobility in an egalitarian society, seemed much closer to the needs of a modern country than Japan's hereditary ranks. Chinese commoners had surnames, and they were not the objects of discrimination and intimidation by a sword-bearing elite, while Tokugawa society was still arranged in the hierarchial order that had been set at the end of the sixteenth century. Samurai, farmers, artisans and merchants made up a hereditary group of descending honor and esteem. Lower groups of outcastes (*eta*) and "nonhuman" (*hinin*) stood outside the principal divisions altogether. Distinctions of clothing, housing and privilege separated the two-sworded, top-knotted samurai with his haughty assertions of superiority from the millions of agriculturalists who had neither family names nor swords and whose taxes supported the warriors.

The samurai class was subdivided into at least ten military ranks. Although some recruitment took place for the lower ranks, the upper grades were difficult to penetrate. Including dependents, samurai numbered around two million, comprising perhaps 6 percent of Japan's thirty million people. Throughout society, hereditary rank and status made the family the continuing entity. It was more important than its members, and its continuity was essential. A pattern of adoption became common to guarantee competent succession. Adoption weakened the rigors of heredity, but although it was sometimes utilized by wealthy commoners to secure rank for their sons, it was more typically arranged between families of comparable status and made for effectiveness and continuity more than it did for upward mobility.

Yet Tokugawa society was less rigid than it seemed, and during the seventeenth and eighteenth centuries it experienced important changes. With no wars to fight, the samurai collected in the castle towns, where they became professional administrators competing for bureaucratic posts. Enfeoffed retainers became stipended functionaries, their lands administered by central fief authorities. Those in the senior ranks were few in number and they held the posts of honor. Effective administrative responsibility tended to be found in the hands of men of middle rank, who were much more numerous. They competed sharply, and the prize of office went to those with ability. Education became essential for office; in early Tokugawa times most samurai were illiterate, but by 1700 this was no longer the case. The classics of China, with their ideology of state service, became the daily fare of the upper classes and, in simplified form, their inferiors as well.

As power and office were the prerogatives of the samurai class, they were conditioned to respond to challenges of service and duty. They were taught that their security of place and income placed them under particular obligation. To an unusual degree among elites, they were also institutionally uncommitted. They were separated from their fiefs, they lived in castle towns and cities, and they had little personal stake in the existing structure of their economy. Indeed, they were often forbidden to travel in the countryside, lest they succumb to temptations of status and cause trouble for their inferiors there. Their counterparts, the Chinese gentry, retained strong roots and contacts in the rural locales. Their attitude toward office was also full of ambiguity between private interest and public demands. Office, in the Chinese system, could be a burden as often as an honor; its lures could corrupt one's values, and its risks and visibility endangered one's patrimony. The honest man accepted office reluctantly and retired early. But for the samurai, public service was everything. Every claim of duty, honor and gratitude bound him to serve the lord who supported him; rustication and retirement had far less attraction. Unencumbered by personal holdings in land and residing in a "company" house appropriate to his rank and formation, the samurai was free and uncommitted, trained and willing to lead in any system, confident of his own capacities and role within it.

Recent studies have shown that the lower orders of Tokugawa society were also remarkable for their ambition and achievement. Although merchants and farmers were restricted to their status, they too developed an ideology that stressed the importance of their roles and called for committed service and performance within them. Seen comparatively, it was probably less important that they were looked down on by their betters than that they learned to respect themselves. There were multiple hierarchies throughout Japanese society, and the "commoners" were by no means a uniformly oppressed and impoverished mass. Merchants and landowners, with their sons, servants and apprentices, matched the pride of establishment and continuity of their samurai superiors. The countryside was dominated by village headmen allied with leading farmers, and "merchants" ranged from powerful concessionaires, who managed and controlled the daimyo's fiscal needs in an increasingly complex economy, to petty hucksters who trudged from hamlet to hamlet for market days with the simple items of peasant need strapped to their backs. Throughout society apprentice-master, student-teacher, and tenant-landlord relationships were usually defined in the family terms also used to describe the bond between retainer and warrior.

The intellectual setting of Tokugawa days also provided significant preparation for the Japanese response to the West in the nineteenth century. Although the shogunate designated the neo-Confucian orthodoxy of China as the official ideology in 1790 and forbade other interpretations in its own academies, the Tokugawa intellectual scene was extremely diverse. Other schools of Confucian learning never died out, although their spokesmen lost official preferment. Works and teachings lost in China during Manchu times survived in Japan to influence Chinese students who came later. It also seems clear that the impress of even orthodox Confucian teaching in Tokugawa Japan differed from its effect in China. In China the official teaching served to confer legitimacy on a functioning political order. Political philosophy and institutional structure reinforced each other, and orthodoxy was more confining. The approved teachings through the civil service examinations provided the only authorized path for social and official achievement. In Japan, however, Confucian teachings of loyalty did more than support shogun and daimyo; they also pointed to the existence of a revered but powerless emperor in Kyoto. Confucian historical scholarship freshened recollections of a time when emperor, and not shogun, had ruled. The thrust of the Confucian message was more complex in the Japanese setting. Furthermore, Japanese Confucianists, however orthodox, were also conscious that they studied *kangaku,* Chinese learning. For many their emphasis on China had the effect of reviving consciousness of the Japanese identity, whether in apology (as when one writer referred to himself as an "Eastern barbarian") or in pride (that, for instance, the Japanese imperial family had never been overthrown by revolution).

In the eighteenth century, Japanese national consciousness was heightened by the spread of a new, "national" learning known as *kokugaku*. Confucian scholarly emphasis on history and philology had the unexpected result of contributing to a revival of interest in Japanese history and antiquity. These studies inevitably focused on the national cult, and the "Way of the Gods" (Shinto), with its emphasis on the divine origins of the Japanese islands and ruling family, made of *kokugaku* a religious movement as well. By the end of the century, national scholars were prepared to dispute the superiority of Chinese learning and morality, and they were insisting that Japan's had been a more pure and perfect order before the introduction of Confucian morality. The battle of books and pamphlets that resulted has sometimes been compared with the romantic movement in eighteenth-century Germany. In both cases there were self-conscious efforts to throw off the incubus of imported, rationalist cultures. In Japan, however, the combination of these traditions became more important than the conflict between them, and by late Tokugawa days the principal schools of thought represented a blend of Chinese and national learning. It was not in any necessary sense subversive of Tokugawa rule, but its focus on emperor and imperial tradition contained important elements of response to future challenges. When the crisis of the Western impact struck the Tokugawa world, the way had been prepared for challenge to that world in the name of the Japanese tradition. That tradition, in turn, so long unrealized in practice, was sufficiently unstructured to permit the greatest flexibility in application. It was the Kyoto emperor who was the beneficiary of the new teachings of divinity and loyalty. Furthermore, the rise of a new and abstract notion of loyalty to him developed after a time of growing separation between feudal lords and their retainers. Long preoccupied by ritual in their Edo and castle residences, the lords had gradually become symbols of power rather than personal leaders. As they became more remote, the way was opened for devotion to a cause even more remote and a loyalty even more abstract.

There were also interesting efforts to learn about the West in Tokugawa years. A school of thought concerned with Western learning, *rangaku*, later *yōgaku* (Dutch, or "Western" learning), developed between 1750 and 1850. Tokugawa Japan closed its doors to all Westerners except a small group of Dutch traders who maintained a lonely outpost of the Netherlands East India Company at Nagasaki. The Dutch, like the daimyo, made regular progressions to the shogun's castle at Edo, and through them the Japanese gradually became aware of the advances that had taken place in Western science, medicine and military technology. This awareness became important in the last quarter of the eighteenth century. It was a time that brought word of Russia's eastward expansion to the islands to the north. From Nagasaki the knowledge of the Napoleonic wars also entered Japan. By the early nineteenth century the shogunate and many of the great fiefs had subsidized translation bureaus in which they tried to avail themselves of Western knowledge. Individual scholars began to see in Western learning an exciting and important avenue to practical problems neglected in their own tradition. Thus the materials for basic revision of Japan's traditional world view were at hand by the time the crisis of the West arrived.

Perhaps the most important point to be made about the intellectual and educational aspects of Tokugawa Japan concerns its amount, for the diffusion of these concerns throughout Japanese society tells a good deal about its vitality and mobility. The Confucian schools were, on the whole, for sons of the samurai elite, and each petty court maintained its official Confucian scholars. But "national" and "Dutch" learning were not at all the preserve of samurai and tended as often to attract men for whom official careers were closed. The seventeenth-century schools were still chiefly for the elite, but throughout Tokugawa years the samurai schools rose steadily in number. Eighty percent were set up in the last century of Tokugawa rule. More interesting still, thousands of parish schools and private academies developed in all parts of the country as the rudiments of literacy became necessary for more and more commoners. Recent studies estimate that by the end of the Tokugawa period male literacy stood betwen 40 percent and 50 percent throughout Japanese society. This suggests that the rush to the government schools in Meiji Japan was a continuation and centralization of trends already present. It also means that a modernizing government could inform and direct its people through the printed word and that alarm about the West and information about countermeasures could spread rapidly. Furthermore, it suggests a society with urban centers in which the stage and printed book could spread values of loyalty and duty, until samurai values were diffused far beyond the elite.

As this account suggests, Tokugawa Japan had changed dramatically in numerous aspects of economic, social and intellectual life during the eighteenth and early nineteenth century. Many of these changes provided important momentum toward the transitions that modernization would require of Japan. But it would be a serious oversimplification to conclude from this that Tokugawa Japan was in any sense "modern," that its major institutional features were more "modern" than those of China, or that, as some have suggested, there was a link between feudalism and modernization. It would be more accurate to emphasize that changes during the Tokugawa years made Japan less "feudal" than it had been in the early seventeenth century and that commerce, education and security concerns had knit together what began as centrifugal forces. Even so, the form of Tokugawa political institutions had not undergone change. Shogun and daimyo, generals and commanders, continued to monopolize prestige and power as their ancestors had. It was this anomaly of a petrification in the political order despite the changes throughout society that made many Japanese, and especially ambitious young samurai of middle rank, impatient with their life and that made Meiji-period Japanese recollect the society of their youth as one of torpor and frustration. It was because Tokugawa institutions were so inappropriate to modern needs that they were so quickly thrown off when the Western challenge came. And that political overthrow opened up a range of alternatives of vital significance for the development of modern Japan.

2. Opening and Overthrow

CHINA AND JAPAN faced the same challenge from the West in the nineteenth century. But there were elements of difference, and these were probably of considerable importance and advantage to the Japanese. Tokugawa Japan operated in a framework of total isolation, one that decreed death for Japanese who returned from abroad and that forbade the construction of ships capable of more than coastal runs. Fear of foreign incursions heightened this uneasiness; an order of 1825 ordered that foreign ships be bombarded when within range, "without a second thought." The appearance of Perry's ships in this setting of total isolation, and his arrival at the commercial and political center of the empire, constituted a challenge immediately recognizable as a watershed of Tokugawa history.

Further, the information that the Japanese had collected about Western technological advances, and their knowledge of Russian and British expansion, helped them to establish the significance of the Western approaches to Japan. The Chinese could, of course, have had as good or better avenues to intelligence about the West through the Canton trade. But Canton was far from Peking, and there was no tradition of public and private concern with Western knowledge comparable to Japan's schools of Dutch learning. As the strategic importance of Dutch study increased, it had also provided an avenue for advancement and prominence for ambitious youths who would have found themselves blocked by the more structured establishment of Confucian orthodoxy. Fukuzawa Yukichi found release for his ambition in the private academy of a *rangaku* pioneer in Osaka, and by 1860 he could secure appointment to the first Japanese embassy to the West. Tokutomi Sohō, more than a decade later, had his family and authorities select a similar course for him when his domain tried to catch up with its more successful competitors.

In the third place, it was significant that the West came to China first. The news of the Opium War caused great consternation in Japan. Dutch study had prepared some for a proper evaluation of the West, but those fully informed through Dutch channels were still few in number. The Chinese defeat, on the other hand, jarred the orthodox and the conservative to the dangers that faced Confucian civilization. When news came in from China, in Chinese, it was available to all who could read. Indeed, some of the publications produced by commentators in China stirred greater interest and alarm in Japan than they did among the Chinese audience for which they were prepared. Writing to subordinates about the news from China, the shogunal counselor Mizuno Tadakuni summed up its significance in these words: "This concerns a foreign country, but I think that it should provide a good warning for us."

The Japanese sense of danger was acute; in fact, it was considerably in excess of what the perils warranted. There was enough foreign pressure to alarm and to goad but not enough to divert or abort the course of Japanese response. The Westerners never thought of Japan as the primary goal of their activities in East Asia. For America, Japan was a way station on the Great Circle route to China and a port of call for whaling ships. The main chance for trade and riches was thought to lie in China, and the British were more than willing to leave the opening of Japan to the Americans. The years during which Japan was opened to intercourse with the West were years of peak disorder on the mainland; it was there that the imperialist story was played out, so that China's misfortune served Japanese advantage.

None of this means that Japan's "opening" was less traumatic than China's. It may well have been more so, in view of Japan's insularity, nationalism and alarm. If the Chinese leaders could not take the West seriously for some time, the Japanese magnified the danger immediately. And those dangers were real enough, for Japan's feudal traditions and hotheaded warriors created an atmosphere charged with the electric tension of provocation. Yet even that feudal division served some purpose in the 1860s, for the autonomy of important principalities permitted them some degree of experimentation with opposition without dragging the whole country along in their wake. Two great fiefs in the southwest, Satsuma and Chōshū, tried to withstand Western demands and retribution and brought on themselves sharp reprisals by Western countries that helped to convince other Japanese of the futility of obscurantist resistance. The young samurai educated by these disasters went on to seize the leadership first of their fiefs and then their country.

The Japanese response to the request that Commodore Perry brought for a beginning of formal treaty relationships in 1853 went through several stages. It is useful to summarize them briefly because of the way they illustrate pressure points in the Tokugawa system. Moreover, the events connected with Japan's opening also provided the heroes, villains and issues for much of Japan's twentieth-century history.

These events are important because the first reaction to the threat from the West was one of individuals who awoke to a sense of danger and opportunity. As Perry's ships neared land, armed units of all the fiefs were called to their guard stations, and the thought of war with the foreigner was congenial to young hotheads who had known no real violence for generations. "I hear there may be a foreign war," a young man named Sakamoto Ryōma wrote his father, "you may be sure I will not return without having cut off a foreign head." For hundreds, and then thousands, of young men there was suddenly a new reason for being a samurai and for perfecting a command of swordsmanship; regional and national tournaments and excited discussions in castle towns and shogun's capital signaled a change in the political climate. No policy and no decision, regional or national, could please all these newly conscious activists, and some governmental responses were sure to goad them into action. The best of them became known to history as *shishi*, "men of high purpose," samurai who chose the higher duty when confronted with apparent contradictions between the constraints of conventional discipline and the demands of the larger challenge.

Perry's arrival served to activate highly placed and responsible officials as well as young hotheads. The first indication of the difficulties that lay ahead came from circles closest to the shogunate. They were brought on by the government, which requested the advice of its vassals because it was aware of its military weakness. In the conflict of differing suggestions that came in, the government could not hope to satisfy everyone. The late 1850s found the shogunate under vigorous criticism from one of its powerful related houses, the domain of Mito, whose lord had sponsored a line of Confucian scholars whose mixture of Confucian and emperor-oriented loyalty became the most persuasive statement of late Tokugawa ideology. Issues surrounding the government's response to the requests of Perry and, especially, Townsend Harris for a commercial treaty became entangled with issues of Tokugawa internal policy, including the question of successor to a shogun who had died. The Mito daimyo lined up support for his program of a strong response to the outside world among other lords and, significantly, went on to recruit support at the imperial court in Kyoto. Thus, major vassals and the court itself had been activated.

The shogunate's response to this was a vigorous reaffirmation of its prerogatives in selection of a successor, the implementation of the decision to grant Townsend Harris his treaty and punishment of the dissident feudal lords. The vigor with which these policies were carried out inflamed the opposition, particularly the vassals of the lords who had been punished. Their criticism now began to bring into question the legitimacy of the shogun's pretensions to protect the emperor when, in fact, by opening the ports to foreigners, he had apparently endangered all that was Japanese. Their anger led to the assassination of the shogunate's first minister in 1860.

By now the ports had been opened, and an embassy dispatched to the West to exchange formal ratification. Traditionalists were in accord with the shogunal initiative but not with its direction; major vassals were critical of assertions of shogunal discretion that seemed to ignore the court and might bring on an even more authoritarian expression of shogunal supremacy. Court nobles willing to work with any of these groups were beginning to surface. Agitation among young samurai who knew little of foreign policy but sensed the possibilities for action made it difficult for their superiors to maintain an even course in these turbulent political waters.

In the early and mid-1860s, national politics was dominated by a struggle for ascendancy between two of the great baronies of the southwest, Satsuma and Chōshū. They vied with proposals for readjustment of the political system which sought to increase the role of the imperial court and of the outside feudatories.

Ostensibly their suggestions were designed to produce a broader consensus of support for foreign policy initiatives, but in fact they also contained increasing requirements for a share in the direction of national policies. While the feudal lords were in disagreement as to what should be done, so were their retainers. Satsuma, Tosa and, especially, Chōshū domestic politics were subject to sharp turns that resulted from conflicting ideological and practical positions on foreign policy. "Radical" acts of antiforeignism brought on the shellings of Kagoshima (in Satsuma) and Shimonoseki (in Chōshū) by Western ships in 1863 and 1864, while "conservatives" preferred the safer course of acceptance of shogunal leadership.

Tokugawa rule came to an end in 1867. In Satsuma, Chōshū and Tosa, radical antiforeignism had gradually changed to a political antiforeignism in which the slogans of *sonnō jōi* (Revere the emperor! Drive out the barbarians!) came increasingly to be used as tactics against a shogunate that could not help itself. Satsuma and Chōshū, with the mediation of Tosa, resolved old jealousies and concluded an alliance. Their forces, some of them armed with imported weapons, were led by spirited young men whose verve and confidence were in contrast to the divided counsels that characterized the Tokugawa houses. Yet the shogunate at the last had also come under able direction. The last shogun, Keiki, was convinced of the need for more effective expression of national unity in the face of the West. He accepted the proposal of Tosa, one worked out by Sakamoto Ryōma, under which he was to resign his powers to take on a role in a new conciliar structure. To his surprise, he was instead outmaneuvered by a group of court, Satsuma and Chōshū leaders who demanded that he surrender his lands as well as his titles. A short and badly coordinated resistance found his vassals defeated by the new "imperial" army of Satsuma, Chōshū, and Tosa. By the fall of 1868 these armies had taken most of Japan, and in the early summer of 1869 the last Tokugawa naval units surrendered on Hokkaido.

The Tokugawa thus fell a mere eight years after the opening of the ports to foreign trade in 1859. The decisions required by the Western challenge had revealed the inadequacies of its institutional structure, and the Western presence had accelerated their destruction. The presence of foreigners had speeded the pace and intensity of a political dialogue that might have required generations to mature without this factor. Weapons for the armies of Satsuma, Chōshū and Tosa came into the port of Nagasaki. Old steamers from the China trade were sold to the same lords, their capacity to move their troops along the coasts increasing accordingly. Other vessels took small but important groups of samurai to Shanghai, where they learned at first hand of the power of the West and the humiliation of China. Still others went on to the West, where they learned of the nature of the modern world's nation-states and became convinced that basic reforms would be necessary to preserve Japan's independence.

Meanwhile the Harris treaty, together with those that followed, reproduced for Japan most of the features of treaty-port imperialism in China. It is natural that young warriors in Japan feared what lay ahead. Nagasaki, Kobe, Osaka,

Yokohama, Niigata and Hakodate were treaty ports; they developed zones of foreign residence and business within which extraterritoriality prevailed. Uniform tariff limitations were watched over by foreign consuls, who doubled as judges. The most-favored–nation clause operated to extend to all countries the benefits contained in the fine print of each clause won by the most recent member of the foreign club. Japanese did not regain control over their own tariffs until 1911, and most features of the system endured until the treaties of 1894. But there were also differences from the Chinese treaty-port system. There were never concessions in Japan, as in Shanghai. In China, Canton and even Shanghai were some distance from the center of national political authority. But in Japan the centralized nature of economic and political activity made the peripheral ports like Nagasaki, Niigata and Hakodate unimportant except (at Nagasaki) as avenues for the import of weapons by wealthy baronies. Yokohama, a new city constructed for the new trade, was only a few miles from the shogun's capital, and it speedily became the most important port. The goods and influence of the outside world thus reached the center of the country and its economy with great ease and speed. In response to those goods and markets, new regional commercial enterprises, often sponsored by daimyo domains, sprang up. The ports helped to integrate the economy and weaken the polity. Foreign trade produced new patterns of movement and weakened the established channels of commercial control. It caused disorientation of a monetary system that had never needed to be adjusted to external valuations, and the inflation that resulted hurt the well-being as well as the disposition of the sworded samurai. Antimerchant and anti-foreign terrorism brought on foreign indignation, indemnities and new indignities for Japan.

Governments that begin modernization programs seldom survive to finish them. They move too rapidly for their privileged supporters and too slowly for outsiders who are without a voice in policy-making. The Tokugawa government had tried to bring its house in order, and its steps toward modernization brought the admiration of Li Hung-chang in China. The vigor with which reforms were introduced under Keiki, the last shogun, had the effect of speeding the schedule for the Tokugawa demise lest the chance be lost. The regime had tried to offset English pressure by looking to France for a program of technical and military modernization. Missions were sent to America and Europe to ratify the treaties and learn about the West, and by 1867 the shogun's own brother was sent to France. Embassies became larger and more purposeful, their mission frankly educational. Satsuma and Chōshū, not to be outdone, sent retainers abroad as well. The shogun's efforts failed, however, because they created new discontent and left old complaints unresolved. Furthermore, the character of the last shogun, his awareness of the problems his country faced and his refusal to challenge the authority of the imperial court operated to prevent a full-scale, last-ditch stand by his retainers.

3. Meiji Modernization

A POLITICAL OVERTURN does not always bring radical changes in policy, but it makes them a great deal more likely. The Tokugawa fall eliminated at one stroke the precedents, institutions and interests that had channeled the center of shogunal politics for two and a half centuries. Initially, to be sure, that overthrow was the work of one regional sector of the old feudal ruling class, and to many it seemed only a coup d'etat. But the fact that it was carried out in the name of the emperor meant that any government that resulted would have a new institutional structure at its center. The first proclamations of the new regime placed great emphasis on a sense of discontinuity with the feudal past. They promised a renewal of more ancient and legitimate traditions and spoke of a "Restoration."

For some time there was great confusion and uncertainty as to what the actual form or thrust of the new government would be. Since the Tokugawa overthrow had been managed by advocates of the exclusion of foreigners, many expected an antiforeign nativist movement and feared a suicidal confrontation with the West. Yet the Satsuma and Chōshū men who were in charge had had practical experience with the dangers of antiforeignism, and their military success against the Tokugawa had been made possible by modern armament and organization. They took immediate steps to reassure the representatives of the West that the new government would live up to the treaty obligations of its predecessor, and edicts from the court explained that just as Japan had had relations with China in antiquity it would now converse with all countries. The new government's ability to make such promises and explanations in the name of tradition, under the rule of a young and impressionable emperor who was ostensibly being "restored" to rule, gave it a bridge between past tradition and future needs and provided a legitimacy for change which even Tokugawa supporters hesitated to challenge.

As reign title for the young emperor, the leaders chose the term *Meiji*, or "enlightened rule." His first public pledge came in April 1868, when the campaign against the Tokugawa forces had just begun. It announced that "absurd customs of the past" would be discarded and learning sought "throughout the world." All classes and groups would be able to realize their just aspirations, and government would be carried out through the establishment of a "council chamber" in order that the "foundations of the empire" might be firmly established. These general statements contained hints of all the Meiji changes: institutional transformation on the basis of international example and national tradition, abolition of the rigid class structure of Tokugawa feudalism, and representative institutions. The "Charter Oath," as it has come to be known, was later cited as authorization for modern constitutions in 1889 and again in 1947.

As each development of this program unfolded, real power shifted more unmistakably into the hands of a small number of leaders from Satsuma, Chōshū and the imperial court. They were an unusual group, bound together by common interests, origin and experience. Most of them were to hold a wide range of official posts. A military specialist like Yamagata served in nonmilitary posts and in fact played a major role in building the structure of local government. Several had been abroad before the Restoration, and within a few years virtually all of them were to go; a large group traveled together in a great mission between 1871 and 1873. They had been trained as youths in the code of the samurai; all had known danger and learned caution in the days when their fiefs and their country had been forced to accept humiliation and defeat. They had learned patience, and they valued practicality over ideology. They also shared a basically Confucian orientation, though they saw no problem in reaching out to the West for solutions and remained free of the cultural ambivalence and conflict that plagued their successors. Their regional and feudal background gave them a sense of cohesion that served to overcome petty disputes and resentments within the group. After assassination, resignation and ill health had removed several particularly strong-minded men who had stood out in Restoration days, the leadership team became a functioning group, oligarchic in fact but ministerial in form, serving with and around the Meiji emperor, whose charisma was essential to their success.

Most of the Meiji leaders were middle- and lower-ranking samurai; none of them were daimyo. So it is not surprising that their concerns with practical problems of national unification led them to begin with the feudal divisions and governance that had hampered them in their rise to power. Of the "absurdities" the Charter Oath had promised to discard, the first to go was Tokugawa feudalism. In 1869 the daimyo of Satsuma, Chōshū, Tosa and Hizen were prevailed upon by their retainers to return their land registers to the throne. Other daimyo quickly followed suit. Provisionally they were appointed "governors" of their domains. In 1871 their fiefs were declared prefectures, which now numbered seventy-five, and later fifty, instead of the several hundred divisions of Tokugawa days. The daimyo were asked to stand by in Tokyo, as Edo had been renamed, and thus found themselves back in the city to which the shogun had restricted them earlier. Later they were pensioned and rewarded with ranks in the new nobility that was established in 1884. Beginning also in 1869, samurai class ranks were simplified and then gradually abandoned. Samurai salaries changed to pensions, and pensions to bonds, which it was hoped would be invested in productive enterprises. Special privileges of rank, dress and hairdo were canceled; sword-bearing was first made optional, and in 1876 forbidden. Post stations and systems, formerly restricted to official use and burdensome to the villagers along the way, became national post and express systems. Commoners received the dignity of family names. The roads would not again be lined with Japanese crouched in the dust as their feudal betters strode past.

That learning was to be sought "throughout the world" meant that inspiration would no longer be restricted to China. Late Tokugawa years had seen a growing number of official and unofficial travelers go to the West; this movement now became far more purposeful and large scale. From 1871 to 1873 most of the government leaders, led by Prince Iwakura, together with students and

Kume Kunitake, the embassy scribe, traveled throughout the United States, Europe and Russia. The fact that this was possible tells something about political stability. The Tokugawa had only recently been overthrown, the Meiji directions were not yet by any means clear; resentful samurai were everywhere, and yet the bulk of the top leadership was able to leave the country for over a year and return to find their jobs waiting for them when they returned. Even in a day of jet planes, few new governments chance such trips. The travels of the Iwakura embassy, like those of the hundreds of students who were sent to the West in the years that followed, proved invaluable in preventing serious misunderstandings about the potential of the West. Meiji travelers returned to Japan convinced that their country had a long way to go before it could gain equality with the Western states that confronted them in the treaty ports. But they were also stimulated by the thought that, as Kume put it, the present strength of the West was the product of the last fifty years. Japan could catch up. It also became clear to them that before the West would agree to revision and improvement of the unequal treaties it would be necessary for Japan to take great steps in institutional reform.

Many Japanese who stayed home, on the other hand, were less convinced of

DEPARTURE OF THE IWAKURA MISSION (1871), a Meiji artist's recreation. Iwakura (center), Ōkubo and Kido stand on the launch taking them to the waiting steamer to "seek knowledge throughout the world."

this. There were revolts by disgruntled samurai, the most important of which, in 1877, was led by the Satsuma Restoration hero Saigō Takamori. There were also numerous rebellions and demonstrations by confused and alarmed farmers. Yet Japan was spared the sort of large-scale rebellion that proved so expensive in men and treasure for nineteenth-century China. At no point in the modern century, in fact, has the government of Japan been unable to collect its taxes or meet its obligations. This stability in administration and economy, like the stability with-in the leadership group, proved of vital assistance in the tasks of modernization.

The Meiji leaders knew that participation and support from the people were as important as direction from above. They drew lessons from their recent past and from Europe to emphasize the need for participation. The disunion of late Tokugawa days had convinced them of the dangers of popular indifference. When British ships bombarded Chōshū in 1864, local farmers had watched the proceedings with interest, and when it was safe they had come down to the shore to help the British demolish the gun batteries that had brought on the mischief. During the war against Tokugawa supporters in 1868, local farmers had followed the fighting chiefly in order to sell refreshments to both sides during lulls in the action. In contrast, in 1871 Japanese in Europe reported with astonishment the way the citizens of Paris had tried to defend their city against the Prussian armies that encircled the city. Clearly, they felt, it was necessary to promote and spread patriotism in Japan. Commoners should feel involved in their country's affairs, and they should be as prepared to serve it as the samurai had been.

To this end, universal education and military conscription were in-troduced in 1873. Several conclusions followed from this. One was that the country would no longer count upon the samurai to do its fighting. Non-samurai contingents had given a good account of themselves in late Tokugawa days. They were more amenable to discipline and training than status-con-scious samurai, who could best be utilized as officers. On the other hand, what was most valuable about the samurai was their sense of commitment and duty, and this could be instilled in all commoners through mass education. By the late 1880s, lesson books focused on figures of bravery and loyalty in the past at the same time that they prepared pupils for life in a modern society. The full effect of these reforms required time. It was easier to announce schools than to staff them and easier to legislate a mass army than to train and equip it. The units that took part in suppressing rebellions in the 1870s showed that much had to be done before Japan could expect to meet a modern opponent with any degree of confidence. But the decisions had been made, and improvement then began.

Because the unequal treaties restricted Japan's opportunities for taxing im-ports or protecting nascent industries, the economic base for Meiji modernization was long restricted to agriculture. The work of the first decade and more of the Meiji period thus centered on efforts to convert a premodern system to a uniform system of agricultural taxation in order to provide a base for later growth. It was necessary to increase the productivity of the traditional sector and to guarantee access to its surplus. The first steps sought to change the tax base from a percentage to a regular and predictable tax yield. In order to achieve this, steps were begun to give farmers full legal title to their land. Under feudalism, the samurai fiefholder had held theoretical title, and customary law had forbidden peasants from leaving or selling their plots. The Meiji government now gave farmers freedom to buy and sell, to move and to grow what they wished. By legislation adopted in 1873 land values were worked out on a basis of average yields, and a percentage land tax was based on the newly derived value of the land. The result was to give the government a predictable income at the same time that it was gradually divesting itself of the burden of samurai support. The land tax was payable in money. It introduced the farmer to the national market. New incentives, more accurate reporting and more efficient agriculture produced a growing agricultural surplus which became the base of government revenue until the early twentieth century. While this was being done Finance Minister Matsukata stabilized the currency and brought order out of the chaos of inflationary conditions that had been produced by the suppression of rebellions and reckless establishment of banks and enterprises. The guarantees for private property that were built into the Meiji Constitution completed the pattern whereby Japan's economy was firmly set on a capitalist base and course.

The Charter Oath of 1868 also spoke of "widely convoked Assemblies." Constitutions seemed an important part of the strength of the modern West. Meiji leaders returned from trips abroad convinced of the importance of such institutions in securing national unity and purpose. They then began to experiment with ways of securing some kind of representation without running the risk of surrendering leadership. If they shared power immediately with their peers, they thought, the modernization program would probably have to be slowed as samurai interests asserted themselves. Had they given way to their critics in the 1880s, when a lively popular demand for "Freedom and People's Rights" formed, the constitutional order would probably have produced a system more responsive to the general will. But the Meiji leaders doubted that their contemporaries were prepared for power, and they were certainly not ready to step aside to see. Instead they set to work consolidating the control of local government while some of their number began work on a national constitution.

The Meiji Constitution of 1889 provided the capstone for the institutional structure of the new state. With its implementation in 1890, and with the preparation of the authoritative statement of national education that accompanied it, the experimentation and reform that had begun in 1868 came to an end. The Constitution set the rules for the exercise of power and channeled all political discussion until 1945. Its distinctive characteristics and specific provisions reflected and determined the strengths and weaknesses of Imperial Japan.

The document was the work of a commission headed by the Chōshū leader Itō Hirobumi. Itō journeyed to Europe for his third trip in the course of drawing it up, and his choice of sources for the new document was reflected in his stops, for he spent the bulk of his time in Germany and Austria. In the institutions of central Europe, he thought, he found precedents that made it possible to combine Western with Japanese traditions of imperial sovereignty. Itō was not narrowly imitative. He discarded the suggestions of some European advisers for establishing Buddhism as a state religion and giving propertied classes special rights. On the other hand, he and his colleagues felt it essential to preserve and enhance the authority of the imperial institution as the essence of the Japanese state, or polity. Representation should be hedged about until it could be assumed that the people would act with responsibility. The Meiji government itself should be above party and competition, and it should represent permanence and prestige. Institutionalized struggle and competition were unflattering terms in the Confucian lexicon. The Meiji leaders saw themselves as an elite leading a poorly prepared people into modernity, and they saw dangers in the willingness of their samurai competitors from other fiefs to court popular favor with appeals to chauvinism. So they designed a constitution that educated and edified but also concealed; it stressed the cooperation of emperor and elected representatives, but it said little about a government of cabinet ministers whose chairs they themselves would fill.

German constitutional thought commended itself to them in a number of ways. It made distinctions between society, constituted out of competing elements, and state. Society was inevitably divisive, class- and status-oriented, and self-seeking; the state, on the other hand, was concerned with the development and advancement of the whole. Only the state could preserve common interests in the face of the conflicting private interests of society, and only the state could provide a higher spiritual and moral focus. This was a useful rationale for avoiding an institutional setting in which public policies could become the playthings of personal and group interests. Party politics and a Diet responsible to the products of such struggle could only produce selfishness and divisiveness. The state, however, should stand forth as the resolution of all problems and the focus of all loyalties. This idealization of the state, later articulated in terms of the *rechtsstaat* philosophy of nineteenth-century Imperial Germany, seemed to fit Japanese needs perfectly.

It also fitted the vague rhetoric of Meiji political theory with its focus upon the god-emperor. For Japan's state could be the highest good of all, bolstered as it was by Shinto belief and hedged with the rationale of a Confucianism now separated from the institutions of the Tokugawa period. Tradition and modernity could thus go hand in hand. Upon the promulgation of the Constitution, the Meiji emperor's oath, made in the precincts of his palace, put it this way: "In accordance with the Grand Design [of the sun goddess], coeval as it is with heaven and earth, and in accordance with this design alone, we have succeeded to the Divine Throne.... In view of the progressive tendency of human affairs and the advance of civilization, it has been incumbent upon us, for the sake of clarifying the instructions bequeathed by the Imperial Founder [to issue this Constitution]...."

The Meiji Constitution was framed in general terms that left much for future interpretation. It provided the first explicit statements of freedom of religion, speech, publication, residence and property that Japan had known, and although all these rights were qualified with possible limitation by law, this marked dramatic evidence of the distance Japan had come from Tokugawa feudalism. It also provided a bicameral legislature, or Diet, with a House of Peers made up of members of a new aristocracy set up in 1884 and a House of Representatives chosen by direct suffrage by an electorate of 450,000 taxpayers who qualified by being over twenty-five, male and paying a direct tax of fifteen yen. Interestingly enough, this was the approximate number of samurai family heads under the old regime. The electors, however, included and indeed were preponderately rural leaders rather than urban ex-samurai. Ten years later this electorate was doubled when the tax qualification was reduced by one-third. The Diet was constrained by the provision that the emperor could dissolve its lower house and force its members to stand for new (and increasingly expensive) elections. The emperor could rule by imperial ordinance which had the force of law until later Diet action. In addition, the government could utilize the previous year's budget if the Diet refused its approval for the current budget.

Despite the mysticism in which its invocation was couched, the Meiji Constitution permitted an important role for representative government, and it had within it possibilities for growth and liberalization as Japan developed into a multicentered society. Even its most deplored feature, the use of a previous budget in case of conflict between government and Diet, becomes unimportant when considered in the light of Meiji history. For the Meiji government, like all governments, constantly asked for increased appropriations, and the Diet's power to approve or reject these increases was in fact critical to the government. The first decade of Meiji constitutional history is a story of continuous and frustrating attempts on the part of cabinets led by the Meiji leaders to have their way with a recalcitrant Diet.

On the other hand, the Meiji Constitution had drawbacks for future development that were real enough, some of which turned out to be a good deal more unfortunate than the budgetary provisions. The first was the lack of any clearly defined executive responsibility. Final authority lay with the emperor, but he did not exercise it. He was declared "sacred and inviolable," and the cabinet system through which he functioned was not clearly sketched lest it interfere with his prerogatives or his splendor, or, no doubt, lest it reveal the role of the real leaders. The emperor was also stated to be supreme commander of the army and navy, and Diet control over the services was restricted to budgetary support. In the first Diet, in fact, the government tried to refuse the Diet any kind of budgetary breakdown for the services on grounds of national security. Meanwhile, the army and navy, which had been organized along the lines of the German high command in the 1880s, enjoyed the right of direct access to the imperial commander. There were, thus, parallel lines of executive authority; civilian, through cabinet, and military, through chiefs of staff. The relationship between these was never made clear. This was not a major problem during the careers of the original generation of leaders; they were all samurai and also, including Yamagata, experienced in civil administration. But thereafter, in the absence of a sharply defined executive responsibility, competitors in the power struggle tended to be those with access to the throne. That this could become a problem was seen as early as 1905 when Itō, as resident general of Korea, saw to it that he would report directly to the throne. These problems became serious because the emperor was not permitted to rule, for inactivity or at least separation from the political process was the condition of the divinity with which he was credited. Later struggles could sometimes be described as rivalry for the right to speak for an all but empty throne.

Imperial loyalty also became more impersonal and ideological as the result of the other major culmination of institutional development, the Education Rescript of 1890. This represented the definitive statement of state loyalty and values. Its contents included Buddhist, Shinto, Western and, especially, Confucian values, and it impressed upon its hearers that imperial loyalty was to be the center of education. By taking upon itself the responsibility of formulating and diffusing such a distillation of values, the Meiji government was playing a traditional Confucian role. The manner in which the document was framed, enshrined and read at formal occasions made it a Japanese variant of the imperial edicts read by local gentry in Imperial China. The process of preparation of the document found conservatives anxious to ward off excessive Westernization and liberals eager to include in the document notes of nineteenth-century progress and ambition. The point on which they agreed was that of national service and priority, and the focus this took was one of imperial veneration, transmitted as something "out of ages past." The Education Rescript meant that the prologue of the Constitution, with its rumbles of tradition, would be as important as the modern privileges and guarantees it contained.

Nevertheless, the Meiji institutions allowed the possibility of growth, and the Constitution's guarantees of privileges, rights and freedom went far beyond what many had expected. This "government of laws," if not yet a government of law, marked a giant step forward from the scene of two decades before. Western observers of the time saw Japan placed firmly in the line of world and modern development. This was important; the Constitution was essential to Western approval of reforms, and that approval was prerequisite to relaxation of the unequal treaties. Itō, certainly, was delighted to discover that the product of his labors met Western as well as Japanese approval. "I feel relieved," he wrote a friend, for "there was doubt in my mind whether Europe and America would accept Japan with a constitution conforming to Japanese national polity." At the same time most Japanese liberals were grateful that their national polity had assimilated so much Western constitutionalism. The young journalist Tokutomi Sohō wrote that "if the spirit of this constitution is not lost and its power is not paralyzed, our people will be forever free."

4. The Road to Shimonoseki

UP TO THIS POINT the account of Meiji modernization has focused upon the workings of the government leaders. Their reaction was one of defensive modernization; their country needed to reform to protect itself from the West, and it could secure release from its treaty handicaps only if Western powers approved its institutional reforms. The government leaders' eyes were turned toward the West.

At first they assumed that the West, on seeing evidence of their intent to reform, would agree to make changes in the treaties that had been imposed on a feudal and antiforeign country. It was a shock to discover that it would take much more and that they were locked into treatment reserved for the weak countries of Asia. Thanks to the most-favored–nation clause, they would have to persuade all countries before they could move any one. Efforts in the early 1870s to discuss the problem had led them to abolish the restrictions against Christianity that had stood since the beginning of the Tokugawa period. During the 1880s a concentrated program of negotiation and reform was carried on to secure Western approval for new treaties. Outward forms of Western civilization were encouraged, and changes in architecture, dress, diet and entertainment were sponsored to show that urban and upper-class Japan, at least, had changed. More basic were the efforts made to recover tariff autonomy, which was seen as essential to plans for industrialization. Twice in the 1880s the government tried to secure tariff autonomy by conceding points on the issue of extraterritoriality. Under Foreign Minister Inoue in 1886-87 and Foreign Minister Ōkuma in 1888-89 it proposed to incorporate Western principles in new legal codes, permit foreign judges to sit in Japanese courts and grant foreigners rights of residence and trade beyond the treaty ports. Twice the powers refused to agree. Each time the government in Tokyo was sharply attacked for its concessions to the foreigners, sufficiently so for the foreign minister to resign and, in Ōkuma's case, face an assassination attempt. As it turned out, it was only after the Constitution had been in use for several years, and on the eve of the war with China in 1894, that the powers agreed to new treaties with Japan. By then there were alarming signs of a new wave of antiforeign sentiment in many sectors of Japanese society and opinion. The war against China thus came at the end of a quarter-century's efforts to throw off the indignities of second-class membership in the Western international order.

The problem of emulation of and resistance to the West colored Japanese attitudes toward their East Asian neighbors as well. East Asia was the only possible outlet for Japanese frustrations and also the most appropriate spot to demonstrate to the West that Japan had learned its lessons. But as the attack on Foreign Minister Ōkuma illustrated, there were deep currents of opposition to the strategies and tactics the Meiji leaders had followed in foreign relations. Throughout all of modern Japan's history tensions resulting from Western and Asian foreign policies have resonated with internal political discontent and provided the catalyst for many political crises.

It was a problem that became clear in early Restoration days. The antiforeign expectations that had been raised by the slogans of the 1860s combined with frustrations of the former samurai to create support for proposals to punish the

JAPANESE ATTACK DURING THE MARCH TO PYONGYANG. During the Sino-Japanese War, woodprints presented idealized accounts of Japanese discipline and valor. In this depiction, the artist focuses on the commanders: Colonel Fukushima, Major General Nozu and Major Oshima.

Koreans for the affronts they returned to Japanese requests for formal treaty relations. The issue had come to a head in 1873, at the time of the return of the Iwakura mission to the West. When the returned ambassadors carried the day with their arguments for the priority of reform over revenge, they produced the first major defection of leaders from the government councils. Restoration leaders from Saga, Tosa and Satsuma resigned together with their followers, and their discontent led directly to several of the major samurai revolts that followed. Government attempts to alleviate these discontents by recruiting samurai units to take part in the invasion of Taiwan in 1874 did little to solve the problem, but they did provide an indication of the direction in which the search for a new consensus might lead.

One group of men who resigned in 1873 channeled their discontent into political organization by issuing a call for an elected assembly, and their agitation helped to confirm the government leaders' views that a constitution would be necessary. In the 1880s two major political groupings developed, and their struggles to organize in the face of restrictive press and assembly legislation produced what became known as the "Freedom and People's Rights" movement. The political party movement of those years was in one sense more "Western" than government policy in that it sought to apply directly the political and social thought of Rousseau and Spencer and criticized the government's reforms as superficial. Yet it was also more Asian-centered. Its concern with transformations within Japanese society and politics made it natural for its leaders to look to neighboring East Asian societies as well, and their rhetoric of liberation and the movement's strongly nationalist tone could easily encompass the needs of neighboring countries.

The 1880s witnessed a vigorous polemic against the backward-looking societies and governments of Korea and China as well as enthusiastic and romantic views of the role a modernized and democratic Japan might play in Asia. Tarui Tōkichi wrote a striking proposal calling for the amalgamation of Japan and Korea into a new country that would be called Great East, one that would be able to withstand the aggressive and threatening West. Other men formed an East Asian Liberal party, although the Meiji government did not permit it to meet.

The leaders of these organizations were also ex-samurai, however, and their ideas of liberation were full of overtones of national mission and leadership for Japan. This was shown most strikingly in one group's abortive plot to stage a filibustering expedition to Korea, one in which they assumed that they would receive the support of Korean reformers and then return to further democratize their own Meiji society. These links between romanticism, activism and nationalism made it easy for the liberal movement to relate to the activist nationalist societies that also sprang up in the 1880s. They could agree on criticism of the Meiji government's imitative and humiliating policies; they shared a dislike of the neighboring regimes in East Asia, and they sought a mission and meaning for Japan and the Japanese spirit. Organizations and activities of this sort provided attractive outlets for the ambition and idealism of young men who wanted something more than the security of position or organization; they made much of Korean and, later, Chinese students and reformers who came to Japan, and they considered themselves unselfish, idealistic followers of the spirit of the Meiji Restoration activists.

The self-styled Asianists were one extreme of the Meiji spectrum of cultural and political affiliation, and thoroughgoing Westernizers the other. But, of course, most Japanese who thought about these things were somewhere between the two, able to respect the evidence of conscience and tradition in the claims of the activist *shishi* and prepared to see the logic of the need to work with the West. And some moved between the two positions. The educator and publicist Fukuzawa Yukichi, for instance, went out of his way in the early 1880s to befriend and educate young Korean students in Japan. He saw the proposed coup of the Korean modernizers in 1884 as beneficial to Japan and to the "civilization" he espoused so strongly, and he kept in close touch with the men who were to carry it out. But after it failed he concluded from this and from the Chinese defeat by France in 1885 that Japan's only possible path lay in separating itself from Asia. "If we keep bad company we cannot avoid getting a bad name," he argued; it was essential that the treaty powers distinguish between a modernizing Japan and a backward "Asia." Thus Fukuzawa led the journalistic pack in calling for strong policies against Korea and China, and his editorials were quick to applaud the success of the war against China. It was, he observed, really a war for civilization.

It was the hope of the Meiji leaders that the Constitution would put an end to the divisiveness that had marked the political struggles of the 1880s. It was to represent the culmination of governmental perfection, a system in which a propertied elite would select representatives willing to cooperate with their government in the interests of furthering the strength and harmony of the nation. Instead, to their surprise, the Constitution only provided new forms in which previous struggles and discontents could be played out in a public and institutionalized setting.

The opening of the Diet in 1890 found Japan's leaders conscious of the historic importance of the departure they were making. No Asian country had yet put a constitution in operation, and many doubted that it would work in Japan. The leaders were afraid that representation might give voice to obscurantist and antiforeign voices, but they had prepared for this event with almost a decade of elective assemblies on the prefectural level. Most of the members of the first Diets had gained experience in local elections first. When the first elections were held, it proved that the majority of the representatives elected were associated with the political parties that had been formed in the 1880s. Both the Jiyūtō, or Liberal, and Kaishintō, or Progressive, parties felt it necessary to stress their patriotism and loyalty. This was not surprising, for they were operating in a setting in which private associations for the expression of political opinion had few roots. From the first, the Diet representatives focused on two issues that were promising and popular. Taxes could be resisted on grounds that they subjected the emperor's subjects to unbearable hardships. Foreign policies could be criticized as subservient and unworthy of a proud nation and tradition. Both tactics struck the Meiji leaders as shamelessly selfish and petty. Yamagata deplored the fact that "many politicians ... favor reducing taxes in order to give respite to the overburdened people. Such a policy serves only the game of politics ... [but] there is need of preparing against international war." Itō too despaired of party politicians, because as he put it, "the thing that drives me to distraction is that there is not one of them who thinks of the nation above self."

Yet the leaders were determined to make the Constitution work. When Diet debates neared dangerous impasses, the opposition leaders were usually equally anxious to prove that Japan could make its constitutional government a success. Thus a certain flexibility marked their stance. The first cabinet, led by Yamagata as prime minister, began with an attempt to restrict the Diet's powers in legislating budgetary matters and promptly found itself with an 11 percent budget cut voted by the lower house. Both government and Diet compromised, but the Diet retreated further. When the fight was continued in the next Diet, the cabinet, now led by former Finance Minister Matsukata, tried to solve matters by dissolving the lower house and calling new elections. This time police interference with the election process produced twenty-five deaths and almost four hundred wounded. Despite this, the parties again returned a majority of elected members. Matsukata resigned to take responsibility for his failure and was succeeded by a cabinet headed by the framer of the Constitution, Itō Hirobumi. Itō subdued the parliamentary enemy by obtaining an imperial rescript which ordered all officials to contribute one-tenth of their salary for six years to defray naval costs. The court also pledged a large contribution of its own for the same purpose.

Thus three cabinets in as many years used unsatisfactory combinations of compromise, pressure and invocation of the imperial talisman in attempts to handle a recalcitrant Diet. The refusal of the Diet representatives to give in before the formidable economic and moral sanctions the government had at its disposal suggests that the Meiji Constitution had granted the opposition a good deal of power to obstruct and influence.

It was in this setting of domestic frustration and foreign policy irritation that the government succeeded, in 1894, in winning approval for treaty reform from the powers. It was also now that the Chinese and Korean governments infuriated Japanese "Asianists" by the murder of Kim Ok-kyun, that the Chinese government risked Japanese reprisal with its intervention against the Tonghak Rebellion in Korea and that the Japanese military decided the time had come to establish their primacy in East Asia. Yamagata Aritomo, in several long and thoughtful memorandums, argued the strategic importance of Korea for Japan and foresaw a Russian-British confrontation in East Asia which would provide danger and opportunity for Japan. It seemed to others that a move against the Peiyang forces of Li Hung-chang would take Korea out of the Chinese sphere and would establish Japan's full membership in the international system. It should also silence domestic critics who were increasingly irritated with their government's inactivity and caution. And so Prime Minister Itō and Foreign Minister Mutsu began by dissolving the Diet to free their hand; they continued by dispatching troops to Korea and finally challenged the Chinese by forcing reforms upon the Korean government.

The war proved as successful in internal politics as in international politics. The treaty-revision success and the popularity of the China war removed military expenditure and foreign policy from the area of political discourse for several years. Military headquarters were set up at Hiroshima, and the emperor moved there to be closer to his troops in the field. The war made significant alterations in the political balance in Meiji Japan. Its success proved the wisdom of the Meiji leaders' caution in deferring action until they were ready. It helped make the government bearable, the army popular and the emperor sacrosanct. The music, writing and art of the war years were full of a simple, unsophisticated joy in action and victory. Japan was unified as it had not been before. Writers spoke of a second Meiji Restoration; the emperor had received the last shogun in audience; the country was as united as its leaders. "For the first time," the journalist Tokutomi wrote, "I realized that this *hambatsu* [fief clique] government I had been criticizing was my government." Chauvinism reigned. After decades of weakness, it was good to be a Japanese and to humble the mighty neighbor that had dominated the horizon for so long.

For a small number of Japanese, the terms of the Treaty of Shimonoseki seemed a betrayal of Japan's war aims of civilization and enlightenment. Uchimura Kanzō, who had hailed a "righteous war" that would liberate China, now regretted his advocacy: "a 'righteous' war has changed into a *piratic* war somewhat," he wrote, "and a prophet who wrote its 'justification' is now in shame." Shiga Shigetaka denounced plans for further armament expansion, argued that Japanese were already the most heavily burdened by military expenditures in the world and warned against harsh treatment of China. Viscount Tani rose in the House of Peers to criticize both the treaty and the pace of armament expansion. But these complaints were submerged in the larger tide of popular euphoria, and they seemed to find convincing answers from the advocates of national interest. Foreign Minister Mutsu wrote in his memoirs that it had always been absurd to think that Japan should extend itself for the benefit of Korea, and the editor of a leading economic review, pointing to the commercial benefits that lay ahead, asked rhetorically, "How could we be so foolish as to destroy our lives and property for the sake of justice alone?"

5. *Japan After the Triple Intervention*

THE EXULTATION of the victories over China soon gave way to resentment that the European powers, apparently at the instigation of the Chinese, had banded together to deny Japan her foothold in south Manchuria. The notes which representatives of Russia, Germany and France delivered to the Japanese minister for foreign affairs a few days after the terms of the Treaty of Shimonoseki became known recommended that "for the peace of Asia" Japan return the Liaotung Peninsula in south Manchuria. The Triple Intervention, as it became known, had profound consequences.

Within Japan it signified the fact that Japan, despite its struggles and achievements, had still not achieved full membership in the inner circle of great powers. It was out of the question for the Japanese to attempt a military challenge to the three imperialist powers, and there was no alternative to capitulation. As was to be expected, the Triple Intervention roused the greatest response among groups imperfectly informed of the contrast between Japanese and Western military might. Japanese government leaders were perfectly aware of this. Civilian leaders, especially Prime Minister Itō and Foreign Minister Mutsu, had feared an unfavorable European response to proposals for territorial acquisitions on the mainland. But they had lost ascendancy in the planning meetings to the military. The Japanese armies had, after all, been victorious, and voices calling for them to press on to Peking had been heard in every quarter. But the civilian leaders had been conscious of the growing pressure among the great powers for a compromise peace. The last thing those powers wanted was to see the Manchu dynasty so enfeebled and discredited as to force its collapse with the consequent overthrow of the profitable order they had brought into being; they were growing suspicious of Japanese ambitions, and they might even disapprove of the seizure of Taiwan. Itō and Mutsu hoped that the powers would permit the acquisition of Liaotung in view of the sacrifices the Japanese forces had made, but when these hopes proved unfounded, they soon agreed that they had to give up Liaotung. There was little choice, for both England and the United States had returned discouraging answers to Japanese feelers for diplomatic support in a possible effort to retain the territory. Perhaps unwisely, Tokyo did not even try to secure a Chinese promise not to lease the peninsula to another power; three years later it was in Russian hands.

Implicit in the decision to give up Liaotung was the admission that because Japan was still weak in relative terms, it was also powerless. "The Japanese," British Minister Ernest Satow wrote, "have the appearance of being thoroughly disheartened, and they do not seem to appreciate the value of diplomacy, except as a preliminary to the use of force." Foreign Minister Mutsu wrote in his memoirs the bitter words, "Unless diplomacy is backed by force it is bound to fail, no matter how sound its case."

The army commanders, on the other hand, were not as conscious of the facts as civilian leaders were. General Yamagata, who had to give up his field command for reasons of health, was commissioned to make a secret trip to south Manchuria to explain the problem to his colleagues and secure their compliance with the government's decision. No doubt they were consoled in this by the knowledge that the blame for this would fall on the civilian leaders. To the Japanese people it looked as though the soldiers had won the war only to have the civilians lose the prize through inept diplomacy.

The emperor thus addressed to his people a special rescript calling on them to avoid rash acts of revenge for having to give up their prize. A better index to his feelings was probably provided by his grandson on the eve of surrender in 1945; he told his councillors that when he recalled Emperor Meiji's distress "I swallow my own tears." The popular mood was best expressed by the bitter phrase *gashin shōtan,* to persevere through hardship for the sake of revenge. Despite the sacrifices and efforts already made, more would be needed; Japan required more guns, more ships and more soldiers before it could expect to reach its goal of world equality. This call to further and increased sacrifice marked a new milestone in the power and effectiveness of the Japanese monarchy.

The Japanese people responded with obedience but not without bitterness for the injustice they felt they had been done. It was among journalists and politicians that the strongest denunciations of the return of Liaotung were to be found. Foreign diplomats in Japan were often scornful of what they considered cheap and uninformed jingoism; Minister Satow, for instance, described much of what he read as "utter rubbish," written by men who were "ignorant of European politics . . . and not aware of the way in which the great Powers pulled together at home and that the extreme East hung upon Europe." But it was precisely this realization that aroused the anger of Japanese journalists, and their effect upon their readers was real enough.

The popular newspaper *Kokumin,* for instance, had responded to the enthusiasm of the war effort by sending some thirty war correspondents into the field. Its publisher-editor, Tokutomi, changed from a position critical of the conservative leaders to become their close friend and confidant. He secured for himself permission to accompany a group of high-ranking generals to Liaotung soon after the armies had taken Port Arthur. When the news reached him that Japan would have to return this spot of mainland territory, he impulsively tucked some Manchurian soil into his handkerchief. This much at least, he vowed, the Europeans would not deny him. "This retrocession of Liaotung," he wrote later, "dominated the rest of my life. After hearing about it I became almost a different man psychologically. Say what you will, it had happened because we weren't strong enough. What it came down to was that sincerity and justice didn't amount to a thing if you were not strong enough." So a deep sense of outrage was left. In practical terms, this meant that many of the most vocal partisans of party politics, who had hitherto seen their chief advantage in contesting tax matters with the government, now became advocates of policies that could only result in greater costs and budgets. The erstwhile advocates of economy now vied with each other to demand greater national strength and joined to criticize the civilian leaders as bungling practitioners of a diplomacy of weakness. The Treaty of Shimonoseki and the Triple Intervention persuaded many Japanese that international law and institutional modernization alone would never bring full respect and equality from the West. Some, of course, had made this discovery well before the Sino-Japanese War. Fukuzawa had written that "one hundred volumes of International Law are not the equal of a few cannon; a handful of Treaties of Friendship are not worth a bucket of gunpowder. Cannon and gunpowder are not aids for the enforcement of given moral principles, but they are the implements for the creation of morality where none exists."

Japanese pessimism about the morality of the international order deepened in the years after the Triple Intervention. The German seizure of Shantung, French gains in south China and English occupation of Weihaiwei were overshadowed by the Russian gains. The Russians began by leasing the Liaotung holdings Japan had been forced to give up, they continued with steps to challenge the Japanese ascendancy in Korea and ended with a bold attempt to dominate all of Manchuria after the Boxer Rebellion. The Russians thus provided the obvious goals for Japanese diplomacy and military planning. After diplomacy failed to deter the Russians, it was used to secure allies against these powerful rivals.

Japan played almost no part in the moves toward the division of China in 1898, except to secure an agreement to safeguard the coast opposite Taiwan. The reminder of weakness that Russia, France and Germany had given them made the Tokyo leaders more cautious than before. They seemed, to English Minister Ernest Satow, demoralized and pessimistic about their ability in world politics. Japan's interests in Manchuria had been taken away, and then taken over, by the Russians. Japan's interests in Korea had been set back by clumsy mismanagement.

It seemed clear to the Meiji leaders that if they remained spectators of the partition of the continent, a partition their victory over China had clearly accelerated, their world would be permanently dominated by a Europe that would never grant them more than a second-class membership. So they gave first emphasis to building greater military and naval strength. General Yamagata wrote his friends that the situation in Asia was sure to grow steadily worse and that another war would probably be necessary within ten years. He provided the leadership in drawing up plans to enlarge the army from seven to thirteen divisions; army expenses rose from approximately 10 to 30 percent of the national budget. A seven-year naval building program was announced. Political party leaders announced that it was urgent for "the whole nation to unite and strive for the enlargement of the military establishment" and to "resolve to face the difficult problems facing us from without." No attempts were made to hide the cost and hardship of this from the Japanese people. *Gashin shōtan,* "persevering through hardship," became the slogan to explain the new sacrifices.

The Sino-Japanese War had, however, provided some important assistance for Japan in this new effort. The Chinese indemnity supplied a large amount of ready capital that made it possible to enter paths of orthodox finance despite expenditures that might otherwise have become inflationary. It also made it possible to funnel government assistance into a new program of heavy industry. The iron and steel works at Yawata on Kyushu were begun in 1896.

Japan also became an important member of the commercial and trading competition in China very quickly. By terms of the Shimonoseki treaty Japan entered the privileged circle of treaty-port powers with "unequal" rights in China. She had extended those rights with provisions for additional ports and foreign-owned manufacturing plants in the ports. Her entry into heavy industry made it appropriate to encourage the production of light and inexpensive goods like matches and cheap textiles on Chinese soil with Chinese labor. As Japanese sources of raw materials for the new iron and steel works proved inadequate, the mainland became ever more important. Interest in Chinese ores was expressed as early as 1897, and two years later the head of the Yawata industries went to China to negotiate the purchase of iron ores from the Tayeh mines, about eighty miles southeast of Hankow.

Thus at the same time that it was assumed that Japan's commercial future lay in south China—an agreement of 26 April 1898 saw the Chinese promise to keep other powers out of Fukien—additional economic interests were developing in central China. In central China, Japan's only hope lay in the maintenance of equal opportunity for all commercial countries. Here, in addition to the ores and coal Japan needed, was a vast hinterland in which the products of plants newly established in Shanghai, as well as inexpensive manufactures from Japan itself, might circulate.

Japan dreaded a premature division of China even more than its better-financed and more heavily armed European competitors. It was natural that the Japanese role from 1898 to 1900 should be one of enthusiasm for the Open Door, of agreement with commercial powers like England and the United States and of exhortation for the maintenance of the territorial integrity of China. The "Preservation of China" became a staple of political oratory in Tokyo, and Count (and Foreign Minister) Ōkuma elaborated what was to be known as an "Ōkuma Doctrine," which held that Japan could not permit European colonization so close to its shores but would instead repay its cultural debt to China by making available political and commercial acumen in the service of Chinese unity and independence.

The Boxer Rebellion of 1900 provided a test for these assertions. Japan had no wish to alienate China: it wanted to prevent or at least delay the partition of China, and it needed to adhere to the policies of the concert of nations. The Boxer movement was anti-Western and largely anti-Christian and not, of course, necessarily anti-Japanese. Yet the murder of a senior Japanese diplomat in Peking gave Japan as direct a cause for intervention as that of any other country. Japan's leaders were, however, eager to avoid the appearance of self-interest in China, and they were aware that precipitate involvement of Japanese troops, which were, of course, the best and most conveniently located of any "allied" troops, could bring reminders of 1895 and the Triple Intervention. Prime Minister Yamagata and his advisers therefore agreed to wait until they were urgently pressed by outside powers before committing Japanese troops. When the call came, they provided more units than any other power, but they did not ask for a position of command in the relief expedition. Japanese troops were under close discipline and behaved with conspicuous moderation throughout the event, and they were among the first to be withdrawn after the siege of the legations had been lifted. The purpose of this was made clear in numerous memorandums in Tokyo. Japan's interests in the north were strategic. A strong Russian presence in Manchuria could embarrass those interests, and nothing should be permitted that might provide an excuse for Russian consolidation in Manchuria. On the other hand, in south China the opportunities were less complicated and more inviting. Administrators on Taiwan, working with Japanese Buddhist missionaries in Amoy who claimed that they had been victimized by an "antiforeign" incident, very nearly created an occupation of Amoy by free interpretation of the instructions they were sent from Tokyo. At the last moment the Tokyo government of Premier Yamagata, alert to the dangers of such adventures, stopped the project. Its eyes were on the Russians and Manchuria, and it did not want its position prejudiced by recriminations in Fukien.

6. The War with Russia

JAPAN TOOK a leading part in diplomatic maneuvers that were designed to relax the Russian pressure on Manchuria. After the siege of the legations at Peking had been lifted, the Russians led in suggestions that the empress dowager and her Manchu court be permitted to return to Peking, but they themselves showed no eagerness to retire from Manchuria. Once before, in 1860, Russian assistance to the Manchus when the powers had occupied Peking had been rewarded by cession of the Maritime Provinces; it seemed possible that this time their price would be Manchuria. In November 1900 Admiral Alekseiev signed an agreement with the Governor General Tseng of Mukden that left the Russians in control of Manchuria for virtually as long as they might consider it necessary.

In February 1901 the Russians presented Peking with their conditions for the evacuation of Manchuria. These were so onerous that the Chinese appealed to all other powers for help in resisting them. The following year the Russians modified their goals and negotiated an agreement that called for withdrawal in three stages, "provided that no disturbances arise and that the action of other Powers should not prevent it." Russia carried out the first step as planned, but in April 1903, when the second step was scheduled, this proviso was invoked to justify failure to continue with the evacuation. A few months later the Russians emphasized their displeasure with moves made against them by reoccupying Mukden, which had been given up in the initial moves.

The importance of Manchuria for the Russians was obvious to all, and although the formulation of measures to protect it became part of a political dispute between powerful factions at the czarist court, all parties were agreed that Russia had special interests and needs in the area. The extension of Russia's Asiatic territories to the Amur area had created the need for an eastern base that was taking shape at Vladivostok. No other Western power had as clear a need for communications and guarantees. The vision and courage that were required to project the Trans-Siberian Railroad to the Pacific were worthy of empire builders. From the time it was begun in 1891, it had been a cause of concern to statesmen throughout the world. To none did it seem as threatening as to the Japanese, and General Yamagata's fears of the way it would alter the power balance have already been noted. Then, after Shimonoseki, the thought of Japanese holdings in Manchuria as well as, perhaps, Korea, which shared a boundary with the czarist empire, seemed sufficiently threatening to dictate the Triple Intervention which forced Japan to give up Liaotung. A few years later, Japanese setbacks in Korea and German grabs in Shantung made it possible for the Russians to take over the Port Arthur and Dairen area. Now a warm-water port and a potentially impregnable base combined to make it possible to anchor the eastern end of the entire Russian empire. The building of the Chinese Eastern Railway brought this home to all parties in Russia.

At the same time, however, these developments raised problems for Russian policymakers. Their country was poor in capital. It was modernizing rapidly but still relatively backward, and it could not expect to compete on equal terms with the great commercial powers of Western Europe. Retention and exploitation of its gains in East Asia therefore seemed to require abandonment of the Open Door in those areas. Otherwise, as Russian leaders pointed out, their efforts in building the Chinese Eastern Railway would only result in opening the hinterland of Manchuria with its extractive wealth to their better-financed Western competitors. It was necessary to maintain control over Manchuria and to deny it to others. (In future years the Japanese would use the same arguments.) As China disintegrated further, other possibilities for territory and for wealth might lie ahead. The question for Russia was one of timing and of tactics. Russia's land bordering the area, and her growing military strength and superior communications, seemed to guarantee her the best seat at the feast.

These issues now became confused with court politics at St. Petersburg. Russia's Far Eastern developments were dominated for well over a decade by the powerful figure of Count Sergius Witte, the minister of finance, who combined managerial talents and broad experience with enormous self-confidence. He developed a personal empire in the eastern empire Russia had obtained. Its nerve center was the Trans-Siberian Railway, its administrative center the new Russian city of Harbin, its officials the bureaucracies of administration, industrial development and finance that gave form to the new territories. Witte's ambition was very great, but his self-confidence was sufficiently firm to free him from timetables and deadlines. Time, and the railways, were on the Russian side; he felt it a mistake to try to rush things and build hostility. He opposed the acquisition of Port Arthur and resisted what he considered premature overcommitment. Some Russian military leaders were even more cautious in their timetables; General Kuropotkin, the minister of war, favored holding only northern Manchuria (to which the Russians had no claims) and granting the Japanese freedom of action in Korea until the Russian military position was strengthened. On the other hand a powerful group of Witte's enemies at the court favored a stronger line at every point and were convinced that this advocacy was the key to destruction of Witte as well as to the construction of Russian greatness in the Far East. By August 1903 they had succeeded in getting Witte fired from his post as minister of finance. ("Now I rule," the czar wrote in his diary.) As a second step, the hardliners established the Viceroyalty of the Far East, centered at Port Arthur.

Although the disagreements between the parties at St. Petersburg were principally those of timing, that timing made a great deal of difference to the dispute with Japan. Japanese miscues at Seoul gave the Russians temporary advantage there. In the fall of 1896, while the Korean king was seeking Russian protection, he was persuaded to grant a concession to a Russian citizen for the organization of a Korean timber company with headquarters at Vladivostok and branches at Seoul and Chemulpo. The charter for the company permitted it a wide range of activities in opening up areas for lumbering and provided a suitable cover for Russian penetration of Korea. The concession area covered a large area along Korea's Yalu River boundary, the river delta town of Yongampo (renamed Fort Nikolai by the Russians in 1903) and an area at the southern tip of the Korean peninsula. Although this concession was not immediately taken up by the Russians, the victory of the hardliners in the years after the Boxer Rebellion guaranteed that it would be. In 1903, shortly before the fall of Witte, the Russian Lumber Company of the Far East was organized, and it soon became known to Japanese intelligence that numbers of the lumberjacks employed were actually military personnel. By then the Japanese had recovered from their errors of 1895-96 to reemerge as the most important political and economic influence throughout the major cities of Korea. Korean markets were now important to the growing Japanese textile industry, and Korean rice mattered to a Japan already at the limit of its own food production. Japanese capital had developed a railroad between Pusan and Seoul, and Japanese investors were anxious to extend it farther north; the Russians saw the approach of this line in much the same light that General Yamagata had viewed the Trans-Siberian.

In its attempts to deal with this problem, the Tokyo government tried first of all to reach an agreement with the Russians. When this failed, they turned to rounding up international support. After the Sino-Japanese War, Japanese and Russian understandings had been concluded by the Yamagata-Lobanov (1896) and Nishi-Rosen (1898) agreements, the last of which had recognized Japan's commercial, residential and industrial rights in Korea. As Russian pressure on Manchuria rose, the Japanese sought reassurances; in July 1900 they proposed the delimitation of spheres of influence in Korea and Manchuria, but the Russians were not prepared to give up anything. There might be differences about how much to claim, but there were few advocates of renouncing rights, or possibilities, even in Korea. There is evidence that the Japanese government considered taking strong measures to assert control over all but northernmost Korea at this time, but that it decided to secure Western backing first.

It was in this setting that the Japanese alliance with England (negotiated after a prior attempt by Itō Hirobumi to reach agreement with the Russians) came in 1902. By its terms both countries recognized the independence of China and Korea, pledged themselves to remain neutral if either became involved with another power to defend those interests and promised to join the war if the other was attacked by a second power in the course of such an involvement. Put in practical terms, this meant that England would exercise a benevolent neutrality if Japan became engaged in war with Russia and would join the fight if a third country should join the Russians. Thus no new Triple Intervention could take place without a general European conflagration, a price Russia's friends were not likely to pay in defense of the czar's Manchurian empire.

Protected from the mistakes of 1895, the Japanese now found their position immeasurably stronger. They posed as the champions of the territorial integrity of China and reached agreement with the United States for parallel agreements with China that provided for treaty ports at Mukden and Antung—measures the Russians refused to concede. Japan's interests in blocking Russian domination of Manchuria were now parallel with those of Washington in its advocacy of the Open Door. Moreover, since President Theodore Roosevelt had come to the conclusion that Japanese acquisition of Korea was in the best interests of East Asian peace as well as of the Korean people (a conclusion implicit in the Taft-Katsura talks), there was no immediate likelihood of a conflict of interests with America.

Japan and Russia now entered a collision course. The attempt by Japan to secure new open-port privileges in Manchuria was answered by Russia's reoccupation of Mukden. In 1903 the Russians presented the Chinese with a series of demands for extension of their Manchurian privileges as the price of evacuation. These were strikingly prophetic of the Japanese Twenty-one Demands of 1915 in the way they were handled and received. The Russians denied to other powers that they had done anything of the sort; the Chinese leaked their contents and refused to sign, and the powers, especially Japan, protested. Russian suggestions that Japan create a neutral zone in North Korea were answered by Japanese demands for such a zone on both sides of the Yalu. The Japanese refused to accept limits on their freedom of political (and military) action in Korea, while the Russians refused to recognize any Japanese interests in Manchuria or to affirm the territorial integrity of China as a whole.

The Tokyo leaders let it be known that they were under consistent pressure from domestic advocates of a strong policy, although they did nothing to discourage, and occasionally seemed to stimulate, the agitation. From 1901 on, popular organizations enlisted men of many affiliations to channel agitation against the Russians. A large popular league was organized to press for action. A new patriotic society, the Amur (Kokuryūkai, in literal translation, the famous "Black Dragon") Society was set up to lead the drive, and university professors (notably the "seven jingoes" of Tokyo University) led public demands for forthright steps. Hara Kei, a leading Japanese parliamentarian, put it this way: "It is a fact that our people didn't want to go to war. But it seems as though the government encouraged the seven professors to call for a strong policy toward Russia, stimulated the formation of the People's Association for Russian Policy and encouraged its advocacy of a hard line, in order to pressure the Russians to grant a better commercial treaty, and then, unexpectedly, found itself forced to go to war."

On the Russian side, important figures felt that an easy victory, as they expected it to be, would help to strengthen support for a faltering regime. Russia was in possession of all it wanted, and the dissatisfaction was Japan's; there were therefore few advocates of war, but overconfidence was too general to produce concerted efforts to head off the war by compromise. In the final negotiations at the end of 1903 the Russians insisted that their side be represented by the Viceroyalty of the Far East, thus guaranteeing a military and proconsular response to Japanese insistence that their minimal requirements be met.

Japan's final decision for war was a sober one, made in full realization of the discrepancy between Russian and Japanese strength. It was dictated by the conviction that the future of the country was at stake and that the odds of success would worsen and disappear as the Trans-Siberian Railroad made it easier for Russia to bring its full strength to bear. At least, the Japanese thought, they could score some important initial victories, and these would enable them to deal with the Russians from a stronger bargaining position. The Meiji leaders' anxiety about the outcome was also tempered by their confidence that their ally and friends among the Open Door advocates would not find it in their interest to see Japan crushed. Diplomatic help could be expected before their condition became desperate. In the supreme command's final presentation of the case for war before the emperor, General Kodama, chief of staff, explained this as follows: "There is a good chance that Japan will win six out of ten victories on the battlefield. If that is the case, we can expect some country to step forward to offer its good offices to negotiate peace."

That country had to be the United States. France and Germany were unsuitable, the one as ally of Russia and both as participants in the Triple Intervention. Great Britain, Japan's ally, could not serve as intermediary. America, on the other hand, had the liveliest interest in the Open Door, which Japan professed to serve. President Roosevelt had formed a great respect for Japan and saw in its rise a much-needed element with which to correct the imbalance of power in northeastern Asia growing out of Russia's developing economic and military strength. Roosevelt's ideas of stability and balance could be expected to make him advocate a negotiated settlement. Destruction of either belligerent would upset the balance, open China to partition and bring dangers for the security of the United States. Therefore, immediately after leaving the imperial conference where the war decision had been made in February 1904, Itō Hirobumi summoned Kaneko Kentarō, a Harvard classmate of Roosevelt's, to his residence and asked him to go to America to stay close to the president. Kaneko met regularly with the president and kept Tokyo fully informed of Mr. Roosevelt's thinking. He also kept the president informed of the nature of Japan's interests and intentions in the war.

With political and military preparations complete, the Japanese informed the Russians that they were severing diplomatic relations on 6 February; they declared war on 10 February 1904. They realized, however, that in a struggle between unevenly matched parties speed and surprise are essential for the smaller, and they planned to have the main Japanese fleet attack Port Arthur and bottle up the principal elements of Russia's Asiatic fleet there. This they did on 8 February. The world was less shocked by this tactic in 1904 than it would be a half-century later at Pearl Harbor; the *London Times,* for instance, hailed the Japanese navy for "an act of daring which is destined to take a place of honour in naval annals."

In the early stages of the fighting, the contestants were very nearly equal in strength. Russia's forces in the Far East were divided, however, between garrisons for Port Arthur (whose forts were still uncompleted) and Vladivostok. They were poorly integrated, imperfectly prepared and poorly led. The Japanese, by their successful action against the Russian fleet, were able to bring their best armies to bear for the early battles, engagements in which they also had a numerical superiority. The first great encounter, one which had considerable importance as the first victory of an Asian army over a European force in modern times, came at the Yalu River in May of 1904. Later that same month another Japanese army, landing at the neck of the Liaotung Peninsula, was able to break through strong Russian positions to advance down the peninsula. Several of its units, constituted as a separate army under the command of General Nogi, then marched south to attack Port Arthur, whose hills and guns sheltered the Russian Asiatic fleet. Port Arthur was strongly held, although its defenses were still incomplete, and at its barren circumference the Japanese troops received a foretaste of the trench warfare of World War I. Semipermanent gun positions utilized every knoll, and concentric trenches gave supporting, enfilade, and cross-fire at every point. Wire entanglements lay in front of the trenches, and machine guns and searchlights, including those of the Russian warships in harbor, combined to complicate the plans of the attackers. The Japanese paid dearly for every foot they gained. The siege began in June, and by the time the fortress was surrendered six months later, Nogi had suffered over fifty thousand casualties, nearly one-half his total strength. A Nogi order of the day applied the samurai code succinctly: "No man must hope to return. Every officer must appoint his successor." Russian losses in total strength and casualties had been about half those of the Japanese.

While the siege of Port Arthur ground on, the main Russian armies hesitated between defensive measures designed to provide time for the arrival of additional armies via the Trans-Siberian and counterstrokes for the relief of Port Arthur. The Japanese armies attacked vigorously but never succeeded in turning the ponderous Russian retreats into routs. Russians retreated along their railroad lines to Mukden, where they were again outmaneuvered in a great battle in March 1905. Each side now had some three hundred thousand effectives in the line; Russian losses were nearly one-third their total forces, the Japanese about one-sixth. The Russians had been defeated but far from crushed, and the Trans-Siberian, which had been much improved in its ability to carry troops during the war, continued to guarantee ultimate advantage for the Russians. After the Battle of Mukden General Ōyama, the Japanese commander, sent General Kodama to Tokyo to warn his colleagues that the armies could do little more without massive reinforcements of men and materiel. This was impossible. General Yamagata and the other leaders realized that Japan, its resources and credit severely strained, could do little more and argued for making peace instead of trying to march on to Harbin or hold extensive defensive positions at Mukden.

One further test remained. In hope of regaining command of the sea, the Russians sent most of their Baltic fleet, a collection of some forty-five vessels, halfway around the world to defeat the Japanese navy. Thanks to the driving energy and determination of Admiral Rozhestvensky, the fleet reached Asian waters in what was a marvel of supply and endurance. Shelter in several French ports (notably Cam Ranh Bay in Vietnam) and Madagascar and coaling assistance from a German shipping line was important. But when the long line of

PRESIDENT THEODORE ROOSE-
VELT AT PORTSMOUTH (1905), with
Witten (extreme left) and Komura
(second from right).

warships tried to make for Vladivostok and repairs, they were intercepted at
Tsushima in May 1905 by the Japanese battle fleet, which scored an overwhelming victory and sank all but three of the Russian ships. It was, as President
Roosevelt wrote Baron Kaneko, a victory more complete and overwhelming
than those of Trafalgar or the Armada.

The Russians had now lost any hope of support from the sea, and though
their armies were strong and growing stronger, their financial crises were scarcely
less serious than those of the Japanese. Their political situation was even more
threatening. With defeat, Russian credit in Paris, Belgium and Berlin had declined; with victory, Japanese credit in New York and London improved. Still,
Japan had no confidence in its ability to break the deadlock of the Manchurian
front. Now was the time to utilize the help of the third power whose intervention General Kodama had predicted.

On 31 May Foreign Minister Komura formally asked President Roosevelt
to provide his good offices. The Russians, troubled by political unrest and
financial pressure, agreed to meet with the Japanese at Portsmouth, New
Hampshire. The conference began in August.

The expensive and impressive victories the Japanese had scored meant
that their price of agreement at Portsmouth would be higher than it had been
in the negotiations that preceded the war. As before, their demands included
full freedom of action in Korea and sharp limitations on Russian activities in
Manchuria. A new priority demand was for transfer of the Russian holdings
and privileges in south Manchuria to Japan. Russia would retain only the
trans-Manchuria crossing of the Chinese Eastern and would have to guarantee

to Japan privileges and opportunities in the north. The impression of unbroken victories that the Japanese public had received made it unlikely that they would be satisfied without additional benefits; territory in the form of Sakhalin, a massive indemnity to cover war expenditures and, some believed, restrictions on fortifications of even Vladivostok.

The Russian delegation, headed by Count Witte, came to America prepared to grant Japan's minimal demands and determined to avoid the indignity of territorial concessions and indemnity. President Roosevelt, working behind the scenes with American purposes of stability and peace in mind, prevailed upon the Japanese to give up their demands for indemnity. The talks very nearly failed, but when the Russians offered Japan the southern half of Sakhalin in place of money, expecting fully to be turned down, they were startled by an acceptance.

Japan had now achieved first-class membership in the concert of powers. She had defeated the largest land power and reclaimed territory and privileges that power had prevailed upon her to give up ten years earlier. She had secured, first from China and then from Russia, agreements to refrain from interference in Korea. She had secured the departure from Manchuria of Russian forces and the recognition by Russia of China's territorial integrity. Her northern borders had been extended, and Hokkaido, once developed anxiously with thoughts of Russian aggression in mind, was now well within the circle of Japanese power. With freedom of action in Korea and ready access to Manchuria, with Taiwan and predominant influence in Fukien and Chekiang, and with equal rights in central China, she need fear no check to her manufactures or acquisition of raw materials. The largest naval power was her ally and banker; the Anglo-Japanese Alliance had been renewed in 1905. England, in turn, had allied with France. The United States had acquiesced in Japan's plan to offset Russian power in northern Asia, and the Taft-Katsura agreements in the summer of 1905 seemed to convey American realization of the inevitability of Japanese control over Korea.

Yet the Portsmouth Treaty aroused much opposition in Japan. Popular ignorance of military and financial exigencies and complacency about favorable military encounters had bred heroic expectations; some popular politicians and journalists spoke confidently of the concession of Siberia up to Lake Baikal, and most expected at least an indemnity. But the senior statesmen knew better, and they would have accepted peace without an indemnity or any part of Sakhalin. Nevertheless, the public, when the terms became known, execrated Foreign Minister Komura as a weakling who had gained nothing at the conference table, had returned only with what the army had seized in Manchuria, and had failed even to retain all of the territory that had been won in Sakhalin. Komura left Japan a hero and returned almost a villain.

Since in any event the Russian presence in the Far East remained strong, one of the first postwar problems to which the government leaders devoted themselves was the security of their newly won position and gains. Agreement with Russia seemed the natural course to the oligarchs who had wanted to solve the problem in that manner from the first. Manchurian and Mongolian interests and rights were delimited by agreement between Japan and Russia, understandings were advanced further in 1910 and 1912 by agreements to preserve and protect each others' interests and zones against outside interference. United States interests had shown the need for this with their unsuccessful attempt to neutralize and utilize the Manchurian railroads for a round-the-world transportation network. Japanese and Russians also cooperated to prevent the new consortium loan to China of 1912 from changing the balance of economic power in their areas. Once the spheres of activities were laid out, in other words, Japan and Russia were fully agreed on the need to restrict the applicability of Open Door doctrines in northeast Asia. Their reasons were identical. Both were low-capital countries, and both would fare poorly in a state of open competition; both felt it necessary to protect their zones by special privileges and favor against more advanced countries. Significantly, in each instance the senior leaders took the initiative in proposing the agreements with the Russians. Itō Hirobumi was in Harbin to talk with the Russian representatives when he fell victim to a Korean assassin in 1909, and Prince Yamagata also was a consistent advocate of better relations with the Russians after the war.

The alternative, in their eyes, was further struggle with Russia. Japan prepared for this while hoping it would not be necessary. The army assumed that a war of revenge would be planned by Russia and set as new goal a peacetime army of twenty-five active divisions (nearly double the thirteen projected after the Sino-Japanese War). The army regarded Manchuria as the center of the nation's defenses, and sharp controversy resulted from civilian attempts, even under the lead of a senior statesman like Prince Itō, to interfere in planning and direction. The Japanese navy, on the other hand, surveyed its new responsibilities and felt that, in view of the possible confrontation with the United States (an awareness sharpened by immigration and school crises, development of bases in the Philippines and the growing talk of "yellow peril" and racial confrontation), Japan required two battle fleets, each headed by eight of the newly developed dreadnoughts, which had suddenly rendered the world's existing naval ships obsolete. The enormous costs of these programs, added to those of the war with Russia, should be kept in mind when considering the disappointment many Japanese expressed with their failure to receive an indemnity from the Russians. Japan was living well beyond its means in paying for the role of a world power, and this time there was little of the ebullience and euphoria that followed the quick, profitable and almost bloodless victory over China in 1895.

7. State and Society in Imperial Japan

THE DECADE between 1895 and 1905 which spanned the period between the wars with China and Russia was critical in the development of modern Imperial Japan. The period was remarkable not so much for specific incidents or move-

ments as it was for the clear evidence that with modernization Japan was beginning to produce distinct interest groups. Despite the rhetoric of national unity
and the undoubted willingness of all to sacrifice more for goals that had not yet
been reached, there now began to develop significant differences in the way
specific groups saw those goals. The oligarchy itself began to develop differences
within its ranks, not merely from personality, but from the influence of groups
that looked to one or another for protection and leadership. After 1900, major
figures like Itō and Yamagata withdrew from front-line positions to let their disciples and protégés take public responsibility. The disciples were soon desirous of
independence. New specialist groups began to be produced; the military were
quite different from the civilian bureaucracy in experience and outlook. Rural-
urban differences increased. And a new business class began to figure much more
importantly in all planning.

At the highest level of government, the decade saw a shift in the balance and
importance of political parties and government leadership. It began with efforts
to recruit party support for cabinets led by senior figures. Itō, the greatest of those
figures, next tried to organize his own party. Thereafter the first-generation
oligarchs retired to the status of genro, senior statesmen and advisers, controlling
major decisions from behind the scenes. When they began to diminish in number
and vigor, the figures and groups who would share the power that had long been
concentrated in genro hands were ready in their places.

These changes began immediately after the Sino-Japanese War, when Prime
Minister Itō invited the liberal leader Itagaki to join his cabinet. His lead was
followed by Matsukata, who enrolled Ōkuma in his cabinet the following year.
Matsukata was followed again by Itō. Itagaki, resentful at Itō's failure to include
him a second time, now turned to his party rival Ōkuma. Together they formed
the Constitutional Government party (Kenseitō, 1898) and mustered a Diet majority so convincing that Itō, who had come to the conclusion that the parties
would never be responsible unless they were trusted with substantial power,
recommended that Itagaki and Ōkuma be permitted to form a cabinet. Itō's suggestion was accepted, and he left for a trip to China shortly after the new cabinet
was installed in office. In his absence the party cabinet fared badly. It was hampered by lack of cooperation from the bureaucracy and the House of Peers, both
of which were controlled by Yamagata. Worse, Itagaki and Ōkuma were unable
to agree on a proper distribution of posts and cabinet seats between the two parties. Ōkuma held the foreign minister's as well as the prime minister's chair.
Itagaki's lieutenant, Hoshi Tōru, who was serving as minister in Washington,
wanted the foreign ministry post and returned to Tokyo against the express orders of Ōkuma. Even worse difficulties followed a slip by Education Minister
Ozaki Yukio, who deplored the rising influence of big business and suggested
that if Japan were a republic an industrialist would head its government. This hy-
pothetical allusion to republicanism was promptly denounced as disrespect to the
emperor, and the cabinet fell during the partisan squabble over Ozaki's chair
after he had resigned. Ōkuma expected a mandate to form another cabinet, but

instead Yamagata saw to it that the resignation was accepted and agreed to head the next cabinet himself.

The period of experimentation with the Meiji Constitution was now drawing to a close. At the outset, the Meiji leaders had not had a very clear view of what the roles of cabinet and Diet would be. They had thought the government would devise policy and the Diet would vote the funds. Their party opponents, on the other hand, were chiefly concerned with lessening the distance between themselves and effective power. They thought in terms of party members serving as ministers, and after 1898 they thought in terms of party cabinets. At first the Meiji leaders had been equally uncertain about the way a cabinet should work. The Constitution said nothing about this, and with good reason, for there was neither precedent nor program. The Meiji cabinets were responsible to the emperor, and at least three ministers reported to him directly; in fact they were responsible to the leadership group collectively. It had not been clear that the prime minister would be more than first among equals, and it was expected that a kind of collective leadership would emerge. The Meiji emperor, in fact, expressed this in one council deliberating the choice of a prime minister by asking why his councillors did not resolve the issue by taking turns in the job. Had there been a clearly designed superior-subordinate position, there could never have been an arrangement like that in 1893, when Itō was prime minister and Yamagata, Matsukata, Inoue and the others served with him. Gradually the cabinets had become divided between oligarchs as divisions between Itō and his group, Yamagata and his, and the Satsuma interest became visible. Meanwhile the service ministers stood to strengthen their institutional stand and backing, for they alone reported back to a fixed constituency. And while the genro leaders, notably Itō and Yamagata, remained cautious and rather slow-moving, their more "professional" juniors like Generals Kodama and Katsura began to show the kind of drive and confidence that won arguments and swayed policy.

Divisions within the elite created new opportunities for differences between oligarchs and the Diet. Itō, who felt most responsible for the success of the Constitution, came to the conclusion that it would be necessary for him to form a political party. He thought of a party made up of established and responsible people: the bureaucracy, wealthy businessmen, intellectuals—a party of "haves" with which the government could withstand the attacks of the jealous "have nots." His fellow oligarchs were not very enthusiastic about the idea of such a party, however; Yamagata was aghast at the thought of anything that would mix "government" and partisan purpose, and the emperor himself expressed his doubts. How much better, others had suggested, to make contact with the more respectable of the party leaders. But the Ōkuma-Itagaki cabinet had been tried and had failed. Itō then determined to go ahead with his party and approached the groups with whom he had worked earlier. In 1900 he announced the formation of the Friends of Constitutional Government party (Rikken Seiyūkai).

For the most part the Seiyūkai was not so much a "new" party as it was an addition of new men to the old Jiyūtō. The senior leaders like Itagaki disappeared from party politics, and a new generation of aggressive and ambitious younger men took their places. Hoshi Tōru was one of these, and his attitude on working for Itō was perfectly frank. "We won't let the old men lead us for very long," he said; "once the foundations have been laid, let's expel them all beginning with Itō, and do as we please." The foundation of the Seiyūkai was clearly a new era in political history in Meiji Japan; the genro had decided that party politics had come to stay.

Not that they were equally enthusiastic about it. Yamagata was prime minister while Itō went ahead with his plans for forming the party, and he took all possible measures to see to it that the new arrangement would not make it possible for party men to inherit power. A revision of the Civil Service Ordinance (1899), an ordinance restricting the service ministries to generals and admirals on the active list (1900) and an ordinance broadening the powers and role of the Privy Council (1899) made it unlikely that the new party would do a great deal of harm. Then, without waiting for Itō to complete his preparations, Yamagata resigned as premier and suggested Itō as his successor. "It's just like Yamagata," Itō grumbled, "to launch a surprise attack before the enemy has prepared his positions."

Yamagata's fears of party power proved exaggerated. Itō now had support in the lower house of the Diet, but he had the hostility of the House of Peers, and for the first time the government's programs ran into trouble in that normally cooperative chamber. Even after he managed to quell that rebellion by a special imperial rescript, he found himself unable to provide the leadership necessary to unify the political and bureaucratic elements in his cabinet. Within seven months he returned his powers to the emperor.

The Itō cabinet of 1900 was the last to be headed by a founding father. The second line of leaders now took over; Yamagata's protégé, Katsura, followed as premier, and Itō turned over his Seiyūkai to the young aristocrat, Saionji Kimmochi. Katsura and Saionji maintained a harmonious cooperation for the balance of the Meiji period, the former serving almost five years, Saionji for three and one half, Katsura another three years, and Saionji a final year. It had been Itō's desire to continue to direct the affairs of the Seiyūkai, but Yamagata, responsive to Katsura's argument that it gave the opposition an unfair advantage to have its man represented in the highest councils, persuaded the emperor to force Itō to retire from active politics to head the Privy Council. From that lofty pinnacle of imperial impartiality Itō was glad to escape to the more interesting task of resident general of Korea in 1905, a post which he held until shortly before his assassination by a Korean in 1909.

"The social history of nations," according to Namier, "is largely moulded by the forms and development of their armed forces"; General de Gaulle added that "the military body is the most complete expression of the spirit of a society." No doubt this is particularly the case when modernization has been defensive against the threat of outside interference.

Japan's modern leadership was drawn from a samurai elite, and this had a double result: an unquestioned agreement on the necessity to build a strong military force, expressed in the ubiquitous slogan *fukoku kyōhei* (Chinese: *fu kuo, ch'iang ping*) and, from the fact that all the leaders considered themselves to have competence in things military, a relatively slow differentiation of a purely military faction. In the first years Meiji "civilian" leaders like Ōkubo Toshimichi had no hesitation in assuming command of the armies to stamp out rebellion. The assumptions and values of the military contest, with its high premium on performance and its goal of total victory, also gave, and give, their tone to political discussions in Japan. Unlike the American newspaper headline, which uses the language of sports for politics and often for war, in Japan the language of the sports page, like that of political discussion, has relied on the terminology of battle. Yamagata and his lieutenants urged parliamentary maneuvers to coordinate information from "spies" and then strike the "enemy" in the "center of the line"; popular calls for action spoke of "annihilation," "destruction" and "utter rout of the opposition." Even a "civilian" like Itō, when he came to the decision to form his own political party, phrased the problem in military terms: "I am tired of mercenaries," he said; "I want my own army."

The beginning of the emergence of a distinct military interest in the Meiji period can be dated from 1878, the date of the decision to form a general staff charged with command functions and responsible directly to the throne. The model for this was taken from Prussia. During the following year a board was set up within the army charged with supervision and education. Its final designation, in 1898, was the Board of Education. Its head, the inspector general of military education, became substantially as powerful and important as the chief of the general staff and the war minister, both of whom reported directly to the emperor, and together they were known as the "big three" of the army. The position of the army and navy was strengthened in the constitutional structure by the requirement that the service ministers be drawn from the services. This meant that they were responsible to the army and navy rather than to the prime minister. As early as 1891, a year after the Constitution went into force, the army informed Premier Matsukata that it would not provide a war minister unless it received the budget expansion it had requested. In 1898, during the Ōkuma-Itagaki cabinet, the army secured a special imperial command for the war and navy ministers to serve to make it clear they were not holding office at civilian behest. And in 1900, as party rule seemed closer, Yamagata secured an imperial ordinance formalizing what had been the practice: war and navy ministers should be chosen from the active list of senior generals and admirals. This provision, relaxed in 1913, was reinstituted in 1936 and formed a powerful lever for the services to use in preventing formation and forcing dissolution of cabinets.

Military education gradually began to provide an officer corps distinct in experience and outlook from the civilian elite. The main path to career ad-

vancement in the army involved leaving the regular sequence of public education after lower school. Middle and high school years found the officer candidate subject exclusively to military instruction and environment, and if he
succeeded in this he could go on to the officers academy and, with luck, the war
college. Military education thus produced a race apart, men who arrogated
to themselves the virtues of the samurai tradition of simplicity and bravery
and tended, all too often, to see simple solutions to complex problems.

The reverse side of military insistence on freedom from civilian and political control was an outward refusal to become involved in politics. The early
Meiji leaders, themselves the products of a society dominated by a military
caste, saw much to praise in Western systems. To Kido Kōin the "fundamental
virtue" of government in "enlightened countries" was "the established distinction between the duties of the civil and the military." For years this meant
keeping the military out of major political decisions; when those decisions included the development of commoner instead of samurai troops and the dis-
banding of the old units, it was important to maintain these distinctions. A
rebellion in the imperial guard a decade after the Restoration gave point to
this. The Imperial Rescript to Soldiers and Sailors (1882) warned them never
to be "led astray by current opinions" or to "meddle in politics"; their duties
were loyalty and bravery, and their role was one of service. But in fact in a
modern nation-state involved in a breakneck attempt to build military
strength, every political decision had military consequences and vice versa.
The voting laws for the new constitution ruled out participation by members
of the armed service, but the military chiefs' participation at the highest levels
of government meant that they would set forth the national defense needs
there in the guise of disinterested patriots. Yamagata, the most political of the
first army generation, never took office without apologies for the fact that he
was a simple soldier who understood nothing of politics. Actually he had had
only one field command, and that a very brief one interrupted by illness, during the Sino-Japanese War.

The military became the core of the regional groupings in the new regime.
Chōshū dominated the army, and Satsuma the navy. Yamagata, the founding
father, was war minister from 1872, chief of staff from 1878, prime minister
twice, home minister and justice minister in two cabinets, head of the Privy
Council and until his death in 1922 the most powerful of the elder statesmen. His
Chōshū disciples dominated the army (including of course, the War Ministry)
into the 1920s, and charges against "Chōshū" favoritism were an important element in factional feuding as late as the 1930s.

With success in war the military was in a position to provide the national
heroes for the nation. They received most of the new peerages that were issued in
1895. Popular suspicions of politicians were fanned by a press that focused on
scandals and corruption and contrasted the simple samurai austerity which
soldiers professed. Japan's startling victories on the seas and on the battlefields

were also contrasted to the less glorious achievements at the conference tables. Interestingly enough, however, the heroes of the Sino-Japanese War were not the commanders, but the commoners who first showed their quality in battle; folk heroes like Shirakawa Danjirō, a bugler boy who was said to have blown the charge with his dying breath, became the Sergeant Yorks of popular culture in late Meiji.

Next to the armed services, the civilian bureaucracy was probably the strongest institutional force in the society of Meiji Japan. Tokugawa times had seen a remarkable proliferation of bureaucratic agencies in all of the domains into which Japan had been divided, and the dissolution of those units provided the new regime with an admirable pool of literate and able bureaucrats. The offices of the early Meiji state were dominated by these samurai administrators. Many of them found it difficult to adjust to the problems of discipline and regularity that are part of modern bureaucratic organization, however, and the emphasis on rationality and regularity in army training may have been one reason why the samurai oligarchs found themselves making such frequent use of their army colleagues for "civilian" tasks. With a view to recruiting and training a modern bureaucracy, the Meiji leaders established the Imperial (later Tokyo) University in 1877 with the specific aim of producing government officials. Its graduates could expect special preferment in salary and position over the graduates of any other school. Graduation from the university's divisions, especially that of law, became the criteria for membership in influential circles in foreign, financial and administrative bureaucracies. In the 1880s Yamagata, as home and justice minister, regularized the procedures for entry and administration. He was as insistent that local administrators be aloof from politics as he was anxious to keep politicians out of the cabinet. "The executive power," he lectured local officials in 1890, "is of the imperial prerogative, and those delegated to wield it should stand aloof from political parties and be guided solely by considerations of the general good in the discharge of their duties." In 1900, as he saw the approaching possibility of stronger political parties, he secured imperial ordinances which closed off the career civil service from outside political interference. As with the military, his assumption was that a group of dedicated career men could represent that higher purpose, theorized in the Hegelian view of the state and articulated in the Meiji language about the emperor. The strength of the career bureaucracy came to stand as an additional limitation on the freedom of action of elective (Diet) or appointed (cabinet) officials. Throughout all this, the Meiji statesmen were anxious to build strength that would not be subject to the whims of popular favor or the will of special interests. Their assumptions were that there was a possible ideal of government, a perfection of institutional pattern which would stand forth as "harmonious" and as "beautiful" as the virtue of the emperor. They envisaged these forces not as divisions of power but as parts of an indivisible perfection. During their lifetime the parts worked well enough, staffed as they were by followers of those who had designed them. Nonetheless the oligarchs were far from satisfied, and as they grew older they became increasingly dismayed by the idea that their countrymen were thinking more about self and less about service.

In late Meiji times a business interest was also beginning to emerge as a distinct interest group. It had required some time for it to stand forth with a program distinct from that of the government. The modern sector of the economy had been dependent upon government help and slow to take an independent stand. It was centered in a few large firms that came to be called *zaibatsu,* or "moneyed clique." These owed their origin to the decade of the 1880s, when the government, as part of its cutbacks under Matsukata, sold its expensive interests in modern enterprise. The two largest firms were the great Tokugawa house of Mitsui, which had been fiscal agent for the Meiji government from the first, and Mitsubishi, which began as a Tosa domain enterprise late in the Tokugawa period and ended in the hands of its chief administrator, Iwasaki. These men and their associates in similar firms were really members of the power elite and remained close to it. Mitsubishi enjoyed excellent ties with one of the political parties and was also close to Matsukata, long a minister of finance, while Mitsui established a particularly close relationship with the genro Inoue Kaoru, an associate of Itō and close to Chōshū centers of power. Mitsubishi grew through close contacts with the government's need for shipping, shipbuilding and coal, and many enterprises grew out of this. Mitsui, in addition to its fiscal services, was a leader in the production of textiles, mining, paper and trading. Inoue's ability to push for contracts with ore producers in China and his ability to mediate with government was central to the firm's growth. Other business interests also required and enjoyed close partnership relations with the Meiji government. Banking, and the productive enterprises that required capital, became the particular concern of Shibusawa Eiichi, whose "No. 1 Bank" (Dai Ichi Ginkō) network girdled Japan. Mitsui and Mitsubishi banks also grew, and the government helped with foreign exchange and industrial banks. Increased armaments and continental expansion brought other large concerns into being, particularly the Yasuda and Ōkura firms. Economic growth in Meiji Japan was so varied and multifaceted—everything "modern" had to be established almost from nothing—that a firm with capital, connections and enterprise almost invariably found itself the center of a bewildering network of businesses producing goods for or supporting its original specialty. The great firms, founder oriented and controlled like great political and military structures, came to straddle the modern part of Japan's economy with colossal conglomerates. The same names reappeared in all markets, and bureaucracies of executives "loyal" to their house staffed the vassal firms. Tokyo University and the great private universities founded by Fukuzawa (Keiō) and Ōkuma (Waseda) educated the officer corps for the armies of commerce.

Shortly after the close of the Sino-Japanese War an article in *Taiyō,* a popular monthly magazine, noted that hitherto the customs of feudalism had remained very much alive. "The officials of the government are considered men of high esteem; the private entrepreneurs are men looked down upon. Even in private banquets where there should be an equality of relations, the officials sit at the head and act arrogantly and the people use humble speech and bow their heads before them; even the powerful entrepreneurs. But recently, even the business men of our country have by degrees advanced their position and have sought to influence by their attitude the position of the politicians." It was now necessary for statesmen and bureaucrats to make private inquiries on many subjects, for it had become clear to all that a government that lacked the confidence of the business group could not hope to succeed.

The Sino-Japanese War marked the beginning of something approaching confidence in the relations between business and government. Government purchases during the war years, the opportunities for continental activities that were incorporated into the Treaty of Shimonoseki, and the Chinese indemnity, which was paid in gold in London, all marked new opportunities for growth. One index of this was the decision to begin the government's Yawata Iron and Steel Works. Far larger and more important, initially at least, were the developments in manufacturing, particularly textiles. These seem to have reached and then exceeded the capacities of the Japanese home market to absorb their product at about this time; together with the need of continental ores for Yawata, the need for additional markets contributed to the new interest in continental contacts. Japan's interests in Korea and China, her crash program of armament expansion that followed the Triple Intervention, and increased international stature after participation in the Boxer Rebellion, all stimulated business activity. The Tokyo government set in movement energetic measures to increase the supply and flow of finance capital. The Yokohama Specie Bank, first established in 1880, was reorganized in 1887 to make it a more efficient instrument of investment and exchange. After the Sino-Japanese War a network of local and national banks was set up to collect and allocate savings and encourage industrial expansion. Agricultural and industrial banks, coordinated with a Hypothec Bank, were established in 1896; the Industrial Bank of Japan came into being in 1900. Similarly the colonial banks of Taiwan (1899) and Korea (1909) were set up to direct economic expansion there. With this improved financial structure, the Chinese indemnity helped make possible the establishment of a gold standard in 1897. Japan's credit rating in foreign money markets improved. Previous discussions of foreign loans had always ended with warnings of foreign control; now there was no longer such danger, and foreign loans offered lower interest and access to large sums that were needed to promote the industrial drive. Nearly half of what was borrowed abroad was used on the continent. Thus the years after the Sino-Japanese War saw the Japanese government take energetic steps to prepare the setting for a substantial increase in the national productive capacity.

The Russo-Japanese War marked a decisive turn in the Japanese economy; for the first time the New York money market was open to Japanese borrowers. Tea and raw silk exports were giving way to manufactured goods: cotton fabrics, yarn, and silk fabrics. Imports of these products fell. A modern investment network had replaced the earlier methods of financing economic growth. Most important of all, the dependence of the modern sector upon the capital and savings of the nonmodern sector of the economy decreased. By 1902 government income from the land tax, which had carried the main weight earlier in the Meiji period, was less than 20 percent of its total income; instead, excise taxes on consumption, on income and business, and customs duties carried the load. The Russo-Japanese War also stimulated modern industry. Military spending increased many times. Heavy industry, still largely committed to armaments, grew rapidly. Change and improvement came in all varieties of manufacturing. "Second stage" enterprises dependent upon more advanced technology grew; electrical engineering, internal combustion motors and rubber processing were developed, and partnerships of various sorts between Japanese and non-Japanese enterprises began to be visible.

The spurt in the modern sector of the economy was reflected in area after area. The system of compulsory national education had been inaugurated in the 1870s. But real growth did not come until later. Figures for expenditure in education tell the story: the government spent less than 7 million yen in 1880, 10.5 million in 1890, 42 million in 1900, and 90.9 million in 1910. Vocational training for the modern sector was incorporated in the Vocational Education Law of 1894; by 1899 schools in fisheries, forestry, agriculture, sewing, midwifery and nursing were established, and in the early 1900s commerce, engineering and advanced technology constituted the core of an entirely new network of special and technical schools that formed an alternative to the university and helped equip young Japanese for the twentieth century.

The business classes naturally responded to all this activity with a positive attitude toward government and state policy. On the other hand, the fact that so much of the modern growth was state induced meant that they had to learn to live with authority and could not afford the luxury of an all-out battle with government. But they did develop strong interests in influencing and channeling political planning. And their cooperation became important to government leaders; "you businessmen can make or break the war effort," one army leader said to a business group in 1904. Leaders in the "modern" business sector also provided important services as mediators between the political parties, who needed their financial help and backing, and the bureaucrats, whose approval counted for a great deal in respect to allocation, currency exchange and regulation. These facts of economic life combined with social conventions of reciprocity and formalized courtesy to encourage a blurring of the line between the public and private sectors in interest and reward. The first decade of the twentieth century was witness to a number of scandals in which business and politics came together. In one, executives of a tottering sugar company bribed Diet members to have the government purchase their firm to make it a state monopoly; in another, textbook publishers were charged with bribing selection committees and school officials. A sharing of power undoubtedly increased temptations for corruption of this sort. Tokugawa Japan had known its full share of influence peddling, but

Japanese tolerance for official corruption was relatively low, with the result that the misdeeds of entrepreneurs and legislators received exceptionally strong denunciation from journalists. Private vengeance sometimes struck public offenders. In 1901 Hoshi Tōru, a prominent jurist, politician and cabinet member, was assassinated by a man who had once been president of a small "college" and the descendant of a house with a military background. Contemporary journals were quick to sympathize with the assassin, who wrote, "I have had no personal acquaintance with Mr. Hoshi Tōru, neither do I bear any personal enmity or ill-feeling toward him [but] ... his arbitrary and dishonest dealing and behavior ... disgusted me so much that I deemed it dishonourable even to discuss with him sacred educational affairs.... Hoshi ... has ... disorganized and corrupted the municipal administration of the City of Tokyo and has caused a degeneration in the moral character of the people of the city ... he has dared to commit the most ignoble crime of receiving bribes, and thus has caused disgrace to the nation, from His Majesty the Emperor down to the mass of the people."

A final, and vital, index of social change was to be found in the balance between rural and urban Japan. Around 1905 Japan became a qualitatively different country. The population picture was changing radically. The first post-Restoration figures for Japan indicate a population of 35 million in 1873. By 1893 the count stood at 41 million; in 1903 it was 46 million, in 1908, 48 and in 1913, 52 million. During the period 1903 to 1918 the population grew by one-fifth, or approximately 10 million. Moreover, since the agricultural population remained largely constant, this population increase meant that the population was being rearranged drastically, with most of the growth in the new commercial and industrial cities of Tokyo, Yokohama, Nagoya, Osaka and Kobe. By the end of the Meiji period the increase in city population was no longer so much the result of a move from country to city, although that continued, as it was a natural increase of the urban population.

The countryside was less and less able to feed these new mouths. Although figures and methods of reaching them are still subject to a good deal of dispute, it is clear that agricultural productivity had risen steadily during the earlier Meiji period. New and improved strains of grains, better farming methods and tools, more and better fertilizers and new incentives had the effect of raising food production steadily until the end of the century. Much of the capital for industrialization came from agriculture, and it was from agriculture that the Meiji government had met its needs for revenue and armaments. Since the franchise was extended to property-owning taxpayers who paid a minimum of 15 (after 1900, 10) yen annually, it was the land-owning farmers and landlords who voted. Professor Scalapino's summary shows that in the 1890 election 129 (of 300) representatives represented the landed groups, and only 19 were listed as coming from "industrial and commercial" backgrounds. In 1898 the count was still 168 for country and 42 for commerce and industry. In 1902, 127 (of 369) were classified as farmers and the next largest group (58) was made up of lawyers. It was because the lower house continued to represent a predominantly rural constituency that the Diet struggle over the land tax always provided such sharp controversy. But gradually the land tax began to take second place to taxes on the modern and commercial economy. A fixed land tax constituted a smaller and smaller proportion of revenue. Central and local government expenditures in 1880 stood at 92 million yen. In 1890, they were 126 million; in 1900, 425 million and in 1910, 834 million. Although land tax totals rose from some 50 million to 126 million yen during the same period, they were progressively less adequate for the growing government expenditures.

Not only did agricultural productivity fail to keep up with government expenditure; it failed to keep up with the growth of the Japanese population. From about 1900, agricultural products began to form a significant element in Japanese import statistics. These imports grew slowly but steadily, until by the years of World War I they constituted an important element of Japanese consumption, and government planners began to seek ways of having the colonies like Taiwan and, later, Korea make good this deficiency. Further problems came within Japanese agriculture. Population pressure and the favorable productivity rate meant that small-scale, labor-intensive cultivation with tenant labor was more profitable than large-scale, capital-intensive production. In the 1880s some of the government leaders argued the advantages of large-scale, Western-type production. In the 1890s such arguments were a thing of the past. Many writers recognized the growing tenancy rate as a national problem. By 1908, 45 percent of the land was cultivated by tenants, and no one could doubt that earlier optimism about a freeholding peasantry had been wide of the mark.

These conditions produced a good deal of social criticism, both forward and backward looking. Many writers deplored the trend toward commercialization, profit taking and seeking, and the destruction of the family and the village. Confucian teachings of the primacy of agriculture, modernized under the slogan of *nōhon shugi* (agriculture-first–ism), came back in a new form and language to argue against a social and fiscal system that seemed to threaten the stability of the countryside. Peasant families in stable villages, it was argued, made good soldiers, provided a guarantee against subversion by foreign ideology and guaranteed a country able to feed itself in wartime. Thus, arguments of morality, polity and strategy combined to emphasize the importance of maintaining healthy rural villages. Advocates of *nōhon shugi* argued for protection for tenants from exploitative landlords, but their arguments against the commercialization of the countryside also contained a nostalgic preference for the traditional status relationships of the countryside.

The significance of all this was that a division between the modern and the premodern sectors of the economy had become visible. The rural setting provided the backbone of the parliamentary strength of the political parties, and it was assumed to be a repository of the loyal, family-centered ethic on which the country had been built. But its importance to the government's fiscal policy had diminished and the real aims of national strength in the modern world meant that the government would place its first emphasis on urban strength and productivity. Both radicals and conservatives tried to deal with this problem, and the social and political thought of the late Meiji period grew in response to this dichotomy between the values of the old society and the importance of the new.

As is often the case, the awareness of a problem between the values of the new and the appeal of the old produced efforts to work out an orthodoxy to affirm the balance with tradition. Late Meiji times witnessed the development of a semiofficial Japanism that drew upon the prologue of the Constitution and the Rescript on Education as its sacred texts. Formulated by ideologists of the state, often in university posts, and popularized by the textbooks of the lower schools, these constructs grew in power. The ideas involved were by no means new, but their selection, emphasis and grouping marked a distinct contrast to the earlier modernization drive. Its concerns had been with things that were new, up-to-date and progressive; now the values were those of continuity and stability.

Central to the new orthodoxy was the view of the family state. Japan's polity, its *kokutai,* was asserted to be unique because its multiple-family hierarchies were but the expression of the national hierarchy. The emperor ruled his people like a father, and loyalty and filial piety, which were distinct (though complementary) virtues in China's Confucian lexicon, were one in Japan. Therefore Japan's was a perfect, a "beautiful," unity in which the individual moved and had his being only as member of the smaller and larger groups. Divisive influences of person, party and profit could not be reconciled with Japanese virtue. "Western" terms like competition, individualism and interest had no place in the life and world view of the family that was Japan. Moreover, since Japan was, it was claimed, uniquely homogeneous racially, the nation was in fact related, however distantly, to the imperial family. And so a religious awe and veneration surrounded the emperor, not in the sense of a transcendent divinity but as the embodiment of the respect that ancestral spirits generate in the hearts of the moral. A 1914 teachers' manual explained this connection:

> Amaterasu Omikami [the Sun Goddess] is not only the ancestor of the Imperial House but also of all Japanese. If we, the Japanese people, all seek our ancestry and parentage the greater part of us will prove to be descendants of the Imperial House. Of the rest, they are the descendants of the various gods who accompanied the Heavenly Grandson, Prince Ninigi, in his descent from heaven, and those who came over from Korea and China, but the numbers of these latter people were very small. . . . The connection between the Imperial House and its subjects is thus: one forms the main house and the others form the branch houses, so that from ancient times we have worshipped the founder of the Imperial House and the heavenly gods. Our relationship to this house is sincerely founded on repaying our debt of gratitude to our ancestors. As the main house it represents the whole nation and we render our devotion wholeheartedly to it.

It followed from this that Japan's structure was unique in its excellence and morality. While the young Meiji Emperor's Charter Oath in 1868 had spoken of searching for "wisdom throughout the world," it now became clear to patriotic Japanese that it was a moral act to extend to neighboring peoples the incomparable blessings of their superior moral order. As with domestic politics, foreign issues came to be seen as moral problems, in which Japan's "sincerity" was obstructed by lack of understanding or positive ill will. The ill will in turn could only be explained by moral lapses on the part of others; the effect of an unfavorable ethical climate, particularly a state of turbulence characterized by revolution and dynastic change (in contrast to Japan's unbroken continuity), the work of selfish and dishonest ruling groups (the Korean aristocrats or Chinese militarists) and the result of outside, non-Asian subversion (the Russians in Korea; Americans in China; world communism.)

The predominating notes in this newly developing code, then, were those of family, virtue and continuity. Japan need no longer "abandon absurd customs of the past," as the Meiji emperor put it in 1868; it had done so in abandoning feudal decentralization and returning to imperial rule. It had sought, and found, foreign wisdom, and that part of it that was acceptable had been enlisted in the service of a dynasty unchanging "from ages past." Concentration upon the uniqueness and morality of that dynastic and moral order provided explanation and understanding of the way family and court, fathers and ancestors, past and present, reinforced each other.

To what degree, and in what numbers, did Japanese believe this? Much of it was misty and at wide variance with the rational world of business and work. No doubt for many it provided a comfortable compartmentalization of faith and experience, convenient summaries of unproven and unprovable belief that only occasionally got in the way of practical action. It is particularly probable that the first generation of Meiji leaders and intellectuals, except for a minority of Shinto enthusiasts, distrusted it. They had received their training in the rational world of Tokugawa Confucianism, one in which respect for facts held sway, and this had been supplemented by the discovery of the inadequacy of their entire world view and the need for its reinforcement by the superior practicality and science of the West. Kume Kunitake, for instance, the chronicler of the Iwakura mission to the West in 1871-73, had become a specialist in historical scholarship, an influential intellectual and professor at the new Imperial University in Tokyo. But he also became an early victim of the new orthodoxy. When he published a reasoned discussion of the Shinto mythology in 1891, pressure to resign was brought to bear on him. It was less an issue of what was "true" or "false" than it was a concern with what was socially and morally appropriate or desirable, what was most desirable in the interests of the larger family that was Japan.

On the other hand, there is no question that the new ideology received its most unquestioning acceptance in the lower schools which began, at the end of the nineteenth century, for the first time to train practically all Japanese. Teachers' handbooks and the lower-school texts, in particular those dealing with "ethics" and history, set forth in romantic and cloying terms the faith of the family-state. Normal schools for lower-school teachers also featured firm discipline and an almost military atmosphere. The teachers were trained as the defenders of official morality and truth. Late in the Meiji period, moreover, the extent to which the content of the educational system was centrally directed increased. Partly as a result of the commercial and fiscal scandals that had been disclosed in the textbook industry, the government began to select and prepare textbooks. State-compiled textbooks became instituted in 1903 because, as the minister of education put it, they "formed an essential part of the moral and civil education imparted in elementary schools ... it was thought advisable to reserve their compilation for the State." In 1907 compulsory schooling for all Japanese was increased from four to six years, and for the first time all Japanese received two years of instruction in Japanese history in those additional years.

The formulation and popularization of this new orthodoxy dated from the promulgation of the Meiji Constitution and the Imperial Rescript on Education. Both, of course, had been in process of discussion for the better part of a decade. But once they were adopted, a standard for conformity and orthodoxy came into being. This applied in numerous and subtle ways. The term "people," *jimmin,* long current in political discussions, for instance, tended to give way to *shimmin,* usually translated "subjects," or, originally, (imperial) "servants." With the religious and mystical overtones that accompanied the popularization of Shinto, it became inevitable that Christianity would be one of the areas of dispute.

In 1891 Uchimura Kanzō, who had accepted a position as instructor in the Tokyo First Higher School, was caught by surprise in an opening ceremony in which his colleagues bowed before the Rescript on Education, which had just been read in a ceremony of matriculation. Uchimura declined out of the feeling that, as a Christian, he should not take part in a semireligious rite. Upon discussion with his colleagues, he was persuaded that the ceremony was a civic and a patriotic one, and not truly religious. But by then his refusal was widely known, and social pressure had brought about his resignation. Uchimura was a patriotic Japanese. He deplored the conversion of Japanese into "universal Christians" who, he said, "turn out to be no more than denationalized Japanese"; he refused to accommodate himself to the dictates or institutions of Western churches and became the founder of the "nonchurch" *(mukyōkai)* movement in Japan. He supported the Sino-Japanese War and thought for a time that "Japan was formed to save the 400 million some Chinese, the more than 250 million Indians, and the other hordes on the continent.... The world looks to Japan, and requires of it revolution." Even after he parted company with Japanese imperialism and deplored the war with Russia, preferring to enunciate a Christian pacifism, he remained insistent that he was a "Japanese Christian." But his act of conscience, as unusual in Meiji Japan as it was unpremeditated, made him the perfect target of hostile criticism.

The task was taken up by Inoue Tetsujirō, a Tokyo Imperial University professor of philosophy who had recently returned from Germany. Inoue leaped to the attack with a series of books on education, religion and the Rescript on Education. He helped give a "modern" setting and language to the mystical cult of nation-as-organism, in which all patriotic Japanese found their place; the emperor's subjects were a father's children; "whether official or not, all are imperial servants"; loyalty and filial piety were one and indissoluble. Christianity, however, was Western, wrong and immoral. It preached equality and denied the principle of proper family structure; it held for universal instead of particular and graded love. It could not serve as moral setting for the unique virtues of the Japanese state structure, and Uchimura and his fellow believers were dangerous. Inoue had the better platform from which to be heard; the Education Ministry circulated his books, and he became, willingly enough, the spokesman of an official cult and ideology. Equally influential assertions of the philosophy of the family state were provided by Tokyo Imperial University Professor Hozumi Yatsuka. The products of this struggle, waged openly enough among scholars and publishers, were grossly simplified and bowdlerized by the time they came to take rest in the textbooks of the primary schools.

It is difficult to estimate the relative strength of forces in the last years of the Meiji period. Despite the formulation of a new and relatively restrictive orthodoxy, there were sufficient opportunities for criticism of the state to admit of a considerable variety of public response. In the famous pollution case of the Ashio mines in the 1890s, for instance, the opposition included almost all possible shades of political discontent. The Christian leader, Uchimura, the conservative Viscount Tani, Shimada Saburō of the political party movement, the young radicals Kōtoku Shūsui, Kinoshita Naoe and Abe Isō all participated; the agitation found echo in the Diet, where Tochigi prefectural representatives forced through a committee of investigation which brought legal recourse including a direct petition to the emperor. More often the bureaucracy won out. When Japan emerged from the unequal treaties, there were those who feared that unrestricted residence for missionaries (theretofore restricted to treaty ports) would result in mass apostasy from Japanism. The Diet passed a law curbing the right to teach religion in private (mission) schools, only to have the Privy Council disallow it as unconstitutional. At this point the Education Ministry implemented the plan anyway as an administrative decision, where it became famous as Ordinance No. 12.

In the years after the victory over Russia, bureaucrats who wanted to accelerate the economic growth necessary to pay for national strength did their best to minimize the social change and counter the radical thought that such growth was bringing with it. It was their hope to avoid the disintegration of social values that industrialization in the West seemed to have produced; as Katsura put it in 1908, "social policy will prevent socialism from taking root." At the level of exhortation, the Meiji emperor issued a Rescript on Thrift and Diligence that called on "all classes of our people to act in unison, to be faithful to their callings, frugal in the management of their households, submissive to the dictates of conscience and calls of duty, frank and sincere in their manners, to abide by simplicity and avoid ostentation, and to inure themselves to arduous toil without yielding to any degree of indulgence." A Local Improvement Movement tried to stay the deterioration of village life that harsh taxation and rapid urbanization had brought about. Credit associations, young men's associations and spiritual guidance all strove to restore social health. Administrative units of villages and of Shinto shrines were consolidated and simplified to increase bureaucratic control. A nationwide organization of former soldiers, the Imperial Military Reserve Association, was set up in order, as one sponsor put it, "to protect the *kokutai* and keep evil and materialistic foreign ideas from flowing into Japan." In General Tanaka's words, a strong populace that respected "cooperation, rules, and discipline" would also be "successful in conducting agricultural, manufacturing, commercial, and other industrial efforts." The reality fell far short of these bureaucratic dreams, but these attempts nevertheless did their part in increasing the divisions between country and city in twentieth-century Japan.

Yet it can not be concluded that late Meiji Japan was despotic and totalitarian. The fully destructive and coercive aspects of ideological compulsion still lay in the future, after orthodoxy had been challenged more thoroughly. Meiji constraints should probably be seen as the fruits of a half-century of united effort under the unchallenged primacy of national service, a generation during which the phrase "for the sake of the country" (*kuni no tame*) satisfied all doubts for a generation one step away from feudalism. This approach helped to create a setting in which the readiness to deplore supposed subversion and to strengthen the comforting orthodoxy through exhortation and enforcement was very great. It is significant that on a number of occasions the pressures for this came not from above, where the government carried on its work of modernization, but from below. Shortly after the Russo-Japanese War patriotic organizations among school teachers campaigned for a uniform and orthodox treatment in school texts of fourteenth-century Japanese history, a period when there were two rival lines of emperors. Editorialists and politicians joined the fray until the cabinet had to intervene with promises to rewrite the texts and label the period and dynasties correctly. The reverberations of this extended to Tokyo University, where the catalogue titles of courses covering the period were brought into line.

Perhaps one should derive from this a new awareness of the ambiguities of the modernization process. Life had become better for millions of Japanese but also less meaningful for some of them. Japan had become far more powerful than it had ever been, only to ask its people for new and greater sacrifices to maintain that position. Japan had become an ideal or model for some of her East Asian neighbors, only to join the Western circle of imperialist powers. Many modern, educated Japanese had had to abandon much of what they had thought of as their national, cultural and intellectual tradition for a Western tradition that proved in important respects unassimilable or inappropriate, and they had worked out a new amalgam of mystical belief in the emperor-centered family state in compensation.

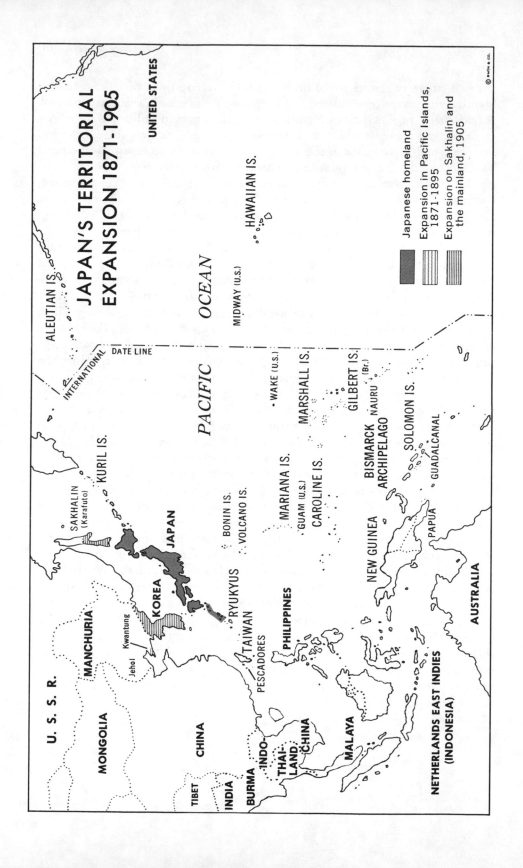

JAPAN'S TERRITORIAL
EXPANSION 1871-1905

Japanese homeland

Expansion in Pacific Islands,
1871-1895

Expansion on Sakhalin and
the mainland, 1905

UNITED STATES

ALEUTIAN IS.

INTERNATIONAL DATE LINE

HAWAIIAN IS.

MIDWAY (U.S.)

PACIFIC OCEAN

WAKE (U.S.)

KURIL IS.

SAKHALIN
(Karafuto)

JAPAN

BONIN IS.

VOLCANO IS.

MARIANA IS.

GUAM (U.S.)

CAROLINE IS.

MARSHALL IS.

GILBERT IS.

NAURU (Br.)

BISMARCK
ARCHIPELAGO

SOLOMON IS.

GUADALCANAL

KOREA

RYUKYUS

TAIWAN

PESCADORES

Kwantung

Jehol

MANCHURIA

U. S. S. R.

MONGOLIA

TIBET

INDIA

BURMA

CHINA

INDO-
CHINA

THAI-
LAND

MALAYA

PHILIPPINES

NEW GUINEA

PAPUA

NETHERLANDS EAST INDIES
(INDONESIA)

AUSTRALIA

CHAPTER 4

Japan and Change in Korea

Korea provided a third variant of East Asian response to the problems posed by the coming of the West and the need to modernize. Its response was warped by the fact that it became the first object of rivalry between Japan and China. It began as China's most important tributary and ended as Japan's most important colony. International rivalries caught the peninsula at a low ebb of political preparedness, and because its leaders were unable to respond effectively, the country became a helpless object of the Sino-Japanese and Russo-Japanese wars before it was swept completely into the Japanese orbit.

Without close examination of Korean society, observers might have been expected to suggest that Korea, like Japan, might well make an effective response to the problems of modernity. The country possessed great national unity, a homogeneous people and one of the world's longest histories as a national unit. It had a single, highly developed language, and in its adjustment to the Chinese writing system and vocabulary it had worked out a system of transcription far superior to the phonetic possibilities of Japanese syllabary. With close proximity to and knowledge of Chinese example, the Koreans had an advanced bureaucratic tradition led by an active and intensely politically motivated elite. The country was smaller and subject to fewer centrifugal forces than China, and its administration was much more united and centralized than that of Tokugawa Japan. Furthermore, the modern world challenged it last, so that it could have learned from both the Chinese and Japanese experience. In fact, the Korean response was less effective than either China's or Japan's. Our understanding of traditional Korean society is still very imperfect, but it is sufficiently informed to permit instructive comparisons and contrasts to the experience of Korea's East Asian neighbors.

1. Korea in the Nineteenth Century

NINETEENTH-CENTURY KOREA was under the rule of the Yi dynasty, which had come to power in 1392. Like Ch'ing and Tokugawa rule, this tenacious structure represented the final development of a political and bureaucratic tradition within the old society. Yi rule had begun with overwhelming authority at the center. The new rulers had nationalized all land and allotted it to tillers in line with the precedents of the T'ang dynasty in China. With time, however, the bureaucratic efficiency that was required to maintain this system in its rigor, with periodic division and review of holdings, had flagged. Fields for official posts, originally held only during periods of service, more and more ended in the hands of those to whom they were entrusted. Deserving officials and court favorites were given lands which became hereditary and often tax-exempt. They added to these by purchase, intimidation and reclamation. Landlordism and absentee ownership became widespread, and as the supply of state lands from which grants could be made dwindled, the competition for advantage became sharper.

These trends were vastly accelerated by great invasions which sapped the vitality of the dynasty. In 1592 and again in 1597 Japanese armies overran the peninsula, and between 1627 and 1637 Manchu armies revenged themselves for the support the Yi dynasty gave Ming armies that had helped them to drive out the Japanese. These disasters destroyed or disrupted the Korean polity and economy. The central government never recovered its control over the land system, and localities over which it exercised effective guidance dwindled by almost three-quarters. The state also lost much of its access to nonagricultural productivity, most of which had come from special guilds of unfree and semifree workers. The loss of population, guild and slave registers in these wars combined to remove the lower classes from central direction and deliver them into the hands of local leaders. If less stratified thereafter, they were not therefore free. Heavy pendants required for travel served as one example of the restraints on personal mobility and freedom that remained in effect.

Korean social standings were organized along the conventional Chinese rankings of scholar, farmer, artisan and merchant. But there were very important departures from Chinese example and Japanese adaptation. These were most immediately apparent at the top of the scale, with the privileged *yangban* class. The Yi dynasty marked the victory of Confucian values over Buddhist emphases in Korea, as did the Tokugawa polity in Japan. Korea went much further than Tokugawa Japan on the Confucian path, however, and indeed helped to transmit Sung Neo-Confucianism to Japan. Civil service examinations like those in China were instituted in Korea, and the ideal of excellence for government service was deeply implanted. The structure of the central government, with its Six Boards, was modeled upon that of Imperial China. Education in the Chinese classics was to provide the avenue of advancement.

But at this point the importance of heredity and the structure of official favor and private interest intervened to change the system. Entry to the examination system was limited for the most part to selected groups who were relatives or beneficiaries of officials. Preparation for the examinations took place in private Confucian academies maintained by large landholders. The *yangban* became a hereditary and privileged class, their concern focused on the family genealogies which formed their claim to privilege and chance of promotion and sponsorship.

During the entire five hundred years of Yi rule, 15,547 men passed the civil service examinations. Many more entered office through sponsorship and favoritism, and *yangban* numbers far exceeded successful examination candidates. Even sons of concubines, although technically excluded from consideration, claimed second-class membership. Estimates of *yangban* numbers range from 100,000 to 400,000. A more rigorous count, made at the time of Japanese annexation in 1910, totals 89,050, with dependents about 3 percent of the population of 12 million at that time. Those with imperfect or second-class membership numbered many times more, and were in fact so numerous as to produce a convulsive and desperate struggle for privileged status. Excluded by pride and standing from productive work, the *yangban* competed for political office. As the dynasty became less effective, positions tended to pass from hand to hand with extraordinary speed. Provisions of the early dynasty were instituted to prevent abuses of tenure; provincial governors held office for only a year, never in their own districts. These gradually gave way to an accelerating rotation in office. The mayor of Seoul, for instance, held office an average of six months throughout the entire half-millennium of the dynasty, and many high officials had as many as one or even two hundred public assignments during careers of three or four decades. This kind of official roulette meant that central government became increasingly superficial. Real power lay with the more permanent local elite, its continuity guaranteed by local and family solidarity. At the capital, meanwhile, kaleidoscopic changes resulted from what Gregory Henderson calls an "unlimited, atomized competition" for office that knew few parallels for ferocity. The central *yangban* families were deeply divided by factions and had long waged warfare on personal grounds camouflaged behind issues of Confucian rites and ceremonies. The proper length of time for mourning for parents, for instance, was important in a social group so intent upon heredity and genealogy, but it hardly suffices to explain the sweeping purges in the early centuries of Yi rule that sometimes took hundreds of lives. On occasion the bitterness was so great that corpses of the losers were dug up for mutilation and dishonor. By the nineteenth century, animosities sufficed to hamper effectiveness, but power was seldom sufficient to remove the opposition.

The political centralization to which the Yi kings aspired was not supported by a centralized market and economy. In the early years of the dynasty, major enterprises like pottery production, in which Korean craftsmen set standards that have seldom been surpassed, were largely restricted to state-run guilds of unfree and semifree workers. With the loss of state power after the great invasions, this central direction diminished, as did the quality of production. A small fraction of the population worked at primitive handicraft occupations. Villages were largely self-sufficient, and farmers had access to goods they could not make or acquire locally through traveling peddlers who moved from town to town for specified market days. The peddlers could serve political use for authorities as sources of information on real or fancied subversion, but their activities did not suffice to knit the economy around major market centers as was the case in Tokugawa Japan. The bars to commercial development were social and economic, however, and not the result of any deficiency in aptitude. Korean traders traveled between China and Japan in medieval times. The Koreans had led East Asia (and consequently the world) in the development of movable type, and the system of phonetic transcription (*han'gŭl*) worked out by a royal commission in 1446 remains one of the world's most efficient. But the greater social attraction of the brush-written Chinese character kept either advance from more widespread use until the twentieth century.

As in any premodern society, some 85 percent of the Koreans worked the land. The rise of local families and decline of central authority made it more difficult for the state to gain access to the land tax. Additional taxes on cloth and other handicrafts were added in attempts to make up the loss. The countryside was increasingly subject to the exploitation of the great families that held most of the best land. Circulation of goods and produce was not sufficient to prevent hardship and famine when crops were poor. Farmers tried to avoid unjust taxes by hiding fields, homes and families and seeking the support and protection of more powerful and wealthy neighbors. Thus the holdings of the powerful and wealthy grew in size. Meanwhile, family, clan and village associations developed in importance as farmers tried to work out some means of protection from their oppressive governors. Many, however, became subjects of economic and social exploitation by the self-styled and nonproductive *yangban* elite. Westerners who came to Korea in the 1880s and 1890s considered the handsome, vigorous people they encountered the most oppressed and misgoverned on the face of the earth. "The Korean official," wrote Mrs. Bishop,

> is the vampire which sucks the life-blood of the people.... Most officials of any standing live in Seoul for pleasure and society, leaving subordinates in charge, and as their tenure of office is very brief, they regard the people with-

in their jurisdiction rather with reference to their squeezableness than to their capacity for improvement.

Small wonder that nineteenth-century Korean chronologies contain accounts of famines, epidemics and similar calamities and that robbery, banditry and rebellion organized around discontented local gentry. The government's military forces were weak, and its low opinion of arms fastidious and extreme. It narrowly survived insurrections in the second and seventh decades of the nineteenth century, and its fear of new disasters in the 1890s led it to request the Chinese assistance that brought on the Sino-Japanese War.

Korea was also the most secluded of East Asian countries. Despite the vigor of the Tokugawa seclusion system, Korea was far more removed from Western influence than Japan. Writers sometimes suggest that Korea's proximity to China and the interest of the Manchu dynasty in maintaining the faltering Yi dynasty with which it had worked out a satisfactory relationship hampered impulses to break out of Korea's pattern of isolation. It is true that the Japanese and Manchu invasions weakened the Yi dynasty fatally without permitting its replacement. During the same period the stabilization of rule by the Tokugawa in Japan and the Manchus in China permitted autonomous developments that Korea was not to experience. Korea remained China's most faithful tributary. Missions went between the courts annually. For a time the Manchus stationed a resident in Seoul and kept Korean hostages at Peking, and throughout the nineteenth century the ceremonial arch north of the Seoul city walls stood as symbol of the importance of the mission from Peking. All Korean official papers and documents were dated in accordance with the Ch'ing calendar as a sign of submission. Yet the Manchus did not normally trouble themselves about Korean affairs or policy, and they did nothing to interfere with internal government. Moreover, the Koreans remained emotionally loyal and partial to the Ming, whose customs they had absorbed. They cordially distrusted and disliked their Manchu visitors and usually found they could turn unpleasant inquiries aside by bribing them discreetly.

Aside from these relations with China, Korea contacted Japan through the island of Tsushima, whose daimyo was permitted a restricted trade with the port of Pusan. Korean relations with the Tokugawa, initially hostile as a consequence of the Hideyoshi invasions, gradually improved, with the result that captives and hostages were returned, but throughout the two and one-half centuries of Tokugawa rule only twelve Korean missions came to Edo.

Through the frequent missions that went to Peking, the Korean elite gained some knowledge of the science that Jesuit missionaries brought to the Chinese capital. As scientific books in Chinese translation found their way into Korea, they became one of the ingredients of the school of "practical learning," which constituted one of the most creative branches of Korean intellectual life. More remarkable was the fact that Christianity came with the Jesuits' science. Without the possibility of direct Western missionary influence, a bookish Catholicism spread throughout Korea until there were thousands of converts. Unhappily, both scholarship and religion seem to have been concentrated in specific social groups that were easily identifiable and politically expendable, so that they made inviting targets for Confucian purists. Several persecutions took place, and in 1839, 1846 and 1866 the Catholic Church was all but wiped out in Korea. Thus Korea ended its traditional period with the same belief in Western subversion and corruption that characterized the first stages of the Tokugawa response to the missionary movement of the sixteenth century. This, too, influenced its rigid rejection of Western contact, and its indignant refusal of a Japanese attempt to establish modern, Western-style relations at the time of the Meiji Restoration.

2. *The Opening of Korea*

IN 1866 A FRENCH SQUADRON attacked the Korean island of Kangwha in an unsuccessful attempt to secure satisfaction for the murder of several French missionaries who had managed to make their way to Korea in time to become victims of the anti-Christian persecution of that year. Five years later several American warships appeared to protest the fate of an American trading ship that had ventured upstream in a Korean river. But these efforts were unavailing, and they were not followed up. China and Japan were the major prizes for the maritime West, and they were already open. Korea was not to know the traumatic shock of the determined Western approach that China and Japan experienced. Instead, its ports were opened as a by-product of the competitive modernization policies of China and Japan. These neighbors' efforts were more intimate and became more intensive. They had the faction-ridden Korean court elite to play and prey upon, and this precluded an effective national response.

At the time of the Korean opening, three fairly distinct factions were taking form in Seoul, and since their central figures continued to dominate the scene until the end of the century, it is useful to identify them. King Kojong, the last of the Yi dynasty, came to the throne in 1864 as an adopted heir. Since he was still a minor, however, his original father, descendant of a minor branch of the royal family, became his regent. The Taewŏngun (or, as often given, Taiwenkun), as regent, worked to strengthen the powers of the ruler by getting rid of encrusted privilege and building for himself a powerful position. As he became head of a faction, a second group of officials naturally centered around his son, waiting for him to attain his majority and hoping to ride into power when he should replace his father. But by the time the king came of age in 1874, a third group of officials had collected around his young queen, who had been selected from a *yangban* family named Min. Queen Min proved to be ambitious, skillful and determined, and her relatives became the center of a powerful political clique.

The issues between these groups were factional and political, not ideological or strategic. As the politics of foreign interference unfolded, each group was to be found in temporary and uneasy alliance with forces for seclusion and opening, reaction and reform, and China and Japan. The Taewongun began with a firmly reactionary and antiforeign position which led to the Christian persecution, the refusal to negotiate with France or America and the decision to rebuff Japan in 1868. But after it became clear that his tactics might bring on Japanese intervention, the Chinese removed him from the scene for several years, between 1882 and 1885, after which he preferred Japanese backing against Peking. Queen Min's group, on the other hand, began as an antithesis to the regent's and espoused relations with Japan for the reform of the country. But after Chinese power removed the regent, who blocked her path, she placed her confidence there and became a threat to Japanese influence until a ruthless representative of Tokyo masterminded her murder in 1895. King Kojong's position as head of the government made his participation essential to the hopes of other factions, but his attempts to balance off outside power while retaining his own made him shift successively from Chinese to Japanese to Russian counsel, each time in hopes of frustrating the plans of the power then dominant in Korea. His last service, years after the Japanese had forced his abdication, was to provide through his death and funeral the occasion for the first nationalist outpouring of modern Korea in the great independence demonstrations of 1919. Traditional Korean foreign relations had been contained in the phrase *sadae kyorin*, "service to the great and friendship with the near." But once the great hegemon in Peking became embroiled in competition with the near rival in Tokyo, no policy short of independence and national self-determination could offer hope. And this did not arise until the desperate play of factions had ended with the loss of independence to Japan and the dissolution of the elite that produced the factions.

The initial Japanese contribution to political instability in Korea was a direct result of political instability in Japan. As has already been pointed-out, the tensions and frustrations of early Meiji Japan, products of social change and national weakness and humiliation, found inviting focus in the thought of diverting them to Japan's weaker and less-modernized neighbor. The Korean regime of the Taewŏngun invited this through its contemptuous rejection of a Japanese proposal for modern diplomatic relations, and it risked drawing lightning by its inability to defend itself. The early Meiji government was confident that even samurai levies could give a good account of themselves in Korea. As samurai incomes and livelihood were abolished, many leaders thought of providing occupation for them in Korea, and a Japan unable to convince the Western treaty powers of its qualifications for diplomatic equality naturally thought of establishing its reputation as a modern gunboat power by avenging the insult from its smaller neighbor. Meiji politics began with the argument of 1873 about a punitive mission to Korea. Samurai rebellions continued the debate with slogans of chastisement for Korea. The political party movement of the 1880s carried on these themes, mostly with charges of governmental indifference to Asian concerns, sometimes with proposals and schemes for associating with progressives on the continent and occasionally with frankly expansionist projects for conquest. These were the product of the ultranationalist fringe of the political party movement. The Genyōsha, a Fukuoka nationalist political party that emerged in 1881, was to provide the nucleus for expansionist organizations and themes for over half a century.

The social upheavals of Japan in Meiji times and the ambitions and discontents that energized a samurai and would-be samurai generation insured that there would be no shortage of adventurers and activists for causes with stakes in Asia. And since all groups, whatever their place in the spectrum of political attitudes, professed to represent a modernizing Japan and to assist a resurgent Asian consciousness, they had the capability of attracting a hearing and following among Asian, initially Korean, groups similarly out of power, similarly frustrated and similarly restless. The divergence of Japanese and Asian nationalisms in the twentieth century must not be permitted to obscure the convergence of sentiment and interest in the earlier decades.

In the face of these pressures for attention to Korea, the Meiji oligarchy worked out a twofold pattern of response. On the one hand, it showed its concern for Korea by pursuing specific complaints and demands with great persistence and determination. Leading Meiji statesmen carried the responsibility of such initiatives: Kuroda Kiyotaka in 1876, Inoue Kaoru in 1885 and again in 1895, and Itō Hirobumi in 1905. On the other hand, until Japan was ready to try its strength with China in 1894, these displays of power were not permitted to deflect the government from its larger purpose and priorities. The proposal for war with Korea in 1873 was rejected on grounds that Western powers would step in to claim the booty. More significant still, the missions of Kuroda in 1876 and Inoue in 1885 to Korea were covered by prior or simultaneous approaches to Li Hung-chang in recognition of the Chinese influence and hegemony. Mori Arinori in 1876 and Itō Hirobumi in 1885 solved the Korean crises of those years in Tientsin with negotiations that prepared the way for seeking satisfaction from Korea.

Although these pressures and the pattern of response to them were consistent, politics in Seoul after the opening of Korea to international relations produced a series of pendulum swings of factional and foreign predominance. The first Korean treaty was that with Japan in 1876. It was modeled on those between Western countries and China and Japan. Although the Koreans negotiated it only after being urged to do so by Li Hung-chang, its language contained the portentous claim that "Korea being an independent state" could negotiate on its own. Japan could now proceed to try to make it so. The treaty gave Japan virtually the same privileges unequal treaties gave the West in East Asia and provided the first claim for Japan's membership in the league of modernizing, opening states. By 1880 there was a Japanese mission in Seoul, and the following year brought the first Korean students to Japan.

Now Li Hung-chang, from his Tientsin headquarters, undertook to repair the damage to China's interests with her principal tributary. He tried to dilute Japanese influence with Western, and especially American, influence by pressing the Koreans to increase their treaty network. The American treaty of 1882, which the United States thought established Korea's autonomy, was actually worked out in China, and its negotiation supervised by Admiral Ting Ju-ch'ang (whose death in 1895 has already been described). Now students began to go from Korea to China's arsenals and schools as well, and the basis for a Sino-Japanese struggle for influence was laid.

The first stage was a Chinese victory. In 1882 traditional Korean army units, disgruntled by the superior attention being given modern units that were under Japanese tutelage, began a murderous riot that ended with Korean conservatives, under the leadership of the Taewŏngun, in secure control of Seoul and the Japanese mission in flight for its life. Chinese military units were rushed in to end the disorder and proceeded to deport the regent to Tientsin. The Japanese mission returned with modest military protection but found far larger Chinese forces present. Japan secured an indemnity and an apology, but the Chinese were in the ascendancy.

That ascendancy was briefly challenged in 1884, when Korean reformers, some of them Japanese educated and all of them Japanese encouraged, decided to move against the cautious regime that had yielded to Chinese dominance. The insurgents, led by Kim Ok-kyun, sparked a rising that took the lives of leading government members and, by controlling the king, seemed to promise a new government and policy. The coup had the implied support of the Japanese legation, which also welcomed the government it produced. It had the strong encouragement and assistance of Japanese nationalists and liberals, including the educator-publisher Fukuzawa Yukichi. Yet it too failed, for the Tokyo government was not prepared to back its representatives with force. The Korean king was returned to Chinese protection, and a Seoul mob once again put the Japanese legation staff to flight. Inoue Kaoru was sent to Seoul to demand satisfaction for damages to Japanese lives and property, while at Tientsin, Itō Hirobumi worked out with Li Hung-chang the arrangements for mutual disengagement and mutual consultation that amounted to a temporary Japanese retreat from the pursuit of dominance in Korea.

The decade between Tientsin and Shimonoseki found China in ascendancy in Korea. On-the-spot supervision was provided by Yüan Shih-k'ai, a representative of Li Hung-chang. The Korean court, uneasy because of the unprecedented extent and intensity of Chinese direction, began to look to Russian and American advisers to escape the persuasive powers of its powerful neighbor, but in vain. Yet long-range trends were working against the Chinese purpose. One was Yüan Shih-k'ai's increasing unpopularity with the Korean leaders. Another, and more important, was the growing domination of the modern sector of Korea's economy by Japanese trade. Korea was becoming important to the growing Japanese textile industry, and its food products were playing a useful role in feeding the growing Japanese population. Japanese grain interests sent representatives through the countryside to secure the crop through loan contracts, well in advance of its delivery. Food exports left periodic shortages in the Korean domestic market. Government officials who hoped for institutional modernization were poorly placed to affront the outside powers and capital whose assistance was essential to that modernization, and poverty-stricken and starving peasants had neither surplus nor sympathy for reforms that threatened to change their way of life. Conditions like those that produced the Taiping and Boxer rebellions in China now produced the Tonghak Rebellion in Korea.

The Tonghaks, or "Eastern learning" group, had their origins in 1860 when Ch'oe Che-u, a scholar repeatedly frustrated in unsuccessful examination attempts, received visions in which heaven instructed him to form a new religion. From this beginning, there were numerous comparisons to Hung Hsiu-ch'üan and the Taipings. Ch'oe drew on all the religions of which he had knowledge: Confucianism (for the five relationships), Buddhism (for heart cleansing), and popular Taoism (for cleansing the body), together with some organizational concepts of Roman Catholicism. The movement's name seems to have come when Ch'oe, asked if his teaching, "The Heavenly Way" (Ch'ŏndogyo), was not really Christian or "Western learning" (Sŏhak), denied this by insisting that it was "Eastern learning" (Tonghak). But the Korean government considered him a troublemaker and his movement heretical; Ch'oe was tortured and executed in 1864. Ch'ŏndogyo survived and spread under his successor. It was still not an insurrectionary movement. Indeed, in 1892 a large group of believers gathered in Seoul to petition unsuccessfully for posthumous reinstatement of their martyred leader. By this time, elements of social and political discontent had entered the movement. It drew its converts chiefly from the lower classes, and its handbills began to call for disestablishment of the *yangban* class, destruction of all slave records, punishment of wealthy and corrupt officials, cancellation of debts and better treatment for the lower classes. Together with social unrest came elements of antiforeign agitation, some of it directed against the Japanese, the most numerous and least popular foreign community. Proclamations placed less emphasis on social wrong and more on xenophobia and called for driving out the Japanese and other foreigners. "The foreign brigands," one read, "are scheming to start a war. Our national capital is full of nests of barbarians.... The Japanese brigands, in particular, still have a warlike heart [i.e., since the 1590s] and are full of intentions for mischief. Poison is everywhere, and danger is constant." Omens circulated that the Yi dynasty, which marked its five hundredth year in 1892, was due to fall.

In the confusion of the times, other interpretations of the Tonghaks came into play. Some credited their strength to the collaboration of embittered and conservative elements close to the former regent, while Japanese ultranationalists later claimed credit for having stirred up political trouble by assisting this antiforeign Korean movement.

In 1893 the Ch'ŏndogyo movement divided into frankly revolutionary and more moderate wings. In February 1894 the revolutionaries rose over issues of peasant impressment, unjust taxes and forced contributions to official coffers. For several months the Tonghaks were highly successful. Their propaganda, with its calls for sweeping measures to bring social and economic justice, found much acceptance, and the government's maladroit combination of brutality and inefficiency did little to undermine the movement's popularity. Ch'oe's writings were reexamined, and their social message was stressed. "In the World of the New Creation," he had written, "those who have been rich and noble will become poor and lowly, and those who have been poor and lowly will become rich and noble." His followers now seemed prepared to use force to fulfill his prophecy. After seizure of an area in which misgovernment had been particularly marked, they consolidated their base by capture of government arms and supplies and quickly moved to abolish much-hated taxes and distribute rice from government storehouses.

By the spring of 1894, the Tonghaks were becoming a recognizable guerrilla movement, designing their tactics to win and deserve peasant support. "Although you are forced to fight," one of the leader's three principles went, "try to avoid injury to life. Do not molest the lives of people in places along the route of march." And, most impressively, "Do not station forces nearer than three miles to a town in which there is a person distinguished for his faithfulness to parents and King." As Tonghak successes multiplied, there were also indications of poor leadership, bad judgment, arrogance and intolerance of the sort that had handicapped the Taipings in China. But Tonghak successes were sufficiently impressive to lead the alarmed Korean court to request the assistance of Yüan Shih-k'ai and the Chinese.

By 1894 Japan had advanced radically in strength over the years since 1885, and it was ready to challenge China for control of Korea. The structure of modern institutions had been completed. In the imperial Diet opposition leaders were still protesting their government's apparent indifference to its position in Korea.

There were also powerful strategic reasons for turning to the continent. By 1890 Yamagata Aritomo, the builder of the Meiji army, had worked out conclusions based on a series of careful studies he had sponsored of the military capability of China. He doubted China's capacity to provide a bulwark against the West, although he was conscious of the strength of some of the naval units that Li Hung-chang had built up. He was even more concerned by what he had learned about the West during a world tour. He had a healthy respect for European ambitions. Two powers, he argued, possessed the capacity to affect Japan's vital interests. The English were moving close to East Asia by building the Canadian Pacific Railroad, and the Russians by a Trans-Siberian Railroad. East Asia would soon be squarely in the middle of a conflict between these giants. War would erupt in Afghanistan, where the Russians would hold the advantage, and then in Korea, where British naval power would decide. Japan could not hope to maintain neutrality in such a struggle. If it sided with Russia, it would alienate England and China; if with England, the Russian threat to Korea would be greater. Clearly, no time was to be lost in building national military and naval strength. All the European countries, even the neutral Belgians, were arming at a frantic pace; Japan, which was all frontier, should work that much faster.

Thus the Meiji leaders now saw Russia looming over the mountains of Korea, a country which was inviting foreign interference by its instability. Korea was defended by a conservative China, but surveys of Chinese arms convinced Yamagata that such a defense would not suffice. Yet it was essential to Japanese security that Korea be kept out of Russian hands. Every tenet of Japanese military doctrine, and the counsel of the foreign advisers who lectured to the Meiji military and political leaders, agreed that Korea, in the stock phrase, was a "dagger pointed at the heart of Japan." This general agreement was now made more specific in Yamagata's terminology. Korea, he wrote, was within Japan's sphere of interest, and it was an essential supplement to Japan's sphere of sovereignty. Its independence was vital to Japan, and that independence was being endangered by the Trans-Siberian Railroad. It followed that Korea could be entrusted neither to hostile Western hands nor to a power unable, as was China, to preserve it for Japan's advantage. Japan's early efforts to win recognition from the reluctant Koreans had changed, in the 1880s, to attempts to influence, direct and stimulate reform in Korea. Now that all this had failed, there seemed compelling reasons to try a different method oriented frankly toward Japan's security interests.

In 1894 Yamagata's strategic conclusions received fresh impetus from the influence of the army General Staff and its chief, Kawakami Sōroku. Kawakami worked closely with ultranationalist groups that were active within Japan and in Korea, and he recognized in the Chinese decision to commit troops against the Tonghaks an appropriate opening for the establishment of a Japanese military presence and claim in Korea. This military determination coincided with political and parliamentary considerations to encourage the civilian government, and especially Foreign Minister Mutsu and Prime Minister Itō, in the decision to intervene in Korea. Any doubts of public approval could have been laid to rest by their observation of the wave of indignation that followed the discovery of the way the Seoul government had murdered and dishonored Kim Ok-kyun, the reform leader of the 1880s. So it was that Japanese troops, once arrived in Seoul, became the basis for proposals for joint intervention for reform that Tokyo made to Peking. When these proposals were rejected, as Japan knew they would be, the war with China for control of a prostrate Korea followed.

3. Korea After Shimonoseki

JAPAN'S VICTORY over China did not solve the question of reform in Korea, but it did serve to make it more urgent. The years of the war saw strong Japanese direction, with sweeping orders that were designed to change the entire institutional fabric of Korean life. Unfortunately for Tokyo, its plans were undone by foreign and domestic complications. Foreign complications followed from the Triple Intervention, in which Russia, France and Germany pointed out that Japanese retention of the Liaotung Peninsula would make meaningless the very independence of Korea for which the war had supposedly been fought. Japanese complications derived from maladroit, strong-arm tactics that served to drive the

Korean court into the willing arms of the Russians, with the result that Japan had to repeat, this time with Russia, the struggle for dominance it had waged with China for control of Korea. Periods of balance between the two contestants provided some opportunity for reform attempts under Korean leadership, but these proved only that the Korean elite was incapable of its own reform.

Japanese leadership began in July of 1894 and intensified as war with China neared. Reform edicts were urged upon the court in July and forced upon it once hostilities gave Japan full control over the king. These sought to undo the worst evils of the social and administrative systems of the Yi dynasty. Official employment was to be open to persons of ability, slavery was abolished, as was the arbitrary despotism of family heads, widows were to be permitted to remarry and the worst abuses of public office were to be regulated by the imposition of clear and rational standards of administrative procedure. During the first stage of their control, the Japanese decided to try to utilize the power and influence of the Taewŏngun because they were distrustful of the weakness of the king and conscious of the hatred with which they were now regarded by the Min adherents. The Japanese legation supported the regent, encouraged the "progressives" and tried to avoid charges of strong-arm methods. But all this was easier said than done, and in the maelstrom of clique and party influence and strategy at Seoul, the Japanese program moved slowly.

In October 1894, with successes against the Chinese in hand, Tokyo strengthened its hand at Seoul and sent one of its senior statesmen to take charge.

"CONFERENCE ABOUT KOREAN REFORMS." An 1894 Japanese woodprint shows Minister Ōtori (center, right) receiving a reply to Japanese demands from representative of Korean kind (center, left). Japanese troops surround the "conference."

Inoue Kaoru was a veteran of Meiji politics, and he had negotiated settlements with Korea in 1876 and 1884. He saw Korea, as he put it, as "a sick man; the question is how to diagnose the disease, give medicine and bring about recovery." It did not concern him that the patient did not like the taste of the medicine: "it is for the recovery of the patient, nothing more." It was clear to Inoue that Korea needed a Meiji sort of renovation. He felt the governmental machinery was archaic and overly personal, and that clear demarcations of authority and role were in order. The Taewŏngun, an anomaly in any neat administrative chart, seemed expendable, and Inoue secured from him a promise to keep out of political affairs.

Like most of his generation, Inoue was inclined to see Confucianism as a backward heritage that had to be overcome. He chided Korean conservatives, who argued that loyalty to king was like filial piety, by reminding them that loyal sons had the duty to criticize when things went wrong. He soon had an impressive list of reforms ready for each governmental department, a list he expounded in wearying detail to Korean officials. Inevitably, he also became convinced of the necessity to work through Korean progressives, although he had been doubtful about their potential ever since the 1880s, when, as foreign minister, he had blocked Japanese who tried to back them. But now a cabinet of pro-Japanese Koreans, veterans of the infighting of the 1880s, came to power. Inoue made every effort to encourage the Korean court to give them its confidence. Many Japanese of great ability and experience accompanied Inoue to Korea. Hoshi Tōru, for instance, a leading figure in the development and practice of modern law in Japan and a politician of note, received the assignment of adviser to the judicial administration.

With Inoue's prompting, the Korean king now vowed to end forever the traditional ties to China. He swore also to reform the governmental machinery and to keep all members of the royal family out of official posts. Soon an institutional structure resembling that of Japan was set up in Seoul. Decrees and proclamations poured out of the palace. The old structure of government, with its Chinese model at the center and encrusted privilege in the country, gave way to modern, functional units. Discrimination against the military arm was declared at an end. The *yangban* class lost its monopoly of office, and the examination system which had served as the symbol of its privilege was swept away. Edicts penetrated to the minutiae of social habit and custom by legislating against the traditional top knot and the white costume, and short pipes were to provide a more efficient substitute for the long symbols of leisure preferred by Koreans for centuries.

Inoue failed not because of his rigidity but because his colleagues in Tokyo decided against supporting the reforms he had in mind. A permanent Japanese influence in Korea required money as well as edicts. Since the Korean government was in no condition to implement a modern budgetary system, he pushed for large loans from Japan, to be predicated upon regional revenues in Korea. With promise of these in hand, he felt he would be in a position to exert the influence he needed in Seoul. But his plans for this matured precisely during the period of the Triple Intervention. The Tokyo government became nervous about Western suspicions of its intentions in Korea. Soon it was under such vigorous attack by domestic enemies that further national expenditure in the service of Korean reform seemed certain to raise new storms in the Diet. Massive rearmament would require all the money there was. Tokyo opted for caution. In September 1895 Inoue was replaced by an army general. The loans had not been made, the favorable climate they might have created was gone, and the powers, especially Russia, were more vigilant about Japanese encroachments in the peninsula than before.

General Miura Gorō, who took Inoue's place, was an old-line soldier who believed in meeting trouble head on. By the time of his arrival the Japanese cause was in serious trouble, for it had been hampered by inability to find Korean leaders through whom stable leadership could be exercised. As soon as people thought to be "progressive" and pro-Japanese came into power, they turned out to be anxious to establish an independent identity for their rule and country and became unwilling to carry out Japanese instructions. The Japanese were quite convinced that their aims and Korean interests coincided, and they tended to conclude that resistance to them could only be laid to corruption or dishonesty. Thus they backed one group and then another, alienated each in turn and by their support discredited the very men whose efforts most deserved the support of Koreans interested in reform. Inoue had begun by dealing· with the Taewŏngun. Having removed him from power, he brought back some of the pro-Japanese reformers of the 1880s and tried to mediate between them and Korean conservatives. The former, however, proved the more powerful and began to assert themselves against Japanese wishes. Since they were at the same time reviled by others as pro-Japanese, it was to be anticipated that the conservatives who intrigued with the old regent against them would soon catch them at a disadvantage. Pak Yŏng-hyo, long a refugee in Japan and now the most powerful of the reform ministers, was unhorsed and found it necessary to flee to Japan again shortly before Miura's arrival. The balance then shifted to conservatives allied with a faction of the Min clique. Miura, tired and confused by all this, was ready to listen to assurances by elements hostile to the Min, chiefly the Taewŏngun, that the real source of anti-Japanese and antireform intransigence was in the palace. He was afraid that the new ruling group was about to dismiss the Japanese advisers, disband the Japanese-trained palace guard and overturn all that had been gained. So he encouraged and provided help for a palace coup early in October 1895. Japanese-trained Korean troops, with Japanese adventurer-toughs, rushed into the palace, murdered the queen and some of her partisans, burned her body and then withdrew.

In 1895 the world was not as used to antigovernment coups and murders of chiefs of state as it was to become. The news of the deed, and of Japanese complicity, could not be covered up for long, and it brought a wave of revulsion. Japanese ministers in European capitals, who were already uncomfortably aware of European feelings about an attempt on the Russian crown prince (who had been assaulted in Japan in 1891) and the attack on Li Hung-chang in 1895, were quick to report the derogatory comments that reached them. The Japanese government, understandably alarmed that the precipitate action by its representative in Seoul might lose all that the war had gained in Korea, recalled Miura and his assistants and put them on trial. The court proceedings made it clear that Miura and his staff had helped to organize the putsch and that they had tried to conceal from their own government what they had done as long as possible. But the court withheld judgment because it lacked hard evidence of Japanese participation in the actual murder of the queen and, more important, did not feel itself fully competent to rule against a properly accredited minister of the Japanese government. It is the judgment of contemporary and later students that the Tokyo government, however much it might have hoped for the queen's demise, was shocked when Miura suited action to words, that it was greatly concerned for its world image and that it had certainly not formulated in its directives the rash steps which Miura took.

Nevertheless, the harm had been done. More than ever before, Japan and "reform" became odious in the eyes of Korean upper classes. A cabinet of near-puppets that followed the queen's murder attempted to bring modernization on by even more forceful acts. In November the king was forced to issue a proclamation informing his people that he had had his topknot cut and that they should follow him on this path to modernization. To the surprise of the Japanese, this became a rallying point for anti-Japanese nationalism. The Japanese had had their own experience with resistance to Western-style haircuts among samurai in the 1870s, but those who protested had done so out of resentment at the loss of a badge of class and privilege, not because they saw it as a moral problem. But for Korean Confucianists, the thought of parting with part of the body that had been inherited from their ancestors constituted a violation of filial piety and loyalty. It did not help to have policemen sent into the streets with orders to cut topknots, and roadblocks set up to corner the reluctant, especially when the drive was Japanese-inspired. In some areas, resistance was organized by Confucian scholars. Everywhere the decree met with patriotic resistance.

While Japan hesitated to press its advantage in Seoul, popular fury and conservative resentment caused the sands to shift under the pro-Japanese in public office. In February 1896 the Korean king managed to slip out of his palace to take refuge in the Russian legation. From there, he issued decrees canceling many reforms, among them the topknot decree. Suddenly, Japan seemed in second place again: Russia now held the advantage. Japan tried to undo the damage through diplomacy. A few months after the flight of the Korean king to the Russian legation, General Yamagata traveled to Moscow to try to reach an understanding with the Russians. The Yamagata-Lobanov agreement, worked out in June 1896, represented agreement on joint Russian-Japanese cooperation in the reform of army and finances. Both parties agreed to withdraw their troops from Korea.

In extension and amplification of these agreements in 1898 (the Nishi-Rosen agreement), both countries pledged to preserve Korean independence, agreed to consult before sending advisers to Korea, and Russia agreed not to obstruct Japanese commercial and industrial interests there. Japan had nevertheless lost its ascendancy. Russian penetration of Korea continued vigorously as the "protection" it provided from the Japanese brought its price. The Korean king stayed under Russian protection for a year. Russian pressure brought British opposition. The British interest was exerted through the administrators of the Korean customs service. In 1897 an English naval demonstration was staged to dissuade the Russians from efforts to replace an English financial adviser with a Russian. United States representatives, especially the missionary-diplomat Horace Allen, also played an important role at the Korean court, which granted profitable concessions to American capitalists in hopes of obtaining leverage against the Russians and Japanese. But American diplomats received little support from Washington. Japanese (and English) diplomats were more convinced than ever that Korea was unlikely to maintain its independence. Korean reformers, tarred with the Japanese brush, seemed to be losing place to conservatives, who enjoyed Russian encouragement.

Yet Russian political manipulation hardly proved more successful than Japanese. In 1897 the Korean king returned to his palace from his refuge in the Russian legation. He now took the title emperor in an effort to assert equality with his more powerful neighbors. Russian dominance had begun to produce the inevitable resentments and countercurrents, and these came to a head in 1898. As a result of maladroit handling by a Russian representative who pushed his advantage too hard, the Russian influence at Seoul was destroyed very quickly. The Japanese plucked up their courage and now suggested that the Russians recognize their ascendancy in Korea in return for a Japanese admission of a Russian sphere of interest in Manchuria. But the Russians refused to go further than the concessions embodied in the Nishi-Rosen agreements, and after Russian influence and presence grew in Manchuria in 1900 even those concessions were no longer acceptable to expansionists in St. Petersburg.

Meanwhile, in 1898 an interesting effort for reform originated within the Korean elite, led by a group of men who were tainted with neither Russian nor Japanese nor Chinese connections. Their efforts were close in time with those of the Hundred Days reformers in China. Like them, they failed because they lacked the political experience, connections and power base necessary for the implementation of their hopes. The Independence Club was led by an American-educated reformer, Sŏ Chae-p'il ("Dr. Philip Jaisohn"). The group produced a newspaper, a fortnightly journal, and it sponsored public debates and discussions designed to awaken Koreans to the needs of the day. Reform became revolution; newspaper articles advocated dismissal of most government officials and election of their replacements. Unfortunately the court still associated movements of this sort with the hated interlude of Japanese domination and had been changing the reforms enacted under Inoue to make things conform with the older, traditional pattern. The Independence Club fared no better. As it escalated its demands for government change in 1898, the conservatives began to organize counter-measures. Mass rallies called by the Independence Club were attacked by irregular but well-subsidized toughs, and by November 1898 Independence leaders had their choice between flight or arrest and torture. Their attempt to influence politics had failed. For many, the interlude would change their careers and attitudes, and some young reformers like Syngman Rhee survived to become symbols of nationalism and independence. But in a larger sense the movement showed the inability of the Korean elite to remake itself and the institutions under which it had developed.

Although the Japanese ascendancy had been threatened by the Russians and seemed temporarily in abeyance, in economic terms the Japanese stake in Korea grew almost without check. Japan began and completed construction of a railway between Pusan and Seoul. Its merchants were far more active in the peninsula than those of any other country, and its Dai Ichi Bank began to issue modern currency in 1902. Japanese received the concession for a gold mine. What was lacking was political authority to parallel the economic lead. This had to wait for alliance with England and victory over Russia.

4. The Closing of Korea

WITH THE OUTBREAK of the war against Russia, Japan moved strong military units into Korea. The Korean government made desperate but futile efforts to secure an international neutralization of the peninsula to forestall the Japanese. Early in the war Tokyo announced an agreement with Korea in which the Korean government expressed its "full confidence in the Imperial Government of Japan" and agreed to "adopt the advice of the latter in regard to improvements in administration." Japan made clear its intentions to "ensure the safety and repose of the Imperial House of Korea" and repeated guarantees of the "independence and territorial integrity of the Korean Empire." As long as the war continued, it was necessary to maintain the pose of defender of a weaker neighbor. But the Portsmouth treaty that ended the war was conspicuously silent on the question of Korean independence. Instead it spoke of Japan's "predominant interests" in Korea and bound the Russians to refrain from interference with the exercise of those interests.

Japan's past failures and present capabilities made it certain that careful planning would go into the formulation of its future role in Korea. Strong pressure groups existed to focus attention on the issue. The imperial army combined the strategic concerns of Yamagata with stubborn militarist assumptions of Japanese leadership and expansion. After the Portsmouth treaty transferred Russian rights in south Manchuria to Japan, Korea, which had up to then seemed an outer limit of Japanese influence, became a supportive base for the new Manchurian involvement.

In Japanese civil society, nationalist political energies had reached new heights in the years immediately preceding the Russo-Japanese War. The Kokuryūkai (Amur or, literally, "Black Dragon Society") had been formed in 1901 as an offshoot of earlier Fukuoka ultranationalist groups. Its members included numerous free-wheeling adventurers long active in Korean plotting. Some claimed close connections with the Tonghak rebels, and they were unceasing in their demands for a permanent Japanese tie with the peninsula.

The Kokuryūkai influence was the more pervasive in that it was part of a generalized affirmation of Japanese values and tradition that enabled it to relate to many groups within Japan. It called for the retention of Eastern values in Japan's blend of East and West, so that it could "lead in the revival of all Asian peoples." It advocated a removal of restrictions on popular rights (an echo of the role of its leaders in the 1880s) and of obstacles to leadership so that all could unite in furtherance of the Imperial Way. Social reforms, it held, were necessary to solve rural and urban problems and promote internal welfare. National defense should find Japan a "nation in arms," a people imbued with the spirit of the Imperial Rescript to Soldiers and Sailors. And the Kokuryūkai also warned that the government's education policy was too imitative of the West. There should, it insisted, be a greater emphasis on teachings about the national polity (*kokutai*) so that the "Yamato race" could rise to new heights.

The society was not secret, although some of its activities were. For propaganda purposes it made every effort to magnify its role and activities. Language schools and research expeditions which could serve intelligence functions were carried on, as was public activity in support of a strong continental policy. The patriots were emphatic Asia-firsters, and one of their most potent issues was the charge that their government was pro-Western and neglected its mission and opportunities in Asia. The leaders of Meiji patriotic societies moved easily between backers high in the worlds of business, armed services and government, and they found it easy to drop in on highly placed government officials to warn or to advise.

Hiraoka Kōtarō (1851–1906), for instance, was active in early plotting for adventure in Korea. He inherited wealth as a coal mine operator, entered politics and served in the Diet after 1894. His contributions made him important to politicians, and his political and journalistic activities were devoted to the theme of a strong foreign policy. It was especially Uchida Ryōhei (1874–1937), the Kokuryūkai founder, who busied himself with Russian, Chinese and Korean policy. He helped organize agitation against the Treaty of Portsmouth in 1905. Uchida began as a disciple of Tōyoma Mitsuru (1855–1944), the most revered figure in twentieth-century Japanese ultranationalism. These men were interested in mining and shipping, and they worked closely with politicians, but it would be a gross oversimplification to make them agents of profit and exploitation. Their business was politics and agitation, and to it they devoted their lives and considerable abilities. And because they were not fixed in their affiliations within Japanese politics, and remained free and indeed contemptuous of their government, they gained for themselves some of the popularity and notoriety due "selfless" samurai. They could profit from Meiji capitalism and at the same time deplore its socially destructive role; they could laud Japanese spirit and patriotism and hamper and embarrass their government whenever it suited their convenience.

The nationalists found themselves particularly central to the development of Korean policy. Convinced that Japan's interests required a close association with Korea, they provided arguments for stronger policies in Tokyo and instruments for those policies in Korea. When they thought that Itō was willing to divide the Korean peninsula into zones in order to avoid war with Russia, they were prepared to threaten his life. Sugiyama Shigemaru (1864–1935), a free-wheeling entrepreneur and politician from Fukuoka, moved easily between unofficial activists and leading statesmen and worked with army and Foreign Office figures to secure forward policies. In 1904 Uchida Ryōhei began work on the organization of a Korean front organization called the Progress Society (Il-chinhoe) that later came to claim many satellite organizations and several hundred thousand members. Itō Hirobumi was constrained to appoint Uchida to a post within the Residency General when he took up his post in Korea. Uchida himself wrote a tract on union with Korea, and the Kokuryūkai later proudly compiled a two-volume work describing its contribution to the annexation of the peninsula.

With pressures of this sort at hand, the Japanese government was not likely to overlook its opportunity. Well before the end of the war with Russia, the senior statesmen in Tokyo agreed that Japan should exercise control of political and military policy in Korea in order to defend Japan's interests. Indeed, as early as 1895 British Minister Satow reported that "Itō replied that the idea of Corean independence was quite impracticable. She must be either annexed, or placed under the protection of some other Power." "We agreed," Satow summarized the discussion, "that 'neutralization' was rather the term to employ than independence." After 1905 Japan no longer faced a rival before whom Korea should be "neutralized," and the question became one of degree and speed of domination.

The determination to annex Korea fully was not reached immediately among Japan's leaders; Hilary Conroy suggests that the oligarchs came to it reluctantly and slowly. Their preference would have been an orderly development of satellite status under the leadership of the Korean court and elite. Their concern with the forms of legitimacy and tradition led them to begin at the center. Yet it was precisely there that Korean leadership had proved itself most wanting in the previous decades. The Japanese thus condemned themselves to frequent frustration, a course that led in turn to stronger demands and direct confrontation. Itō and his civilian staff thus prepared Korea and Japan for the full emergence of Japanese military imperialism in Korea.

Outside modernizers have a strong tendency to project the institutions and values of their own society onto objects of their attention. If United States administrators counted on schools and elections to transform the Philippines, Itō and the Japanese in Korea were bemused by the work of the Meiji Restoration.

They put their first efforts toward raising the prestige of the Korean court and separating it from politics. But the Koreans' skills in evasion, and their commitment to politics, made these goals impossible to attain.

In November 1905 Itō was sent to Seoul to secure Korean acceptance of a status as protectorate of Japan. By terms of the agreement, Japan took full control of Korean foreign relations "until the moment arrives when it is recognized that Korea has attained national strength." A Japanese resident general, with right of access to the Korean throne, would be stationed in Seoul. Japanese would also be stationed at Korean treaty ports and elsewhere as needed. The treaty was resisted by every device of temporization and evasion that the Koreans could muster, but Itō coerced enough ministers into approving it to declare it accepted. Other countries were informed that "the unwise and improvident action of Korea, more especially in the domain of her international concerns, has in the past been the most fruitful source of complications," and they were invited to close their legations and downgrade them to consulates. Without exception, they complied. The Korean court was now unable to manipulate foreign diplomats in its efforts to stave off Japanese advice.

In December Itō accepted appointment as first Japanese resident general. He took up his duties in February of the following year. He saw to it that his base in Japan would be a strong one. He demanded for the Residency General full command in Korea including that of the armed forces and reported directly to the emperor in Tokyo.

Nothing could better illustrate the importance the Japanese government attached to its hopes in Korea than the sending of Itō. For him personally, Korea meant a new venture in the evening of a career as the emperor's right-hand adviser. Korea had broken many Meiji careers and reputations, and it was not a task Itō can have undertaken with any great confidence. He may have seen the peninsula as his ultimate challenge. He may have wanted, and sought, a new power base for his domestic political confrontation with rival oligarchs. By accepting the task, he forestalled its delegation to members of the Japanese armed forces. He knew that the imperial army had been insisting since 1902 that nothing less than full annexation of Korea would suffice. Itō himself was neither pacifist nor idealist, but in Korea and in Manchuria he recognized the dangers that Japan would run if the soldiers were given a free hand.

Itō began with efforts to separate the Korean ruler from politics. Modernization efforts had been slowed and warped by the way domestic and international issues revolved around the person of the sovereign. Itō hoped that by establishing "modern" services under advisers and by separating the throne from rule it would become impossible for conservatives to ambush programs and leaders from the shelter of the court. But in fact the activities of the court had gradually become restricted to such maneuverings, for the weakness of local rule and external interference had long since robbed the government of whatever effectiveness it might have had. Therefore, Itō's efforts were in effect a call to the court to give up its last area of importance. Predictably, it resisted. The efforts to institute "modern" and centralized policies were also bitterly resented throughout the country. Koreans had a long-standing and well-grounded suspicion of government. They were now able to couple this with sentiments of loyalty and devotion to the throne. The ironic result was that Itō, whose rise to power in Japan had been accompanied by a campaign calling for return of power held by military usurpers to the throne, now placed himself in a position in which he represented a new shogunate.

It seems clear from the recollections of members of Itō's entourage that the marquis spent an inordinate amount of time in maneuverings at the court. It is equally clear that the Japanese advisers' measures to modernize the administrative structure were bitterly resented as imposing new and burdensome obligations on many sectors of Korean society. Modernization in Korea required some of this, however equitably conducted it might have been, but when it was done by Japanese it could not be accompanied by the slogans of nation building and independence that had won over the Japanese people in the 1870s and 1880s. Itō and his staff directed their efforts at the central government and the upper classes. But they were soon followed by a large number of Japanese carpetbaggers who were out to make their fortunes, exulted in their pride of nationality and treated the Koreans like colonial subjects. The available literature leaves no doubt of the hatred and contempt the Koreans reserved for Japanese of this sort in day-to-day contact.

Yet it is instructive to note the amount of moral support the Japanese received as they began their work. Yale University historian F. W. Williams wrote of Korea as a "derelict state" that was in need of a Japan to perform "the world's work" in extending the "benefits of modern civilization." The American traveler and journalist George Kennan, writing in *Outlook* in 1905, called attention to the fact that

> There is now in progress in the Far East a social and political experiment which, in point of interest and importance, is not surpassed, I think, by anything of the kind recorded in history. For the first time in the annals of the East, one Asiatic nation is making a serious and determined effort to transform and civilize another.

The Koreans, he noted,

> are not undeveloped savages; they are the rotten product of a decayed Oriental civilization ... The most competent foreign observers in Korea attribute the intellectual degeneration of the *yangbans* largely to the benumbing and paralyzing effects of Chinese education. ... Japan has finally undertaken to stop the process of decay; remedy the evils of bad government; encourage honesty, industry, and public spirit; and substitute modern enlightenment for the gloomy darkness of semi-barbarism. It is a gigantic experiment, and it may or may not succeed; but we, who are trying a similar experiment in the Philippines, must regard it with the deepest interest and sympathy.

Before very long the same observer had come to the conclusion that the Japanese effort to work through the highest levels of the Korean government was not working. Japanese advisers, he reported, were blocked at every turn by the crafty velocity of men in high office. As Kennan put it,

> What are you going to do with a government which ... avoids action and evades responsibility by allowing its Ministers to resign at the rate of one or two a week? The Korean Emperor has a set of twenty or thirty men who may be compared with the court cards in a whist pack.... Every time the cards are shuffled and dealt the same old knaves turn up, but in new places. Just as you have laid your plans to capture the jack of spades in the Foreign Office, the Emperor grabs and shuffles the cards, deals them afresh, and the jack of spades appears in the Ministry of Agriculture, or smiles at you blandly from the Ministry of Home Affairs.

The first clear evidence of failure came in 1907, when the Korean ruler managed to get a message to the peace conference meeting at the Hague through the help of the American missionary, Hulbert. Itō took this as sign that Emperor (formerly King) Kojong would have to go. Under intense pressure from his pro-Japanese ministers and urged on by demonstrations of Ilchinhoe members in the streets outside the palace, the emperor reluctantly stepped aside in favor of his son. The Japanese had now succeeded in transforming an unrepresentative and colorless ruler into a national symbol and martyr. The change in the palace was followed by a new series of Japanese advances. That same year the Korean army was disbanded and all peace-keeping machinery entrusted to the hands of Japanese. Some units rose in mutiny and protest, but more melted into the countryside to join groups that styled themselves the "Righteous Army." Itō tried to offset this opposition by providing a regular monthly subsidy to the Ilchinhoe. Nevertheless, insurgents multiplied in number and posed a serious problem to the Japanese military. Estimates of their numbers ranged between fifty thousand in 1907, seventy thousand in 1908, and nineteen thousand in 1910. Their leaders included local scholars and *yangban* who had been pushed aside by the social reforms the Japanese were instituting and also traditional bandits, tiger hunters and other malcontents, all armed with antiquated weapons. The guerrillas clearly could not have been so numerous and fought so well if they had not had the active support of the countryside. But since leadership came from former elite and from demobilized army units, it is probably correct to conclude that the object of the resistance was restoration of the old order and that it became a preponderantly conservative and often antiforeign movement. Perhaps the most important effect of the resistance movement was the sanction it provided for a constantly greater role for the Japanese military in policing and ultimately ruling Korea.

As the controls of the Residency General increased and those of the Korean government withered, the former gradually expanded to become a shadow government. It now controlled virtually all aspects of central government, key functions at intermediate levels and all police powers. Stringent new rulings were implemented to control publications and the press in order to prevent the enlistment of Korean intellectual opposition. Japanese authorities became more watchful and suspicious of foreign activities in Korea and began to credit the large and growing Christian movement with a role in the maintenance and encouragement of Korean nationalism. Striking increases in the numbers of missionaries and their converts in Korea came during the years the Japanese were strengthening their control. Itō himself welcomed missionary activity as an aid in the modernizing of Korean consciousness, but his subordinate administrative and police officials did not. Their treatment of Koreans under their charge often made missionaries critical of them and so strengthened Japanese suspicions of mission hostility. The result was that in Korea, alone in East Asia, Christianity and nationalism went hand in hand, and church and compound often served as relief from a foreign invader.

By 1909 Itō was ready to resign and return to his position as head of the Privy Council in Tokyo. He continued to hope, against available evidence, that policies of paternalistic reform might secure Japan's purposes in Korea, but powerful forces within Japan were demanding full control. Ironically, Itō provided a justification at the last. In October 1909 he was assassinated at Harbin, where he had gone to negotiate with Russian representatives, by a Korean, An Chung-gun. After the end of World War II, the assassin, who had become a national hero, was honored by a statue at the site of Itō's old Residency General in Seoul. There must be few other cases in which the assassin of a neighboring country's leading modern statesman has been similarly honored by his countrymen.

Itō's Korean experience furnishes a valuable perspective for consideration of the relative differences between modernization from within and without. Many of the same measures that were accepted as necessary in Japan became the work of a hated oppressor in Korea. Part of the difficulty lay in the lack of Japanese sensitivity to Korean sentiment. Measures that had aroused difficulty in Japan—ending the privileges of the elite, changes in dress and hair and changes in landholding—could have been cautiously introduced in stages. Instead, they were rushed through with impatience and frustration when once Japanese power permitted it. Too little attempt was made at explanation. In Meiji Japan, school, paper and noticeboard reassured doubters about what was being done, and in the early years the government hired propagandists who appeared in all sorts of public places. Little of this tolerance was shown to Korean conservatism. The *Mainichi Shimbun* put it graphically: "The world," it announced, "can enjoy peace only when all countries reach the same level of civilization. . . . It cannot permit such a thing as countries with low civilization." This contemptuous intolerance of diversity stood in sharp contrast to the early Meiji efforts to emphasize the liberation and challenge of modernity.

Itō had furthermore dealt chiefly with the elite, whose powers he nevertheless set out to destroy. In the end many of them came along, for lack of an alternative. The commoners, however, who in Japan had been the objects of government education, training and encouragement, in Korea became the chief victims of many of the changes. They were able to transfer their ancient distrust of government to the modernizers and their agents, men who spoke a foreign tongue and treated them with condescension. Nothing better illustrates this than the program to modernize and regularize land registrations. Under the old society, ownership had been shadowy, but tenure reasonably firm. The Japanese now began a large-scale land survey that continued well after the annexation. While many large tracts had been attached to the royal house, palaces, government offices and *yangban* families, with intermediate levels of agents operating as tax farmers, and while other areas had known a communal pattern of holding, the Japanese now set out to create a capitalistic system in which land would become a commodity of exchange subject to regular taxation. Units of measurement had been extremely irregular. In the effort to establish title, it was decided that owners of land would have to claim and establish their title within a fixed time limit. Failure to do so meant that land was placed in trust, and much of the territory that was involved ended in the possession of the Oriental Development Company, a large Japanese-run enterprise. *Yangban* who were aware of their opportunity often became major landowners. Illiterate peasants, however, usually found themselves without clear claim or title to the land they had been farming and became subject to expropriation or recruitment as tenants on new and onerous terms.

Thus, the number of the unfortunate and indigent grew, and no real attempt was made to develop or find substitute employment for them. For some years, the chief contribution of Korea to the Japanese economy was the provision of the agricultural supplies in which Japan was deficient. While production of rice went up as Japanese established agricultural test stations, improved strains and expanded acreage, average consumption of rice declined, because of a growing population and growing exports. Cheaper substitute grains, especially millet, took the place of the rice that was sent to Japan. Under these circumstances the rationalization of Korean administration, the series of social and legal reforms and the slow development of educational innovations meant little in terms of the welfare of the Korean commoners.

Shortly after the murder of Itō, the Tokyo government decided that the time had come for the full annexation of Korea. Japanese patriotic societies redoubled their efforts to speed the process. Their Korean friends in the Ilchinhoe submitted public petitions for full Japanese annexation. The Tokyo government replaced the man Itō had designated for the Residency General and entrusted the new task to a Chōshū general, Terauchi Masatake. In August 1910 the Meiji emperor announced that

> We, attaching the highest importance to the maintenance of permanent peace in the Orient and the consolidation of lasting security for our Empire and finding in Korea constant and fruitful sources of complication ... have now arrived at an arrangement for such permanent annexation.... All Koreans, being under Our direct sway, will enjoy growing prosperity and welfare, and with assured repose and security will come a marked expansion in industry and trade.

With future cooperation and compliance, it concluded, "Our subjects may long enjoy the blessings of peace and tranquillity."

In 1910 the imperialist order in Asia seemed complete and reasonably stable. Vague and poorly marked borders in Northeast Asia had become distinct. Japan and Russia had agreed on their respective limitations and rights. Agreements between them in 1907, 1910 and 1912 made it unlikely that Manchuria or Mongolia would provide the cause for a new struggle. Russia seemed unlikely to try a war of revenge. It had instead accompanied a withdrawal from East Asian competition with a new interest in the Balkans.

The balance of foreign influence in China seemed to have reached a stage that, if not stable, was nevertheless more so than it had been. There was less talk of division. British Minister Satow had foreseen this earlier. In 1903 he commented to his French counterpart at Peking:

> We talked about the absurd reports in the newspapers about an English Viceroy of the Yangtze, and he said that Chang Chih-tung had sent Liang to him to ask if it was true! I again affirmed my opposition to a partition of China and so did he. How could we possibly find the men to carry it out, and then just think of the difficulties among ourselves.

Except for the Japanese and the Russians, the major powers were now engaged in cooperative loans and consortiums; these were designed for profit, but they nevertheless seemed to foreshadow the end of unilateral ambitions. The Manchu dynasty was finally entering the path of institutional reform.

The imperialist powers were neatly balanced. The Japanese and English were allies, as were the English and the French, and the French and the Russians; also, the Japanese and the Russians had resolved their pressing disagreements in treaties. The United States, a newcomer to the power balance, had secured the Philippines and was willing to grant Japan its lead in Korea in exchange for mutual guarantees. Korean instability no longer tempted the ambitious. A stable order seemed to have been reached between Western imperialism and East Asian development. But the international order Japanese leaders had spent a half century in studying and joining came to an end just as they found themselves able to profit from it.

CHAPTER 5

Japan and Change in China

Japanese efforts to sponsor change in Korea led to the struggle with China for control over the peninsula and ultimately to the annexation of Korea itself, but the story of Japan's impact in China is more complex by far. It is one affected by deep-seated attitudes on both sides but also influenced by outside opinions and evaluations. It is much more a story of change within China. The story is more important because its consequences are larger. Its ramifications remain visible in the kaleidoscopic shifts of Western, and especially American, judgments about Japan and China in the second half of the twentieth century.

Direct and large-scale contact between Chinese and Japanese has been a product of the twentieth century. Before then, if one excludes the isolated military encounters—the thirteenth-century Mongol invasions, the fifteenth-century pirate raids on China and the sixteenth-century encounters between Ming and Japanese armies in Korea—Sino-Japanese contacts were restricted to the diplomatic and learning missions of early Japan, to travelers to and from Buddhist temples and to limited commerce carried on between coastal traders from Fukien and southern Japan. However important these contacts were for the development of Japanese culture and, at times, for the Chinese and Japanese economies (through the export of Japanese copper for minting Chinese coins and the import of Chinese coins into Japan), they remained restricted to fringe groups of the elite and to a small number of merchants. The Chinese elite were superbly condescending toward the Japanese when not completely indifferent to them; the Chinese masses were unaware of their existence. The Japanese elite, however, were caught up in more complex emotions toward their continental neighbor. China was for them a Greece and Rome that remained powerful, a Renaissance Italy and a classical France, all rolled into one; a single, unitary and unique cultural colossus that had known no real competitor. It posed no political or security problem, but in its overwhelming proportions it blotted out all possible competitors. It even mediated and strained the influences of Indian Buddhism and much Western science through transmission and translation. No educated Japanese could be indifferent to a China whose culture was so much a part of his own "tradition," and the development of modern Japanese and Shinto nationalism was necessarily accompanied by a process of disengagement from and resistance to this Chinese cultural incubus. Yet modern Japanese nationalist ideology also retained important elements of Confucian political culture as "Japanese" tradition, and this conservatism came to recommend it to Chinese reformers who were anxious to avoid a complete break with the past.

The nineteenth-century modernization drives in East Asia brought the first possibility of real competition between Japan and China. The judges were the observers in London, Paris, Berlin and New York whose techniques of industrial and political development were being applied, and the rules were those of political and military competition the imperialist order had worked out. As early as the 1860s Japanese travelers to Shanghai expressed shock at the flagrant evidence of European violation of Chinese sovereignty there, and their letters from the West provide evidence of their eagerness to separate themselves from the Chinese in European and American estimate and evaluation.[1] Although there was a fair amount of talk of cooperation against the agressive West, most discussions of "cooperation" were basically competitive in nature and assumed either Chinese or Japanese leadership. Thus Li Hung-chang wrote in 1863 of the advantage of having the Japanese "attach themselves to us, and watch the shortcomings or strength of the Westerners." That same year the Tokugawa naval commissioner, Katsu, was talking to his associates about his belief that the very existence of all Asian countries "depends on banding together and building a powerful navy"; Japan, he thought, should "start with Korea, our nearest neighbor, and go on to

---

[1] There are many accounts of the annoyance Japanese travelers experienced on being mistaken for Chinese in the West. Besides the affront to their patriotism, their emotions were affected by the fact that most Chinese had come in as laborers and that China itself was considered less progressive. Uchimura Kanzō worked out one device to counter a florid, vested and watch-fobbed gentleman who accosted him at the Brookyn Bridge in the 1880s with "Well, John Chinaman, there's nothing like this in your country, is there?" "No," admitted Uchimura, "but neither is there in your home in Ireland." When his interlocutor sputtered that he was not Irish, Uchimura coolly replied that he wasn't Chinese.

include China." Yet within two decades Japanese assumptions of hierarchy and the disastrous course of affairs in China led Fukuzawa and others to believe that Japan, and not China, would have to lead in any alliance that resulted, while Li Hung-chang had altered his initial optimistic forecast to predict that Japan would become China's greatest problem instead of its satellite.

The Sino-Japanese War was a contest for foreign opinion as well as for control of Korea. Its results demonstrated the superiority of Japan's modernization, and Japan's reward was to be admitted to the imperialist club. Extraterritoriality disappeared in Japan, while Japan joined those who enjoyed its benefits in China; tariff autonomy returned to Japan while Japan joined in depriving China of its own tariff autonomy; Great Britain shifted its reliance from China to Japan in its search for an East Asian counter to Russian power. Mutual attitudes inevitably changed also. Chinese condescension toward Japan became grudging admiration, and Japanese respect for China changed with extraordinary speed to condescension and even contempt.

Basic to this extraordinary change was the fact that thousands and hundreds of thousands of Japanese received firsthand, direct experience of the neighboring continent for the first time. The armies of the Sino-Japanese and, especially, the Russo-Japanese wars brought back, in thousands of diaries, letters and conversations an intimate account of Chinese poverty, misery and backwardness. Soldiers tend to consider the misery they see and cause as standard to the areas they blight, and Japanese foot soldiers who took part in the dreary campaigns in Korea and Manchuria saw little of the Chinese culture their forebears had respected. For Tokugawa painters and poets, "China" had been a land of mountain retreats peopled by Zen and Taoist sages. But the farmers' sons who slogged through the dusty villages of the north wrote their families in Japan about dirt, disease and backwardness. The result was an almost complete turnabout of attitudes. In 1868 the Meiji government had issued an edict telling its people that Westerners were not, as some had had it, beasts; they should in fact be treated with the same respect that was given to Chinese. But by the end of the century it would have been more appropriate to warn that Chinese were not to be scorned and might well be given some of the respect that was by then reserved for Westerners.

1. The Hundred Days

AS LIANG CH'I-CH'AO put it, China "was awakened from the dream of 4000 years by the defeat in the war of 1894." Just at this time of shifting Japanese opinion, large numbers of Chinese leaders began to give serious thought to the possibility of utilizing the Japanese example of modernization for their own country. To be sure, there were only two real models of rapid modernization for observers in late Ch'ing times. In 1896 K'ang Yu-wei put it this way: in all the world, only two countries had carried out political reforms and rapidly become strong countries: Japan and Russia. But, he went on, Russia was far away, its politics were obscure and its writing was unrelated to China's; Japan was the country to study. A decade later, after the Japanese had defeated the Russians, Japan seemed the most appropriate model for the Chinese.

The timing of the Japanese changes encouraged this. Peter the Great belonged to history, but the Meiji emperor was a living reminder of the speed of the Japanese leap to modernity. In 1872 the Japanese secretary of the Iwakura mission, Kume Kunitake, had drawn comfort from the fact that the modernity of Europe was a product of the nineteenth century. Chinese now looked to Japan's advance as the product of a mere thirty years and concluded that they could do as well or better themselves. Indeed, in a memorial of 1898 K'ang Yu-wei saw an accelerating pace of change; what Europe had done in three hundred years Japan had done in thirty; China, with many times the resources of Japan, could do it in three years. This view of accelerating change through adaptation and derivation would reappear in the writings of Sun Yat-sen thirty years later.

The Chinese reformers were not pro-Japanese in any basic sense. Theirs was a reactive nationalism comparable to the urge which had sent the Japanese to study in the West. Virtually all of them were bellicose and hawkish critics of the Treaty of Shimonoseki; they agreed that Li Hung-chang had erred both by the inadequacy of his policies and the craven nature of his surrender to the enemy. Mention has already been made of the memorial that K'ang Yu-wei drew up with 603 of his fellow examination candidates in 1895 calling for continuation of

K'ANG YU-WEI (1858-1927), reformer, political philosopher, and prophet of a future utopian commonwealth.

the war, and K'ang's was only one of many. Memorials of protest signed by thousands of indignant literati of less exalted rank were presented as well, and a number of outstanding officials, including Chang Chih-tung and Liu K'un-i, added their voices to the calls for resistance. With Li Hung-chang in decline and near-disgrace after Shimonoseki, the Peking court came under the influence of these opponents of appeasement. China was urged to follow Japanese example in order to avoid disgrace from Japan.

Yet the sources of knowledge about Meiji Japan were still few. K'ang Yu-wei himself visited Japan only after the failure of the reform attempt, and it is unlikely that he had personal knowledge of many Japanese writings. There were, however, writings in Chinese by Meiji scholars which circulated in China, and some of these went through additional Chinese printings in Shanghai. But most of Japan's literature was in the Japanese mixture of Chinese characters and Japanese phonetics, and Liang Ch'i-ch'ao later recalled that it took him the better part of a year after his flight to Japan to establish reading speed. Therefore K'ang and his fellow reformers had to draw on writings which were produced in China.

These were few enough to permit mention. Wang T'ao, a pioneer advocate of reform, worked with English missionaries in Shanghai, collaborated with James Legge in his pioneer translation of the Chinese classics in Hong Kong and studied in England. In the course of these travels he visited Japan for several months in 1879. His travels there introduced him to a wide circle of literary, political and, especially, journalistic figures and familiarized him with the course and content of the early movement for constitutional government in Japan. In his travel account Wang praised the selective nature of the Meiji reformation by stressing that it did not represent indiscriminate use of imported institutions. He was emphatic in his approval of some of the friends he had made (like Nakamura Masanao, the translator of Samuel Smiles's *Self Help* but also an enthusiast for Chinese and Confucian studies), and he was aware of the importance of private, nongovernmental efforts for enlightenment and reform. Like Japanese Sinologists who visited China, Wang T'ao was able to establish a level of discourse and intimacy far greater than most Westerners could expect to find in either country. Evenings were spent at banquets solemnized with poetry and calligraphy, and all the advantages of a shared cultural tradition came into play. Yet it remains true that this activity had no more bearing on political opinions than did the Western culture which Europeans shared. Wang T'ao was highly critical of Japan's conduct in seizing the Ryukyus. Takezoe Shinichirō, Japan's minister at Seoul during the 1884 incident, was a renowned Sinologue who had himself toured China.

Huang Tsun-hsien's account of Japan was the principal Ch'ing source for Japanese developments. Huang went to Japan in the suite of Chinese Minister Ho Ju-chang in 1877, when modern diplomatic relations between the two countries began, and he remained there until 1882. The Chinese legation in Tokyo became the center of attraction for old-style Sinophiles, and Huang made many contacts there. His account of Japan, begun in 1882, was finished in 1887, but it was not circulated until the time of the Sino-Japanese War and published only in 1897.

The book was a political history of Japan from the Restoration until 1882, the time of the author's departure, and it stressed particularly the opening stages of the movement for constitutional government—a movement crowned with success in the Meiji emperor's 1881 promise of a constitution. It praised Japan's selective use of Western institutions, with particular emphasis on the merits of the drive for freedom and people's rights. This book made a great impact on K'ang Yu-wei, and it clearly served as one of his principal sources.

Another writer and individual of influence was Cheng Kuan-ying, a comprador whose reformist writings stressed the importance of selecting and rewarding ability. Cheng argued from Western example, but he was in touch with Wang T'ao and helped to subsidize a missionary-sponsored journal which provided a principal source for the Ch'ing reformers. In his own writings he held up the Japanese achievement in the abolition of extraterritoriality and praised the Meiji government's intelligent attitude with regard to the protection of private entrepreneurs.

A fourth major source of information about Meiji Japan came from the writings of Western missionaries in China, particularly through the pages of magazines of international news and commentary like *Wan-kuo-kung-pao* (*International News*), published in efforts to "instruct and elevate the people, especially through the more intelligent and ruling classes," as the "Society for the Diffusion of Christian and General Knowledge among the Chinese" expressed its purpose. The pages of this journal were filled with articles by missionary educators like Young J. Allen and Timothy Richard, themselves close to the reform leaders. They praised the Meiji emperor's decision of 1868 to "seek wisdom throughout the world," emphasized the importance of a national system of education and of representative government and urged similar steps upon their Chinese readers. Indeed, in 1895 Timothy Richard, in a meeting with the Viceroy Chang Chih-tung, warned him that "God demanded reform on the part of China, and that if she neglected it God would appoint some other nation to reform her, as had been the case in India, Egypt, and other nations."

These were the principal sources of advice for the Chinese reformers. Wang T'ao became acquainted with Huang Tsun-hsien in Japan; Huang Tsun-hsien befriended the youthful Liang Ch'i-ch'ao in China, and K'ang Yu-wei read Wang, Cheng and Huang. Timothy Richard, when consulted on the matter of reforms by K'ang Yu-wei in Peking, told him that "as Marquis Itō had been so successful in converting Japan into a strong Power, the best course would be for the Chinese Government to invite him as one of its foreign advisers."

K'ang Yu-wei's first memorial of advice to the Kuang-hsü emperor was written in 1888 and held up the example of Japan for emulation. Like the next memorial, that of 1895 excoriating the Treaty of Shimonoseki, it was not forwarded to the emperor by the palace officials. Later in 1895, however, K'ang, who had now attained *chin shih* status in the metropolitan examination and was to be offered a minor post, tried a third memorial. This one reached the emperor. It was still a product of K'ang's bellicose mood and held up the Japanese model of military and political reforms as example with the express purpose of crushing Japan. Since China's resources, size and population were ten times those of Japan, properly carried out reforms should enable China to control the world itself and reach a point at which an insignificant Japan could pose no problem. The emperor is reported to have read this with gratification and enthusiasm.

Later in 1895 K'ang joined with other reform-minded officials to form the Society for the Study of Strength. Timothy Richard was associated with this group, as were Huang Tsun-hsien and Liang Ch'i-ch'ao. After conservatives forced its dissolution, Huang invited Liang to join him at Shanghai as editor of a news and commentary magazine. The *Shih-wu-pao* had a Japanese people's rights movement enthusiast as a staff translator, and it popularized much of the Meiji literature about constitutionalism for its readers. Huang also took Liang with him to Hunan, and Liang's enthusiasm for the Meiji story was now sufficiently intense for him to think of Hunan as providing a center for reform and strength comparable to the examples of Satsuma and Chōshū in late Tokugawa days. His friend and associate, T'an Ssu-t'ung, an advocate of radical political thought, he compared to the Meiji writer Ueki Emori. Liang was increasingly drawn to the example of scholar-activists in Restoration Japan, and upon his flight to Japan in 1898 he took the name and example of Yoshida Shōin as his own. His poetic shipboard farewell to China as he neared Japan held out the hope that he might himself become a *shishi* for his country and equated restoration sacrifices with Meiji successes: "Precious blood was shed over Mito, Satsuma, and Chōshū, [but] Meiji governance now shines over all the world, to the extent that Japan has surpassed Europe and America." At that time the Japanese minister to Peking was the politician, novelist and journalist Yano Fumio, and Liang undertook the translation of Yano's political novel based upon Epaminondas of Thebes, *A Noble Tale of Statesmanship*. The lure of Meiji Japan was powerful.

K'ang Yu-wei's fifth memorial came near the beginning of 1898. Now he compared Peter the Great with the Meiji emperor but reserved his chief enthusiasm for the latter. Among the emperor's traits he lauded was his habit of reading books about the West. The Kuang-hsü emperor now started reading not only memorials by K'ang but also a new version of his earlier study of the Meiji Restoration. The emperor, as K'ang recalled, was pleased to learn of Japanese methods and successes and waited eagerly for new installments of K'ang's account. K'ang wrote that

> At that time the emperor had repeatedly pressed the Grand Councilors for the books that I had written on political reforms in various countries. Thus I spent day and night adding annotations to the "Study of Reforms in Japan." There were in all twelve chapters concerning the events in Japan from the first to the twenty-fourth year of Meiji [i.e. 1868-91], to which I appended a resume in one chapter and a governmental table in one chapter. In these annotations I made use of each innovation in the governmental system in Japan to expound a single idea.... As soon as I had completed one chapter, it was immediately presented to the emperor who would then press me to send another chapter....

In June K'ang had his first audience with the emperor, just five days after the Hundred Days (actually 103) began. The flood of edicts that emerged from the palace was based principally upon the twenty-one additional memorials that K'ang Yu-wei provided during this period. But it must be remembered that K'ang was not very specific or practical in his suggestions and that his suggestions were not fully followed. He praised, in the Meiji achievement, the emperor's wisdom in assembling men of ability and in arranging institutions for them to work through. He pointed to the significance of the Charter Oath with its promise to seek wisdom throughout the world, and he lauded the abolition of classes and ranks and the effort to base government upon the entire Japanese populace through institutions of representative government. But he minimized the practical difficulties of doing this in China and argued on a high level of generality with emphasis upon symbol more than substance. The edicts that emerged from the court in Peking took insufficient account of K'ang's desire to democratize Chinese institutions. Indeed, since China had known neither feudalism nor the rigid class structure of Tokugawa Japan, it may have been thought that the task was a simple one of exhortation. K'ang also pointed to the advantages of the Japanese network of public education, yet little mention was made of his educational and cultural proposals. He praised the economic policies of the Meiji government with their provisions for firm guarantee of property, the separation of public and private and the promotion of new products, techniques and exports. But Peking paid only lip service to this with the announcement of central and provincial agricultural and industrial offices. As Liang Ch'i-ch'ao was to put it, K'ang, the "Martin Luther of Confucianism," was more educator than statesman and more idealist than educator. Peking's efforts utilized only the top of this frothy brew. One further caution is important: although K'ang admired what the Japanese admired, there is little reason to think that Meiji nationalism, with its narrow focus, or Meiji social structure were his goals. As Professor Hsiao observes, his long-range goals were more egalitarian and democratic, and in the course of his career he moved from constitutional to titular monarchy as a goal.

The Hundred Days stirred great optimism in Meiji Japan. In 1898 Japanese leaders were anxious to block Western imperialist expansion in China and eager to assist Chinese resistance and reform. Ōkuma Shigenobu, one of the leaders of the political party movement, was prime minister and foreign minister, and his lieutenant, Yano Fumio, was minister to Peking. Ōkuma contributed a rationale for government policy and assistance by espousing as the "Ōkuma Doctrine," the concept that Japan, so long a recipient of China's culture and spirit in the past, was at last able to repay its debt by holding the West at bay in order to give China the time it needed to reorganize under new leadership and institutions. *Shina hozen ron,* "the preservation of China," became a cause that combined self-interest with altruism. Itō Hirobumi visited Peking during the Hundred Days of reform and, perhaps at Timothy Richard's urging, was received in audience by the Kuang-hsü emperor, who asked him about the nature and successes of the Meiji Restoration.

Itō was hailed as a modernizing sage, and some enthusiastic memorialists went so far as to suggest his employment as first minister in a modern Chinese government. He was cordially received by the emperor as Teng and Fairbank document: "The government of your honorable country after its reforms has been praised by all nations," the emperor said.

> The two countries, yours and ours, are geographically situated on the same continent and are nearest to each other. At the present time reform is pressed upon our country by necessity. We are willing to hear an opinion expressed by your Excellency, and we request your Excellency to tell our princes and great ministers of the *Tsungli Yamen* in detail the process and methods of reform, and give them advice.

The collapse of the reform movement in the aftermath of the empress dowager's coup found the reformers in danger for their lives. Itō instructed Japanese representatives to give assistance. K'ang Yu-wei received English protection as far as Hong Kong, where he boarded a Japanese vessel that took him to safety in Japan. Liang Ch'i-ch'ao, who fled to the Japanese consulate at Tientsin, proceeded from there to Japan on a Japanese gunboat. His emotions on nearing the country he associated with reform and reconstruction, revealed in his shipboard poem, have already been mentioned:

> Here is a land of superior men.... its culture and people identical with ours.... I come to ask for help, and I am confident that a country so great will hear my request.... I have studied Japanese history and I enjoy telling again the stories about Japan, ... where countless *shishi* sacrificed their lives for their country's cause.

In October Liang sent Ōkuma a long letter comparing the Hundred Days to the Meiji Restoration. Kuang-hsü was like the Kōmei emperor, Tz'u-hsi the shogun; the Manchu nobility were the Tokugawa partisans. Unfortunately, in China things had gone the other way. Where the *bakufu* had respected the court, Tz'u-hsi had coerced her nephew; where the *bakufu* and court had separate centers, in China the struggle had had to be carried out within the imperial palace; and while the Japanese court had been able to rely upon the strength of some domains, whose rulers then accepted its thanks and titles, Kuang-hsü had possessed no independent source of power with which to oppose the selfish advocates of the old regime.

The reformers were soon established in Japan as leading figures in Japan's growing Chinese community. Their contacts were with highly placed Japanese. Ōkuma personally received K'ang Yu-wei and corresponded with him thereafter. Prince Konoe Atsumaro, scion of the Fujiwara house and head of the House of Peers, talked with K'ang and later saw to his journey to North America with a Foreign Office subsidy. Inukai Ki and other parliamentarians prided themselves on friendship with their distinguished Chinese guests. As a growing student movement began to swell the Chinese community in Japan, the reformers, with their intellectual and moral prestige, seemed even more important. Liang Ch'i-ch'ao particularly came into his own as a publicist and spokesman. He was the central figure in the selection of educational administrators for a school that was established for Chinese youths in Japan. He plunged into the study of Japanese, translated vigorously and began to draw on European jurisprudence via Japanese sources to argue the case for constitutional monarchy against his younger countrymen who were partisans for republicanism.

2. Manchu Reforms

THE FALL of K'ang Yu-wei and the eclipse of the Kuang-hsü emperor did not bring an end to Japanese influence. Japan remained the logical model for all Chinese who wanted change carried on within traditional patterns. K'ang's more conservative contemporaries, the great viceroys who disapproved of the rashness of the Hundred Days, were even more persuaded of the advantages of the cultural conservatism they saw in the Meiji synthesis. This was prefigured in the document Chang Chih-tung forwarded in 1898, his *Exhortation to Learn.* Chang's conclusion was that "that which should not be changed is our human relationships and fundamental principles, not the system of laws; it is our sages' way, and not their implements; it is the principle of the mind, and not technology." Consequently the court continued to issue edicts encouraging continuation of reform suggestions, although it now combined these with calls for discretion and caution with respect to local conditions and actualities. Unfortunately those local conditions and actualities also encouraged the development of xenophobic resistance to modern reforms and finally led the court to base its hopes on the irrational frenzy of the Boxer movement. As in 1898, however, important governors general ignored the directives they received from Peking and retained their maneuverability for the post-Boxer future.

Japan's apparent moderation during the Boxer interlude, and the disappearance from the scene of Li Hung-chang once the Boxer settlement had been negotiated, meant that chief influence in advising institutional changes for China now came to rest with Chang Chih-tung and Liu K'un-i. Chang Chih-tung had already familiarized himself with the nature of the Meiji system. Although Chang had been bitterly opposed to concessions made to Japan at Shimonoseki, he had established personal relations with several Meiji leaders, and he was prepared to take an optimistic view of cooperation with Japan and the utilization of the Japanese example. As he wrote to Itō Hirobumi, who had recently requested his advice for Japanese policy during the Boxer crisis, "Japan has common interests with China and common sentiments, because both peoples are of the same race and of the same continent.... Japan's policy toward China should be different from that of other Powers." So it is not surprising that Chang also placed great emphasis on the advantages of studying in and learning from Japan in the years that followed.

The setting in which the principal institutional reforms of late Manchu years were developed began with the humiliation of the Boxer suppression and the flight of the court to Sian. From Sian, in late January of 1901, the empress issued an edict urging all higher metropolitan and provincial officials to submit proposals for reform.

The most important response to this case was a series of memorials submitted jointly by Chang Chih-tung and Liu K'un-i six months later. Both men had been advocates of moderate reform for several years. They had opposed the Boxer madness. They were neither antiforeign nor antitradition, and they thus escaped the censure of both foreigners and court conservatives.

The memorialists began with emphasis on the education process.

> We presume to say that China is not poor in wealth but poor in men of ability; she is not weak in troops but in morale. The dearth of men of ability is owing to our limited knowledge and unsubstantial learning....

After these conventional arguments came the application for the twentieth century: civil and military schools should be set up like those of Germany and Japan; the civil service examinations should be reformed by elimination of the stereotyped essays; students should be encouraged to go abroad, especially to Japan; and the new education system should be related to the examination system to make modern education the standard path for state service as literary elegance had been in the past. "Unless ability is trained," the memorialists argued, "It is impossible to strive for national subsistence; unless schools are opened, it is impossible to train ability; unless the civil and military examinations are reformed, it is impossible to open schools, and unless students study abroad, it is impossible to make up for our delay in opening schools." Chang and Liu went on to criticize the empty formalism and inefficiency in the Chinese bureaucratic system. They also emphasized the importance of economic change and wrote of agriculture, industry, mining, currency and communications. They warned that "people's feelings are not the same as thirty years ago. They admire the richness of foreign countries, and they despise the poverty of the Middle Kingdom.... We must entirely wipe out the various defects mentioned before we may expect a permanent consolidation of the popular mind."

Military reforms naturally received high priority. Some had begun immediately after the conclusion of the Sino-Japanese War. Yüan Shih-k'ai (at Tientsin) and Chang Chih-tung (at Nanking) had begun to form modern-trained and modern-equipped units that were meant to be used against the Japanese but were not ready in time. It is interesting to read the searing criticism by memorialists of the "new" forces that had been formed in Taiping suppression efforts; the same arguments had been used at that time in criticism of the superannuated Manchu military organizations, and these criticisms were to reappear until the 1940s. They charged that soldiers were not paid and were inadequately fed, that they became a rabble and oppressed the people they were meant to protect and that their officers were ignorant and useless. Just so the late Ch'ing "modern" units that now developed became the warlord rabbles of the 1920s, and some Kuomintang armies, formed in efforts to restructure this archaic military system, themselves became ineffective participants in the civil war that led to the Communist victory.

Yüan Shih-k'ai's efforts were designed to build up better continuity and contact between army and countryside. He tried to secure local guarantors for soldiers and build up local units in which men would know each other, and he tried to see to it that the pay was regular and that part of it was regularly sent home. Foreign observers noted that Yüan's picture hung in every barracks and correctly concluded that he was trying to build up a personal as well as a regional loyalty.

Administrative reforms were needed at all levels. In 1901 an imperial decree ordered the abolition of special military examinations. The significance of this was that the idea of military service as a separate and inferior route was now given up and that the close relationships between military education and modern knowledge were recognized. In 1903 the government established a Military Board in response to numerous memorials that had argued the many advantages of the German and Japanese General Staff system. Study abroad for military specialists received high priority.

Nevertheless these reforms did little to strengthen the dynasty. Indeed, in some senses they hastened its fall. They were underfinanced. The government was limited by its antiquated tax and budget system, it carried a crushing burden of foreign debt and it had only limited access to provincial resources. Consequently, local governors usually had to work out their own financing for their reforms. Thus the new military groups became personal instruments of power like those of Taiping days. By the last years of the dynasty virtually every province had a provincial army, more or less properly equipped, and staffed at least in part by officers who had studied abroad, usually in Japan. But as these men had been exposed to radical and innovationist thought, they often became central figures in spreading revolutionary thought. Among the commanders no one put these possibilities to better use than Yüan Shih-k'ai. His youth coincided with the period of modern military training, so that he experienced a longer continuity with his lieutenants than did any competitor. Thanks to his central role in the dismissal of the reformers of 1898, he gained the full support of the empress dowager and unusual opportunities for favoritism and patronage. As a result he was able to resist the transfer of units from his command to other or central jurisdictions until the ties between him and his lieutenants were unbreakable. At the end of the dynasty the Manchus had no choice but to call on him for help, only to find him choose the classical path of the dynastic founder who worked in his own interest. Even after his death his lieutenants dominated Chinese politics. His first battalion produced five presidents and two premiers of the infant Chinese republic that was to come, as well as most of the warlords who dominated north China in the years that followed.

No area of reform was more difficult than that of education. Traditional education had prepared men for the civil service examinations and government service. Education for specialists in unorthodox areas such as Western learning had earned men like the translator Yen Fu only second class official careers, and even students like Ma Chien-chung, a man whose service under Li Hung-chung might have been expected to qualify him for important office, fared poorly despite the profound knowledge of the West he acquired during his study in England and France between 1877 and 1880. Yet the slogans of reform always emphasized the importance of retaining the Chinese core of wisdom while adding Western practicality. It was essential to safeguard the morality of the classics while providing incentive and reward for the techniques of modernity. Western education would never know real success until it could bring men to public office, and all the memorialists agreed on the need for better-educated public servants. Thus, if the new education was to provide government servants, some way had to be found to integrate it with the examination system. This was attempted by making changes and additions to the body of material tested by that system, by rewarding graduates of modern schools with examination degrees and, finally, by abolishing the examination system entirely.

Proposals for change within the examination system became specific from the time of K'ang Yu-wei, who proposed dividing examinations into several categories in order to make them test more specific subjects. In addition he favored giving academic degrees to men who had distinguished themselves through achievements of national importance. K'ang sought to retain the unity of morality and wisdom by adding another category of examinations, one concerned with ethics and religion. It seemed to him that since China lacked a religious bureaucracy like the clergy of Europe, it would require the continued propagation of Confucian doctrine. K'ang's concerns for a balance between morality and practical knowledge were shared by all thoughtful conservatives in twentieth-century China and Japan. In 1906 the dynasty, which had just given up the examination system, directed that Confucius be given the same offerings as heaven and earth. A quarter century later, Nationalist China attempted to utilize traditional ethics in the New Life movement of the 1930s.

By the time China had absorbed the lessons of the Boxer Rebellion, the traditional civil service examinations had few defenders. Chang Chih-tung, as early as 1898, had urged their abolition. The reformers of 1898 had projected plans for a national system of schools. In 1898 governors and governors general were directed to establish middle and elementary schools in provincial capitals and prefectural, subprefectural, departmental, and district towns. The new schools were to build on the basis of Confucian academies, and their curricula were to combine Chinese with Western learning. Officials were ordered to encourage local gentry to establish schools in ancestral halls. An imperial university was described as the pinnacle of this new system.

After 1901 new effort was put into the implementation of these plans, but for some time it was not clear how all this would relate to the civil service examinations. Many reform memorials proposed a simple equivalence of old degrees for new schooling: university degree holders would receive the *chin shih* formerly awarded after the metropolitan examination, high school graduates the *chü jen,* and lower school graduates would be admitted to the bottom rung of gentry privilege. But this change could not be made easily, and it was 1904 before a single, comprehensive structure designed by Chang Chih-tung was decreed by the court. Only now did China receive its equivalent of the Meiji school regulations of 1873. Chang's plan envisaged a system of nationwide lower, middle and higher schools, with graduated awards for scholars according to their academic achievement. Significantly and ominously, however, the highest awards awaited those with the most foreign experience. This experience was graded as study in Japan and the West for three years, tours of two Western countries for two years, a tour of one Western country for one year, and a period of study in Japan for one year. The coveted civil service *chin shih* degree was to be awarded university graduates.

At the same time, Chang's plans called for combining Chinese with Western learning in Chinese schools. By including Chinese learning in the curriculum of the new schools he felt that there would be less danger of producing officials inadequately grounded in their own culture and values, while the gradual shift within the schools would substitute a new emphasis on content and ability for the old concentration on literary style. Memorials had urged that the court appoint official examiners for graduation from the higher schools, so that their function would resemble those of the old metropolitan examinations. Nothing short of this, they argued, would give the new schools the backing and prestige they lacked. Next, in 1903, it was proposed that the examinations be abolished in stages, between 1903 and 1911, by which date the schools should be sufficient to their task.

In 1905 this schedule was greatly accelerated. Japan's striking success in the war with Russia persuaded a number of high officials, many of them authors of earlier reform memorials, to petition that the system be abandoned immediately in favor of the new school system that was now getting underway. For the first time, as W. Franke shows, these men expressed their interest in a larger school system, one dedicated not only to the production of government officials but also designed to create an educated citizenry. "The establishment of schools is not merely for the training of men of ability," they wrote; their chief purpose is "the dissemination of knowledge among the people, so that all may receive a universal education and have general knowledge and abilities. Thus, in one direction they can devote their loyalty to the country, and in another pursue their own livelihood."

As a result of this urging a court edict of September 1905 ordered discontinuation of the examination system as of the following January. The structure of degrees and titles remained unchanged, but the only path to their acquisition was now to be through the new schools. The edict stressed the continuity with the classical past before there had been an examination system. "In essence," it explained, the school system is the same as the system of schools in ancient times. The encouragement of talent by rank and degree is also the same as the rewards hitherto obtained by the old style of literary compositions.... We are certain that the official classes and gentry throughout the empire, on learning of this, will enthusiastically set about to start as many schools as possible, and thus give the advantages of modern education to every subject of the throne.... We command our viceroys and governors to insist that their subordinates, the prefects, sub-prefects, and district magistrates, shall make haste to establish primary schools in all the towns, hamlets, and villages within their respective jurisdictions....

The abolition of the civil service examinations meant a permanent change in the institutionalization of rewards and sanctions for ability and application in China. It triggered the great rush of Chinese students abroad. As Liu K'un-i and Chang Chih-tung had memorialized earlier, "We have found that the prosperity of Western countries has been preceded by travel." The search for foreign wisdom at its sources now loomed uppermost. But however inevitable the abolition of the system seemed to late Ch'ing reformers with their despair of the amelioration of the stereotyped "eight-legged essay," it is important to remember that the principle of the civil service examinations China now abolished had become accepted in most of the modernizing states whose institutions Chinese were preparing to investigate. The rejection of the system also brought with it some disadvantages. A turn to foreign education as the new criterion of advancement brought with it a reliance on criteria that were usually divorced from any moral content and encouraged a new intensity of careerism and bureaucratism that widened the gap between officials and people. The fact that the new system was not adequately prepared by a national system of schools further exaggerated the reliance upon the outside world.

This meant, among other things, a decline in equity and regional balance. Examination quotas had been set by central authority, and examination content was known and available to all. But the rush abroad brought increased advantages for the affluent. As central authority weakened, new reliance was placed on provincial and local support, with a centrifugal effect that was intensified by the already decentralized pattern of political and military institutions. China seems also to have suffered from the lack of a clear priority of public over private goals of the sort that characterized the ambitious young men of Meiji Japan. The samurai ideal of service may have served to mitigate some of the worst aspects of Meiji bureaucratic careerism. It is also possible that the Chinese change, coming a full generation later, proved correspondingly more destructive. What is certain is that by the time Chinese students required foreign study to establish their careers in the public or private sector their Japanese counterparts could desert the security of school and peer group only at grave danger to their careers. As China turned outward, Japan was turning inward. China was abandoning structure for variety, while Japan was fashioning structure out of earlier experimentation with variety.

Finally, the abolition of the examination system represented acknowledgment that Chinese tradition, as well as Chinese institutions, would have to be remade if China was to modernize. It was not just that the old institutions did not work but also that the old wisdom was not true. The late Ch'ing reformers, like their nineteenth-century predecessors, did their best to get around this by assuring one and all that both spirit and function, body and use, Chinese learning and Western techniques would be taught in the new schools. But the uniqueness of their tradition had been that Chinese learning *was* practical and that it was in fact the only worthwhile method for governing. Morality must flow from learning, and before morality and learning, the most untutored head must bow as grass before the wind. But now moral and political truth were no longer one; virtue and science had become two. China was not to see them united again until the thought of Mao Tse-tung became acclaimed as unifying truth for the pluralistic world of the twentieth century.

The Japanese example also bulked large in the area of Manchu governmental reforms, and it was particularly important in the argument about a constitution for China. Projected legal and administrative reforms were closely related to constitutional efforts, and as work went forward on new codes drawn from German and Japanese practice, a number of Japanese legal scholars of later eminence began their careers as consultants and advisers in Chinese employ.

If the Japanese victory over China had seemed to provide evidence of the superiority of constitutional government, the Japanese victory over Russia settled the argument for many Chinese. Russia, as the last great European empire without a constitutional system, had in this key respect proved incapable of marshaling national support for the war effort. Chang Chien, a leading industrialist, visited Japan in 1903. Upon his return, he presented the court with what must have been its favorite book by then, a copy of the Meiji Constitution, and went on to write a discussion of it as well. A letter he wrote to Yüan Shih-k'ai during the Russo-Japanese War illustrates his application of its lessons. "It would be futile," he said,

> to change a little bit here and there without having a fundamental reform of the political body, and it would be useless to attempt a humiliating appeasement policy while the Russo-Japanese War has not yet been concluded. The outcome of this war depends on which nation has gained a constitutional government. In Japan Itō, Itagaki, and others worked out a constitution and magnificently achieved the great goal of respect for their emperor but at the same time the protection of their people; that is really fortunate for Japan. As far as your ability is concerned, you are not inferior to them.

Between 1906 and 1911, study missions to Japan and Europe heard the same sort of cautious advice from Japanese that the Japanese had heard themselves. They concluded that the Ch'ing constitution should be conferred by the court and that democratic enthusiasms should not be allowed to outrun the more sober judgment of the government modernizers.

Administrative preparations kept pace. In November 1906 the Six Boards became ten ministries, as greater diversification and specialization of function were recognized. By the summer of 1907 a constitutional commission was in being, traveling, studying and searching for devices appropriate to a Ch'ing constitution. In 1908 the empress dowager was ready with the announcement of a nine-year program under which provincial assemblies would meet in 1909 and a national assembly in 1910. A parliament would convene in 1917. The nine-year schedule (later modified to advance the parliament to 1913) was taken directly from the Japanese experience of 1881–90. The Manchu court had come to see constitutionalism as a possible way of tapping gentry support and cooperation. The national assembly, it hoped, could be structured in such a way as to make disruptive activity unlikely. Half its representatives would be metropolitan bureaucrats appointed by the emperor, and the other half, selected by provincial assemblies, would be men who would function as representatives of local officials and local gentry. The Peking reformers were similarly cautious with regard to public education and preferred to think of academic and bureaucratic rewards as the culmination of a school system that chiefly would produce officials. The constitutional apparatus would give voice to lower officials and gentry, who would then support the central elite.

In the first elections, which were held in 1909, the proportion of representatives for provinces was set at 5 percent of degree-holding graduates of the examination system in each province, augmented by large property holders. Candidates could qualify for election if they were teachers, graduates, degree holders, officials or large property holders. Ninety percent of those who were elected were degree holders, so that the assemblies were controlled by local gentry. It was inevitable that these assemblies would become instruments of local interests, and their leaders soon saw the possibilities of utilizing the new institutions as safeguards against new efforts for centralization. Their first activities took the form of petitions for advancing the effective date of the ultimate constitution. Thus the new institutions threatened to work at cross-purposes with the modernization plans and needs. The difference between the Meiji Constitution, which was given by the government from a position of strength, and the Ch'ing constitution drafters, who sought to build strength by granting a constitution, was thus very great.

The late Ch'ing years were also marked by accelerated efforts for industrial development. These are of considerable interest for the way political direction was intertwined with industrial administration, usually to the disadvantage of both. China's parlous international condition also meant that the new developments were threatened by foreign capital and control as well as by bureaucratic direction. In several cases, enterprises designed to provide strength against Japan ended under Japanese control.

The development of modern industry in late Ch'ing years showed some comparable developments and important contrasts with the experience of Meiji Japan. As in Japan industrial and bureaucratic careers often overlapped, but in China the bureaucratic role was larger. Thus Chang Chien (1853–1926), whose enthusiasm for constitutionalism has been mentioned, was both a leading advocate of educational reform and a modern industrialist. Chang devoted a good deal of the first half of his life to efforts to win success in the examination system, and he was over forty before the coveted *chin shih* degree was his. After a period of service as assistant to Li Hung-chang, he formed the Ta Sheng Cotton Mills in 1898. Its purpose was to hold back the tide of Japanese textile imports, its capital came from government sources, and its official patron was Chang Chih-tung. Like his Meiji counterparts, Chang Chien made good use of Confucian slogans of exhortation as well as traditional ideas of organization and service in getting the best out of his workers and managers. His efforts prospered. By 1910 he had three mills in addition to a land reclamation company and steamship interests. From this base he was able to assume a considerable burden of local philanthropy, and he became a leading citizen-scholar-official in the movement for constitutional innovation.

All things considered, Chang's role was not unlike that of semiofficial and Confucian-minded entrepreneurs like Shibusawa Eiichi on the Japanese scene some decades earlier. Chang spent a great deal longer struggling for government and official status than Shibusawa, who left the Meiji bureaucracy early in his life out of a conviction that Japan needed a modern-minded and independent business class, but in their views of worker relations, Confucian ideology and national service, Chang and Shibusawa shared a great deal. What was different was the institutional setting. Shibusawa had the support of the entire governing elite, which saw the need of giving him and his counterparts maximum freedom and were confident that they were advancing the national interest. In turn the elite could count on Shibusawa's full effort in furthering larger plans; the Dai Ichi Bank was the leading Japanese institution in Korea before the establishment of official channels of Japanese fiscal policy there. But in China, leadership lay with officialdom, and development was hampered by personal, factional, institutional and regional frictions. The career of a Chang Chien was much more closely tied to the official standing of Chang Chih-tung than Shibusawa's was to any one group of Japanese leaders.

Japan's modern industries had been able to benefit from firm guarantees for private property, ultimately incorporated in the Meiji Constitution, and from the uniformity of a strong national administration that was the product of political centralization. In China, however, modern enterprises required bureaucratic favor that often led them along uneconomic paths which consequently blighted their growth, while modernization policies risked offending local interests that were vested in the hands of the regional gentry and merchants. One sees this most clearly in Chang Chih-tung's coal and iron complex at Hankow, the Hanyehp'ing enterprises, that were entrusted to the leadership of Sheng Hsüan-huai (1844–1916). Chang ordered an arsenal designed for him while he was at Canton, but he took everything with him when he was transferred to Hankow. Unfortunately neither coal nor iron could be found nearby, and supply arrangements finally worked out for iron from the Tayeh fields (eighty miles away), and coal from P'ing-hsiang (two hundred fifty miles away) proved expensive and uneconomic. By the time the firm was finally in working order, it proved so burdensome that it was a logical target for Japanese loans designed to secure access to the iron ore and pig iron it produced.

Sheng Hsüan-huai, its manager, was the most spectacular example of a bureaucratic industrialist in China. The China Merchant Steam Navigation Company, the telegraph network, the Tientsin customs, the Hua Sheng Cotton Mills, the Imperial Railway Administration and a government bank all had to compete with Hanyehp'ing for his attention. Local merchant capital was available only at cost to the central government affairs that were Sheng's first priority. Consequently· government tax or customs revenue, and when those failed, foreign loans, proved—superficially—more manageable and attractive. To keep Hanyehp'ing afloat, Sheng found himself resorting to Japanese loans that were made in search of ores for the Yawata iron works, which had been built with the indemnity China agreed to pay at Shimonoseki. Sheng negotiated contracts with Japan in 1899, and loans in 1903, followed by other, larger loans in the years that followed. When the entire development was formally incorporated as Hanyehp'ing Company in 1908, over half of its foreign debt, seven million dollars, was with Japanese creditors. Sheng was not scrupulous about transfers of funds between his several responsibilities, and in the process he undoubtedly amassed a considerable private fortune. (One of his descendants posted, through the Hong Kong government, a claim to the Senkaku Islands in 1971.) This, plus the inability of court conservatives to see why any official funds should be diverted into ostensibly private enterprise at all, made official impeachment an inviting tactic for bureaucratic rivals. One finds Sheng repeatedly accused of corruption. In 1905 he was forced to resign his post as director of the imperial railways. In 1908 Yüan Shih-k'ai seemed to be successfully pressing an attack upon him for having mortgaged the Hanyehp'ing Company so heavily to Japan, but the fortuitous death of the empress dowager in that year, and the emergence of forces hostile to Yüan, reopened the path of official preferment to Sheng. He now became minister of posts and communications, once more in charge of telegraphs and railroads, and initiated efforts to bring under closer central control the many disparate and local efforts for railway construction throughout China.

Several points stand out from even a cursory investigation of industrial developments of the last years of the Ch'ing rule. The contrast with the case of Japan is real enough, as is Japan's role as an aggressive industrial imperialist. Yet considerable gains did in fact take place in China, more, certainly, than in any comparable period of time theretofore. Had these been accompanied by institutional changes in the direction of rationalization and centralization, there is no reason why these efforts should inherently have been doomed to failure. Unfortunately the lack of strong direction at the center of the political process condemned such efforts to dependence upon the outcome of personal and bureaucratic struggle. Worse still, efforts at centralization created sharp conflict with deeply entrenched and justifiably suspicious local groups. That Sheng was not scrupulous about his books is, therefore, less important than that he was never secure in his support. Innovators had always to keep their guard up, and this could be done with shares, money or gifts as well as by diversifying their efforts and security. Clearly, as Albert Feuerwerker has put it, an institutional change would have been worth several steel mills.

Furthermore, the conditions under which the modern enterprises had to be carried on made them vulnerable to foreign control and rendered them even more insecure. Sheng Hsüan-huai, for instance, worked out an agreement with the firm of Russell & Company during China's war with France in 1884 whereby the ships of the China Merchant Steam Navigation Company were ostensibly purchased by Russell to give them immunity from French seizure; after the war they were returned to Chinese hands. Similar devices had to be utilized during the Sino-Japanese War in 1894 and the Boxer Rebellion in 1900. At the Kailan coal fields in north China, an enterprise begun in 1878 to provide coal for the Steam Navigation Company vessels, other problems arose. These fields were reincorporated as a Sino-British firm called the Chinese Engineering and Mining Co., Ltd. during occupation of the fields by Russian and Japanese units during the Boxer Rebellion. Later, the foreign investors, represented by a young American mining engineer named Herbert C. Hoover, and the Chinese managers worked out additional agreements designed, the Chinese thought, to protect their interests. But it soon developed that the foreign firm had the bulk of the control, as of the stock, which had furthermore been badly watered. When Yüan Shih-k'ai memorialized to impeach the Chinese officials who had permitted this to come about, they brought suit in London to reverse the agreement, but although they gained some points, the final disposition was indecisive. In 1906 Yüan began a competing firm, in the hope of arriving at agreement by sharp competition, and one was finally worked out in 1912, when both the original and the newer firm were put under the control of a Chinese Kailan Mining Administration.

Even this has to be considered a happy outcome compared to the fate of the Hanyehp'ing Company. As the Manchu dynasty came to an end, the Japanese, in need of constantly greater quantities of iron ores for the Yawata Works, were making vigorous efforts to strengthen their control over the company. The Chinese Revolution of 1911 provided a setting in which Japanese financiers worked out an agreement for joint control and capitalization of Hanyehp'ing; the head of the firm was to be Chinese, his second in command Japanese, with a board of directors of six Chinese and five Japanese. The return of Yüan Shih-k'ai as political leader of the Chinese Republic spoiled this promise, however, and it lay dormant until the Japanese built it into the substance of the Twenty-one Demands in 1915. Before many years had passed, the Hanyehp'ing Company was overshadowed by other enterprises. Its constituent elements were uneconomically located and inadequately linked by low-cost, volume transport. It had become bound to deliver its production to Japan at fixed prices (as return for the loans), so that it was unable to adjust to changing conditions and needs.

The last decade of Manchu rule nevertheless saw significant progress, partly because of the relative weight the great regional viceroys managed to throw into the struggle. The foreign powers, too, tended gradually to shift from the unsettling competition of individual loans to a larger cooperation in consortiums whose conditions could be met with greater safety and stability. These, in turn, required the assertion of more effective control by the central political power in China. The late Manchu years began to provide growing confidence that China could survive as a national unit. Yet the reform efforts that have been described were also producing trends that could not be contained within the bounds of Ch'ing institutions for very long. Institutional reforms were alarming the local elite, while educational reforms were producing a new and disaffected intellectual elite. The movement of students abroad combined with the discontent of local gentry to produce a contradictory and unstable balance.

3. *The Student Movement to Japan*

LARGE-SCALE MOVEMENTS of students overseas are a product of the twentieth century, and the Chinese student migration to Meiji Japan provides the first instance. Students went abroad to study earlier, of course, and among them Japanese students to Imperial China. But these were few in number, they were selected by and representative of the elite, and they went abroad for the study of universal truths in a universal language. In Meiji Japan hundreds of students were sent overseas, but numbers were still limited by cost and distance. The twentieth-century movements have been far larger, and they have been a part of the modernization process. Students have gone not so much in search of universal principles as in search of specific techniques and things, the products of modernized societies, which they might expect to apply to the development of national strength upon their return home. Chinese students in Japan, and African students in the Soviet Union, have visited and seen cultural repositories, temples and churches. But that is not why they went abroad. Thus the interest of the Chinese movement is that it was the first truly large-scale modernization-oriented migration of intellectuals in world history.

The first thirteen Chinese students proceeded to Japan shortly after the Sino-Japanese War in 1896. A special school was set up for them in the Kanda district of Tokyo. Since they had no knowledge of Japanese, they had to begin with language training. Seven of them persevered to finish their course and became the first of the Japan experts who began to produce texts and guidebooks for their successors.

As the European advance in China stepped up in 1897 and 1898, Chinese leaders began to emphasize the importance of study abroad. Japan was close by, inexpensive and familiar. European imperialism was China's great danger, and Japan's resistance a logical object of emulation. Chang Chih-tung, in his *Exhortation to Learn*, wrote that "it is better to study in the west for one year than to read western books for five years; it is better to study in a western school for one year than to study in Chinese schools for three years." Japan had obvious advantages as a place to study:

Japan is nearby and inexpensive for travel, so that many can go; it is close to China, and students will not forget their country. Japanese writing is similar to Chinese, and it can be translated easily. And western learning is extremely varied, and the Japanese have already selected its essentials.

The Japanese had shown the way. "How did Japan rise, although it is only a small country? It was because men like Itō, Yamagata, Enomoto, and Mutsu were students in the west twenty years ago." Liang Ch'i-ch'ao added other arguments: Japanese was an easy language for Chinese, its vocabulary was related to Chinese, and 60 to 70 percent of it was written in Chinese characters.

In 1899 there were over a hundred Chinese students in Japan. Representatives of Chang Chih-tung were making surveys of study facilities. A study guide prepared under his direction remained a standard guide for some time. The Boxer disaster added new urgency and arguments. The number of publications about Japanese educational opportunities grew. Arguments for the reform and eventual abolition of the examination system became common. Perhaps most important, a tie-in between study in Japan and employment in the bureaucracy developed to provide a direct payoff. Study abroad gradually became the basic requirement for entrance into the Chinese official elite. After Japan defeated Russia, the examination system was abolished in China. Henceforth, officials would be drawn from students in the modern schools and graduates of study overseas.

The effect on the movement of students to Japan was immediate. By the end of 1905, estimates of the number of Chinese students in Tokyo rose to eight and even to ten thousand, and for 1906, the peak year, estimates range between six and twenty thousand. This range of possible error shows the problems of counting; neither passports, visas, nor school or course registrations provide reliable estimates, and there have to be numerous instances of overlap. A leading authority on the student movement, using very conservative contemporary estimates, has arrived at these totals:

1901	280	1907	7000
1902	500	1908	4000
1903	1000	1909	4000
1904	1300	1912	1400
1905	8000	1913	2000
1906	8000	1914	5000

These are enormous numbers. They decline in years of political friction and dip at the time of the Republican Revolution of 1911, but they provide impressive testimony of the attraction of the Japanese model. The student tide included entire families, as fathers sometimes accompanied their sons.

Since movement back and forth to China was so easy, a migration of these dimensions had to be of pivotal importance to the experience of an entire generation of Chinese. From the wide range of student publications, diaries and reminiscences now available, it becomes possible to see the connections between local encouragement in China and the decision to travel. Students often returned home to encourage others to follow their example. It was a pattern that would continue into more recent times; an account of 1921 speaks of celebrations and send-offs for departing students that remind one of community farewells for Japanese recruits at the time of conscription. Provincial organizations and networks provided financial support as well as encouragement, and in a time when local taxation was provincially controlled this was of great importance. One recent study estimates that in 1906 over half of the students in Tokyo were there on provincial government scholarships. Networks of provincial groups encouraged, informed, housed and organized the students in Tokyo. Students came from all parts of China, but the wealthier, more conveniently located, and more politically prominent provinces of Kwangtung, Hunan, Kiangsu and Chekiang—future revolutionary centers—supplied far more than their share.

Few educational structures would have been prepared to deal with this human tide, and Japan's system, itself only beginning to adjust to the needs of Meiji modernization, was swamped by it. Many thoughtful Japanese recognized the importance and opportunities offered by the student movement. They called for special programs, schools and funds for Chinese students and urged the importance of efforts to acquaint the students with all aspects of Japanese life. Many new schools were set up for Chinese students, and private institutions like Ōkuma Shigenobu's Waseda enrolled many hundreds. Special schools with names like East Asian Commercial, East Asian Unity and East Asian Common Culture attracted many. One such, the Kōbun Gakuin, enrolled Huang Hsing, Lu Hsün and Ch'en Tu-hsiu—respectively a hero of the 1911 revolution, modern China's greatest novelist and the founder of the Chinese Communist party— among the 3,810 who completed its course. Special schools for women were set up to prepare mothers for modernity. Opening ceremonies, with their references to the mothers of Mencius and George Washington, would have reassured Chang Chih-tung of the advantages of study in the "Eastern country."

Most students were ill prepared for work in Japan. Many went to cram courses or seminars, and most were probably not formally enrolled at all. Undoubtedly most students fared poorly. Their stays were irregular and often of short duration, and their dissatisfaction and restlessness were quickly communicated to their relatives and friends in China. Although special schools set up for Chinese graduated large numbers, the Japanese schools to which most students sought admission graduated far fewer. Some figures will suffice to show the time that was required to produce significant numbers in this category:

1901	40	1909	536
1902	30	1910	682
1904	109	1911	691
1905	15	1912	260
1906	42	1914	366
1908	623	1915	420

One reason for the gradual decline of student numbers after 1906 was a growing dissatisfaction with the quality of education many students were getting. Japanese observers, for their part, watched the confusion and disorganization of their student guests and began to wonder whether superior students were not being sent to other and more expensive countries and only the less qualified coming to Tokyo. There may have been some grounds for this; the United States made its remission of Boxer indemnity funds available for educational interchange in 1908, while Japan did not do the same thing until 1924. Chinese government surveys and representatives began to indicate alarm over the unstructured and chaotic nature of the student tide in Japan and worked out cooperation with Japanese educational bureaucrats to prescribe criteria for selection of students and institutions, but regulations designed to manage the student guests usually irritated them. The quality of schooling clearly improved as numbers fell, as the figures of school graduates indicate, but so did the intensity of disaffection. In 1907 agreements were worked out to open up the best Japanese state higher schools to Chinese students on a regular basis, and during the next two years over 460 Chinese students were enrolled in them. In 1911 the Chinese government scheduled the establishment of a preparatory school in Peking to prepare students for the Japanese special higher schools (as Tsing Hua later did for study in America), and there was also a rise in the number of Japanese teachers going to China, both to open new schools and to teach in Chinese schools. Japanese teachers numbered some 600 at their peak in late Ch'ing times. Western, and especially American, missionary educators, who numbered several thousand in the 1920s, were more numerous even if less frequently invited to employment in Chinese government schools. In 1909, for instance, of 356 foreign teachers invited by the Chinese government schools, 311 were Japanese.

At any rate it is certain that the students' experience counted for more than their formal education. It was often full of irony. The future anarchist leader Ching Mei-chiu, who came in 1903, wrote later of his astonishment at finding that Japanese houses were more like ancient than contemporary Chinese dwellings. "The inns were built of wood," he recalled,

> and you had to take off your shoes before coming into the room. Here we had crossed the seas and gone abroad to study in order to prepare for the future, and the first thing we had to do was go back to antiquity.

Virtually all the students were in Tokyo, and most of them in the Kanda district. They left their mark on the lodgings, business establishments, and restaurants of the area. Specialty shops for printing textbooks proliferated, and pawnshops that catered exclusively to Chinese students appeared. Some of the major publishing houses of twentieth-century Japan began as enterprises to publish translations for the students. Barbers worked out something called a Fuji hairdo by piling up the queue on top of the head in order to permit students to look modern without becoming revolutionary. But many did not stop there. The same anarchist, Ching Mei-chiu, recounts an early attempt at conversation with

Japanese students as they scribbled notes in Chinese characters to each other. "Why don't you cut your hair?" they asked him. "We call it a pig tail!" Overcome with shame, Ching headed straight for the barber shop and, in sign language, ordered his queue cut off.

The fact that so many students were so close together with so little to do made their experience more intense. They became conscious of their Chinese nationality in a new way in the foreign setting of Tokyo. Japanese condescension and discrimination helped to accelerate this process. The Sino-Japanese War had begun a period of popular contempt for Chinese weakness. Japanese chauvinism grew steadily in the decade that followed and reached a new apogee with the victory over Russia. "At the time of the war against China," as the anarchist leader Kōtoku Shūsui put it in his treatise on imperialism,

> the patriotism of Japanese developed to extremes that had never been known before. They despised the Chinese, scorned them as effeminate, and they were hateful to them. It did not end with words; from white haired elders to little children, everybody was full of bloodthirsty intentions toward the four hundred million.

This did not end with the war, and students were inevitably treated to a good deal of amusement and contempt. The term *chan chan bozu,* a slighting chant with some earlier currency in reference to the queue and dress of Chinese, now became common, and street urchins often followed students to hoot at them.

The setting of a triumphant and militarist Japan was a constant reminder of Chinese weakness and failure. A Chinese novel about student life had the very rickshaw coolies turning in their shafts to ask Chinese student passengers whether they realized that Japan was defeating Russia and whether that did not make them jealous. "Why is your country so weak?" was a concern already at the forefront of student consciousness and must have been reinforced by daily slights and sights. Attitudes of deprecation came to be associated with the very term for China that Japanese used. "Shina" as a term went back to T'ang times; and for a time it had a certain attraction for students through its silencing of reference to the Ch'ing dynasty. But as it became associated with insult and taunts, it gradually connoted weakness and scorn, until the later Chinese Republic made diplomatic representations in 1930 to persuade the Japanese government to give up use of the term. Yet it remained standard in Japanese reference and writing until the end of World War II.

Japan also made positive contributions to Chinese nationalism through example. The late Meiji surge of pride in Japanese achievement produced a patriotism that made a deep impression on even profoundly nonpolitical Chinese students. Many diarists recorded their astonishment at Japanese patriotism. The stories of General Nogi's loss of his sons, one under his own command at Port Arthur, won universal admiration. Liang Ch'i-ch'ao wrote of his emotions on witnessing a scene at Ueno Station as relatives and friends arranged festive send-offs for recruits entering the army, and particularly on seeing a great banner inscribed "Grant death in battle." "On seeing this," he wrote, "I was astonished and respectful and unable to put it out of my mind." He decided that China needed a "China spirit" comparable to Japan's *Yamato damashii* to stress the identification of self with country. Participation could only follow identification. When a work by a Japanese scholar entitled *The Spirit of Patriotism in National Education* appeared, it was promptly translated and issued by Peking University Press as a textbook.

The student movement thus served as a breeding ground for Chinese nationalism. Authorities in Peking and Tokyo agreed that the students were becoming increasingly self-conscious, emotional and vigilant. Each affront served to heighten their nationalism, and each response showed an increasingly emotional and romantic, at times almost hysterical, response. The student population produced ever larger numbers of heroes of resistance. The principal issues were those that affronted the students' national identity. At times, these developed in harmony with Japanese sympathies, especially when China seemed threatened by European power. But as often the issues took the form of resistance to Japanese efforts to restrain and channel student enthusiasms, and in such cases student nationalism turned against a Japan which seemed to be in league with the Manchu government in Peking.

In 1902 a group of students led by Chang Ping-lin, later a prominent revolutionary leader, scheduled a rally to honor the last Ming emperor as a gesture of anti-Manchu sentiment. Japanese authorities ruled against it. That same year the Chinese minister to Tokyo ruled that private Chinese students could not enroll at a Japanese military academy. When student representatives demanded a meeting with the minister to protest his stand, the legation called in Japanese police to arrest them. On this occasion, Wu Chih-hui, later a prominent revolutionary leader, tried to resist arrest and deportation by an attempted suicide in the moat of the imperial palace as he was being led away. Sympathetic Japanese quickly sponsored a military academy for privately supported Chinese students.

In 1903 students successfully protested the inclusion of Chinese minorities and products among products of aboriginal societies in an Osaka exposition on the "Races of Man." During that same year, Japanese cooperated with students in organizing resistance to the "Seven Demands" (curiously prophetic of the later Japanese "Twenty-one") which the Russians had issued on Manchuria. A Resist Russia Volunteer Corps and, later, a student army had obvious political and revolutionary potential. Amid scenes of intense emotionalism, students enrolled with announcements of their determination to die, and they commissioned representatives to return to China to urge the authorities to resist the imperialist aggressors. This movement produced among its leaders the revolutionary heroes Huang Hsing and Ch'en T'ien-hua.

Student ties with centers of discontent in Shanghai and other coastal treaty ports in China were close, and the publications of these centers were beginning to produce an embryo press and public opinion. In 1894 there had been 12 papers in all China; four years later Shanghai alone counted 15. In 1895 there were 8 magazines; three years later there were 25 in Shanghai alone. Within a few years there were 179 papers and 82 magazines; 34 of the latter were published in Tokyo and 4 in Yokohama, illustrating the importance of the movement overseas. Most of these were small publications with limited circulations, but they provided the beginning for a network that carried indignation and concern from one student center to another with astonishing speed. In 1905 came the first modern Chinese boycott, directed against the United States in connection with negotiations for renewal of the restrictive immigration treaty of 1894. Stories of mistreatment and discrimination in America aroused exactly the same coastal areas that produced the emigration and students, and this modern problem, fought with modern weapons and publications, saw a vigilant Chinese response.

A fiery anti-Manchu pamphlet, entitled *The Revolutionary Army,* by Tsou Jung, was published first in Shanghai in 1903 (with a preface by Chang Ping-lin) and again in Hong Kong and Tokyo; some authorities credit it with a million copies in these and later printings. Other publications that circulated in large numbers included Chang Ping-lin's attack on K'ang Yu-wei's reformism and two tracts by Ch'en T'ien-hua (of the Resist Russia movement), entitled *Wake Up!* (*Meng-hui-t'ou*) and *Alarm to Arouse the Age* (*Ching-shih-chung*).

In 1905, students came into direct conflict with Japanese educational authorities over a set of regulations entitled "Problems in Controlling Ch'ing Students." Articles 9 and 10 specified that schools would have to have their students reside in authorized dormitories and maintain control over them and called on schools to monitor student conduct and terminate students who violated rules. Chang Chih-tung, who had helped activate these restrictions because he had become alarmed over student unrest, warned of revolutionary consequences of student organization in a setting in which the most vocal dominated the more studious. "Nine out of ten are intimidated," he wrote, "while the instigators and troublemakers do not number more than one in ten." But the students charged that the new regulations discriminated against them and denied them constitutional freedoms enjoyed by Japanese. Provincial organizations organized protests that grew into a general strike in response to the new rules. The flow of students into Japan slowed and virtually stopped for a time, and many returned home and urged others to follow their example. Meanwhile the Japanese establishment began to weary of student unrest and complaints. On 7 December the influential Tokyo *Asahi* remarked that these strikes were caused by the students' misunderstanding of the regulations and their purpose and went on to castigate unruly students as typically Chinese. "The strike of more than eight thousand Chinese students in schools in all parts of Tokyo has become a great problem," it announced.

> It is based on flimsy grounds, on discontent growing out of a very narrow and one-sided interpretation of the Education Ministry's regulations by the students. It also derives from a self-indulgent and petty self-will that seems peculiarly Chinese.

This slur drove Ch'en T'ien-hua, who had so far taken little part in the strike, to spend much of the night writing a statement in which he drew the attention of his fellow students to the unfavorable characterization of the *Asahi;* unless they disproved this view, he argued, China was lost. "If the students are really self-indulgent and petty, isn't China doomed? Never forget those four characters [self-indulgent, petty]," he charged, "work to make them inapplicable, and work to build a country in which they have no place. Study for your love of country." Early the next morning he gave emphasis to his words by committing suicide in the ocean at Ōmori. The strike continued and grew, until Japanese Diet members and politicians entered the discussion. In January of 1906 the Education Ministry weakened its residence requirements for Chinese students, and a solution was gradually reached.

In the next few years, revolutionary organizations and propaganda increased among the students, and the Japanese government's attitude became more conservative and concerned. In 1908 came the first Chinese anti-Japanese boycott. This was triggered by the offensive way in which the Japanese government had reacted to a complaint of the Peking government that Japanese vessels had been engaged in smuggling weapons into China for revolutionary groups. Thus even activities nominally congenial to student radicals—weapon smuggling—could not be brooked if they were accompanied by actions or attitudes offensive to nationalist susceptibilities. Throughout the remainder of the years allotted to the Ch'ing dynasty, provincial and national organizations of Chinese students in Tokyo kept a vigilant eye on real and fancied insults to Chinese sovereignty and dignity. In the steady sequence of loans and rivalries over spheres of interest, the students found no lack of issues with which to maintain their political consciousness.

In the long run, the cultural importance of the migration to Japan was probably greater even than its short-run political significance. As Kuo Mo-jo summarized it in the 1950s,

> We studied Western culture through Japan.... At the same time that the study of Japan broke the feudalistic conventions of the past, it served to further China's progress toward modernity.

The student movement meant a great surge of translation from Japanese. Most student journals and newspapers had sections reserved for translations. By 1900 a group of Chinese students in Japan (a group that included two future prime ministers and two future ministers to Japan) had organized a translating and publishing firm, and within a few years enterprising publishers had put together an encyclopedic shelf of one hundred Japanese texts in translation. The search for the secrets of Japanese modernization led logically to translations of a good deal of Japanese modern history also, and lists of works translated are rich in biographical studies of Meiji leaders and political history.

The Chinese turn to Japan was of particular importance because it came at a time when Chinese interests in outside literature were shifting from the purely practical to the institutional and political. From 1902 to 1904, for instance, almost half of the books translated into Chinese were concerned with history and with institutions. From 1880 to 1940, over two thousand works were translated from Japanese, and of these nearly half were in the social sciences, history and geography. Japanese translations made up only 15 percent of the total from 1850 to 1889, and 18 percent from 1912 to 1940, but they totaled 60 percent of the total in the years around the Russo-Japanese War.

This flood of translation from Japanese affected Chinese vocabulary. There was a massive infusion, amounting to three-fourths of the new vocabulary of those decades, of new terminology into Chinese in the form of Chinese character equivalents the Japanese had first worked out for themselves. But the translation vogue went far beyond the purely institutional and political. Romantic and political novels of the Meiji 1880s were translated by men as important as Liang Ch'i-ch'ao.

It must be remembered that the Chinese student movement to Japan marked the beginning and not the end of a movement of young Chinese abroad. Japan was by no means its only focus, but it was long the most popular, and always the least expensive, goal. Chinese students in other countries became numerous also, particularly in later decades of the twentieth century. A recent study gives the figure of six thousand for France in 1920 (although this includes two thousand worker-students drawn from the labor corps sent to help on the western front during World War I) and three thousand for the United States in that same year. Europe and America became relatively more attractive after 1915 and the Twenty-one Demands. Students there were sufficiently numerous to draw some of the same complaints about disorganization and lack of motivation that characterized Japanese grumbling in the late Meiji period. But the Meiji movement was the first, largest and most concentrated, and it remained of permanent importance. Its size may be placed in further perspective if the later Russian experience is taken into account. When the Soviet Union announced in October 1966 that it was expelling all Chinese students from Russia, there were only sixty-five to expel, and in all the seventeen years of Communist power in China, the Russians could claim only ten thousand Chinese as entirely or partly Russian trained.

Because China's twentieth-century history was so largely one of civil war and disorder, it is particularly worthy of note that Japanese military education attracted so many students. Throughout the 1920s and 1930s Japanese military attachés and advisers serving with warlord and national armies in China were dealing with officers whose educational background was close to their own. This had its origin in the Meiji movement and particularly in a recommendation by the minister to Tokyo in 1903 that "Japanese military education stresses loyalty and patriotism and subordination to superiors ... and contains no dangers of unbridled indiscipline or opposition to government." Regulations already provided for the selection of one hundred students for military education on government scholarship support. This number grew, and it was supplemented by the products of private education in Japanese military academies. Y. C. Wang has pointed out that by 1907 there had been 521 graduates of Japanese military academies, that 350 were currently enrolled in military courses and that most of China's military leaders of the next two decades came from the Japanese-educated group. As late as 1932, he writes, one-half of the military commissions in Kuomintang armies were held by men who had received at least some of their education in Japan. Curiously, it was in letters and in arms that the Japanese-educated predominated; China's future leaders in the sciences were predominantly Western-educated.

The late Ch'ing rush to overseas schools marked the beginning of a foreign orientation that continued to characterize twentieth-century China until the Cultural Revolution of the 1960s. By the Chinese government regulations of 1904, all teachers in colleges and universities were supposed to be foreign-educated or products of foreign-modeled research academies in China. The graded series of rewards, correlated with length of study overseas, that was announced has already been noted, but this was not limited to government and teaching service. There is a striking example in the case of China's leading private publishing firm in the second decade of the twentieth century: salary, office space, desk size and length of book shelves were all correlated with length and location of study abroad. Along with this went a steady decline in the importance and rewards attached to the mastery of traditional Chinese culture in the educational system from lower schools through Peking University. From serving as the center of education, the classics were gradually eliminated in lower schools and relegated to a part of the faculty of literature in higher schools.

It is interesting to contrast this process to the methods the Japanese had used to appropriate Western learning for the Meiji state. Early Meiji also saw a large-scale movement of Japanese students abroad. But there was no nearby and inexpensive alternative to studying in the West. As a result, a much smaller number of students could go and those who went were on the whole better supported and connected. Upon their return they were worked smoothly into places and positions of leadership. Foreign professors were hired at high cost for institutions of higher learning, at first in order to free them from excessive "voluntary" Western, and especially missionary, influence, but at the same time their future Japanese successors were dispatched abroad for education which equipped them to replace the foreigners as soon as possible. This process was first completed in the sciences. By the turn of the century, when Natsume Sōseki was sent to England to prepare him to succeed Lafcadio Hearn, it was extending to foreign literature. Thereafter Japan's government universities were virtually closed to products of foreign institutions, unless they had first qualified through the orthodox paths of Japanese academe. Some foreign experience after graduation was highly desirable, but a foreign degree was of little practical importance in a system that had become self-sufficient and self-perpetuating. China's student movement, in contrast, was done without, or in advance of, the development of an institutional framework which could accommodate this tide of ambitious young men. Until the establishment and consolidation of the Republic of China in the late 1920s, China's uncoordinated and diversified academic migration provided an educational analogue to the centrifugal forces that were at work in politics and economics.

4. The Revolutionaries

JAPAN AFFECTED CHANGE in late Imperial China in at least a half-dozen ways. Japan's defeat of the land and naval forces of Li Hung-chang in 1894 revealed the inadequacy of Chinese attempts to appropriate Western material and military strength and showed the need for more thoroughgoing institutional reforms. Japan's revelation of the military weakness of the Chinese empire, its seizure of Taiwan and its attempt to alienate part of Manchuria triggered the imperialist rush in which Britain, France, Germany and Russia established exclusive spheres of interest and advantage for themselves. The resulting sense of despair and crisis led to the Hundred Days of 1898 in which reformer-literati tried to emulate the Meiji example to create a country that would not suffer foreign insult and humiliation. Thereafter, Chinese students began to seek in Japan the secrets of rapid modernization.

In rural and especially in coastal China, meanwhile, the Japanese defeat of the Ch'ing armies, and the discontent of Chinese levies disbanded after the Treaty of Shimonoseki had ended hostilities, increased the potential for local disorder and insurrection. Rebellion had broken out in Manchuria while the war was still going on; in south China, where units were hastily recruited only to be disbanded again, these groups demanded back pay, refused to disband, and often scourged the countryside. All of this vastly increased the potential for traditional forms of insurrection by secret societies. These groups were always an index of political and economic health of the Chinese social order. They had proliferated mightily during the half century that began with the Taiping Rebellion. They drew upon folk belief and religious syncretism, combined sorcery with ritual and constituted regional networks capable of enlisting and dispersing large numbers of men almost overnight. The Boxers, who rose in opposition to the imperialist penetration of north China, were the most celebrated instance of this because their targets were foreign. But throughout central and south China, groups like the Hung Society and its branches, the Triple Harmony (San-ho hui, or Triad) organization and the Elders (Ko-lao hui) Society, provided the human material for subversive planning and activity. Even their numbers and organization, important as they were, constituted only the peak of the vast iceberg of human power that was available for rebellion in the setting of social and economic crisis in which China found itself. Bankrupt peasants, ex-soldiers, rural and urban poor, vagrants, unemployed and underemployed farm labor were everywhere ready at hand for those with some resources and the courage to challenge existing authority.

There was a climate of rebellion. The number of official executions and the estimates of incidents of "revolt," which totaled between eighty and one hundred annually, suggest the volatility of the late Ch'ing social setting. After the suppression of the Boxers in the north, conditions in south and central China—along the Yangtze and in the mountainous and poorly policed areas of Kwangtung—were most appropriate for insurrection. These were the areas with minority groups like the Hakka (who had manned the early Taiping armies), numerous Triads, Elders and smugglers, groups to which the new leaven of demobilized soldiers added a new spark after 1895. These were also the areas from which most overseas Chinese had emigrated and which had produced large numbers of overseas students. Setting and area thus encouraged experimentation with revolt. The Japanese had not created this, but their defeat of the Ch'ing contributed to it. Their occupation of Taiwan, with the resulting flight of many islanders to the neighboring province of Fukien, had also stimulated it. This was the area of Sun Yat-sen's first revolt of 1895 in Canton and of his major insurrection at Waichow in 1900, and it was also the setting for secret society risings in the central Yangtze by reformers who worked with secret societies in 1900.

Japan's contribution had also, as has been shown, extended to the institutional reforms the Manchu court undertook after the failure of the Boxer uprising. These reforms began to create new interests and new classes without providing adequate channels or opportunities for them. In Harold Schiffrin's words,

> selective modernization ... created a chain reaction which could no longer be contained within the traditional political and social setting. Projects involving modern industries, railroads, and the renovation of the armed forces and the educational system had created new functions, roles, and interests, which required institutional change.

Or, as Lucien Bianco adds,

> the officers ... students ... businessmen ... were not only modern, they were new: ... They did not yet constitute a class that could challenge the old ruling class, but were at most social groups in the process of formation, groups beginning to define their identity in response to stimuli introduced into the Middle Kingdom by recent history.

In no area was Japan's contribution more important or direct than that of the student movement. By example, precept and pressure, as we have seen, it had helped to create a disaffected intelligentsia.

In addition to these contributions there was one additional Japanese-inspired dimension to change in late Ch'ing China that requires discussion. This was the direct participation of Japanese in a revolutionary movement. For in addition to the officials and would-be officials of the Ch'ing government with their ideas of institutional reform, there was a large and growing number of Chinese determined to overthrow that government altogether and start out anew. Some of these were men who knew they had no chance of serving the existing government, while others were convinced that government had no chance of serving China.

Students trained in modern learning were most likely to have such attitudes. Their experiences in the treaty ports, Hong Kong, or Japan exposed them to dramatic contrasts with the communities they had left. The large number trained in Christian schools had additional grounds for discontent with the traditional society and government of their country. Most surely cut off from personal advancement, most intimately aware of the contrasts between their countrymen's self-image and outside repute, they could not fail to give thought to the ways in which their country might be brought to measure up to the Western world. After 1895 the revelation that China had fallen behind its island neighbor added urgency to such reflections.

Christianity added other things: programs for social amelioration, ideas of personal dignity, of equal treatment and of liberation for women. To some opportunists it offered also the hope of protection by foreigners if they should find themselves in trouble with their government. One might, from what has been said, construct an ideal revolutionary leader. He would be from south China, the area of emigration overseas, to provide him with ties to overseas Chinese resources and continental Chinese secret societies. He would be Christian, to provide him with contacts and sympathy with powerful foreigners and give him the standing from which he could reassure his fellows about foreign purposes and promise foreign support. He would have enough foreign experience and reading to be able to interpret Western experience to suggest its applicability to the problems that China faced. Without this evidence of intellectual input, he would have little to offer the new student generation. Superficially, at least, he would need, in Y. C. Wang's phrase, to reverse the old slogan of "Chinese as essence, Western knowledge for practice," with "Western as essence for practice in China." This construct of an effective revolutionary salesman happens to describe Sun Yat-sen perfectly. But it leaves out one important ingredient: his ability to appeal to and, at times, deliver Japanese contacts as well.

There were many reasons for Japanese and their government to maintain direct contact with politics in China. The danger of a Manchu collapse and a partition of China was a constant theme in Japanese writings after the Sino-Japanese War. For the conservative leaders of Meiji Japan, the first choice of method in influencing the course of events in China was through advice and assistance to the legitimate imperial government. Military missions and educational programs provided irrefutable evidence that Japan was ahead in the race for modernity and provided a feeling of Japanese leadership in an Asian restoration. On the other hand, Japan had achieved its successes through affiliation with the West, and many Japanese felt it wise to steer clear of any obvious ties with Asia. They maintained this concern through at least the Russo-Japanese War, when a Chinese tie was avoided lest the West think of the war in racial terms. Thereafter Japan's full participation in imperialist politics reduced still more the attractions of an "Asian" stance.

But there was also widespread opinion that some ultimate confrontation between East and West, nonwhite and white, was inevitable. This conviction was particularly current in the last decade of the Meiji period, in large measure because there was so much published in the West about the inevitability of a racial struggle. The echoes of Western "yellow peril" argumentation produced a new Asian consciousness in Japan. From this perspective Japan's need to affiliate with China was clear. And if the Chinese government should prove incapable of response or inflexible in assumptions of Chinese leadership, the cultivation of possible alternatives to that regime became wise.

This view of racial struggle and the fear of Western dominance characterized most of the Meiji period and it crossed most political positions. Shadings varied and, with them, tactics, but the root sense of kinship and commitment to an Asian cause—expressed as "common culture, common race"—was seldom denied. By the twentieth century the principal Meiji leaders were entering the status of genro and becoming more conservative. Some of them, especially Yamagata Aritomo, were much concerned about a coming clash between the races, but the responsibilities of power usually sufficed to keep their eyes on the side of the navies and industries of the West. Yamagata's position overlapped with that of the military specialists, whose leader he was; the army leaders were particularly aware of China's lack of power to stop the West, and they were quick to take upon themselves the responsibility for protecting the continent—in Korea, in Liaotung, or "south Manchuria," and in Taiwan, so that they could make up for their neighbor's weakness. Their concern with China's borders on the north made them particularly eager to help train China's new armies, and it helped account for the decision to permit Chinese government-sponsored students to enroll in Japanese military academies.

Over against Yamagata and the power elite, there were also influential Japanese who were tired of their country's apparent second-class citizenship in the international order and who became articulate advocates of nationality and of Asia. As self-appointed guardians of the national conscience and without the responsibility of power, they were persuasive spokesmen of a national reawakening that had followed the advocacy of emperor, nation and culture. This group included the spokesmen of the nationalist societies that had grown out of the era of party organization in the 1880s, such as Tōyama Mitsuru's Genyōsha (1881). In the twentieth century its most powerful organization was the Kokuryūkai ("Black Dragon," or Amur River Society), formed in 1901 by Uchida Ryōhei in pursuit of a strong anti-Russian policy in Manchuria. The nationalist leaders were advocates of nationalism and morality, of "Asianism" over against Westernization, and they had ready access to men of influence and to youths of courage and fanaticism. Their government, which was working out a new cultural orthodoxy of emperor and state, could scarcely contradict their propaganda, and it was careful about the ways it chose to control them. So the nationalists produced activists in Korea, China and Manchuria; they sheltered agents of intimidation and terror at home, and their top leaders had such ready entry into government circles that Itō Hirobumi, as has been mentioned, thought it wise to take Uchida with him to Korea. Consequently a statement by Tōyama or Uchida that Sun Yat-sen should receive shelter in Japan was not lightly set aside.

At the turn of the century, the "preservation of China" meant its preservation from Russian imperialism, for it was the Russian armies that were refusing to evacuate Manchuria and had succeeded the Japanese in the occupation of Liaotung. Asianism and agitation for a stand against Russia went hand in hand in

Japan. Both commended Japan to the Chinese student thousands in Tokyo, and the Resist Russia Volunteer Corps the students organized in 1903 had the enthusiastic support of Japanese jingoes who wanted a "fundamental solution" of the "Russian problem." The nationalist and Asianist movement intersected at the highest level of the elite in the activities of Prince Konoe Atsumaro (1863–1904), the father of the premier of the 1930s. Konoe had impeccable social credentials, he was head of the House of Peers, and he had been educated in central Europe. He made it his mission to warn his countrymen of the nature of racial conflict, to sponsor the study of Asia and especially China and to work for a strong line against Russia. In 1898 he sponsored, subsidized and headed the East Asian Common Culture Association (Tōa Dōbun Shoin); through its educational centers in China and its research centers in Japan, it made important contributions to cultural exchange and cultural diplomacy. That same year Konoe wrote, in a much-quoted article, his arguments for Sino-Japanese cooperation and association. He argued that the root causes of Western aggression were racial and that Japan had no alternative to helping China oppose them. "The survival of the Chinese people is by no means a matter of some one else's welfare," he wrote; "it affects the vital interests of the Japanese themselves." Japanese would have to study China, travel to China and meet Chinese, and only then would they be able to adopt policies appropriate to the danger both countries faced. In 1901, the year Uchida Ryōhei founded the Kokuryūkai, Konoe set up a National League of Those United on Russian Policy (Kokumin Tairo Dōshikai), an organization that drew its supporters from the top of the Meiji political, journalistic and nationalist establishments.

One would expect to find Chinese refugees and students in Japan the recipients of friendship and attention appropriate to their station in Chinese society. The reformers of 1898 were a natural elite among the political refugees, and they received the care and hospitality of high-ranking Japanese. Support for the escape of K'ang Yu-wei and Liang Ch'i-ch'ao to Japan was arranged at the highest levels of the Meiji government. Prince Konoe was intermediary for much of this and close to all of it. K'ang Yu-wei met leading Japanese, enjoyed the hospitality of Ōkuma Shigenobu and had a long talk with Konoe himself before his departure for Canada was arranged by Konoe with Foreign Office funds. Liang Ch'i-ch'ao also met with Konoe and other highly placed Japanese. In 1899 Konoe himself traveled to China, where he talked with top-ranking officials like Chang Chih-tung and discussed his favorite themes of Sino-Japanese cooperation and concern.

A liberal and Christian reformer like Sun Yat-sen, on the other hand, found natural friends among Japanese of the liberal left. Miyazaki Tōten was acclaimed by Sun Yat-sen as

> a chivalrous hero. His knowledge is extensive, his ideals are out of the ordinary; he is one who hastens to help another's need, his heart warm with benevolence and righteousness. He always laments the oppression of the yellow race by barbarians, and grieves because of China's increasing weakness.

Miyazaki and his brothers came out of the early liberal movement, experimented with Christianity, studied the single-tax solution of Henry George and devoted their lives to the service of the Chinese revolution.

Because these themes of crisis, commitment and conscience were so basic to the Meiji scene and because the turn of the century brought so many of these to fruition in quick succession, it is natural that the groups and themes that have been mentioned should intersect at many points. For instance, Ōkuma Shigenobu was premier and foreign minister during the Hundred Days' reform. It was possible for Miyazaki and an associate to find government interest in their desire to cultivate contacts among Chinese revolutionaries and for them to be willing to accept funds without fear of compromising their ideals. The crisis of the Western imperialist advance in China seemed to reduce most differences between Japanese to minor proportions. Thus the years 1897–98 brought Sun Yat-sen to Japan; Ōkuma and Inukai were in power in Japan, and the reformers of 1898 came to power and then to Japan in flight; Konoe founded the Dōbunkai, and Chinese students began to come to Japan in significant numbers; the same years saw the launching of the life work of Miyazaki Tōten as a lieutenant of Sun Yat-sen.

Sun Yat-sen was born in a village near Canton in 1866. His area was one of heavy emigration. At the age of thirteen he was sent to Hawaii to join an elder brother, and there he entered an Anglican school. When he returned to Kwangtung three years later, he had the opportunity to compare late Manchu China with conditions in the Western world. He returned to his village a Christian, contemptuous of local superstitions and backwardness. In 1883 he was sent to Hong Kong, where he continued his education in an Anglican school and, later, Queen's College. After another trip to Hawaii, he began medical training in Hong Kong in 1886 and completed it in 1892. Sun's formative years and his educational experience thus served to separate him from the values and attitudes of traditional China. His observations of life in Hawaii, Hong Kong and in his village, his Christian orientation and his modern education combined to make him associate Manchu China with backwardness and the West with progress.

Sun Yat-sen made little use of his medical training. He practiced briefly in Macao, only to run afoul of a statute that required local doctors to have Portuguese diplomas. But medicine had not been his main interest anyway, for he would have entered a military academy if the opportunity had presented itself. His real profession was that of salesman and spokesman for revolution. During his period in Macao he came into contact with friends who proved to be members of secret societies espousing overthrow of the Manchus. Yet his first expressions of political interest fell in the conventional area of reform. In 1894 he set out for Peking with a friend in an attempt to present Li Hung-chang with a memorial to urge reforms. Sun's suggestions were unexceptional: proper employment of human abilities, of the soil, of goods, and freer circulation of currency would all bring China wealth and strength. He denounced traditional learning,

SUN YAT-SEN (center, holding coat) returning to China in December, 1911, after the outbreak of the revolution. Directly behind him in this welcoming party is Miyazaki (bearded), his most important Japanese associate.

urged new efforts for expanding agricultural production and concluded by pointing out that Japan, which had begun later, had pulled ahead of China.

The Sino-Japanese War provided the opportunity for Sun's first revolutionary attempt. Once the war was on, Sun returned to Honolulu, where he joined with friends to form the Hsing-Chung hui, or "Rise China Society." Its first members, about one hundred Kwangtung men, were tradesmen, clerks, workers, farmers and tailors, the sort of overseas Chinese whose contributions remained central to Sun Yat-sen's later revolutionary work. Their membership oath stressed themes that became frequent in the decade that followed: "Our descendants may become the slaves of other races! China can only be restored by men of determination."

Sun returned to Hong Kong, where he founded a branch of the new organization. In addition to cash contributions, he sold shares, or bonds, redeemable at profit once the revolution came. The war with Japan was nearing its conclusion, and Sun and his associates began planning for a rising. Their goals were still extremely vague, and in releases for the English press it was not clear whether they planned a new dynasty, a local power, or a Chinese republic. The important thing was to get rid of the Manchus. It was hoped that foreign interests would support, or at least not impede, attempts to organize an insurrection from Hong Kong. The revolutionaries were all young, modern educated, and nongentry in origin; most had been abroad and contrasted what they knew of the outside world and the "modern" treaty ports with the disorder of the Manchu mainland. They planned to seize Canton in October of 1895. The scheme was far from elaborate; it was assumed that·it would suffice to throw a match into the tinder of Manchu disorganization. Local Christians were prominent in the plans. But everything went wrong. A shipment of arms was discovered, secret society "revolutionaries" were delayed, and the leaders fled for their lives. With the exception of an overnight stay on the border of China in 1907, Sun Yat-sen was not to return to the Chinese mainland again until 1911. But this pattern of improvised revolt, inadequately prepared, armed and financed, based upon the recruitment of secret society toughs and mercenaries, would be repeated many times in the next fifteen years.

Sun Yat-sen fled to Japan with a price of one thousand *taels* on his head. There he cut his queue, grew a mustache, and passed for Japanese. As he later recalled,

> After the Japanese war, when the natives of Japan began to be treated with more respect, I had no trouble, when I let hair and mustache grow, in passing for a Japanese. . . . otherwise I should not have escaped from many a dangerous situation.

Sun moved on to Hawaii and then to London. There his escape from capture in the Chinese legation, which planned to send him home for certain execution, made him famous. He published his story as *Kidnapped in London* and overnight became the most famous Chinese revolutionary. His own sense of destiny and mission strengthened, Sun returned to the Orient, his determination to topple Manchu power greater than ever.

Sun's optimistic expectations of support from Western, and especially English, Christians proved unfounded. He was in fact banished from Hong Kong, and he would not be permitted to return there for the next fifteen years. But he fared far better in Japan, where he spent the next three years. The first friends he made were two men named Miyazaki and Hirayama. They had originally been asked by an official close to the Ōkuma government to keep track of the revolutionary movement in China, and they had just returned from frustrating attempts to get in touch with Chinese secret societies. In Sun Yat-sen they found a friend and guide who soon mattered much more to them than their government subsidy, which stopped with the fall of the Ōkuma cabinet. From Miyazaki's account of his first talk with Sun, one can get some idea of the idealistic rhetoric with which the revolutionary inspired the confidence and invited the support of his hearers. "Alas," he said,

> our territory is so huge and our people are so numerous that we are like a piece of meat on the butcher block! The ravenous tiger who devours it will grow so strong he will come to dominate the world. But now if somebody with moral principles responds to this challenge, he will find himself in harmony with the principles of humanity. . . . You have come to help me. It is up to us to see that we do not fall short of your expectations. And you have to do your part to help us gain our objectives. The way to help the four

hundred million of China's masses, the way to wipe out the insults that have been heaped on the yellow peoples of Asia, the way to protect and restore standards of humanity throughout the universe—all this can be done by helping the Chinese revolution. If this one cause succeeds, all other problems can be taken care of quickly.

As is clear from arguments like these, Sun Yat-sen considered Japan a natural ally, and he could address himself to his Japanese friends with a warmth and eloquence he could never achieve in appeals to Westerners. His Japanese friends like Miyazaki, moreover, were his comrades in a special cultural sense. Like him, they stood somewhere between tradition and modernity, alienated from a society which denied them a role, and yet resentful of a West that threatened their identity and independence. Politically, culturally and socially they were between worlds and traditions. Sun's Japanese friends were indifferent to personal comfort and position and neglectful of family responsibilities. They styled themselves as activists of an Asian Meiji Restoration, and they were eager to associate themselves with a leader and cause that might rejuvenate and awaken the world's largest country and oldest tradition. This seemed to them the supreme challenge of their age. In Sun Yat-sen they felt they had located such a person. And so they busied themselves in mediating between Sun and the Japanese elite, in raising money for the revolutionaries, in reporting to their countrymen through word and in books the activities of the revolutionaries, and in utilizing for the cause the relative immunity to arrest and assassination that was theirs as citizens of a great power. Miyazaki Tōten, Sun Yat-sen's closest Japanese friend, spent years in his service and published in 1902 an autobiography, *The Thirty-three Years' Dream,* that was soon translated into Chinese and contributed importantly to Sun's fame. Hirayama Shū was constantly on the travel lanes for Sun, and another, Yamada Yoshimasa, was killed in the Waichow revolt in 1900. Kayano Chōchi was an intimate of the leaders of the late Ch'ing revolutionary movement and provided an important contribution to its history in his memoirs. The Japanese who participated in the movement thus provided protection and prestige. The contacts they made were important to Sun Yat-sen, and his obvious ability to influence Japanese stood him in good stead among Chinese revolutionaries as well.

For most Chinese, Japanese imperialism was not yet a major problem. Young Chinese, whose formative years had been dominated by Western imperialism and Manchu incompetence, saw in Meiji Japan a nation that resisted the former and humbled the latter. From Japanese friends they heard the language of Pan-Asianism, and it was as difficult for them to conceive of a thoroughgoing commitment to imperialism on the part of Japan as it was for many liberals in the 1930s to believe that the Soviet Union could sponsor its own brand of imperialism.

The events of 1899 and 1900 illustrated this spirit of Pan-Asianism perfectly. Sun Yat-sen and his Japanese friends worked on a futile effort to get weapons to Emilio Aguinaldo, who was resisting the substitution of American for

Spanish imperialism in the Philippines. "For Sun Yat-sen," as one of the Filipino participants put it,

> the problems found in the various countries of the Far East presented them-
> selves in such form that he could study them together.... Sun was one of the
> enthusiastic advocates of a group of young oriental students from Korea,
> China, Japan, India, Siam, and the Philippines.

It is significant that it was Sun Yat-sen, and not the Japanese, who provided the means, who was the leader and organizer of this effort. But it came to nothing, and the hopes went down with the antiquated and overloaded ship that headed for Aguinaldo with Japanese weapons. Thirteen men, three of them Japanese, were lost. A small party of six Japanese got to Luzon and Aguinaldo, but they had nothing to bring or to promise.

The next year provided new opportunities in south China while the atten-tion of the world was fixed on the siege of the Western legations by the Boxers in the north. Sun and his secret society allies in Kwangtung launched another rebellion there. He was optimistic at first of British and then of Japanese assis-tance from Taiwan. Neither was forthcoming, as wiser counsel overruled the short-sighted enthusiasm of local administrators in Hong Kong and Taiwan. The expectation of Japanese support led Sun to order an overland march from Waichow to Amoy for which his supporters were not prepared or equipped. Sev-enteen days after the fighting had begun, he had to send word that there was no longer hope of substantial Japanese help. Yet the Waichow Rebellion, as it is known, was of considerable importance. Its initial successes provided convincing evidence of the inflammable social discontent in the Kwangtung area; the rebel leader soon had several thousand men, armed with weapons captured from lackadaisical Manchu resistance, under his command. It marked also the apogee of Japanese assistance. A provisional government that was sketched out before things began included several Japanese among its members.

The rebellion also showed the limits of secret society organization. There was little to distinguish the revolutionaries from traditional peasant rebels; Sun and his lieutenants could ignite, but they could not structure, insurrection. For a time, disillusion was profound. Miyazaki made the rising the culminating chapter in his autobiographical account, *The Thirty-three Years' Dream*. Parallel attempts at insurrection farther north in the Yangtze region found other Japanese involved, and equally unproductively. Partisans of the reformers K'ang Yu-wei and Liang Ch'i-ch'ao organized a rising in Hunan and Hupeh that was based mainly on manpower provided by the Society of Elders (Ko-lao hui). Chinese students returned from Tokyo to take part in insurrections that were planned for five cities in three provinces. But while the rebels waited for their funds, Chang Chih-tung discovered the plot and moved in to crush the conspira-tors in August. Twenty leaders were executed.

Although Waichow marked the high point of Japanese participation in ac-tual rebellion, Sun Yat-sen's friends' importance continued in other respects. One of these was in a series of efforts to get the revolutionaries and the reformers to cooperate. Both groups competed with the same overseas Chinese communities for financial support, and in 1900 both groups used the same secret society networks for manpower. Leaders of both groups were receiving refuge and support from the same sources in Japan, and it made sense to try to get them to cooperate.

These attempts failed, and the reasons for the failure show a good deal about both movements. K'ang, Liang and their student followers were members of the scholar-gentry and considered themselves natural heirs to the official tradition. As they saw it, Sun Yat-sen and his friends were bandit and secret society types, drawn from rural China and poorly educated in the Chinese tradition. Their distrust of the violence that marked the revolutionaries extended to their Japanese friends, and they as often expected assault as they did assistance from Sun's adventurer-associates. As a result every effort to reconcile the two groups of Chinese fell afoul of fundamental social and cultural differences. When Sun Yat-sen tried to approach K'ang Yu-wei in Singapore by sending Miyazaki to see him, K'ang assumed that his would-be visitor planned to assassinate him and denounced him to the British police. K'ang is quoted as having said, "Sun himself isn't such a bad fellow, but he is uneducated. He doesn't understand the things you say to him." Sun finally dismissed K'ang with contempt by saying "That rotten Confucianist is hopeless." Many of the student leaders and radical intellectuals had the same unflattering view of Sun Yat-sen's intelligence. He had his work cut out in making them take him seriously. Chang Ping-lin later said of Sun Yat-sen that "He was quite well known to the foreigners and Chinese . . . but the Chinese students in Japan thought he was an uncultured outlaw." Wu Chih-hui, another leading revolutionary, was surprised to find Sun of "good appearance and gentle manner"; "I suspected him of being illiterate," he said; "only later did I realize that Sun was very fond of reading." And Sun himself, when a new follower complimented him upon the style of a document he had drawn up, assured him that "Why, I have read a great many books." The assumptions and criteria of the gentry elite died hard.

Relations between Sun Yat-sen and Liang Ch'i-ch'ao were better for a time, but after 1900 they parted company permanently. From now on, the principal source of support and focus of opportunity lay with the growing student population in Tokyo. In the early stages of this competition Liang held all the advantages. He was a brilliant stylist, his literary connections in Japan were superior, and young students naturally gravitated to his standard of reformism. Liang was able to draw on the entire Meiji school of constitutional law which drew its examples from German and Austrian theory to argue the case for constitutional monarchy. His influence crested with the publication of *Enlightened Despotism* in 1905. Although Liang continued in his advocacy of the monarchy, it was a monarchy headed by a Kuang-hsü emperor who was the prisoner of the empress dowager. His innovative and even revolutionary import should not be overlooked.

Yet there were important psychological and political problems inherent in the position maintained by Liang. Mounting a revolution in the name of the ruling dynasty had its problems. If one opposed the dynasty, he was also unlikely, by

HUANG HSING (1874-1916), after Sun Yat-sen, the most important of the leaders of the 1911 revolution.

1905, to propose establishing another in its place. To be sure, there were partisans of a Ming restoration, and there might be other candidates for the throne. But because the Manchu dynasty ruled as well as reigned, action undertaken to topple it was likely to result in the abolition of monarchy and not its reform. Here the contrast with Japan, where there had been the inviting alternative of a powerless court, was important. The Chinese tradition had little that was appropriate as an alternative to republicanism. The Manchus, who grew continuously more protective of their prerogatives, did little to help.

Another reason for Liang's temporary ascendancy among Chinese overseas was Sun Yat-sen's discouragement and indecision after his failure at Waichow in 1900. Sun lived quietly reading and thinking in Yokohama for a time; he began organizing a few Chinese students into a military academy with the help of Japanese army officers, he experimented unsuccessfully with support from French authorities in Indochina to start something on the Yunnan border, and he traveled to Hawaii and America to try to wean Hung and Triad Society leaders away from their support of Liang Ch'i-ch'ao.

But the times were on Sun Yat-sen's side. The student movement saw revolutionary discontent and activity rise in intensity and made it possible to work with representatives of the elite or would-be elite instead of secret society plotters. The volunteer army against Russia of 1903, for instance, was transformed into a frankly revolutionary organization. Huang Hsing returned to Hunan as instructor in a Japanese language school, but in addition he printed and distributed the revolutionary pamphlets of Ch'en T'ien-hua. The revolutionary organization he founded, the Hua-Hsing Hui, was made up entirely of present or former students in Japan. When Manchu suppression of Huang's planned revolt forced him to flee to Japan in 1904, he was quickly contacted by some of the same Japanese who worked with Sun Yat-sen. Japanese liaison efforts that had failed to bring reformers and revolutionaries together worked better in uniting the revolutionary movement. Sun's contacts, long restricted to southern Chinese emigrants and secret society representatives, now began to extend to central Chinese revolutionaries and intellectuals.

To equip himself for working effectively with these men, Sun needed new arguments and a more impressive image. The years 1900–04 were also years of intellectual growth for him as he experimented with revolutionary programs and slogans. A swing through Europe in 1905 on his way back to Japan from the United States gave him the opportunity to try his ideas on Chinese students there. By now he was talking in terms of his future "three principles" of nationalism, democracy, and socialism. He added devices from Chinese tradition in adding an examination and censorate to a proposed "five-power constitution." And he began to see the merits of working through returning students, especially military students, when once they were part of Manchu China's new army. At a Brussels meeting Sun succeeded in having himself accepted as the leader of a new revolutionary party, in which he combined his new and Western political ideas with thoroughly traditional conspiratorial symbols of loyalty oaths sealed through special handshakes, passwords, and other secret society rituals. Sun's persuasive powers were never more in evidence; we read of one student who pledged half of his (Manchu government!) scholarship to the new organization. In addition, Sun was gaining considerable exposure through an English tract he had written, *The True Solution of the Chinese Question.* Thus he returned to Japan in 1905 known among students and foreigners as the leading advocate of revolution in China.

Sun returned to Japan by way of Suez, and twenty years later the memory of the new confidence that Japan's victory over Russia had given Asian nationalism was still fresh in his mind:

> On my way home, in going through the Suez Canal, I met an Arab. Looking at my face, he said 'Are you a Japanese?' I told him, no, I was a Chinese. He told me he had observed vast armies of Russian soldiers being shipped back to Russia from the Far East. . . . the joy of this Arab, as a member of the great Asiatic race, seemed to know no bounds.

Several hundred Chinese students were waiting to welcome Sun at the dock in Yokohama. Soon his Japanese friends introduced him to Huang Hsing, the Hunanese hero. The two became firm friends, shared their funds and followers, and set to work creating a new revolutionary organization.

The T'ung-meng hui, or Revolutionary Alliance, was inaugurated late in August 1905. Regulations and membership oaths showed the ties of the new organization with the tradition of secret societies: "I swear under Heaven," these went,

> that I will do my utmost to work for the expulsion of the Manchus, the restoration of Chinese sovereignty, the establishment of the Republic, and the equalization of land rights. I swear to be faithful to these principles. If I betray my trust, I am willing to submit to the severest penalties imposed by my comrades.

Recently published lists show the names of 963 members who joined the league during its first year. In Tokyo 863 joined; the rest joined in Europe, Hong Kong, and Southeast Asia. All the provinces of China except distant Kansu were represented. It was basically an organization of students and intellectuals, in contrast to Sun Yat-sen's earlier groups of overseas Chinese and Kwangtung natives with limited education. This time Hunan (with 157 in that early T'ung-meng hui register) outnumbered Kwangtung (112), and new leaders such as Huang Hsing and Sung Chiao-jen played major roles. That Sun Yat-sen could dominate the organization as he did is therefore impressive evidence of his powers of leadership. His Japanese friends were full members of the new organization, and several had authority to negotiate on its behalf for purchase of arms and supplies.

The T'ung-meng hui did not offer its members a very distinct vision of the China that was to come, but its propagandists were quite specific about the things they were against. *The People's News* (*Min Pao*) listed a basic program of six points. These were: the overthrow of the Manchus, a republican government, world peace, nationalization of land, cooperation with Japan and world support for the revolutionary cause. The most important of these prefigured the subsequent Kuomintang's "three principles" of democracy, nationalism and peoples' livelihood.

The slogans about nationalization of land reflected the search for an answer to the political and economic crisis of China. The single-tax plan of Henry George was well known in Japan, and one of Miyazaki's elder brothers was in fact one of its most enthusiastic advocates. The plan made sense to Chinese who, like Sun, had seen the values of land mushroom in the modern sector along the treaty ports, and the notion that such "unearned increment" should go to the state seemed to offer an equitable way of financing the costs of government. It was the larger social organism that counted, and individual rights would have to take second place. As a writer in the first issue of *The People's News* put it, "What we seek is the freedom of the group; we do not seek the freedom of the individual." This view would continue in later Chinese thought; in 1924 Sun Yat-sen would say, "On no account must we give more liberty to the individual; let us secure liberty instead for the nation."

It was nationalism that was at the center of the program that united the Revolutionary Alliance. For most of its student members, imperialism was the main enemy. Liang Ch'i-ch'ao and other publicists had drawn on John Hobson and the Japanese writer Kōtoku to argue that expansive tendencies in modern economies generated imperialist pressures and that expansion provided one way for Western governments to allay domestic discontent and hardship. After 1900 Liang went on to dismiss the rhetoric of the Open Door policy as "economic aggression" and as a policy whose dangers were no less great although less immediately recognized. The fear that the powers would swallow up a helpless and prostrate China was at the heart of a great deal of emotional and even hysterical writing that circulated among the student agitators, and no group could have gained their allegiance without taking note of it and condemning Western imperialism.

Yet the Boxer experience had also seen the powers pass up their opportunity for division and agree to cooperate in support of a suppliant Manchu court. As Lord Curzon put it for the British, the aim was "to preserve in an age of competition what we had gained in an age of monopoly," and in this advocacy of Open Door and equal opportunity the danger of China's actual partition receded. Nationalist indignation shifted, logically, to attack the Manchus. They were charged with setting a higher price on the continuation of their despotism than on affiliation with their Chinese subjects. Memories stretched to recount again the outrage and horror that had accompanied the original Manchu occupation of China. A fine example of this anti-Manchu, and basically racist, Chinese nationalism was to be found in the inflammatory booklet by Tsou Jung, *The Revolutionary Army*, which was immensely popular throughout the decade. It called upon its readers to

> Sweep away millennia of despotism in all its forms, throw off millennia of slavishness, annihilate the five million and more of the furry and horned Manchu race, cleanse ourselves of two hundred and sixty years of harsh and unremitting pain, so that the soil of the Chinese subcontinent is made immaculate, and the descendants of the Yellow Emperor will all become Washingtons.... Revolution is inevitable for China today. It is inevitable if the Manchu yoke is to be thrown off; it is inevitable if China is to be independent; it is inevitable if China is to take its place as a powerful nation on the globe; it is inevitable if China is to survive for long in the new world of the twentieth century... Stand up for revolution!... Revolution is the universal principle of evolution.

So the revolutionaries turned their indignation against the Manchu rulers. They attacked them as oppressors of the Chinese people, and they called attention to the humiliations of the queue and Chinese exclusion from the highest posts in government. They assailed the Manchus as barbarians, and they warned that the proposed constitution was little more than fancy talk designed to head off discontent. Small wonder that in 1905 a student was inspired by his reading in these revolutionary materials to throw a bomb at an imperial mission about to leave on a tour to study foreign constitutions. Throughout this debate, as Michael Gasster has shown, writers like Wang Ching-wei argued that states ought to be set up along ethnic and cultural lines, thereby signaling the turn whereby China was beginning to be thought of as a nation-state, instead of a universal oecumene. Modern nationalism was taking root. The development and implementation of ideas and suggestions contained within these polemics would require decades, but when they neared completion they presaged a radically different view of Chinese nationality and culture.

The Manchu focus was the more important because after the Japanese victory over Russia, which had seemed the principal threat, China's "outside" danger seemed less acute. No doubt this, plus the fact of the Japanese setting and protection for the early T'ung-meng hui activities, accounted also for a platform plank about Sino-Japanese cooperation. But this was not without its problems. *The People's News* readers occasionally had to be reassured about Japanese intentions. Hu Han-min, in one editorial, found himself explaining and apologizing for some of the condescension and arrogance implicit in the "favor" of Count Ōkuma and the more explicit disfavor of the Tokyo government and tried to distinguish between the Japanese leaders and the Japanese people. Some of the Hunan radicals, notably Sung Chiao-jen, never accepted Sun Yat-sen's optimistic view of Japan.

Sun's partiality toward Japan suffered severe setbacks in 1907. By then the Peking government was becoming alarmed about revolutionary activities in Japan and began restricting the flow of students to Japan. The Tokyo government, for its part, was becoming sensitive to the existence of the radical and hostile element in the mounting tide of student agitation and activity. It had made its peace with its former Russian enemy, and in agreements of 1907 and after resolved the border conflicts that remained. Now, conscious of its dignity and duty as a great power, it found it undesirable to arouse Manchu and Western suspicions of subversion by seeming to harbor eccentrics and revolutionaries. In 1907 Sun Yat-sen was asked to leave Japan and given a sum of money to ease the pain of parting. In the next few years, he and Huang Hsing attempted several revolts based on French territory in Annam, but despite promising beginnings insufficient amounts of money and ammunition doomed them to failure. Thereafter Sun found himself banned from French territory, as he already was from British territory, in Asia. He visited America again. Meanwhile the unity of the T'ung-meng hui had been much weakened by Sun's banishment from Japan. But the more important trends inherent in the steady accretion of education, nationalism and discontent among young Chinese went on as before, to the ultimate benefit, though not the direct credit, of the revolutionary movement.

Japanese influence declined as the dynasty neared its end. Miyazaki, Kayano, and other agents of the revolutionary party became the objects of government surveillance and distrust. So did their Chinese friends during secret visits to Japan. The image of a friendly Japanese government gradually changed to that of a dangerous imperialist power, the more feared for its proximity and ease of access. The outbreak of revolution found Sun Yat-sen far removed from the scene, in Denver, Colorado, and his immediate move was not to return to China but to go to London, in hopes of securing loans and deterring threatened Japanese government intervention against the revolution. The Tokyo government itself was so unsure of its course that it succeeded in alienating almost all candidates for power in China. In Manchuria, army-backed adventurers launched an attempt to set up a separate pro-Japanese buffer state under a Manchu prince. Sun Yat-sen's old friends were active in his support but unable to deliver or guarantee Japanese help. Kita Ikki, a socialist and nationalist, was close to Sung Chiao-jen, but he also managed to send daily cables that reported the political situation to Uchida Ryōhei, the Kokuryūkai head. He later turned to write a thoughtful explanation of how it was that the Japanese bourgeoisie had failed in its great opportunity to establish a position of leadership and trust with a Chinese republic struggling to be born. Others, including Miyazaki and Kayano, were so close to Sun Yat-sen that they shared in his speedy eclipse upon the failure of the revolutionary government. Sun himself, thrown back upon the hospitality of Japan after his brief moment of glory, proved more willing to make compromises with regard to Japanese interests in Manchuria than he had before.

Yet these personal and political misfortunes should not be permitted to obscure the enormous role the Japanese had played by image, by example and by effort in affecting change in late Ch'ing China. The "Revolution of 1911" can readily be denigrated in any search for historical change. Its centrality to the political history of modern China is in part a product of the political mythology of official nationalist historiography. It was an incident in, and not the occasion of, the birth of modern China; its partisans created, in Mary Wright's words, a tradition rather than a revolution. That tradition itself becomes, with its attendant mythology, a fact for later historical evaluation. The Japanese role, in turn, has been obscured by a second, and unhappy, tradition that began with the Twenty-one Demands of 1915. Before turning to these important shifts, it is worthwhile to pause and imagine the possibilities of the role the Japanese began and failed to finish as agents of change in twentieth-century China.

CHAPTER 6

Changing of the Guard

The second decade of the twentieth century brought decisive changes in the international relations of East Asia. The pattern of imperialist stability in which Western empires cooperated to force their will upon a prostrate Chinese empire disappeared as first the victim and then the contenders disappeared as empires. The concert of power and privilege that Japan had spent a half century in trying to join disappeared virtually at the moment of Japanese success. The Manchu empire, which had become increasingly important to the balance and structure of East Asian international relations, collapsed and gave way to a series of contending local hegemonies that brought on a new and more confusing contention for influence. The principal European contenders fell into a half decade of suicidal warfare that all but removed them from East Asian competition. New terms were to be set by the rivalry between a newly powerful United States and a newly industrialized Japan.

It would be wrong to emphasize the stability of the order that was overthrown. The treaty-port system had existed for only a half century and had known constant change. Cooperative efforts to win favors from the Manchus at mid-nineteenth century had given way to the struggles for exclusive privileges at century's end, only to have the post-Boxer collapse convince the powers that they had best cooperate on the basis of what they already had. But the dictates of military and maritime superiority remained unchallenged, and Japan's victory over Russia had found her join rather than challenge the circle of the favored and industrialized few. A pattern of privileged trade, regularized and administered by an internationally staffed customs service and balanced by the operation of the most-favored–nation clause, rewarded all contestants equally. The post-Boxer years had seen competitive loan contracts gradually replaced by cooperative consortiums. The powers seemed to have worked out the rules for joint exploitation of the Chinese market.

Still, the first decade of the century, during which these arrangements had been worked out, was also full of tremors that signaled the imminent fall of imperialist giants. In the Near East the Turkish empire was in process of collapse, and the struggle this precipitated between Austria-Hungary and Russia signaled the start of Europe's instability. A new and powerful Germany had entered the European system. Feared by all its neighbors except Austria-Hungary, it was not absorbed into the European system, which instead organized against it. Its ambition and discontent precipitated the short-lived imperialist grabs in China in 1898, helped ignite the rush for empire in Africa and ultimately led to World War I. Japan's rise, meanwhile, had removed Russia from contention in Manchuria and Korea only to force it back to Eastern Europe, thereby bringing the European system closer to collapse. Japan and Germany, the two latecomers to the competition, had also worked out zones in which they brooked no competition from their imperialist colleagues in China. South Manchuria and Shantung were exceptions to the pattern of shared advantage and collaborative exploitation that was developing. Nor did Japan and Germany, both more equipped with military than financial resources, become full members of the consortium club that replaced the treaty-port competition.

After 1905 the cutthroat competition of earlier days nevertheless seemed long past. East Asia, as Professor Iriye has pointed out, had been a world dominated by empires and not by nation-states. The East Asian policies of the great powers had long remained a factor of their mutual hostility and fear as much as a result of specifically East Asian concerns. Great Britain had seen in Japan a check against Russian imperialism, Germany had seen in Russian expansion an outlet for energies that otherwise would turn to Europe, and France had recognized in Russian expansion encouragement for a European concert against Germany. Japan worked itself into this system. In Korea it profited from British conclusions that China could not stand against Russia; in Manchuria it profited from Britain's need for allies against Russia, and in China it worked out useful additions to the privileges the treaties accorded Western powers. On overcoming Russian threats to dominance in Korea, Japan had moved swiftly to conciliate its recent enemy on the territorial concerns that remained.

Unlike the other powers that competed in East Asia, Japan had its own security involved in each step of its progress. Japanese had concluded that south Korea was essential to the security of the home islands, that north Korea was to south, that south Manchuria was essential to the whole, and finally came to see that north Manchuria and Inner Mongolia were strategically linked as well. "Security" is always a relative term, but in an age of clearly established national borders countries seldom develop territorial ambitions unless they are led by personally ambitious leaders or fanatical ideologies. The Meiji leaders did not fit this pattern. Their concern was with the insecurity and disorder on their borders, a condition which they sought to improve by extending their "line of sovereignty," as Yamagata called it, to their "line of interest." With the Russo-Japanese War and the annexation of Korea, they had achieved a good part of these goals.

However numerous the sources of instability in East Asia, there seemed some sort of equilibrium in the years after the Russo-Japanese War. The Japanese government, after several years of sheltering the Chinese revolutionaries among the students who thronged to Tokyo, turned them out in 1907 and maintained its relations with the Peking court on an official level. The revolutionaries had failed repeatedly, they were now deprived of a base in Japan, and they were very short of funds and support. The powers were organizing to provide broad backing for consortium loans to underwrite Chinese modernization measures, not out of a late-blooming sense of obligation, but from the realization that cutthroat competition would no longer benefit them. Although the Japanese in south Manchuria and the Germans in Shantung remained reluctant or unable to participate fully in these measures, they too maintained agreement with the general principles of Open Door and equal opportunity elsewhere in China.

Most important in the impression of stability in late Ch'ing China was the performance of the Chinese government itself. The action of the powers in returning the Manchus to rule after the flight to Sian in 1900 seemed to indicate that there was no real alternative to continued Manchu rule within China. The Manchus also seemed essential to the stability of China's border areas. The border tributaries, and especially the Mongols to the north, were loyal to the "Ch'ing" and not to a generalized "China." The performance of the court under the empress dowager until her death in 1908 gave encouragement for hopes of stability. The vigorous program of institutional change that was set in motion seemed to hold some promise of corrective and preventive reform that might thwart both revolutionaries and outsiders.

Of particular interest are recent studies of the manner in which senior Chinese officials now maneuvered to restrict imperialist advances in their areas. Many of the leading governors and governors general showed skillful and increased understanding of international law and a developing concern with modern conceptions of sovereignty. This is shown particularly in John Schrecker's recent study of German activity in Shantung. Senior officials in Shantung developed tactics of evasion, legalism and communication to hold the Germans to the letter of the treaties with which they had expected to be able to dominate the entire province. Successes of this sort owed much to the institutional reforms of late Manchu years, because those reforms held out the hope of participation by a provincial elite whose personal interests were involved in the maintenance of Chinese sovereignty. An increasingly awakened and confident body of local gentry and merchants thus stood prepared to contest and protest additional incursions of Chinese sovereignty.

Such efforts were supplemented and helped by the pervasive sense of nationalism and of national danger that was beginning to spread through all sectors of China's literate population. Professor Mary Wright's studies of local journals and papers have shown how intense and desperate this sense of imminent disaster was. The emotionalism of the student revolutionaries provided only one aspect of this sentiment. The powers had had one experience of illiterate peasant and proletarian xenophobia in the Boxer disaster. They did well to hesitate to affront similar emotions in better informed, more communicative, more widely traveled and more widely read students and semiintellectuals. Ironically, this intense fear of foreign division of China developed only after that danger was virtually a thing of the past. As the post-Manchu days were to show, China's greatest dangers of disunity and collapse were to come not from without, but from within.

1. The End of Imperial China

THE FIRST COLLAPSE was that of the Ch'ing empire. The Revolution of 1911 marks the beginning of Republican China and provides the start for modern Chinese dating. But in fact its origin and course are full of ambiguities, and its importance has been obscured by several decades of nationalist historiography which has been devoted to the apotheosis of Republican heroes. It is probably more accurate to say that the imperial system collapsed than to say that it was overthrown.

The empress dowager died in 1908, and with her end the Manchu court found itself poorly provided in leadership. Chang Chih-tung died the following year. Prince Chun, father and regent for the infant emperor Pu-yi, was vacillating, incompetent and ignorant. One of his first acts was to dismiss Yüan Shih-k'ai, probably the only powerful official who might have steered the dynasty through the next few years. Yüan's troops remained loyal to him, and he quietly bided his time. The Manchu court perversely sought comfort in more Manchu, non-Chinese appointments and grew more restrictive, and less national, toward its close.

But in several key respects, financial and political need combined to encourage continued measures of modernization and centralization. One of these came under the leadership of the industrialist-bureaucrat Sheng Hsüan-huai, who was recalled from retirement and entrusted with the direction of a campaign of railway centralization. The unification of a multiplicity of lines begun under local sponsorship and management was the price for a badly needed foreign loan to which Great Britain, the United States, France and Germany had agreed to subscribe. Also in 1909, the movement for constitutional government produced the preliminary step of provincial assemblies. These provided a focus and platform for local expressions of opinion and indignation.

Trouble began in May 1911, when steps were undertaken to nationalize the Szechwan-Hankow railway. The terms seemed unfair and disadvantageous to the local elite who had invested in, and often mismanaged, these enterprises, and they charged that the government was selling Szechwan to the foreigners. Thus once again an issue of imperialism roused widespread indignation in a manner that could combine the fury of the lower classes with the more directly involved interests of the local elite. There was nothing remotely revolutionary about the motivations of the Railway Protection League, although the indignation it helped stir, fanned by clumsy Manchu efforts at repression, roused coarser and simpler emotions of xenophobia. Thus a movement begun by "gentry, literati, large landowners and wealthy merchants" had the potential of arousing the passions of poor peasants whose complaints had little or no connection with the railway issue.

The emergence of disorder in Szechwan suggested to revolutionaries the possibility of yet another attempt to topple the dynasty. But the revolutionary movement had fared extremely badly since Sun Yat-sen had left Japan in 1907. He had alienated many of the elements within the T'ung-meng hui, and that organization itself, barely kept alive by student scholarship support, was close to dissolution. Arguments about tactics, about funds, about leadership and even about a revolutionary flag produced sharp splits between Sun Yat-sen and revolutionaries from central China. In 1910 Sun Yat-sen had formed a group in San Francisco which he called The Revolutionary Party, and he entrusted more and more of his business to his Japanese friend Miyazaki Tōten instead of utilizing the Revolutionary Alliance shadow headquarters in Tokyo. In turn the Yangtze province revolutionaries had formed a Mutual Aid Society that looked to Huang Hsing and Sung Chiao-jen for leadership. In central China the dissidents were often drawn from landholding families, and their manifestos made less point of promises of livelihood. In April 1911 a disastrous uprising in Canton had taken the lives of seventy-two revolutionaries. Discouragement was general, and revolutionary strength there badly depleted for a time. Along the Yangtze, however, student and ex-student elements in the new army units provided a core of several thousand revolutionaries from which something might yet be hoped. Nevertheless as late as 7 October 1911 a Central Executive Council of the revolutionaries decided that "the disturbances in Szechwan are quieting down, and Hunan and Nanking are not reliable . . . arrangements for revolts should naturally be slowed down."

The "Double Ten" of revolutionary fame was three days away. Sun Yat-sen was in Denver, Huang Hsing in Hong Kong, and other leaders widely scattered. What happened was that a premature bomb explosion forced the hand of revolutionaries in Wuchang, who had no intention of starting their revolt; sympathetic units of the new armies on the spot were able to overcome the incompetent traditional levies which the Manchus sent against them, and Wuchang, to the revolutionaries' surprise, was suddenly—and temporarily, as it turned out—in their hands. That this sufficed to become the start of something serious was possible only because the Manchus had lost all support from the elite. Local assemblies, dominated by local gentry, were indignant because of new taxation and governmental policies, modern army units felt themselves under suspicion and little inclined to fight for the dynasty, and officials of the central government chose to take a wait-and-see attitude before announcing their position. The typical pattern was one in which provincial governments announced their independence rather than endorse a revolutionary government. Thus in Szechwan local gentry and members of the Provincial Assembly conferred with the viceroy to effect a peaceful transfer of authority; on 27 November they formed the Great Chinese Military Government of Chengtu and declared the province independent. Similarly the governor of Shantung declared the independence of his province, then telegraphed Peking to explain that he had little choice and promised to reverse his action as soon as it proved practicable. If the officials had little revolutionary sentiment or loyalty, the commoners did not have a great deal more. New institutions of local self-government and many provincial assemblies had become unpopular because of the new taxes they had instituted for modernization measures like schools, and many local riots destroyed schools and local bureaus. It was important for the local elite in most areas to head off or to forestall real revolutionary sentiment.

None of this needs to obscure the devotion and courage of revolutionary leaders who had been working for a comparable opportunity for more than a decade. But their success at this time was, as Sun Yat-sen later described it, "sheer accident." And this explains their strategic and economic weakness in dealing with the events after 10 October. They had been geared to fight the Manchus, and when the hated foreign dynasty suddenly collapsed, their preparations and backing proved seriously inadequate to their purposes. The Wuchang revolutionaries, in fact, forced a reluctant colonel in one of the new army units to serve as their leader and then found themselves stuck with him. He later explained his role in these words: "I was quickly arrested and asked to become the commander of the revolutionary army. I was surrounded by guns at the time, and I might have been killed instantly if I had not complied with their request."

The Manchu court saw no alternative to the recall from retirement of Yüan Shih-k'ai. Yüan, concerned chiefly with his own position and power, obliged slowly and carefully. He scored enough points against the revolutionaries to establish his importance to the dynasty but not enough to crush them prematurely.

He had China's best troops in his Peiyang army, but the revolutionaries remained strong along the Yangtze and had the loyalty of many of the modernized units there. By 12 February 1912 Yüan had persuaded the Manchu court to announce its abdication. The child emperor and the Manchu court were left in residence in the Forbidden City. A final proclamation guaranteed Yüan's position: "Let Yüan Shih-k'ai organize with full powers a provisional republican government, and confer with the republican army as to methods of union, thus assuring peace to the people and tranquillity to the Empire."

Sun Yat-sen arrived in Shanghai on 25 December 1911. He was soon elected provisional president by the leaders of the revolution. But by the time of his arrival, peace talks between representatives of the revolutionaries and Yüan Shih-k'ai were already underway. Yüan's role in this process was clearly central. He provided the image of the "strong man" the powers felt was essential to order in China, and thus he had access to foreign backing. The optimistic revolutionaries and the despairing Manchus also accepted him. On 15 February 1912 the Provisional National Assembly at Nanking installed Yüan as provisional president. As vice-president it retained Li Yüan-hung, the reluctant colonel who had been persuaded to "lead" the revolutionary armies at Wuchang.

With the exit of the Manchus, Yüan's problem was simplified to one of agreement with the revolutionaries. An agreement whereby Sun Yat-sen renounced the presidency of the Provisional Government specified that the capital of the new regime would be at Nanking, an area in which the revolutionaries were strong. Yüan, however, secured the backing of the foreign powers for his preference of Peking, and a "rebellion" of his troops at Peking served to convince him, as he explained it, that he could not possibly leave the capital. Many historians cite this as further proof of his dishonesty. In fact, however, the dependability of troops in those months of confusion was seldom certain. The Nanking revolutionaries also approved the move to Peking until countermanded by Sun Yat-sen. Even at the time of the military "disorder" in Peking, a delegation of Nanking leaders who were in Peking to urge Yüan to come to the south accepted his explanations as sound. Early in March the fledgling legislature at Nanking approved Yüan, and on 10 March he was inaugurated as provisional president at Peking.

With provisional government and constitution arranged, Yüan had to contend with political opponents. Nothing in his background had prepared him for this, and he reacted harshly to the criticism and program proposed by Sung Chiao-jen, a follower of Huang Hsing, who formed the Kuomintang as China's first modern political party. Liang Ch'i-ch'ao reorganized the former reformers into a Democratic party, while a third group calling itself the United Republican party formed around a young army man educated in Japan, Ts'ai Ao. All these groups, however, represented little more than new organizations of old revolutionaries and reformers trying to accustom themselves to a new setting in which organization and opposition were not only legal but necessary.

For a time the Kuomintang leaders cooperated with Yüan Shih-k'ai. They had little alternative, for they were unable to sustain their troop strength for lack of funds. In the spring of 1912 Huang Hsing disbanded his forces. Both Huang and Sun Yat-sen were treated with dignity and courtesy by Yüan, and the latter was asked to draw up a plan for railroad development. Sung Chiao-jen carried on the main job of political organizing and electioneering. In 1913 the first election of Republican China was held. The Kuomintang was easily the most successful among the three competing groups. Shortly afterward Sun Yat-sen went to Japan in connection with his plans for railroad development. The former exile and refugee now returned to the land that had sheltered him a democratic leader, and he was given a hero's welcome.

Meanwhile Yüan negotiated with the Western powers for a loan to enable him to get his administration organized. The conditions fixed by the powers, in view of China's instability, were onerous, and President Woodrow Wilson made it one of his first decisions to withdraw American participation in the consortium, which then became five instead of six powers. But Yüan, eager to have money available, was willing to accept conditions that seemed shameful to the revolutionaries. They themselves had made numerous promises to foreign powers, but they were now aware that success in this matter would greatly strengthen Yüan's hand. The Reorganization Loan, as it became called, was negotiated in April 1913. It was for 25 million pounds sterling, but after discounting and bank interest were deducted China received 21 million. Repayment, at 5 percent interest, would bring this sum to more than three times that by the maturity date of the loan in 1960. But by 1960 China was no longer honoring such debts.

The Chinese government had contracted for loans at onerous terms before. In this case, the consortium demanded and received a monopoly of loans to China and reserved the salt taxes as security; like foreign customs, they were to be collected by a mixed commission. What was new about the arrangement this time was the vehemence of the criticism that it aroused. The Chinese negotiators who arrived to sign the final contract were forced to enter and leave through the back door of the building to escape pickets. One of those responsible, the finance minister, fled to the foreign concession in Tientsin shortly afterward. Meanwhile, the new National Assembly had demanded a say in matters of such serious national concern.

A few days earlier Yüan had provided evidence that he would not brook party opposition to his plans. Sung Chiao-jen, the popular and courageous Kuomintang leader, was assassinated by hirelings of Yüan in Shanghai. With his death the first period of optimism and idealism of the Chinese Republic came to an end. Yüan now used his funds, some of them from the Reorganization Loan, to buy Assembly votes as long as it suited his purpose. When the senate exercised its prerogative to turn down some of his appointees to cabinet posts, its members were subjected to abuse and intimidation. Placards appeared denouncing individual legislators; offers of rewards for their heads were posted, and on one day over one hundred legislators received bomb threats. Clearly the machinery of parliamentary democracy was going to work poorly in a setting dominated by Yüan and his military henchmen.

Discontent was first to flare among the revolutionary republicans, and in the summer of 1913 Huang Hsing and Sun Yat-sen announced and launched their "second revolution." It was a total failure. The country was tired of strife, none of the convenient racial animosity that could be turned against the Manchus lay at hand for agitation, and the elite, whose disaffection had been crucial two years before, were not aroused. Huang Hsing had disbanded his revolutionary troops, so the dissidents had the assistance of only a few discontented provincial commanders. Within a very short time Huang and Sun were once again in Japan, once again dependent upon the hospitality of their Japanese friends. Yüan had won, in part through his ability to utilize the foreign financial backing the consortium loan had given him, for the rebellion centered in the Yangtze area and, when the Chinese navy showed signs of sympathy for the rebels, the consortium made payments available for the government to buy up doubtful supporters. The foreign powers were convinced that Yüan was a practical realist, Sun Yat-sen an impractical idealist and professional revolutionary, and they preferred to support the "existing government."

The revolutionaries were overcome. The southwestern provinces, however, farthest from Peking, were still uncertain in their support for Yüan. During the second half of 1913 and 1914 Yüan set himself to improving his control over his military subordinates. In doing this he alarmed some and antagonized others. He tried to cover his followers by making parallel or overlapping appointments, but he was unable to control enough territory or money to provide adequate rewards to the commanders who had fought against the second revolution, and he would not again be as confident in their cooperation. He anticipated less trouble with politicians. By the fall of 1913 he was asking for changes in the Constitution that would strengthen his hand in affirming his presidential powers. War, peace and treaties (including, of course, loans) would all be made on his signature. At the same time he enlisted the support of provincial military figures to vilify the Assembly, the Provisional Constitution and especially the Kuomintang. In November Yüan outlawed the Kuomintang and besieged its headquarters, and thereafter the Assembly ceased to have meaning. Next came the announcement of a Political Council which suggested dissolution of the Assembly and which granted Yüan, inevitably by unanimous vote, whatever he requested.

Yüan's powers and image now grew rapidly, and he inched steadily closer to imperial aspirations. At his 1914 New Year reception, "twenty generals with sky-blue uniforms with acres of gold lace across their chests unrolled a carpet for him to tread on as he entered the Palace Hall," and his chief officials donned court robes formerly used for Manchu ceremonies. He was surrounded by a claque of self-seeking hangers-on who kept him from knowledge of what the popular response would be. It is also probable that his son was anxious to see his own position stabilized as heir apparent. But what should have been clear to both of them was that his generals, who had a chance to succeed him as president, would have none if he became emperor.

When he took power, Yüan Shih-k'ai promised in a message to Sun Yat-sen that "we shall never again allow monarchical government in China." Yet by 1915, after he had negotiated with some success to keep concessions to Japan at the minimum and after he had the word of an American expert (Dr. Frank Goodnow, later president of The Johns Hopkins University) that constitutional monarchy seemed more appropriate to China's traditions than republicanism, Yüan developed monarchical ambitions. In doing so Yüan neatly fit the stock image of the end-of-dynasty militarist who had succored the imperial family only to betray it. The experience of instant republicanism in many "new nations" since World War II provides a useful perspective from which to consider Yüan and his task. He could agree with the revolutionaries on the necessity of getting rid of the Manchus. On the other hand, there was nothing in his cultural or political background to prepare him for representative government. The revolutionaries had acceded to his leadership but chiefly in the expectation that they would be able to control him. The European powers had been gratified by his emergence as leader but chiefly because he stood for stability. The modern armies were his best card, and these were for the most part officered by generals whose loyalty, however questionable, was more committed to Yüan than to anyone else.

Inevitably his thoughts ran to power and his hates to opponents. Like Nkrumah and other mid-century leaders, Yüan sought to extend and make permanent the period of his control. Sweeping powers, president for life, and finally emperor—these were the terms in which he saw his political future. On the other hand, his emergence had also helped assure a relatively safe passage from monarchy to a shadow republicanism. Manchus were not, except in isolated instances, objects of hate. The opposition was threatened, bribed and its leaders murdered, but no mass hunts of suspected dissidents took place.

Yüan was a traditional figure operating in a setting for which China had no precedents. He was president of a republic with virtually no republicans. When he tried to solve this by making himself monarch, he found out that his country also had no monarchists. As K'ang Yu-wei wrote him, "From the point of view of the Manchu Imperial House you are a usurper, and from the point of view of the Republic you are a traitor." Consequently Yüan's imperial aspirations failed; yet the symbolism of his attempt is full of interest for the cultural and the political historian. Yüan spared no effort to combine the sanctions of tradition with those of the present, and while he was mediating between heaven and his people, he was also trying to mediate between antiquity and modernity. He rewarded his generals with ranks of nobility. He issued an Audience Act as president, gave regular audiences, and announced, and carried out, regular worship ceremonies at altars to Heaven and to Confucius. His trip to worship at the Altar of Heaven was begun in an armored car, continued in a vermillion coach, and ended in a sedan chair. He began in his field marshal's uniform and changed into sacrificial robe and headgear. Succession posed similar problems. Before ascending the throne he had the presidential election law changed to permit his reelection and even allow continuous service without reelection. It fell to him to nominate three candidates, their names written on a golden plate locked in a gold casket, to which keys were kept by the president, his minister of state and the Speaker of the Council of State.

But Yüan also wanted expressions of popular will and approbation. Generals and governors were ordered to send delegates to the capital to discuss the proper political order for China; it was considered desirable to convene a National Congress of Representatives to take up specific suggestions, and messages urging the president to "rectify his name and position" began to come in. Next, the generals and governors were ordered to write Peking "Respectfully urging the present President, Yüan Shih-k'ai, to assume the title of the Emperor of the Chinese Empire." By late 1915, "consensus" was overwhelming. Yüan ordered the imperial kilns to manufacture forty thousand porcelain pieces for his palace, organized a popular front called "Planning the Peace Society" and prepared for his enthronement. His reign began on New Year's Day 1916. Early in 1916, a "divine dragon" fossil, a happy augury, was discovered. But it was one of the few of Yüan's reign, which lasted eighty-three days and ended 22 March. Yüan was dead on 6 June.

Yüan's monarchical attempt failed in the first instance because of the opposition of generals and governors of the southwest, led by Ts'ai Ao. Ts'ai led his forces out of Yunnan into Szechwan, and although not successful against the government troops, he rallied enough support and used up enough time to make many of his neighbors doubt the success of Yüan's moves. Yüan furthermore misjudged the temper of his supporters badly and changed the assignments of generals of whom he was not quite certain, thereby alienating some and warning others of the fate in store for them. The generals' chief aims were safety and survival. Several, like Feng Yü-hsiang, who made his first appearance in the wars as a front commander at this time, fought well against the southerners only to change sides and protest that they had had to play along with the government for the time being. In the second place, Yüan's effort failed because of hostility abroad, particularly in Tokyo. By denying him the foreign aid he had foolishly expected, the Japanese played a significant role in convincing Yüan's enemies that his position was hopeless. But third, and most important, was the fact that the temper of the times no longer allowed an imperial attempt to succeed. The reaction of popular hostility and abuse that Yüan reaped marked the difference between the fall of the Manchu dynasty and the fall of all earlier dynasties. China had not yet modernized, but neither was it traditional any longer.

China was to see one further effort at an imperial restoration, this one carried out in Peking by General Chang Hsün in 1917 on behalf of the young Manchu emperor Pu-yi. Chang, a deeply conservative servant of the Manchu throne who had refused to cut his queue at the time of the revolution, seized the opportunity offered by a dispute between the premier, Tuan Ch'i-jui, and President Li Yüanhung to occupy Peking with his troops on 1 July 1917. K'ang Yu-wei, who had responded to Yüan's failure by publishing a long work which argued the case for Manchu restoration, now reappeared and began drafting imperial decrees in classical style for the young emperor. But none of them were followed. This attempt, too, did not last long. All the provincial military leaders sent telegrams denouncing it, and army forces within striking range of Peking prepared to attack Chang Hsün. In two weeks the "restoration" was over. Both K'ang Yu-wei and Chang Hsün fled to the shelter of the Dutch legation. Chang's troops, about twenty thousand in number and most still wearing queues, ceased to exist as organized units. In his autobiography, the "emperor," Pu-yi, recalled how suddenly the mood of the shadow court in the Forbidden City changed from jubilation to dejection as Manchu hopes glimmered. In later years, he recalls, people told him how

> Ch'ing clothes that had not been seen for years reappeared on the streets worn by people who looked as if they had just stepped out of their coffins. The papers brought out special issues for the restoration at a higher price than usual, so that amid the strange sights one could hear news-vendors shouting, as they sold the Edicts of Hsüan T'ung, "Antiques, six cash only! This nonsense will be an antique in a few days—six cash for an antique!"

Others insisted that there was, nevertheless, genuine enthusiasm. In the words of Pu-yi's English tutor, "in this instance there is no doubt that the lavish display of bunting was an outward manifestation of popular sympathy with the re-establishment of the monarchy." Yet at most it remained the enthusiasm of the moment, a touch of nostalgia devoid of meaning. That it ended there provides renewed testimony to the importance of 1911 in the political history of modern China. It marked the end of the longest continuity of governmental organization and function in the history of the world. Yet as Joseph Levenson phrased it, the successor republic, while not a mistake, was nevertheless a failure.

2. The End of Meiji Japan

ALTHOUGH IT was a good deal less spectacular than the end of the Chinese imperial system, the close of the Meiji period had consequences that were of decisive importance for Japan's response to the changing challenges of the international order. The Meiji political order had developed in response to a very particular set of personalities and circumstances. The root purposes had been those of strength and wealth with reference to equality with the powers, *fukoku-kyōhei*, in the phrase of the generation. The emphasis of this had been unity of effort and thought, achieved through the leadership of the sacred emperor, *tennō shinsei*. Unity and effort had been achieved and rewarded through devices of conservative constitutionalism, expressed in the phrase *rikken kunshusei*. The government had selected from the West those institutions and techniques that contributed to this drive, rejected those that threatened it, and retained from its own past, and

indeed embroidered from that past, ideas and institutions to achieve these purposes. Emperor and constitutionalism provided the keys to the system.

The government that had developed around these ideas was bureaucratic to
the core. It was dominated by Satsuma and Chōshū strength at the top, but in its
middle and lower levels it had been opened to ability from all parts of the country. The bureaucrats at the top were responsible to the Diet for some of their procedures, particularly with respect to finances, but they were totally responsible
only to the emperor, who symbolized the entire polity. The Diet could be denied
information and kept in the dark, but the emperor could be denied nothing. Yet
he trusted his servants and advisers and normally contented himself with asking
questions of his ministers. The Satsuma-Chōshū inner group shared his fullest
confidence and he their full devotion, with the result that central executive
authority had developed in a peculiar pattern that could not be recreated once
the original group was gone. The founding fathers, who became genro after 1900,
were privileged to ask what questions they would of the top bureaucrats and
could interfere almost at will. Thus, the constraints on bureaucratic government
were essentially personal rather than institutional. With the diminution of the
original group, the process of questioning and approval became formalistic, and
unless and until a constitutional and parliamentary alternative to such constraints
developed, Japan would be entirely bureaucratic in its administration.

The departure of the first team therefore resulted in a sharp decline of the
central unity in the Japanese government. The genro were omnicompetent, and
during their long careers they had participated in the bureaucratic process at
numerous points. Their successors were more narrowly specialized, and they
faced problems more "modern" and more complex. At the center of the whole,
the Meiji emperor, who had been a participant in the decision process, was
replaced by a vastly junior and less competent—in fact, for a time, incompetent—successor who could serve only to dramatize the difference from the original setting. The difference in the human balance amounted to an institutional
change.

The Meiji generation had also been characterized by caution and by
deference to the West. The caution was in large measure the result of formative
years spent in the realization of national weakness and backwardness. Attitudes
toward the West had developed in a period when Western and especially European power and prestige were at their zenith. The Meiji leaders grew up in a
world dominated by Europe. Consequently the English tie was essential, and the
protection of the British fleet sufficient for Japan's ultimate security. Imperial
alliances after the victory over Russia cemented this conviction of European primacy. The Meiji leaders were more comfortable with the frankly imperialistic
powers of Europe than they were with the emerging entity of American
diplomacy. Mixed as it was with democratic egalitarianism and racial discrimination at home and idealistic diplomacy abroad, the American polity presented
many more problems for them than the frankly realistic, often cynical, monarchies of Europe.

The last years of the Meiji period found additional currents that augured future changes. One was an increasingly racist strain in Western writing and thinking about the rising presence of East Asia. Another was a feeling that in the presence of a burgeoning America Japan's true interests lay closer to the empires and kingdoms of Europe. There was substance to the growing fears of confrontation with the United States that characterized the years after the Russo-Japanese War. Theodore Roosevelt's efforts to restrain the anti-Japanese sentiment on the Pacific Coast and his decision to send the American battle fleet to East Asia coincided with a period in which both American and Japanese general staffs for the first time found their strategic planners taking account of the possibility of future hostilities between their countries.

The imperial navy began plans for a larger fleet that was required to meet the threat from America's access to its Pacific interests through the Panama Canal. The imperial army had its own plans, worked out for General Yamagata by Tanaka Giichi in 1906. These focused on the need to prepare for a possible Russian war of revenge and the security requirements of the new continental responsibilities in Korea and Manchuria. Four additional divisions were immediately required. Two were soon authorized, but civilian reluctance to authorize the expenditures for the next two brought on the cabinet crisis of 1912 and the "Taishō Political Change."

While preparing for the worst, Japanese leaders were also doing their best to mend fences with recent enemies. The late Meiji years saw the aging genro discussing the wisdom of combination with the "old world," of which they considered themselves a part, against the "new," dominated by the United States. It was partly in response to such thinking that Itō Hirobumi went to Harbin for talks with Russian representatives in 1909. It was there that he fell victim to a Korean assassin who saw in him the thief of his country's independence.

The death of Itō removed the most important of the Meiji emperor's entourage. Thereafter leadership fell increasingly to Yamagata Aritomo, the founder of the modern army, who lived until 1922. But Yamagata's presence and role were increasingly remote, as he himself became the center of a miniature "emperor system" in which his military and political subordinates probed for his intentions and claimed to speak on his behalf. More and more real leadership passed into the hands of the second echelon, the younger and the more vigorous exponents of a distinctly Japanese interest. Thus Premier Katsura was inclined to accommodate E. H. Harriman's dream of a round-the-world transportation empire that would include Manchuria after the Russo-Japanese War, only to have his agreement canceled by his combative young diplomat back from Portsmouth, Komura Jutarō.

In June of 1912 the Meiji emperor himself died. His death symbolized the end of an era. Countless expressions of grief showed the force which the ideology of the family-state had assumed for Japanese. "A dense mass of humanity," reported the *London Times,* "thronged the great open spaces outside the Palace walls last night, continually moving up to the Emperor's gate, there to kneel in prayer a few minutes and then pass on once more. The crowd was drawn from all classes, and all preserved the highest degree of orderliness and silence, save for the crunching of the gravel under wooden sandals and the low continuous murmur of prayers."

The emperor's death was followed by a spectacular act of ritual suicide by General Count Nogi, the victor of Port Arthur. He and his wife chose to follow their sovereign in the excruciatingly painful rites of *junshi* (following in death) by hara-kiri. Nogi's testament related his suicide to the shame he incurred during the Satsuma Rebellion of 1877, when as a young regimental commander he had lost his banner, then regarded as the very incarnation of the emperor, to the enemy. After the battle he requested permission to atone through suicide, but General Yamagata, after first agreeing, ruled that he should continue to serve instead. Nogi asked permission again after the fall of Port Arthur, where he lost 59,000 of the 130,000 men in his command. Now he asked the emperor to permit him to atone through death for the loss of so many of his loyal soldiers. The emperor, his biographers tell us, pondered the question and replied that it was still too early; if Nogi continued to desire to immolate himself, he should wait until his own death. Nogi was thus waiting for his emperor's death as the proper time to atone for his own lapses.

But he was also doing more. The custom of *junshi,* in which a faithful retainer accompanied his lord in death, played an important role in feudal morality in medieval Japan, though it had been ordered stopped in the seventeenth century. By reviving it so dramatically, Nogi was publicly calling the nation back to its sense of traditional duty and values. Until the end of Imperial Japan, soldiers were taught to consider their rifles and swords entrusted to them by the emperor, as Nogi did his banner. Thus, the Guam straggler from World War II, Yokoi, who surrendered only in 1972, brought his rusted rifle stock back with him with apologies to his ruler. And the spectacular ritual suicide of the author Mishima in 1970 provided for many a modern echo of the Nogi death and testament. Nogi's wife accompanied the general in death. This bizarre but moving tragedy struck the *Times* as

> a striking reminder of the persistence in Japan of the spirit to which our ally owes her greatness. To this latest manifestation of its profound but stern appeal, the Western world, even if it cannot fully comprehend, must bow in respectful silence. Men like the late Count Nogi were the mainspring of the era of Meiji, or enlightenment, which may be passing in fact as well as in name with the death of the great ruler whom he served.

In Japan its effect was great. Nogi societies formed to call the nation to patriotism and service, and a shocked, silent sense of guilt and shortcoming seems to have been widespread.

It remained for a great novelist to use these deaths as the leitmotif of the greatest novel to be written in modern Japan. Natsume Sōseki (1867–1916) lived almost his entire life under the Meiji emperor's rule. After gaining a thorough training and skill in the traditional culture of his youth in Japanese poetry and

Chinese literature, he made his way to Tokyo University, where he specialized in English. After a brief period as English teacher, he was ordered by the Ministry of Education to go to London in 1900 to study English. For two and a half lonely years he tried to reconcile his East Asian cultural orientation with the study of English literature. His dream of achieving for his country and culture a mastery of English literature faded, and his hopes gave way to concern with his own personal and psychological needs. Natsume became obsessed by problems of the individual in society, the problems of loneliness and alienation and the difficulty of meaningful attachment and love. After he decided that the Western and Eastern literary traditions were not going to be bridged by him or anyone else, he began to express his dilemma through creative writing. It was still a calling of national service, however, and almost mystical in its compulsion: "I feel a strong impulse," he wrote a friend, "to engage in novel-writing with the same fervent spirit as the Restoration activists who staked their lives for the realization of their cause." He gave up his post in English literature at Tokyo University (Lafcadio Hearn's chair, in fact) and accepted a newspaper post that permitted him to publish his stories serially. All his novels struggled with the theme of man and individuality, a problem taken up against the background of his Confucian training and his modern, fragmented existence. He concluded, in the words of one authority, that man has the choice of madness or self-annihilation. Lacking either possibility, there is no alternative to endurance in loneliness and isolation.

Kokoro (*Heart*), published in 1914, set these themes against the deaths of the emperor and his general. Its principal figure is a man outwardly serene but inwardly tormented by the realization of the destructive force of his own egotism. To share his dismay with others, even with his wife, would only burden them without relieving him, and he sees no way out of the private struggle he must wage. Into this consciousness comes, like a temple bell bringing enlightenment to the Zen acolyte, the news of the Meiji emperor and General Nogi. As he wrote his disciple,

> Then at the height of the summer, Emperor Meiji passed away. I felt as though the spirit of the Meiji era had begun with the Emperor, and had ended with him. I was overcome with the feeling that I and the others, who had been brought up in that era, were now left behind to live as anachronisms.... A month passed. On the night of the Imperial Funeral I sat in my study, and listened to the booming of the cannon. To me, it sounded like the last lament for the passing of an age. Later, I realized that it might also have been a salute to General Nogi. Holding the extra edition of the paper in my hand, I blurted to my wife, "*Junshi! Junshi!*".... It was two or three days later that I decided at last to commit suicide.[1]

Not all, and not even most, Japanese reacted this way. The importance of the Meiji and Nogi deaths was precisely the realization they brought that a generation that had given its all "for the sake of the country" was passing from the scene. In 1911 a sensational trial and quick execution of anarchists charged with

---

[1] *Kokoro*, trans. Edwin McClellan (Chicago: Henry Regnery, 1959), pp. 245–46.

plans for the very murder of the Meiji emperor had shocked most Japanese, but even then some, whether in doubt of the justice of the procedures or in dismay for a generation increasingly nonpolitical, were drawn to praise the rebels while condemning their plans and to eulogize the spirit of rebellion without endorsing its practice. Natsume Sōseki himself, in an essay on individualism, ridiculed those who posed as though every act, from eating to going to the bathroom, should be performed "for the sake of the country." Old shibboleths long unquestioned were now in disrepute, and conservatives were dismayed to learn from newspaper polls that contemporary Japanese now thought more about themselves and less about their country.

Thus it was appropriate that the political structure was convulsed by a procedural and constitutional crisis almost immediately after the death of the Meiji emperor brought the Taishō emperor to the succession. The Taishō Political Change was precipitated by a refusal on the part of the army to provide a minister of war for the cabinet unless its demands for two additional divisions were accepted. In an attempt to provide transitional leadership, Prince Katsura, who had earlier retired from active politics to serve the court as grand chamberlain and lord privy seal, returned to accept the prime minister's chair. Unfortunately, Katsura's reappearance focused long-lingering doubts about Chōshū army leadership, and his "abandonment" of the newly enthroned emperor's service to resume the premiership was denounced as selfish, corrupt, clique- and army-dominated politics. Katsura encountered difficulties from the naval ministry, which wanted its quid pro quo in the form of new battleship authorizations, and he proved a perfect target for political party spokesmen who denounced his practice of palace politics. A clumsy attempt to silence opposition with an imperial pronouncement, which had never failed before, now served chiefly to feed the flames of opposition; quite obviously, it could be argued, the fledgling emperor who had just taken over could be no more than a mouthpiece for the experienced and wily Katsura.

A League for the Protection of the Constitution gradually became a mass movement against Katsura. Old-style politics were the first target of new-style organization, and Japan's most popular parliamentarians led the fight. In particular, Inukai Ki and Ozaki Yukio, soon to be dubbed "the gods of constitutional government" by their admirers, proved colorful and effective with the masses. They led in the charge that Katsura had entered the court to establish control there, destroyed the civilian cabinet through manipulating the army's demands, issued himself imperial orders to return as premier, and finally issued an additional rescript to force the reluctant navy to provide a naval minister for a cabinet in which it expected to fare poorly. Public meetings of denunciation were based upon the local political party organizations. Katsura tried to fight back by attracting politicians to a rival party and finally resorted once again to the tactic of an imperial rescript ordering the Seiyūkai to withdraw its vote of nonconfidence. On 9 February 1913 Itō's old party refused to heed the emperor's request. No prime minister would again dare to use an imperial rescript to cow a hostile House of Representatives. The next day riots broke out all over Tokyo. It required several thousand police, companies of mounted soldiers, and bloodshed and casualties to restore order. Katsura was forever pilloried by Ozaki in a vehement Diet speech as one of those who "use the throne as their rampart and Imperial Missiles as weapons to strike their enemies." He resigned and died shortly afterward.

Despite the spectacular fall of Katsura, victory went not to the colorful "gods of constitutional government" but to the careful planners of Seiyūkai strategy, who profited from quiet agreement with the surviving genro. A new cabinet was formed under Admiral Yamamoto. Prince Saionji, recently resigned as premier, joined the group of genro and became the last and longest lived of that prestigious body. Even Inukai and Ozaki soon found themselves forced to seek shelter with stronger organizations. Inukai began to trim toward the Seiyūkai, which he joined in 1925 and later came to head, while Ozaki gravitated toward the very party that Katsura was striving to build at the time of his death.

These same shifts marked profound changes in the Meiji pattern. Power still lay in organization and planning, not in popular demagoguery or emotional appeal, and victory went to those who were willing to compromise and give up the romantic dreams of total capitulation of the oligarchy that had animated the first generation of party politicians. But the political parties now defined the path to power. The Seiyūkai was now so entrenched that although its enemies within the power structure made one more desperate effort to curb it, they failed totally.

In January 1914 the revelation of corruption in connection with naval building contracts brought public demonstrations against the Yamamoto cabinet, which had to resign. The genro now met in the evening of their lives to select one of their original number, Count Ōkuma. After he was carefully sounded out for strategy and purpose and properly briefed, Ōkuma was given three charges. He was to destroy the power of the Seiyūkai, cut down government spending but give the army its two divisions and improve relations with China. Ōkuma's popular support came from the adherents of the Dōshikai that Katsura had begun to form at the time of his death.

The initial enthusiasm for Japan's cheap victories of World War I helped Ōkuma immediately after he took office, and the profits of Japan's new ability to supply military goods for the Western powers made for prosperity. But the genro's major hopes proved misplaced. The China solution that Ōkuma and his foreign minister reached was that of the Twenty-one Demands, and their reception, as will be described below, stirred deep fears. Budgets, far from declining, continued to rise and even to accelerate under the impetus of wartime spending. And while the Seiyūkai proved weaker when separated from power and patronage, Ōkuma's own electoral victories were accompanied by corruption and resulted in the duplication under his auspices of most of the objectionable features of Seiyūkai patronage and practice. As Yamagata began to veer toward the Seiyūkai, it was clear that the future belonged to the political parties.

The end of Meiji Japan had not brought anything like the institutional collapse and revolutionary consequences that followed the fall of the Ch'ing. Nevertheless it signified a period of transitional organization in which the long-revered sanctions of the period of nation building no longer met unquestioned acceptance. Japan met unprecedented opportunities and responsibilities just at this time of political and personal transition. They began with the border problems that accompanied the collapse of the Ch'ing empire. They intensified with the coming of World War I and the collapse of the entire European imperial system. And they climaxed with the effort to resolve problems that were outstanding with Republican China. This led to the Twenty-one Demands, an episode that cast a longer shadow over future Sino-Japanese relations than even the Sino-Japanese War.

3. The Collapse of the European Order

BY THE TIME of the Chinese Revolution of 1911, the international order in East Asia seemed to have reached a point of stability. Russian and German ambitions and energies had been diverted to Eastern Europe, North Africa and the Middle East. Great Britain and Japan had worked out a pattern of cooperation in East Asia, and France was more intent upon consolidation of its rule in Indochina and revenge in Europe than it was on further competitive advantages within China. Japan's absorption of Korea had removed an important cause of contention and instability from the international bargaining table, and despite the clear case of Japanese aggression the Korean representatives could have made at the Hague Conference in 1907, the powers preferred to look the other way rather than open a Pandora's box of instability. Japan and Russia had agreed on a delimitation of their interests in Northeast Asia. The United States had worked itself into this new cooperative system. The Open Door policy had come to stand for the interests of all the maritime and commercial powers in the face of further territorial ambitions. American interests in the Philippines made Washington's policy judgments subject to the strategic requirements of that distant outpost. Presidents Roosevelt and Taft, in the Taft-Katsura agreements, had seemed to acquiesce in Japanese leadership in Northeast Asia. Roosevelt had turned a deaf ear to Korean requests for diplomatic assistance against Japan. Taft encouraged American capitalists to enter the Western consortiums formed to provide Manchu centralizers with the funds they needed. Competition was now orderly and structured. It took place within a system to which the Japanese had learned to conform and the Chinese had become accustomed.

But a stable China was essential to that system, and with the collapse of central government in China changes within the system were certain. When China's collapse was followed by the collapse of several of the principal European imperialist competitors and when still other participants were fighting for their lives in Europe, the imperialist order in East Asia had to be restructured.

The first effect of the Manchu collapse was to encourage bordering powers to revise boundaries and peripheral peoples to declare their independence.

Mongolia and Tibet had acknowledged a tributary relationship not to "China" but to the "Ch'ing." China now became weak and divided, and the Ch'ing sovereign remained titled and enthroned but powerless in the Forbidden City. It was a setting to encourage declarations of independence by subject peoples.

In the last years of the empire, Chinese assertions of control had been strengthened under the pressure of imperialist rivalry. As a result, grudges against Chinese dominance were fresh. They received encouragement from the imperialist giants. In Tibet the Manchu emperors had asserted full control only at the end of the eighteenth century, when they sealed the country to Europeans and controlled the trade between western China and the windswept plateau that lay around the mountains at the Tibeto-Indian border. During the same years England was establishing relations with the hill kingdoms of Sikkim and Nepal, whose Gurkha mercenaries made up some of her finest Indian forces. Tibet remained Chinese-dominated until 1904, when the British Indian government, under Lord Curzon, sent a military mission which fought its way to Lhasa at a time when it seemed that Russian influence might be penetrating the remote kingdom. British pressures were relaxed after the Japanese victory of 1905 reassured the British about Russian power; in 1906 the British again recognized Chinese suzerainty of Tibet. The last years of Manchu rule saw vigorous and effective Chinese measures to control the dependencies that remained, and in 1910 a Ch'ing army suppressed revolts in border Tibetan provinces and marched to Lhasa. The Dalai Lama, the spiritual potentate who ruled there, fled to India, as his successor would do again in the 1950s.

With the fall of the Manchu dynasty, Chinese moves for the control of dependencies came to an end, for Yüan Shih-k'ai was unable to occupy the areas he desired to retain for China. In 1913 the Dalai Lama declared Tibetan independence, and in the following year negotiations between Britain, "Tibet" and "China" clarified the border along the lines that would later become known for one of the negotiators as the MacMahon Line. Among the negotiators, the British, with their Indian borders in mind, were of course in the strongest position. The Chinese representatives, in fact, refused to recognize either the border or the principle of Tibetan independence. The negotiators agreed that eastern or Inner Tibet, incorporated in the modern provinces of Hsi'kang and Ch'ing-hai, remain Chinese. (Here the matter rested until the emergence of a militarily strong Chinese state in the 1950s again made possible assertion of full Chinese control over Tibet. China's border war with India in 1962 resolved the rest of the MacMahon Line disagreements. In neither case did the Nationalist regime on Taiwan disagree with the Peking government's assertions of Chinese control.)

In Mongolia, as in Tibet, Chinese dominance had been importantly affected by the fact of Ch'ing rule in Peking. The Mongol nobility received special attention in Manchu policy, and Chinese statesmen were at all times careful about their country's special relationship with Mongolia. Lamaist Buddhism, itself controlled through Tibetan centers, helped keep the Mongols in line; possible slurs against Mongols were a major concern in Manchu censorship of Chinese publications. Moreover, the Russian advance in Central Asia had made it essential to be particularly careful about Mongolia. Russian moves had resulted in the treaties of Nerchinsk (1689) and Kiakhta (1727). Thereafter the Manchus, while maintaining relations of near-equality with Russia, sealed off north Manchuria and Outer Mongolia from Russian interference as much as possible. The treaty relations included permission for camel caravans to come from Russian Central Asia to Peking. There a Russian church and governmental mission which included language students was established; all this added up to more of a concession than anything the maritime powers were permitted before the nineteenth century. On at least two occasions Manchu missions traveled to Russia, where they were treated by the court with much the same courtesy as Peking granted the Russian missions.

After Russian acquisition of the Maritime Provinces along the Amur in 1860, the border problem became more urgent. In the 1870s armies under Tso Tsung-t'ang had crushed Moslem dissidence in Sinkiang and made it possible for Ch'ing diplomacy to contain the Russians in negotiations over the Ili Valley. Shortly thereafter, Russian development of the Trans-Siberian Railroad once again altered the picture to Ch'ing disadvantage and guaranteed border problems in the future. The late Ch'ing reformers strove to offset these by administrative measures. In 1902 Mongolia was opened to Chinese settlement. The Japanese victory of 1905 also helped to contain the Russians, and thereafter the dynasty restructured its control over Manchuria. In 1907 the area was divided into three provinces administered from Peking, and railway construction was begun to facilitate the introduction of Chinese nationals and products. Japanese agreements with Russia helped to stabilize imperialist competition. An agreement of 1907 proposed that north Manchuria and Outer Mongolia should be considered a Russian sphere, while south Manchuria and eastern Inner Mongolia would be within the Japanese zone.

The Ch'ing abdication immediately stimulated Mongol separatism. The Mongols were quick to seize the opportunity offered by the Revolution of 1911 to throw off Chinese control. In December 1911 the Living Buddha of Urga was declared ruler of Mongolia. Thus, both Tibet and Mongolia reacted to Chinese weakness by declaring themselves independent theocratic states. The Russians used this for their own advantage. They declared their recognition of Mongolian autonomy, though under Chinese suzerainty. This left the Mongols dependent upon Russian guidance in modernization. Under a series of agreements with Urga, the Russians now began to train, arm and modernize Outer Mongolia, which soon became a Russian protectorate. The early Chinese Republic was thus victimized by loss of its frontiers to the north and to the southwest. With the exception of the Tibetan and Mongolian borders, however, the Manchu passing had not resulted in major shifts of imperialist influence in China. The system of mutual restraints that had been worked out operated to balance out imperialist rivalries in the period following 1911, and in Tibet and Mongolia it required a combination of minority nationalism and imperialist ambition to activate change.

World War I, however, brought down the entire structure of Western imperialist control. The principal contenders for influence were soon immersed in their suicidal struggle for survival in western Europe. Under these circumstances the German holdings in Shantung, the heart of historic China, became the object of Japanese ambitions. Japan's participation in the war was delayed somewhat by an inability to believe in the reality of the European suicide and by the longstanding admiration on the part of the Japanese military for German military and institutional example. On the other hand, Japan was activated by old scores dating from the Triple Intervention of 1895 in which German participation had been particularly offensive and insensitive. Japan's involvement was finally triggered by a British request under the terms of the Anglo-Japanese alliance.

Upon the outbreak of war in August 1914, the English asked Japan to help destroy German men-of-war in Chinese waters. The Japanese government, however, decided that if it was to cooperate at all its role should be larger and more profitable than this. It also determined that it should not be drawn into the conflict in Europe. The German holdings in Shantung therefore became the principal objective of Japanese participation in World War I. When the Japanese decision to seize the Shantung port base was communicated to the British government, the British strove to discourage such extensive Japanese involvement. It would be better, London thought, for Japan to limit herself to German shipping in Chinese waters; further involvement might disturb the situation in the Far East unnecessarily. Tokyo's response, predictably, was that Japan had no territorial ambitions and that the situation would not be disturbed: Japan would demand transfer of Tsingtao to Japan for eventual return to China, for to allow the Germans to restore it directly to China would risk enabling the Germans to force the Chinese to return it after the war. The British gave reluctant agreement to this and tried to limit the Japanese activity to Chinese waters. By 15 August Japan's ultimatum was served on Germany; the Germans were given a week to respond. When no answer was forthcoming, Japan declared war on 23 August and immediately began military and naval preparations for the seizure of Tsingtao. A British detachment joined the Japanese forces in the effort to make it an Allied operation. Bombardment of Tsingtao began in October, and the fortresses surrendered on 7 November.

Japan had now revenged herself on Germany for the Triple Intervention and had succeeded it as the principal political force in the Shantung peninsula. Although the initial demand for German surrender specified that Japan was taking Shantung for eventual return to China, the Japanese were later to argue that their forcible seizure of the German holdings had created a new situation in which they were no longer bound by that intention. In any case it was unlikely that Japan would return its military gains to the Chinese without some guarantees of economic advantage. In September Foreign Minister Katō refused to respond to Diet questions about the return of Shantung on grounds of diplomatic security, and by December he was assuring the Diet that the Foreign Office had made no promises of any sort to return the German leaseholds to China. Japan had utilized the Anglo-Japanese alliance for its own purposes, and it had no intention of joining in the European slaughter. But its willingness to help with strikes against German shipping extended to the South Pacific. During the fall of 1914 Japanese naval forces occupied the German islands in the South Pacific; the Marshalls, Marianas, Palau, the Carolines, Yap, all names that would become household words during World War II, shifted from German to Japanese hands. By 1917 Japanese naval units controlled the entire South Pacific and Indian ocean areas. Repeated English requests for Japanese help in the Mediterranean area brought a convoy force in 1917. Further French and Russian requests for Japanese army units to join the ground fighting in Europe fell on deaf ears.

World War I thus saw Japan develop a strong bargaining position in international politics. Before the dispatch of Japanese naval units to the Mediterranean in 1917, secret agreements with England, France, Italy and Russia brought guarantees that Japan's claims to the German leaseholds in Shantung and to the Pacific islands north of the equator would be honored in the peace settlement. As a result of Allied support, the Pacific islands were mandated to Japanese authority and Shantung left to Sino-Japanese settlement. The Japanese thereby thwarted the efforts of the struggling Chinese republic to influence the postwar settlement by a token declaration of war and the shipment of thousands of Chinese laborers to the western front. Japan's limited involvement in the war was surrounded with none of the mystique of the Sino-Japanese and Russo-Japanese wars. In the weeks after the initial ultimatum to Germany, the government encountered pointed and often hostile responses in the imperial Diet, and after the seizure of Shantung, army and naval expansion bills encountered rough treatment in the lower house, growing out of the Taishō Political Change. Government dissolution of the Diet and new elections in the spring of 1915 changed the Diet representation and votes on these matters, but it remained true that the unity of earlier days was giving way to political partisanship.

It was above all the Russian Revolution, even more than the Chinese Revolution or the European war, that laid open the northern boundaries of East Asia and led to the combination of cupidity and concern that characterized Japanese attitudes there for the next decades. The full import of this must be reserved for a later discussion of Russian challenge and Japanese response, but in the context of World War I the Russian collapse must stand as the final solvent of that international and territorial order to which the Japanese had struggled to conform. As was to be expected, Japanese political and military leaders saw in the Russian emergency possibilities for greater security and gain for themselves. When the Russians, cut off from their Western allies and desperately short of munitions which Japanese industry could supply, came to Tokyo with requests for help, the Japanese military were ready to talk. In 1916 the Japanese concluded a treaty whereby Russian support for the Japanese position in China was accompanied by Russian purchase of Japanese munitions. In addition, the Russians agreed to move the meeting point of the South Manchurian and Chinese Eastern railroads, thereby extending the Japanese zone in Manchuria to the north. The Japanese press, aware of the desperate Russian need for assistance, discussed Russian cession of north Sakhalin and even, in moments of euphoria, Siberia up to Lake Baikal. When Allied officers met early in 1917 in London to discuss further contributions and asked for a half-million Japanese soldiers, Japanese representatives set extremely stiff terms: north Sakhalin, control of the Chinese Eastern Railway as far as Harbin, and the demilitarization of Vladivostok. Japan would thus have been militarily dominant along the entire Pacific coast.

The collapse of the Russian government in 1917, its replacement by the ineffectual Provisional Government and its overthrow by the Bolsheviks in November changed the picture completely. Pressures for Japanese involvement grew, for now the Western Allies expressed interest in the idea of an expedition to Siberia. Japan would obviously have to play the leading role in this. The setting was one to make Japanese political and military leaders give thought to the structure of postwar Asia. The old order was gone or, if not gone, irreparably damaged. The Chinese empire, so long the focus of international rivalry and cooperation, had crumbled. Germany, one of the principal maritime forces in East Asia, was out of the picture. Imperial Russia, the menace to the north, was no longer so. Both Germany and Russia had led in imperialist seizures. Now both were to lead in the new shape of things. Germany renounced extraterritorial rights and special privileges in China in 1921, and the Russian Bolsheviks, after early announcements about renouncing all czarist gains, reached the same decision in 1924. The influence of Germany disappeared with its ships. But China's land frontier with Russia, the completion of communications lines through Siberia and the movements of Russian settlers meant that whoever gained power in European Russia would have influence in Asiatic Russia also. Bolshevik calls to partisans in Khabarovsk and Vladivostok to seize power underscored this point for the Japanese.

Japanese leaders were thus forced to rethink and to restructure their world order. They failed to do this successfully. Before showing how they failed, however, it is useful to turn to closer examination of their response to the Chinese Revolution. For the collapse of Imperial China, followed by that of European imperialism, presented the Japanese with an important challenge to their ability to conceptualize the new order. This challenge came precisely at the end of the Meiji period. It came to a Japanese society increasingly complex and multicentered, at a time when its leadership group was giving way, and before the makeup of its successor group could be known. Japan was entering an era in which old structures were collapsing before new rules were in sight.

4. Japanese Foreign Policy

AT THE END of the Meiji period, a new group was coming into positions of authority in Japan. The emerging generation of leaders was only partially and gradually able to exercise its independence. Of the original group it was particularly General Prince Yamagata Aritomo who dominated. Neither Matsukata, Inoue, nor Ōyama, the other surviving members of the original band, had the kind of influence or following that Yamagata had established. They lacked the disciplined followers that Yamagata had installed in the bureaucracy and army, and they did not have the personal confidence and contact with the court that Itō had established with the Meiji emperor.

Within the political order the generational change was demonstrated by the growing confidence and ambition of the political party leaders. It was especially Hara Kei, the leader of the Seiyūkai, who had gradually established his personal and institutional influence in preparing the day when Japan might be governed by political party cabinets. When the surviving oligarchs, alarmed by the growing power of the Seiyūkai, entrusted Count Ōkuma Shigenobu with the responsibility of forming a cabinet in 1914, they discovered to their dismay that Ōkuma's following, the future Minseitō, would develop the same ambitions and potential as the Seiyūkai.

As with the political parties, so also with the armed services. A new generation of leaders was emerging which was close to openly challenging its Meiji sponsors. Within the Seiyūkai the succession was from Saionji, now become genro, to Hara; within the Minseitō it was from Ōkuma to Katō Kōmei, his foreign minister. The service succession was within the confines of Chōshū orthodoxy, but it was no less real for being regional. Already in 1901 General Katsura Tarō had expressed to intimates his desire to get out from under the influence of "old men" like Yamagata. For Katsura the realities of power condemned him to satellite status under Yamagata. But as the old men withdrew increasingly into the shadows, a third generation of army specialists emerged in the generation of the future general Tanaka Giichi, one much less patient about accepting the leadership of its seniors. It was Tanaka, in the General Staff, who would make policy with respect to Japan's response to the Bolshevik revolution, while a still younger Araki Sadao was serving as attaché within Russia and accumulating the horror of communism that would characterize his leadership in the army of the 1930s.

The emergence of these new groups coincided with Japan's need to make policy and decisions at a point when the orderly universe the Meiji oligarchs had known was crumbling in the collapse of empires all around Japan. For some leaders, particularly those in the political parties, the responses were more truly internationalist than ever before. Others, like Tanaka and his associates, proved more nationalist. But neither group had known the discipline of weakness, poverty and fear that forged the caution of the first generation of oligarchs. They were probably more institutionally cautious than their predecessors, more in awe of arrangements they had inherited, particularly the Constitution and a throne increasingly sacrosanct. But intellectually they often shared and even magnified the fear of their elders that an almost unbridgeable gap lay between East and West. Rampant Western racism of the years of World War I and after affected the new generation the more because it had less reason to receive treatment as the representatives of a second-class civilization or nation. Nor could the suicidal war in Europe fail to carry its own cost. The concerns of these new leaders consequently came to focus first on the problem of Japan's relations with its mainland neighbor, for China assumed special importance if one accepted gloomy views of East-West antipathy. It also required new decisions in the wake of the collapse of its established order, and it presented new possibilities and even temptations during the lapse of European dominance and leadership. Finally, the leap of Japanese industrialization during the war years put a new premium on access to and mastery over China's markets and materials. These themes and potentialities dominated Japan during the decade between the Meiji emperor's death and the Washington Conference of 1922.

It is useful to begin by an examination of the way Yamagata viewed the world during these years. He was first of all convinced of the inevitability of racial conflict. Like so many of his generation, he saw the Western advance into Asia as a form of racial imperialism. He was less impressed by Western generosity than he was by reports of the treatment accorded Oriental immigrants in the West. The strident tones in which many announced the coming "yellow danger" were not lost on him. The slowness with which Europe had accorded Japan a status of equality despite the success of the modernization campaigns and the quickness with which Japan's initial gains in Manchuria had been seized by a group of European powers, only one of whom had a direct interest in the area, all served to strengthen Yamagata's youthful recollections of Western contempt for Asian weakness.

The product of these fears was a conviction that Japan could trust no Western power or group of powers to serve her interests. Europeans were ultimately undependable. On the other hand, it was vital for Japan to be on good terms with as many powers as possible in order to ward off a racial lineup against Japan. The English alliance had served Japan well against Russia, but immediately after the war began Yamagata started to work for an agreement with the Russians. His advocacy was an important factor in Japan's conclusion of the alliance of 1916 with the Russians. Yamagata saw World War I itself in racial terms and believed that "the real cause is the struggle between the Slavic and Germanic races. Seeing this, it is easy to imagine how much more fierce the struggle between the yellow and white races will be." He wrote his fellow genro in 1915 that Japan would have "to make plans to prevent the establishment of a white alliance against the yellow races." Now that the Russians were beginning to be grateful for Japanese help in munitions, Japan should ally with them. With other countries alliance might not work out, but that did not mean they should be antagonized; America was sure to be a growing influence in East Asia, but "for the realization of our China policy it is advisable not to aggravate America's feelings toward us needlessly." Yamagata was not seeking enemies, but his world was a hostile one, and he sought to hold off as much of it as he could. He had little respect for those who trusted the West. Foreign Minister Katō, who had served as ambassador to London, seemed foolishly oriented toward English approval, and

Yamagata scornfully dismissed him as "that Englishman." No country's propaganda was more racist than that of Imperial Germany, but Yamagata would always have preferred a German tie to the alliance with England. He trusted no
Western power, but he had some confidence in a country whose institutions were
similar.

The corollary of this distrust of the West was Yamagata's conviction that
Japan and China had to learn to live together. Yamagata played an important
part in the policies that brought Tokyo closer to Peking in the closing days of the
Manchu dynasty. The banishment of the revolutionary leaders had his warm approval, and the steps of Manchu reformers to appropriate some Japanese institutions seemed full of promise to him. By the end of the Meiji period, as Europe
prepared to commit suicide, Yamagata began to stress more than ever the need to
work out a close partnership with China. "The principal aim of our plan," he
wrote in 1914,

> should be to improve Sino-Japanese relations and to instill in China a sense
> of abiding trust in us. . . . If the colored races of the orient hope to compete
> with the so-called culturally advanced white races and maintain friendly
> relations with them while retaining their own cultural identity and indepen-
> dence then China and Japan, which are culturally and racially alike, must
> become friendly and promote each other's interests.

Moreover, he went on, "if we fail to dissipate China's suspicion of us, she will
rapidly turn against us and turn more and more to America." Yamagata's conclusions from all this were necessarily cautious, for he realized the practical demands
of the international setting. "Our politicians must be sternly warned against raising the issue of racialism. . . . it would be more prudent not to raise the issue of a
league of colored people. . . . China must be won over by hints and suggestions . . .
before we can realize our plans." There was more strategy than tactics in these
sentiments, but the main emphases would have had the approval of most
Japanese.

The confusing scene that followed the outbreak of revolution in China in
1911 made these principles a good deal easier to affirm than to apply. The revolution caught the Japanese government as unprepared as it did the revolutionaries,
and Japan's twists of policy reflected both the confusion on the mainland and the
disagreement within Japan. There were at least three fairly distinct groupings in
Tokyo. The first was that of the government, which was most responsive to the
conservative promptings of the aging genro. The second was more popular and
less powerful and represented the sentiment of the liberals who had associated
themselves with Sun Yat-sen and the other revolutionaries. Since they were
strongest in central and southern China, they were able to attract support from
Japanese business groups with interests in those areas. Many business and political
leaders were prepared to agree with Ozaki Yukio when he predicted that in the
long run south China would count for twice as much as north China in Japanese
trade, and even the Kokuryūkai chief Uchida Ryōhei warned publicly that
Manchuria was not all of China. The third interest group was within the army

and found expression in men like Tanaka Giichi of the General Staff who believed that Japan's true interest lay in helping along what seemed an inevitable breakup of the Manchu empire into its constituent parts and obligating each sector to Japanese financial and military assistance. A brief review of these three interest groupings as they affected Japanese policies toward the early Chinese revolutionary years is essential to consideration of the Twenty-one Demands of 1915, and those demands in turn came to stand as a political and psychological watershed for modern Sino-Japanese relations.

Government policy toward the emerging Chinese republic went through several distinct phases. During the first stage it seemed that the revolution might fail and that timely assistance to the Manchu government would obligate it to Japan. A new cabinet, the last to be formed by Prince Saionji before he joined the genro, had just taken power in Tokyo; Foreign Minister Uchida had not taken over his post until after the revolutionary outbreaks at Wuchang. The new government was consequently no match for the deeply entrenched conservatism of Yamagata, who wanted Tokyo to respond quickly to Manchu requests for military supplies. The cabinet adopted a policy that was no policy, the conclusion that it should work for a "paramount position in China" while conciliating the Chinese and securing their trust; it should work within the confines of its alliance system and also "make every effort to enlist the United States as our friend."

The reemergence of Yüan Shih-k'ai as a Manchu minister in mid-November seemed to promise a return of stability, and Tokyo, with the other powers, welcomed the return of the necessary "strong man." The Japanese minister in Peking considered Yüan a personal friend and predicted the establishment of a constitutional Manchu monarchy under Yüan's leadership. Yamagata now approved approaches to London to suggest that Japan and England jointly coordinate their efforts to speed this process. But although Tokyo put its trust in Yüan and in London, neither side returned the compliment. The British, without consultation with their Japanese allies, helped mediate the compromise between Yüan and the revolutionaries, while Yüan, on receiving Japanese assurances of support, bought time by asking about its details and then apologetically explained that the urgency of the situation had not permitted him to delay his acceptance of the presidency of the new republic. As a result the Japanese government, which thought it was working in tandem with its principal ally, found itself in isolated support of a defunct monarchy and distrusted by other world powers and other factions within China. (Some Japanese were prepared with rueful comparisons to the position of Premier Satō's government after President Nixon's direct approach to Peking in 1971 seemed to leave Tokyo isolated in its support of the Republic of China on Taiwan.)

The Tokyo government's policy was also constrained by the enormous popularity which the Chinese revolutionaries enjoyed in Japan. The revolutionaries' comparison of their role with that of the activists who had worked for the Meiji Restoration was not lost on their Japanese friends, and many Japanese retained a paternal approval of the revolutionary movement from the days of its growth among Chinese students on Japanese soil. The revolutionaries' Japanese friends were popular and romantic figures in Japan. Sun Yat-sen himself had become known through the best-selling account of Miyazaki Tōten. Most Japanese were conditioned by over a decade of print and propaganda to think of the Manchus as corrupt and reactionary, and they had several decades of vilification of Yüan Shih-k'ai as a slippery and crafty opponent. The popular press was overwhelmingly favorable to the revolutionaries and their cause, and leading politicians like Inukai and Ozaki soon took their stand in approval of the revolutionary cause. Government proposals to intervene in favor of the Manchus or to back the new cause of Yüan Shih-k'ai were strongly attacked. The China adventurers, Miyazaki among them, were with the revolutionaries, reporting back in syndicated columns their fears of Japanese intervention and betrayal by Yüan. Consequently Japanese General Staff planners had little hesitation in responding to requests for economic and military help from the revolutionaries. Ironically, the idealism and courage which Japanese associated with the revolutionary cause served to bridge military and commercial efforts to advance other interests.

The revolutionaries needed arms and money desperately. Material of war was made available to them through the same cartel of firms that provided some assistance to the Peking government; Mitsui trading interests served the revolutionaries while Ōkura operated in north China. Some weapons were made available to the cartel directly by the Japanese War Ministry, while others were purchased from Japanese manufacturers. There were at least four major transfers of weapons between December 1911 and February 1912. The same commercial interests provided loans to the revolutionaries against pledges of Yangtze Valley assets. The most important of these was the Hanyehp'ing Company. Loans made in 1904, 1907, 1908, 1910 and 1911 had brought the company into close relationship with Japan. So it was entirely natural for Board President Sheng Hsüan-huai to ask the Japanese to do what they could to protect the plants when the revolution broke out and for the Japanese to warn the contenders of the importance the plants had for Japan. The Japanese admiralty instructed its warships in the Hankow area to provide protection for Japanese nationals, and in the event of threat to the Hanyehp'ing plants they were "to extend protection in the name of national defense. Be sure that in protecting our nationals you protect also our national interests." These interests were in the heart of the area controlled by the revolutionaries. When Sun Yat-sen returned to China in 1911, he was met by the local Mitsui official (and later South Manchuria Railway head), Yamada Junsaburō, who suggested an arrangement for joint Sino-Japanese control of Hanyehp'ing. The discussions soon included Board President Sheng, who had fled to Tokyo. Contracts were drawn up to reorganize the company. Its board of directors would include six Chinese and five Japanese, and it would be headed by a Chinese national with a Japanese assistant. Sheng sent out letters to the stockholders to explain the advantages of the agreement in providing a base for modernization of the firm. But soon after Sun retired in Yüan's favor, the latter advanced national bonds to the Hanyehp'ing Company to keep it out of Japanese hands. Japanese saw in this a victory for Yüan Shih-k'ai, backed by British money. Japanese liberals and socialists like Kita Ikki, however, felt that their influence with the revolutionaries had been betrayed by the capitalist greed of their countrymen. They were to have even better grounds for this in the negotiations Sun Yat-sen would carry on in Japan after his unsuccessful attempt to unseat Yüan Shih-k'ai in 1913.

The third interest group involved in the formation of Japanese policy toward the Chinese Revolution was within the imperial army. That force had grown under Yamagata's jealous care and patronage, but it was no longer to be identified with his wishes at every turn. Its middle and junior echelons were full of confidence drawn from the victories of 1905, which grew in imagination as they receded in time. It was particularly the General Staff, to which the Kwantung army in south Manchuria was responsible, that was the home of proconsular ambitions and concerns for Northeast Asia. Its leaders saw in the Chinese Revolution an important opportunity to strengthen Japan's strategic and political position. The War Ministry was dominated by a grumpy old Satsuma veteran, Uehara Yūsaku, who had never bothered to hide his impatience with parliamentary government. Fukuda Masatarō, a Kyushu man from Saga, was chief of staff of the Kwantung army military zone and, hence, central to plans for Manchuria; so was Terauchi Masatake, Yamagata's most trusted general at this juncture, who was governor general of Korea. These men were by no means automatons or carbon copies of their mentor. They were agreed, however, that in strategic terms Japan's position in Manchuria was of first importance and that the gains the Russians had scored in Outer Mongolia after the Manchu abdication should be balanced by some equivalent Japanese advance in northern Manchuria and Inner Mongolia.

Early probings in Manchuria included a suspicious explosion on the Peking-Mukden railway that served as reason for moving an additional number of Japanese troops into the area. By 1912, after military men in Tokyo had given up all hope of particular favor or gratitude from Yüan Shih-k'ai, a plot developed that was based upon cooperation between elements in the Imperial General Staff, a China adventurer named Kawashima Naniwa and Manchu and Mongol princes. Kawashima first discussed with General Terauchi the prospect of moving troops into Manchuria from Korea. Since Yamagata and Katsura were urging the government to take a similar course, it can be assumed that the plan had very powerful backing at the outset. The Foreign Office opposed this successfully, however, and thereafter Kawashima turned to more covert plans to form a Manchu state in Manchuria. He had important elements in the General Staff with him. His candidate for puppet was a Manchu Prince Su, a man who had once headed the Peking Police Bureau where Kawashima had served as instructor. Prince Su was brought to Port Arthur in south Manchuria. Kawashima now worked out "treaties" with Mongol princes from Inner Mongolia whereby the latter, in return for Japanese military and financial help, agreed to virtual

Japanese domination of that area. Kawashima cabled the General Staff on the last day of January 1912 that the outcome would "resemble independent action on the part of Manchus." If things were coordinated with the Russians, Japan need not fear outside interference, and "when the inevitable break-up of the Manchu Empire comes Manchuria and Mongolia will be found virtually in our hands." The Port Arthur house in which Prince Su was sheltered soon became a meeting place for Kawashima, his army friends and Chinese, Manchu and Mongol partisans. But after Japanese consular officials in Manchuria reported to their Foreign Office superiors the suspicious activities that were going on, Foreign Minister Uchida succeeded in getting the army to stop its cooperation with the plot. Kawashima was recalled to Tokyo, where he learned to his dismay that Japan was planning to enter the international consortium that was backing a reorganization loan for the new republic under Yüan Shih-k'ai.

The momentum of the preparations that had been made was not immediately broken. Projects to smuggle arms to the Mongol bands continued. A shipment of "agricultural machinery" that included fifty wagons of arms and ammunition was taken across the mountains of Jehol by young Japanese army officers, and when they were intercepted by Chinese troops fifty lives were lost in the skirmish that took place. This ended Tokyo's efforts to back separatist movements for the time being. The Saionji cabinet had succeeded in blocking both direct and covert action, but it was under sharp criticism from the military for its failure to make greater provision for defense of Japanese interests in Korea and Manchuria. The cabinet fell when War Minister Uehara refused to accept its decision to postpone expenditures for two additional divisions in December of 1912. The army's refusal to provide an alternative war minister precipitated the Taishō Political Change that has already been described.

In the course of all this activity the Chinese inevitably became confused about the Japanese purpose, and many Japanese were never entirely clear on it either. The scene was full of busy figures: China adventurers, professional patriots, agents of the military and economic establishments, all known to each other and all contacting the same Chinese, and yet each seeing his purpose in a different way. From freebooting to filibustering, from talk of sacrifice to concern for security, Japanese explanations began to ring a little bit hollow. And the Tokyo government, as we have seen, was never entirely free to proceed on the basis of its own reading of the situation. Constraints of genro and army power meant that people not charged with implementing a policy were constantly devising one for others and criticizing them when it failed. The Foreign Office, struggling to work within the constraints of the Anglo-Japanese alliance, was particularly subject to attack.

The collapse, or at least the distraction, of the principal European states then made this even more complex, while the collapse of Chinese unity increased the avenues for action, for disunity and for discontent within Japan. These conditions and frustrations, combined with the fortuitous possibilities of the international situation, served as prelude to the Twenty-one Demands of 1915. But there was an intermediate step, one furnished by the aftermath of the 1913 revolution in China and Taishō change in Japan. Both increased the expectations of many Japanese for gain in a settlement with China.

In 1913 Sun Yat-sen, who had been appointed by President Yüan Shih-k'ai to plan railway development for China, visited Japan. The former revolutionary and refugee came as an important statesman. In addition to his old friends among the China adventurers, he was sought out by important industrialists and politicians who now saw him as a leader of China. More often than not, the conversation between Sun and his Japanese hosts focused around the possibilities of Japanese trade relationships with China and the arrangements for joint enterprises in the Yangtze Valley. Sun Yat-sen greeted his Japanese hosts as friends and benefactors. "The patriots of your country," he would say, "have led and taught me, and I deem Japan my second fatherland and your statesmen my mentors. China awaits your saving help." He stressed at every turn the similarity of culture between China and Japan and the logic of economic cooperation between the two countries. His hosts did their best to recreate the pattern of business cooperation that had been snatched from them by the intervention of Yüan Shih-k'ai in 1912. In June of 1913 a China Industrial Company, with Sun as president and Japanese among its directors and its capital provided by the great Japanese trading companies, was set up for the purpose of developing sources of raw materials in China. Sun Yat-sen also met with General Katsura Tarō, whose unsuccessful attempt to form a cabinet had precipitated the Taishō Political Change a few months earlier. Katsura spoke with enthusiasm of a Sino-Japanese cooperation to liberate India and rescue the colored races of the world. This done, he explained, Japan would "never have to worry about land for colonization and commerce, and it would never pursue crude policies of conquest." This made sense to Sun, and upon his return to China he sent telegrams to Peking and to the provincial capitals assuring Chinese leaders of Japanese goodwill. As he put it to reporters,

> I have visited Japan for the purpose of ascertaining what foundations suspicions of Japanese motives have, and I have realized that the protestations of friendly sentiments are not superficial but come from the bottom of their hearts. . . . What Japan wants in China is not territory, but trade.

Sun returned to China in the summer of 1913. Yüan Shih-k'ai's murder of Sung Chiao-jen and his suppression of the Kuomintang power had embittered the revolutionary camp, and Sun and Huang Hsing announced their "second revolution" in July. But they failed completely. Yüan was bolstered by the monies of the Reorganization Loan, and the Chinese elite, who had risen with the revolutionaries in discontent with Manchu centralization policies in 1911, had no comparable reason to break with Yüan. The revolution was badly planned and inadequately financed, and within a very short time Sun Yat-sen and Huang Hsing found themselves refugees in Japan once again. Japan now seemed farther from influence in China than ever, and soon an increasing number of voices calling for a "forceful" or "fundamental solution" of Japan's China and Manchurian-Mongolian "problem" were to be heard. Exponents of these views found fresh arguments for their positions in the course of the summer of 1913. Yüan Shih-k'ai's armies committed a number of anti-Japanese outrages in the course of suppressing the "second revolution." In Shantung a Japanese army captain was assaulted; in Hankow a second lieutenant was beaten, and in Nanking, early in September, old-style troops commanded by Chang Hsün sacked the city with violence that took the lives of three Japanese civilians. Two months later, when American Minister Paul S. Reinsch visited Nanking, the old capital seemed to him "forlorn and woeful," its streets lined by

> huge, black-uniformed, pig-tailed men, "guarding" the streets along which the native dwellers were slinking sullenly and in fear. Everywhere charred walls without roofs; the contents of houses broken and cast on the street; fragments of shrapnel in the walls—withal a depressing picture of misery.

This reminder that premodern forces had crushed the hopes of what might have been a pro-Japanese rebellion served to ignite Japanese dissatisfaction with the government's China policy. Public meetings of denunciation were held, and one great gathering in Tokyo in September 1913 very nearly ended in riot. Within the government opposition to proposals for stronger action in Manchuria and Mongolia was led by an official named Abe Moritarō, who was head of the Foreign Office's Political Affairs Bureau. He had scoffed at talk of separatism for northeast China and had argued that the effort would bring Japan nothing but trouble. Early in September, at a time when the indignation over the government's China policy was at a peak, Abe was murdered in a spectacular gesture of protest by a young man who then seated himself on a map of China and committed hara-kiri so skillfully that his blood poured out over Manchuria and Mongolia.

The government was now forced to secure satisfaction from China for Nanking. An indemnity was demanded and received, rights to additional railway lines to the north were demanded and granted, Chang Hsün's troops were made to line up in front of the Japanese consulate in Nanking while the Japanese national anthem was played, and Chang himself was forced to call on the Japanese consul to present his personal apologies. "This he did," Minister Reinsch recalled, "saving his face by arranging to call on all the foreign consuls the same day."

Abe was succeeded in his post by Koike Chōzō. Koike was on far better terms with the China adventurers like Kawashima and with the General Staff advocates of a positive policy than Abe had been. His office became a message and meeting center for army men and civilian "China-firsters," and his assumption of office marked the beginning of a strongly anti–Yüan Shih-k'ai policy by the Japanese government. It would fall to him to draft the text of the Twenty-one Demands in 1915. His chief, Foreign Minister Katō, was also on good terms with the military. Katō, when asked whether it was true that he paid a good deal of attention to the China enthusiasts, answered disparagingly that the army men were a good deal more important. Under such circumstances the likelihood of a change in Japan's China policy was great.

5. The Twenty-one Demands

THE TWENTY-ONE DEMANDS which Japan served on Yüan Shih-k'ai in 1915 marked a milestone in Sino-Japanese foreign policy. The process of their formulation and negotiation illumines all the complexities and pressures of the Japanese internal political situation. The Demands also marked a milestone in the Chinese response to imperialism. The date on which Yüan submitted to a Japanese ultimatum became commemorated as National Humiliation Day, and the inability of Chinese representatives at Versailles to secure reversal of the clauses affecting Shantung led directly t the May Fourth outbreak in 1919. The presentation of the Demands can be interpreted as one response of Japan to the breakdown of the international order in East Asia. Finally, the American response to the Demands marked the assumption on the part of the United States of a role as the spokesman of a new, moral authority in the postimperialist order and signaled America's assumption of a special protective role toward Republican China, one tinged with romanticism and paternalism. In a larger sense these American tones of sentimentality and protection characterized American attitudes toward Republican China until the communist victory, when they were transferred to postwar Japan and, less successfully, South Korea and South Vietnam.

It is useful to distinguish between the Demands as process in Japanese policy formulation, as fact in Japanese penetration of the continent and as symbol in Chinese and American thinking, and they will be taken up in that order.

Enough has been said about the disappointments Japan experienced in the years after the 1911 revolution to make it clear that the opportunity for a full-scale review of relations with Yüan Shih-k'ai would be welcome. The China negotiations were in fact a direct charge to the Ōkuma cabinet by the elder statesmen. Yamagata and his colleagues had had bad luck in their selection of cabinet leaders since the death of the Meiji emperor in 1912. In the Taishō Political Change Katsura, a Chōshū general, and Yamamoto, a Satsuma admiral, had both failed. Both had to contend with intense criticism of their China policies as well as parliamentary dissatisfaction with their domestic tactics. As a result, the genro had turned for leadership to a surviving member of the Restoration group in 1914.

Ōkuma Shigenobu had favored the encouragement of constitutional government. His university at Waseda had trained many of the most articulate modern Japanese journalists and politicians. He maintained connections with Chinese reformers. Two of his associates, Inukai and Ozaki, were among the most vocal and popular politicians of Meiji Japan, and both were champions of the

YŪAN SHIH-K'AI, surrounded by his generals, at the time he was named Provisional President of the Republic of China in 1912.

cause of Sun Yat-sen and "modern" China. Ōkuma himself was a garrulous and popular figure, the antithesis of the silent Yamagata, and his appointment was greeted with enthusiasm. Before he took up his task he was questioned closely by Inoue Kaoru on behalf of the other genro. Ōkuma agreed that it was time to break the power of the Seiyūkai and was confident that a period of power would enable his organization to break the links to local power that were essential to Seiyūkai influence. He was also agreeable to retrenchment of government spending; the genro were worried by political party pork-barrel politics. But he agreed to the army's desire for two additional divisions, the issue that had toppled the Saionji cabinet in 1912. The genro retained reservations about Ōkuma's foreign minister, Katō Kōmei, and later came to resent his tactics deeply. Once in office, Katō was more careful about his relations with the General Staff than he was about the genro. His director of the Office of Political Affairs, Koike Chōzō, also maintained connections with military and civilian advocates of forceful measures in China. As a result the army did not complain about Katō to Yamagata, and it was well satisfied with Ōkuma's promise of two additional divisions. Since Katō was dedicated to independence of action from octogenarian interference, Yamagata and his colleagues soon found themselves ignored. A long memorandum from Yamagata on the China question did not get the courtesy of a reply from the foreign minister. Important telegrams on foreign affairs, always shared with the senior statesmen, now stopped coming, and as Katō had his way in leading Japan to the side of the Allied Powers in World War I, the complaints of the genro became increasingly frequent.

The outbreak of war in Europe in 1914 made it possible for Katō to combine cooperation with the British with destruction of the German position in China and preparation for an overall settlement with Yüan Shih-k'ai. After Japanese troops captured the German installations on Shantung, Japan had new bargaining power with Yüan. By December, Katō was telling the Diet that Japan had made no promise about retrocession of Shantung, for although the ultimatum to Berlin had spoken of "eventual retrocession," German refusal to heed that ultimatum had created a new situation. The Shantung holdings had a long period to run, but Japan's Manchurian rights did not. The agreements for Port Arthur and Dairen were to expire as early as 1923. So Shantung provided leverage for Manchuria, and Europe's preoccupation with war seemed to rule out interference. Yamagata's preference for an overall settlement with China stated the general sentiment rather than a solitary opinion. But methods differed. The genro suggested sending an outstanding leader, possibly one of their number, to China as evidence of Japan's sincerity. Yamagata also urged explicit renunciation of any interest in the revolutionary movement in order to reassure Yüan. Other genro suggestions included the convening of a conference to examine the conditions under which Japan might return Kiaochow Bay to China and liaison with Japan's European partners for establishment of international arrangements to finance Chinese development. Probably none of this could have bridged the gap between Japanese and Chinese interests, but some or all of these steps could have created a more constructive atmosphere. Katō chose to act alone in attempted secrecy.

The Foreign Office had the benefit of a good deal of unsolicited advice in preparing its plans for negotiations with China. The Kokuryūkai, for instance, prepared a long statement which was presented to Premier Ōkuma late in November 1914. Uchida Ryōhei argued that the first requirement for Japan's position in China was the overthrow of Yüan Shih-k'ai. Revolution against Yüan was certain anyway, he wrote, and Japan should cultivate and encourage groups with whom it could work. Uchida favored support for the revolutionaries in the south, but he also sought help for the Manchu royalists, led by Prince Su, in the north. Uchida's concerns were first of all political, and although he went on to spell out desirable economic concessions he never lost sight of the essential shift of government in China and the substitution of a friendly for an unfriendly regime. Although the Kokuryūkai approach was simplistic and poorly reasoned, in some respects it proved more consistent than Katō's disregard for political and psychological considerations.

Uchida addressed himself to the highest levels of government authority, and sent copies to the genro as well as to government leaders. Sun Yat-sen, the revolutionary refugee, addressed his own suggestions to Premier Ōkuma and more particularly to Koike Chōzō, the Foreign Office official with ties to China adventurers. Shortly after Ōkuma took office, Sun Yat-sen sent him a letter pleading for Japanese help in driving Yüan Shih-k'ai out of office and promising in return a lasting Sino-Japanese alliance. Japan was assured elaborate commercial benefits, unrestricted residence, a customs union and, in fact, overall commercial leadership. Sun argued that chivalry, idealism, profit and security should all impel

Japan to oust Yüan Shih-k'ai and set up a friendly government under his leadership.

Sun was in desperate straits by now, farther from power than ever, shorn of the glamor and youth that had made fund raising so easy for him, bitter and disillusioned about the prospects of spontaneous regeneration for China. If power required bargaining, he would match Yüan; if it required power, he would seek it by the establishment of a new revolutionary party whose members were forced to take oaths of personal loyalty to him. "Unless the comrades are united and obey me personally," he wrote in 1914, "the revolutionary cause is doomed to failure." Many of his former colleagues refused to follow him in this course, and this hardened him further and made him the more dependent on outside assistance. Sun became so desperate for financial support that he tried to raise money from an American admirer by proposing to appoint him to a department store trust which would buy cheaply in the wake of the revolution's confusion and sell at profit, thereby sparing "the grateful people" from heavy taxation. The American, Dietrick, was further authorized to "close up a deal" to undertake work "in such industrial lines as Mining, Iron, and Steel Works, Transportation, etc."; he might even

> use your judgment as to disposal of districts to various persons and for such sums as may be deemed prudent and fair.... In case of cash transaction you will have the money deposited in a bank in my name.

Nothing came of this, but it can serve to illustrate the low state of Sun Yat-sen's morale and ingenuity at this time.

It is not surprising that when Sun Yat-sen got wind of the Twenty-one Demands in 1915, he addressed a letter to Koike Chōzō to try once more for Japanese help. He warned that it was no good to try to arrange something through Yüan Shih-k'ai's "evil government." The revolutionaries, on the other hand, would gladly build cordial relations with Japan once they were in power. With Europe preoccupied in war, it was a perfect time for Japan to get rid of Yüan Shih-k'ai. To encourage the Japanese, Sun included a sample of the kind of agreement that should be possible. By its provisions China and Japan would be closely allied, with China giving Japan priority on arrangements for munitions, military advisers and governmental advisers. Outside capital would be extended through a Sino-Japanese bank that should be set up with branches throughout Japan and China. Japan was to provide the help needed to remove China's "evil government," reform it, modernize it and help China in the tasks of attaining independence and equality in the world. Neither country would ally with any other power.

The benefits for Japan of such an arrangement would be immense. Yet one notices in Sun's proposal that both parties would promise not to ally with other powers. This condition would run counter to all of Yamagata's and, indeed, all modern Japanese policy. The Japanese government always wanted it both ways, for it was convinced that ultimate security could only come through alliance with Western countries. Japan's gains had been scored under the protection of the British fleet, and such a relationship ruled out the fraternal and symbiotic ties many Japanese sought with China. In economic matters also, a large and growing amount of Japan's trade was with the Western world, particularly with the United States. Thus Sun Yat-sen's proposal entailed dilemmas that have persisted in Japanese policy formation. Increasingly a part of the modernized, trading maritime world and yet also convinced of the necessity of a special relationship with neighboring China, Japanese have never willingly accepted exclusive ties with either. At the time of the Twenty-one Demands, however, the Tokyo government tried to browbeat the Chinese government without weakening Japan's ties with its Western allies. As a result modern Chinese nationalism came to be directed chiefly against Japan, as the governments of modern China, instead of showing "gratitude" for Japan's "leadership," instead turned to the United States, itself Japan's largest customer in the Western world, for help against their persistent neighbor.

The Twenty-one Demands were worked out in consultation with senior government, army and business leaders. The specific contribution of adventurers and ultranationalists cannot be estimated, but they were no doubt kept informed. Katō instructed his representative in Peking, Minister Hioki, to assure Yüan Shih-k'ai of Japan's concern for Chinese territorial integrity and to prepare the setting for important talks. The occasion came in January 1915, when the Chinese government requested the return of the special transit and military rights that the Japanese had required for their operations in Shantung. Minister Hioki presented the Demands personally to Yüan Shih-k'ai and asked him to maintain complete secrecy during the discussions.

The Demands were arranged in five groups of which the first related to Shantung province. All of Imperial Germany's rights there were to be transferred to Japan. Group II extended the lease and the privileges in south Manchuria and east Inner Mongolia which the Japanese had taken over from Imperial Russia in 1905. Group III confirmed the pattern of joint Sino-Japanese administration of the Hanyehp'ing Company that had been sought earlier by Japanese interests. In Group IV China was to promise not to alienate any port or island along the China coast to any other country, in "the interest of preserving China's territorial integrity." None of these went much beyond previous requests that had been made of China. Group V, however, contained more difficult problems. It consisted of seven items that were offered as the "desires of the Imperial [Japanese] Government," and Minister Hioki was instructed that the items

> in this category are entirely different in character from those which are included in the first four groups. An adjustment, at this time, of these matters, some of which have been pending between the two countries, being nevertheless highly desirable for the advancement of friendly relations between Japan and China . . . you are also requested to exercise your best efforts to have our wishes carried out.

In fact the Japanese negotiators pushed hard for Group V. By its terms Japanese would be employed as political, financial and military advisers; Japanese hospitals, schools and temples would have the right to own land in the Chinese interior; Japanese would be appointed to police positions where needed; China would purchase Japanese arms or approve the establishment of a Sino-Japanese arsenal; Japan would be permitted to construct railways connecting the Yangtze Valley with the south China coast; Japanese capital would be given first call for the development of Fukien province; and Japanese would be permitted to do mission work in China.

Foreign Minister Katō seems to have been convinced that the Demands did not, for the most part, create a new situation. They were designed to tidy up the diplomatic scene and forestall future misunderstandings. They were also designed for domestic capital in Japan by showing that Japanese missionaries and schools now had the same privileges as their Western counterparts. But in several crucial respects new situations were indeed created. The clause pertaining to railway connections between the Yangtze Valley and Japan's zone on the south China coast was one such, for it affected the heartland of what the British considered their own special zone. Ironically, Katō's commitment to the Anglo-Japanese alliance did not keep him from alarming his British allies, and his desire to avoid future friction with China did not keep him from providing Chinese nationalists with their most inflammatory anti-Japanese arguments. There was no real basis, even in British imagination, for the British minister's verdict that "Japan's action toward China is worse than that of Germany in the case of Belgium." Several recent studies go far to deny the standard textbook claims that the Demands threatened China's existence as a sovereign state. Japanese arms were in keen demand everywhere in China, Japanese advisers were already in the employ of all sectors of the Chinese government, and in the deteriorating conditions of political unification and order in China competing candidates for foreign aid had made such generous offers that, as the British minister observed, it seemed almost as though the whole of China were up for auction. Minister Hioki was also directed to assure Yüan that Japan would not support his revolutionary adversaries.

Yet the symbolism of the Demands, and their permanent place in modern Chinese political folklore, is that of a crafty Japan seizing the momentary advantage of World War I to serve sweeping demands upon its helpless neighbor. The explanation for this is to be found in the extraordinary insensitivity and maladroit diplomacy of the Japanese negotiators and their government as contrasted with the masterful political and psychological defensive action of the Chinese. It was one in which they received important foreign, especially American, assistance and one in which they utilized to the full the Japanese mistakes. Yüan Shih-k'ai summed up his views in a friendly conversation with the British Minister John Jordan after it was all over; he did not have a very high opinion of Baron Katō as a diplomat, he explained, "considering his disadvantages in material strength, he [Yüan] had come out fairly well. The concealment of the 5th group of demands he considered a strategic blunder which he had recoiled upon Japan's head." The explanation thus lies in part in a closer examination of the diplomatic process as it worked to Chinese advantage.

Japanese handling of the negotiations provided an object lesson in the evils of old-style, imperialist diplomacy that World War I was supposed to bring to an end. Yüan Shih-k'ai was warned to keep his silence. When word got to Washington and prompted questions to the Japanese ambassador, he confirmed to Secretary of State Bryan that Japan had indeed made some "propositions" to China, but he revealed only Groups I to IV. In Tokyo Foreign Minister Katō assured American Ambassador Guthrie that the "propositions" were "not contrary to China's integrity or to the rights and interests of other nations." But if not contrary to China's, the "propositions" proved to be contrary to Japan's "integrity," for neither the ambassador nor the foreign minister said anything about Group V, which was being forced on Peking together with the others. Not until Washington, on 19 February, expressed to Tokyo its relief that the existence of a fifth group, which had been discussed in the press, was spurious, did the Japanese Foreign Office admit that there was such a group. But these, Tokyo explained, were "requests" and not "demands." It was thus more than a month before Tokyo admitted the contents of its entire document that had been presented to Yüan Shih-k'ai. He, in turn, seized the opportunity to refuse to discuss Group V at all.

Yüan Shih-k'ai proved a resourceful and able negotiator. His first tactic was that of delay. He scheduled meetings for once a week, on Saturday; points were taken up separately instead of by groups, as the Japanese wished. In two months the discussions got through Groups I and II. The exasperated Japanese began to talk of force, and by 17 April Minister Hioki was urging Tokyo to issue an ultimatum. During March the Japanese army increased the pressure by sending large numbers of "railway guard" units into Manchuria, and Foreign Minister Katō was close to losing his control over the negotiations.

The Chinese president also made the most of foreign support. Although he could have revealed the Japanese demands immediately to China's treaty-port masters, he chose instead to leak them quietly to selected journalists and to American Minister Paul Reinsch. Reinsch, a University of Wisconsin legal historian and student of Far Eastern affairs, had been selected by President Wilson for Peking because he wanted for China someone firmly Christian in outlook; he felt that the contribution of Christian missions had been one of America's most important contacts with the new China. Reinsch shared to the full Wilson's idealism and sense of mission. This, plus a certain naiveté about his role, made him an ideal spokesman for the Chinese interest. Reinsch accepted at face value Yüan's assurances of his intention to model Chinese political life upon that of the United States. "As I represented the Republic upon which it [China] had been largely modeled, whose spirit the Chinese were anxious to follow," he later wrote,

> it fell to me to counsel with Chinese leaders as if I had been one of their number. The experience of a great American commonwealth which had itself successfully endeavoured to raise its organization to a higher plane was

of unending assistance to me in enabling me to see the Chinese problems as part of what right thinking men were struggling for throughout the world.

Reinsch took up his duties with the view that Japan might give leadership in modernization in the Far East, but his period in Peking persuaded him that Japan "employed every device of intrigue, intimidation, corruption, and force in order to gain a position for itself in flagrant disregard of the rights of the Chinese people itself, and in oblivion of the rights of others." His warning of the threat of Japan stirred the head of the Far Eastern Division in the State Department to warn President Wilson and Secretary Bryan that it was in the American interest to "ask explanation from Japan and *insist firmly upon our rights* ... [or else] we are in danger of *losing our influence in the Far East* and adding to the dangers of the situation...." Japan, which was not "restrained by the scruples of the West," was becoming "a greater menace than ever to the U.S. She has given us fair warning that she will not tolerate what she considers race discrimination against her people." And E. T. Williams went on to argue that America, having forced Japan to reduce the Demands, should next "insist upon China's putting her house in order and making herself able to defend herself. We *can* and *ought* to assist her in this, and in so doing we shall be building up *a strong defence for ourselves.*" These notes would all be repeated in the 1930s and 1940s, when a disciple of Minister Reinsch was influential in the formulation of American Far Eastern policy.

The American response was slow in taking form. Secretary of State Bryan was inclined to give the Japanese the benefit of the doubt and wanted to believe the Japanese ambassador's assurances that Minister Reinsch's reports were erroneous. But by 18 February the Chinese Foreign Office had transmitted the full Japanese document to all China's treaty powers and thereby helped precipitate Foreign Minister Katō's assurance that Group V was in a separate category. By 13 March the State Department was ready with a long note to Japan which reviewed American policy and rights in China. Washington was prepared to grant that Japan's territorial contiguity created special relations between Japan and Shantung, south Manchuria and east Mongolia; it thus accepted Groups I and II, also IV and said nothing about Group III, and the missionary, hospital and railways provisions in Group V. But of the provisions for advisers, munitions and loans in Group V the note warned that "The United States ... could not regard with indifference the assumption of political, military, or economic domination over China by a foreign Power."

Katō's response, as might have been foreseen, was to express pleasure with America's willingness to grant that territorial contiguity made for special relations and to reassure Washington on the points at issue. Secretary Bryan now came close to accepting the Japanese position. "Japan and China must remain neighbors," he said to Wilson. "It is of vital importance that they should be neighborly, and a neighborly spirit cannot be expected if Japan demands too much, or if China concedes too little." He then suggested several points of compromise: let the Chinese promise not to discriminate against Japan in seeking advisers and buying munitions and let the Chinese agree to use Japanese police supervision in Manchuria and Inner Mongolia. When word of this reached Peking and Minister Reinsch, his explosive reaction was a long wire of protest which ended that

> it would at any rate be more expedient to follow a course of passive acquiescence rather than to intervene in such a manner as could scarcely fail to cause revulsion of Chinese feeling against the United States and put an end to our influence here....

Two weeks later, Reinsch wired that Minister Hioki had been warning the Chinese "that they would be foolish to expect any support from the United States, since the American government had approved the Japanese demands."

At this juncture President Wilson personally took over direction of American policy in the matter. More distrustful of the Japanese than Bryan and fully sympathetic with Reinsch's ideals, he concluded that "I am convinced that we shall have to try in every way practicable to defend China. We shall have to be very chary hereafter about seeming to concede the reasonableness of any of Japan's demands or requests either...." Early in May a public statement announced that

> This Government has not only had no thought of surrendering any of its treaty rights with China, but it has never been asked by either Japan or China to make any surrender of these rights. There is no abatement of its interest in the welfare and progress of China....

And on 10 May, after the conclusion of the negotiations with the offensive demands of Group V eliminated, Wilson ordered the release of a declaration announcing that

> the Government of the United States has the honor to notify the Imperial Japanese Government that it cannot recognize any agreement or undertaking which has been entered into or which may be entered into between the Governments of Japan and China, impairing the treaty rights of the United States and its citizens in China, the political or territorial integrity of the Republic of China, or the international policy relative to China commonly known as the open door policy.

Yüan would not have been able to make use of Washington's support without the clumsy deception that swung Washington from sympathy to hostility and the direction of policy from Bryan to Wilson. The evidence of Japanese intimidation in Peking brought Yüan support from the modern sector of China, an area where he had been weak. Student and shopkeeper indignation resulted in boycotts of Japanese goods and in a virtual exodus of revolutionaries from Japan to China. Yüan also made skillful use of a Japanese adviser, Dr. Ariga Nagao. Ariga's career illustrated the official purposes and rewards of higher education in Meiji Japan. After graduation from Tokyo University, he had taught there before entering government service in the Secretariat of the Privy Council and the prime minister's office. With the outbreak of the Sino-Japanese War, he was attached to imperial headquarters to advise the field armies on problems of international law. He repeated this role at the siege of Port Arthur in 1904. After each conflict he wrote a study of its relevance for international law. He also became head of the Japanese Red Cross, a delegate to the first Hague Conference in 1899, and a professor at Waseda University. In 1913 he went to China to become legal adviser to Yüan Shih-k'ai, a post he held until after Yüan's death. During Yüan Shih-k'ai's ill-fated monarchical attempt, he bore the title "outside [foreign] minister." As the negotiations over the Twenty-one Demands neared their climax, Yüan sent Ariga to Japan, where he talked with Yamagata and the other genro and described to them the damage that the Japanese procedure was doing to Japan's image in China.

Early in May, after a compromise plan of Katō's had failed to win Chinese approval, the discontent of the genro, fed by Ariga's warnings and by knowledge of the reaction in Washington and London, became focused against the foreign minister. Men who had spent so much of their adult life making sure of the esteem of Europe were quick to sense alarm and failure, and in several stormy meetings they prevailed upon the government to abandon Group V for a list of irreducible demands which were to be the subject of a final ultimatum. As a result the ultimatum that reached Peking on 7 May 1915 contained little the Chinese had not already agreed to; indeed, it probably achieved less than it could have. It may be accounted a last victory of Yüan Shih-k'ai's that he had forced the Japanese into a show of force that would highlight his dislike of the document he signed on 25 May. The Japanese received important gains in Manchuria, and their future history there was one of safeguarding the position they had won. In Shantung, in Hanyehp'ing, and elsewhere they had also gained concessions. But the Shantung rights were later surrendered after the Washington Conference and the other concessions were worth little without a stable government to permit access to them, and China was not to have that for many years. The economic gains the Japanese achieved were poor return for the psychological cost they accumulated in providing Chinese nationalism with a National Humiliation Day.

A few months later Yüan Shih-k'ai began the preparations for his monarchical attempt. He seems to have had some expectation of Japanese support, but the caliber of his resistance to the Twenty-one Demands ruled this out as a possibility. On the governmental level the Japanese Foreign Office took the lead in a joint Japanese-British recommendation and diplomatic initiative against the monarchical attempt in October 1915. Within the Japanese army anti-Yüan sentiment was organized by General Tanaka Giichi, now deputy chief of staff. Tanaka sent trusted assistants (including the future General Matsui Iwane) to China as his representatives and secured Foreign Office agreement to a January 1916 memorandum that called for the government to refuse recognition for any monarchical attempt Yüan might make. Meanwhile armed resistance to Yüan had developed in southwest China, where Ts'ai Ao, a disciple of Liang Ch'i-ch'ao, was taking the lead. Unofficial groups, coordinating their efforts through the businessman Kuhara Fusanosuke, began providing funds for Sun Yat-sen in the hope of coordinating attacks against Yüan. Kuhara had strong Pan-Asian and anti-Western sentiments, and he found much to discuss with Sun Yat-sen. He was also on excellent terms with General Tanaka and with Koike Chōzō of the Foreign Office, who later resigned his government post to go to work for Kuhara on a full-time basis. In all Sun Yat-sen and his associates received close to two million yen from Kuhara to help their revolutionary plans. With these funds they were expected to stir rebellion in south and central China, and even to buy off some of Yüan's armed forces. But Sun was not Japan's only candidate for assistance. The once-discredited plans of Kawashima Naniwa to promote a separatist movement under Prince Su in Manchuria and Inner Mongolia were resurrected by Tanaka also, and army and private funds were channeled there. The military detachment that was sent to the north to supervise the allocation of funds and munitions included the future General Koiso Kuniaki.

Tanaka and his associates thus saw the possibility of surrounding Yüan Shih-k'ai with enemies. But their enemy proved weaker than they thought, for his own generals were not prepared to support him in the face of foreign disapproval. Sun Yat-sen proved unable to do anything of consequence with the assistance he had been given, and the Manchurian plans came to nothing when Yüan died in June 1916. Important voices in the Foreign Office, including the then consul and future Foreign Minister and Premier Yoshida Shigeru, warned of the folly of antagonizing Chinese nationalism through clumsy filibustering expeditions. Still, the tendency of propositions of this sort to assume a life and momentum of their own was illustrative of problems that would bedevil Japanese policymakers in future years.

All of this Japanese activity achieved very little except the demise of Yüan Shih-k'ai, who might better have been left to his Chinese opponents. For his warlord followers, now regional rulers, did not maintain their interest in his plans when they proved to conflict with their own. Foreign approval, upon which Yüan Shih-k'ai depended for funds, was essential to his ability to command the loyalty of his generals. After Britain and Japan offered their "friendly advice," Yüan was denied even the income from the British-controlled salt tax, and efforts to raise alternative monies were unsuccessful. Yüan finally gave up. A decree of 22 March announced the end of the era of Glorious Constitutionalism. In April Yüan's ambassador to Japan begged for relaxation of the pressure on him from Tokyo, but Foreign Minister Ishii's only response was to offer him sanctuary with his family in Japan. A few weeks later Yüan was dead.

Soon Japan, too, had a new government, this one headed by Yamagata's nominee, the Chōshū general Terauchi Masatake. Terauchi came to power in October 1916, and he tried to use Japan's World War I opportunity and profits to build order out of the warlord chaos that followed Yüan's death. His efforts brought Japan's initial adjustment to postimperial China to a close. They also solidified the opposition of Chinese nationalism to Japanese imperialism.

Terauchi brought with him a group of men with whom he had worked in Korea; all were concerned to speed a "forward" policy which would advance Japan's continental interests. He could hardly have found a more inviting setting for such plans than the China of his day. The relative unity of Yüan Shih-k'ai's rule had been replaced by cliques of warlords who maneuvered for position and profit behind the screen of legitimacy of the constitutional drafts that changed with the incumbents of power. All the generals needed help and money, all of them hoped for a chance to unify and lead, and Japan was the readiest source of money. A group of *tüchun,* known as the Anfu clique, led by Tuan Ch'i-jui came to be associated with Japanese desires.

In 1917 the prospects for Japanese freedom of action in China were better than ever. The distress of western Europe brought suggestions of Chinese participation on the Allied side, a participation encouraged by European belligerents with hopes of access to Chinese food and Chinese manpower. Ambitious plans for training an army of several divisions, or a half-million, or even a million, men were discussed. In the end China contributed a small army of laborers to the western front. For the Anfu generals, participation in the war seemed to promise access to capital and munitions, both desperately needed, and a seat at the conference that would decide disposition of the German assets the Twenty-one Demands had transferred to Japan. Japan opposed and then encouraged the Chinese decision for "war," first taking the precaution of securing guarantees of its gains from the principal European allies. Chinese belligerency offered new ways of channeling military and economic aid to Chinese allies through what became known as the War Participation Bureau. After the Bolshevik revolution these plans had new urgency. Terauchi and his advisers talked of a Sino-Japanese military alliance that would secure the northern border against the communist infection that was following the revolution in Siberia. China needed all it could get, but only Japan stood ready to lend and direct. Thanks to its booming trade during World War I, Japan was a capital surplus nation for the first time. Great Britain, France and Russia received Japanese loans; Japan enjoyed a favorable trade balance of two billion yen, and it was providing almost half of China's imports in a field that was suddenly free of significant competition. Naturally, Japan expected to play the leading role in helping China to take part in World War I.

Terauchi had several aims. One was to secure American acknowledgment of Japan's position in China. The Lansing-Ishii notes, signed and released in November 1917 (and eliminated by negotiations only in 1923), seemed to serve this purpose. Worked out without the knowledge of American Minister Reinsch in Peking, the notes acknowledged "that Japan has special interests in China, particularly in the part to which her possessions are contiguous." This time the Peking government felt constrained to declare, in language reminiscent of America's recent nonrecognition statement, that it could not recognize any agreement other powers might enter into relating to China. On the other hand, the notes went on to pledge Japan not to use its special interests in such a way as to "discriminate against the trade of other nations, or to disregard the commercial rights heretofore granted by China in the treaties with other powers." Thus the document could be used to argue the Open Door or its partial closure; the Japanese felt well served by it, and the Chinese rather poorly.

Terauchi also sought a specific military alliance with the warlords who controlled north China in order to buttress Japan against danger from the Russian north. Particularly after the Allied decision of August 1918 to intervene against communism in Siberia, most of the military aid that went to China was for operations on the northern frontier. The Peking militarists were expected to put their full reliance on Japan for arms and funds. Most were Japanese educated, and many had Japanese military advisers at their headquarters. With military and economic support, Peking might be expected to enter some kind of economic union with Japan. These were the most ambitious, coordinated and expensive plans Japan had yet had for China.

Terauchi's plans did not have the approval of all Japanese leaders, but as prime minister he was able to work his way around his opposition. The popular press was bitterly hostile and pictured him as a militarist backing militarism in China. "The Middle Ages supporting the Middle Ages," was the way the popular *Asahi* put it. But by controlling the sources of information, Terauchi was able to keep much of his activity out of sight. He also selected his channels and agents in order to bypass the bureaus in the Japanese government that should have been consulted most closely. Instead of working through the Foreign Office and the Yokohama Specie Bank, Terauchi chose to send an old acquaintance and former director of the Bank of Korea to China. Japanese companies like the Mitsui and Ōkura trading firms and the several China-Japan industrial organizations that had been organized at the time of Sun Yat-sen's Tokyo visit in 1913 were used. On the Chinese side, the principal contact was Tuan Ch'i-jui's minister of communications, Ts'ao Ju-lin, himself a graduate of Waseda University in Tokyo. A fellow Waseda alumnus, Lu Tsung-yu, was president of the Exchange Bank of China.

Nishihara Kamezō, Terauchi's agent, went to China in December 1916. His first loan with the Communications Bank was signed in January the following year. Soon Peking was rife with rumors about Japanese financing. Minister Reinsch described Nishihara as an "unofficial financial agent ..., a borer in the rotten trunk of Chinese finance." Certainly he was successful in placing a great deal of Japanese money. His activities were kept secret, and even the Japanese minister in Peking charged that he and his officials were being bypassed in negotiations that vitally affected Japanese policy toward China. The Wilson administration, for its part, decided that the influence of the Nishihara loans was becoming so great that it would reverse its earlier position and allow American participation in a new consortium for Chinese loans in order to offset Japanese activities.

The Nishihara loans totaled approximately 150 million yen (about $80 million), double the amount of American loans and investments to China at that time. They were intended for currency and financial reforms, the satisfaction of foreign obligations, the political needs of central and provincial governments, development projects and above all military assistance. In addition, other, and more publicized, formal loans were extended to the Chinese government, often through then Finance Minister Liang Ch'i-ch'ao. The Yokohama Specie Bank was also a member of an international consortium that was lending money to prevent the dominance of the Nishihara mission. For its pains its autonomy was drastically cut by Prime Minister Terauchi late in 1917, and the bank was forced to limit itself to short-term loans.

For a time Japan seemed to achieve many of its purposes in China. After Tuan Ch'i-jui resigned as premier in November 1917 (partly because of criticism of these policies), he became head of the War Participation Bureau, which became a powerful organization with virtual control over police, finance and national resources. In some measure the commanding position the Japanese secured in this bureau might be said to have given them the control they had sought through Group V of the Twenty-one Demands. For a time Chinese currency seemed likely to become pegged to the Japanese yen. Official Chinese government opposition to the Japanese position in Shantung weakened. International interference in Japanese plans in China was greatly reduced, and the Siberian intervention seemed likely to leave Japan in virtual control of northern China.

But the gains proved ephemeral and insubstantial. The loans were predicated upon an administrative rationalization that never took place. They were given without security. Most of them were wasted, and they left little more than bad debts. "War participation" swallowed more and more of them, and this usually meant expeditions against rival warlords of China. The modern divisions they made possible were soon to be destroyed in China's civil wars. The end of the fighting in western Europe in November 1918 sobered the *tüchun,* who had come to think of the flow of foreign money as endless, and it affected the Japanese equally drastically by putting an end to their war profits and services. Premier Hara Kei, who succeeded Terauchi in September 1918, refused to continue the wasteful disbursement of funds and put an end to further political loans. As Japan's wartime boom gave way to postwar slump, the Nishihara loans came to an end.

In retrospect the lavish use of Japanese money, which worried many foreign observers, did little good and much harm to Japan. It increased the warlord confusion and delayed the date of stability in China. It prolonged the dissatisfaction with China policy within Japan. It became an almost totally unproductive trap for the use of Japan's wartime surpluses and made it impossible to utilize them to modernize, rationalize and lighten Japan's own fiscal structure. Most importantly, in political goals the Japanese were building on sand. Their warlord allies were little more than elaborately decorated and plumed political birds of passage, and as they left the Japanese inherited chiefly dislike and resentment for their efforts to collect interest on the loans.

The warlords themselves were well hated within China by the most modernized sectors of Chinese society. Japan's aid to them associated Japan with backwardness and imperialism instead of with reform and nationalism. The boycotts that began during the negotiations of the Twenty-one Demands should have served to warn Terauchi. The Nishihara loans brought student demonstrations in Peking, where Peking University students marched to government buildings to demand an end to participation with Japan in the war. Popular meetings soon were held all over China denouncing Tuan Ch'i-jui. When in 1919 the fourth anniversary of the forcible signing of the Twenty-one Demands approached and when word came from Versailles that the Peace Conference had honored the Japanese interpretation of the Shantung settlement, a gigantic demonstration on 4 May, directed against the officials who had accepted the Nishihara loans, ushered in the era of modern Chinese nationalism. "China," as Minister Reinsch had surmised, "was divided only on the surface."

CHAPTER 7

The New Generation

World War I marked the end of the great age of imperialism in East Asia. That age had been dominated by Europe. Japan had developed imperialist policies out of fear that others would preempt areas vital to its interests, and the United States entered the imperialist race very late. The powers had worked out a pattern of mutual abstention in which their interests lay in maintaining reasonably equal access to the markets, railways and materials of China. Mutual rivalry, as well as Chinese resistance, had prevented the partition of the Chinese empire into zones. By 1914 the partition of China, which many had once assumed to be inevitable, had become unlikely. European powers were preoccupied with rivalries closer to home. Chinese statesmen, operating with considerable skill from positions of weakness, had evaded fatal commitments. And the Chinese people themselves had developed a growing capacity for united protest. By the time the dynasty fell in 1911, it was clear that although fringe areas might be compromised China would not be parceled up among the powers.

World War I removed the possibility of colonial expropriation by any country other than Japan. Thereafter the decline of the European states in terms of real power was rapid. The physical, financial and moral destruction of Europe during the years of slaughter on the western front left the principal contenders in poor positions to resume their ambitions of the 1890s. Germany was removed from the lists altogether and no longer acted as spur to the others, while Imperial Russia disappeared as a threat. Great Britain and France were fully occupied with tasks of reconstruction at home, and they no longer possessed the surplus of investment capital that had drawn international bankers to development consortiums in China. Early Republican China seemed in any case a far less secure and promising outlet for capital.

1. Areas of Change

FOR THE GENERATION of modernizers, the Europe that had threatened them had lost prestige as well as power. Their firm commitment to the Spencerian assumptions of progress disappeared in the mud and blood of western Europe. It was no longer clear that science and progress were destined to rule a world of increasingly rational men. Many of the first generation of translators and writers drew lessons from this. In the case of Yen Fu, who had interpreted Adam Smith, John Stuart Mill and Charles Darwin to nineteenth-century China, Benjamin Schwartz concludes that "the enormity and scale of destruction of World War I filled him with alternating moods of awe and horror." "The West's progress during the last three hundred years," Yen wrote, "has led only to selfishness, slaughter, corruption, and shamelessness. When I look back on the way of Confucius and Mencius, I find that they are truly the equivalent of heaven and earth and have profoundly benefited the realm. This is not my opinion alone. Many thinking people in the West have gradually come to feel this way." Liang Ch'i-ch'ao agreed that writers like Darwin, with their apotheosis of struggle and competition, might have led Europe to disaster. "This great European war," he wrote, "nearly wiped out human civilization; although the causes were very many, it must be said that the Darwinian theory had a very great influence." He now called for a synthesis of Chinese culture with Western civilization.

But the most important changes did not lie with the disillusionment of the elder generation. They were to be found in the emergence of a vocal, idealistic and critical generation of students and writers who continued to draw on Western thought without always subscribing to it as fully or uncritically as some of the earlier modernizers had. For these young people, "tradition" and "modernity" were no longer the absolute contrasts they had been for their elders, for their "tradition" already included the generation of effort at "self-strengthening" and reform. They were more likely to react to the disruption of the second decade of the twentieth century in East Asia by criticizing the West as well as their own tradition rather than by retreating into praise of Confucius and Mencius. They reached out eagerly to new definitions of social and national problems, and many of them moved steadily to the Left.

This growth of radicalism took many forms. In Korea, most recently subject to modern changes and unified rule under despotic foreigners, its main thrust was toward national identity and self-determination. In China, where the disunity of militarism was compounded by foreign intrigue, notes of national unity and social and cultural revolution predominated. And in Japan, where the ideology of nationalism had run its course and unity had been achieved, tones of democracy and social reform replaced those of achievement and national equality that had inspired the Meiji generation. In Imperial Japan nationalism was in the service of the state. Imperial loyalty was maintained by education, the military and the press, each reinforcing the other. Inevitably Japan's student generation found less self-expression in nationalism, and its thoughts turned instead to social and political reform and more universal goals. In China national sentiment was directed against the militarist leaders who were unable to maintain their position without the help of foreign money and arms. The world knew a surplus of armaments in the years after World War I, as it did after World War II. Thus Chinese student nationalism became critical of the political society in which it lived and struggled against the international as well as the domestic structure so that nationalism led to social revolution. In Japan it worked against social revolution.

It was the setting more than the constituency of discontent that determined its course in politics and ideology. There was not so much a shift of class as a growth of tension between generations. Chinese student groups were still part of the social elite and still a small minority. But they were impatient with old restraints, pieties and clichés. Chinese students found their aspirations to influence blocked by the irrationality of the warlord era in which they lived. Korean students, on the other hand, found themselves disadvantaged by their Japanese rulers. But Japanese students were scarcely less impatient, for the mobility and aspirations of Meiji times, when the educated were still a small elite, had been replaced by a slow upward climb in the carefully structured bureaucracies of the new society. They found themselves a more numerous group and less a true elite, less able to influence the world they had to enter. Examinations came to dominate young lives in Japan at a time when they ceased to do so in China. The conflicts of the 1920s and 1930s in East Asia took on new meaning against the sources, channels and outlets of the new radicalism.

The first important external source of the new generation's enthusiasm was the United States. In one sense this was an unlikely source of inspiration. America was a late entrant into the imperialist race and held its Philippine empire only after 1898. It experimented with ideas of coaling stations on the China coast during the years of imperialist expansion, but it had not pursued these operations with any amount of tenacity. At home its immigration and racial tensions might have been expected to limit the United States's powers of attraction.

Yet America's espousal of the "Open Door," although talked about a good deal less in China than in America, and its willingness to take the lead in converting part of its Boxer indemnity debt to educational purposes helped to balance the picture. More important than this were American attempts to restrict Japan's successes during the Twenty-one Demands in 1915; these helped to improve the American image in the eyes of Chinese students.

Yet it was not so much its policy that made the United States important as it was the development, during the period of European decline, of a new image of the United States as harbinger of democracy and self-determination in a part of the world that had known neither. These were goals with which youth everywhere could affiliate. Students sensed in these goals a new idealism. Nothing could have served better than the rhetoric of Woodrow Wilson to provide an alternative to the political actualities of East Asia. It was the American image and not the American performance, and it was Wilson's rhetoric more than his policy that made the American contribution to the new generation so important. Yet there was also enough effort devoted to the implementation of self-determination and democracy to guarantee a major place for Wilson in the enthusiasms of the period. These were not restricted to the educated; indeed, they often assumed more heroic proportions among the ignorant. At the time of the independence movement of 1919 in Korea, rumors were rife that Wilson would arrive by plane to direct the fight for independence, that American battleships were on the way, that American troops had landed on the coast and that the peace conference in Paris had recognized Korean independence at Wilson's insistence. Peking students were no less certain that the Paris Peace Conference would recognize China's rights in Shantung and cancel out the Twenty-one Demands, and Japanese students were scarcely less convinced of Wilson's powers. When it became clear that Wilson's power was a good deal less sweeping than his promises, the simple expectations of American intervention came to an end. Even so, the broader pattern of American influence and inspiration remained, and although separated from the United States as a polity, it remained important in the cultural stimulants for the student generation.

It is a good deal easier to speak about cultural influence in general terms than it is to specify its sequence and content. The praise of "Mr. Science" and "Mr. Democracy" that was to be found in the writings of young radicals in Peking was not necessarily American in origin, and yet it was unlikely that any one using these terms would be unaware of the country in which industrial science and political democracy were most advanced. More specifically American, of course, was the vogue of baseball in Japan; introduced as early as 1878, it had become so popular by the first decade of the twentieth century that American college teams came to meet the great private universities of Keiō and Waseda (the University of Hawaii in 1907, the University of Washington in 1908 and the University of Chicago in 1910). The annual Keiō-Waseda games, which were inaugurated in 1903, stirred such warlike emotions that they had to be suspended between 1906 and 1925. For the most part it would be wrong to attribute political importance to such historical curios. Yet the pervasive spread of industrial mass society and spectator sports provided a broader base for cultural enthusiasms than Japan had known before. Even the appearance of merchandising techniques imported from abroad (as when the Matsuzakaya Department Store named its "bargain sale" in 1908) is not without significance.

The attributes of mass culture in an industrializing society naturally affected Japan first and most powerfully. But China, too, was producing, especially in Shanghai and Tientsin, important features of this society. More important than sports and sales was the multiplication of communications media. The growth of a metropolitan press and of periodical publications affected all of Japan and much of China. Korea, where Japanese administrators suppressed hundreds of publications in the years after the annexation, was affected less. Significant numbers of Chinese and Korean students were also found in the university centers of Japan. In 1917 Korean students in Tokyo numbered 659, and Chinese between 3,000 and 4,000. The tight police laws of the Shōwa period were still unknown in early Taishō Japan, and the experience of the groups was of great importance. Chinese and, especially, Korean students were able to find support in the relatively liberal setting of Japan which they would have had difficulty finding in militarist China or occupied Korea.

The other external source of influence was revolutionary Russia. This is an influence difficult to assess, in part because contemporary conservatives and later radicals were so quick to exaggerate it. It could not be backed by very specific and practical policies, for Russia was too beleaguered by foreign enemies to be able to exert much power in East Asia. As with Wilson, rhetoric counted for more than action. More important, there was the appeal of a revolutionary ideology that gradually gained relevance from its implementation in the Soviet Union.

The Russian appeal operated on several levels. One was the peculiar attraction and relevance that Russian revolutionaries had long held for Chinese conspirators against the Manchus. Japan had played its part in transmitting this tradition to young Chinese. In late Meiji times intellectuals of the socialist left found many occasions to express their disenchantment with parliamentarianism in speech and publication. Works on Russian nihilism had been published in Japan as early as the 1880s, and after 1902 a growing interest in anarchism developed in Japan. A Waseda professor wrote a work, which influenced Chinese revolutionaries, about the Russian revolutionary movement; the book emphasized a three-stage periodization of revolutionary literature: propaganda and agitation; assassination; and terror. The Russo-Japanese War increased Japanese radicals' interest in Russia. After the February Revolution, a number of Russian refugees and revolutionaries made their way to Nagasaki. Sun Yat-sen met them through Japanese intermediaries, and for a time a magazine designed to speed both the Chinese and Russian revolutions was published. A climate of vigorous left-wing publishing developed in Japan, though the police never let it get out of hand. *Hikari* (*The Light*), *Heimin Shimbun* (*Commoners' Press*),

Chokugen (*Straight Talk*) and other journals indicated by their titles the tide of social criticism.

This development coincided with a major shift toward anarchism within the Japanese socialist movement. The term and concept entered Chinese language and thought through Japanese translations. The individual heroics of Russian revolutionaries began to seem unusually appropriate models for Chinese students, and the idealization of suicide and bravery in the Chinese revolutionary movement owed much to the Russian example. These influences continued in post-1911 China. They were not purely derivative, of course. Denunciation of the evils of capitalist society in the West owed much to philosophical currents in the East Asian tradition hostile to bourgeois materialism, but they were certainly reinforced by Russian example and literature. Thus it was natural that upon hearing the news of the Bolshevik success in 1917 Sun Yat-sen should have sent Lenin a message of congratulations.

On a more general level, the great works of Russian culture of the nineteenth century came to replace the simplistic success literature that had entered Japan and China from Europe and America. Chinese and Japanese readers came to see in their themes of struggle and survival, individuality and collectivity, and freedom and despotism ideas that spoke directly to their condition and tradition. The impact of Russian literature on the modern Japanese novel was direct and impressive, beginning with Futabatei Shimei, a man who began with translating from the Russian. The cries of protest and desperation against the stupidity of governmental bureaucracy common to Russian writers also found echo in figures like Lu Hsün, a creator of the modern Chinese novel. It was inevitable that a sudden change in the condition of the society that had produced these powerful human statements would move Chinese and Japanese readers.

Prior to 1917 anarchism seemed to win out over Marxism. However, the power of the Bolshevik victory and example gave Marxism a new and sudden relevance for East Asian radicals, who had thought its applicability was limited to the industrialized societies of the West. Now it seemed possible that a small elite, one with which students could associate themselves, might jump in as leaders to speed the operation of the dialectic even in undeveloped and only partly industrialized countries. It is not surprising that Marxism stirred more interest in Japan, where the injustices of early industrialization gave it particular relevance. In 1904 the *Heimin Shimbun,* or *Commoners' Press,* tried to publish a translation of the *Communist Manifesto.* The Kyoto University scholar Kawakami Hajime began lecturing on classical economics in 1908 and first proposed altruism as a cure for the poverty he saw under capitalism. But Kawakami announced his commitment to Marxism in 1919 and began a full translation of *Das Kapital* that appeared in 1927. Lenin was first translated into Chinese in 1919. But for the most part the "communism" of the years around World War I was still an eclectic acceptance of many theories of discontent and reform. Intense and serious young men knew that something was very wrong with their world, but they had not yet settled on one doctrine to the exclusion of others.

They talked and wrote with a romantic intensity and burning curiosity. As one Japanese put it later, "I lived among passionate young people with vague ideas, in the realm of anarchists, bolsheviks, Christians, and radical liberals." Mao Tse-tung's recollections in 1936 were not very different: "At this time [1918] my mind was a curious mixture of ideas of liberals, democratic reformism, and Uto-pian Socialism. I had somewhat vague passions about 'nineteenth century de-mocracy,' Utopianism and old-fashioned liberalism, and I was definitely anti-militarist and anti-imperialist."

The radicalism of the student generation was not Bolshevik in origin, and it became communist only gradually under the pressure of events. As radicals became more discouraged, the Russian model seemed to have more to offer, and Marxist ideology made that appeal universal and not narrowly Russian. Li Ta-chao, a Peking University professor and future communist leader in China, hailed the end of World War I in these terms in a much-quoted panegyric. The Allied victory, he said, was one for "humanitarianism, of pacifism; it is the victory of justice and liberty; it is the victory of democracy; it is the victory of socialism; it is the victory of Bolshevism; it is the victory of the red flag; it is the victory of the laboring class of the world; and it is the victory of the twentieth century's new tide. Rather than give Wilson and others the credit for this achievement, we should give the credit to Lenin, Trotsky, Collontay, to Lieb-knecht, Scheidemann, and to Marx. . . ."

This readiness to associate the future with the Russian Revolution received powerful support from the political skill the Bolsheviks showed in appealing to antiimperialist emotions. Surrounded by enemies, unable to profit from or uti-lize any of the gains their czarist predecessors had won abroad, the Bolsheviks tried to deny the profit of these positions to their White Russian enemies. In Manchuria the revenues from the Russian-controlled part of the Chinese Eastern Railway and the payments of the Boxer indemnity due the Russians were going into the treasuries of counterrevolutionary armies. Thus it made sense for Chicherin, the commissar for foreign affairs, to propose in July 1918 that the Soviets renounce all conquests "in Manchuria and restore the sovereign rights of China in this territory" and that they also "renounce all indemnities." A year later the Council of People's Commissars issued, through Karakhan, the proposal that made this a formal offer to the Chinese people. Though long delayed in transit for reasons never wholly clear, this proposal stirred the stu-dents of Peking mightily just when they were most frustrated by their country's inability to make any headway with the Allies at the Paris conference. That Rus-sian magnanimity declined as Russian power returned was less important than the fact that these pronouncements, when coupled with Lenin's theoretical assault on imperialism, seemed to substantiate the Russians' claims to inaugurate the postimperialist era.

The period after the great war is an extremely difficult one to study or de-scribe. We know what came out of it and run the risk of exaggerating the con-temporary importance of currents that later became dominant. It is easy to remember the anti-Japanese currents in modern China and overlook the large areas of mutual stimulation between the young generations of China and Japan. Much of the story could have turned out differently, and if it had, historians would now stress quite different themes in studying the same years. Yet they would in any case have to begin with the intellectual and student world, for it set the terms of dialogue for decades to follow.

Issues and problems resonated with each other, and maladjustments that might have remained minor instead became sympathetic vibrations and ended by becoming uncontrollable oscillations. The pattern of internal reaction and response, of resonance, must occupy the historian. Thus the Russian Revolution came at a time when Japan under General Terauchi was able to influence a warlord government in north China. It led to Japanese intervention in Siberia, an alliance between Terauchi and the warlord Tuan Ch'i-jui and massive financial assistance for Tuan, already the richer for Nishihara's work. Warlord acquiescence strengthened the Japanese hand in maintaining their Shantung holdings at the Paris Peace Conference. News of the failure to oust the Japanese from Shantung at Paris sparked the great student demonstrations of the May Fourth movement in China. Wilson's promises and presence in Paris also brought independence demonstrations in Korea. Dismayed by waves of anti-Japanese sentiment on the continent, discontented with the intervention against the Russian Revolution and impatient with the continuation of Chōshū rule in Japan, a new student left began to organize in Tokyo. The Chinese demonstrations, together with the pressures from Japanese militarism and setbacks in Europe, led the Russian revolutionaries to reconsider their priorities of revolution in Europe and to sponsor the slogans of Chicherin and Karakhan in China. Within a few years Russian representatives were working smoothly with Sun Yat-sen and the new nationalist leaders in China, while Japanese conservatives associated that nationalism with communism. Bit by bit national, political and social revolutions drew nearer to each other in China. The background for this entire process began with cultural revolution among middle and upper class students.

2. Intellectual Trends in Taishō Tokyo

THE MEIJI EMPEROR was succeeded by his son, who adopted the era name of Taishō, in 1912. The first decade of his brief reign was a period of profound change in Japanese intellectual life. The world that Tokyo students knew in those years was complex, and the conventional antithesis of soldiers and politicians does it little justice. Power had passed from the hands of the first generation of modernizers, for whom goals of national equality had merged with ideals of self-achievement. This group of nation builders had been replaced by a generation that had come to maturity during the years when Japanese were working out a sense of identity and role in the modern world. The new generation had been educated in Japanese institutions. Foreign study had come later and was no longer the center of education. By this time every facet of Western thought and writing was available in Japanese translation. Japanese institutions were substantially adequate to modern needs, and the Taishō generation had readied itself for positions of responsibility in the agencies devised by the first-generation modernizers. Many of them knew more about the West than their fathers had, but they knew it less directly and less at first hand. They were entering a structured society, one less tolerant of nonconformity than that of Meiji. The ideas of imperial rule and authority had become an ideology that permeated most areas of Japanese life. "We believe," said the founders of a church that was formed in Tokyo in 1907, "that all authorities are sanctioned by God as taught in the Bible and are presided over by the line of emperors for ages eternal." Leading thinkers faced the problem of reconciling their views of nationality and nation with the growing complexity of life and thought.

Because Japanese intellectual as well as institutional life was structured, it is useful to begin at the top. Japan's leading philosophers strove to find an integrated pattern of thought in a synthesis of traditional and Western ethics. The most eminent was Nishida Kitarō, of Kyoto University, whose *Study of the Good* (1911) is probably the most important work of philosophy in modern Japan. Nishida was unwilling to accept either the orthodox insistence on national uniqueness or the individualistic ethics of the West. Instead he reached back to Zen Buddhism for mystical insight that he related to aesthetic experience. The Zen concept of negation was central to his approach, and he combined this with German idealistic philosophy. While insisting upon individual experience, Nishida had no place for individual control of that experience. He had no role for the remaking of society by the individual, and he had little to say to young men impatient with their society. Although his ideas were expressed in the vocabulary of modern philosophy, they owed more to traditional thought than they did to Western sources. Yet, as a philosophical exposition of the powerlessness of the individual to alter his destiny, Nishida's work is central to modern Japanese experience. His emphases superseded and canceled out the facile optimism of the Meiji cult of Spencer, Darwin, Smiles and the other high priests of the religion of progress. In this respect Japanese intellectuals were simply keeping step with their Western counterparts, for whom the years around World War I meant the end of the conviction of endless progress. Thus the philosopher Watsuji Tetsurō, a colleague of Nishida's at Kyoto, translated Shaw as well as Byron, introduced to Japan existential thought with books on Nietzsche in 1913 and Kierkegaard in 1915, and then returned to the study of early Japanese culture.

Just as the principal schools of philosophy in Japan tended to draw attention away from problems of political and social action, widely read authors showed the same preference for aesthetics and aloofness from the world of politics. Natsume Sōseki's concern with individual loneliness has already been mentioned. More striking is the fact that a school of naturalist novelists limited its efforts to description and made little attempt to arouse indignation or response from their readers. They produced, in the words of T. Arima, a kind of "urban-pastoral melancholy" in their treatment of twentieth-century Japan. A larger and still more influential school of literary men eschewed social criticism altogether. Neither nationalism nor protest interested them; instead their concerns were entirely subjective and personal. This left them poorly equipped with standards for social values and judgment; instead individual purity, honesty and sincerity became all that mattered. To quote the same critic, these men placed the individual in the center of the universe but endowed him only with the faculty to feel. Mushakōji Saneatsu, one of their number, wrote in 1917, "I am the only man given to me by nature. Unless I have a desire to fulfill this life of mine, how could I care for the lives of others?... Since I can neither love nor care for the lives of the others, nor influence their fate, it is a blessing that I can remain indifferent to the affairs of other people." To balance this aesthetic restraint, however, Mushakōji organized a utopian community based on the humanitarian ideas of Kropotkin, Tolstoy and idealistic socialists. Its members shared their property and tried to remove themselves from a world of contention and dispute. The movement aroused a lively interest on the part of a number of radical intellectuals in China in the period around the end of World War I.

YOSHINO SAKUZŌ (1878-1933, left). An educator and political philosopher, Yoshino was a key voice of democracy in Taisho Japan.
NATSUME SŌSEKI (1867-1916, right). Beginning as a student of English literature, Natsume taught at Tokyo Imperial University and became the foremost novelist of twentieth-century Japan.

Theoretical disputes within schools of law were particularly important because those schools, and especially Tokyo Imperial University, had been established as centers for training the people who ran Japan. By ordinances of 1887, Tokyo graduates were exempt from civil service examinations; their professors held bureaucratic status, and they themselves received better salaries for government posts than their fellows from other universities. Inevitably Tokyo law students thought of themselves as future officials. Their professors' intellectual orientation was therefore of particular importance for the future bureaucrats.

From the days of its first president, the Imperial University had been oriented toward German political thought. That thought centered on the concepts of *staatslehre* and *staatsrecht,* the philosophies of state and state law. These views were originally the products of a search for a systematic theory of state sovereignty. The state was seen as the incarnation of the national spirit, personified and credited with a substantive purpose. It was the agent of unification, liberation and preservation. It came to have an existence quite exterior and anterior to that of groups or agencies within it.

German *staatslehre* had much to commend it in Japan. The sources for the Meiji Constitution had been overwhelmingly German in origin. Itō and his colleagues had been especially receptive to the advice of Stein and Roesler. The intellectual and institutional tradition of the Imperial University owed much to German instructors and precedents. Their view of the mystic entity of the state had similarities to the mystique of *kokutai* (though there were also important differences) to make it seem the most appropriate approximation to the Japanese tradition.

Toward the end of the nineteenth century the theories of Georg Jellinek (1851–1911) came to emphasize the idea of the state as a juridical person possessed of sovereignty which it exercised through the persons or bureaus which constituted its organs. It was this cross between absolutism and constitutionalism that became the inspiration for liberal Japanese jurists. Jellinek was also a favorite source for Chinese students in Tokyo who wrote on political theory in late Meiji days. Alternatives to the strict-construction Shinto school of imperial absolutism also derived from the formulations of Jellinek.

The "organ" theory of the emperor, as it came to be called, could be traced as far back as Prince Itō, the father of the Constitution. "The monarch," he wrote at one point, "is not the ruler of the state, but is an organ of the state.... However, he occupies the highest position in the state. Besides, he possesses the public power.... The fact that the monarch is the possessor of the nation's constitution definitely does not mean that his rights and powers are unlimited ... [he] must first conform to fixed usages, and second, must accept the participation of other organs." It is not completely clear how Itō meant this to be taken, and he certainly said nothing of the sort in his official *Commentaries* on the Meiji Constitution.

By the turn of the century, the organ theory had found its official statement in the work and career of the jurist and educator Minobe Tatsukichi

(1873–1948). A graduate of Tokyo Imperial University, Minobe had several years of study and travel abroad before he returned to take his post as a professor of law at the university in 1902. By 1912 he was engaged in a vigorous polemic with a more conservative colleague, Uesugi Shinkichi, on the applicability of the organ theory to Japanese constitutionalism. "In present day legal terms," Minobe argued, "Japan's national policy does not differ in pattern from the constitutional monarchies of Europe ... the state alone is the subject of governmental power, and the monarch is an organ of the state." For Minobe priority lay with the power of the state, which belonged to the nation as an everlasting community; "to say that in a monarchical system the state power belongs to the monarch," he wrote, "means that the monarch as an organ of the nation possesses the power of governance. But the sovereign is an organ of the nation; in other words, governance is not his private possession but the public affair of the nation." This does not seem very radical in the 1970s. But in early Taishō Japan it was remarked that Minobe's views were somewhat difficult to reconcile with the words and claims of the Meiji Constitution, whose imperial prologue made it clear that "the rights of sovereignty of the state, we have inherited from Our Ancestors, and We shall bequeath them to our Descendants."

More striking than this view was Minobe's tendency to group Japan's state structure with that of all other countries and consequently to make the Meiji constitutional order one which might be compared to others without specific reference to the mystic aura of Shinto deity and eternal succession. Such, at least, was the view of Minobe's scholarly colleague, Uesugi, who denounced him as a sort of traitor. Oddly enough, Uesugi had studied with Jellinek, while Minobe had not. Uesugi was a Western dandy, Minobe ungracious and pugnacious; he was an unprepossessing lecturer, remote and aloof, who usually wore Japanese dress. Uesugi, who graded examinations more generously, was somewhat the more popular of the two. Between them these men educated a generation of Japanese jurists and public servants.

It is not surprising that the clash between Minobe and Uesugi in 1912 had its political ramifications. That year was one of popular outrage over the dumping of the Saionji cabinet by the military and Katsura's abortive effort to form his own party and cabinet. It was the first time the imperial Diet had failed to heed an imperial rescript. Minobe was with Saionji and the political party men, while Uesugi was with the bureaucrats of the old school. Uesugi took alarm when Minobe, in talks to lower-school teachers, used the ideas about the emperor as organ that he had expounded in university lectures, and charged his rival with poisoning the minds of the public. Uesugi became the constitutional authority of the old guard and lectured at the service academies, while Minobe was widely sought by private universities. The times were with Minobe. Uesugi found himself isolated as the great war shattered Germany and the cult of state power, and Minobe won the support of his colleagues, who no doubt feared the effects of Uesugi's attempts to rally extrauniversity support for an intellectual battle. Minobe's victory was accompanied by a strong tide of journalistic and popular interest in democratic doctrine. Movements for universal manhood suffrage, labor organization, tenancy reform and curbs on militarism were in the air, and Minobe's formulation seemed to provide an approved and conservative mandate for limitation of the state structure.

It is possible to exaggerate Minobe's liberalism. The attack of ultrarightists on him in the 1930s derived more from their need of an academic-intellectual target than it did from the "dangers" inherent in his writings, and when he was one of a group charged with constitutional revisions after the Japanese surrender in 1945, his suggestions proved much too modest to satisfy postwar democrats. This may, however, have reflected his alarm at the radicalism of that day as well as his belief that the Meiji Constitution itself, properly interpreted, had room for the development of party government under a limited monarchy. Whatever the case, there is no doubt that the prevalence of Minobe's opinions in the early years of the Taishō period signified a willingness on the part of members of the Japanese elite to consider relatively liberal interpretation of the Meiji Constitution as a natural prelude to government by political parties.[1]

Minobe remained within the confines of approved academic and political orthodoxy. This was not as true of his younger colleague at Tokyo Imperial University, Professor Yoshino Sakuzō. Yoshino combined greater orthodoxy in political theory with far more thoroughgoing and radical suggestions for political action. Yoshino (1878–1933) came from a merchant family in northern Japan. Like many others of his generation, he became and remained a Christian. This, it may be noted, was also true of many "outsiders" from the northeast who were educated in a world dominated by Satsuma and Chōshū men. Christians had also been numerous among the leaders of the social democratic movement. Five of the six who founded the first organization in 1901 were Christians. Yoshino graduated from Tokyo Imperial University in 1906 and accepted a post in China. For three years he served as tutor for Yüan Shih-k'ai's son, as adviser to Yüan and as consultant for the formation of the Peking University Law School. Yoshino's China years were important to him, for they sensitized him to Chinese nationalism. He learned about the activities of Sun Yat-sen's Japanese friends like Miyazaki, and when he was asked to prepare a history of the Chinese revolutionary movement in 1916, he found sources and contacts among the group of liberals and idealists who had given their enthusiasm and lives for Pan-Asianism.

Yoshino returned from China in 1909 and began lecturing at Tokyo Imperial University. Soon afterward he left on a tour like the one Minobe had taken, spending three years in America and Western Europe. He seems to have been strongly aware of the rising strength of the world social democratic movement, of the labor movement (he experienced a general strike in Belgium) and of the shrinking of aristocratic privilege (he saw the Lords lose their legislative power in England). Yoshino returned to Japan to resume his teaching in 1913. It

---

[1] In 1974 Minobe's son, an economist, was the popular governor of Tokyo.

was a year of political turmoil in Tokyo, the year of Sun Yat-sen's second (and abortive) revolution, and it was the eve of the great European war. Yoshino now began writing for the popular *Central Review* (*Chūō Kōron*), and it was in that journal that he leaped to fame in 1916 with an article entitled "The True Meaning of Constitutional Government and Methods by Which it can be Perfected."

Yoshino was not an enthusiast of the *staatslehre* school of Minobe, and he spent no time disputing the source of sovereignty under the Meiji Constitution. He granted that popular sovereignty was totally inappropriate to Japan, which had always been monarchical and where loyalty was the essence of the national polity. Japan might not have democracy (*minshushugi*); but it did, or should, have *minponshugi*. The distinction between the terms lies in the second element; the first implies popular sovereignty, while the second means that the people and their welfare are the state's first concern. The term was not new with Yoshino. Its origin is found in the Confucian classics, it was urged upon rulers by Tokugawa Confucian advisers, who credited it to the first emperor of the T'ang dynasty, a contemporary journalist had used it in contrast to militarism and even Uesugi Shinkichi, Minobe's rival, used the term to indicate the concern of the sovereign for his people. But Yoshino used it as a Japanese variant of Western democracy, and in modern usage it came to retain the meaning which he gave it.

Yoshino's concerns were pragmatic. If it could be taken as axiomatic that good government, and therefore Japanese government, made popular welfare its principal concern, then it had to follow that expressions of popular will and concern would provide authorization for what that government did. Furthermore it was clearly part of the task of government to raise popular political consciousness by education and participation in decision making through representative government. Yoshino thus proceeded from somewhat conventional postulates to invoke a sanction for political modernization and reform of the Meiji constitutional system. Conservatives like Uesugi were quick to take alarm; they attacked Yoshino's focus upon parliament and the will of the people and implied that this was tantamount to interference with the imperial prerogative. Radicals, meanwhile, attacked Yoshino for avoiding the issue of sovereignty and deprecated his views as a new form of elitism. Yoshino's replies showed his readiness to work from practical grounds toward changes in the political order. He had no quarrel with expositions of the emperor's sovereign powers, he wrote, but direct imperial rule was no longer feasible in the complex society of his day. To deny limitations on the emperor was therefore to provide a carte blanche for despotic power for those who could claim to represent the throne. Any emperor, he argued, needed assistance, and "if one wished validly to reject democracy, one would have to go a step further and prove that it is always bad to take counsel with many men and always good to take counsel with few men."

Yoshino went on to criticize the "few" of his day, the new plutocracy, the elder statesmen, and the military. He advocated ways of educating the electorate so that its opinions would be sound and its actions wise. He was a leading figure in the fight for universal manhood suffrage that was successful in 1925, and he was a powerful force in arguing for greater powers for the lower house of the imperial Diet. He called for legislation to reduce the corruption and manipulation of the election process by the party in power, and he wrote about the need for an independent judiciary. In 1922, when he was at the top of his journalistic influence, Yoshino drew on the experience and disgust with Japan's Siberian intervention to argue against the special channels to imperial influence which the Meiji structure had reserved for the supreme command of the army and navy. "Dual government," in which the military could arrange things their own way with the throne and bring down civilian cabinets that refused to cooperate, he described as "Japan's unique parliamentary disease," and he deplored the "arrogance" of the military. The emperor and nation should be one, he argued; they should speak and act as one, and divided or dual government could only distort the picture. To abandon the military's privilege of direct access was "to stop this abnormal system, to include all national responsibility in the sphere of the advice of the government, and then to hope for the unified activity of the sovereign."

Yoshino's analysis did not end here. He went on to advocate stripping away the special prerogatives of military privilege, the military ordinances that did not require the prime minister's countersignature, the restriction of service ministry posts to active duty (and, since 1914, retired) professional officers, the original Cabinet Organization Ordinance which removed military affairs from the area of collective ministerial responsibility and the independence of the general staffs. He argued that these things had been instituted at a time when it was feared that ignorant commoners would have no idea of national goals and danger. They had been strengthened when the military saw personal danger in the growing democratic movement. But now that the electorate was more mature, and now that Japanese constitutionalism had come of age, it was time to regard these institutions as anachronisms and get rid of them. Yoshino, operating from an impeccable basis of imperial sovereignty, thus went further toward practical reformation than Minobe did.

These were not sheltered academic arguments. Yoshino took full part in the public controversies of his day. In 1918 a group of superpatriots took umbrage at a presumed slight to the imperial government contained in one of his articles. Some toughs of the Imperial Nation Youth League (Kōkoku seinen kai) assaulted the publisher and tied him to a stone lantern with a placard explaining that heavenly punishment (a cliché of Restoration activists) had been visited on the traitor. Yoshino denounced this as hooliganism, and soon young stalwarts from the Great People's National Essence party were visiting his classes and seminars. In November a public debate was arranged with members of the Rōnin Association. On the day of the debate several thousand people, many of them university students who were championing Yoshino's cause, jammed the hall. Yoshino carried the day with his eloquence and emerged to a hero's welcome from the jubilant crowd that trailed along behind him as he slowly made his way home.

As with Minobe, so with Yoshino: progressive opinions stirred the fears of conservatives that old values were being abandoned. The collapse of monarchy in China, Germany and Russia alarmed Japanese conservatives, but the consciousness of change exhilarated Japanese students. The end of Japan's wartime profits brought unemployment, strikes and massive urban riots directed against the high price of rice. University students were likely to question goals that had long been taken for granted. Political office, once the goal of every ambitious young man, now appeared to be the preserve of mediocrity. Yoshino provided a link between theory and organization.

Shortly after the debate just described Yoshino and other liberal scholars formed the Dawn Society (Reimeikai). At first it had twenty-three members, and even when it disbanded two years later it numbered only forty-two. This was still a small elite. Monthly lecture and discussion meetings were held to rouse support for liberalism and to "eradicate dangerous bigoted thought." Then in December 1918, young law students at Tokyo Imperial University organized the "New Man Society" (Shinjinkai) to "collaborate with the new movement for the liberation of humanity which is the cultural trend of the world" and to "engage ourselves in the rational reform movement of present-day Japan." Within three months the group was publishing a magazine and trying to organize a labor union. In 1921 the group's activities and membership were limited to make it a purely student organization. By the mid-1920s it had become a largely communist front group, and in 1929, after extensive police raids, its remaining members agreed to dissolve the organization. Yet the Shinjinkai, Tokyo Imperial University–centered, was the most important student group of those years. Branches or parallel groups with the same or similar names flowered on other major campuses in Japan. Many of them tried to make contacts with labor and tenants, but their principal focus remained on students. This represented an enlightenment movement among the new and future elite, and it stands as the forerunner of the modern Japanese, and in a sense the East Asian, student movements.

The Shinjinkai's roots were in the confused ideological setting of its day. In the recollections of one member, "The ideologies of political democracy, bolshevism, social democracy, syndicalism, the IWW, guild socialism, anarchism, Fabianism, and national socialism were all blooming at once, like spring in the north country, presenting a beautiful scene of many colors." Members included future communist leaders like Nozaka Sanzō, Miyazaki Ryūnosuke, the son of the China adventurer Miyazaki Tōten, and a wide spectrum of future leaders in Japanese society. Their enthusiasm was for self-realization and participation in a new, romantic and intensely humanitarian movement. "While we do not believe in the whole of Marx's material view of history," said one article in the organization's periodical, "we are deeply moved by the example of his moral life, he who sacrificed everything and died a martyr for the great cause of human emancipation."

Yoshino and his student followers were also part of the antiimperialist tide of their day, even though the imperialism they knew was their own. Yoshino was highly sympathetic to the Korean independence movement and encouraged Korean students in Tokyo in every way he could. The Shinjinkai periodical predicted that "at the proper time the pent-up resistance of the Korean people will turn to riot. This is not the fault of the Koreans, but of the privileged, militaristic Japanese rulers. We are deeply ashamed that this sort of rule is being conducted in Korea ... we feel shame that Japanese should possess the sort of ruthless disposition that seeks its own gain through the unjust plunder of others, and that oppresses the weak through force. True victory can be won only with an encompassing love and broad mind." Yoshino's China experience had also made him aware of the importance of Chinese nationalism. After the May Fourth movement he organized a tour of Chinese student leaders to meet with their Japanese contemporaries, and he published articles pointing out that anti-Japanese sentiments in China were directed at the Japanese bureaucracy and militarism and not at the Japanese people. He warned that

> China's ominous anti-Japanese feelings will not be assuaged by aiding the pro-Japanese faction ... and thereby oppressing the Chinese people. Instead, we must try to restrain the policy of the military and financial leaders toward China and communicate the peaceful desires of the Japanese people to our friends in China. It is for these ends that we have worked for many years to liberate our beloved Japan from the bureaucrats and the militarists. Are the aims of the Chinese student movement any different from ours?

To a Chinese friend at Peking he wrote, "Aggressive Japan is not only opposed by the youth of your country, but also by us."

Immediately after the May Fourth incident, the Reimeikai exchanged messages with the Student Union of the Republic of China. The daily *Asahi* had also been bitterly critical of Japanese government policy since the Terauchi loans to the Peking warlords; it charged Terauchi with efforts to crush democracy in Japan by helping to stifle democracy in China and described military assistance to Tuan Ch'i-jui and Chang Tso-lin as the Middle Ages in Japan reaching out to perpetuate the Middle Ages in China. One is struck by the consciousness of common interests and problems between the emerging middle-class, liberal groups in Japan and in China. Coincidentally, but also symbolically, the Shinjinkai met in a house that had been entrusted to Miyazaki by the Chinese revolutionary Huang Hsing.

Before very long, other Japanese intellectuals went beyond Minobe and Yoshino to challenge the very bases of modern Japanese society. Kawakami Hajime moved from Mushakoji's humanitarianism to Marx's materialism. Nozaka Sanzō began in the New Man Society and persevered into the Marxist effort for an entirely new society. The communist movement as a social and political force belongs to a later date in Japanese history. During the first decade of Taishō, however, modern Japanese liberalism was in its springtime of idealism and optimism. In 1924 Yoshino decided to resign his Tokyo Imperial University post to become a free-lance writer and critic for the *Asahi,* a post he held only four months before leaving formal employment altogether for a life of scholarship and political commentary. He continued to warn against the dangers of militarist and undemocratic influences in Japanese government, and his overall orientation remained Christian and humanist. In 1926 he helped organize the Social Democratic party.

However real the ferment among Japanese students in the years after World War I, the numbers of those actively involved in organizational effort remained modest, and their efforts to reach out to other groups in Japanese society were abortive. Their intellectual mentors were for the most part members of the academic establishment. What distinguished this movement from its counterparts in Korea and China was a lack of intensity born of national outrage and humiliation. Japan had achieved its national goals, and its young men knew a reasonably modern and structured society in which they could expect to function. There was nothing comparable to the unifying force of national humiliation that produced the movements of Korea and China.

3. *The Korean Independence Movement*

MODERN KOREA dates its national consciousness from a nonviolent protest against Japanese rule in 1919. On 1 March of that year, thirty-three leading citizens met in Seoul to issue a declaration of independence they had drawn up. They met for dinner, drank a toast to independence, read their declaration and then sent copies to the governor general and telephoned the police that they were ready for arrest. Similar demonstrations came elsewhere throughout Korea; the group in Seoul represented the apex of a national movement. In all, over two million Koreans were involved.

As was to be expected of the country last opened, soonest conquered, and most slowly modernized, the Korean story was very different from those of China and Japan. The nationalist protest was expressed in part as respect for a regime that had disappeared, and it found powerful support among the groups most affected by the Christian teachings which modern Chinese youth were finding objectionable. Yet in timing, language and organization the protest was entirely a product of the twentieth century. It was the first great demonstration of nonviolent resistance in the twentieth century, and its suppression by the fearful Japanese gendarmerie was accompanied by practices more appropriate to Hideyoshi than to Hara.

The rise of nationalist consciousness in Korea was in large degree a product of Japanese rule. Japan's administrators unified the peninsula by an arbitrary and uniform process of administration. They were often impartially brutal and indifferent to Korean sensibilities. Their conduct had the effect of lessening the deep divisions of status, class and region that had operated to limit the response to earlier challenges to sectional and regional groups. Earlier imperialist rivalry in Korea had had the effect of creating divisions within the elite oriented toward Russian, European, American or Japanese assistance, but the occupation of the peninsula by Japan changed most of this into an "either-or" confrontation in which attitudes toward Japan became the principal issue.

The harshness of the military administration which General Terauchi inaugurated in 1910 accelerated this process. Within three years, over six hundred publications were closed down. Japanese police, both civil and military, were given administrative and judicial responsibilities from which there was no appeal. A vast army of minor functionaries fastened Japanese control upon even local and minor institutions. As customary tenure gave way to "modern" legal titles, an Oriental Development Company that had been established in 1907 came to hold enormous grants of land through purchase (often regarded as confiscation by Koreans) and reclamation. Improvements in irrigation resulted in increased productivity, but the benefits were often for Japanese. It did not seem to Koreans that, as the Meiji emperor's annexation rescript of 1910 had promised, "All Koreans, being under Our direct sway, will enjoy growing prosperity and welfare," although it was undeniable that "with assured repose and security will come a marked expansion in industry and trade." By 1919 official Japanese sources reported that acreage of arable land had increased by 54 percent. A good deal of this was probably the result of more efficient taxation surveys. But even if production increased, "forced savings" of state-directed modernization projects prevented any great rise in per capita well-being from becoming apparent.

Nationalism grew in response to Japanese methods. By 1913 a "New People's Society" headed by a Western-educated Christian leader had become sufficiently successful in spreading ideas of national independence through schools, books and clubs for the Japanese authorities to stage a series of "conspiracy trials" in attempts to prove that the organization had conspired to assassinate Governor General Terauchi. After Terauchi succeeded Ōkuma as prime minister of Japan in 1916 (to preside over the Nishihara loans to China and the rice riots of 1918), his successor, General Hasegawa, continued the same stern repression of civil liberties and freedoms in Korea.

Japanese influence also made for an increase in modern education and a modest, though steady, increase in the numbers of Korean students in Japan. In 1917 these numbered over 650. As Japanese educators were added to the considerable numbers of Western, often missionary, teachers in Korea, the sources of modern learning and consciousness grew steadily. Since Japan was one of the Allied nations during World War I, the Japanese press reported war developments and major pronouncements for Koreans. This, added to the strong American mission movement, meant free entry into Korea for the Wilsonian phrases of "self-determination" and "democracy." A group of American sympathizers even prepared large printings of inexpensive editions of Wilsonian statements. Groups of exiled nationalist leaders formed to exploit whatever opportunities these phrases and the world climate might offer for the reassertion of Korean independence. Major centers for such groups were the United States, Hawaii and China, especially Shanghai. Efforts were made to send Syngman Rhee to Paris to plead the Korean cause at the peace conference, but these were discouraged by the Department of State. Kim Koo Sic, another nationalist leader, was successful in fulfilling his travel plans, although his political goals were equally unattainable.

The text of the Korean independence declaration of 1 March 1919 was put together after it was clear that the Wilsonian rhetoric in the Treaty of Versailles had no carry-over for Koreans. Yet it contained unmistakable evidence of the effect of the wartime slogans. It made reference to the new and promising role of the United States in the Far East, as it did to Wilson's Fourteen Points, and emphasized their importance for the emergence of new nations. Only then did it rise to its peroration: "Think, our compatriots! Now is the great opportunity to reform the world and recover our ruined nation. If the entire nation rises in unity we may recover our lost national rights and save the already ruined nation ... rise!"

The independence movement was remarkable for the evidence it provided of Korea's progress toward a sense of nationhood. The cooperation of the several religious communities in Korea was particularly impressive. Of these, the Buddhist had been moribund until the Japanese occupation had breathed new life into it. Buddhism had been virtually proscribed by the Confucian rigor of the Yi dynasty, and its clergy had been assigned a particularly low social rank. But the Japanese had not only removed all restrictions upon Buddhism but encouraged mission efforts by Japanese Buddhists in order to strengthen the bonds between the two nations. Buddhist abbots were thus included in the Preparatory Committee that began planning for an independence day demonstration in Seoul late in 1918.

More important than Buddhism by far was the national cult of the Tonghaks who became renamed the Ch'ŏndogyo (The Religion of the Heavenly Way) in 1905. After its proscription by the faltering government of the Yi dynasty the Tonghak movement tended to seek increasingly close ties with Japan. Its leader, Son Pyong-hi, had assumed the title of "Holy Teacher" in 1898. Like his predecessors, he desired the elimination of Korea's discriminatory class structure and consequently saw much to approve in some of the modernizing measures the Japanese were forcing upon the Seoul government. He devoted his early efforts to reorganizing the Tonghak movement, including a return to its earlier patterns of nonviolent resistance. In 1901 Son moved to Japan, where he resided for the next five years. At that time association with the Japanese was still to be preferred to persecution by the Korean government. Son favored Korean support for the Japanese in their struggle with Russia and saw in this the best guarantee of Korean independence.

These hopes were not fulfilled; in 1905 the Korean government was forced to accept the Japanese protectorate of Itō Hirobumi, as has already been described. But when part of the Tonghak organization chose to continue its cooperation with Japan despite the hazards of Japanese control, and when one group went so far as to amalgamate an indigenous Progress Society with a Japanese-sponsored Advance Society (Ilchinhoe) under Japanese sponsorship and to permit its utilization to demonstrate "popular" support for Japanese annexation, Son Pyong-hi renamed his organization. He also "modernized" his movement by incorporating practices suggestive of Christianity. These included a regular ritual, a baptism with water, a regular offering in "sincerity rice," prayer and the setting apart of Sunday as a day of rest and worship. Vigorous evangelization and a new organization transformed a movement of the superstitious and disadvantaged into a formally organized and officially tolerated cult. Middle and upper level schools trained future leaders for Ch'ŏndogyo.

The Ch'ŏndogyo movement enjoyed Japanese toleration because its leaders and predecessors had cooperated with the Japanese until the time of the Russo-Japanese War, and some of its offshoots continued to serve Japanese purposes even after that time. Under the reforms of Son Pyong-hi its rationalization paralleled some of the modernization the Japanese were bringing to the land. Its resources helped provide the expenses involved in the Independence Day protests of 1919, and Son Pyong-hi himself was among its representatives on the National Preparatory Committee for that day.

But it was the vigorous and vital Protestant Christian community of Korea that was the major element in the independence movement. Principally Methodist and Presbyterian in origin, its roots were American and its tradition was one of local self-government. The message of Christianity had a particular relevance to Koreans who suffered the humiliation and injustice of a foreign non-Christian oppressor. Christians had led in modern learning and education. Japanese authorities were suspicious of the native Christian community because of its American friends, and they usually assumed that Christians were at the bottom of whatever trouble they encountered in Korea. The ability of missionaries and the Christian Church to identify with Korean nationalism in opposition to foreign oppression thus made conditions for proselytizing dramatically different from those to be found in China or Japan. In Japan nationalism was in the service of the state, and in China the Church seemed an extension of Western cultural subversion and control.

By the fall of 1918 groups of Koreans representing the major religious communities agreed that it was important to bring their country's plight to the attention of the outside world by sponsoring an orderly, nonviolent and nationwide demonstration that would dramatize Korea's desire for the return of its independence. A national headquarters was set up in Seoul with branch offices in each of the provinces. Each cooperating group took the responsibility for enlisting its own people. The Christians were the natural channels for communication with President Wilson and other Western statesmen at the Paris Peace Conference. Ch'ŏndogyo representatives charged themselves with preparation and distribution of the declaration of independence and of memorandums to the Japanese government. Korean students in Tokyo met to coordinate their efforts with those of their fellow nationals at home, and ties with Korean communities and leaders in China and elsewhere were utilized extensively. Remarkably, in a setting in which defectors could have earned rich rewards by informing the ever-suspicious Japanese police, this nationwide effort escaped Japanese detection.

The timing of the demonstration was provided by the defunct royal house. The former Yi dynasty emperor died suddenly in January 1919 amid rumors that the Japanese had poisoned him because of his refusal to sign an assurance that it was his desire that Korea remain united with Japan. His funeral was set for 3 March, and as it neared, white mourning garments were seen all over the country. Children were kept home from school, traditional New Year festivities were suspended and thousands of mourners began converging on the capital city of Seoul. In Tokyo, at a meeting of Korean students, one speaker related the emperor's death to the slavery of his people, stressed the opportunity provided by the Paris Peace Conference and capped his eloquence by cutting his finger to write in blood a petition asking the Japanese Diet for national independence. The day selected for the demonstration was 1 March. It could be anticipated that Seoul would be crowded with mourners for the royal funeral. The signers of the declaration of independence met together, read their declaration and awaited arrest. Similar ceremonies were held throughout Korea, and the movement did not subside until the latter part of April.

The Japanese response was quick, direct and brutal. Japanese records make note of 848 "incidents" and 26,713 arrests. Japanese estimates of Koreans killed and injured are 553 and 1,409 respectively, while postindependence Korean historical compilations produce figures of 7,645 killed and 45,562 wounded. Since only 2 Japanese civilians and 6 gendarmes were killed, these figures reveal the brutality of Japan's treatment of an unarmed and largely unresisting movement for national liberation. Japanese methods drew protests throughout the world and left a legacy of hatred for Japan in Korea that has become part of the story of the independence movement. On the Korean side, the evidence of organization. moderation and courage provided, as the organizers had hoped it would, remarkable evidence of the desire for independence, although it was achieved at great cost in suffering. Thereafter the principal burden of agitation for independence had to be carried by Koreans outside their own country. A provisional government had already been selected by a small group which met secretly in Seoul before the Independence Day demonstration. The first group was organized in China and operated there until the Japanese defeat in World War II. Other groups supplemented it. It was from this shifting, unsatisfactory base that the nationalist leader Syngman Rhee carried on his attempt to bring the cause of Korea to the attention of the world's statesmen until 1945.

It is apparent that in range and depth the Korean movement was very different from those of Japan or China. Nevertheless the statistics of participants establish it as a Korean version of the generational ferment that was so marked elsewhere in East Asia. One-third of those arrested by the Japanese were under the age of twenty-five. Large numbers of women participated. The role of Korean Christians was particularly marked, and Ch'ŏndogyo was able to participate only because it had remodeled its organization on the Christian model. Conspicuously absent was any indication of Confucian ideology, participation or organization. The movement thus marked a new era and beginning in Korean culture. It was one in which Japan would play a role and one which Japan, by its occupation, had helped universalize. But it was also one that would focus on the Japanese presence as the first and greatest of Korea's problems.

It should be added that the brutality of the Japanese suppression of the independence movement drew protests in Japan as well as from abroad and that it provided part of the spark for the opposition to militarism and imperialism that characterized postwar Japanese youth movements. Under Prime Minister Hara the Japanese government attempted to civilize its administrators and their methods. The army governor general was replaced by a retired admiral, and Hara sought reforms that would demilitarize the Japanese police, establish local self-government and introduced the applicability of Japanese constitutional guarantees. Unhappily Japanese extremism drew a Korean response with attacks on several leading Japanese, including the new governor general, and prevented the implementation of much of this program. Instead the foreign community in Korea was wooed with receptions and rewards, a few pro-Japanese Koreans were appointed to high office and a limited number of Korean newspapers were allowed to publish. The budgetary pressures caused by Japan's postwar economic setbacks restricted reforms to inexpensive ones, with the result that substantial moves toward improvements in schooling and communications were long deferred. The major reforms became those working for law and order, with an impressive increase in the number of Japanese police. With more intensive and pervasive control, sporadic and irrational brutality became less likely and less possible. For Korean youth, however, the Japanese presence remained the great fact and barrier to self-realization and self-expression.

It is important to note that Japanese control of Korea constituted one of the great exceptions to the ebb tide of imperialist control that has been described. Moreover, it represented imperialism on a scale that was unknown in East Asia before the twentieth century. European control and occupation of subject areas was everywhere nonintensive, and the European presence was relatively light. Throughout Southeast Asia it came to areas in which national consciousness was little advanced, and it usually operated to knit together areas that had not known modern communication or administrative unity. Affected, however modestly, by Christian and modernizing consciences at home, Western imperialism also emphasized its benefits in education and well-being. Western control furthermore meant, for modernizing Asian intellectuals, control by a more "advanced" and consequently "esteemed" people, however complex the ambivalence of attitudes might be.

None of this obtained in the Japanese occupation of Korea. Japan's proximity and population density made possible an occupation of unusual density and intensity, one which was certain to rouse opposition. The poor and the carpetbaggers could afford to go to Korea and seek their fortunes in a way that was not true for English in India or French in Vietnam. Korea already had a fully developed national unity and tradition, one that was at least as old as Japan's. Its attitudes toward Japan were never those of admiration and esteem, and consequently Japanese occupation became more comparable to that of Britain over Ireland than to that of Europe over the non-West. Moreover it proved to be of short duration, a mere thirty-five years. Thus the mid-century decades found survivors of the original opposition to Japanese control mingling with young people who knew Japan only as the oppressor during World War II. Finally, a large and growing Korean minority in Japan contributed, through the discrimination it met, to the dislike of Japan in Korea. The antiimperialist concerns of young Japanese were more often expressed in theoretical and political opposition to their government's actions than they were in relations of personal warmth and cordiality with their Korean contemporaries.

4. *The Cultural Revolution in China*

THE RADICALISM of postwar days in China owed something to the stirrings in Japan, but there were many differences between them. In both cases there were strong currents of antimilitarist sentiment. There was a new freedom and liberalism, a beginning of feminism and a halting attempt, still imperfect, to reach out from the security of middle and upper class university contacts to reach workers and peasants. There were the same convictions that the war had spelled the end for autocracy and despotism and that the future belonged to democracy and liberalism.

Yet the movements were as different as Chinese militarism was from Japanese. Patriotic stirrings in a country as harassed by imperialist pressures as China meant that student rebellion there would embrace nationalism, while in Japan it began to reject it because it was in government service. Domestic disorder intensified the contrasts. From 1915 to 1922 China knew ten major civil wars, and fighting raged for more than forty-eight months. Japanese military activities in Siberia were more distant, less destructive and far less important in their effect. The sense of national humiliation was also very different. China had partaken in a European war that did not concern her in hopes of gaining relief from the pressures of imperialist, especially Japanese, demands. Instead Japan's secret treaties and its bribery of the Peking government denied her any gain. Chinese student frustration was the greater because it followed exuberant hopes. Nor were the stages of modernization in which these stirrings took place comparable. Japan's was a "second stage" awareness, coming as it did early in the final push for full-scale industrialization, operating on the basis of a functioning though still imperfect constitutional order, and set within the consciousness of the achievement of all important national goals. The intensity of the revulsion that young Chinese felt for their tradition could have been approximated only if the Meiji reforms had failed and if Japan had been struggling painfully to turn in new directions while handicapped by foreign pressures.

Many date the true birth of modern China from the events which centered around the great demonstrations of 4 May 1919 in Peking. These stand as symbol of the wider "May Fourth movement" which encompassed a literary revolution, a new tide of thought and philosophy, strikes and boycotts by students, merchants and workers and a modern nationalism. It brought with it a reevaluation of the Chinese tradition and a new emphasis on Western science and democracy. Above all, it provided in great student demonstrations the prototype of later student political activity in Asia. Its successes were claimed by many groups and factions, but its makeup was so many-sided that no single group can lay claim to all of it. The movement was nationalist and antiimperialist, but it was not in any important sense anti-Western or even, in more than the most immediate political sense, anti-Japanese. Ch'en Tu-hsiu, the most important figure among the intellectual leaders of the day, criticized "selfish nationalism and patriotism" as shoddy Japanese products that should be boycotted together with other Japanese imports. If China was to be subdued anyway, he thought, it did not make much difference who did it. But he preferred ideals like humanitarianism and justice to nationalism or patriotism. The Shinjinkai members in Tokyo, where Ch'en had studied, would have agreed wholeheartedly.

Again, the May Fourth principals were indeed radical in the sense that they went to the roots of problems, but they were not therefore Marxist and, still less, communist. They hardly ever used the terms of feudalism or imperialism in their Marxist sense, and their leaders, among them Ch'en Tu-hsiu, entered the Marxist fold only well after 1919. Nor, although the demonstrations were the closest China had yet come to a "national" movement, did they go far beyond the ranks of students, most of them upper class, in the modern schools of China. As laborers gradually joined the struggle, the focus was still on the modernized cities. In scale of participation, the May Fourth movement reflected the limited level of modernization and participation that was so large a part of China's problems in those years.

The cause for the outbreak of the demonstrations on 4 May is easily understood. Chinese had expected that their participation in World War I, which included a labor force of nearly two hundred thousand men that was sent to Europe, would entitle them to an honorable seat at the Paris Peace Conference and with it the opportunity to undo Japan's gains in Shantung. They had faith in the intentions and power of Woodrow Wilson to prevent Japan from violating "self-determination" by "annexations" and "secret diplomacy." The exact opposite proved to be the case. Secret treaties skillfully utilized by the Japanese enabled them to retain the German holdings in violation of Chinese desires.

China's mission to the Paris Conference contained representatives of both a "republican" south Chinese regime and the original Peking, now warlord-dominated, regime. Among the members of the latter group was Lu Cheng-hsiang,

LU HSÜN (Chou Shu-jen, 1881-1936, left). Educated in Japan, Lu Hsün was spokesman of the League of Chinese Left-Wing Writers and foremost novelist of the 1930s.
HU SHIH (1891-1926, right). Educated in the United States, Hu Shih was a philosopher and educator, and a leading advocate of pragmatism, scientific thought, and *pai-hua* style of writing.

who, as Yüan's foreign minister, had signed the capitulation to the Twenty-one Demands in 1915. In Paris these negotiators found their hands tied by two factors. One was the Japanese disclosure that they had come prepared with secret treaties whereby Great Britain, France and Italy had promised, in February 1917 (at the time when Chinese participation was being discussed) to support Japan's claims to Shantung. (The Bolsheviks had already exposed, and denounced, a similar Japanese agreement with the czarist government.) But equally damaging was the disclosure of an agreement of September 1918 that had been entered into by Peking officials in connection with the Nishihara loans to Tuan Ch'i-jui. The Chinese minister to Tokyo, Chang Tsung-hsiang, had gone on record that China "gladly accepted" Japanese proposals for Shantung railway management. The grounds for frustration were thus threefold. Japan had outmaneuvered, and America had failed, the Chinese, but in student eyes the real fault lay with traitorous officials who had bartered away their country for Japanese money.

Numerous autobiographical accounts spell out the despair and fury that possessed young Chinese when they heard this news. China's hopes of the peace had been betrayed everywhere. Spheres of interest, foreign troops, foreign post offices and telegraph communications, consular jurisdiction, extraterritoriality, leased territories, foreign concessions and fixed tariffs all remained in effect. It was in vain that Chinese had waited for the peace; in vain that they had celebrated the Allied victory; in vain that they had, in triumph, torn down the Peking statue of German Minister von Ketteler, long symbolic of the Boxer disgrace. Student meetings were held to endorse a statement lamenting that "They have been told that in the dispensation which is to be made after the war nations like China would have an opportunity to develop their culture, their industry, their civilization, unhampered. They have been told that secret covenants and forced agreements would not be recognized. They looked for the dawn of this new era; but no sun rose for China. Even the cradle of the nation [i.e. Shantung, homeland of Confucius] was stolen."

This disillusion was directed in good part toward America, for Woodrow Wilson had helped to dramatize the hopes now blasted. On 4 May, four student representatives tried to call on Minister Paul Reinsch. "The United States, whose hands were free, could have saved us all," they said, "by insisting on the right solution." "Probably nowhere else in the world," Minister Reinsch wrote, "had expectations of America's leadership at Paris been raised so high as in China. The Chinese trusted America, they trusted the frequent declarations of principle uttered by President Wilson, whose words had reached China in its remotest parts. The more intense was their disappointment and disillusionment due to the decisions of the old men that controlled the Paris Conference." "We had nothing to do with our Government," one participant wrote later, "that we knew very well, and at the same time we could no longer depend upon the principles of any so-called great leader like Woodrow Wilson.... Looking at our people and at the pitiful ignorant masses, we couldn't help but feel that we must struggle." [2]

Struggle they did. The target date for action was 7 May, "National Humiliation Day," the fourth anniversary of the Japanese ultimatum in 1915. As it became probable that political groups would use that day for other protests, the students decided to advance theirs, lest they be associated with causes not their own. On 3 May student leaders held a planning meeting in the Law School of Peking University. Plans were made to cable the delegates in Paris urging them not to sign the treaty, to send telegrams to all parts of China to arrange demonstrations, and to form a giant student demonstration at the centrally located Gate of Heavenly Tranquillity (T'ien An Men, the scene of Party spectaculars in the People's Republic in Peking). Emotions were taut. One law school student cut open his finger and wrote on the wall in blood, "Return our Tsingtao."

The Fourth of May was Sunday, and thirteen thousand students from thirteen colleges and universities gathered. Their manifesto denounced the Shantung settlement and warned that China would soon be annihilated. They called for demonstrations, protests and action against the "traitors at home." "Today we swear two solemn oaths with all our fellow countrymen: (1) China's territory

---

[2] Similar though less personal betrayal can be found in writings by Shinjinkai members studied by Henry Smith. Miyazaki Ryunosuke, criticizing division of the Turkish lands in Asia Minor in 1919, referred to Wilson as an "oppressor of humanity."

may be conquered, but it cannot be given away; (2) the Chinese people may be massacred, but they will not surrender. Our country is about to be annihilated. Up, brothers!" After an hour of speeches the demonstration moved toward the legation quarter. It carried great funeral scrolls dedicated to the "traitorous" ministers. Students shouted demands for death to those ministers as well as for refusal to sign the peace treaty; they demanded self-determination, justice and the return of Shantung. After failing to reach Minister Reinsch (and also the British, French and Italian ministers), the students became impatient and unruly under the irritation of police and gendarmerie. They now headed for the home of Ts'ao Ju-lin, where they surprised and badly beat the minister to Japan, Chang Tsung-hsiang. They narrowly missed Ts'ao himself who fled in disguise.

These events were the beginning, not the end. Students proceeded to organize sympathetic demonstrations in other areas and to persuade merchants to boycott Japanese-made goods. The response they received was sufficient to make it impossible for the Chinese commissioners to Paris to sign the Treaty of Versailles. Struggle and strife had now become the center of the students' values. The street demonstrations provided the focus for hitherto undirected feelings of frustration and rage at their impotence in the face of brute force. In the considerable amount of public and even covert police sympathy they evoked, the students helped to create a political consciousness in areas that had been politically dormant. It is impossible to consider the great demonstrations of the 1920s, or of the 1960s in Korea and Japan, or even the Red Guard movement of 1966, without thinking back to this first great explosion of student anger and enthusiasm in East Asia. Yet it was only the tremor of a cultural revolution that was ultimately far more important.

The cultural revolution was made possible by the growth of the modern academic sector in China. More Chinese than ever before were receiving education in modern knowledge. More of them were receiving it in Western countries. The student movement to Japan peaked shortly after the Russo-Japanese War. In 1918 it was estimated that perhaps 40 percent of Chinese who had been educated abroad had been to Japan, but in absolute numbers they had declined to perhaps one-fourth of their 1906 high. Movements of protest whereby large numbers returned, as at the time of the Twenty-one Demands and in 1919, served to emphasize the students' number and cohesion. On the other hand, by 1918 the growth of the Japanese educational plant and the superior preparation of Chinese students for their education in Japan had changed the chaotic conditions of Meiji years and produced a far more meaningful education. Still, the intellectual leaders of the postwar cultural revolution included proportionally more who had studied in the Western world. America's remission of its Boxer indemnity had made it possible for large numbers of Chinese to come to America. In 1911 Tsing Hua College was organized in Peking to prepare students for schooling in the United States; after 1914 women students were included as well. After the United States, France played the most important role in the education of Chinese students in the Western world. The presence of large numbers of Chinese laborers at the western front during World War I brought efforts to teach them to read in order to assist them in communications with the homeland. Shortly before the war Chinese students began experiments in cutting the cost of studying in France by combining work and study there. Although it is an area little studied, it seems reasonably clear that the community of Chinese students in Paris had an influence far beyond its numbers on later Chinese radicalism.

It is useful to compare these students, or at least their leaders, with the early Meiji Japanese who traveled to the West for prolonged periods of study. Like them, they went at an early age, and they often completed their formal education abroad. They drank deeply of modern knowledge at its source and seemed, and probably were, more "Western" and "modern" to non-Chinese who met them than did their Japanese contemporaries of the Minobe and Yoshino generation for whom foreign travel and study had become the reward for success in their own educational system. Upon returning to China they were advantaged by the directness of access they had enjoyed to Western schooling, rather than handicapped, as would have been true for Minobe if he had taken all his training abroad and returned without a Japanese degree. During the world war a remarkable group of Chinese returned to head their country's principal university. Ts'ai Yüan-p'ei, who served as minister of education after the founding of the Republic, returned from Leipzig to become chancellor of Peking University. His first appointment, as dean, was Ch'en Tu-hsiu, recently returned from Japan. Hu Shih and Chao Yuen Ren returned from the United States to professorships at the university. In age and intellectual vigor these men were quite different from the senior academic statesmen who controlled the Japanese university structure of their day. One writer considers Ts'ai's reorganization of Peking University as the "cause and symptom" of the cultural revolution. But if the Chinese scholars gained by not having to make their peace with deeply entrenched educational bureaucrats and with official ideology, they proved in the end the poorer for having to operate in relative isolation, cut off from influence in a society whose political problems brought increasing reliance upon military means to maintain the essentials of unification and direction.

Nevertheless these men exerted enormous intellectual and moral influence on young Chinese from their university posts. Theirs was a time of intense discussion in lectures and in periodicals. The most important of these publications was edited by Ch'en Tu-hsiu. Ch'en, like Hu Shih, reacted against a tradition in which publications seldom went beyond stultifying homilies on stereotyped themes. As Hu put it upon his return to China, "As a whole, the world of publication in Shanghai—the world of publication in China—has not produced in the last seven years two or three books worth reading! Not only is there no single book with a high standard of scholarship, but also not a single book one could read for pleasure while traveling. I felt like weeping when I discovered this peculiar situation." All of this changed as a sudden "periodical fever" produced hundreds of magazines which proceeded to tilt against all the windmills on the cultural landscape. The most important one of them was Ch'en's, and it was titled, and addressed to, *New Youth*.

Ch'en began with a "Solemn Appeal to Youth" in 1915. He exhorted them to give up servility for independence, conservatism for progress, retirement for aggressiveness, nationalism for world-consciousness, ceremony for practicality and speculation for science. In issue after issue he fought against the old society that made people weak, passive and subdued. His arguments provide in capsule form the principal attitudes that distinguished the May Fourth movement and the new culture.

All of this meant the demolition of much of China's traditional culture. Ch'en derided the heroes of traditional Chinese morality and spoke of his revulsion for the weaklings who were extolled as filial sons and respectful subjects. He held up instead a new idea of independence: "I have hands and feet and can contrive to make my own living. I have a mouth and tongue and can state my own views. I do not recognize any other man's right to meddle in my affairs. I shall never allow him to lord it over me and shall not allow myself to become enslaved to him. I consider myself an independent and autonomous personality. I shall not slavishly follow other men's flaws. The morality of loyalty to superiors, filial piety, and fidelity is a morality of slaves."

This set of attitudes did not leave very much room for the Confucian view of hierarchic social relations and obligations which had been the cornerstone of the traditional culture. "The pulse of modern life is economic, and the fundamental principle of economic production is individual independence," Ch'en announced. But "in China, the Confucianists have based their teachings on their ethical norms. Sons and wives possess neither individuality nor personal property. Fathers and elder brothers bring up their sons and younger brothers and are in turn supported by them. . . . This is absolutely not the way to personal independence. . . . Confucius lived in a feudal age. The ethics he promoted is the ethics of the feudal age. The social mores he taught and even his own mode of living were teachings and modes of a feudal age. The political institutions he advocated were those of a feudal age. The objectives, ethics, social norms, mode of living, and political institutions did not go beyond the privilege and prestige of a few rulers and aristocrats and had nothing to do with the happiness of the great masses. . . ."

Views of this sort led to a vigorous polemic. It was the sharper on both sides because the disorders of early Republican China had strengthened the opinions of many conservatives that a revival of Confucianism was desirable in order to provide an ethical core for Chinese life. During these same years "sponsored Confucianism" was also making considerable headway in Japan as financiers, Education Ministry bureaucrats and elderly conservatives all saw in it a desirable way of moderating attitudinal change. On the other hand, the modernizers saw as their problem the very spirit of harmony and submission that the conservatives found so admirable. Fukuzawa Yukichi, for whom Ch'en Tu-hsiu had a high regard, and other publicists had denounced traditional Confucian morality in similar, though less vehement, terms in the 1880s. Men like Fukuzawa had charged that traditional East Asian religions were unprogressive and that Christianity was to be preferred if there had to be a religion at all. But the Japanese had never gone so far as the May Fourth publicists, for they had never been as frustrated. Their anger had not remained pent up as long. Perhaps equally important was that they had been restrained by the renewal of an imperial mythology that drew on important elements of the old morality. No such restrictions operated in what Hu Shih came to call the Chinese Renaissance. Directness and practicality were the goal, and honesty and irreverence essential. A Young China Association that was organized after the May Fourth demonstrations adopted as its four watchwords "strife, practicality, endurance, and thrift."

These goals dictated changes in the language as well. The traditional preference for the archaic forms of the written language seemed to have no place in a new China in which men of letters tried to communicate with as many of their contemporaries as possible. The great novels of China had been written in a vernacular known as *pai hua*. Hu Shih now argued that this should become the medium for all self-expression and that writers should sacrifice elegance for practicality and directness. This movement began in America, when Chao Yuen Ren and Hu Shih wrote a series of articles in the *Chinese Students' Monthly* in 1916. Chao, one of China's first specialists in modern linguistics, initially advocated alphabetizing the Chinese language and abandoning the time-consuming though prestigious and beautiful script. He later worked out a romanization system that incorporated the tonal inflections essential to spoken Chinese. Hu Shih hesitated to go this far, but he did take the lead in advocating abolition of the old written form and replacing it with the vernacular. "What we call our literary language," he wrote, "is an almost entirely dead language.... We must free ourselves from the traditional view that the spoken words and the spoken syntax are 'vulgar'.... The criterion for judging words and expressions should be their vitality and adequacy of expression, not their conformity to orthodox standards. The spoken language of our people is a living language; it represents the daily needs of the people, is intrinsically beautiful, and possesses every possibility of producing a great and living literature...." He exhorted his readers to "Speak only when you have something to say. Speak what you want to say and say it in the way you want to say it. Speak what is your own and not that of someone else. Speak in the language of the time in which you live." This is sound advice, and that it was considered revolutionary in China in 1918 tells a good deal about the pace of change there. Yen Fu, for instance, had used the formal literary language for all his translations from Western authors. Sun Yat-sen was distrusted by figures like K'ang Yu-wei precisely for his failures in the traditional culture, which centered on the written word.

In Japan the change had been less abrupt. During the Tokugawa period, writing in formal Chinese (or what Japanese hoped was formal Chinese) was plentiful, but it gradually became less general. Poetry was always written in vernacular Japanese, although a considerable body of Chinese verse also developed. In the Meiji period the needs of mass education produced a great simplification of vocabulary and forms. The literary style gradually gave way to complete colloquial, although some of its grammar survived in correspondence and in better class newspapers because of its greater economy of space. *Pai hua* could not, of course, drive literary Chinese to the wall immediately; but its ultimate victory was certain when the Education Ministry made it the instrument of instruction in 1920.

This insistence on strife and resistance and the revolt against outside influence meant that Christianity would not play the role in China's intellectual reform that it had for Japanese or Korean modernizers. Christianity had in fact faced a more concerted and official opposition in China from the first. Given its identification with the Taiping rebels and with the gunboat diplomacy of the imperialist powers and given the frequent interference of missionaries in internal matters, Christianity was in any case severely handicapped. Ch'ing officials and gentry popularized a large literature against heterodoxy, often focusing specifically on the ruinous social effects of Christian doctrine. In Japan, official disfavor, symbolized by the Education Ministry's measures against religious instruction in schools, did not come until the end of the century; by then an entire generation had been educated, many of them in Christian schools. It was furthermore the students from politically "outside" areas, men who faced difficulties in competing with Satsuma and Chōshū products, who were often drawn to Christianity. Yoshino Sakuzō, among many, was a product of northern Japan. The same was true of Uchimura Kanzō, Nitobe Inazō and many others. But in China the staying power of the old society ruled out intense and direct experience of Western values for all but a few, and they, lacking the proper scholar-gentry pedigree of education, were not likely to achieve high estate. By the time of the Republic and the cultural revolution the full anti-Christian tide of twentieth-century secularism was at hand to provide Chinese skeptics with newer answers than Confucianism had for combating Christian and missionary influence. Christianity could be now derided as irrational and unsuited to the needs of the modern world, and, in addition, new theories of imperialism made it seem a form of cultural imperialism.

As a result the May Fourth movement coupled with its attack on Chinese tradition an equally virulent charge against the Christian tradition of the West. In 1920 the executive committee of the Young China Association approved a proposal submitted by its Paris branch that all people with religious faith should be excluded from membership. Lecturers like John Dewey and Bertrand Russell brought Western sanction for warnings against Christian proselytization. The anti-Christian tide reached its height in 1922 when an anti-Christian movement was formed to oppose a meeting of the World Student Christian Federation scheduled for Peking.

If the May Fourth movement was so firmly opposed to the modern base of cultures, East and West, its positive goals were those of science and democracy.

Ch'en Tu-hsiu held these up as the final arbiters of value judgments. Replying to criticisms of conservatives, he wrote "We committed the alleged crimes entirely for the sake of supporting the two gentlemen, Mr. Democracy and Mr. Science. In order to support Mr. Democracy, we are obliged to oppose Confucianism, the code of rituals, chastity, traditional ethics, old politics; and in order to support Mr. Science, we are compelled to oppose traditional arts, traditional religion; and in order to support Mr. Democracy and Mr. Science, we have to oppose the so-called national heritage and old literature." He went on to argue that it had required much blood and pain to establish these in the West and that Chinese should not shrink from the cost of enshrining them in China.

To fight for Mr. Democracy meant to oppose militarism and imperialism; to work for Mr. Science meant to resist the old patterns of culture, the "morality of slaves," religion and metaphysics of all sorts. In the lively pamphlet and periodical war that was waged over articles of belief, victory tended to go to the advocates of materialism and pragmatism. The mechanistic materialism of Wu Chih-hui, who was educated in Paris, restricted itself to the affirmation of what could be proved scientifically; that man "has a brain which weighs four pounds and two ounces along with 5,048 nerve connections. Comparatively speaking, he is an animal with a large supply of brains and nerves." Hu Shih praised this as representing solid ground and wrote whimsically: "With one stroke of the pen he wipes out God, extinguishes the soul, and punctures the metaphysical idea that 'man is the most spiritual of all things.' He thus raises a real challenge. We would like to see those who believe in God come forward and defend God against our venerable Mr. Wu." It was Hu Shih's opinion that this scientific view of life should achieve a unity through education and propaganda that might replace the unity which religion had given the philosophy of life in Europe for so long.

In addition to democracy and science, the principal journals and writers stood for a host of humanitarian ideals. In 1919 *New Youth* published a manifesto of belief that explained that "our ideal new era and new society are to be honest, progressive, positive, free, equal, creative, beautiful, kind, peaceful, full of universal love and mutual assistance, and pleasant labor; in short, happiness for the whole society. We hope that the hypocritical, the conservative, the negative, the bound, class-divided, conventional, ugly, vicious, warring, restless, idle, pessimistic elements, happiness for the few — all these phenomena will gradually diminish and disappear."

How was all this to be brought about? Not by the politics of their time, although "we recognize that politics is an important aspect of public life ... we recognize political parties as a necessary device for political practice, but we will never tolerate membership in parties which support the interests of the few or of one class rather than the happiness of the whole society." By thus holding out for pure and humanitarian politics, the intellectuals of the Chinese Renaissance resigned themselves to educational activities while other groups, usually less humanitarian, took over the politics of their time. Moral elitism often cost them the opportunity to influence the society of their time.

It can be argued, as some have done, that this sort of reasoning provided more support for the demolition of the old order than it provided pattern for the new. Not all the modernizers were content to wait on the sidelines for the coming of a situation that could be pragmatically and scientifically described as appropriate for their participation in political action. Marxist study groups developed in these same years. In December 1919 a society for the study of socialism was founded at Peking University. In 1920 the Russians, impressed by what they had heard of the May Fourth movement, began efforts to encourage Chinese intellectuals to organize a Communist party. This was formally set up in 1921. Ch'en Tu-hsiu was elected secretary, and thereafter he made the Communist movement his chief business. Similarly, in Japan the Shinjinkai members began to slip into diverse political and cultural activities. Nozaka Sanzō was one of the founding fathers of the Japan Communist party, which was established, after several false starts, in July 1922. Hu Shih, however, refused to endorse movements aimed at overthrowing the Peking government and scornfully dismissed ideologues with the comment that now that "the slaves of Confucius and Chu Hsi have decreased in number, the slaves of Marx and Kropotkin have appeared." After 1923, the Peking militarists became more reactionary and began to suppress reformers and liberals; political activity, necessarily secret, gradually became forced into the communist mold of illegal operation unless liberals chose to emigrate to Canton.

In dealing with the struggle in this brief compass, it is easy to exaggerate its emphases. The May Fourth movement was by no means unanimous. Ch'en and Hu parted company emphatically because the latter was not interested in the dogmatism of Marxist ideology. Undoubtedly many students and intellectuals were thoroughly confused, though generally optimistic about the prospects for social and political betterment in China. Many well-known writers were aghast at the extremism of the day. Since they tended to be of the elder generation, they serve admirably to illustrate the conflict between generations in the second decade of the twentieth century.

Liang Ch'i-ch'ao was one of those who drew different conclusions from the destruction of World War I. Western Europe had entered a blind alley, he thought, and its vaunted progress was limited to a grasping competitiveness and search for material goods that had finally led to its own destruction. China would be well advised to think twice before jettisoning any more of its traditional culture. Even Westerners, he thought, were beginning to realize the value and importance of Chinese culture. Europeans had come to realize that the shadows thay were trying to reach disappeared just as they came into sight. "What is this shadow? It is this Mr. Science! The European people have had a big dream about the omnipotence of science. Now they are talking about its bankruptcy. This is a great turning point in the change of modern thought."

Similarly Liang Sou-ming, who believed that the agrarian basis of China made the European order permanently inappropriate for it, wrote of three different types of civilization. That of Europe's was dominated by a Faustian will, which produced science, democracy and the desire to conquer nature. That of China preferred contentment, harmony and moderation. That of India and Buddhism counseled retreat and withdrawal. The world of the future, he thought, would come to recognize in the Chinese value structure and approach a suitable middle ground between rash destruction and self-defeating withdrawal. Many Western writers like Renan and Bergson were interested in some of these ideas, and the Indian poet Tagore traveled to China and Japan to study and popularize an antimaterialist "East." But his reception was mixed and his disappointment keen.

Hu Shih responded to conservative rebuttals in trenchant terms. He warned that they risked appealing to inertia, conceit and vanity. What, he demanded to know, was so spiritual about a civilization that bound the feet of its women, that practiced cremation of widows and endured the caste system? Eastern civilization, he suggested, was built on human labor, and Western civilization on the power of machinery. The use of inanimate means of power seemed to Hu a quite satisfactory measure of idealism and spirituality in a civilization. As he put it, "Let all apologists for the spiritual civilization of the East reflect on this: What spirituality is there in a civilization which tolerates such a terrible form of human slavery as the 'ricksha coolie?'"

5. The Appearance of Communist Parties

THE THIRD DECADE of the twentieth century brought radical movements to East Asia. After 1921 Marxist patterns of analysis and communist patterns of organization appeared in each country. Communism was one of the theories that had come flooding into the thought world of young intellectuals around the years of World War I. Although the Bolshevik success in Russia had given it new relevance, it did not become structured and supported until the 1920s. Even then it was only part of the general ferment of idealistic discontent that moved young people. But in the frustrations of warlord China it was the chief gainer of the radicalization of politics. Positions became polarized, and the discontented moved beyond radicalism to organization and discipline. Political turbulence and frustration created a disorder in which the priority of political order and pattern seemed higher than ever before. Unless the country was unified by a government that could become master in its own house, nothing could be accomplished. National unification brought communists and nationalists together in an alliance against imperialists and warlords. In Japan the rise of an industrial labor force and a tenant movement in the setting of conversion from a wartime to a peacetime economy provided the setting for large-scale development of what the Japanese called a "social movement." It required several years for social democrats to separate themselves from the amorphous but increasingly communist left. It is possible to exaggerate the contemporary importance and number of the communist groupings that emerged from all this, for they were only a fraction of the intellectual elite. But they must be taken up first because they precipitated the separation and polarization of opinion and policy.

Why did so much of the radicalism and discontent end in the communist camp? To answer this question one has to begin with consideration of the nature of the social outlook of intellectuals in East Asia. Most of them, and particularly those in China, were determined to bring an end to what they considered the intolerable injustice of their society. Their immediate predecessors had looked to the inevitable processes of evolution and progress to bring this about, and the grand symmetry of the plans of Darwin and Spencer had seemed to promise solutions. But World War I had punctured this optimistic and facile expectation. The tools of science and technology could be self-destructive as well as creative, and they offered no panacea for the organization of society. For Ch'en Tu-hsiu "Mr. Science" and "Mr. Democracy" had promised to provide answers during World War I. When John Dewey was lecturing in Peking in 1918 and 1919, pragmatism and democracy still seemed within reach. But at best they were slow to come. At worst, they were inappropriate for an environment terrorized and brutalized by physical force and poverty and constrained by imperialism. They served better to break down the old moralism of Confucius than they did to provide an alternative around which men could unite. Japanese intellectuals had already begun to bring home other fare from their study years in Germany. German philosophical idealism, with its lofty abstractions of the state, with Hegel's ideas about the role of the dialectic in the making of history and, finally, with Marx's emphasis on economic forces, seemed to provide more inclusive and comprehensive weapons for thought and analysis. Marxism itself was a product of this holistic, sweeping categorization, and its "wholeness" seemed to hold out more hope, and more wisdom, than the piecemeal pragmatism to which Dewey and Hu Shih remained committed.

It must be remembered that the intellectuals we have discussed were only one generation away from a wholehearted commitment to Confucianism, and most of them had imbibed Confucian ideals in youth. This was as true of a Yoshino Sakuzō, who reached out for Confucian terminology and values in defining his Japanese-style democracy, as it was for a Ch'en Tu-hsiu, who raged against the Confucian tradition. Whether accepted, modified or rejected, Confucianism continued to serve as bedrock of the world view of virtually all the men we have considered. Seen from this perspective, Marxism, however iconoclastic, offered certain continuities in values. It was Marx the social prophet who attracted followers in East Asia. For some it was "the example of his moral life," as the Shinjinkai student journalists put it, "he who sacrificed everything and died a martyr for the great cause of human emancipation," that was admirable. The Marx who denounced the inhumanity of early nineteenth-century English factory conditions and who made this out to be a result of the greed of factory operators who must soon fall victim to the workers they had exploited was a writer who struck responsive chords in the minds of young readers who were inclined to scorn material values and who, with an outlook inherited from earlier East Asian elites, saw themselves as custodians of public morality and decency. This was true in Japan as well as in China. The Meiji generation's unexamined drive for achievement was giving way to a more introspective and questioning search for values. A plutocracy that had come to life on the profits of World War I was beginning to be able to buy its politicians, and sharpening disputes in factory and farm seemed to be giving point to Marx's warnings about the dislocations modern industrial organization would bring.

The complexity and solidity of the Marxist theoretical armory had further attractions for East Asian intellectuals who saw so much of their idealism and ambition frustrated by power brokers drawn from the military and plutocratic elites. No competing system had as structured a system of analysis. On the other hand, discontent did not necessarily run to Marxist solutions. Many of the Japanese rightists were equally indignant for their less successful countrymen, equally determined to deal with exploitation in the modern sector of the economy and equally dubious about the wisdom and unselfishness of their military contemporaries. The situation encouraged extremism of either variety. It contributed to a polarization of thought far more than it encouraged the expectation of reform through parliamentary means.

Radicalism in an unstructured social setting was difficult for most intellectuals, and the consolation and discipline of the group were important. Government repression, of course, made it difficult to maintain an independent standard of criticism without some sort of social base for personal security. It was also necessary to secure a psychological base in group decision and solidarity. The intimacy of the communist cell, the security of the Party thesis and directives and the intensity of the intramural family arguments about points of doctrine contained important appeals. In a setting in which much philosophical speculation was centered around issues of self-awareness, and much literature around themes of loneliness and anomie, the role of the communist communicant as family member is worth keeping in mind.

An equally important area to examine in connection with the rise of organized communist parties in East Asia relates to international politics. The enthusiasm of young people in East Asia for the ideals and language of Woodrow Wilson had brought them little in the way of concrete results. The United States discouraged Syngman Rhee from getting to the Paris Conference. It accepted the rebuff which Australia delivered to the proposal that the League of Nations Covenant incorporate a clause calling for racial equality, and it was unable to get the Japanese to do more than agree to take up their Shantung holdings with the Chinese at some future date. America itself withdrew from the Siberian intervention it had helped initiate, but it was long unable to get the

Japanese to leave. It refused to take part in the new international organization that had been created, and the American electorate willingly exchanged the noble utterances of Wilson for the platitudes of Harding. Soon afterward, immigration legislation discriminated against all East Asians.

On the other side, the Bolsheviks were overcoming tremendous handicaps of war and famine and developing a system that seemed to have particular promise for the backward parts of the world. They had made basic additions to the Marxist theory and practice. Both were the work of Lenin. The first was his view of the Communist party as the vanguard of the proletariat. Marx and Engels had assumed that communism could succeed only in highly industrialized settings, and they made Western Europe, especially England, the center of their concern. Marx lived in exile in London and thought he saw there the fullest working out of the laws of historical development connected with the rise of an industrial proletariat. In the twentieth century the deprivation and exploitation he described were better duplicated in the new industrial cities of Asia than in the England of which he wrote. By Marxist laws of historical materialism, the discontent of Western European workers should have sufficed to make them loosen their chains, in the words of the Communist Manifesto, and seize the modes of production from their capitalist masters. The entire apparatus of industrial management counted for little in Marxist economics; the difference between what workers received and the value of the products they made was "surplus profit" that their employers had sweated out of them. But in World War I it had become clear that Marx's predictions were nowhere borne out. Workers had not risen in revolt. They had instead worked overtime to help their capitalist employers outproduce the enemy instead of joining, by strike and insurrection, workers across the lines to overthrow both ruling classes. If revolution had not come in Western Europe, what possible relevance could Marxism have for the less industrialized parts of the world?

The answer lay in two parts for Lenin: one of practice and one of theory. The practice lay in the discovery that in the Russian setting there was as much revolutionary fuel to be found in the discontented peasantry as in the exploited workers. The immediate source of the Bolshevik coup in November 1917 was the soviets of factory workers, but what made it endure and succeed was the revolutionary ferment of the conscript peasants, to whose demand of "land and bread" the new regime was responsive. The only way to account for so un-Marxist a revolution was to credit its Bolshevik managers with a class role. The communists were therefore defined as the "vanguard" of the proletariat, qualified to act on its behalf and to organize and lead. Communist party members became an elite, schooled and trained in ideology and practice, armed with the knowledge of science and history and qualified to interpret and apply these on behalf of their less awakened countrymen. The attractions of this innovation for a country like China, where the industrial proletariat was minute and where intellectuals (traditionally trained in the ideology of Confucianism as instrument of power) took their role as a cultural and political vanguard seriously, were very great.

The Leninist explanation of the Bolshevik success made Marxist theory relevant for East Asian radicals.

Lenin's other great contribution was through his theory of imperialism. It seemed to explain why the revolution had not come to the imperialist powers of Western Europe and why the contrast in well being between the West and the East was so striking. In *Imperialism the Highest Stage of Capitalism* (1916), Lenin explained that the capitalists had succeeded in delaying the domestic revolution by bribing their workers with the wealth of the underdeveloped world. As capitalist systems matured, he argued, they faced a declining rate of investment profits because of the limitations capitalist exploitation placed upon the workers who constituted the home market. "Monopoly capital" therefore had to find backward countries that offered a high investment return, and in the competition between capitalist giants for control of such backward areas imperialist competition and war became inevitable. Success in this competition enabled the capitalist country to put off the operation of the dialectical contradictions that would otherwise bring it to class revolution.

Lenin's version of imperialism represented a polemical adaptation of earlier twentieth-century approaches. Polemics were not new. The Japanese anarchist Kōtoku Shusui had written a study of imperialism as "the twentieth-century monster" almost two decades earlier. What was different about Lenin's approach was that he hinged his entire analysis upon the concept of monopoly capital investment and thus seemed to give it a securely "scientific" explanation. Moreover he internationalized the class struggle at one stroke. Now the colonial countries were an exploited proletariat, and their Western masters "capitalists." In similar manner, a half-century later, the Chinese leader Lin Piao transferred the imagery of the revolutionary "antiimperialist" war to the sphere of the rural and the urban, with the capitalist powers constituting the "cities" that would be surrounded and slowly strangled by the "country."

As polemic, Lenin's *Imperialism* scored telling points. It was translated into Chinese in 1919 and swiftly became the most important weapon in the arsenal of communist writers in Asia. The disparity between Western wealth and Asian poverty could now be traced to imperialism and the West's ability to bleed the East. The difference between Western power and Asian weakness seemed reducible not to the virtues but to the iniquities of the social structure of the oppressors. The result was a call for resistance and not for emulation. The argument lent itself equally well to a racist view of Western rapacity and deceit. Slightly camouflaged, it served Japanese propagandists in the 1930s almost as well as it did their communist enemies.

A logical consequence of Lenin's association of imperialism with capitalism was the conclusion that the way to fight the capitalist class war was to deprive imperialism of its profits overseas. Attacks on imperialist countries and on the entire system of imperialism could most conveniently be mounted in the non-European world by attracting nationalist forces, even though they might be bourgeois rather than proletarian, to a "United Front" against the imperialist enemy. In Asia even the middle classes, if nationalist minded, could be a revolutionary force. Direct struggles inside the European capitalist countries had fared poorly, and so the Bolshevik leadership resolved to strike the West through the East. In 1920 Lenin announced to the Second Congress of the Communist International that the struggle would shift from support for oppressed classes to support for oppressed peoples against the oppressing countries. Seventy percent of the population of the world, he said, was suffering from imperialist injustice. To focus the struggle on those countries would result in the weakening and ultimate collapse of the capitalist centers. With the Communist party to act as vanguard, the proletariat of Asia might be able to bypass the turn from capitalism to socialism that seemed to be taking longer than anticipated in the West. It might be possible to advance directly into socialism. Nothing could fit better with the ideas of K'ang Yu-wei and Sun Yat-sen for bypassing the tedious sequence of historical change the West had gone through.

In September 1920 a Congress of the Peoples of the East met in Siberia; in January 1921 a second congress met at Moscow. It now seemed that the greatest opportunities lay not in Japan, which had a large and growing proletariat, but China, where political disruption and intellectual disillusion offered revolutionary possibilities. Comintern agents and money therefore traveled to the East. In 1920 an agent named Voitinsky began meeting with a small group of Chinese intellectuals which included Ch'en Tu-hsiu. By the summer of 1921 a small group of intellectuals had met to organize the Chinese Communist party. Ch'en Tu-hsiu, although not present, was chosen head of the Central Committee. A young man who had assisted in the library of Peking University during the stirring days when Ts'ai Yüan-p'ei and Ch'en Tu-hsiu reformed that institution, was among the original group. His name was Mao Tse-tung. Another Comintern agent, Janson, helped to organize a group of Japanese radicals as the Japan Communist party the following year. Similar beginnings were made in Southeast Asia and among refugee Koreans. Some promising young communists were given periods of training at the University of the Peoples of the East, which was established in Russia in 1921. The training of disciplined groups of young activists had been begun.

The appearance of professional, disciplined and dedicated groups of revolutionaries under communist leadership marked the beginning of a new stage of intellectual and political history in East Asia. At the outset, of course, their number was insignificant, and their base was limited to intellectuals. In the testing that followed, only some of the original group were willing to pay the price that membership in the Communist party involved. Aside from personal submission to the Party line and subordination to tactics and controls imposed from Moscow, there was enormous personal danger from the watchful gendarmerie of Japan and the ruthless police agents of Chinese warlords.

Despite this, the movement grew. In Japan, where it was denied the nationalist and imperialist issues that engaged a generation in China, it found itself limited to intellectuals, often bookish, theoretical, isolated and vulnerable. In

China, where social and political conditions provided issues that none could ignore, it soon grew beyond the boundaries of the intellectuals with which it began and continued to engage workers in the industrial towns and peasants in the tension-laden countryside. In both countries it continued to grow among men of books and letters. In China "the intellectual activity of the country between 1930 and 1937," Lucien Bianco insists, "was indisputably dominated and shaped by Marxism and the hope of revolution." Men of the May Fourth generation moved in a setting dominated in the early 1920s by the struggle of the Creation Society, which strove for artistic expression, and the Society for Literary Studies, which called for social emphases, until in 1930 a League of Left-Wing Writers included both the future cultural commissar, Kuo Mo-jo, and the idol of a generation of writers, Lu Hsün. In Japan the insistent aesthetics of the art for art's sake movement, championed by organizations like the White Birch group of writers, also became overshadowed by the advocates of proletarian literature by the end of the 1920s. This powerful movement found its themes in factory and tenant exploitation in the capitalist Japan of its day.

In the social sciences Marxism, after a slow start, gradually won its way in Japan until by the 1930s the epochal struggle for definition of the sources of Japanese militarism resulted in the symposium series, *Studies in the Development of Japanese Capitalism.* Japanese student and intellectual radicalism was forced by its setting to remain theoretical, but within those limitations its domination was scarcely less important than it was in China. In volume it was submerged under the tide of approved scholarship, in which the theory of empire and history was an often uncritical chronology of facts. But social science writing after the end of police repression in 1945 left no doubt of the victory of earlier decades that had had to remain covert and disguised.

In writing of the young and the intense, one inevitably emphasizes the radicals who mark the greatest break with their past, and who can, in retrospect, be seen as spokesmen of the future. Two warnings must be offered. The first is that in the setting of their day these radicals did not loom nearly as large as their subsequent victory made them seem. That victory was a product less of intellect and theory than one of history, in which the flames of war and extremism destroyed the moderate and the pragmatic who might otherwise have prevailed. A second is that the emphasis on radicalism forces one to take up the Left, often at cost to the Right. In both China and Japan other young men, equally intense and equally able, no less committed to their nation and no less convinced of its present wrongs, sought their answers in other areas. The immediate future, in fact, would belong not to academic Marxists but to anti-Marxist militarists. These were men equally contemptuous of bourgeois politics and equally indignant because of imperialist restraints. They too fed on foreign doctrines, those of national socialism and of modern war. The young officers the Japanese army sent to study in postsurrender Germany played a role no less important than the young intellectuals the communist parties sent to postrevolutionary Russia.

They were full of enthusiasm for revolution and liberation, as when Ishiwara Kanji led his little group of men out of a garrison town in Korea to climb a hill to give three banzai for the Chinese Revolution of 1911. Nor can one find a stronger excoriation of the evils of imperialism for Chinese politics, economics and morals than in the writings of Chiang Kai-shek. Educated in Japan, traveled in Russia, and committed to "modern" military tactics and organization, he too, like Ishiwara, represented a new generation about to make its play for power. The generation gap within the Japanese military was particularly important. Mark Peattie says of Ishiwara and his friends in Japan, "They had contempt for the maneuverings of the older political generals and chafed at the lingering deference paid at the army's highest levels to the interests of the Chōshū and Satsuma cliques. As most had either observed the war in Europe at first hand, or had become acquainted with current western military doctrine through study tours in Europe after the war, they were more familiar with the principles of the new military technology and more willing to question the tactical doctrines of the past. This new professionalism made them impatient at the apparent inability of their leaders to deal effectively with the problems of modern war and resentful of the new tides of public opinion eroding the material and moral position of [Japan's] armed forces."

CHAPTER 8

China Under the Republic

China's first decades under the Republic constitute an important part of the prism through which contemporary China sees its history. These were years of shattered hopes and humiliation, of collapse, cruelty, disillusion and dismay. Chinese and foreigners contributed equally to these disappointments; imperialism could not be thrown off without internal order, but imperialism itself also tended to prevent such order. The denunciations of China's cultural past that make so large a part of the May Fourth movement need to be considered against the miasma of corruption and militarism through which young Chinese saw their tradition throughout those decades.

These conditions affected foreign as well as Chinese judgments of the Chinese tradition. They contributed to despair among China's friends abroad as movements began with firm intentions of restoring diplomatic equality to China only to find that there was not yet a "China" with which the outside world could negotiate. In 1925 a Tariff Conference met at Peking and worked out important steps toward tariff autonomy only to have the Peking government overthrown in the spring of 1926. China's disorder reinforced the conviction of many Japanese that unless Japan stepped in China would never know development and that the Chinese themselves must be so tired of disorder that they would welcome any governance, even non-Chinese, that brought order. Other and more perceptive observers realized the force of the new nationalism that was stirring young Chinese.

Republican China is a period little studied and imperfectly understood. Our knowledge of the institutions of the late dynastic period of Chinese history has only recently begun to permit assurance about what it was that changed, and the significance of that change could not be estimated without some confidence that the base line of institutional development was clear. There are numerous chronologies of the wars of the Chinese militarists, there are studies of the policies of the foreign powers, and there are studies of the Communist and Nationalist parties. But it is much more difficult to find out what was happening to the vast majority of the Chinese people.

There is also no general agreement on the interpretation that should be held of the 1911 revolution. Some historians see in the overthrow of the Manchus one more dynastic overthrow. Several decades of disorder usually followed the overthrow of a dynasty, they argue, and the interlude of war and hardship that came between Ch'ing and Communist power should be seen as another interregnum of the sort that Chinese history has known. They would argue that there was a minimum of social change in the countryside, where most Chinese lived, and that the real revolution came much later. Yüan's assumptions that he would inherit the imperial throne, and the prolonged hopes of Pu-yi that he might be restored to the throne, illustrate traditional expectations in the twentieth-century situation. The 1911 revolution, goes the argument, meant little; if a date for the beginning of substantial movements for modernization has to be selected, that date ought to be 4 May 1919, when genuinely new sentiments began to appear.

The formal conventions of political history argue against this assertion. The calendar in modern China has been dated from the establishment of the Republic in 1912. The restoration attempts of Yüan Shih-k'ai and Chang Hsün were failures, and the abolition of a system of rule that had endured for two millennia proved permanent. Chinese of many classes and persuasions felt there had been a revolution.

Since the sequence in which events are treated reflects the weight they are assigned, it may be useful to make explicit the view upon which this presentation is based. Despite all its incongruities and inadequacies, 1911 did mark the end of the imperial system and therefore constituted an event quite different in character from earlier dynastic changes. This was shown in the proclamation of the Republic. Imperialism marked another major difference; the consciousness of the outside world as a factor in Chinese history led to experimentation in titles, institutions and ideas with which to forestall outside interference. The failure of monarchy in much of the West after World War I helped guarantee that judgments made in 1911 about possible forms of statecraft for China proved lasting. On the other hand, social institutions changed far more slowly. In numerous areas far removed from the centers of political and economic collapse life went on as it had before the revolution. Changes in local government and economics came later. It was especially for the young and impressionable, those who were receiving training in the new schools, that transformations became revolutionary. The May Fourth movement remains the great symbol of these shifts, and one need have no quarrel with assertions that these changes marked the true beginning of national reconstruction. Political reconstruction lagged behind intellectual, and social reconstruction came last of all. The imperfect unification under the Nationalist government between 1927 and 1937 marked a great step over the chaotic efforts of military leaders. That reconstruction was helped, then hampered and finally destroyed by the Japanese presence in China. Therefore, 1937, the date of the outbreak of the war with Japan that destroyed the gains that had been made by the forces under Chiang Kai-shek, is the appropriate point at which to terminate this discussion.

1. *The Countryside*

THE VAST MAJORITY of the Chinese people lived in the countryside, and twentieth-century China's crisis was first of all a crisis in rural well-being. The manner of life that Chinese peasants knew in 1911 was beginning to change but their conditions of life had worsened. Throughout the eighteenth and nineteenth centuries population growth had produced smaller holdings, greater utilization of marginal land and higher rents. Lucien Bianco sums up one view by stating that "poverty, abuse, and early death were the only prospects for nearly half a billion people." Many have argued that China was too poor to save and therefore to invest and that it was caught in a vicious circle of poverty. More recently other scholars have questioned these assumptions of universal misery and found evidence that China produced a substantial surplus that was not available to the government because it went for consumption by the well-to-do. (It has been the ability of the People's Republic to command and allocate that surplus, they go on, that has made possible a growth in investment and in per capita consumption since 1949.) Whatever the size of the surplus in earlier China, however, it was not concentrated in cities but scattered widely throughout the countryside, and the central government's ability to channel this surplus diminished as its authority declined.

Political disunity was accompanied by decline of the communications network. Modern communications were limited to railroads and the steamers that plied river and coastal routes. Unfortunately China's railway network declined with the central government, and the number of locomotives and passenger coaches decreased throughout the 1920s. Thus "modernization," limited largely to the major communications lines that had begun to connect the major coastal cities, affected the hinterland in only a few areas where conditions of order and stability prevailed. Motor roads of any quality were to be found only around major cities. In 1928 there were only about 15,000 miles of dirt roads usable for motor vehicles, and these did not even suffice to connect Shanghai with Nanking and Hangchow.

The cyclical alternation of the agricultural year found rural village life organized around market centers. These have been analyzed by William Skinner, who finds that standard market towns serviced about eighteen villages, populated by perhaps fifteen hundred households whose members lived within walking distance of the market town. Itinerant tradesmen came on a regular schedule of, on the average, every five days. The tradesmen operated out of a larger market center and could service four or five market towns. The market town provided more than goods; it had a temple with festivals, voluntary associations and lodges and a tea house, and it provided a setting for organization and recreation. It also required unity in weights and measures and dialect. More than the nuclear village, it constituted a culture-perpetuating unit of social organization. Within this unit the male representatives of rural families were likely to be acquainted with each other since they met at markets seventy times yearly. Within it they sought brides for sons and supplements for their diet. The market town constituted the horizon of rural experience. It connected with larger and central markets to form one of some sixty thousand units.

The structure of effective rural administration paralleled this structure of livelihood. Under the imperial government of the Manchus, central government had reached to the level of the *hsien*. These were large zones encompassing a walled city and a dozen or even scores of marketing systems, and they contained a population that might vary from tens to hundreds of thousands of households. Hierarchies were not identical. The *hsien* seat might function as a large marketplace, the center for many standard and intermediate marketing centers, but such a central marketplace could also be outside its walls. What is more important is that there were never more than fifteen hundred district magistrates under the imperial order. Their immediate staffs were small. Since they all were "outsiders," forbidden to serve in their home provinces and rotated regularly, their involvement in the life of the area they governed was slight. On the other hand, each *hsien* government had a large staff of regular bureaucrats. Clerks might number from one hundred to over a thousand; runners, who also numbered in the hundreds, provided police, communication and security functions. There were also the magistrate's personal servants and private secretaries, the men he thought he could trust. Of all this host, only a handful of private secretaries had status and honor, and only they were personally known to the magistrate.

For most practical purposes, in other words, local government had been in the hands of local men. Though they received little salary, their income was based on payment for "services" at rates that were regulated by local custom and fear of official retribution. These local functionaries had long held the upper hand over the magistrate and his retinue. They knew their area and its problems, they knew the dialects, the tax and water allocations, and they could make or break their magistrate. It was the magistrate's job to keep their income and corruption within bounds, and it was their job to keep the official system moving.

If, as these estimates indicate, the administrative district had within it as many as thirty to fifty marketing systems within which the farmers' life was carried on, it becomes necessary to ask how the system of status and authority had been structured before it is possible to estimate the impact that political revolution could have on such a structure.

Status in Imperial China had been gained through success in the civil service examinations. Even those who purchased rank to qualify for office did so by purchasing the equivalent of academic rank. But by no means all of those with rank aspired to public office. Large numbers of those who emerged from the civil service examination system with status had no intention of leaving their localities for service under the empire. Rather, by obtaining and maintaining their standing, they could, as "gentry," improve the conditions of life for themselves and their families. Thus it becomes necessary to distinguish between "local gentry" and "officials" or, in William Skinner's useful distinction, the "nonofficial elite" versus the "bureaucratic elite." It is probable that the vast majority stayed on the bottom rung of the privileged class, content to maintain their status and utilize it at home.

The real system of local government—working with the magistrate's instructions, ceremonial reading of the Confucian precepts, guarding against the low-ranking official runners and servants who could be counted on to appear as locusts whenever they had the excuse—lay with the local elite. Ordinary commoners were not even permitted to approach the magistrate, and they did not stand much chance of resisting the demands of his minions. On the other hand, this local power structure, made up of nonofficial gentry and retired official gentry, could, with its special immunities, prestige and dignity, intercede and protect its neighborhood.

In *hsien* capitals, the world of the bureaucratic elite was important; in provincial capitals it probably dominated. But in village life the local elite was what counted; in market towns and intermediate-sized cities, where they were more numerous and where their wants and needs were served with specialty products and luxury goods, their role was central. Traditional China thus did not have a sharp dichotomy of urban wealth and rural misery; its elite was found in all parts of the country.

This local elite, the nonofficial gentry, came into the republican years with growing strength and confidence. As the central network of control weakened, local networks gained in power. It has already been noted that the great governors general of late Manchu times established strong networks of gentry support. Their terms of office were longer, and their power structures correspondingly stronger. Li Hung-chang served at Chihli for twenty-five years, Chang Chih-tung at Hukuang for eighteen, Liu K'un-i at Nanking for twelve, and

Yüan Shih-k'ai in Chihli for seven. It is natural to expect that tenures were correspondingly lengthened all along the line in the areas they controlled.

Efforts to change this administrative pattern in the direction of stronger central control were doomed to failure. The Hundred Days of 1898 as it had been conceived by K'ang Yu-wei and Liang Ch'i-ch'ao, for instance, might have weakened the gentry greatly. But when reform did come in the final stage of Manchu rule, the local gentry managed to live with it and utilize it. When the traditional system of examinations was given up in 1905, the court ordered that academic ranks were to be given to the graduates of the new schools instead of successful products of the examinations. Local elite naturally turned to patronize the new schools and sent their sons to study in them. Again, when the provisions for election to provincial assemblies were announced in 1908, the qualifications for candidacy incorporated provisions for education, rank under the old system and property. This effectively defined the local elite. Small wonder that the new assemblies championed local autonomy and the "rights recovery" movement, which fought for the return of privileges (such as railroad construction) to local hands. Small wonder also that the outbreaks that precipitated the political turnover of 1911 began with gentry-instigated risings in Szechwan. The few local studies that have been completed in recent years indicate that local gentry took over the revolutionary movement very quickly after the anti-Manchu revolt. Gentry-led local assemblies provided essential legitimacy for the new regimes. The great majority of the new governors who emerged were local men; almost overnight, Manchu regulations against locals were reversed by local insistence.

If, on the basis of these analyses, one asks what the effect of the 1911 revolution was on the Chinese countryside, certain conclusions quickly suggest themselves. The first, most strongly stated by Professor Ichiko, is that local power as represented by local gentry replaced central influence. Or, as John Fincher has put it, 1911 represented less a "revolution" than it did a "devolution" of power downward to the provincial elements of the structure. As central control was weakened, the middle and local elite, which had been kept in check and under some kind of control by the central system, suddenly found itself without significant competition.

But if this was so, then the sanctions and checks and balances that the old pattern of official alternation and Confucian ideology had provided were also lost. Ichiko holds that, as gentry power grew, patterns of local protest in late Ch'ing years began to move against the gentry; increasingly, he suggests, local riots, previously utilized by gentry against officialdom, had come to be directed against local gentry instead. Furthermore as the dynastic decline continued and culminated in the Republican government, the traditional norms and values invoked by the central government to restrain the local elite began to lose their force altogether. As their bureaucratic protectors and peers lost power and office the local elite began to look to different areas for security. Primary affiliations in family, clan and market network became more important. Governmental checks and sanctions became ineffective. Ultimately, coercive power replaced normative and exhortative power. Sometimes the autonomy of the province was paralleled by the increasing autonomy of the locality. At other points sustained local distinction of provincial affairs reduced the autonomy of the rural elite and forced upon it taxation demands that brought into question its moral aegis over the peasantry. As coercive arrangements grew in frequency, traditional restraints withered. Corruption, exploitation and oppression became more naked. A Confucian-oriented elite began to transform itself into a profit-oriented landlord class. And then, as order weakened, many found it prudent to move to nearby urban centers where they could be safe.

If there is merit in these suppositions (for they are not yet facts), the Revolution of 1911, to the degree that it affected rural China at all, operated to retard modernization by increasing the power of the local elite at the expense of

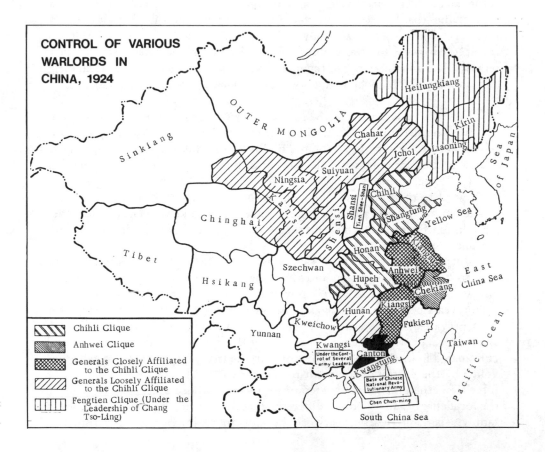

that of the central authority. In some areas, meanwhile, the development of modern transportation and the provision of outside goods and services continued the process of transforming the marketing network of the traditional countryside. This process saw a gradual shift in importance from local, first-level markets to higher, intermediate and central market areas. A growth in the radius of mobility brought increased commercialization of agriculture with a consequent decline of traditional markets. Paradoxically enough, as William Skinner has pointed out, this change meant an "expansion of social horizons" as areas of travel, contact, trade and even marriage broadened, but at the same time it produced a "contraction of social community" and a new "importance to the village." Cooperation that had been focused upon the standard market became irrelevant to livelihood, yet the larger area, too vast to permit meaningful involvement, tended to throw the peasant back upon his village.

Political decentralization and partial economic centralization consequently posed perplexing difficulties for the vast countryside of China. These were made the harder by the destruction and rapacity of the warlord armies in a setting of dense population.

2. The Warlords

THE MILITARISTS who ruled most of China and ruined a good deal of it during the first two decades of the Republic are usually called warlords. Military governors were called *tuchün;* collectively, they were referred to as *ch'ün fa,* "army clique." The term is one of opprobrium. No one ever spoke of himself or his friends as member of a *fa;* in its Japanese reading, *batsu,* it was used to characterize military, academic and administrative cliques and above all the business oligarchy (*zaibatsu*) as a term of reproach. In short the term meant chiefly that the army generals who strutted across the land were unpopular.

In earlier Chinese history the fall of a dynasty had usually been followed by a period of competition between military leaders. Military rule constituted a denial of the normative values of Confucian thought and was considered an aberration and the earmark of a time of troubles. In the end one of the competitors would manage to set up a new dynasty. Yüan Shih-k'ai, in his ill-starred attempt to mount the throne in 1916, was playing a completely traditional role.

The importance of military specialists in the disorders that always accompanied a downward turn of dynastic efficiency was supplemented in late Ch'ing times by the specter of modern imperialism with its new instruments of violence and war. Militarism was to some degree dignified by the addition of an aura of Western modernity. The great governors general of the late nineteenth century were also specialists in recruiting and equipping modern troops. The armies that suppressed the Taipings became, as we have seen, personal instruments of power. When the court in Peking ordered the governors general to support Li

Hung-chang against the Japanese in 1894 or the Boxers against the foreign legations in 1900, those officials chose to ignore the orders and conserve their armies,
which constituted their administrative and bureaucratic capital.

But the army leaders who appeared after the fall of the Ch'ing were not by
any means restricted to men who had known the advantage of status and education in the old order. Some, to be sure, were led by disciples of Yüan Shih-k'ai.
He created, in the Paoting-trained officers, the largest single group of modern
general officers, and the leaders in the first stage of warlord influence were by
and large drawn from his following. The disorder that followed the dynasty's
collapse also made it possible for men of lower status to rise rapidly. The
warlords of the 1920s included among their number men whose forebears had
been peasants, who themselves had begun as peddler, fiddler, bandit and foot
soldier. No calling has more absolute sanctions against incompetence than war,
and as the ne'er-do-wells were weeded out by defeat or carelessness, others were
always ready to take their place. Warlordism included a form of social mobility
that helped to mark the overthrow of the old bureaucratic elite.

It was also powerfully affected by international constraints and opportunities. Some twenty arsenals in China produced weapons, but small arms from
abroad were also plentiful in the years after World War I (as they would be after
World War II). Although the principal foreign manufacturers of weapons
agreed to a Chinese Arms Embargo Agreement in 1919, the Soviet Union was
never party to that embargo, and the Japanese military were willing to look the
other way in the case of Manchuria. Outside powers could affect the course of
events in China in a number of ways. The Nishihara loans strengthened the
northern warlords. The Japanese could also act to bar enemies of their favorites
from pursuing them into their zone in Manchuria. In 1924 they prevented Kuo
Sung-ling from taking Mukden and overthrowing Chang Tso-lin. The powers
often provided sanctuary for the defeated. By the terms of the Boxer Protocol no
Chinese troops could be stationed within seven miles of Tientsin, and that city
thus became a favorite place of sanctuary. In 1925 twenty-six former warlords
were to be found living there. More direct help was also possible. The Russians
aided Feng Yü-hsiang with weapons, and they provided Chiang Kai-shek and
the early Kuomintang with most of its military equipment. Occasionally foreign
powers could reduce internal discord by providing new threats of outside imperialist aggression. Major civil wars were several times delayed (but seldom
abandoned) because of uncertainty over the possibility of foreign action to
avenge some antiforeign outrage.

The warlords have had a very bad press from historians, but recent studies
by James Sheridan and Donald Gillin help to provide a more balanced picture
and relate the turmoil of the period to the larger course of social and political
change. Both remind us that as individuals the warlords were not without charm
and ability. "Without exception," Sheridan quotes Pearl Buck, "the war lords I
have known have been men of unusual native ability, gifted with peculiar personal charm, with imagination and strength, and often with a rude poetic

quality. Above all, they carry about with them, in them, a sense of high drama.
... The war lord is a creature of emotion; cruel or merciful, as the whim is; dangerous and unstable as friend or enemy; licentious and usually fond of luxury."

When one looks at the warlords as a group, it is easy to see what some of the requirements for success were. First, and probably most important, was something of the presence and imagination that would make men take them seriously and follow them into battle. Courage, presence, a flair for the dramatic and a belief in individual destiny were part of the makeup of the successful militarists. There was truth in Pearl Buck's reminder that they saw themselves as great "in the traditional manner of heroes of ancient fiction and history." Their survival also required shrewdness, a willingness to let bygones be bygones, and the ability to avoid being trapped by ideology or principles; they were opportunists with the ability to jump from one side to another at the moment of danger and profit. The best of them also had a good sense of publicity. Since China lacked good communications on land, the telegraph played a large role. From the time of the Revolution of 1911, China's new telegraph system became an essential tool of political ambition. Political and military moves were prefaced by circular telegrams to all corners of the land as warlords used them to announce their intentions, to call upon their opponents to withdraw and to rally support. A warlord also had to be practical. He seldom fought last-stand battles, and he did not expect his opponents to do so. Enemies were often permitted to withdraw from inextricable impasses, usually in the hope that they would retire to Tientsin or travel abroad. But tolerance could also give way to highly personal malevolence when necessary. A favorite way of getting a particularly difficult or dangerous opponent out of the way was to lull him into carelessness, invite him to a splendid banquet and then have him murdered when he was least expecting it. When young Chang Hsüeh-liang, about to become ruler of Manchuria, decided that he would have to get rid of his adviser and possible rival, Yang Yü-ting in 1928, he shot him personally. His uncle, who was then "governor" of Fengtien, is said to have praised him: "Didn't I always say you were a splendid boy?" In 1921 Feng Yü-hsiang, entertaining an enemy at an elaborate banquet, stationed so many assassins around the garden that pressure on the wall caused it to collapse, with the result that the intended victim would have made good his escape had not his host personally seized him and held him for his soldiers to behead.

A successful warlord needed a geographical base. Its income was essential to his cause, and its peasants, usually "recruited" by force, were his only source of manpower. A near-perfect base, like the highly defensible province of Shansi, provided Yen Hsi-shan with the longest tenure any warlord enjoyed. A poor base, difficult to defend and deficient in produce and men, meant that the man who held it would have to come to terms with outside sources of help. Warlords often had "foreign" relations with each other through emissaries who approximated ambassadors. Money was all-important. It could undermine the loyalties of subordinates. At times it could hire entire units, who fought as mercenaries.

Sun Yat-sen had recruited secret society leaders in this manner, and after the revolution he occasionally tried to line up his own troops. No one could be quite sure of his own subordinates, and few abandoned hope of winning over or buying their rivals. As a result the "international" relations of warlord satrapies resembled those in the Indian model of Kautilya; immediate neighbors were enemies, while the next, outer, ring of warlords constituted potential allies against the intervening rival.

Since money was essential, the warlord pressed the inhabitants of the areas he controlled as much as he dared. Cases of collecting—or at least demanding—taxes many years in advance were common. But there was a limit to what could be squeezed out of a given area. Revolt or famine could make excessive pressure dysfunctional. The early 1920s were years of tragic famines in China, and the International Famine Relief Commission was organized to provide help for the starving and homeless vagrants who moved through the Chinese countryside. The rural elite had never been so closely oppressed by so numerous a body of soldiers, and the traditional sanctions against excessive pressure no longer operated. Warlords often threatened to permit their men to loot if they were not given the money they needed. At its worst, warlordism was close to banditry. It represented a larger scale, and somewhat more systematic, exploitation of a region. Nationalist and Communist polemicists consistently referred to each other as bandits.

Tax yields could be supplemented with other sources. Warlords who held Peking could claim to be China's legitimate rulers and gain access to the maritime customs and, in the days of Nishihara, outside loans. The Canton area provided another source of customs income. Salt-producing areas were also lucrative. Many warlords profited from the growth and marketing of opium, frequently forcing farmers to substitute the poppy for food crops. Tax-collecting units of many sorts could be set up; one *hsien* had sixty-four such units in twenty-two different centers, and *likin* was collected at over seven hundred stations throughout the land. The eighty miles between Tientsin and Peking had seven revenue stations that taxed goods in transit. When "legal" recourse failed, measures closer to "banditry" could be tried. Feng Yü-hsiang, needing pay for his men, held up a "government" money train on its way to Peking in 1921. There were also real bandits. In 1923 an entire train was held up in Shantung and over three hundred passengers, including foreigners, were held for ransom. Chinese travelers suspected of having wealth or access to wealth were favorite targets for kidnappers, with relatives encouraged to do their best to raise money by threats of torture and mutilation.

Yet the warlords were not bandits. During the entire time of their notoriety most of them maintained the pretense of national unity and a national government. Each of the major figures saw himself as a real or future leader of the entire country and refused to settle for purely regional status. Even Yen Hsi-shan in Shansi, who was most nearly a provincial satrap, made one major attempt at national hegemony. Control of Peking would provide access to greater income, prestige and legitimacy. It promised to bring a kind of foreign recognition and, consequently, control over customs receipts. It also made it possible to determine the shape of the civilian government in Peking, which the generals were supposed to serve. Thus, struggles for Peking gave form and polarity to the affiliations of the military leaders. They also accounted for the kaleidoscopic changes in the Peking governments. In the decade that began in 1916 there were six heads of state in Peking and twenty-five cabinets. The "national" government was so badly in arrears that in 1923 Chinese ministers and consuls abroad threatened to return home unless their government sent them their salaries.

The major wars of the period can be grouped. Until 1916 the scene was dominated by Yüan Shih-k'ai and his subordinates. Upon his death the northern (Peiyang) faction of Yüan's lieutenants emerged as a counterforce to a comparable group in south China. Two years of desultory warfare between north and south, with most of the action in central China, followed. Strains of battle weakened loyalties in both camps, and the northern group divided into an "Anfu clique" and a "Chihli clique," the latter led by Wu P'ei-fu and the former by Tuan Ch'i-jui. In the wars for north China that began in 1920, important contributions came from Chang Tso-lin, the Japanese-backed ruler of Manchuria. Chang was a member of neither group, and he soon developed his own ambitions for national hegemony. When he was driven back to Manchuria, the Japanese blocked his pursuers and thereafter they tried—unsuccessfully—to keep him there.

In 1924 a second round of warfare found Feng Yü-hsiang, theretofore subordinate to Wu P'ei-fu, deserting him for the opposition. For several years Feng and Chang Tso-lin were the major figures in north China, but Chang finally defeated Feng, who had to retreat to the far west of Kansu where he secured Russian backing. During all of this south China was also unstable. The dissatisfaction of the southerners with the mockery of the constitutional government in the north resulted in a round of battles between southern generals for control of the area between Canton and the Yangtze Valley. Sun Yat-sen entered into this struggle politically and militarily. A second parliament met at Canton and was harassed by southern warlords, especially a group known as the Kwangsi clique. In the 1920s national loyalties sometimes gave way to ambition as second-rank militarists tried to ensure their membership in a winning clique. It would serve no useful purpose to detail the lightning shifts that took place. It has already been remarked that from 1915 to 1922 China had ten major civil wars that ran a total of forty-eight months.

Because of difficulties of transport and supply, warlord armies, although the largest in the world at that time, were usually divisible into smaller, self-contained units which could break off from the parent force and live off the land. In 1929 it was estimated that 1,620,000 men were under arms in China. Recruitment was forceful and brutal in emergencies, and stupendous hosts could melt down to a few of their better equipped and more professional units with remarkable speed. One of the most successful of the militarists, Feng Yü-hsiang, became known for the quality of his troops because of the way he drilled and in-doctrinated them. The core of his effectives, the best-drilled units, probably did not exceed one or two divisions. But with success came numbers, until by 1929 Feng had 220,000 men under him. Reverses saw his army dwindle to a core of his well-trained groups. In 1930 setbacks led to the defection of his old com-manders, who had become confident by the responsibilities incurred in leading large forces. There was thus a natural rhythm in the accumulation of warlord strength. Personal courage and leadership in the maneuvering of small bodies of troops led to the accumulation of forces that were less responsive, less trained and less controlled. Finally the general's personal qualities proved useless as he became more remote and institutionalized. His future then depended upon dis-cretion and diplomacy. If in addition to these qualities he had geography on his side, he had some chance of surviving into the 1930s. By then his discretion often resulted in a decision to proclaim himself a lieutenant of Chiang Kai-shek and the new republic.

The warlords were for the most part nonmodern. With the possible excep-tion of Ch'en Chiung-ming in Kwangtung, they had little sense of popular par-ticipation and popular support. Ch'en Chiung-ming brought the Peking educa-tor (and communist leader) Ch'en Tu-hsiu to Canton as educational adviser; he sent students abroad and did his best to stimulate the establishment of schools and newspapers. If Sun Yat-sen and the new Kuomintang forces had not driven him off the stage in the 1920s, he might have provided a rallying point. Yet even Ch'en Chiung-ming did his best to prevent the assertion of rights by labor and peasants. He utilized wall posters to warn against strikes, and he was responsive to local gentry requests to help them suppress peasant movements. Ch'en also quoted Mencius with approval, and he seems to have seen himself in the role of a Confucian paternalist who ruled for the benefit of the masses. Feng Yü-hsiang's peasant background and populism made him more socially oriented. His self-discipline and ostentatious adherence to Methodism won him the title of "Christian general," and he gained fame as a scourge of dishonest officials and corrupt social institutions. Again, Yen Hsi-shan is described by a recent biographer as more traditionally oriented in his values in that he supported the gentry of his province against rebellions but also repressed their efforts to take advantage of disorder to increase their own power.

In other ways, however, the warlords demonstrated a crude and imperfect awareness of some of the needs of twentieth-century China and strove to dem-onstrate their aptitude for directing modern changes. Feng Yü-hsiang trained his soldiers in praise of the common people and drilled them by repetition of a simple catechism in the importance of treating commoners decently. He called his troops the "people's army" (*kuominchün*), and in their early stages their behavior marked a notable exception to the usual rapacity of warlord armies. Feng even tried to treat his soldiers decently. His officers were given instructions that under eight circumstances they were not to beat their soldiers (if they were new, tired, sick, etc.), and the soldiers themselves were equipped with moral ditties set to hymn tunes to help them maintain discipline and morale.

Feng also attempted, and Yen Hsi-shan did more, to promote forms of industrialization essential for military independence and local economic growth. In Shansi the building of a narrow-gauge railway line highlighted a ten-year plan of industrial development that saw Yen's regime take the lead in control of the economy in order to increase investment. The plan included technical colleges, laboratories, machine-tool works, increased outputs of coal, a locomotive factory, an iron foundry, a small steel mill, a small petroleum refinery and repair shops of many kinds. Provincial governments in Kwangtung, Shantung, Hunan, Kwangsi and Szechwan also made efforts to encourage modern industrial development. In the 1920s Chiang Kai-shek incorporated these beginnings into a more ambitious five-year plan of his own.

Although the warlords were uniformly anticommunist, those that have been studied were impressed by Soviet tactics of modernization and quite willing to learn from them. None of them had any understanding of capitalism or liberalism, and many of them saw the gentry leaders of their areas as hoarders of wealth and a potential threat to their own leadership and initiative. Yen Hsi-shan, for instance, was particularly critical of the limitations the Shansi gentry seemed to place on his ability to organize his province.

Nor were they in the slightest impressed by individual opposition to their projects. Crude measures to recruit popular support and cooperation served chiefly to forecast the need for more effective and large-scale mobilization by later governments. Thus Feng Yü-hsiang and Yen Hsi-shan forced people to cut their queues, often by stationing squads of soldiers at the city gates. Motion picture theatres also provided captive audiences for checks on hair length. Inoculation could be handled in the same effective manner at bridges and traffic points. Feng and others plastered the walls of their cities with moral maxims to inspire those who could read and put on morality plays to instill resentment of foreign, and especially Japanese, humiliations. Footbinding was forbidden, and the populace was recruited in periodic fly-killing campaigns. Yen Hsi-shan retained the Manchu system of collective responsibility in his area and encouraged people to report the misdeeds of their relatives, employers or landlords to the police. Children were urged to tell on their parents. Volunteers knocked on Taiyuan doors early in the morning to get the names of those in bed after six o'clock, and schoolchildren, prophetic of the Red Guards, were encouraged "to gather outside the homes of malefactors and curse the occupants until they came out and promised to mend their ways." Still others were reformed through compulsory labor in state-managed factories and work camps.

The warlords were not insensitive to burning issues of national reconstruction. Their methods were idiosyncratic and self-centered, but they used the slogans of national strength and social reform that were part of the political discourse in their China. They were also quick to denounce imperialism and foreign humiliations. The example of Tuan Ch'i-jui's hapless stand in the face of the wrath of the students on 4 May was not lost on men as able as the major warlords. Feng Yü-hsiang provided belts for his officers and men with the slogan, "Remember the National Humiliation of May 7," printed on them, and he encouraged his soldiers to perform crude dramas to keep indignation against the Twenty-one Demands alive. Feng scheduled meetings on 7 May each year, and he had maps hung in the barracks to indicate how much of China's territory had been taken away from her.

Yet warlords could not afford quixotic patriotism either. Wu P'ei-fu, who refused first Russian and later Japanese assistance and who was the most thoroughly traditional of the group, would have had little difficulty fitting into a conventional situation between dynasties. His classical scholarship also set him off from most of the militarists. Feng Yü-hsiang, on the other hand, willingly accepted Japanese assistance when he decided to turn on Wu P'ei-fu in 1924. As a result of that coup, which saw Feng seize control of Peking, Tuan Ch'i-jui, who had been in control during the Nishihara loans in 1918, returned to the center of the stage. But when Feng and an ally developed hopes of full Japanese support, utilized a Japanese military adviser and tried to extend their sway to Manchuria, they ran afoul of the preference the main leaders of the Japanese military had for Chang Tso-lin. The Japanese Kwantung army declared the South Manchurian Railroad right-of-way off-limits to Chinese armies and provided security for Chang in Mukden, denied his enemies the opportunity of defeating him and forced Feng into defeat. He then turned to the Russians, who were anxious to have a friendly force on their border in northwest China and also tried to secure his cooperation with the communist forces in south China. As this happened, Feng's emphasis on anti-Japanese sentiments and National Humiliation Day observances grew stronger again.

Domestic bickering was a luxury that could be indulged only during a period of relative foreign calm and relaxation. On several occasions, for instance, civil war was averted or postponed because of fear of foreign exploitation of its opportunities as when, for example, the large numbers of foreigners kidnapped in Shantung raised the fear of outside punishment. But the 1920s were by and large a period of relaxation in foreign pressure on China, and the season was conducive to civil war. As Japanese pressure renewed in 1931, the possibility and safety of such warfare diminished, and after the Sian incident in 1935 Chinese armies stood together against the invader. It would seem that Japanese moderation contributed to Chinese disunity, while Japanese aggression speeded the unity of the 1930s. That unity, in turn, brought on the full Japanese attack in 1937.

It is useful to ask how the decade of militarism from 1916 to 1926 affected the several groups within Chinese society. Certainly the difficulties the agricultural sector of Chinese society had been experiencing in increasing degree since the middle of the nineteenth century were vastly increased by the disorders and turbulence of the warlord era. Levies increased sharply. Every time a province or district changed hands, the new occupant was almost certain to begin with tax demands. The warlord armies, swollen by agrarian hardship and hopes of loot, were extremely unpleasant neighbors for farmers. The fame that Feng Yü-hsiang (like Mao Tse-tung later) gained through the novel strategy of curbing arbitrary demands against peasants provides some idea of the popular image of the other warlords. The 1920s were years during which services of communications and flood control diminished as a result of the intermittent warfare. Partly as a consequence, they were also years of crop disaster and regional famine. Feng Yü-hsiang's Kansu was a scene of desperate want, and the hardships of his area were made worse by a racial and religious war between Chinese and Moslems that was encouraged by Chang Tso-lin from his secure base in Manchuria.

The effect of all this on the countryside varied by time and place. A province like Yen Hsi-shan's Shansi, which was under more or less continuous rule, was not subject to the same ravages of competing armies that cursed the more traveled routes, but its farmers were the object of a more systematic program of taxation. Yen saw the local elite as competitors for the wealth of his province, and he did his best to strip them of power and influence. After several years he gave up this attempt, however, as he found them too firmly based and necessary to his rule. The disorders of the period make it difficult to study the actualities of the class stratification and well-being of the countryside, and it was not until the relative peace of the Nationalist era in 1927 that serious efforts were made to study the agrarian setting. Patterns of tenure and rates of rent and taxation varied enormously throughout China, and the extent of hardship and indignation is illumined spectacularly but poorly by occasional accounts of rural uprisings. Mao Tse-tung's famous account of the situation in Hunan in 1927 has properly drawn the attention of all students of the countryside, but it would be difficult to have much confidence in the universality of the conditions he described.

Still, there is some significance to the rule-of-thumb definition of "middle peasant" the Communists adopted—those who could make out without debts in a normal year—while a "rich peasant" was one who rarely ran into debt. Tenancy probably rose throughout the period, while individual plots declined in size under the pressure of population growth. On the other hand, commercialization provided increased opportunity for cash crops and side employment, and the diffusion of kerosene lamps, tile roofs and manufactured products can even be argued to provide evidence of a modest rise in living standards. Thus the dismal picture of "preliberation" misery that characterizes mainland Chinese writing since 1949 is probably open to serious question. Yet it is also certain that the disorder of warlord, Japanese and civil war added crushing burdens and that local governments, unchecked by national administrations, became increasingly rapacious. In this sense the failure of government to meet rural needs was critical, making it possible for Bianco to conclude that "The class that listened to the revolutionaries, the class they cultivated, the backbone and flesh of the Chinese

Revolution, was the poor peasant class, which is to say the backbone and flesh of China herself."

The modern cities with their Western enclaves were less affected by the political disorder that cursed inland China. Most of the warlords were too anxious to avoid trouble with the West to take chances by harassing foreigners. Thus the Westernized cities along the riverways and coast remained protected, and they proved attractive for Chinese as well as foreign capital. If anything they grew more rapidly than they might have done under a more equitable and orderly administration.

One result of this was the rapid growth of a manufacturing sector and of a working class that often knew brutal exploitation. The cities also became the base for nationalist and radical movements, since much of the industry was under foreign control. The May Thirtieth movement of 1925 represents this perfectly, for it was a series of strikes and demonstrations sparked by the killing of a worker by a Japanese foreman. The demonstrations resulted in ten deaths from overreaction on the part of the International Settlement police in Shanghai, and were soon directed against the British. Meanwhile the membership of the Chinese Communist party, theretofore largely urban intellectual, increased tenfold in six months until it numbered ten thousand in November 1925. During the revolutionary years of 1926 and 1927 the workers registered in the Communist party grew in number. Warlords like Wu P'ei-fu were as quick to crush worker discontent in areas they controlled as were the treaty-port police.

Student and intellectual movements that have already been described continued to grow and in fact grew considerably faster because of the frustrations and humiliations of the political picture. Partly because the principal campuses were in the modernized cities that were less subject to warlord action, but also because the intellectuals were still an elite, warlords tended to leave universities alone. No warlord besieged or invaded a campus, and though the personal safety of intellectuals known to take part in political proceedings hostile to the militarists might occasionally be in jeopardy, intellectuals were on the whole free to continue their writing and criticism. University campuses, abetted now by worker discontent, increasingly became the center of the nationalism of the younger generation in China.

Nationalism grew steadily throughout the period. Even the major warlords made frequent mention of their country's sufferings, and none of them entered fully into a relation of permanent subjection to outside powers. Chang Tso-lin was never fully responsive to Japanese desires, a fact that ultimately cost him his life. Workers and students, dismayed by the perpetuation of an order they cordially detested, were humiliated by the spectacle of Chinese disunity and were determined to reverse the state of affairs.

The reverse side of the nationalist coin was republicanism. It is striking that despite its shallow roots in Chinese tradition and history no one really lost faith in the applicability of republicanism. The restorations under Yüan Shih-kai and Chang Hsün were crashing failures, and Feng Yü-hsiang had an accurate eye to public favor as well as personal profit when he drove Pu-yi out of the Forbidden City in 1924. Pu-yi fled to Tientsin, where he joined the exiled warlords, and he later reappeared as a Japanese puppet in Manchuria. But the chance that he or anyone else could again occupy the Dragon Throne in Peking was gone. Parliaments continued to sit in Peking throughout most of the period. When national unity seemed remote in 1922, the only alternative suggestion to receive any favor at all was one of federalism on a basis of provincial autonomy. More than nine provinces and five completed provisional constitutions, documents in which modern Chinese history is rich, were involved. Significantly the assumption was that such an order could serve as a bridge over which regional militarism could be changed into true republicanism. Chinese concerns remained with legitimacy and unity: some new way of reaching the goal might be needed, but everyone realized that the old idea of monarchy was dead.

Republican China thus presents the picture of a society in which many trends for change and modernization that had been set in motion earlier continued to operate. It lacked unification and a political ideology that could provide a way of reaching its goal. It was the function of the veteran revolutionary Sun Yat-sen, supported by the organizational work of the Communist party and the material resources of the Soviet Union, to articulate these needs.

3. The Reorganization of the Kuomintang

IN THE EARLY 1920s Sun Yat-sen seemed an unlikely choice to become the political philosopher for a united China. His course had been erratic. There were reports that his mind had begun to fail. His five-year effort to champion the first republican constitution and parliament as instruments of his return to power had damaged his prestige in China and abroad. But the turmoil of the warlord years had not produced an alternative to Sun Yat-sen, and it had discredited and removed other major figures from contention. Sun's unbroken string of failures and disappointments gradually made him seem sincere and honest in comparison to his more successful contemporaries.

The earlier Sun Yat-sen had had relatively little to say about the problems of Republican China. His nationalism had seldom gone beyond attacks upon the Manchus as foreign barbarians. There was little in the record of the T'ung-meng hui to suggest a thoroughgoing opposition to imperialism, for its propaganda had talked about cooperation with the foreign powers and with Japan. Until World War I, at least, it had seemed more important to assure the foreign powers that a republican China would carry out its treaty commitments and that they would have less difficulty with a modernized China than they had had with the old.

Nor had the earlier Sun Yat-sen had very much of a social message for his countrymen. He had spoken in general terms about equal landholding but without specifying how it should come about. He had talked of the general poverty throughout Chinese society and implied that since extremes of wealth were not marked China ought to be able to do without a social revolution if it instituted a political revolution. He had nothing to say to the very poor who made up the revolutionary armies at Waichow in 1900 and little to tell the city inhabitants he knew better. His ideas and programs had not sprung from a Chinese setting. They were, like Sun Yat-sen himself, foreign oriented.

Organizationally Sun Yat-sen had talked in Western terms, but in action he retained a preference for the more traditional forms of the secret society organization and loyalty. The T'ung-meng hui was little more than a league of such societies. After Sung Chiao-jen's failure to build a modern, democratic Kuomintang party in 1912, Sun concluded that tighter organization was the first requirement for success in China, and he tried to reorganize his followers in a closely controlled Revolutionary party in 1914. In the course of this effort he lost many friends. His ambivalent attitude toward Japan in 1915 cost him more. In 1919 the Kuomintang was reorganized once again as an open political party in an attempt to appeal to the modern sector of Chinese society. The final reorganization in 1924 restored the central controls more congenial to Sun.

Quite aside from these shifts, Sun Yat-sen made disastrous errors in judgment. In 1917 he moved to Canton after giving up on political progress in Peking. The southern members of the Parliament followed him. Under the aegis of a "Movement for Protection of the Constitution," he had himself named generalissimo of a Chinese National Military Government and tried to unify China from Canton. His government declared war on Germany in order to deprive Peking of the claim to represent China and then ordered his armies to march against Peking. Unfortunately Sun's base in Kwangtung was not secure, for the armies were not really his. The generals who commanded them preferred to restrict their operations in accordance with their own interests and had little intention of risking their forces in quixotic drives against larger forces to the north. In 1918 Sun Yat-sen found it necessary to return to the French concession of Shanghai. After peace talks between the northern and southern governments in 1919 failed he returned to Canton but soon found himself outclassed by the militarist Ch'en Chiung-ming, who had an army.

In 1921 Sun Yat-sen had himself declared provisional president of China. His platform showed that his goals were still limited. He espoused local autonomy, peaceful unification, the Open Door and the development of industry. But once again he ran afoul of his military colleagues. When he tried to enter into negotiations with Chang Tso-lin of Manchuria in hopes of forming an alliance against the militarists situated between them, Ch'en Chiung-ming turned against him and forced him to flee to a gunboat in the Canton harbor. Sun spent much of the summer of 1922 aboard it trying to work out a new strategy. Before long the northern militarists were fronting with constitution and parliaments again, with the result that Sun Yat-sen's play for legitimacy came to nothing. Enraged and frustrated, he hired Yunnanese and Kwangsi

民國六年九月十日孫大元帥就職拍照紀念

SUN YAT-SEN (center, front) WITH FOLLOWERS in Canton observance of his assumption of military command as Marshal in 1917.

mercenaries to drive Ch'en out of Canton, which they did in 1923. Unfortunately, they decided to stay in the city to enjoy its sources of income and diversion. Sun's record was not one to encourage Chinese or foreign support.

Outside help had always been important to Sun, and now it was essential. He tried again to get Japanese support, but the Japanese were doing well enough with Chang Tso-lin in Manchuria and had little confidence in Sun's ability to organize the rest of China. He sought European, especially British, and American support, and his real preference would have been some sort of international organization to support a united Chinese government. But he had no government to back; his needs were more fundamental. Sun's desperation coincided with a new search by Soviet Russia for a foothold in Chinese politics. The Russians were actively seeking groups to back, and of all the candidates for leadership in China, Sun Yat-sen seemed the only one who might command the large-scale support that would qualify him for Russian backing.

Sun Yat-sen's endorsements of Soviet Russia did not contain praise or admiration for specific features of Russian communism. Instead he reverted to earlier themes of "Asian" unity and justice. It is probably fair to say, as one of Sun Yat-sen's Japanese colleagues wrote, that his real ideology was that of Pan-Asianism. In his final speech in Japan in 1924 Sun said that Russia had decided "to separate from the white peoples in Europe. . . . she insists on the rule of Right and denounces the rule of Might." As a result Russia had been "expelled from the family of nations by the white races of the whole of Europe." Russia had joined with the Orient. Pan-Asianism was, for Sun, a moral revulsion from imperialism; the problem was "how to terminate the sufferings of the Asiatic peoples and resist the aggression of the powerful European countries. In a word, Pan-Asianism represents the cause of the oppressed Asiatic peoples." To the end of Sun's life, he continued to think that Japan too might still side with the code of "Right" instead of that of "Might."

Sun Yat-sen had always been unusually dependent upon foreigners, but at the end of his life he came to blame most of China's ills on those same foreigners. Antiimperialism and Pan-Asianism were the reverse side of his personal disillusion and frustration. "The Peking Government could not stand twenty-four hours without the backing it receives from foreign governments," he told an interviewer in 1923. "The people could easily overthrow the whole military system if not for this backing of foreign countries." Consequently "We have lost hope of help from America, England, France, or any other of the great powers," and now "The only country that shows any signs of helping us in the South is the Soviet Government of Russia."

The chronology of Sun Yat-sen's turn to the Soviet Union for support is not completely clear, and the details of the agreement he reached with the Russians have never been published by either party. By the time of the Second Congress of the Chinese Communist Party in July 1922 that organization had accepted the idea that, in countries like China, communists would have to work through a two-stage revolution. The first would be directed against imperialism and feudalism, and in this revolution support from "bourgeois" forces as well as "democratic" militarists could be utilized. The second revolution would follow military victory and would bring the social revolution. For the first revolution, communists could profit from a united front with the nationalists. During the same period the Russians were scouting out "progressive militarists"; Ch'en Chiung-ming, Feng Yü-hsiang, and even Wu P'ei-fu were all considered.

But none of these had Sun's credentials as a national figure and leader of a party that could, with proper reorganization, become a mass nationalist movement. For his part Sun needed to firm up the control of his territorial base in Canton to qualify for assistance—hence his desperate efforts to secure that base by the use of militarist mercenaries. The late months of 1922 were a period of tremendous activity for him. Efforts to rejuvenate his party following negotiations with the Russians and simultaneously with northern warlords like Chang Tso-lin, and a spate of telegrams, press interviews and letters showed that, whatever outsiders might think, Sun himself was not prepared to give up his fight.

During the same period the Russians returned to the Chinese diplomatic arena. The Peking militarists had given up their recognition of the nonexistent czarist government only in 1920. Shortly afterward the Russians again published an offer by Karakhan proposing renegotiation of all Russian rights in China.

And in August 1922, Adolf Joffe, a Soviet envoy, arrived to an enthusiastic welcome from Chinese students in Peking. Joffe's negotiations with Wellington Koo, the foreign minister and acting premier, went badly because of Koo's insistence that Russia withdraw from Outer Mongolia and renounce all rights to the Chinese Eastern Railway. In January 1923 Joffe left Peking and proceeded to Shanghai, where he met with Sun Yat-sen.

Sun had already been in contact with one or more Comintern representatives there. At least one Communist, Li Ta-chao, had already accepted an invitation to join Sun Yat-sen's Kuomintang, although he insisted on retaining his Communist membership. Precedents existed for Sun Yat-sen to refuse a united front of equal parties and to insist on Kuomintang leadership of the national revolution. Communists would join his party as individuals, he ruled, but Kuomintang members were forbidden to join any other organizations. Work began on a new manifesto for the Kuomintang. It emphasized nationalism, a revised party program and new party regulations. In January Sun Yat-sen conferred with Joffe over a period of ten days and reached agreement with him on the details of Russian aid.

The only public result of this was a statement Sun issued with Joffe on 26 January 1923. In this release Sun Yat-sen appeared as the head of a government. "Dr. Sun Yat-sen and Mr. A. A. Joffe, Russian Envoy Extraordinary and Plenipotentiary to China," it began, "have authorized the publication of the following statement." The statement itself was not very explicit. It expressed agreement that the "Communistic order or even the Soviet system cannot actually be introduced into China, because there do not exist here the conditions for the successful establishment of either Communism or Sovietism.... China's paramount and most pressing problem is to achieve national unification, and attain full national independence." Joffe reaffirmed the principles expressed in the Karakhan declaration and affirmed Russian readiness to enter into negotiations looking toward the renunciation of czarist rights in China, including those relating to the Chinese Eastern Railway. The statement noted Sun's desire that Chang Tso-lin should be consulted on this point. Furthermore Joffe categorically declared that "it is not and has never been the intention or purpose of the present Russian Government to carry out imperialistic policies in Outer Mongolia or to work for Outer Mongolia's independence from China. Dr. Sun therefore does not deem the immediate evacuation of Russian troops from Outer Mongolia to be urgently necessary or to the real advantage of China...." Thus Joffe, rebuffed in Peking by Wellington Koo, had won Sun Yat-sen's endorsement of the Soviet position, while admitting to Sun that China would not qualify for communism. More important, certainly, was his implied agreement that the Kuomintang would be the vehicle of the national revolution in China, and most important to that intention was the promise of the support of Russia for Sun's drive for national unification.

The Sun-Joffe agreement set the stage for future Kuomintang cooperation with the Chinese Communist party. For both sides to that agreement it was a good bargain. Sun Yat-sen's control over even Canton remained very imperfect.

His mercenaries were reliable only as long as he could pay them, and in December 1923 he tried to seize the Canton customs office in the hope of getting a secure source of money. The treaty powers, who relied on the customs as security for the 1913 Reorganization Loan they had given Yüan Shih-k'ai, denounced this as piracy and Sun as a troublemaker. Sun also did his best to raise money through loans and exactions from the Canton business community. His government taxed quite as ingeniously and harshly as did most of the warlords. He resorted to the sale of government land and buildings and expropriated and confiscated religious and institutional buildings when necessary. Despite his best efforts, he was almost driven out of Canton again in November 1923 by the armies of Ch'en Chiung-ming. He clearly needed a more solid base and better ways of winning popular support within it. He could expect no help from the Western powers and from the middle and upper classes in Canton. The Russian model of organization, coupled as it was with promises of arms and military training, was attractive.

For the Communists, on the other hand, the tie with the Kuomintang provided the opportunity of political participation on a scale they had not known before. They eagerly seized the assignments for which they were best fitted, the organization of worker and peasant groups. Party membership grew rapidly, and the rapid successes of the years 1924 and 1925 would have been impossible without the tie with the Kuomintang.

The Kuomintang-Communist merger was made official at a Kuomintang reorganization conference in January 1924. From this time on, the chief Moscow representative was Michael Borodin, who had been sent to Sun Yat-sen by the Kremlin in October 1923. This veteran communist was a man of great drive and ability. He had lived in the United States (as Mike Gruzenberg) from 1906 to 1918, and thus he could work with Sun and his lieutenants in English. He had served on communist missions in Spain, Mexico, America and England. He was perfectly suited to serve as an agent of the recommendations which Soviet Foreign Minister Chicherin sent to Sun Yat-sen in December 1923. Chicherin's advice was that the Kuomintang should build a popular movement, for which propaganda and organization were the prime requirements. The contrast between the Kuomintang and the warlords had to be made obvious.

Borodin set to work to suggest ways of building and strengthening the Kuomintang. He utilized the near-panic caused by Ch'en Chiung-ming's advance on Canton in November 1923 to urge the development of a radical social program. His job was not easy. The Chinese Communist party numbered barely three hundred. Of these only a few had joined the Kuomintang, and many must have had grave reservations about casting their lot with a group of politicians they had known and distrusted for many years. In Canton some two hundred thousand troops were attached to generals who were not in sympathy with the movement at all. The workers were divided and unorganized, the peasants were apathetic and distrustful. The Kuomintang was little more than a loose society scattered all over China, and the income of the Canton government was not more than a few hundred thousand (Mexican) dollars a month.

The first efforts were to strengthen the organization of the Kuomintang and to make it responsive to central direction. Borodin urged, and Sun Yat-sen grasped at, the model of the Russian Communist party. Sun had always had his doubts about an open and democratic party structure in China, and he saw instantly the advantages of the new model. Under Borodin's recommendations the Kuomintang changed from the personal following it had been to a carefully structured and authoritarian body. Local cells sent representatives to a regional Congress, which selected regional executive committees, which in turn formed the National Party Congress, which named a Central Executive Committee with the real power of decision. Policy was controlled from the top in accordance with communist principles of "democratic centralism." Sun Yat-sen was made party president, and the reorganization was approved by the Party Congress, not without some murmurings from old members who resented the new communist structure, in January 1924.

Sun Yat-sen's old followers dominated the Central Executive Committee, but some of the new communist members were the logical candidates to head the new divisions of propaganda that were set up. Provision was made for registration of members (and exclusion of those who opposed the new policies), establishment of a weekly paper to disseminate the ideology and a propaganda school.

SUN YAT-SEN (1866-1925) in his mature years.

In evaluating the organizational tie the Kuomintang formed with the Russians, it is important to avoid exaggeration. The Russians and the communists needed Sun Yat-sen fully as much as he needed them. There was a negligible communist membership in China and no indication that Chinese society could sustain a communist revolution. Sun Yat-sen was a world-known figure who had in the past enjoyed great respect in the Western world and among Chinese all over the world. During interludes of success he had been treated as an honored guest by authorities throughout the world. His fame made him a particularly attractive figure for the growing student population of China. Therefore he was able to drive a rather hard bargain with the Russians. The united front did not dignify the Chinese Communist party with equality with the Kuomintang. Kuomintang members were not permitted to join the other organization. Sun Yat-sen was, as always, serenely confident in his own destiny and ability to handle any problems that might arise. In earlier days he had not worried about the costs of Japanese support, and he was not about to fret over Russian intentions now.

4. The San Min Chu I

CHICHERIN HAD POINTED OUT to Sun Yat-sen that propaganda and organization were the first necessities, and it was partly at Borodin's urging that Sun Yat-sen set himself to elaborating his views of the nationalist revolution. These were given as a series of lectures in 1924 and published as the *Three Principles of the People* (*San Min Chu I*). The ideas were not new, for Sun had used them in unstructured fashion for some time. His manuscripts were destroyed in the attack on his headquarters by Ch'en Chiung-ming, however, and consequently the lectures come to us in rough form. "I do not have the time necessary for careful preparation nor the books necessary for reference," Sun apologized. "I can only mount the platform and speak extemporaneously." The historian can be thankful for this. The lectures have freshness and immediacy, and their homely illustrations and irrelevancies tell more about Sun Yat-sen than a finished product would have.

The idea of three principles was derived from the Gettysburg Address, with its reference to government "of the people, by the people, and for the people."[1] Sun Yat-sen saw these ideas as translating into national independence, government and livelihood, and he organized his talks around those concepts. Under his first principle, nationalism (*min-tsu*), Sun stressed the importance of freeing China from the restrictions of imperialism and the unequal treaties. China's sense of racial spirit and pride had been lost under the centuries of

---

[1] It lives on also in the postwar Japanese Constitution, with its introductory statement that "Government is a sacred trust of the people, the authority for which is derived from the people, the powers of which are exercised by the representatives of the people, and the benefits of which are enjoyed by the people."

Manchu rule, he felt, and it was essential to restore it. Several barriers stood in the way. One, curiously, was population growth in other countries as opposed to what Sun believed to be China's stagnant population. The Chinese, he warned, were about to be submerged in a world dominated by peoples who were increasing more rapidly. Furthermore China was threatened by a process of foreign pressure and control. Sun stressed particularly the dangers of economic penetration, and he warned that these were greater than those of political penetration because they were less obvious. Foreign trade could seem beneficial to both parties, but the unequal treaties kept the Chinese from reaping their share of the profits. The powers, by such slogans as "Open Door," magnified their own profits at China's expense.

In this emphasis on economic imperialism it is possible to recognize the influence of Sun's new Russian allies, for his earlier treatments of nationalism had concentrated far less on imperialism. Yet these ideas had stirred a generation since Lenin had put them in persuasive form. China, said Sun Yat-sen, was worse off than a colony, since China was the colony of every country that had an unequal treaty with her. (In this he was reverting to an idea of Liang Ch'i-ch'ao.) He suggested the term "hypocolony" to depict China's prostration and exploitation. It was essential for the Chinese to recapture their sense of autonomy and independence so that they could enter the international community on a basis of dignity. Most of the world's millions, he argued, were under the oppression of a small minority. China, by freeing herself, might then be able to help others free themselves from imperialism. If it failed to do so, it faced national extinction; China was in desperate danger, and foreign imperialism was the enemy. Whatever Sun's consistency or logic, his performance now provided extremely persuasive propaganda. For "propaganda and organization on the biggest scale," in Chicherin's words, nothing served so well as an attack on the affluent and privileged imperialist giants.

Sun's second principle, usually translated as democracy, was literally people's rights or powers (*min-chüan*). In the lectures devoted to this subject he began with the assumption that there was no real alternative to democracy in the twentieth century, since its predecessors (royalty, theocracy and brute force) had been discredited. But Sun lingered over the growing dilemmas of democratic government in the world of his time. It seemed to him that total popular sovereignty made no allowance for inexperience and inability and that people everywhere, while wishing their government to be strong, were at the same time afraid of giving it too much power.

Sun's solutions were simple. He made a distinction between sovereignty, which lay with the people, and ability, which was to be found with the few. He had a modern illustration. The owner of a motor car had power but no ability to drive it. His chauffeur, on the other hand, might have ability but no power. Just so, said Sun; the people have the power, or sovereignty, but they must allocate it to those with ability who will drive the machine of government.

Sun Yat-sen proposed to keep all things in balance by a new enumeration of powers. The people's powers would be expressed in suffrage, recall, initiative and referendum, all of which were to be found in the West. The government, for its part, would have five powers: executive, legislative, judicial, civil service examination and the censorate, China's ancient device for correcting bureaucratic arbitrariness. "With these nine powers in operation and preserving a balance," said Sun, "the problem of democracy will truly be solved and the government will have a definite course to follow."

One trouble, however, was that the Chinese people, despite their limited electoral experience, would be asked to manipulate institutions like those of initiative and recall that had been tried in only a few of the most enlightened and experienced electorates. Sun's answer for this was a stage theory of democracy. The first thing on the agenda was military unification, during which the army would rule. Next would be a period of Party tutelage, during which the Kuomintang would educate the nation in the workings of the promised institutions. Only then would the transition to *min-chüan* be possible. Sun had believed in the need for such stages for two decades, but in earlier schemes he had specified set lengths for each. In 1924 he no longer did this. As it worked out, the period of military unification ran into the Japanese war and that of tutelage came to an end only in the desperate attempts to stave off the Communist victory in the last stages of Nationalist rule on the mainland.

An examination of Sun Yat-sen's views on government shows how great an influence the traditional heritage of elitist government had on even so Westernized a man as Sun. Into these views elements of the Leninist view of the Party as vanguard fitted very well. Sun Yat-sen was convinced, as he said, that "freedom" was not really a problem for China. China had never known despotism of the sort that Europe had suffered. The problem was rather that the Chinese had known so much freedom that they were like a "sheet of loose sand." What they needed was the cement of organization and discipline to make them take their place in a modern society. Sun's earlier efforts had failed because of weakness and individualism. As he said in the speech with which he opened the Reorganization Congress of the Kuomintang, "There is one thing of the greatest importance in a political party, that is, all members of the party must possess spiritual unity. In order that all the members may be united spiritually, the first thing is to sacrifice freedom, the second is to offer ability. If the individual can sacrifice his freedom, then the whole party will have freedom. If the individual can offer his ability, then the whole party will possess ability . . . ." Lincoln would have had some difficulty in recognizing his "by the people" in the reminders that "on no account must we give more liberty to the individual; let us secure liberty instead for the nation." For Sun Yat-sen, as for so many of his generation, national wealth and strength were the standards against which all political projections had to be measured, and "democracy" was really a subcategory of the "nationalism" with which the *San Min Chu I* began.

Sun Yat-sen's third principle, livelihood (*min sheng*), explained what the new order would mean "for the people." It was not a subject he had dealt with before in detail. He needed a middle path to keep his past supporters' loyalty without losing his ability to attract young radicals. Already in the fall of 1923, when Ch'en Chiung-ming's troops were threatening Canton, Borodin had urged a radical policy to win over peasants and laborers. He had proposed that Sun announce the confiscation and distribution to tenants of landlord holdings, an eight hour day for workers and a minimum wage. As long as the danger from Ch'en was great, the Kuomintang leaders had agreed, and announcements of the new policy, advertised by a new propaganda apparatus, helped win popular support for Canton. But after the danger was past, Borodin found that his proposals were under attack. He had to be content with rent reductions and the establishment of peasant and tenant unions.

Sun Yat-sen was not prepared to institute a program of class hostility between landlords and tenants. The social problem, he said in one lecture, was new: it "arose with the invention of machinery and with the gradual substitution of natural power for human labor in the most civilized nations." Unfortunately "men who possessed machinery have taken wealth away from those who did not have machinery." China, fortunately, was still in a position to avoid this problem, for "all the Chinese people must be counted as poor. There are no great rich among us, only differences between the fairly poor and the extremely poor. How can we equalize this condition so that there will be no more extreme poverty?"

The problem therefore was to encourage modernization without worsening this situation. Sun came prepared with two slogans, one calling for equalization of rights in land and the other for the control of capital. His ideas on land turned out to be directed almost entirely to the treaty-port centers which were the China he knew. He proposed the application of Henry George's tax on land-value increments. Each landholder would be asked to appraise his holdings, with the government having the option of purchasing it at the appraisal figure. Thereafter all "unearned increments" in land value would revert to the government, for it was the larger society that had made the parcels of land take on added value. Sun's other approach was to encourage industrialization through state planning. State capital would rule out the rise of a wealthy class of capitalists like those who were responsible for the social problems in the industrialized countries of the West. In a separate lecture Sun Yat-sen bore down more heavily on the problems of tenantry and the landless peasantry. But beyond a general call to state action he did not provide the specifics of a program.

Throughout his lectures on livelihood Sun Yat-sen took care to distinguish his program from the Marxist or Russian examples. He repeatedly disavowed communist intentions and stressed a basic disagreement with Marx as to the motive force of history. He rejected Marx's materialist philosophy of history, wherein the "contradictions" between the owners of the modes of production and the workers generated struggle and revolution and accepted, instead, the views of a little-known American dentist, Maurice William, that the struggle for livelihood was the motive power in history. History was thus determined by social, not economic, forces.

The *San Min Chu I* lectures provided effective propaganda for the nationalist revolution. They offered simple answers to complicated questions. They were full of engaging, though often irrelevant, illustrations. They were strongly nationalistic, from the initial cry of alarm at the coming extinction of the Chinese race in a sea of non-Chinese to the separation of the Kuomintang purpose and program from those of any other countries. Sun's excoriation of imperialism as the bane of Chinese political and economic problems and his elaborately programmed scheme of future government seemed preferable to the selfishness and opportunism the major warlords displayed in their search for outside support.

In logic and in content the *San Min Chu I* left much to be desired. It had much more to say to coastal, urban China than it did to the vast interior of rural China. Its arguments about the coming extinction of the Chinese race, about urban land values and about China's degrees of poverty do not stand up. Nor do its proposals that a powerful, sovereign people should hand over their powers to self-delegated experts who will run the vehicle of government. But these failings did not hamper the Kuomintang in 1924. Nor need they have hurt it later, except for the fact that Sun's sketchy notes became the basis for a new orthodoxy and ideology after the death of their author in 1925.[2]

Sun Yat-sen's popularity with young Chinese grew with his denunciations of imperialism. His failure to secure a share of the customs receipts for Canton embittered him against the imperialist powers. To the American Minister Jacob Schurman he talked about a coming conflict between great powers and the Asian countries they were oppressing. To another interlocutor Sun said bitterly that there could be no republic in China until foreign interference came to an end and that he did not think that could end until there had been a drastic change in the governments of the principal treaty powers. The oppressed peoples of the world would have to overthrow the oppressive governments. On his final trip to Peking, Sun seemed so dangerous to the treaty-port newspapers that they urged their authorities to exclude him. They denounced him as a demagogue, "his hands still stained with the blood of his fellow citizens," and "surrounded in the eyes of urchins [the students] with all the glamour of triumph." In Japan, his last stop before Peking, he gave a number of speeches on Pan-Asianism which urged the Japanese to join their natural allies in the struggle for "right against might."

Sun Yat-sen went to Peking to negotiate once more with an advocate of Might rather than Right, the warlord Chang Tso-lin. He hoped to form an alliance with him against the forces of Wu P'ei-fu in central and north China. Instead he was stricken with cancer and died on 12 March 1925. A will he left began, "I have devoted forty years to the work of Nationalist Revolution, the aim of which is to secure the freedom and independence of China. After forty

---

[2] One might compare the ideology of emperor in Meiji Japan. A positive factor for unification in that generation, it became a barrier to progress for the next.

years of experience I am profoundly convinced that in order to reach this aim we must wake up the masses of the country and unite with those races of the world who treat us in equality, and struggle together.... All my comrades must continue to exert their efforts according to the General Principles of Reconstruction, the Outline of Reconstruction, the Three Principles of the People written by me, and the Declaration of the First National Congress of the Kuomintang, until this aim is realized." Sun's imposing mausoleum at Nanking and the state cult the Kuomintang built around him made the hastily prepared lectures of the *San Min Chu I* a binding document for the edification and inspiration of future citizens. Courses in the Three Principles remained compulsory in the curriculum on Taiwan fifty years after Sun's death. The logical fallacies of the document and the uses to which it was put should not be allowed to obscure its merits. Not only was it excellent propaganda for the revolution, it was also the first document produced by a popular leader in China that set out a generalized goal and proposed a method of reaching it. It was the first document to include mention of social and economic problems and to treat the task of political modernization as something more complicated than the writing and enforcing of yet another constitution. Its eclectic nature, its echoes of the Chinese past and the Western present and its refusal to follow any line to its logical conclusion made it a document around which men of many opinions could gather. Nor was it designed as a closed system of canonical perfection. It left plenty of room for later commentary and exposition. Although the *San Min Chu I* had many drawbacks as ideology, it is hard to see why these should have cost the Kuomintang its right to rule in China. Many writers have tried to establish such a link, but the successes and failures of the Nationalist period have to be sought elsewhere.

5. *The Northern Expedition*

AT THE TIME of Sun Yat-sen's death in Peking there were several possible candidates for succession. One was the gifted essayist Wang Ching-wei. Wang had been one of the principal editors of the revolutionary journal *Min Pao,* and he had become famous as the result of a daring attempt at political assassination in late Manchu times. He was with Sun Yat-sen at the time of his death in Peking and helped draft the impressive will Sun left to the party. Wang's relationships with other Kuomintang leaders were never easy, and his career was to end ingloriously with his leadership of the Nanking government installed by the Japanese military during World War II. There was also Liao Chung-k'ai, who was in some ways the architect of the cooperation with the Soviet Union. Liao carried on conferences with Adolf Joffe in Japan for Sun Yat-sen, and Sun appointed him governor of Kwangtung when that was the only province under his control. Liao became recognized as a leader of the left wing of the Kuomintang, and he was convinced of the necessity to organize workers and peasants through

CHIANG KAI-SHEK (1888-), the young leader of the Kuomintang armies.

a program of practical reform and political propaganda. Conservative groups within the Nationalist party were responsible for his assassination in April 1925. With his death the program of cooperation with the Communists lost one of its strongest supporters.

Ideas without arms could get nowhere in China in the 1920s, however, and the leader of the Kuomintang armies came to inherit the Kuomintang party. This was Chiang Kai-shek. Chiang was born in 1887 in Chekiang province, the son of a farming family that had entered the salt trade. Through the help of relatives who made up for his loss of parental support in the early death of his father, he was educated in Yüan Shih-k'ai's military academy in Paotingfu in 1906. In 1907 he went to Japan for further military training, and there he joined the revolutionary league of Sun Yat-sen. The years of the revolution and the early Republic found him in the Shanghai area. Although the exact nature of his activities can no longer be discovered, it is logical to suppose, as most authorities do, that he established himself as a figure of some importance in the shadowy area between Shanghai business and revolutionary politics. The chaos of those years required qualities of strength and ruthlessness in those who survived. Sun Yat-sen recognized in Chiang a devoted and able military follower. Chiang remembered in the treaty-port world he knew so well the source of moral and political rot that was responsible for many of China's ills. Chiang was only one of

Sun Yat-sen's lieutenants in the early days of Russian cooperation, but he was entrusted with the building of the military establishment. In a China beset with problems of civil war this gave him the inside track for power.

In October 1923 Chiang left Shanghai with three companions for Moscow. A letter from Sun Yat-sen to Karakhan explained that the purpose of sending his chief of staff was to discuss the preparation for military action against the warlords in north China. Chiang Kai-shek seems to have become disillusioned with the sincerity and intentions of his hosts in Moscow very quickly. While there, he learned about Borodin's arrival in Canton. Years later he recalled that he had become convinced that "Soviet political institutions were instruments of tyranny and terror" and that the Russians "had not given up their aggressive designs in Outer Mongolia." But the details of Russian aid were generous and promising. Trotsky assured Chiang that Russia would help his program of unification through weapons and economic aid.

By mid-December Chiang was back in Shanghai. In a report to Sun Yat-sen upon his return, Chiang Kai-shek warned that "the Russian Communist Party cannot be trusted.... It is the Communists' policy to convert the Northeast Provinces, Mongolia, Sinkiang, and Tibet into parts of a sovietized domain. It may even harbor sinister designs on China's other provinces." So he saw his problem as one of using the Russians without being used by them. Until he controlled the modern cities and could attract outside support, however, he had no alternative to utilizing the Russians. The two partners in the pattern of cooperation had different schedules and objectives. Chiang wanted to use the new military machine as soon as it was ready in order to get away from his benefactors. The Russians wanted to delay the military campaign as long as possible in order to give the Communists time to build up the dynamics of a revolutionary movement that would be irreversible.

The core of Russian military assistance was the Whampoa Military Academy that was opened in Canton in May 1924. Chiang Kai-shek was its head. With him he brought old friends and fellow students from Paotingfu, and in it he produced the core of a personal military following for the next half-century. Initially about five hundred students were selected from over two thousand applicants. Since it was clear that the academy and its graduates would be central to the political future of the Nationalist movement, there were sharp struggles for the control and content of its programs. It was probably in this connection that Liao Chung-k'ai lost his life. But the more important struggle came between Chiang Kai-shek and Communist party representatives. Chiang resolved this struggle by a tactic he would utilize again on several occasions in the future. He resigned in protest and returned only when the lines of power were securely placed in his hands. His cooperation and leadership were recognized as important by all groups.

In October of 1924 a shipment of eight thousand rifles, with five hundred rounds of ammunition for each, came from the Soviet Union. For the first time the basis of a modern force could be constructed; up to now the total stock available for training had been thirty rifles. Later additional shipments of fifteen thousand rifles, machine guns and artillery came. However, the ideological controls of the academy were as important as the hardware that began to come in. Chiang saw to it that Confucian values of sincerity and loyalty were stressed. He selected students from all parts of the country. The cadet core became a personal rather than a regional clique. It was a highly motivated group, dedicated to the national revolution. Rules of collective responsibility were set. Retreat was to bring punishment by death. Early engagements between units from Whampoa and the warlord Ch'en Chiung-ming brought resounding successes for the Nationalists, although they were sometimes gained at great cost of life because of Chiang's insistence on morale and his reluctance to countenance even tactical retreat. Similar tactics in future years against the northern warlords and later against the Japanese cost the regime dearly in the lives of its most committed and dedicated military men. But they also served to inspire emulation and to intimidate enemies. The Whampoa corps became the nucleus of a large force that absorbed many of the provincial troops with which it came in contact. Some of those commanders, especially the southern warlord generals Pai Ch'ung-hsi and Li Tsung-jen, played important roles in the military history of mid-twentieth-century China.

Russian help included tactical and strategic suggestions. A General Blücher, who had earlier used the name of Galen, came to direct the Russian advisers. By 1925 there may have been as many as one thousand Russian military and naval personnel in China. On the advice of these men, a military council was established to parallel a political council. In July 1925 a national government for the stage of military unification was set up, and the army was named the National Revolutionary Army. The political council was considered superior to the military council, however, and a political commissar was attached to fighting units for each one hundred fighting men. The armies grew rapidly. In 1924 they numbered less than one thousand; in January 1925, fifteen hundred, six months later there were nine thousand, and in November 1925 there were thirty thousand. When Pai Ch'ung-hsi and Li Tsung-jen joined in February 1926 the total rose to eighty-five thousand men. The need for arms now began to outrun the supply lines from Vladivostok, and the Nationalist leaders were anxious to start the advance toward the arsenals of the industrial cities along the Yangtze.

By the early days of 1926 a split between Kuomintang members anxious to continue the cooperation with Russian and Chinese Communists and others who opposed these policies was clearly visible. Conflicting resolutions were adopted at the Second Kuomintang Party Congress in Canton in January 1926, and a rival Party Congress was called at Shanghai by groups who had earlier agreed to oppose the Russian tie at a meeting outside Peking that has become known as the Western Hills Conference. Both sides could claim a link with Sun Yat-sen. His last visit to Peking had been to work out cooperation with Chang Tso-lin, and on the way he had made one more attempt at cooperation with the Japanese. Yet he had never renounced or given any evidence of distrusting the arrangement with the Russians and the Chinese Communists.

The Russian advisers had their own priorities. A situation in which rural and labor agitation was organized by Communist efforts and in which the military establishment continued dependent upon Russian military assistance was clearly to their advantage. They did their best to delay the military expedition and tried to combine it with measures that might serve their purpose to the north. Thus the "Christian general," warlord Feng Yü-hsiang, was bailed out with Russian help in 1926 after a defeat by Chang Tso-lin. He withdrew to the northwestern province of Kansu, where he could count upon a friendly Russia at his back. Feng went on a pilgrimage to Moscow in the summer of 1926. Upon his return he oriented his efforts to the commoners even more than he had before. Sun Yat-sen now took the place of God in invocations that featured Feng's unique prose. A catechism in which his troops were drilled took on revolutionary tones.[3]

> Q. Whose troops are you?
> A. We are the troops of the common people.
> Q. Why do we want to wage war?
> A. In order to abolish the unequal treaties.
> Q. Whom do you want to fight?
> A. We want first to overthrow the traitorous warlords, and second, to overthrow imperialism...
> Q. Why do we wage war?
> A. In order to overthrow imperialism, the traitorous warlords, grasping and corrupt officials, local bullies, and bad gentry.

In Kansu the Russians tried to develop a military academy that would be the northern equivalent of Whampoa. Russian advisers were sent. Fifteen thousand infantry rifles, nine thousand pistols, and thirty thousand hand grenades were shipped. Crude plays put on by newly "indoctrinated" and educated soldiers brought home the story of national humiliation at the hands of imperialists and warlords.

All of this made it appropriate for Chiang Kai-shek's Russian advisers to propose that the Kuomintang troops try to link up with those of Feng Yü-hsiang, perhaps through an amphibious movement to the north China coast where Feng could try to meet them. No damage would be done to the Kwangtung base that was being revolutionized so satisfactorily. Both armies would still be dependent upon their Russian sources of supply.

But Chinese nationalism was genuine, and the Russians found that they were unable to manipulate it to their advantage. When it came to the test, Feng Yü-hsiang chose to throw in his lot with Chiang Kai-shek instead of maintaining his Russian ties. And Chiang, who correctly saw the Russians' intention to squeeze him "like a lemon" (to use the phrase Stalin used), chose to squeeze first. In the spring of 1926 he picked a time when Borodin was away from Canton to arrest the Russian political advisers and take over full military control. Wang

---

[3] James E. Sheridan, *Chinese Warlord: The Career of Feng Yü-hsiang* (Stanford: Stanford Univ. Press, 1966), p. 212.

Ching-wei, whom he considered doubtful, was dismissed as head of the Nationalist party and government and was driven out. Chiang then called a meeting of the Central Executive Committee. It named him Kuomintang head and called for the beginning of the Northern Expedition. He next turned to mollify Borodin and the Chinese Communists. They had nowhere else to go and accepted his reassurances and continued their cooperation. But thereafter their authority was much reduced.

In launching the Northern Expedition, Chiang rejected the strategic suggestions of the Russian advisers and chose to drive north and east to the modern cities of the Yangtze Valley. There he would be placed in contact with the great industrial and financial centers of Wuchang, Nanking and Shanghai, and he would be able to liberate himself from further dependence upon Russian assistance.

The Northern Expedition began in July 1926. The Kuomintang forces were successful everywhere because of the political preparations that had been made. The cooperation of the inhabitants of the countryside through which the armies passed was as important as the enthusiasm the Whampoa cadets showed in the military engagements. The armies had been drilled against theft and rapine. They behaved, and were greeted, like liberators. But the political campaigns served Communist as well as Kuomintang purposes, and the military successes led to political crises. Labor and peasant movements mushroomed. As the armies conquered the warlords, the political competitors prepared to set up rival governments.

In 1926 a left-wing group set up a joint council in Wuhan and began to move the political headquarters there from Canton. Chiang Kai-shek recognized in this development a threat to his own dominance. The Central Executive Committee in Wuhan reversed many of the decisions that he had taken at Canton after his suppression of the Communists there. In the spring of 1927 worker organizations in Shanghai delivered that city into his hands, and he was able to capture China's largest city without having to fight for it. He then decided on a counterstroke and swiftly undertook a bloody suppression of the labor and communist organizations in Shanghai. These massacres of April 1927 crushed the left-wing strength in Shanghai so thoroughly that it could play no further role in Chinese politics for the next two decades. On 18 April Chiang then set up his own government in Nanking and prepared to compete with the left-wing government in Wuhan.

Chiang's hand was strengthened by foreign approval. When the Nationalist armies took Nanking in March 1927, the political commissars had unleashed violence against the foreign settlement. Earlier, at Hankow, the British concession had been seized. Antiimperialist and especially anti-British propaganda had provided an inviting focus for agitation among urban laborers. Consequently the emergence of a "moderate" noncommunist Chiang Kai-shek in opposition to forces that seemed intent upon making the nationalist revolution a virulently antiforeign movement brought him foreign support. English customs inspectors in Shanghai delivered to Chiang's government an advance of three million dollars in customs income, and foreign and domestic banking concerns added generous loans. The foreign powers also lifted their embargo on arms to China. His position fortified by foreign arms, money and the approval of the business interests in the modern port cities he had just taken over, Chiang now stood prepared for a struggle with his enemies. Against this strength, Wuhan, with its inadequate trickle of Russian arms and enthusiastic but weak labor and peasant forces, could not prevail.

The principal warlords were still in existence, and both sides devoted their first efforts to the task of unification. The Wuhan councils were divided. Some, like Borodin, advocated military moves in the hope of beating Chiang Kai-shek to the control of the north. Others wanted to give first priority to establishing control over the territory Wuhan already held. In Moscow tactics in China were becoming a dimension of the struggle between Stalin and Trotsky for power after the death of Lenin. Chinese Communists were handicapped by uncertain directives from a distant leadership that was imperfectly acquainted with the complexities of the Chinese situation.

The Wuhan leaders counted on the cooperation of Feng Yü-hsiang and wanted to combine a northern push with a move by Feng along the principal east-west rail connection. They rushed into battle and sacrificed their best units in fighting against Chang Tso-lin. Then at the key moment, and after the Wuhan troops had paid the price of battle, Feng Yü-hsiang moved into the communications centers that were their goals and announced his adherence to Chiang Kai-shek. The political miscalculations of Wuhan had resulted in expensive military successes that prepared the way for political control by Chiang. Neither Feng Yü-hsiang nor Yen Hsi-shan, who also shifted to Chiang Kai-shek, had any reason to expect much from the Wuhan government with its worker-peasant and left-wing sympathies. The accession of these two generals combined with the bloodletting that the Wuhan forces had suffered to bring Chiang an almost painless victory.

It should not, however, be thought that the Wuhan government was Communist dominated. The bulk of its leaders, men like Wang Ching-wei, were quite uncertain about the proper lines of an agricultural program and undecided what the Party's line on landholding and rents should be. When a formal choice between Moscow and Nanking became necessary, they would surely stay with Nanking. In June 1927 this choice suddenly seemed necessary. Wang Ching-wei was shown a telegram from Moscow in which Stalin called for an immediate agrarian revolt to recapture the leadership of the national revolution from Chiang Kai-shek. The next month the Wuhan government dismissed its Russian advisers and Communist allies.

It is clear that the Moscow part of the story in China deserves to be entitled, as one author does, "Stalin's failure." But it is less clear that Trotsky or Lenin himself could have succeeded with the tools that were at hand. The situation in China could not be controlled from Moscow. The decision to restructure the

Kuomintang on centralist lines meant, in the first instance, that control of the masses, unless they were under arms, would not necessarily lead to control of the Kuomintang. The Communists never came close to controlling the military machine of the Kuomintang. It served their purposes to have that machine destroy the principal warlords, but they only succeeded in replacing them with the much stronger order of Chiang Kai-shek, whose modern structure was more to the liking of the imperialist powers. Stalin, completely out of touch with realities, suggested at one point that the Wuhan leaders seize and "try" Chiang Kai-shek, ignoring the fact that they would need a larger army than Chiang's to do this. Trotsky, for his part, later clarified his position to make it one of constant support for a "proletarian" party which would fight under its own banners. The trouble with this was that the proletarians in China were few and weak, and Trotsky-style revolt could only lead to brutal, warlord-style repression. The Kuomintang, a broadly based national movement, was the only sort of framework within which large-scale organization and agitation could be carried on with anything approaching success. The astounding degree of success that the Communists did reach testified to the depth of discontent and latent fury within Chinese society. But the fate of the Communist movement once it had to give up the shelter of Kuomintang leadership also showed the limitations of its capabilities.

In Moscow the summer of 1927 was one of agonized argument about the course to follow in China. Stalin was not prepared to adopt a line of revolution immediately, for this would have borne out Trotsky's analysis of the situation. Instead, he insisted on the continuation of an alliance that had already failed. Then, in August, a rising in Nanchang that was supposed to capitalize on a wave of revolutionary enthusiasm was ordered. It was promptly crushed by the Wuhan leaders who had been expected to encourage it. In the fall of 1927 a series of desperate revolts tried to reverse the losses of the previous months. The symbols of cooperation with the Kuomintang were sacrificed. Communist leader Ch'en Tu-hsiu gave way to Ch'ü Ch'iu-pai, and he, shortly afterward, to Li Li-san. Borodin was recalled. "Autumn harvest" insurrections tried to win and hold a revolutionary center. They were unsuccessful everywhere.

Stalin's need for victories led to a final, massive, miscalculation in 1928. In Canton a large-scale commune was organized and led an insurrection that resulted in the slaughter of the core of Communist strength there. In a desperate attempt to wrest victory from disaster, Moscow then proclaimed that capitalism in China was finally disintegrating. Li Li-san, newly elevated to the leadership of the Chinese Communist party, led a revolution at Changsha. The city was taken in July, held briefly and then given up again. The Communists had sacrificed their best followers and had lost their principal centers of organizational strength in a vain effort to meet Stalin's needs in the power struggle within the Kremlin. The domestic revolution that might have stood as a continuing reproach to the military was temporarily over. Its leaders were scattered; workers were demoralized and the peasants cowed and discouraged.

But the swift and often savage repression of the Communist movement provides indirect confirmation of its astounding success. The sources for revolution were clearly present in a China that could mount the worker insurrections in Canton and Shanghai. They were even more visible in the agricultural sector. In the spring of 1927, a young Mao Tse-tung had studied the peasant movement in Hunan, and his report provides a monument for the identification of agrarian injustice and anger. Mao pointed to the clear evidence of hatred, conflict and violence he saw on every side and described a setting filled with revolutionary potential. "Revolution," he wrote in a famous phrase, "is not a dinner party, nor literary composition, nor painting, nor embroidery. It cannot be done so delicately, so leisurely, so gentlemanly, and so 'gently, kindly, politely, plainly, and modestly.' Revolutionary insurrection is the violent action of one class overthrowing the power of another." He went on to describe the tensions between landlords, "gentry," and peasants. "Believe it or not," he wrote, "some gentry in the adjacent districts who refused to turn in their opium pipes were arrested and paraded through the villages by the Peasant Associations. Some big gentry in the cities were even killed. . . . at the general celebration of the victory of the Northern Expedition more than 10,000 peasants raised banners of various sizes, amidst poles and hoes, and paraded in great strength."

Mao argued that a real revolution in China could only be managed by seeking out and exploiting divisions of interest and of class in the countryside. In the fall of 1927, when he led the unsuccessful Autumn Harvest Uprising in Hunan, however, the effort fared poorly. Repression and wholesale executions of the Party cadres made it possible to crush the uprising within a week, and Mao himself barely escaped with his life. With the few followers he could salvage he headed for the mountains on the border between Hunan and Kiangsi, where, in October of 1927, he established his first revolutionary base area. As the unsuccessful putsches carried out at Stalin's orders failed, additional Communist forces came to join Mao in the hills. It was there, poorly armed and fed, that the Chinese Communist party organized what was to become the future People's Liberation Army and developed the strategies of guerrilla warfare that made possible its survival under Kuomintang attack and Japanese aggression. The first phase of collaboration with the Kuomintang, of rapid success and even more rapid disaster, had come to an end. Chiang Kai-shek had triumphed.

The international dimension of the Northern Expedition was of great importance and complexity At the time of the antiforeign incidents in Nanking in 1927, Chiang Kai-shek was occasionally described in the West as a dangerous and fanatically antiforeign nationalist. Within a few months he emerged as a "moderate" nationalist leader, denounced by Chinese Communists as a captive of the imperialist powers. A very short time later he became a symbol of resistance to foreign imperialism and the hope of Chinese patriotism against Japanese aggression.

The base line for a discussion of these changes must lie with the Washington Conference of 1921 and 1922 in which the United States, Britain, France and Japan tried to work out a new relationship in the Pacific. The Anglo-Japanese alliance was replaced by a network of treaties designed to protect the national interests of each power and protect China's territorial sovereignty. It was agreed to schedule conferences to arrange for increases of tariff rates for China. Japan agreed to restore to China the Shantung rights she had taken from Germany in 1914 and held on to in the Twenty-one Demands of the following year, and a new consortium was worked out to cooperate in future loans to a Chinese government anxious to reform and reorganize itself. The problem was, of course, that warlord China did not possess such a government and that the Peking government's jurisdiction scarcely extended beyond the walls of the city. A major effort to correct tariff inequalities in 1925 collapsed with the fall of the current Peking government.

A second major difficulty was that the Washington treaties ignored the existence of the Soviet Union. While the Pacific powers that initiated the Washington treaties struggled to work out some pattern of cooperation, the Soviet Union moved forward on its own with assistance to the Kuomintang. At the same time it denounced its imperialist privileges of czarist days, granted China tariff autonomy, remitted the Russian part of the Boxer indemnity and ended extraterritorial rights. Thus Russia unilaterally indicated the direction that future relations with a resurgent Nationalist China would have to take. During the Russian ascendancy antiimperialist emotions fanned by the May Thirtieth incident and the Northern Expedition reached new heights, and the Pacific powers feared for the safety of their nationals and despaired of the security of their investments in China. Chiang Kai-shek's break with the Communists and the eclipse of Russian influence thereafter brought many of these fears to an end, but they also damaged Chiang's image as a nationalist and antiimperialist figure. It fell to Japan to come to Chiang's rescue by proving that he was no captive of imperialist, and least of all of Japanese, purpose.

The Northern Expedition was deeply divisive in Japanese politics. The policies of internationalism that had resulted in Japan's participation in the Washington Conference and the Tariff Conference that followed were threatened when the Northern Expedition seemed likely to unify all of China, including the strategic north, with its importance for Japanese holdings in Manchuria and Korea. The moderate and noninterventionist stance of Foreign Minister Shidehara was the target of bitter attacks by advocates of a "positive" and "independent" foreign policy, with the result that the Russian initiative of the early Northern Expedition was followed by a Japanese initiative against the continuation of that same expedition. In June and again in July 1927, small forces of Japanese troops were moved from Manchuria to Shantung to provide protection for Japanese nationals in the event of military action between Kuomintang and warlord troops there. These moves were taken by Prime Minister General Tanaka, newly in office, who had based much of his criticism of the previous government upon the "weakness" of its China policy and who felt obliged to make a public show of force to rule out another Nanking incident.

The troop movements were of brief duration, however, and they did not yet poison the relations between Nationalists and Japanese.

Chiang Kai-shek's position was still not firm. He could not be certain that a strong reaction against Japan would not do him more harm than good. The Japanese interventions came while the Wuhan regime was parting with the Communists. In an effort to rally national unity both Chiang Kai-shek and his Wuhan counterpart, Wang Ching-wei, resigned their posts. Chiang himself traveled to Japan, where he met with Premier Tanaka in November. Tanaka urged him to return to political life in China and argued the importance of consolidating his gains south of the Yangtze, while Chiang in return argued the necessity of extending the revolution to the north. Tanaka was under the impression that his talks with Chiang Kai-shek had gone well, but the fact was that basic differences in interpretation separated them.

On the Chinese side there was no longer any real alternative to Chiang Kai-shek. His temporary withdrawal from the scene gave rise to fears of a resumption of warlord disorder and full-scale violence. Late in December 1927 Chiang Kai-shek resumed the Northern Expedition by advancing on Peking through Shantung. The Japanese government of Premier Tanaka again decided to send troops to protect its nationals in Shantung. In April, five thousand troops under a commander who was intent upon his honor and dignity initiated hostilities with Chinese units in Tsinan. From May 1928 to the following January, Japanese military government ruled over Tsinan while the two governments tried to find some way out of the impasse that would satisfy homefront jingoes without permanently alienating the other. The Japanese, who were out of bounds, got the worst of this struggle in prestige and propaganda. Their foolish insistence on "face" cost them agreement with Chiang Kai-shek on Manchuria, and it encouraged Chang Tso-lin to think of himself as a leading contender for power in Peking. His Japanese backers, he thought, would always be there to help him out. Thus Tanaka's Shantung intervention brought Chiang Kai-shek squarely into conflict with the Japanese and made him a symbol for nationalist Chinese who might otherwise have been less inclined to trust him.

Throughout all of the disorders of the 1920s, Manchuria had been under the control of Chang Tso-lin and his Fengtien army. Chang had begun as a bandit chief, and he began receiving Japanese support during the Russo-Japanese War. He gradually became an instrument of the Japanese desire for order and stability in Manchuria. Japanese military and political protection was occasionally extended to other warlords in China but usually to prevent the development of forces that might challenge Chang's control of Manchuria. Thus in 1924 Feng Yü-hsiang seems to have had some hope of Japanese support, but the army figures who dominated Manchurian policy were distrustful of Feng as a radical and insisted that Chang Tso-lin be left in charge of the northeastern provinces. When Feng Yü-hsiang became a recipient of Russian help, Chang Tso-lin could make a plausible case for Japanese help against him. After 1925 Chang, from his secure Manchurian base, began to dominate Peking and north China. The warfare between rival warlords now contained a concealed expression of Japanese-Soviet rivalry. When the struggle seemed to be going in Feng Yü-hsiang's favor in 1925, the Japanese denied him victory by forbidding entry into the South Manchurian Railway zone, thereby guaranteeing Chang Tso-lin the security of his base. Thus there were precedents for resistance to the Northern Expedition. But Chiang Kai-shek was no ordinary warlord.

As the Kuomintang armies approached Peking, held by Chang Tso-lin, in 1927 and 1928, they seemed to constitute a most formidable threat to Japan's ability to affect events in north China. Since the Northern Expedition had been supported by the Soviet Union and since it was strongly antiimperialist as well, there was reason to expect the Japanese to try to bar it access to the area of Japan's prime interest. Chang Tso-lin thought the Japanese might leave him in control of Peking, but the Japanese were eager to separate Manchurian affairs from those of north China. They were anxious that Chang establish himself as a Manchurian power to guarantee the necessity of separate negotiation and struggle before Manchuria could be added to the territory of Kuomintang China. Chang, however, had little desire to become a Japanese puppet, and he preferred to bargain for a foothold in Peking in order to improve his ability to bargain with the national regime. As the Kuomintang armies neared north China, the Japanese Kwantung army authorities in Manchuria grew more anxious to separate Manchuria from north China. They wanted to disarm all Fengtien troops that crossed the mountain barrier to the north in order to preserve it as a neutral zone. Differences developed between elements of the Japanese government and military over whether it would be wise to back Chang Tso-lin in Manchuria, or whether Chang, deeply involved as he had been in the politics of Chinese unification, might not better be sacrificed.

The government of Premier Tanaka, after some hesitation, decided against unilateral action in Manchuria. But shortly thereafter, extremist elements within the Kwantung Army, exasperated by their superiors' hesitation, decided to force the issue. On 3 June 1928 a unit of Japanese army engineers carried out a project that had been conceived by a Colonel Kōmoto Daisaku to bomb the train carrying Chang Tso-lin as he withdrew from Peking to Mukden. Kōmoto had hoped for disorder that would bring Japanese intervention. But the disorder did not materialize. Chang's son, Chang Hsüeh-liang, succeeded his father as warlord and commander of the Fengtien troops. This Japanese action thus removed Chiang Kai-shek's most important competitor for military unification in north China from the scene and replaced him with a son who was to show himself resentful of his father's murderers and later to cooperate with Kuomintang power.

On 6 June 1928 Chiang Kai-shek entered Peking. He announced an early end of the unequal treaties and called for their substitution by new treaties or the application of Chinese law. Chiang was riding a crest of popularity and esteem that was in good measure the product of the anti-Japanese feelings that had arisen after the intervention in Shantung. With Soviet advisers dismissed and Japanese military on the defensive, Chiang's new government seemed to be in a good position to speak for a more united China. The next decade saw the Kuomintang build China's first modern government.

6. *The Nationalist Decade*

THE PERIOD from 1927 to 1937 provided a decade of growth and organization between Chiang's victory in the Northern Expedition and the full onslaught of Japanese militarism. It is in this decade that the achievements and shortcomings of the Kuomintang government and leadership must be evaluated. After 1937 Nationalist China was fighting for its life against Japanese invasion, and after 1945 it was subject to special problems of war-produced inflation and destruction. Thus it is only in the decade after 1927 that any fair kind of balance sheet can be drawn up. At this writing it is only possible to sketch the problems of making such an evaluation. The period is still inadequately studied and understood, and passions of recent politics have entered to distort the judgments of much of the writing on the subject.

Chiang Kai-shek's problems centered around three sets of goals. The first concerned the completion of unification. National unity continued to be threatened by militarists who had combined with, but not really submitted to, his rule; it was complicated by civilian associates who chose at times to combine with these men, and it was threatened by the growing size and strength of the communist enclave in the hills of the southeast. The second goal concerned problems of reform. The ravages of the warfare that had swept China since the Manchu collapse had created towering obstacles to economic and political modernization. Communications, finance and education all required heavy investment and central control that had national unification as prerequisite. A third set of problems concerned China's recovery of national sovereignty. Unequal treaties and fixed tariffs, treaty-port zones and daily reminders of international inequality, extraterritoriality and foreign control of customs income brought growing irritation and impatience with the Nationalists' moderate course in foreign policy. Finally, affecting all three areas of need and achievement, there was the problem of Japanese aggression. The murder of Chang Tso-lin in 1928 was followed by the full-scale occupation of Manchuria in 1931, and in the next half-decade Japanese armies slowly moved closer to the full-scale warfare of the "China incident" of 1937. Japan ultimately guaranteed Chiang's success in the struggle for national unification by providing an enemy against which all could unite. But the resources and effort required for this struggle also doomed the nationalists' efforts to conduct an effective program of internal reform. Japan, one may suggest, created and then destroyed Kuomintang China. It is possible to do little more than indicate the dimensions of each of these areas of inquiry.

The success of the Northern Expedition did not bring an end to warfare in China. Chiang Kai-shek found himself surrounded by militarists who were far from ready to submit to the will of a central government, and many combinations between Kuomintang dissidents and rival warlords followed.

In January 1929 a conference was convened to discuss the demobilization and disarmament of warlord armies. In province after province these forces had been consuming 80 percent and more of the tax income, and it was clear that nothing could be done about technological and political modernization until they were controlled. But in every case local rulers hesitated to give up their forces without the assurance that their enemies would do the same. The armies sometimes were put to use to contest with Chiang the direction of the new national unity.

The principal warlord contenders were the generals of the southwest, north, and northwest. Chiang's own forces controlled only the Yangtze Valley, with its ports and modern cities, and four provinces: Kiangsu, Chekiang, Anhwei and Kiangsi. The first challenge came from the Kwangsi generals, Pai Ch'ung-hsi and Li Tsung-jen, who tried to launch their own northern expedition. Chiang managed to put them down with the help of Feng Yü-hsiang. The next round saw Feng Yü-hsiang try his luck. He teamed up with Yen Hsi-shan, but their coordination was far from perfect, and Chiang was able to strike first at Yen and then at Feng. The fighting in north China involved approximately a million men, and it extended Chiang's name and authority considerably.

Ironies abounded. In 1928 Peking had been seized by Yen from Manchurian troops in the name of the Kuomintang. Now those same Manchurian armies retook it from Yen, still in the name of the Kuomintang government. But Chang Hsüeh-liang, unlike his father, soon acknowledged the primacy of Chiang Kai-shek and accepted from him designation as commander of a Northern Pacification army. Things also went poorly for Feng Yü-hsiang, who had declared the Kuomintang government illegal and designated his army as the "Party-Safeguarding and National Salvation Forces." Some of his best commanders responded to urgings of patriotism and money and joined Chiang. Feng never regained a position of independent command and authority.

In addition to military challenge, there was the possibility of combining Kuomintang dissidence with warlord ambition. Some party regulars thought that since the Northern Expedition had achieved military unification the way was now open to the second of Sun Yat-sen's stages, that of political tutelage. An Organic Law of the Kuomintang government was promulgated in October 1928, and this specified that the Political Council of the Central Executive Committee would exercise executive power. In preparation for democracy it was to do this through the five branches of the ultimate government: the Executive, Legislative, Judicial, Examination, and Control Bureaus. A confusing plethora of ministries and agencies swiftly led to an inflation of bureaus and officials. A Provisional Constitution, worked out in 1931 through a National People's Convention whose members were appointed by the Kuomintang, continued the basic complexity of this structure. Chiang Kai-shek countered by giving up the presidency, but he retained control of the armies. The complexity of governmental organization and the inflation of ministries served to emphasize that the military remained the clear and unambiguous arbiter of power. Since Chiang Kai-shek more than anyone else had been the creator of the Kuomintang armies, they were loyal to him. A strong sense of group spirit, personal loyalty and national purpose distinguished Chiang's group. What was lacking was any sense of popular participation and activation. Instead, the generalissimo, as Western writers came to call him, worked through manipulation and balancing of personal and group interests to maintain his own primacy.

Chiang's immediate following included several important elements. There was the so-called "C. C. Clique," the brothers Ch'en Li-fu and Ch'en Kuo-fu, nephews of the military leader Ch'en Ch'i-mei, who had been Chiang's associate in Shanghai days. The brothers Ch'en came to be considered Chiang's strongest supporters in the party; they directed a number of programs of ideological and educational content, and they were responsible for the party police and secret files. Chiang's ties to the modern sector were symbolized and strengthened by his marriage to Soong Mei-ling, the daughter of a Shanghai banking family, in 1927. Through her sisters, the wives of Sun Yat-sen and financier-official H.H. Kung, and her brother, T.V. Soong, Madame Chiang brought her husband into intimate contact with persons who had great power and influence in the Chinese economy.

The combination of personal and military following which Chiang Kai-shek possessed in army, party and government made it impossible for men less fortunately endowed to challenge him successfully. Two important figures did their best. One was Wang Ching-wei. His oratory and eloquence proved inadequate substitutes for Chiang's military strength, but he had had the advantage of a close relationship with Sun Yat-sen, at whose bedside he had helped compose the will that became part of the Sun Yat-sen cult. Wang wanted civilian leadership for the new regime, and in it he would have occupied a central place. He was out of power from 1928 to 1931, but in that year he utilized popular discontent with Chiang and the ambition of the northern warlords to associate himself with an effort to unhorse Chiang Kai-shek. A Kuomintang government with claims to national authority was set up in Canton. Wang Ching-wei and Ch'en Yu-san (Eugene Ch'en) were its two most prominent personalities. Ch'en went to Tokyo to try to get Japanese help for the new regime with suggestions for compromise with Japanese policies in Manchuria, but several interviews with Foreign Minister Shidehara netted him nothing. At the same time, however, the Japanese army in Manchuria spirited Yen Hsi-shan back to his Shansi domain in hopes of adding alternatives to Chiang Kai-shek. But after September 1931 the Manchurian incident made it impossible for Chinese leaders to court Japanese assistance. The Canton leaders had already begun compromise talks with their Nanking counterparts and agreed to dissolve their government. Chiang Kai-shek was to return to power, while the Shanghai area would be garrisoned by a

Canton army to guarantee Nanking's compliance with the agreement. It was the unexpected resistance of the Canton army in Shanghai in the spring of 1932 that made the Shanghai incident of that year so costly for the Japanese. From this time until 1935 Wang Ching-wei worked with Chiang Kai-shek, but it was a frustrating relationship that came to an end with an attempt on Wang's life in that year.

Chiang Kai-shek also faced opposition from another follower of Sun Yat-sen, Hu Han-min. Hu's position was considerably more conservative than that of Wang, and he moved to the Right after Wang appropriated the Left for himself. Chiang worked closely with Hu in the years immediately after his break with the Communists in 1927. Hu then associated himself with the Kwangsi generals in a vain effort to have Kuomintang leadership in civilian hands. In the spring of 1931 a suspicious Chiang Kai-shek had Hu Han-min arrested. The negotiations for national unity that brought the Canton and Nanking governments together secured Hu's release, and for a time plans for a new coalition called for them all to serve in Nanking. But Hu Han-min refused to trust his old associates and remained in Canton, where he died in 1936.

These complex shifts illustrate a number of points. One is that military power, of which Chiang Kai-shek had the most, was still the key to survival in Chinese politics. Advocates of civilian leadership under the Kuomintang saw no inconsistency in teaming up with Kwangsi generals or Yen Hsi-shan to gain their ends. The personal vendettas of the warlord era continued. Chang Hsüeh-liang felt obliged to personally ambush and murder his father's chief of staff before he felt confident in control of his armies. No one trusted Feng Yü-hsiang. Chiang Kai-shek himself was often referred to as a dictator. His bloody repression of the Shanghai labor organizations in 1927 and alleged assassinations thereafter made him seem a ruthless ruler.

In addition to this, and recognized by Chiang Kai-shek as more dangerous than ordinary militarists, were the Communist leaders. Mao Tse-tung, Chu Teh and their followers had succeeded in establishing a remote and relatively secure base in Kiangsi in the winter of 1927. By the fall of 1929 their armies were beginning to win local successes, and the area under Communist control was growing. The warfare between Chiang Kai-shek and Feng Yü-hsiang in 1929 and 1930 seemed to open the way to direct action again, and led to the Communist insurrection in Changsha, a reckless action that cost the Communists many lives. They were much harder to track down in the countryside, where the precepts of Mao Tse-tung and Chu Teh about guerrilla warfare were beginning to produce effective tactics. It was Mao Tse-tung's view that the Changsha mistake saved the Red Army from subsequent large-scale rashness, and he came to a firm decision to concentrate on a remote, rural base. This area, stabilized by land-reform measures and organized by a strong party and defended by the Red Army, was able to maintain itself and offer hope for prolonged resistance and warfare. Chiang Kai-shek used his best units to reduce this area. It required a series of "extermination campaigns" before sufficient pressure could be brought on the soviet area to force its abandonment in 1934. In the "Long March" that took the Communists to Yenan in that year, Chiang's armies, following and harassing, had the opportunity to bring many more areas under his control.

Thus almost up to the eve of the Japanese invasion of north China, Chiang Kai-shek was preoccupied with military measures of unification. As his campaigns progressed, the areas under his effective control grew. But some resisted until the end. Shansi, for instance, under the rule of Yen Hsi-shan (who withdrew after his defeat in 1930 but soon returned), was a virtually autonomous area. Yen did his best to keep national government currency out of his domain, he minted his own coinage, and he carried out his own taxation, education and industrialization policies. Ultimately it was Japanese aggression that "solved" the problem of national unification; Japanese armies emphasized the importance of national unity in the face of foreign danger. But the Japanese presence also made it impossible for Chiang Kai-shek to carry on a thoroughgoing campaign for unification, and numerous gradations of local control survived the foreign invader. One major contender for national leadership, Wang Ching-wei, sacrificed his career and reputation in an effort to collaborate with the Japanese at Nanking.

The second major goal of Kuomintang leadership centered around problems of domestic reform. Efforts to deal with these were complicated by the political and jurisdictional confusion that has been described. But the urgency of the reforms was apparent on every side. *Likin*, the tax on goods in transit that had been instituted during Taiping times, was collected at more than 700 stations in 1927. A bewildering succession of taxes and surcharges had proliferated in all parts of China; there were, in fact, more than 130 tax bureaus in Shanghai alone. When the government secured provincial agreement to abolition of *likin* in 1931, an abolition that was prerequisite to rationalization of government customs revenue, it had to compromise by allocating local taxes to provincial governments. Government revenue was thus restricted to areas of the "modern" and coastal economy. Customs made up over half of this, and the salt revenue provided another quarter. Miscellaneous taxes on tobacco, yarn and the like provided the rest. Customs returns were burdened with debt payments to foreign powers, and government income was drawn in roughly equal parts from customs, salt and other internal taxes. Agrarian China's government was denied the income from its chief commodity, agricultural produce.

The government's achievements included impressive steps toward fiscal responsibility and management. The plethora of foreign debts that China had accumulated was rearranged and restructured. Accounts long defaulted were rescheduled and rationalized. By 1937 few debts were in arrears, and most of those would soon have been settled but for the hostilities with Japan. One set of accounts whose settlement proved particularly troublesome for nationalistic reasons were the Nishihara loans which China had contracted with Japan in 1918. The Manchurian invasion understandably sidelined all efforts to reach an acceptable settlement on those accounts.

Nationalist China's economic gains, while impressive under the circumstances, were nevertheless far short of what was needed. To begin with, they were distorted by the exigencies of the military situation. Communications received urgent attention. The rail network received important additions, and some of the major north-south and east-west trunklines were only connected at this time. Unhappily it was precisely along these lines that the Japanese chose to advance, with the result that these routes became avenues for invasion and served to divide rather than to unite the country. A road system, of great urgency for military unification, was also an important by-product of the military campaigns, and the 1930s saw vastly improved networks of roads that totaled more than one hundred thousand kilometers of highways. Air service also began, and postal and telegraph networks were further improved and expanded. The vast hinterland of China made problems of communication immensely more complicated than any Japan had ever known, and the proportion of investment required made this a chapter for which Japan, with its small number of heavily traveled trunk lines, had known no parallel.

The financial and banking systems were much improved under a group of modern financier-bureaucrats headed by the generalissimo's brother-in-law, T.V. Soong. But the Chinese, beginning late, had little of the success of the Meiji bureaucrats in getting banks, insurance, finance and shipping under national control. Added to foreign handicaps were the interests of local and provincial banks in areas where Kuomintang control was less than adequate. The Nationalist government found itself forced to develop a series of official banks, all of which issued notes and whose functions were largely specialized in the areas of development and growth. The policy of the United States in supporting, at the behest of senators from silver-producing states, an artificially high price for silver also complicated the Nanking government's efforts to establish a stable currency. Not until 1935, when a national paper currency based upon silver was substituted for the silver coins, was a solution worked out. The American silver-buying spree, although it came close to bankrupting Nationalist China, ultimately forced it to modernize and rationalize its currency. Unfortunately the new currency also had ominous potentials for future inflation. The more China struggled for equality, the more it became clear that outside help, hard to come by in the depression years, was required. The National Economic Council, established under League of Nations auspices, and the special loans for currency reform discussed in London and Washington illustrated the fact that the Nanking government was leading in a new and "modern" role, that of the "underdeveloped" country whose plight was an object of international concern. It may not be an exaggeration to suggest that the psychological results of the Meiji leaders' "bootstraps operation" were consequently denied the Kuomintang leaders even in their elements of success.

A major handicap in planning development measures was that they had to be carried on under constant pressure from military requirements. While the Meiji modernizers were able to defer major military expenditures until the substructure of the modern economy was complete, the Kuomintang leaders faced constant and growing demands for funds for the military. Military commanders were usually paid in lump sums for their troops, and the opportunities for peculation that this offered were infinite in number. Military needs also received higher priority than development.

Against the advice of counselors who suggested developing a "model" base of agrarian reform that would serve to advertise and attract others to the government's intentions, Chiang chose to wait until effective unification and pacification had been achieved. As a result his advisers' principal efforts in debt management, a balanced currency and a rising revenue failed to offset the larger failure to attend to the urgent needs of rural China. This did not seem urgent, because the Kuomintang was dependent upon and based upon the modern economy and the coastal area of China. After Japanese invaders drove it inland into the arms of its provincial allies, however, it lost much of its "modern" potential. Consequently Nationalist financial and economic planners never found themselves in a position to engage at first hand the livelihood of most of the Chinese people who farmed. Their pattern of legislation included prohibitions on rent gouging and established the legal rent at a maximum of 37.5 percent of the yield, but in view of the relatively superficial influence of the Kuomintang administrative structure upon the countryside, this meant little or nothing. After the loss of coastal and modern China, the likelihood of the government's reforming rural relationships, on which it was now dependent, was very much reduced.

Flood, famine and war continued to take their toll. When the Nationalists dynamited the banks of the Yellow River to block the Japanese advance on Chengchow in 1938, as many as several million peasants may have been caught in the swirling muddy waters. Population growth continued to worsen the ratio of men to land. In modernized sectors the flow of machinemade goods undercut handicraft income. The impact of an unseen and dimly understood world market puzzled and angered farmers who had shifted from consumption to cash crop agriculture. It was this combination of political instability, natural disaster, population increase and market disruption that caused the chief hardships of peasant life. A national government that had its eye on other priorities was in no position to deal with these basic needs, and it left them for the Communists to exploit.

However real the shortcomings of the Nationalist program and performance, it is important to emphasize that its achievements were nevertheless substantial. For the first time in the twentieth century China seemed to be drawing closer to solutions for real problems. National dignity and confidence were returning. The most visible sources of this new spirit were the steps the government was able to take toward the recovery of national sovereignty. The establishment of the national government at Nanking was welcomed by the powers, and it received quick recognition. Even the Japanese, who had obstructed the Northern Expedition in Shantung, joined in this recognition by 1929. Tariff autonomy, a goal toward which China had striven since the imposition of the unequal treaties, became fact in 1933. The new tariffs provided significant assistance in raising the national budget and increasing the government's capacity to deal with its problems of modernization. For the first time in several decades China was represented by officials who were able to speak for a united government in international councils. Movements toward the abolition of extraterritoriality were undertaken, but the Japanese aggression of the 1930s made it seem wise to delay these until they bore fruit in 1943, at a time when Japanese occupation made it purely symbolic. The pace of recovery of national sovereignty was rapid. Foreign concessions in Hankow, Kiukiang, Amoy and Weihaiwei were reclaimed. Debt management and modern budgetary methods provided a more inviting climate for growth and development. The political writ of the Nanking government was gradually increasing in effectiveness. Had it not been for the Japanese pressure and invasion, the historian's estimate of the Nanking government might well be very different. The causes of its destruction must be sought not in its inner contradictions, though those were real, but in the hostility of its neighbor.

CHAPTER 9

Problems of
Modernization in Japan

The years between the wars brought a new and puzzling stage in Japan's modernization. "Economic problems, social unrest, a sense of malaise, and difficulties in the decision-making process in government," as E. O. Reischauer summarizes its aspects, replaced the firm consensus on goals that had characterized the Meiji period. These problems combined to create a consciousness of domestic dilemmas and foreign difficulties in which economic problems and continental opportunities somehow became inextricably linked. Problems which should have been manageable for a country that had overcome sharper challenges so recently now combined to plunge Japan into a desperate search for national unity and imperial conquest. Both of these were unattainable. Both constituted a denial of the course of Japanese diversification and of Chinese nationalism and modernization. The question of the degree to which Japan's failures in these years constituted a reversal or a result of the Meiji changes has dominated many historians' approach to the modern century. Put in this way, however, the alternatives are put too sharply and simplistically. The problem is rather one of trying to indicate the point and manner in which reversible trends became linked to produce irreversible oscillations and vibrations that destroyed the possibility of peaceful and constructive growth.

The questions raised by Japan's problems have drawn more than their share of simple answers. The International Military Tribunal for the Far East that sat in Tokyo to identify and try Japan's leaders for "conspiracy to wage aggressive war" looked for guilty individuals. American occupation policy in postwar Japan was designed to eliminate guilty groups from influence. Japanese and foreign historians have been writing since the 1930s to identify and explain the causes of Japan's undemocratic development, and a particularly startling piece of historical detective work has recently tried to pin the entire blame on the unlikely person of Emperor Hirohito. For the most part these efforts have not been much more successful than the episodic violence of terrorist gangs of the 1930s who tried, by selective assassination, to remove men they thought were the central pillars of the existing political and social structure in Japan.

A first task is to understand the diversity of twentieth-century Japan. The Meiji thrust for national strength had been led by a samurai elite. Convinced of the urgency of their task in the face of foreign danger, they rallied support and dedication by stressing national over personal goals as justification for the sweeping changes they forced upon their countrymen. At the same time they left social relationships relatively undisturbed, for they were anxious to retain as much of the fabric of the previous society as they could. For the most part they were not distracted by large-scale public expressions of discontent. The samurai rebellions were crushed by 1878, and the movement for representative government was dealt with through a combination of repression and concessions that culminated in the Constitution of 1889. The great mass of the Japanese people took little part in political agitation or activity. The decades of steady growth and the gains in international dignity and standing undoubtedly satisfied the needs of the first generation. The economy showed growth and provided opportunity. By 1900 the political parties had been incorporated into the constitutional order, the country was beginning to reach its goals of international status, and the leadership still agreed on the goals, though not always on the details of its programs.

The twentieth century brought changes in this picture. The indemnity from the Sino-Japanese War helped to accelerate the process of large-scale industrialization. New managerial groups began to be absorbed into the elite. A larger worker class began to show signs of being restive with its share of the gains. The Ashio mine case, in which industrial pollution poisoned an entire agricultural area, symbolized the discontent that now began to surface. In agriculture the ceiling of growth under existing techniques of agronomy had been reached, and by the 1920s the agricultural sector was falling behind the rest of the country. More and more signs of disparity between landlords and tenants, and wealthy and poor, began to draw comment.

With new and different impulses to political participation the political picture changed as well. Education was beginning to spread to all parts of Japanese society. By 1890 50 percent of all children were receiving some modern schooling, and in 1908 six years of schooling became compulsory and also free, so that over 90 percent of children attended school. Communication networks could operate to bring awareness of public issues and problems to all parts of Japan. One product of the boom that accompanied the Russo-Japanese War was a rise in the number of voters able to pay the ten-yen voter qualification tax from 760,000 (in 1904) to 1,590,000 (in 1908). Urban masses, with or without the financial qualifications to vote, also began to find their voice.

One phenomenon of the late Meiji period was an increasing tendency to take to the streets—not for organized, planned campaigns but in spontaneous, sporadic and inchoate expressions of mass dissatisfaction. Riots requiring martial law came in 1905 after the revelation that the Treaty of Portsmouth would contain no indemnity. Demonstrations reached new heights in the efforts of Katsura to organize a government in 1913, riots followed the reports of mistreatment of Japanese nationals at the hands of Yüan Shih-k'ai's armies in China in the wake of the abortive revolution of 1913, and they flared again in 1914 with reports of corruption in navy contracts. In 1918 the discontent of urban workers over the sudden rise in the price of rice touched off the largest riots of all. Over 700,000 people in 36 cities, 129 towns and 145 villages took part. If these riots were neither organized nor democratic, they nevertheless indicated a rising awareness of public issues, and their extension throughout the country was one reflection of the way industry and mass communications were creating a single citizenry. "It is a fact," the *Asahi* declared in 1919, "that the attitude of the majority of our people is completely different from their attitude when they have met with so-called hardships in the past ... the people are not asking 'What will become of the country?' but they have risen to cry out, 'What will become of us?'"

The government that had to deal with these more complex and large-scale problems was itself no longer as united and flexible as it had been during the earlier part of the Meiji period. The problems that now arose were no longer the sort that could be dealt with on the basis of common sense or simple warrior loyalty. They required statistical preparation, specialist training and bureaucratic depth. The original statesmen themselves were fewer in number, older and, in part, had become the instruments of the special interests they had helped create. This was true of Yamagata, at once the leader and the instrument of the military. But the Meiji elite was not, in any event, able to endure or to reproduce itself. The society in which it spent its last years was one in which new special interests in the form of political parties, specialized bureaucracies, professional military, large industrial firms and modern intellectual elites struggled for a share in the national leadership. The new men entered the lists as products of specialist education rather than as Confucian-educated generalists. And yet Confucian moral outlooks were very far from dead. Twentieth-century Japan constantly tended to judge contemporary crises by traditional criteria. One result of this was a deep distrust of government and particularly of professional politicians.

1. Bureaucrats and Politicians

THE FIRST EVIDENCE of professionalization that requires attention came in government. Under the constraints of the Meiji constitutional order and the opportunities offered by the social and economic changes of modernization, the political parties changed from small bands of ex-samurai and rural leaders to professional bureaucrats and politicians. The first decade of constitutional government, from 1890 to 1900, saw the party leaders experiment with the powers that had been granted them. On the part of some the tendency to continue frontal attacks on the Meiji government and to treat it as the "enemy" was still strong. But concern for the national prestige, satisfaction with the victories in war and the need to reward party faithful gradually produced a willingness to consider alliances with government oligarchs. On the part of the government, the realization that a stable base in the House of Representatives was the first requisite of orderly government had led Itō, the author of the Constitution, to organize his own party, the Friends of Constitutional Government, in 1900. The next two decades were remarkable for the change in tactics, strength and standing of the Seiyūkai, until it came to power under the leadership of Hara Kei in 1918.

Seiyūkai tactics and leadership were provided not by Itō, who soon retired from active participation in politics, nor by Prince Saionji, his aristocratic successor as party head, but by Hara Kei (1856–1921), who exemplified the new type of leadership Japan was to receive. Hara failed to make his mark through orthodox paths of bureaucratic or military preferment in the early Meiji years. He entered a law school, only to be expelled, and then became a newspaper reporter. In the 1880s he entered the Foreign Office as a protégé of one of the oligarchs, and after fifteen years as a bureaucrat—he rose to be vice-minister of Foreign Affairs in 1895—he became editor of the important *Mainichi.* From this strategic post he moved to the secretariat of the new Seiyūkai. Since party head Saionji was little interested in the give and take of practical politics, it was Hara who held the party together by maneuvering between factions and groups. Effective leadership centered in the secretariat which he headed. Within a few years he was the party's chief negotiator with the government of Katsura, with opposition parties and with the genro. His goals and outlook were party centered, and he was determined to build a Diet majority as a base of strength.

It would have done Hara little good in the political world if he had developed the art of public speaking as a democratic spokesman. He rewarded his party faithful but often ignored their opinions, while he courted the views of Peers, genro and military with caution. Gradually they came to see in Hara an alternative to popular demagoguery and, indeed, democracy. Yamagata, at the end of his life, assented in 1918 to Hara's emergence as the first "party" prime minister. He was the first, that is, to hold a seat in the lower house and to serve as head of a political party at the same time.

As Najita shows, Hara saw clearly that the path to power in Japan lay in control over the bureaucracy. He was home minister for approximately half the time between 1906 and 1915 and thus had it in his power to control the prefectural governors and bureau chiefs. He allocated patronage and public funds to build a strong base of interest and gratitude for the Seiyūkai.

During these same years the bureaucracy was changing rapidly. It was becoming the special preserve of graduates of the law division of Tokyo Imperial University instead of a patronage reward for men from Chōshū and Satsuma. In 1902 only 2 (of 7) vice-ministers were from the university; in 1916 all 7 were. Again, in 1902, 9 bureau chiefs (of 27) were from Tokyo Imperial; in 1916 26 (of 29) were from the university. Until 1905 the number of university graduates who were prefectural governors was almost negligible; in the next two decades almost all of the important governors were from Tokyo Imperial. These men were "new" types. They were professional civil servants, and they were younger. Their outlook was national and not regional, and they included more and more of nonsamurai background. The bureaucracy as a whole also grew rapidly in size. In 1890 it numbered about 29,000. By 1907 there were 58,000 and, in the following year, 72,000. World War I brought a further growth in the size of the government, and by 1922 the bureaucracy numbered 162,000 men. A force this large was necessarily selected by more equitable standards. The makeup of the Tokyo Imperial University student body had also changed strikingly in its inclusion of students of varied backgrounds.

As home minister Hara gradually strengthened control over the selection and performance of the governors. He suspended unfriendly or incompetent men ruthlessly and promoted his own supporters, with the result that local administration became increasingly tied in with changes in the central government. The replacement of a pro-Seiyūkai cabinet by one hostile to Hara would also result in large-scale reshuffling. The Seiyūkai's political party opponents were themselves gradually forced to organize in self-defense against Hara's generalship. The remnants of Ōkuma's party gradually began to form an anti-Seiyūkai organization, one which Katsura himself tried to utilize after 1911. The consequence of all this was that administration and officeholding became increasingly related to political parties, and links between the parties and the bureaucracy became essential to both. Moves from bureaucratic to ministerial posts became standard.

Hara also made it his business to expand party influence throughout the countryside. Years earlier Yamagata had designed units of county government with the preservation of traditional social stability in mind, but Hara saw these as inimical to central government influence and after a long struggle succeeded in doing away with them in 1921. Well before then, he had done his best to expand party influence throughout the countryside by the implementation of what he called a "positive" economic policy. This meant a carefully planned program of public works and pork-barrel legislation to build a solid party base in all parts of the country. Seiyūkai candidates could promise and deliver on requests addressed to them through local rallies and leagues. Through effective implementation of patronage Hara was able to starve out the opposition. To make this possible he was willing to challenge the military on occasion, as when Katsura fought hard to change Japanese railway lines from narrow to standard gauge in 1909 in order to tie them in with the lines in Korea and Manchuria. Hara preferred the additional miles of trackage that narrow gauge lines made possible, and he had his way. The Japanese Government Railways were not to have standard gauge lines until the advent of the high-speed trains of the 1960s. Under Hara's policies railroad trackage rose from 7,595 miles in 1906 to 13,475 miles in 1915. The army had its way in the nationalization of the principal lines in 1906. On the other hand, Hara resisted approval for the additional two divisions that the army demanded in 1912 because it would interfere with his domestic plans. It was Prime Minister Saionji's agreement with this stand against the army that brought on the cabinet crisis of 1912 and the Taishō "Political Change."

The Taishō political crisis was resolved by the appointment of a cabinet headed by the Satsuma admiral, Yamamoto, under which Seiyūkai predominance continued. It was in response to this long tenure that the genro turned to Ōkuma Shigenobu for the premiership in 1914, with the specific wish that he destroy the political power of the Seiyūkai. Ōkuma's cabinet extended through the years of World War I and the Twenty-one Demands on China. When he resigned in 1916, Yamagata arranged to have him succeeded by General Terauchi. During Terauchi's stay in power the Nishihara loans to China and the Siberian intervention were undertaken. Perhaps more important domestically were the rice riots of 1918 in which Terauchi's government failed lamentably. During the whole of this period Hara maneuvered skillfully to ingratiate himself with Yamagata. He visited him periodically to listen to him express his disillusionment and disappointment with the incumbent governments, and by 1918 Yamagata was ready to agree to Hara's appointment as prime minister.

As prime minister, Hara's achievements were not inconsiderable. He lowered the tax qualification for voting from ten yen to three, thereby increasing the electorate to three million and adding a numerous class of small landholders, thereafter firm Seiyūkai supporters. He promoted higher education by establishing new universities and larger budgets. He abolished the county system and established small electoral districts to increase the stability of precincts. He devoted very large sums to railroad expansion, harbor dredging and bridge building. He maneuvered cautiously between Peers, Privy Council and military to loosen military control over colonial administration in the aftermath of the repression of the Korean independence movement of 1919, and he did his best to pull the army out of the Siberian intervention. He changed, to some extent, the context of political power by so relating the party to the bureaucratic structure that thereafter transfers between the two became the established path of preferment. Symbolically, he was on his way to a regional Seiyūkai rally when he was stabbed by a young rightist in 1921.

After the death of Hara the political parties entered a period of confusion and frustration. For one year (1921–22) the premiership was held by Hara's successor as party head, a finance bureaucrat named Takahashi Korekiyo, who lacked Hara's skill in maneuvering between the several elements of the power elite. In 1922 Yamagata died. Saionji was now the only active genro and he found himself a reluctant kingmaker and cautious experimenter. Saionji had none of Yamagata's antipathy toward the political party government, and his youthful experience of Western liberalism had left him somewhat inclined toward responsible party government as the most stable system that Japan could develop. On the other hand, he saw no obvious leader among the Seiyūkai contenders, and he was unenthusiastic about the opposition. The descendants of the Ōkuma faction, now the Dōshikai, had grown in strength and had come under the leadership of Katō Kōmei, and Saionji was not prepared to trust him until a coalition of party leaders united behind Katō in 1924 and left him no alternative.

In the meantime problems of international relations and disarmament made it desirable to conciliate other forces. In 1922, with the convening of the Washington Conference, to which Hara had committed Japan, Saionji gave the nod to a retired admiral, Katō Tomosaburō, in the belief that the navy would view a program of reduction of armament spending more acceptably if it also had executive responsibility. He proved correct. Under Admiral Katō, Japan subscribed to the treaties for naval reductions, agreed to give up most of its World War I gains in Shantung and also cut back schedules of army and administrative spending that had soared during the years of World War I.

On 1 September 1923 Tokyo was devastated by fires that followed one of the great earthquakes of Japanese history. Over 130,000 persons died, and in the wake of fires, disorder and social distress, a cabinet headed by Admiral Yamamoto (who had, it will be remembered, served briefly in 1913 and 1914) was installed. Yamamoto served only a few months before he resigned to accept responsibility for an anarchist's attack on the prince regent and future emperor, Hirohito. Saionji replaced him by an aging Chōshū bureaucrat, Kiyoura Keigo, who lasted into 1924.

During these strange and unsuccessful experiments in alternatives to party government, the party leaders banded together in a Movement to Defend the Constitution. With vigorous press and magazine support, supplemented by activities of the newly founded labor unions, they were able to muster an overwhelming majority against the Kiyoura cabinet in 1924. Katō Kōmei now became prime minister and headed a three-party coalition until 1925, when he formed his own cabinet. The Katō government contained many past and future prime ministers, and its links to Mitsubishi were sufficiently close for it to be termed by some a Mitsubishi cabinet.

Katō had served as foreign minister under Ōkuma in 1914. He was a man of ability, ambition, and confidence. A graduate of Tokyo Imperial University, he had experience in business with Mitsubishi and had risen in the Foreign

DEMONSTRATION FOR UNIVERSAL MANHOOD SUFFRAGE in Tokyo prior to Diet passage in 1925.

Office to become foreign minister (under Itō) at the age of forty; he had held a Diet seat, served as ambassador to England (earning Yamagata's dislike for becoming an Anglophile) and headed the Dōshikai after Katsura's death. He made no attempt to ingratiate himself with the masses and was reserved with his associates, but he won respect for his ability and determination.

The achievements of the Katō cabinet included a bill for universal manhood suffrage that was passed in 1925. By its terms suffrage was finally separated from financial qualifications, although requirements of age (twenty-five) and residence still provided safeguards against the masses. The suffrage campaign, which had begun in the early years of the twentieth century, had received overwhelming popular and press support by the 1920s and represented the finest fruit of "Taishō democracy." Under the new provisions the electorate rose from about three million to nearly ten; by the time of the 1928 elections it was twelve and one-half million, and it continued to keep step with the population rise thereafter. Woman suffrage also began to be the object of concern in the 1920s, but it made little headway then and less in the 1930s. It was realized only during the American occupation of Japan after World War II.

Katō had been ambassador in London during the campaigns to reduce the power of the House of Lords, and he also turned his thoughts to the structure and makeup of the House of Peers. His caution made him give up plans for changing the Constitution to curb the Peers' powers, and he even backed away from a plan to change the system of elections to membership in the upper house. But he was able to change the composition of the House of Peers by increasing the number of imperial appointees for special merit. Persons of civil or academic eminence now augmented their numbers and moderated the influence of the hereditary peers.

The need to reduce government expenditures saw Katō reduce the civil bureaucracy by twenty thousand positions, and it also brought him into contact with the army. His minister of war, General Ugaki, was a transitional figure in the high command. Although he was not from Chōshū, he wàs acceptable to Chōshū interests and was firmly committed to modernizing the army. Ugaki managed to modernize and trim at the same time. Four divisions were disbanded, and the savings that resulted went to improve equipment and training for the units that remained. The Japanese army now took its first steps toward armor and motorized transport. The officers of the four divisions, however, could not easily be returned to civil life. A solution was found by introducing military drill into middle and higher public schools. These changes were not very popular with the military, and even less so among the students. The 1920s were remarkable for strong antimilitarist currents of thought in Japan. The army's stubborn refusal to get out of Siberia and the currents of liberalism and radicalism made soldiering and soldiers unpopular. Servicemen took to wearing civilian clothes when off duty. There were complaints about difficulty in finding suitable marriage partners, and there were numerous incidents of revolt and discourtesy against military instructors by students.

The Katō cabinet also took cautious steps in the direction of a program of social reform to curb some of the injustices that had accompanied Japan's early industrialization. Initiative in this area came from the bureaucracy rather than from the Diet. Laws that had operated to forbid the formation of labor unions were abolished. Steps were taken to set standards for working conditions in factories, to provide health insurance for workers and to provide mediation of labor disputes. There was also a good deal of discussion about problems of tenancy. The problem was not new, but the realization of its importance was. Already by the turn of the century, 45 percent of all farmland had been tenant occupied, and one cultivator in four owned no land. In the years after World War I tenant-landlord disputes rose at a rapid rate, and there was widespread concern lest the peasant base of Japanese society deteriorate. Unfortunately the Diet with its strong ties to landlords throughout the country proved an unlikely rostrum for discussions of either rural reform or tenant disputes mediation, and little was done in this regard.

Katō's were also years of internationalism despite the provocations to nationalism provided by the American Immigration Law of 1924 and the anti-imperialist propaganda of the Northern Expedition in China. During the years of the Katō cabinet the army was finally induced to withdraw from north Sakhalin. With the withdrawal of Japanese forces from Russian soil it became possible to resume relations with the Soviet Union, a step that was taken in 1924.

Simultaneously, however, Katō's cabinet took steps to counter possible subversion. A Peace Preservation Law was passed in 1925 to checkmate the dangers that might result from nonparliamentary movements in the new liberal atmosphere. The law sternly forbade the formation of groups advocating the abolition of private property and change in the "national polity," which was left undefined, and stiff fines and imprisonment were provided for those who formed or abetted the formation of organizations advocating such steps. Three years later, under the Seiyūkai cabinet of General Tanaka, the fines were strengthened to include capital punishment. This law, together with the Special Higher Police Force that was established to investigate "dangerous thought," provided the legal framework for the immediate repression of communism and the subsequent repression of liberalism. The fact that this legislation went almost unquestioned in the Diet, although it drew vigorous criticism in the liberal press, is indicative of the political atmosphere in Japan during the 1920s. Too often the ruling groups, with their heavy stake in the existing order of things, were prepared to equate suggestions for change with subversion of the entire panoply of institutions that led to the throne and to group them all under a "national polity" that had once signified only the throne itself.

Katō died while still in office in 1926. His tenure as prime minister had seemed likely to mark the beginning of an unquestioned predominance of political party governments, but it proved to be the high point rather than the inauguration. After Katō's death the leadership of the Minseitō government passed into the hands of Wakatsuki Reijirō, who had entered the party organization from a high position in the Finance Ministry. Wakatsuki proved to have little of Katō's ability to conciliate competing interests, and he found himself particularly hard-pressed to defend Foreign Minister Shidehara against charges of a "weak" policy in the face of the Kuomintang revolution in China. When a disastrous series of bank failures and business reverses was added to this in 1927, the way was clear for the Seiyūkai again.

In its search for powerful leadership the Seiyūkai had turned to General Tanaka Giichi. Tanaka, the last in the main line of succession of Chōshū generals, had served in the General Staff since the early 1900s and had drawn up defense plans for Yamagata in 1906. He also had had close ties with the political parties since his service as war minister under Hara. He had an expansionist past that stood him in good stead with military jingoes, for he had managed the Siberian intervention from the General Staff. By the mid-1920s, however, he tended to accept more moderate goals while cloaking them in extravagant statements about the need for a "forceful" and "positive" policy toward the mainland. Tanaka was far less expansionist than his supporters, but his rhetoric—and his interventions in Shantung—did in fact change the climate within which Japan's China policy was conducted. Under Tanaka the Peace Preservation Law was strengthened to add the death penalty for crimes against the national polity. In a series of swift raids in 1928 the police broke the power of the fledgling communist apparatus for years to come. Tanaka fell in 1928, after officers of the

Kwantung Army in Manchuria engineered the murder of Chang Tso-lin in hopes of forcing a stronger Japanese policy in that area. Tanaka was in agreement with the position taken by the emperor and court officials that the guilty parties should be disciplined, but he was unable to carry this argument with the army high command. He died shortly after resigning his office.

Power now returned to the Minseitō, which had scored well (as had a new Social Mass party) in the first election conducted under the provisions of the new suffrage laws. Shidehara returned as foreign minister in a cabinet led by Hamaguchi Osachi, an able and strong-willed party leader who had, like Wakatsuki, entered politics from the Finance Ministry. Hamaguchi exercised strong leadership in forcing a reluctant navy to accept the agreements for reduction in cruiser strength that were reached at the London Conference. Convinced of the economic necessity for political understanding with the Western powers, he withstood bitter criticism from the Privy Council, the House of Peers and the opposition Seiyūkai to have his way. His effective performance in this struggle neared the limits of the possible in the exercise of personal leadership in Japan, and in 1930 he was fatally wounded by a right-wing fanatic who felt he had betrayed his trust.

Hamaguchi's period in office unfortunately coincided with the world depression. During those months a sense of crisis growing from depression, the collapse of the silk market and a disastrously timed return to the gold standard by Japan just when Western powers were taking inflationary moves to relieve distress did much to undermine confidence in the government. Wakatsuki, who succeeded Hamaguchi, reaped the whirlwind of military discontent in Manchuria. Inukai, one of the "gods of constitutional government" in 1913, followed as new head of the Seiyūkai, and the era of party government ended with his murder by young naval officers determined to bring about a "Shōwa Restoration" in 1932.

An analysis of the period of party government in Japan between the wars shows that the achievements were modest but also steady within the limits of the permissible. At the time of his death Hamaguchi was contemplating ways of making further changes in the makeup of the House of Peers and the General Staff. The suffrage had been expanded impressively. A start had been made in the direction of social legislation. The parties had gained respectability and acceptance at the top of the Japanese structure. Unfortunately they had done this without comparable acceptance and respectability at the base of that structure among the common people. More ominous still, three effective party leaders died at the hands of assassins.

Much of the party argument for reform had been phrased in terms of preventing popular democracy and dissatisfaction instead of in terms of popular welfare and participation. At the top of each of the Japanese elites, there was a general reluctance to trust the judgment of commoners, hence the effectiveness of arguments advanced by army leaders that it would weaken popular faith in the army to discipline the perpetrators of the murder of Chang Tso-lin. That faith needed to be total and unqualified, they argued, for the nation to be secure. Most of the men who ran Japan continued to think in terms of a Confucian and paternalistic view of government, and they retained in broadened form much of the elitist consciousness of their Meiji and Tokugawa forebears. Essential controls continued to be clustered around the throne. Prime ministers were nominated from above. Elections tended to come after cabinet changes, and they were usually plebiscites to ratify changes rather than referenda to settle issues.

If Japan's leaders retained many Confucian norms, the same was true of their critics. Most agreed that government should be above party and interest. Textbooks and Confucian rhetoric derogated power seekers as corrupt and selfish and competition as unworthy. The emperor and the system he had ordained were by definition moral and good, as his people were loyal and long-suffering. Whatever went wrong could have no other explanation than the moral defects of those in government. Party politicians fared poorly by these standards. Their popular image was seldom a flattering one, and the advantages all lay with the critics.

It has to be granted that the politicians did little to help improve their image. Beginning with Hara's "positive economic policy," the association of promise and reward was a carefully enforced axiom of domestic politics. The two great parties competed for influence and wealth. The Seiyūkai reviled the Minseitō as Mitsubishi oriented and, in turn, was charged with serving the house of Mitsui. With the growth of the electorate, elections became much more expensive, and government surveys and press exposures provided graphic evidence of vote buying. Professor Peter Duus shows that election law violations soared from 1,427 in 1908 to 23,208 in 1917 and remained near 15,000 in 1924. Campaign expenditures rose from eight thousand yen per candidate in 1915 to more than twenty thousand in the 1920s, a sum far beyond the means of most candidates and larger than they could recoup on their salaries. For incumbents the expenses of an election often had to be avoided if at all possible, and deals to extend the life of a Diet and avoid its dissolution were the expected order of business. The background of candidates for office also changed. Men who moved from local assemblies to the national scene declined in number. By 1908 over half of the new members of the Diet were men with business connections. Business, in other words, became a route to power, as power was based upon affluence at election time. The use of money was often open and frank. One writer, recalling his activity during the days of Tanaka, recalled that "when you went into Tanaka's reception room there were always one or two hundred yen notes which had fallen under the desk. That's how much money was thrown around." It is not surprising that many voters formed a poor idea of elective politics. Hara's first budget was nearly 50 percent larger than Terauchi's, and the following years made that seem modest. Few were willing to relate this to the growing population and to the responsibilities of government in a modernizing society. It was simpler to relate it to issues of personal morality.

Significantly, even liberals like Yoshino Sakuzō had only modest expectations of the Diet system. Radicals and rightists could agree that the Diet showed a lack of propriety and decorum. Policy came from above, the work was done in committees, and what remained for public view was too often a scene of disorder that contributed to public distaste for competitive institutions of representation. Quite aside from issues of corruption and decorum, furthermore, it would be erroneous to see the Diet as a force for civilian control and responsibility over against a power-hungry military. All too often Diet debates found civilian hardliners taking stands that called for military action. Mori Kaku, a powerful Seiyūkai figure, saw himself as an empire builder and played a prominent role under Tanaka, and he later sabotaged efforts that Inukai was making for peace with China.

But it has been less often noted, though it is directly relevant to Japan's later experience, that Japan somehow had domesticated parliamentary institutions during a period of rapid social and economic change under an institutional structure that allowed for modest but continuous advances in representation. If domestic economic stability had remained at reasonable levels, and if the shortcomings of the system had not coincided in time with disorder and temptation on the mainland, Japan's party system might have survived. Instead, when once the whirlwind of depression and militarism combined with the mounting international crises of the 1930s, the parties abdicated their responsibility and gratefully entered a single national structure, the Imperial Rule Assistance Association, that promised to serve the national rather than the parochial interest.

2. *Workers and Farmers*

JAPAN'S POLITICAL STRUCTURE between the wars reflected the mixture of tradition and change in the society of the time. Compromises and shifts that came in the institutional structure reflected the uneven and often disjointed rate of modernization within Japan. Large-scale industrial growth came rapidly and late, with much of its ownership concentrated in a few firms. The countryside, which had produced the agricultural surplus of the early Meiji years, reached the peak level of output that was possible under the technological and social conditions of the time and had become a problem area for the larger economy. Despite the steady growth of urban populations the rural districts continued to be thickly populated. The stability and continuity of family and society in the villages provided impregnable electoral bases for the political parties, and the narrow ownership base of modern industry supported a political structure that served the upper classes. But Japan's economy was remarkable for the extreme diversity of its patterns of ownership, size and efficiency, and small-scale, family enterprise retaining artisan traditions had also grown alongside the modern industrial structure. Part of the Japanese economy competed with the most modernized sectors of the West, but much of it was carried on in the manner of an earlier generation. The gap between the very large and very small, and between the modern and the traditional, was pronounced, and it was reflected in the contrast between the modern appearance and traditional content of much of the democracy of the 1920s.

Japan's modern industry got under way only in the twentieth century. Before then there had been a start in textiles, which were capable of mechanization relatively cheaply and in which the supply of cheap labor gave Japan a competitive advantage it badly needed in view of the unequal treaties. The international climate changed dramatically in the first decade of the twentieth century. The unequal treaties came to an end, and final restrictions on Japanese tariffs were lifted in 1911. Thereafter it became possible to protect Japanese firms and products from the plants of the West. The indemnity of the Chinese war, paid in gold on the London market, went in part to found the Yawata steel and iron works, which began production in 1901. By the time of the Taishō Political Change, Yawata was meeting almost half of Japan's needs in iron and steel. Foreign trade grew rapidly. Silk exports, themselves a mixture of agrarian craft organization and relatively simple factory operation, increased eightfold between 1900 and 1929 and provided an important source of foreign currencies with which to finance the imports of raw materials and foreign technology.

Japan's great boom in industrial growth began with the Russo-Japanese War in 1904–05. Government expenditures increased six times between 1905 and 1913 and provided a powerful expansive force in the economy. The activities and resources that were opened up in Korea and south Manchuria provided new stimulus for industrial and intellectual horizons. The country was knit together physically and economically by the vast expansion of the railroad network that marked Hara's "positive economic policy." Government investments in rails, bridges, utilities, iron and steel, international banking, industrial development in the empire, and in the constantly growing military and naval budgets provided almost half of total investment for the decade after 1905. Japan's new confidence and security made it safe, in government eyes, to resort to foreign loans after the Russo-Japanese War, and thereafter the money markets of London and New York were an important port of call for Japanese diplomats. These possibilities and obligations contributed to the influence of internationalism between the wars. Government bonds and higher government taxes, as well as government monopolies in commodities like tobacco and salt, siphoned off popular capital and diverted it from consumption to investment in industry.

If the Russo-Japanese War provided the "takeoff," World War I brought a recognizable boom. The war cost Japan little. It brought cheap glory in the seizure of the German holdings, and it provided an interval of competition-free opportunity to dominate the markets of Asia and even to supply the giants of the West, who were locked in suicidal conflict. Overnight Japan changed from a debtor to a creditor nation. Overnight new fortunes mushroomed, providing pejorative terms for newly rich *(narikin)* to the vocabulary of resentment. Between 1915 and 1920 the Japanese shipping fleet nearly doubled in size. The number of factory workers doubled from 845,000 in 1914 to 1,777,000 in 1919; the percentage in metal, machine and chemical industries increased from 13.6 in 1909 to 24.2 in 1919. The percentage of workers in factories that employed more than one hundred workers rose from 43 to 55.

It is probable that the uneven rate of modernization that has been mentioned helped make this growth possible at the same time that it was itself made more conspicuous. The modern sector was characterized by a narrow base of ownership. Beginning in the 1880s, when government pilot plants were made available for sale to private firms, a small number of firms—Mitsui, Mitsubishi, Yasuda, Ōkura, Sumitomo, and a few others—had been willing to accept the risks of modern economic opportunity by getting in on the ground floor of the new developments. They dominated the modern sector collectively, but not individually, and developed a pattern of cooperative oligopoly instead of competing for individual monopoly. Like their political counterparts, the financial magnates shared control; they did not concentrate their investments in any one industry. A pattern of tolerance and association tended to characterize their relations. Mitsubishi might be strong in shipbuilding, but driving its competitors out of that market risked subjecting it to comparable treatment in an area of manufacture, trade, or finance in which Mitsui or Yasuda held a comparative advantage. Executives and managers were usually committed and loyal, for horizontal mobility between structures was unthinkable. The structure that emerged was not something distorted and irrational but one deeply in harmony with Japan's patterns of family and personal loyalty. In a sense it served Japan well; the narrow base of ownership, coupled with tremendous capital accumulation, made it more likely that the proceeds would go into investment rather than conspicuous consumption.

This probability was the stronger because it was reinforced by Japan's traditional code of values. The Meiji invocation of national service and loyalty was part rhetoric to inspire the lower classes, but it also contained a personal commitment. The traditional ethic of restraint, austerity and simplicity meant that the industrial nabobs, while by no means self-denying hermits, nevertheless stayed away from extreme ostentation and extravagance. Even if they had chosen to pursue this path, most of them would have found themselves bound by the constraints of the family system. At all levels the traditional Japanese family was thought of as a continuing institution with legal status. Like administrators of a firm or university, those who headed it did so as stewards and not as absolute owners. Senior family members and collaterals often constituted a governing council that could depose an unworthy heir and replace him by an adopted son. Like landed patriarchs, industrial capitalists had full honors but limited initiative, and in this they resembled the apex of every other hierarchy in Japan, from emperor on down. Confucian and samurai traditions added their own sanctions against self-indulgence and ostentation. Modern Japan, like contemporary China, was a land of slogans. In the 1920s, Katō's cabinet declared four "Thrift and Diligence Weeks" a year, and throughout the land posters blossomed exhorting Japanese to "Be Frugal!" "Let's Work Hard!" and "Let's Save a Lot!" And as late as 1967, in Kōchi Prefecture, the visitor was greeted with posters mounted by the "Society for Saving Time": "Let's All Save Time!"

The 1920s showed that the profits of World War I were not a lasting phenomenon and that it would require sustained effort and rationalization to consolidate the industrial gains that had been made during the war. The government made poor use of the influx of foreign capital of the war years. The Nishihara loans of 150 million yen were soon in default, and other dealings with Chinese warlords proved equally unremunerative. Most of these led to further diplomatic difficulties as Japanese statesmen tried to press successive Chinese governments for satisfaction. The costs of the Siberian intervention, which was liquidated only in 1922, exceeded one billion yen, almost two-thirds the cost of the Russo-Japanese War. Here again international trust was endangered without any corresponding economic or political advantage.

The end of World War I brought Western competitors back to the scene long before Japan was ready for them. Shipbuilding was the first to feel the pinch, and in 1930 it still stood at half its 1919 figure. The first postwar industrial labor disputes centered in shipyards. Japan had experienced serious inflation in the years of growth during World War I, and as a result the wage structure became seriously distorted. Many people experienced a loss in real income despite the general prosperity. This was the significance of the rice riots of 1918, in which urban poor revolted against the spiraling price and growing shortage of food. Postwar years found Japan entering a new era of competition with a distorted price structure. Deflationary measures that were undertaken resulted in a slowdown of economic growth and the first sustained depression since the 1880s.

Urban distress and social unrest were visible everywhere, but the events of the 1920s also made it difficult for the government to adhere to its deflationary program. On 1 September 1923 Tokyo was laid waste by fires that leveled almost the entire Tokyo-Yokohama plain after a violent earthquake, and the government was forced into renewed inflationary spending for reconstruction and relief. In efforts to remedy its position Japan left the gold standard in 1924 and returned to it in 1930, a move that proved disastrously timed because it coincided with the world depression and the loss of Japan's principal export market for silk in America. Professor Patrick has recently surmised that "the Japanese government's muddled objective to return to the gold standard at pre–World War I par, and the attendant deflationary fiscal and monetary policies taken in the 1920s, were responsible for much of the retardation of growth in that decade.... Slower growth caused, or at least exacerbated, the stresses of industrialization and the social and political conditions which put the militarists in power." In December 1931 Japan left the gold standard again.

The growth of the Japanese economy after World War I was also complicated by the fact that the modern sector of the economy was no longer able to profit from growth in the traditional sector of handicraft and agricultural production. The low levels of per capita income in those sectors, which still employed the great majority of Japanese workers, made it necessary for the modern sector to seek other markets. Imports changed, with consumer goods giving way to raw materials for the modern sector, and exports changed from tea and raw silk to cotton fabrics, cotton yarn and silk fabric, all of which were products of modern organization and technology. Export competition brought the need to increase productivity through more improved technology. This meant higher investment, but it did not bring the increased employment and the generally high level of economic activity that had accompanied the first period of industrial expansion. The process also contributed to concentration in the modern industrial sector. During the decade of depression and uncertainty after World War I only the best-financed enterprises survived. Approximately one-half of Japan's banks disappeared during the period, and a major banking crisis, accompanied by political tremors, followed the collapse of the Bank of Taiwan in 1927. Expansion and improvement capital became increasingly controlled by great nationwide networks of banks, each of them the core of an economic empire. As their wealth and visibility increased, these firms were natural candidates for popular resentment and distrust. The term *zaibatsu,* "money clique," became a pejorative cliché that infected all discussion of Japanese economic relationships.

Professors Ohkawa and Rosovsky show that in the traditional economy neither productivity nor real wages were rising. Agricultural production had leveled off, and investment in the traditional sector was no longer as attractive as investment in the modern sector. A differential, two-level economic structure became clearly visible. Earlier, wages in the two sectors had been roughly comparable, but now the productivity gains in the modern sector resulted in a growing wage differential. The role of modern industry, especially in terms of output, now became much larger. The impact of this on politics, particularly in expressions of discontent by those who claimed to speak for the disadvantaged countryside, was considerable, and the impact of this dual structure on Japanese perceptions of their society and its problems was even greater.

The two structures were intimately related. Traditional demand remained high, and it was satisfied by the traditional sector. Many of the great concerns tended to put out simple jobs to the tiny shops that were everywhere to take advantage of their wage rates. Each sector to some extent presupposed the other. Their existence in combination was not the result of capitalist or *zaibatsu* plotting with conservative party politicians, as it seemed to right- and left-wing critics, but rather a consequence of rapid industrial rationalization under conditions of population growth in a time of international competition.

One should not conclude from the use of terms like *modern sector* that Western-style relationships characterized that part of the Japanese economy. In the provision and training of a modern labor force one sees once again an amalgam of traditional practices and the needs of modern productivity and enterprise. Particularistic loyalties sometimes reproduced in modern form the paternalistic relationships that operated throughout Japanese society.

Labor for the first factories of the Meiji era had been organized and recruited through labor middlemen and contractors. The labor boss, referred to in familistic vocabulary as *oyakata* (parent), tended to have a clearly defined group of followers, referred to as *kokata* (children), whose dependence on him was the result of their need for employment in a society with an abundant labor supply. Laborers were drawn from villages and often returned to them, so the *oyakata* could supply and move them at will in response to demand. The modern sector, however, came to require discipline, continuity and training. Businessmen pressed the government for the establishment of vocational schools, which multiplied rapidly around the turn of the century. In a transitional period there remained a function for the labor contractor. The *oyakata* was sometimes introduced into the enterprise and given status and tenure to serve as a sort of foreman. His services were gradually supplemented by in-service training programs for products of the vocational schools. Then, as the needs of modern enterprises for a stable labor force became a condition of higher productivity, a system of modern labor relations developed that put great emphasis on enterprise loyalty and reciprocal obligation. Companies guaranteed tenure and provided housing and other fringe benefits. Employees served for life, and their remuneration was scaled by seniority rather than function. Though restricted to "modern" plants and trained employees within them, these practices did much to stabilize the skilled labor market. Large enterprises also cooperated to share the labor market as they did other markets. The major spinning companies often cooperated to divide the labor supply on a geographical basis to simplify procurement.

If one relates these institutions to their political expressions, the modernity of the social scene in the 1920s becomes more traditional. The development of a labor movement was made particularly difficult. Between 1897 and 1907 the early labor movement was characterized by intellectual leadership that was heavily influenced by anarchism and syndicalism. Article 17 of the Peace Police Law of 1900 forbade organized action on the part of workers on the grounds that it would constitute a disturbance of public peace. A Social Democratic party was founded in 1901 only to undergo immediate dissolution by police action. In 1912, a Friendship Society (Yūaikai) was organized by a young Tokyo Imperial University graduate. It began as a mutual aid society for workers, and it was supported by progressive capitalists. Its publications and pronouncements were heavily moralistic and showed a blend of Christian and Confucian values in which harmony was emphasized. Managers were urged to be thoughtful and to treat their workers as fellow humans, while the workers were encouraged to show traits of sobriety, promptness and efficiency. At the same time, however, labor analysts have noted that a large number of the small "unions" then formed were the products of *oyakata* leadership, easily organized in view of the labor contractor's personal following and often expressive of his resistance to the gradual takeover of his functions by factory employment agents and vocational schools. After World War I, says one authority, there was "a substantial conservative trade union wing ... that had its origins in *oyakata* resistance to management's take-over."

Visible aspects of the labor movement in the years after World War I centered on the consequences of depression and unemployment. In 1918 there were 417 disputes involving 66,457 workers. Labor unions grew to number 300 in 1920 and 500 in 1927, and their members increased from 103,000 to 309,000. Most were enterprise unions rather than craft organizations, and most strikes, like the giant Kawasaki Shipyard strike of 1921, alarmed conservatives more than they satisfied workers.

Perhaps it is natural that under such conditions the labor "movement" remained in the hands of intellectuals who, without firsthand contacts with laborers, tended to turn to social theory. By the early 1920s Marxist currents of analysis and thought were overwhelmingly dominant. A bewildering succession of parties, programs and theses all served as evidence of the impotence of the movement and as explanation for the alarm of its opponents. The conservative governments did their best to slow the continued growth of radical movements and ideologies by universal manhood suffrage, labor and factory legislation, and the Peace Preservation Law. For the labor movement parliamentary tactics became relevant only after universal manhood suffrage prevailed in the election of 1928. By then the character of the labor movement was firmly set, but within a half-decade the fires of continental war and terrorist assassination had obscured the outlines of peacetime progress.

If the left wing was affected by problems of the industrial sector, the right wing capitalized on the difficulties of the villages. By the 1920s it was apparent to almost everyone that Japanese agriculture was in serious trouble. Its growth had come to an end, and population pressure kept marginal land in use. Tenant rates of 45 percent remained in effect for all cultivated land. The tiny scale of operation was more important. In 1934 68.4 percent of all farm families worked less than one *chō* (2.45 acres) of land, while only 3.7 percent worked more than two *chō*. Agriculture was incapable of contributing more to Japanese growth under existing conditions of tenancy and technology. Imports of food made up larger proportions of imports until they neared one-fifth of the total, and government subsidies were required to keep rice within the income of the city poor. Japanese agriculture was producing almost double the amount of food that it had in Tokugawa times, and it was doing so with fewer agricultural laborers, but it had ceased to grow.

Although living conditions ceased to improve for agriculturalists, their education and expectations knew steady advance. Elementary education was universal and high school was available to most. The metropolitan newspapers brought word of the larger society into all but the most backward areas. Bicycles, buses, trains and an electrification program were bringing rural Japanese into closer touch with nearby towns and cities. Inevitably they were affected by the currents of thought and agitation of their counterparts in the cities.

The tenant movement was necessarily small. Landlords, who often lived on their holdings, usually owned only small plots of land. Their presence and close supervision operated to maintain patterns of tenant subordination and obligation. Informal or formal contracts spelled out the familistic relationship between tenant and landlord, with the former often referring to his superior as his "parent" *(oyakata)*. Traditional authority and Confucian values were strongest in the countryside, and the virtues of harmony and status tended to perpetuate stratification. Rents averaging 50 percent of the crop remained common, and the organization of tenants proceeded slowly.

Despite all this, rural organization developed in the postwar years, and it provided telling evidence of pervasive social and intellectual change. Farmers' unions grew in all parts of Japan, their organization encouraged by Christian socialists and Marxist intellectuals. Recorded instances of disputes between tenants and landlords numbered 85 in 1917 and 2,206 in 1925. By that year there were 3,496 tenant unions with a total membership of 307,000. This was only a minute proportion of Japanese tenant farmers, but it was a significant development, one which the radical parties tried to exploit by labor-farmer coalitions.

To meet this development, the conservatives who governed Japan tried a variety of measures. Police measures were vigorous. In Aichi Prefecture, for a time, regulations forbade the assembly of more than three farmers without a permit. Patterns of village authority operated to restrain individual protest, but they could also make that discontent villagewide when discontent became pervasive. Politicians found their strongest electorate in the countryside, and they operated through village heads and "men of influence," who were usually landlords. Japanese voted in multimember constituencies, and election strategy and management depended upon the proper allocation of votes. A crashing majority for one candidate would constitute a waste of votes that could have gone to elect his party colleague for the second of the several seats at issue. Election management depended upon being able to predict votes, allocating certain villages to certain candidates and establishing "iron constituencies." The vote manager with his *kaban,* or satchel, traveled through such a *jiban* with promises designed to keep the district safe for his candidate. Duus's summary of the election disbursements of a candidate in a rural district in 1915 shows payments to five village heads, eleven village assemblymen and a number of town assemblymen and other local figures of influence.

At the end of the 1920s problems in the countryside took on crisis proportions. The world depression destroyed the market for the farmers' principal currency earner, silk; the price of silk cocoons fell by two-thirds within a year. Within Japan a bumper harvest in 1930 coincided with food imports from the colonies of Korea and Taiwan to depress food prices. Vegetables and fruits, luxuries in many diets but important sources of farm income, plummeted in price. Home industry declined, lessening the cash income available from part-time or family-member labor. Taxes remained unchanged. In the hardship that resulted, class division and discontent were less important than an overall concern for agriculture and village welfare. Tenant disputes grew in number, but since owner-farmers and landlords shared in the disaster of the countryside there was less emphasis on rural reform and more talk of national reform than would otherwise have been the case. All this had important consequences for politics and thought, for the hardship was related in the popular mind to the policies and personalities of government by the business and political party elite.

3. Books and Bullets

THE MOST POWERFUL CURRENTS of protest in Taishō and Shōwa Japan ran in nonparliamentary channels. Japanese radicals had little hope of parliamentary solutions for social problems. Most of them were disillusioned by the limitations of the liberal philosophy with which they had made contact and were strongly influenced by the moral absolutes of the Confucian society of their fathers. They applied traditional standards of sincerity and purity to the institutions of their day and found them wanting, and they imagined a dim future in which selfishness and avarice would give way to communal harmony. The "radicals" were thus profoundly "traditional" in their emotional response. A strongly moral and almost prophetic tone distinguished all Japanese radicalism, both Left and Right.

World War I and the Russian Revolution replaced the simple activism of early anarchist terrorists with the more complex and structured vision of the communists. The holistic philosophy of Marxism found support in much of the modern intellectual establishment. The preference for holistic philosophy that began with the German view of the state led easily via Hegel to Marx. Communist organization and activities were, however, dealt quick blows by the police. The Japanese Communist party was soon discovered and its members rounded up. The Peace Preservation Act of 1925, strengthened three years later, provided the basis for a sweeping roundup of fifteen hundred communists and suspected communists in 1928. Times of crisis saw other means employed. When rumors swept Tokyo that radicals and Koreans had started arson and looting after the 1923 earthquake, police quickly rounded up radicals and labor leaders. Several were murdered in their cells by police officers, one of whom explained to the court of inquiry that he was unable to restrain himself when he thought of what his victims were doing to the national polity. On the whole, however, terror was less effective than reeducation. Once Japan entered paths of peril that brought international disapproval, police efforts to win radicals back to the familial unity of Japanese society were often strikingly effective. Significant numbers of radicals forswore their heresy and embraced Japanese expansion as the working out of a historic tide that would efface Western imperialism in Asia.

Organized communist activity was dealt crippling blows by these means, but this did not mean the end or even the ebb of Marxist thought. During the 1920s and 1930s Marxism became entrenched as the leading alternative to official thought. Government suppression reduced the communists to theoretical disputes, most of which turned on the question of where Japanese society now found itself in the transition between feudalism and socialism. Since the polemicists were, for the most part, academic intellectuals, their disputes were waged with vigor and style. Successive "theses" sent or endorsed by Moscow and designed to set the tactics for political struggle became springboards for scholarly dispute. Had the Meiji Restoration been a bourgeois movement? If so, Japan was ready for a socialist transformation, and the Communist party should work for an early revolution. Had the Restoration been a mere coup d'état by one element of the samurai class, which fastened its rule on the people through an absolutist monarchy? Then political revolution was premature, and Japan would have to abolish remnants of feudalism before moving on to socialism. The monument of this debate, a many-volumed *Studies in the History of Japanese Capitalism,* became at once the name of a school and faction (the *kōza* studies group) as well as a point of departure for much social science analysis until well after World War II.

Writers as well as social scientists were attracted by the prophetic sweep of Marxism. Since the late Meiji period, many of the finest works of modern Japanese literature had reflected the dilemmas modern society posed for the individual. Some writers retreated from an unpleasant reality into a world of aestheticism, and others into a private world of introspection and withdrawal. But in many ways the most representative works were those produced by a group known as "proletarian novelists." During these same years the literary world of China was also moving to the Left. In Japan, Nakano Shigeharu, writing in 1927, explained that "our art—the art of the workers themselves—should publicize the shame of our country." That "shame" was portrayed in novels that ground out the hardships of workers and peasants. Thus many of the best minds and most courageous spirits of late Imperial Japan saw in Marxism a resolution for problems of personal commitment and protest. Their courage and the hostility of the government they execrated helped to make them symbols of intellectual freedom and democracy in the days after World War II.

But there were as many critics of the status quo to be found on the Right. They too had no confidence in the parliamentary machinery of the modern state and looked for other ways of setting the world straight. Some of them were out of tune with all forms of modernity and associated all the things of which they disapproved with the influence of the West. The appearance of the Tokyo that replaced the preearthquake city, Western dress, Western architecture, feminism, equality, cabarets and movies all seemed expressive of the selfishness, avarice and immorality of modern materialism. These aspects of modernization had long been present, but postearthquake Tokyo made them more visible and made the contrast with the Japanese countryside more startling than ever before. Conservatives deplored all this as a departure from the true Japan. The national foundation, or *kokuhon,* was being eroded. Its preservation was the object of the Kokuhonsha, a society formed by conservatives headed by Baron Hiranuma in 1924. Many similar, though less important, groups formed.

The tenets of this new conservatism began with an affirmation of the primacy of emperor and empire. The loyalty due the sovereign was his right as head of an extended family hierarchy. Loyalty and filial piety were the cornerstones of personal morality and social cohesion, and departures from them would bring national disaster. Japan's unique "national polity" (*kokutai*) made possible this identity of person and nation. Individualism was by definition selfish and egalitarian. For Sun Yat-sen, it will be remembered, individualism was a long-standing Chinese weakness. But in Japan it seemed to deny familial primacy, and it was denounced as foreign. The obedient sacrifice of a country girl who accepted her sale to a distant brothel to save her father's farm was an act of moral beauty, and it contrasted with the disgraceful pursuit of pleasure by modernized young men and women on the dance floors of city hotels. Enthusiasts of the Taigyōsha (Great Achievement Society) felt called upon to invade a ball at the Imperial Hotel in 1924, seize the microphone and harangue the hapless dancers about the evils of their ways. (Their detractors suspected them of being financed by brothel interests.) Filial piety and the family system were the focus of the elementary school morals textbooks. Children began by learning that "our country takes the family system as its base: the nation is a single great family, and the Imperial family is the main house." Family loyalty led to the throne.

Shinto nationalism furthermore maintained that the Japanese were a divinely ordained race. They had polluted their tradition with the material effects of modernity, but if they would only return to the simplicity of their ancestors other countries would bow before their virtue and example. Indeed, as D. C. Holtom phrased it, the doctrine that divine governance is the noblest state of man has as corollary that it is an act of benevolence to extend its blessings to neighboring peoples. Thus the Shinto phrase *hakkō-ichiu*, "bringing the eight corners of the world under one roof," was a proper mission for the chosen people. An Education Ministry booklet issued in 1938 explained the *kokutai* as the blessings of emperor, filial piety and harmony and combined these with Japan's martial spirit, which did not have for its object "the killing of men, but the giving of life to men. This martial spirit is that which tries to give life to all things, and is not that which destroys."

The other principal concern of Japanese conservatism was for the primacy of the agricultural village. In the village family, order and personal dedication were maintained most perfectly. There the community of men in harmony showed true beauty. Agriculture was the base of society. *Nōhonshugi* enthusiasts saw the ideal society as made up of the self-sufficient communities that once dotted the landscape. They were against all influences of capital, of government and of thought that operated to change this. The modern system, wrote Gondō Seikei, "made those who profit without working and the members of the privileged classes the pampered favorites of the state. The bureaucracy, the *zaibatsu* and the military became the three supports of the state, the political parties attached themselves to them, and the scholars fawned upon them. . . . When the plutocrats conspire with those who hold political power, the resources of the people fall under their control almost before one is aware of what is happening ... the common people fall upon evil days; they are pursued by cold and hunger, and unless they work in the midst of their tears ... they cannot stay alive." Tachibana Kōzaburō, sometimes described as a Tolstoian philosopher, wrote of the beauties of peasant life. The state, he asserted, could survive only under agrarian communalism, and "Japan cannot be herself if she is separated from the earth." Like Gondō, Tachibana deplored the modernity of Tokyo, which seemed to him "a branch shop of London." For Gondō, Japan was a branch shop of the Prussian bureaucracy. The agrarians were primitive utopians. They did little to provide a program of structural reform, but they struck powerful and responsive chords in Japan. The contrast of rural poverty with urban prosperity was evident to all, and the statistics of rural tenancy and income demonstrated to the most skeptical that something was wrong in the countryside.

These themes provided the material for dissidents, but they did not constitute a program. Agrarian communalists were not normally military expansionists, though they did call for changes in society. Nor did family loyalty necessarily lead to imperial arrogance. The connections were provided by the Education Ministry, the custodian of Shinto nationalism, through popular indoctrination. The dynamics of discontent were supplied by individual terrorism and organized disruption. The latter was often quietly supported by elements of the military who took alarm at the commitment to internationalism represented by the Washington and London Conference agreements. The military's share of the budget had declined sharply in the 1920s (from 981 million yen in 1919 to 437 million yen in 1926), and during the same period its share of the national product fell by more than 50 percent. The suspicions that the businessmen-politicians were selling the military short, combined with the army's espousal of the "plight of the villages," provided important elements in the popular response to the extremism of the 1930s. Individual terrorist activities, in addition, drew on the traditions of strongarm tactics that had distinguished modern Japanese politics since the middle of the nineteenth century.

On 3 September 1921 Asahi Heigo, a member of the Shinshū Gidan (Divine Land Righteousness Band), assassinated the head of the Yasuda *zaibatsu* at his home. Asahi's political testament, which he sent to fellow nationalists, called for a "Restoration" that would free Japan from capitalist politicians just as the Meiji Restoration had freed it from feudalism. "This is a time of danger," he warned; "foreign thought contrary to our national polity has moved in like a rushing torrent. The discontent of the needy masses who have been mistreated for long years by this privileged class ... is being stirred up. The cold smiles and reproachful eyes of the poor show that they are close to brutality." Asahi himself was already there. He called on his fellows to bury the traitorous millionaires, crush the political parties, bury the high officials and nobles, bring about universal suffrage, abolish the inheritance of wealth, nationalize the land and big business, confiscate all large fortunes and reduce military service to one year. "Do not speak," he concluded, "do not get excited, and do not be conspicuous. You must be quiet and simply stab, stick, cut, and shoot. There is no need to meet or to organize. Just sacrifice your life." True to his word, he committed suicide after murdering Yasuda. He sent copies of his statement to Uchida Ryōhei of the Kokuryūkai, Kita Ikki, of the Yūzonsha, and Fujita Hisamu, the publisher of the *Mainichi.*

This was still individual and unplanned terrorism, for Asahi had seen no need to "meet or organize." Prime Minister Hara noted in his diary that "Yasuda was a very unpopular man, but the assassin seems to have aroused a very pessimistic murderous mood. He doesn't seem to have had any particular hatred for Yasuda himself." A few months later a young man named Nakaoka Ryōichi stabbed the prime minister. Nakaoka wrote that "when I read in the newspapers that Asahi had killed Yasuda and then committed suicide I was powerfully moved ... public opinion of his final statement seemed if anything, to praise Asahi." The press had, in fact, deplored the bearing of the arrogant capitalists that brought on such terrible retribution from an intense and selfless youth. It was, the *Jiji Shimbun* observed, "impossible to sympathize with Yasuda." Thus within a year terrorism had deprived Japan of her leading statesman and an influential capitalist. This was still a full decade before the Manchurian incident set the match to the fuse that led to Pearl Harbor.

Asahi's unstructured call for a "Restoration" was given substance by a group of men who may be called a "radical Right." The 1920s were a period of rightist organizations. The prolixity of names and causes suggests the lack of rightist unity; each group tended to be the product of one personality. There were the "Great Reform Society," the "Self-Government Study Society," the "Continuity Society," the "Anti-Bolshevization League," the "Great Japan Morality Society," the "Establishment of the Nation Society," the "Heavenly Swords Society," the "Patriotic Society," the "People's Battle Society," the "Advancing Patriots Party" and many others which showed the tempo of conservative concern and enthusiasm.

The most interesting individual among these founders was Kita Ikki. Kita combined the fervor of Nichiren Buddhism, the experience of Meiji China adventurers and the reformist ethic of Marx. He began as one of the band of enthusiasts who sought to support the Chinese Republican Revolution through cooperation with Sun Yat-sen. As the 1911 Revolution neared its climactic days, Kita was particularly close to Sung Chiao-jen and reported to Uchida Ryōhei in daily telegrams about the progress of the fighting. After the emergence of Yüan Shih-k'ai, Kita was dismayed by the role that Japanese big business had played in compromising Japan's image among the Chinese revolutionaries. The attempts to secure concessions in Hanyehp'ing and Manchuria seemed proof of the inability of a bourgeois Japan to ally with Asian nationalism. And since that nationalism was the path of the future, it was incumbent upon Japan to restructure its institutions. Kita was powerfully affected by the currents of socialism of the early twentieth century, and he combined this criticism of capitalist immorality with his experience of Asian realities during the Chinese revolution. In his

Unofficial History of the Chinese Revolution he gave free play to his misgivings about the Japanese future in a revolutionary Asia and laid the groundwork for his political philosophy. Kita was also a believer in Nichiren Buddhism. He saw a future united Asia under the leadership of a divinely ordained Japan. He argued the necessity of restructuring Japan to fulfill its destiny with the apocalyptic fervor of a Nichiren.

In 1919 Kita completed the text of an *Outline for the Reconstruction of Japan.* The following year he founded the National Continuity Society. His book was printed secretly and passed from hand to hand until, in 1920, the police took note of it and forbade its distribution. In 1923 the book was published, with major excisions, only to be banned again. A third edition, also soon banned, was issued in 1926.

Of all Japan's rightists, Kita came closest to the national socialism that was coming to the fore in Italy and Germany. Like his European counterparts, Kita had been influenced by Marxism, and like them he distrusted parliamentary democracy as an instrument of the privileged classes. The welfare of Asia depended upon Japan's reconstruction. "Our seven hundred million brothers in China and India have no path to independence other than that offered by our guidance and protection," he wrote, while "for our Japan, whose population has doubled within the past fifty years, great areas adequate to support a population of at least two hundred and forty or fifty millions will be absolutely necessary." Class struggle would no longer suffice as an operating principle; it had to be combined with a national struggle.

In short, he argued, the "Greece of Asia" should take the leadership in a world federation, "proclaiming to the world the Way of Heaven in which all are children of Buddha," and it should "set the example which the world must follow." Reconstruction and armament, morality and world leadership, were all related. Kita proposed that the "people's emperor" suspend the Constitution and declare martial law. He should then abolish the House of Peers and replace it by a Council of Deliberation, made up of "distinguished men in many fields of activity, elected by each other and appointed by the Emperor." The House of Representatives should be elected by universal manhood suffrage ("Women will not have the right to participate in politics"), and the numerous ordinances by which Yamagata and the genro had weighted the Meiji political order (civil service, press and police laws) should all be abolished. A National Reorganization Diet then would nationalize Japan's principal industries, confiscate large fortunes and enforce limitations on individual property. The sovereign, in order to become a "people's emperor," would give up his property and live on a stipend provided by the Diet.

Kita was radical but not egalitarian. He believed in the supremacy of Japan, and he wrote that "the inequality of men in all other respects makes it impossible that they can be reduced to one level of economic ability, one level of consumption, or one level of economic destiny. Hence the coexistence of small landlords and tenants may be considered to accord with the will of the Gods." But he was unusually specific in his program and proposals. His preface to the

1926 edition of his book praised Asahi Heigo as a man who, through the murder of Yasuda Zenjirō, had shown an affinity for his own goals. Kita's close associations with young military extremists in the 1930s undoubtedly helped stir them to acts of violence, and his China experience in 1911 had shown him the importance of military radicals.

Right-wing theorists had importance only as they could find organizations willing to work for their ends. Individual terrorism could shake, but it could not topple, much less replace, established patterns of government. For that, there had to be power and organization. The best source for this was the army. It, too, was worried about the plight of the countryside, the source of its recruits and noncommissioned officers. In the nationwide organizations of reserves it had powerful transmission lines for the receipt of information and diffusion of propaganda. It was worried, even indignant, about cutbacks in military spending, and it associated growing freedom in Japan with anarchy and foreign subversion. Nor did it have confidence in parliamentary government. Unlike the civilian rightists, the military men had access to money and influence, and they possessed the support of troops that had been trained to trust and obey. Garrisons in Manchuria, China and Korea also produced proconsular ambitions that would produce important pages in the development of policies that were to come.

Thus it is worthy of note that Kita's greatest influence came only after his thought had penetrated the officer corps in the 1930s. In the late 1920s, action was possible chiefly for military hotheads, like those who assassinated Chang Tso-lin in 1928, and for discontented members of the elite like those who planned the March incident of 1930. In that abortive coup the chief instigator was a collaborator of Kita's, a graduate of the law faculty of Tokyo University named Ōkawa Shūmei. Ōkawa held an important position of managing director of the East Asian Research Institute of the South Manchuria Railway Company. In 1930 he got together with a group of military officers, field grade in rank, who had organized a "Cherry society" of "selfless patriots" for the "cleansing of the army" and the "reconstruction of the country." This was to involve the establishment of military government, a "solution" of the Manchuria and Mongolia "problems" and the reorganization of the army by reform-minded generals. The plan was simple and crude. A crowd of ten thousand men would be organized to demonstrate around the Diet building. Generals Tatekawa and Koiso (important names in later military politics) would stride to the Diet rostrum and call for replacement of the cabinet by an emergency cabinet headed by General Ugaki. The emperor would then give his approval, and the renovation of Japan would be under way. Money to buy explosives and to hire demonstrators was provided by a businessman and by a scion of the house of Tokugawa. The demonstrators were to be imported from as far away as Fukuoka, which had long been a center of right-wing enthusiasm.

Despite the backing it had, this plan came to nothing. Ugaki, who was optimistic that the political parties were about to ask him to take over anyway, saw no need of dynamiting a system that seemed likely to bring him to power on its own. Without his backing, the plot petered out. The same fate met an even more ambitious plan that called for the use of army dive bombers to blast the prime minister's residence during a cabinet meeting the following October. But one month before, in September 1931, the Manchurian incident had opened the way to mainland adventure which received the priority of the responsible military figures whose cooperation was essential to success of a coup. Individual assassination plots continued in the years ahead, but they were important only when allied with the dynamics of the discontented military.

On 15 May 1932, after the Wakatsuki cabinet had been replaced by a Seiyūkai cabinet under the venerable Inukai Ki, a group of young navy officers, their spirits raised by fighting in which they had recently taken part in China, rushed into the prime minister's residence and murdered the old man in cold blood. Inukai was personally popular, but he was sacrificed as a symbol of party politics. One of the assassins, Koga Fujito, reminisced in 1967 about his part in the incident in these terms: "What did we achieve besides the death of Prime Minister Inukai and one policeman? In the first place, we spread before the people the true meaning of the national renovation movement. Appraisals of the Blood Brotherhood League [Inoue's organization] also changed. People began to think of Onuma Tadasu [who killed Finance Minister Inoue Junnosuke] and Hishinuma Gorō [who murdered Mitsui financier Dan Takuma] as patriots instead of as traitors."

The assassins themselves developed a type of reverence for death and self-destruction that has often characterized terrorism. "My act of assassination was a mysterious one," wrote Hishinuma. "When I had achieved my purpose I seemed to realize who I was, and for the first time I realized the meaning of brotherhood. [The group called themselves the Blood Brotherhood League.] It was as though the brotherhood was myself, and I the brotherhood. It is impossible to know this feeling on the basis of observation or from explanation; it has to be experienced."

As Japan became mired in war on the continent and as foreign criticism mounted, its domestic crisis deepened. After the death of Inukai, Prince Saionji decided that it would be unwise to invite further violence by naming politicians to head cabinets. Instead he twice selected former admirals as premiers. The second of these, Okada, became the victim of the largest uprising of all when a group of army captains and lieutenants (influenced by Kita Ikki) staged a revolt on 26 February in 1936. A carefully coordinated series of murders had as targets cabinet members, senior servants of the Imperial Household Ministry and the aged Saionji himself. A number of outstanding leaders were killed. Although Saionji and Okada escaped, the death knell of moderate, party-centered politics had been sounded. For three days the rebels held the center of Tokyo with fourteen hundred men. At first they thought they had succeeded; civilians and police, one of their number recalls, "came up to us and asked 'why did you spare so and so?' and gave us information about the other side." But the "other side" stood firm. At the emperor's insistence the army managed to convince the troops that their officers had acted without official approval.

By 28 February the insurgents were denounced as rebels. After their surrender the officers were herded into the War Ministry building where they were provided with stationery for last testaments and permitted to keep their swords and encouraged to use them to commit suicide. But only one officer shot himself, and the others decided to try to continue their struggle in the courtroom. Soon afterward trials brought speedy justice to the leaders, although some lesser figures survived into the 1960s. The civilian rightists who provided the ideas were quietly executed. The deaths of Nishida Mitsugu and Kita Ikki marked the end of the peak influence of civilian rightists. Their influence had proved destructive, but it had not sufficed to bring about a reconstruction of society. What had been destroyed was Taishō democracy and Taishō internationalism. They proved fragile plants, for no one cared as much about their preservation as some cared about their destruction.

4. The Army

RECONSTRUCTION WAS SUPPOSED to be undertaken by a "purified" army. The army was, after all, best suited to meet the expectations of the rightists. Its men were dedicated to sacrifice rather than selfishness, they served emperor rather than party, their roots were rural rather than urban, and their values were nationalist rather than internationalist in nature. The soldier symbolized all the ethical and moral values of the code of Bushidō. Because "the soldier exists only for battle," Ishiwara Kanji wrote, "he is essentially an idealist."

Nevertheless army idealists had their own frustrations, and these had an important bearing on army officers' participation in political plots and rivalries. Most basic was a sharp generational conflict between the surviving members or protégés of the Meiji generation and younger outsiders. This took three forms. First, exponents of military modernization doubted the adequacy of Japan's preparedness for conflict along the lines that had been indicated by World War I. Second, advocates of preparedness for total war had little patience for the compromises political generals had worked out with political parties and big business. The realities of the post–World War I world seemed to point to the Soviet Union and the United States as Japan's future adversaries; abolition of the Anglo-Japanese alliance and the United States' immigration laws and protective stance on China policy all showed the way planning had to be directed. Third, priorities between technological modernization and spiritual mobilization provided new issues for controversy. All of these issues became embroiled in regional, generational and personal factionalism.

By the 1920s the Japanese army had not been seriously challenged for two decades. Its tactics and equipment were far behind those that other powers had been forced to develop during World War I. The army had provided a means of ascent for commoners from all sections of Japan, and it had played an important role in national integration, but its leadership in the 1920s was still in the hands of the Chōshū clique that had been founded by Yamagata. Prime Minister Tanaka, the last lineal descendant of this tradition, was seriously hampered in his efforts to investigate the murder of Chang Tso-lin by the accumulated animosities of non-Chōshū outsiders.

Lateral organization by rank and graduation class in the Officers Academy and War College developed in response to favoritism in the assignment system for top posts. Fittingly enough, it began outside Japan. In 1921 three majors—one a military attaché in Switzerland, one on his way to a post as attaché in the Soviet Union, and one on leave from a tour in China—met at the German resort of Baden-Baden. The three were classmates of the Sixteenth Class of the Officers Academy; two had been class and club mates at the War College, and the third had had two years at the War College. They were "outsiders" disadvantaged by Chōshū favoritism; their origins were in Nagano, Kōchi and Tokyo. This was the beginning of the Futaba Kai, a group dedicated to overthrow of the Chōshū clique. Nagata Tetsuzan, the most important and brilliant member of the group, played a central role in the decade and a half that ended with his assassination in 1935.

There were other groups. By 1929 some forty officers of the rank of colonel and major, graduates of classes fifteen to twenty-five, organized an Evening Club (Isseki kai) that became the center of the anti-Chōshū force. With members powerful in all branches of the army bureaucracy, though none were at its summit, they managed to block Tanaka's efforts to enforce discipline. But their purposes went well beyond this. Depressed by the inflexibly conservative system of seniority in the army, they were determined to change the system of personnel administration. Disturbed by Chinese nationalism and the Manchurian army's failure to follow through on the murder of Chang Tso-lin, they wanted a "solution" of the Manchuria and Mongolia problems. Simultaneously stirred by Pan-Asian thought and anti-Western nationalism, they were impatient with their government's internationalist stand and cooperation with the imperialist powers. Tired of the Chōshū conservatives who blocked change at the center, they pinned their hopes on generals like Araki Sadao, who was from Saga, Mazaki Junzaburō and Hayashi Senjūrō. In these meetings men like Tōjō Hideki, Nagata Tetsuzan, Itagaki Seishirō, Ishiwara Kanji and others of the most restless spirits in the Japanese army came to the fore as leaders. They did their best to get their comrades in important posts in the War Ministry, the General Staff and the Inspectorate of Military Education so that they could influence policy through those agencies. In turn, the opportunity to make appointments to the staffs of units serving overseas, especially in south Manchuria, provided the opportunity for direct implementation of plans. At times meetings became highly emotional and expansionist. Utsunomiya Tarō, who had organized a group of "Saga outsiders" that included Mazaki Junsaburō, Araki Sadao and Yamashita Tomoyuki in the 1920s, summoned his friends to his deathbed in 1922. Pointing to a world map that hung in his sickroom, he had a

General Staff captain draw a red line around all of Siberia, India, Southeast Asia, Australia and New Zealand. With his dying breath, he asserted "That all belongs to Japan."

As was true in Meiji politics, the army's Chōshū clique was not limited entirely to men from Chōshū, and the Saga men were by no means all from that prefecture. Their assumption of the name signified only their opposition to the men who stood at the center of the army's decision-making process. By 1924 the Chōshū group selected General Ugaki, who was from Okayama, as war minister, and he, as future leader of the Chōshū faction, was reviled by Saga men who were not from Saga. Ugaki moderated, although he did not end, favoritism. He recognized ability in Nagata Tetsuzan and placed him on the road to power and influence. This was important, for Nagata was an advocate of total national mobilization.

The issue which now received priority was that of modernization of the army. Ugaki's elimination of four divisions in 1925 was designed to provide funds for mechanization and air power, and Nagata, a brilliant staff planner, supported this fully. But no one could have disbanded thirty three thousand officers and men without making enemies. Nagata seemed, to his old friends, to show great caution in implementing their program, and many of them turned against him in the 1930s. The Araki, or Saga faction now turned from technical overhaul to spiritual renovation for its countertheme and stressed the importance of ideological indoctrination, fighting spirit and the invincible characteristics of the "Imperial Way" (*kōdō*). Araki had served in Russia during the Russian Revolution, and he was intensely concerned about bolshevization and the preservation of Japan's *kokutai*.

Further divisions became apparent between graduates of the War College, who were on the main escalator to rank and success, and the more numerous groups limited to attendance at the Officers Academy. The former received the top commands abroad, they wore special insignia, and they were treated as the military elite. The latter could hope for little more than field-grade commands, usually in uninteresting posts. They made up the majority of those who formed the lower level action groups within the army.

The most interesting of these groups was the Cherry Society (Sakurakai) that was begun by three lieutenant colonels in 1931. Most of its members were young officers from line units, career schools and army offices. The first meeting resolved that "the renovation of our country is our aim, and we will not rule out the use of military force to bring it about." The Sakurakai leaders were direct, brusque and simplistic in their approach. Some held for individual heroics to demolish Japan's existing institutions of government and felt that reconstruction would take care of itself. Others thought it desirable to think more about construction before going into action, and still others favored keeping destruction to the minimum. The leaders, like Hashimoto Kingorō, were War College graduates, and well placed; they included men responsible for the China and Russia desks in the General Staff. The organization provided the impetus and the ammunition for the abortive March incident of 1931. As has been mentioned, that incident failed when General Ugaki refused his support.

The failure of the March incident led to important results within extremist circles. Influential middle-ranking army bureaucrats decided they should give top priority to military action abroad to compensate for their failure to carry out reforms in Japan. At times these views seemed to extend to the top of the army pyramid. When General Ugaki retired as war minister in April 1931, he addressed his last meeting of division commanders with this warning: "It is essential that we work out a solution to the Manchuria and Mongolia problems, because our economic position is unsatisfactory." The main current was beginning to put first priority on action overseas.

Almost immediately afterwards, Finance Minister Inoue Junnosuke submitted plans for reducing the strength of the army by another four divisions. At approximately this time Hashimoto and his friends in the Sakurakai, their expectations of direct action by their superiors shattered by the failure of the March incident, turned their attention to company-grade officers of line units— the lower samurai of the Shōwa Restoration—with a campaign of inflammatory agitation. This activity coincided with writing, agitation and organization by civilian rightists. The new war minister, General Minami, inherited a situation in which some of his General Staff officers were strongly influenced by Ugaki's failure to back them in March. The heads of the China and Russia desks were in fact the main figures in the Sakurakai. Situation judgments and policy papers drawn up by these men were not likely to contribute to a tranquil attitude on the part of their superiors. In July an additional Little Cherry (Kozakura) Society was formed by Officers Academy graduates of the twenty-eighth to thirty-first classes. Manifestos from this group, signed by more than 140 members, were sent to Prince Saionji and to all company-grade officers. The thirty-fifth class chose to circulate a separate statement, which announced that "the Shōwa Restoration means the overthrow of government by political parties" and called on captains and lieutenants all over the country to become the "standard bearers" of the Shōwa Restoration.

The year 1931 thus brought a situation of rising, though temporarily frustrated, extremism among army planners and junior officers. Army leaders shared their alarm and resentment at threatened budget cuts. In addition there were factions at the very top of the army structure. Younger officers distrusted their seniors for cooperating with civilian politicians, and among the most senior generals Araki and Ugaki engaged in bitter arguments about the course Japan should follow. The lower officer "revolt" that journalists described was thus in actuality one that reached into the highest quarters, and its staff work was carried on by men in responsible positions within the General Staff. But when it came to disciplinary action, all groups stood as one against "interference" by civilians. Even Prince Saionji was some months finding out about the March incident, and by then the fever chart had risen so rapidly that disciplinary measures that might have been effective at the time could no longer be undertaken.

The growing discontent of the military reached the point of fusion on the Manchurian mainland before it did in Tokyo. There were sound reasons for this, and the full politics of Manchurian intervention receives treatment in Chapter 10. In the context of army insubordination, it will suffice to point out that staff officers in field commands had far greater opportunities for action than their counterparts in Tokyo.

The rising tide of Chinese nationalism and the anti-Japanese agitation that followed the Shantung intervention alarmed military men everywhere in Japan. For Ishiwara Kanji, who thought in global terms, it was essential for Japan to control Manchuria and the north of China to prepare for the drawn-out struggle with the United States that was to follow. But even for officers with less-exalted prophecies of apocalypse, it was intolerable for Japan to suffer indignity in a sphere where it should be dominant. The indignities themselves were the fault of craven civilian leadership and helped to explain the need to reform Japan. They could never have taken place, asserted General Araki, "if Japan had been Japan." In 1931 the overseas command of the Kwantung Army contained staff officers like Ishiwara Kanji and Itagaki Seishirō, who had the ability to convince their Tokyo counterparts and the nerve to act when opportunity came. The Tokyo high command tried to restrain them by arguing that it needed time to prepare political and public opinion, and when it was presented with the evidence of the deed, it was in a weak position to countermand.

The Manchurian incident of September 1931 was thus less an act of insubordination than it was an acceleration of plans the high command had approved in the proper manner. Civilian moderates proved unable to reverse it. When Prince Saionji replaced Wakatsuki with Inukai in December 1931, the post of war minister went to General Araki. He swiftly replaced the Chōshū, Ugaki partisans with Saga exponents of "The Imperial Way." Araki made many enemies with his ruthless purge, and he alarmed others by the encouragement he gave to younger officers whom he compared to the patriots of the Meiji Restoration. Within the army, planners like Nagata Tetsuzan worried about Araki's apparent preference for "Japanese spirit" over modern military equipment and thought that both his tactics and his beliefs were bad for the morale and efficiency of the army. During 1934 Araki and General Mazaki, whose subordinates were involved in a plot to carry out more assassinations, were removed from office.

The extremists, temporarily without top-level support, were now moved to direct action. In 1935 Lieutenant-Colonel Aizawa walked into the office of Nagata, now again high in the General Staff, and hacked him to death with his sword. The judges at his trial permitted him to turn it into a review of the entire structure of Japanese society. The defense called financial executives as witnesses to let them display the moral lapses that had driven the defendant to action, and Aizawa himself apologized only for his lack of skill as a swordsman.

While the trial was still in process, the mutiny of 26 February 1936 broke out. Although the mutineers enjoyed temporary popular sympathy, the high command, after a period of hesitation, accepted the emperor's instructions to control the rebellion. The mutiny marked the high point of insubordination and factional in-fighting. Advocates of military discipline now took a firm line. The Araki-Mazaki faction was finally removed from influence, military police were more vigilant, and the plotters and mutineers, including Aizawa, were dealt with swiftly. Control of the army came firmly into the hands of the group that had been collected around Nagata after the departure of Ugaki. Men like Tōjō, Mutō, Yamashita and the other leaders of Japan's armies in World War II came into prominence, and they kept controversial targets of factional dispute out of office. When General Ugaki was proposed as prime minister in 1936, the army refused to provide a war minister to complete the cabinet for fear of reviving the hatreds of the years before. Araki reappeared as minister of education under Prince Konoe but not as a leader of the high command.

Nevertheless, personal feuding continued. Generals Ishiwara Kanji and Yamashita Tomoyuki, who incurred the dislike or jealousy of General Tōjō, found their careers blocked. Ironically, many of the original leaders of army extremism and outstanding civilian ultranationalists were out of action by the time Japan entered the long trauma of the China incident of 1937, and some of them survived war-crimes trials and returned to deplore the failure of their associates to follow their advice.

The cost of army factionalism was very high. It served to raise the temperature in which political and policy decisions had to be made. Some men turned from it with relief to face a foreign enemy against whom unity could be achieved. None dared to resist, and many tended to accelerate, the rising trend of hysterical orthodoxy in defense and praise of the Japanese *kokutai*. In 1935 Professor Minobe, whose theories about the emperor as an "organ" of the modern state had gone unchallenged for a generation, was singled out for spectacular humiliation, in part as a deliberate effort on the part of Araki extremists to embarrass their competitors. Army pamphlets, passed out on street corners, called on the nation for patriotism and orthodoxy and painted a grim picture of the dangers of internal subversion and external concession. In 1938 the Education Ministry issued an explanation of *kokutai* which served as a textbook for study groups in schools for the next seven years. The mysteries of the national polity, described in archaic language that pleased the ear but puzzled the mind, were contrasted with the disorder that individualism, selfishness and democracy had caused in the West. Fortunately, as the book reassured its readers, major powers in the Western world had also seen the light and had moved away from individualism. In these years *kokutai* became a major category of literature, and so many books were published about it that libraries reserved a special classification section for the category.

Despite all this, the Japanese electorate, in the opportunities that were given it to express its opinion, never deserted the trends that began in the 1920s. In the elections of 1930, 1932 and 1936 most voters stayed with the Seiyūkai and Minseitō. The military premiers of the period found themselves hard-pressed to govern without Diet support. Moderate socialism, represented by the Social Masses party, grew to hold thirty-seven seats in 1937, when it received almost a million votes. It may, in fact, have been this combination of electoral failure and ideological frenzy that helped to drive the activists on. The Japanese people had to be increasingly exhorted to show their patriotism because of their relative apathy. The few were full of conviction, the many fearful for the times.

On the other hand, enthusiasm for the party cause was also slight. In 1937 Prince Saionji, searching for a symbol of unity amid the confusion of society and politics, selected Konoe Fumimaro as premier. Konoe was a member of the old court aristocracy and hence above faction. He was urbane, popular and articulate. He had had ties with the rightists in the 1920s and also with the Marxists. He had few enemies. He had written a much-quoted article to warn of Anglo-Saxon domination of the world in 1918, and he was acceptable to the military. Unfortunately he also lacked conviction or courage. Accustomed to reticence, ambiguity and compromise, he met militarist pressure with strategic retreats. Larger budgets and stronger policies followed for the military, and in time General Araki reemerged as minister of education. In 1937 the China incident led to full-scale war on the continent, and under wartime conditions the parliamentary system made adjustments. By 1940 Konoe thought Japan needed a superparty, one that might provide a check for the military and serve as symbol of national unity. Instead the Imperial Rule Assistance Association, as it became known, provided for the final integration of political activity in a single, government-controlled party that ruled out serious political competition and debate until the end of the war. Thus a succession of terror, militarism, ideological fervor and war had brought to an end the democratic gains of the years between the wars.

5. *Japan in the 1930s*

SOME ASPECTS of the political changes in Japan during the 1930s were comparable to those in the fascist states of Europe, but there were important differences. European fascism grew on the basis of mass movements led and organized by skillful demagogues. One looks in vain for such developments in Japan in the 1930s. Instead the dynamics came from the military, although they were supplemented by uncoordinated plans of civilian terrorists which encouraged moderate counselors to turn to responsible military leaders in hopes of curbing extremism. European fascism prepared for war with rigid controls and organized popular frenzy; in Japan it was the war that led to the totalitarian structure rather than the reverse. Japanese theories of *kokutai* also inhibited the development of popular leaders, for any assertion of individual authority would have been deeply abhorrent to loyalists who professed to serve their emperor and who denounced the political parties for obscuring his virtue. The path to power in prewar Japan did not lie through popular agitation. Japan had not yet been modernized to that extent. Neither the party leaders nor their militarist adversaries could hope to do more than create a setting conducive to behind-the-scenes maneuvering that might bring their ideas to bear. The military, who were able to arouse patriotic enthusiasm by creating international tension, had the advantage, but they never thought of trying to rule through a mass party. Effective popular participation was still limited, and civilian rightists and militarists thought of themselves as a dedicated elite rather than as popular leaders. They had been too contemptuous of politicians who courted popular favor to choose that route for themselves.

On the other hand, the theoretical basis of Japanese ascendancy was a good deal more direct and simplistic than was that of European fascism. In Italy and Germany the riches of Roman power and Teutonic strength had to be exhumed in efforts to stir the masses to action. Skillful and often cynical politicians conducted a willful retreat from rationality and modernity. But in Japan ideological "modernity" had been built on the basis of just such myths of Shinto divinity and *kokutai.* Except for an intellectual and Western-oriented elite, these myths had been the substance of education, and they seemed related to basic forms of communal sanction and belief. Japan thus possessed, as General Ludendorff noted in the 1920s, what Germany had to construct. The pattern of ideology that had served to discipline the national will in the race to modernity now served to deny the fruits of that modernity. Imperial ideology had been a means for many of the Meiji leaders. For their successors, it often became an end in itself.

The structure of despotism that scarred the face of Germany with concentration camps for political prisoners and racial minorities was not to be found in Japan. Individual moderates like Professor Minobe were hounded to disgrace, and suspected radicals were imprisoned, mistreated and sometimes tortured, but the full application of draconian codes to enforce orthodoxy was not necessary. Just as freedom had not been absolute, despotism did not need to become explicit. Communal controls, social conformity, family loyalty, group ostracism and mutual policing through the block or village leader made the booted storm trooper unthinkable. Japanese society bent with the gale, but it did not break. The institutional structure of the Meiji state remained intact, ready to serve for implementation of the surrender in 1945.

The struggle that counted thus took place at the top and behind the scenes, in a quiet alteration of the balance of forces between bureaucracies. When one sees the advantages that were held by the "moderates" like Prince Saionji at the start of the process, it becomes necessary to ask in a different way what went wrong and why these men could not halt trends that they clearly deplored.

No doubt one can begin by saying they were lesser men than their Meiji predecessors, the genro. But that is not enough. They also worked in a very different and far more complex situation. They were themselves the product of the bureaucracies the Meiji structure had brought into being, and they spoke as representatives of these interests and not as their creators. They lacked that body of shared experience, confidence and trust that distinguished the first generation. Instead it is striking to find the degrees of misunderstanding, distrust and indirection that characterized Japanese leaders in the 1930s in discussions and decisions of the greatest moment.

Until the end of the decade there were few who were fully conscious of the importance and irreversibility of the decisions that were being made by indirection. The conservatives thought in terms of temporizing, optimistic that there would be future opportunities to set things straight. "If you could be sure this was the point of no return," Saionji said, "this would be a very interesting time. But it's no good to be always saying, 'How terrible!' or 'Whatever will I do!' " Forthright resistance, they thought, might create a crisis in which their cause would be forever lost, while gradual, strategic retreat would leave them a field for future maneuver.

The danger they saw was one of greater institutional change. It was above all concern for the safety and prestige of the imperial institution that kept the men around the throne from using the emperor, their strongest weapon. Once his prestige was thrown into the battle, there could be no retreat, but there might well be defeat. The court advisers feared the extremism of the young officers and the anarchistic tendencies of individual heroics that made it possible to serve the emperor by "protecting" him from bad advice. Memories of the way the Diet had refused to heed an imperial suggestion in 1913 and more recent evidence of military willingness to risk insubordination made it dangerous to involve the emperor's prestige unless it was absolutely essential to do so. Only when he himself insisted, as in the 1936 revolt, and when the danger of total destruction of Japan and its society in 1945 became clear, was the emperor's participation permissible. Had that resource been squandered in a premature effort there might have been no way to engineer the final surrender.

Another element that must be kept in mind was the fact that the Meiji state structure obscured responsibility. The genro kept final controls in their own hands, and until his death Yamagata was distrustful and resentful of prime ministers who were too successful or too long in power. A complex structure of behind-the-scenes controls and limitations on executive authority concealed the entire decision-making process. With responsibility diffused, final determination was not likely to be assumed by any one element because charges of arrogance would surely follow. With responsibility diffused, men were more likely to take risks. The military was responsible only for defense, and it was insensitive to foreign opinion. The civilians could stick to their business and leave security to the military, and senior statesmen found themselves fully occupied in resolving mutual differences without setting directions. The setting made for irresponsibility.

In such a complex structure the advantage lay with the simplistic, fervent advocates of action. In a setting that distinguished between abstract authority at the top and effective, though nonresponsible, power at the middle, the importance of section and division chiefs in all bureaucracies became greater. No doubt it is true in every bureaucracy that middle echelons prepare the papers for their superiors and that the advantage lies with the document as it proceeds up through the establishment. A document can only be met by a counterdocument. Failing that, it is qualified, or postponed, or obscured in its language. In the Japanese bureaucracies, qualifications and postponements were sometimes added by the men at the top, but they usually acted to delay and not to cancel. Advocates of action usually got promissory notes for the future. The Kwantung Army staff's plans for action were delayed but not denied by the General Staff. A decade later, military deadlines for action against America were moved forward but not ruled out. When the action came, it was possible to assert that the decisions had been normally worked out. Japan in the 1930s experienced neither a "revolution from below" nor strong leadership at the top; indeed, there was more often "abdication at the top." Isolated explosions had not ripped the fabric of its institutions, but maladjustments and vibrations produced the irreversible oscillations that sent the nation careening to destruction without full realization that it had entered a path from which there were no exits.

These institutional and structural weaknesses of Japan's between-the-wars government were clearly important. They had been there from the beginning of constitutional government, although crisis management in the Meiji period had been carried on in a more structured world order and by surer hands. In summing up the interwar period, it is therefore useful to distinguish, as E. O. Reischauer recently has, between Japan's objective problems and Japanese perceptions of those problems.

The objective problems were real enough. They were related to the growing divisions within Japanese society caused by uneven rates of growth. The difficulties of the economy are more clearly seen than those in the intellectual world, but there the maladjustments were no less serious. The economic difficulties of the 1920s came closer to solution in the 1930s than did the intellectual difficulties. Massive government spending and vigorous export management reversed the deflationary trends of the 1920s, and on statistical evidence Japan emerged from the depression well before many of its competitors. The intellectual maladjustments, on the other hand, grew worse rather than better. Even so, it is easy to exaggerate their contribution. Conservative and reactionary thought had always been present in modern Japan. Although intermittently persuasive, it was basically antimodern and often antimilitary. Agrarians were more often dropouts from modernization than they were supporters of the kind of national structure that a modern war would require.

The performance of the political party governments was uneven and often unimpressive but not necessarily more so than was the case in many other countries. A major problem was the lack of a vigorous intellectual rationale for party government. Instead throughout Japanese society there remained assumptions of an achievable perfection of governmental structure. The parties' performance was more inadequate as the standards set were more unrealistic.

On the other hand the perception of these conditions, especially by the military, was very gloomy. Politics seemed corrupt, business demoralized, and countryside impoverished. Imperfection, disunity and injustice provided opportunities for advocates of a basic reorientation of Japanese society and policy. The net effect, in Reischauer's words, was a "virtual military dictatorship with strong totalitarian overtones" which was scarcely a "naturally harmonious, unified society." This led in turn to a "drive for imperial conquest that in retrospect is seen to have made little economic sense and in any case led shortly to military disaster."

If one accepts this distinction between objective problems and their perception, it is probable that the tie between perception and product—between what the military thought they saw and what they did—is to be found in their awareness of the "China problem." The perceptions that proved central to the whole course of Japanese militarism were those based on foreign affairs and especially those that related to the development of Chinese unity and nationalism. It was the "China problem," as much as any other, that destroyed Taishō democracy in Japan, just as it was the "Japan problem" that destroyed the Nationalist government that took power in China in 1927.

CHAPTER 10

The Road to the Pacific War

*Japan's political rise had been achieved at the expense of neighbor-*ing states whose governments were incapable of effective reform. The political cost of early Japanese imperial expansion had been slight, for Korean and Chinese modernizers were as likely to side with Tokyo as with regimes that had no tolerance for them. But the twentieth century saw the old regimes overthrown. Twentieth-century Chinese nationalists found their problem less with the old regime than with external conditions that seemed to hamper the development of modern successor states. For these men Japan now stood as problem and not as promise.

Japan's rise had been carried out within the rules of nineteenth-century imperialism. The gains any power scored in China stood to benefit its competitors under the most-favored–nation clause. The rise of a European-style state in Asia had served as a useful counterpoise to the territorial ambitions of the Russians, and the chief requirement for acceptance by the maritime powers had been effectiveness in political maneuvering. The Japanese had given evidence of this in diplomacy and in war. At the end of the first decade of the twentieth century,

Japan seemed secure in every position. She was allied with Great Britain. She had replaced Russia in Manchuria and occupied Korea, and treaties with Russia seemed to rule out the danger of a war of revenge. Treaties with France supplemented those with England and Russia, and repeated agreements with the United States seemed to promise mutual recognition of essential interests. Japan's military rise had been carried on in the shadow of the British fleet. So long as the Anglo-Japanese alliance stood (and it was renewed, for ten years, in 1911) Japan was in little danger of attack. In World War I the Japanese skillfully set the limits of their involvement with their allies, and they had no difficulty in securing a round of treaties which guaranteed new gains. The elimination of German influence in the Pacific was quick and total. Japan's dominance in Northeast Asia replaced an earlier and less amenable Russian presence. Throughout this period Japan's tactics and goals had been fully compatible with accepted practice.

The post-Meiji state was managed less skillfully, but what changed was not so much Japan as the international order. The Japanese leaders had devoted a half century to the realization of goals no longer possible under the demands of twentieth-century nationalism. The situation, alternatives and rules changed almost at the moment of Japanese success. The situation had changed first with the fall of the Chinese imperial order. The possibility of a republican order in China was particularly welcome to America. It was greeted with hope by Woodrow Wilson, who told the Congress that "changes scarcely dreamed possible in our lifetime have suddenly transformed the Chinese empire." Throughout the travail of warlord disorder and corruption that followed, official Washington and unofficial America never abandoned this hope of political regeneration. American representatives in Peking often shared the impatience and disillusion with China of their diplomatic colleagues, but in the Department of State the determination to sponsor and support Chinese autonomy and integrity remained firm.

The decline of European imperialist powers during and after World War I provided the second major change. Germany left the Asian scene, and France never fully regained its prewar potential. Britain survived but no longer stood as the strongest maritime power. The war left the United States the strongest Western power in East Asia. Financially and politically it was now Washington that ruled the roost, and the moral tone of Wilsonian diplomacy counted for more than the conservative tone of London. Japan's principal antagonist among the maritime powers was, thus, the United States. Since England would not lend Japan the protection of its fleet against the danger of a confrontation with America, the Anglo-Japanese alliance came to an end.

The destruction of the Russian empire and its replacement by the Bolshevik revolutionary order completed these changes. There no longer seemed a Russian imperialist alternative to Japan. Instead there was a new republican and revolutionary challenge that stirred young China after 1919, one that found echo in Japan as well.

To put it differently: in the Asia of the 1920s Japan suddenly represented conservatism and the old order. The real competition for youthful enthusiasm lay between Russian and American ideals. The allies the Meiji statesmen had courted so carefully disappeared. The position and territories they had seized became objects of danger instead of security. Japan's world had changed at the moment that it had been completed. This was the meaning of the consternation with which old soldier Yamagata regarded the international and domestic order at the end of his long life.

1. The Washington Conference Order

SINCE WORLD WAR I had destroyed the frame of reference for international relations in East Asia, efforts to work out a new form of organization became necessary. The years after the war saw Japan and the United States saddled with expensive naval building schedules which neither side wanted to maintain. The American navy had become one of the world's most powerful forces, but it had not figured in the planning of the Anglo-Japanese alliance. Japan faced new security responsibilities with the German holdings in East Asia, but at the same time its prewar security within a network of imperial alliances came to an end. What was worse was that it faced evidence of American opposition to its course in China. The expensive and unpopular Siberian intervention had also shown the difficulty of working out security needs through independent action. Japan had to be prepared to work out its security alone, without British protection, or enter a new international system of guarantees. The imperial navy had advocated the former course and worked out the schedule for a massive buildup. But the costs of this combined with uncertainty that it would prove effective in the face of probable American countermeasures. The internationalist inclinations of the business-supported governments of the 1920s made international cooperation more attractive and logical.

The same course commended itself to Great Britain, which desired to maintain its ties with Japan without antagonizing the United States. The United States, however, had different aims. Washington wanted to put an end to the diplomacy of imperialism and secret agreements. It was anxious to prevent Japan's launching on a course of independent action in East Asia, and it wanted to create the conditions for order and stability in China. The United States was also anxious to end the ruinous arms race before congressional budget cutting limited it unilaterally. The solution seemed to be a set of agreements that would legislate the continuation of the existing order of things.

At the Washington Conference, which met from November 1921 to February 1922, nine maritime powers were represented. But while Italy and Portugal were present, the Soviet Union, which the United States had not yet recognized, was not. The conference thus addressed itself to problems of the maritime nations rather than to those of territorial powers, of which Japan and Russia were the principal representatives. It worked out a network of interrelated treaties that provided the principal framework of international relations in East Asia for the next decade.

The first agreement reached was a substitute for the Anglo-Japanese alliance. Both England and Japan had thought of inviting the United States to join in that agreement, England to obviate the possibility of conflict with America, and Japan to checkmate the American fleet. The United States, however, was more interested in reforming "the old structure of power diplomacy" than it was in joining it. In order to get rid of the Anglo-Japanese alliance, Secretary Hughes agreed to a more general and consultative pact which would include France. In his thinking, the pact now seemed less imperialistic and more likely to gain Senate and public approval. In the Four Power Pacific Treaty, America, England, Japan and France guaranteed each other's rights and possessions in the Pacific and promised to consult if those rights should be threatened. The wording of the agreement was vague and general; if rights were "threatened by the aggressive action of any other power," the parties were to "communicate with one another fully and frankly in order to arrive at an understanding as to the most efficient measures to be taken, jointly or separately, to meet the exigencies of the particular situation." It was hardly necessary for the U.S. Senate to add the reservation that "under the terms of this treaty there is no commitment to armed force, no alliance, and no obligation to join in any defense."

What Japan lost in security in the Anglo-Japanese alliance it regained in the five-power Naval Limitation Treaty that was signed in February 1922. This was designed to end the competition in battleships and aircraft carriers. Future conferences were scheduled to deal with cruisers, submarines and destroyers. Under a complicated formula England, Japan and the United States agreed to scrap obsolete battleships, to cut back building plans and to work toward a level of 15 capital ships for America and Britain and 9 for Japan by the year 1936. The overall ratio of strength in capital ships for America, England, Japan, France and Italy was set at 5:5:3:1.75:1.75. This was the most ambitious and specific plan for disarmament yet worked out. Capital ships to be scrapped and to be kept were specified by name. Agreement on smaller ships was never reached, nor were efforts to abolish submarines and restrict military aviation. Nevertheless the agreement on capital ships brought security to each power by limiting the heavy equipment that would be available to launch long-range attacks.

The restrictions on shipbuilding were made effective by promises the United States, England and Japan made to maintain the status quo in naval bases and fortifications in the area between Hawaii and Singapore where their Pacific interests were contiguous. If Britain did not build a base at Hong Kong, the United States in the Philippines and Japan in the mandated islands of the South Pacific, the powers could not easily launch an offensive attack on each other. Japan thus secured safety in its home waters, and it had been spared the cost of an armaments race for naval strength. Nor had the Western powers made sub-

stantial concessions. Neither Britain nor America had any plans to fortify their
Pacific possessions, and their legislatures would hardly have provided the money
to do so. Insofar as a multilateral disarmament agreement could, the Washington Conference succeeded in its goals.

China remained the most troublesome problem for East Asian stability, and
Secretary Hughes also sought what he called a "substitute for all prior statements and agreements" about China. This became the Nine-Power Treaty, to
which China was a signatory. The powers agreed to respect China's sovereignty,
independence and territorial integrity, to help China gain territorial and administrative stability, to work for an Open Door of equal opportunity and to keep
from taking advantage of China's turbulence to seek special rights or privileges.
This generalized affirmation of morality could expect to have meaning only so
long as national interests did not conflict. But in addition, during the Washington Conference sessions, Japan and China agreed on the return of the Shantung
port of Kiaochow and the Tsingtao-Tsinan Railway to China. The Japanese also
stated themselves as ready to modify some of the provisions of the Twenty-one
Demands and to withdraw altogether Group V of the Demands, to which
China had never given agreement. In discussions of advisers and railway rights
the Japanese also showed a new preparedness to work within new international
rules. They furthermore indicated Japan's intention of making an early withdrawal from the Maritime Provinces and north Sakhalin, and they agreed to
American cable rights on Yap in return for American approval of Japanese administrative authority in the former German-held islands in the South Pacific.

The agreements affecting China were destined to be the least successful of
those worked out at Washington. The Nine-Power pact did not wipe out the
record of earlier Chinese diplomacy in the manner that Secretary Hughes had
hoped it would. Japan agreed to modify its stand, but it was not prepared to start
over again. There was a more basic misunderstanding. Secretary Hughes interpreted the Nine-Power pact as canceling earlier agreements in which the
United States had seemed to recognize Japan's special interests in Manchuria.
But Tokyo interpreted that part of the Nine-Power pact in which the powers
agreed "to refrain from countenancing action inimical to the security of such
states" to connote continued recognition of Japan's special security interests in
Manchuria. Maintenance of the existing order meant Open Door to America
and special privilege to Japan, with the result that the future of the Open Door
in northeast China depended upon Japan. Throughout the 1920s no Japanese
statesman, whatever his background or position, ever compromised on the fact
of his country's special rights in Manchuria.

The China issue was further complicated by the recognition by all the
Washington powers that China was not yet a modern state. Chinese delegates at
Washington demanded full sovereign status and an early end to the unequal
treaty system, only to be countered by the "Root resolution" wherein the other
delegates pledged to "provide the fullest and most unembarrassed opportunity
to China to develop and maintain for herself an effective and stable govern-

ment." It was planned to restore tariffs to a general 5 percent (in fact they were closer to 3 percent in 1922 and seriously limited the Peking government's ability to raise revenue) and to convene special tariff conferences to provide additional income for China. In addition a factfinding commission on extraterritoriality would try to help work out reforms that might "warrant the several Powers in relinquishing, either progressively or otherwise, their respective rights of extraterritoriality." For all their rhetoric the Western powers were no more prepared than Japan to grant China full membership in the international order and insisted on setting requirements of stability and modernization.

Nevertheless Japan's participation in the Washington Conference network of treaties signified a conscious commitment to international cooperation. Her minimal security needs had been met, and there was optimism that the gradual modernization of China could somehow be combined with the retention of Japan's rights. Even Henry L. Stimson, no great admirer of Imperial Japan, later granted that for the next ten years Japan had "given an exceptional record of good citizenship in the light of the international world."

Yet the Washington Conference failed to set up a new order of cooperative diplomacy in East Asia. One element in this was the turbulence of China in the 1920s. The revolutionary and communist movements and the speed with which they turned upon the imperialist powers as scapegoats for the frustration of Chinese nationalism made it both more necessary and more difficult for the foreign powers to work together. Foreign diplomats and even the most determinedly pro-Chinese observers were often confounded by Chinese disorder. China was too far from defining its "national aspirations" for the powers to be prepared with assistance for reaching them.

If the Chinese had been more united, they would have been able to show the lack of unity among the Washington Conference powers. There was very little effort to develop a cooperative approach. Instead the principal powers showed a tendency toward individual positions and bilateral diplomacy that would emphasize their goodwill toward the "Chinese people." Secretary of State Kellogg instructed American negotiators in 1925 to "avoid the possibility of any charge that the American Government is taking sides for or against any other government represented at the Conference." With the strongest of the conference powers taking this position, the possibility of a cooperative approach was nonexistent. Instead a situation was created in which the Soviet Union, a lone outsider, could encourage Chinese distrust of the powers. Ultimately a Chinese nationalist government moved with skill in exploiting antagonisms and distrust among its self-appointed protectors.

Japan's commitment to international cooperation was never adequately exploited or fairly tested. Where it was tested, it drew a sharp line between Manchuria and China. Cooperation and internationalization applied to China but not to Manchuria. Japan's civilian governments moved cautiously and intelligently to keep from contributing to the antiimperialist furor of the Northern Expedition in China. But in Manchuria the insistence of the Japanese military on backing Chang Tso-lin affected the outcomes of campaigns between the warlords of north China. It was one such operation that caused the overthrow of Tuan Ch'i-jui and the flight of the Chinese delegates to a tariff conference in 1926.

Japan's participation in the discussions for tariff reform in China itself found Tokyo maintaining a firm line on Chinese obligations to Japan. Since these included, in the Nishihara loans, obligations incurred by venal warlord regimes whose peculation had helped bring on the riots of 1919, they were not likely to be recognized by a nationalist Chinese government. Japan's participation in the tariff negotiations that had been envisaged at the Washington Conference also found the Japanese working for the adoption of a schedule that would benefit Japanese exports to China rather than the more expensive manufactures of the West. Since Tokyo furthermore tied in tariff assistance with debt consolidation, Japanese negotiators were never able to reach agreement with their Chinese counterparts. As Chinese nationalism grew and the Chinese bargaining position hardened, Japan's conception of its "rights and interests" thus came to lie athwart Chinese "national aspirations." Shidehara's commitment to moderation was never total or unconditional. It would be unreasonable, he told the Diet in early 1927, for Japan to use force to protect its rights and interests before all peaceful and diplomatic means had been tried. Japan would view China's reasonable demands with sympathy, but it would also expect the Chinese to show an equal understanding of Japanese interests in China.

At the same time, the Japanese willingness to experiment with adherence to a pattern of relative cooperation with the Washington Conference powers reflected the broader trends toward internationalism in Taishō Japan. Foreign affairs, as James Crowley puts it, now had priority over national defense in the ultimate determination of national policy. This furthered the dominance of civilian leadership and the growth of parliamentary government. It meant more responsible and more powerful cabinets. In the absence of determined genro leadership after the death of Yamagata, the civilian statesmen were challenged only by the military, and as the cabinet rose in influence the ministers of the army and navy together with their ministry staffs gained in power relative to the army and navy general staffs. The Washington Conference, which permitted military expenditures to decline from 49 percent of the national budget in 1921 to 30 percent in 1923, showed the importance of the new priorities. National defense, statesmen now pointed out, meant more than guns and warships; it included productivity and diplomacy. National defense was becoming everybody's business.

The growing democratization of Japan and the extension of party influence into all aspects of national policy also had the effect of making the political aspects of foreign policy important. Foreign, and especially China, policy became the subject of political debate, and it was no longer the exclusive property of a small elite. Shidehara and Tanaka were more subject to political constraint than their predecessors had been, and the debate usually operated to fan rather than to diminish disagreement.

Even in areas in which there could be no disagreement, debate could operate to lessen public confidence in government policy. The gratuitous insult delivered by the United States Congress with the passage of the Exclusion Act in 1924 convinced most Japanese that the international order to which their government was trying to subscribe contained built-in reminders of second-class citizenship for Japanese. Japanese had been aware of racial discrimination against emigrants in the United States since the Meiji period, and their negotiators' failure to secure clauses calling for racial equality in the negotiations for the League of Nations had seemed to confirm the gloomy views of future racial conflict that became general around World War I and borne out in the shameful treatment accorded Japanese Americans during World War II. The Exclusion Act particularly weakened the positions of Western-oriented liberals like the Quaker, Nitobe Inazō, who vowed that he would not again set foot in the United States until its repeal.

Issues of this sort had their ramifications in China policy, where they affected the influence of civilian leaders like Shidehara who were closely identified with the new internationalism. Within a few years the attempt of civilians to control defense policy in the name of the totality of national strength had given way to the return of the military, who demanded controls on civilian life under theories of "total national defense." Prime Minister Hamaguchi's success in dominating the navy after the London Conference of 1930 was followed by army and navy determination to control political priorities theretofore allocated to civilian authorities. The development of a responsible Japanese internationalism would have required unusually salubrious weather. In fact, the currents of Soviet policy and Chinese nationalism provided unusually difficult conditions for maturation.

2. The Russian Return

SOVIET RUSSIA was not invited to participate in the Washington Conference, and for some years its representatives were not eligible for conventional diplomatic courtesies. The Soviet Union posed a new problem for the powers. It was at once a revolutionary force, eager to subvert existing governments and overthrow the societies they governed, it sponsored political parties designed to do so, and it was the source of revolutionary propaganda and ideology that made a profound impression throughout East Asia. At the same time it was a great power with its own territorial and security interests. At times revolutionary and security interests combined. Antiimperialist hostility was directed primarily against Britain, whose Asian policies had always conflicted with Russian interests. At other times security took precedence over revolution, as when Russian diplomatic interests dictated temporary support of anticommunist governments instead of support for local communists. At such times the interests of the Soviet Union, as the heartland of the proletarian revolution, came first. Policies could also be justified in terms of promoting war among the imperialist powers. "We would be ... safer," Lenin said in 1920, "if the imperialist powers were to start a war among themselves.... The capitalist thieves sharpen their knives for use against us; it is our duty to see that their knives are directed against one another." It was in the Russian interest to work for a conflict between America and Japan, and so Lenin tried to encourage American capitalists to invest in Siberian development.

More basically, Lenin saw it in the Russian interest as well as in the interests of the world revolution to promote the nationalist movement in East Asia, even though it might not be communist led, in order to weaken the capitalist homelands of Western imperialism. As he put it, "The separation of colonies and a proletarian revolution at home will overthrow the capitalist system in Europe. For the achievement of complete success of the world revolution, the co-operation of these two forces is essential." Thus aid to the Chinese nationalist revolution would be both an "episode in the history of the downfall of the international bourgeoisie" and an advancement of Russian security against Japanese imperialism, which would be an early target of Chinese nationalism.

The necessity for the powers to develop individual and unilateral approaches to the great land power that remained outside the Washington Conference system discouraged the development of the cooperative approach to East Asian international relations that the Washington system required. From the first, efforts to develop multilateral checks on the new Russian state proved failures. The Siberian intervention provided the clearest example of this. At the time of the Bolshevik revolution the Tokyo policymakers were poorly informed about the situation and first considered the Bolsheviks as German agents. They tended to see the problem chiefly in terms of utilizing opportunities to extend their influence in northern Asia, with particular reference to gaining control over raw materials. But their counsels were divided. Army hardliners, influenced by the reports their military attachés sent home, wanted unilateral Japanese intervention and the establishment of a pro-Japanese regime in Asiatic Russia. Most civilian policymakers, more oriented toward Western opinion, held out against this course, and the Tokyo government agreed to intervention only after a joint approach was signaled by suggestions from Washington in July 1918. But after the intervention began, Japanese army leaders exaggerated the strategic requirements of the situation and as a result Japanese forces far outnumbered those of their allies. In the field, Japanese commanders sponsored anti-Bolshevik governments under right-wing figures and created serious doubts about their intentions.

The success of civilian leadership in Tokyo in stopping this marked one of the first victories of Taishō democracy. Premier Hara and his successors

cautiously did their best to restrain the military. By refusing to establish a
Supreme Headquarters for the expedition, Hara kept formal control within his
own hands. In December 1918 his government decreased army troop strength in
Siberia instead of increasing it, as the army had demanded. Japanese intervention
had provoked hostile responses among the Russian population in Siberia, and it
eventually created pro-Soviet sentiment. Tokyo planners were also alarmed by
reports of subversion of their units by communist propaganda, and the management of the expedition was contributing to antimilitarist currents in Japan. The
defeat of the anticommunist armies in Russia and the costs of the expedition to
Japan made it necessary for Japan to devise a plan for extricating itself from an
unpopular and unsuccessful involvement. It took several years before this was
successful. There was growing concern among Japanese conservatives that
Bolshevik ideology was making headway in Japan as well as in China. The army
saw the Japanese rice riots of 1918, the Korean independence movement of
1919, and the May Fourth movement in China as Bolshevik inspired and hesitated to give up whatever leverage the intervention might give them with the
revolutionary government.

In 1922 the challenges provided by the Washington Conference finally
made it possible and indeed necessary to come to terms with the problem. On
the Russian side Lenin provided a face-saving measure by the establishment of a
buffer state, the Far Eastern Republic, in 1920. The Republic was established
with a facade of democratic institutions to shield its subservience to Kremlin
control. Japan granted de facto recognition to the Far Eastern Republic and did
its best to derive economic benefits as the price of military withdrawal. In October 1922 the Japanese evacuated their forces from all Russian soil except northern Sakhalin. A month later, its mission accomplished, the Far Eastern Republic
lowered its flag to be incorporated into the Soviet Union.

The way was now open for the resumption of formal relations between
Russia and Japan. The same Russian negotiators who made the offers to Sun
Yat-sen and the Kuomintang represented their country in exploratory talks
with Japanese statesmen. In 1923 Adolf Joffe, who had just talked to Sun Yat-
sen in Shanghai, came to Tokyo for talks with Tokyo Mayor Gotō Shimpei.
Gotō believed strongly in the necessity of friendly relations with the Soviet
Union as "instrumental in forestalling the plot the Chinese are now engineering
and . . . bringing about a favorable situation for us to get easy access to economic
concessions." Just as Japan had managed friendship with Czarist Russia, Gotō
argued, it could work things out with the Soviets. Any other course would lead
to a Russo-Chinese alignment and the isolation of Japan in East Asia. Gotō's
views triumphed over those of more conservative men in the Foreign Office. In
1924 Gotō's work was taken over by Foreign Office representatives who dealt
with Soviet Minister Karakhan in Peking. Out of this came the resumption of
formal relationships between Japan and the Soviet Union in 1925.

The treaty pledged each party to refrain from interference in the internal
affairs of the other. Trade relations maintained fishery rights that Japan had

gained at Portsmouth in 1905. Japan agreed to evacuate northern Sakhalin by the end of May 1925 and in return received rights to oil and coal. The Russians, now temporarily relieved from pressure from Japan, found themselves able to turn the full force of their politics and propaganda against British imperialism, and Great Britain served as principal whipping post for the propaganda of Communist-Kuomintang collaboration during the early part of the Northern Expedition. This setting must be kept in mind in considering the moderation of the Shidehara policies at the middle of the decade. The principal antiforeign thrust in China was reserved for Great Britain. The great strikes of 1925 began in Japanese-owned textile mills, but they swiftly became demonstrations against the British. Propaganda slogans called on people not to work for British firms, not to use British banknotes, not to buy British goods or insurance, not to study in British schools and not to sell to the British. Hankow and Nanking felt the same anti-British fury, and Hong Kong was virtually blockaded for almost a year and a half.

Despite all this, the Japanese and the Russians continued to regard each other warily. Comintern activities in Japan were carefully followed and ruthlessly suppressed. The same period that saw the resumption of relations with Russia brought the Peace Preservation Law of 1925. Japanese rejected Russian proposals for a neutrality pact in 1926 and for a nonaggression pact the following year. For the most part, Japanese planners were more concerned with the effects of communist activity in China than they were with direct threats from the Soviet Union. But the inauguration of the first Soviet Five-Year Plan in 1928 awoke once again the fears of Japan's military leaders of Russian preparation for a war of revenge, and they began to speak of the 1930s as a period of danger and national crisis. Nor was Russia's accommodation to Japan in the 1920s ever more than tactical. Russian planners were aware of the northern orientation of the Japanese military, and they saw Japanese influence as the principal counter to their own in Mongolia and northern Manchuria. Some authorities suggest that Russian willingness to gamble as heavily as they did on the success of the Kuomintang and Northern Expedition can be traced to their desire for a firm political ally against and buffer to Japanese expansion on the continent. (This continuing distrust remained a feature of Japanese-Russian relations until World War II, and it is far from dead in the cautious three-way relations between Japan, the Soviet Union, and the People's Republic of China in the 1970s.)

3. *Japan and Chinese Nationalism*

STUDENT NATIONALISM and radicalism found perfect soil for growth in the troubled political conditions of warlord China. The bearing this had on Chinese politics during the years of the Northern Expedition created problems for all the powers. Russia sought to exploit it and succeeded for a day. The Japanese, whose stake in the old order was far larger, never worked out a consistent and integrated approach to it. In failing to do so, they lost their chance for success in mid-century East Asia.

Japanese modernization had posed a constant challenge for change in China. Japan had provided the stimulus of example in its own political reforms and had added the shock of defeat in 1895. In the years that followed, Japanese liberals and activists brought encouragement and cooperation to the revolutionary movement. The Boxer settlement was followed by the movement of Chinese students to Tokyo, a tide that crested at the time of the Russo-Japanese War. After the Tokyo government adapted its policies to the trends of the imperialist giants, Japan added new stimuli to hostility for Chinese nationalism by the Twenty-one Demands in 1915. Although it was this final path that was to dominate, alternate courses were never foreclosed completely. Japanese radicalism influenced Chinese radicalism throughout the early stages of the anarchist and communist movements. Japanese liberals maintained ties with their Chinese friends. Miyazaki Tōten responded to a request from the young Mao Tse-tung to come to his school in Changsha. To the end of his life Sun Yat-sen retained hope that Japan would choose the road of nonmilitary Pan-Asianism, and after his death Wang Ching-wei trusted his reputation to the possibility of cooperating with a Japan that seemed certain to dominate the Asia of his lifetime. Chiang Kai-shek was by no means firmly anti-Japanese throughout the 1920s and 1930s. He repeatedly risked his political fate through determined efforts to reach an understanding with Japan, and Japanese leaders themselves remained sufficiently optimistic about reaching a settlement with Chiang to limit their support of Wang Ching-wei.

Japanese and Chinese were too aware of the things they had in common, including a shared ambivalence toward the West, to reject cooperation precipitately. Japan's "Asianists" were no doubt guilty of great exaggeration in their constant reiteration of the "values, tradition and culture" they claimed they shared with China, but there was something to the arguments they used. It is a misreading of history to see the alienation of Japan from China as the working out of a deeply set historical inevitability, but it is even more obvious that the Japanese assumption that history and proximity made for friendship and cooperation was wrong. Proximity has seldom made for friendship anywhere in the world, and the sudden inversion of the traditional relations of power and prestige between China and Japan was more likely to make for resentment and suspicion than amity. Still, these were long-run probabilities. In the short-run picture of the 1920s it required very specific Japanese provocation to alienate Chinese nationalism.

The intimacy of contact and participation with the scene in China gave the Japanese much more knowledge than any other nationals possessed. The Japanese had access to a mass of information; they had more facts, more names, more contacts and more contracts than others. They had more China experts and more China scholarship than the rest of the world could command. But there were also important drawbacks. One may have been that the proximity of writing systems made it too easy for Japanese Sinologues to read Chinese without taking the time to learn it properly. The presence of Japanese residents in China and the numerous Chinese with Japanese educations further reduced the necessity for verbal communication in the Chinese language. A great—perhaps the greatest—avenue into Chinese thinking and psychology, that of the spoken colloquial, was too frequently overlooked. Instead Japanese learned to know China and Chinese writing through the traditional focus of classical knowledge and writing. Since those classics were, furthermore, an important part of their own thought and ideology, they had a particular and often idiosyncratic significance for them; they thought themselves closer to Chinese than they actually were. As a result the Japanese view of China was largely traditional, innocent of the social science approaches of the twentieth century and anchored to the classical tradition in which the Chinese elite had been steeped. The dominant schools of Sinological interpretation in Japan popularized the view of an "unchanging" Chinese cultural tradition at the very time that young China was taking its lead from the revolutionaries of the May Fourth movement in determined efforts to overthrow that cultural tradition.

This being so, the mass of information about China that came pouring into Japan did not often receive an appropriate or consistent framework of analysis. Popular syntheses of Chinese change, like that of Professor Naitō of Kyoto University, spoke of the "decay" of Chinese government and civilization rather than of its transformation. Professor Yano, also of Kyoto, stressed the enduring aspects of China that resisted change. A China scene viewed through such prisms was quite different from the one seen through the less distinct, but more timely, prisms of American observers. Japanese saw the warlords, with their Confucian talk of governmental responsibility and their repression of student and worker radicalism, as traditional dynasts of transition. To the national socialist Kita Ikki, mentor of army fanaticism in the 1930s, Sun Yat-sen himself was little more than a bit of Western, republican froth on the surface of the deeper current of Chinese history. Most of the warlords, many of whom had received their military education if not their equipment in Japan, had Japanese advisers at their headquarters. These men reported to Tokyo regularly, and they often became spokesmen for the headquarters to which they were accredited. One of the reasons Japanese policy, even army policy, could not be more closely integrated in the 1920s was that there were so many persuasive advocates of different lines of action. Thus in the middle 1920s there were advocates of cooperation with Feng Yü-hsiang, who had a measure of influence until he broke with Chang Tso-lin, who had the Kwantung Army on his side. At that time Feng was jettisoned and cast on the mercy of the Russians. A superfluity of advice and contact made policy consistency difficult. Business, Foreign Office and army lines were numerous but far from unanimous, and divided counsels often resulted in great confusion within Chinese politics. Thus Tanaka's Shantung intervention encouraged Chang Tso-lin to think that his position in the competition for Peking had improved, delayed his acquiescence to the Northern Expedition and ended in action against Chang by exasperated Kwantung Army officers.

Japanese adjustment to change in China was complicated by several other factors. There was a heritage of bitterness dating from inadequately secured loans to warlords. There was also a rapidly growing realization of the importance of markets in south and central China, the areas of Kuomintang strength, that seemed to contradict the priority attached to the extractive riches of Manchuria and north China. The new school of geopolitical strategists within the army saw the raw materials of the north as essential to any autarchic hopes for a future "national defense state," but Japanese traders saw brighter futures in the market provided by the giant populations of the areas under Kuomintang rule. Exporters and traders, with their contacts in the Japanese political world, stood prepared to face the realities of politics in south and central China and to support the policies of nonintervention which Shidehara espoused in the mid-1920s. It was they who felt the brunt of anti-Japanese boycotts that accompanied the early nationalist movements, and they were well pleased to have those movements focus on British imperialism instead. As the Chinese share of Japanese manufactures grew slowly from 15.6 percent in 1900 to 23.8 percent in 1910 and 26.6 percent in 1920, the trade lobby in Japan stood to gain in authority. But while traders stood for nonintervention, they were not prepared to sacrifice favorable tariff arrangements, hence the Japanese interest in a tariff schedule for China that would favor Japanese textiles over the more expensive manufactures of the West.

As long as China was divided, differing views and interests in Japan could avoid conflict. Shidehara could refuse to intervene in Nanking without immediately alarming the advocates of a strong line in Manchuria. But as the Kuomintang came closer to its goals of uniting all of China, it forced a resolution of disagreements in Japan. This resolution was complicated by the fact that Japanese politics had become more open and democratic in the 1920s. In the Meiji period the complaints about policymakers had been quite constant, but the political structure kept the opposition from having much weight. But once it was tacitly agreed that the majority party in the lower house of the Diet ought to form a government, and as the political parties, bureaucracy and business structures became more intimately interrelated, popular emotions and political gamesmanship combined to make the adoption of moderate policy more difficult. Policies became argued in terms of "positive" and "direct," "forceful" and "basic," and in this debate the advantage lay with those who favored action rather than restraint. The democratization of Japan in the years after World War I combined with the radicalization of China to threaten the course of Sino-Japanese relations. In ironic fashion the supremacy of civilians over the military in the years of the Washington Conference came full circle at the end of the decade as military leaders accepted the challenge to include the nonmilitary structures of industry and the polity as elements in their estimates of national defense projections.

These considerations make it clear why the Japanese response to the political changes of the 1920s in China was so complex. It is convenient to discuss this in the sequence of Chinese crises.

In May 1925 strikes against Japanese and English textile plants swept China's modern cities. Japanese Foreign Office officials stressed the importance of moderation and conciliation on the part of the industrialists, while army circles stressed the need for measures to salvage the empire's prestige in China. As it happened, the Peking government realized that it would itself become a target for the new radicalism and combined efforts to control disorder with overtures to Japan in the hope of isolating Great Britain as the target of discontent. It called for a new round of treaties to replace the outmoded pattern against which the students and workers were demonstrating. The tariff negotiations that took place at Peking in 1925–26 resulted from this. The Japanese interest, ably set forth by Foreign Office emissaries under Shidehara, was to call for selective tariff relief for China, calculated to operate least against "ordinary" goods like Japanese consumer exports and increasingly against "luxury" goods. Shidehara also hoped for guarantees that increased Chinese customs income would be used to fund loans in default. In short, as Professor Iriye summarizes the issues, "Japan would consent to a change in the economic order of the Far East only if the change insured against the loss of China as a market for Japanese goods and capital." But the Peking conference ended in failure when the Chinese negotiators had to flee the city in 1926.

Japanese negotiators next inaugurated bilateral negotiations with representatives of the Peking government in January 1927. The Northern Expedition was now six months old, and Peking no longer controlled the south. The Chinese had given notice of their intention to abrogate the treaty of trade and commerce which the Japanese had negotiated with them after the Sino-Japanese War. Shidehara instructed his negotiators to hold to a hard line where Japanese interests were concerned, and he preferred to delay agreement of any sort pending clarification of the political confusion in China. Despite his rhetoric of prosperity and cooperation, in other words, Shidehara held to concrete points of negotiations with considerable rigidity.

On the other hand, Shidehara carefully avoided participation in the various moves for cooperative action against the antiforeign incidents that accompanied the Northern Expedition. He did not want to associate Japan with the unpopular reminders of treaty-port diplomacy the Western powers were providing, and he was willing to risk denunciation by those who wanted revenge for the loss of life and property Japanese nationals suffered at Nanking in March 1927. Shidehara's moderation was based on possession of more accurate information about the forthcoming Kuomintang-Communist split than his Western counterparts had; many of them saw Chiang Kai-shek as a Russian puppet. Shidehara was optimistic about the possibility of reaching a working agreement with

Chiang, and he was eager to avoid alienating potential allies. His refusal to take a strong line on the Nanking incident was motivated in part by a desire to gain leverage in dealing with the future Nationalist government.

Unfortunately for Shidehara, Chiang Kai-shek also needed leverage with Chinese nationalism, and this kept him from making the formal apologies that would have been required to mute the torrent of criticism that Shidehara received for his "spineless" diplomacy. As a result the Minseitō government was replaced by that of the Seiyūkai under General Tanaka on 20 April 1927.

Prime Minister Tanaka Giichi has earned himself a place in the textbooks as the epitome of Japanese militarism. He is credited with reversing the Shidehara diplomacy, with setting Japan on a course of continental aggression, and with articulating the rationale for this with the "Tanaka Memorial" in which he charted Japan's steps toward war. There is very little hard evidence for this and not a scrap of evidence to authenticate the so-called "Memorial," which became a convenient item of anti-Japanese propaganda before and during World War II. The document even became a subject of anti-Tanaka and anti-Seiyūkai propaganda within Japan itself. Tanaka's reputation can best be understood as the joint product of Japan's partial political democratization and the military response to Chinese nationalism.

Tanaka had been a hardliner on Siberia in 1918. As prime minister in 1927, he made the fateful decision to transfer Japanese troops from Manchuria to Shantung a month after he took office. It seems apparent that this step seemed politically necessary to the Seiyūkai, which had come into office calling for stronger measures to protect Japanese lives in China. Tanaka's overall view of China policy up to this point had not been significantly different from that of Shidehara, but his hasty decision to send a token force to Shantung constituted a shift from Shidehara's reluctance to intervene. Combined with the second intervention in April 1928, it created a climate in which the Minseitō and Shidehara charged that domestic considerations were being allowed to dominate foreign relations, while the Seiyūkai leaders, especially expansionists like Mori Kaku, tried to gain political advantage from forceful measures. But this polarization of opinion changed politics more than it did policies at the top of the decision structure. There were Foreign Office officials who favored the stronger show of force (and non-Japanese diplomats who applauded it), while the Army General Staff (as opposed to line commanders in China) tended to oppose minor involvement in continental maneuvering. Tanaka's "forceful" measures prompted nationalist responses on the part of the Chinese in boycott and agitation. These promoted radicalization on both sides and made it less likely that the Japanese public would side with "moderation."

Even so, the first Shantung intervention would have done no lasting harm. The shifting balance between Nanking and Wuhan and the decision of the left wing of the Kuomintang at Wuhan to dismiss Borodin and the Russian advisers obscured and all but obliterated the event. Japanese troops were withdrawn as had been promised. Tanaka hoped for a working agreement with Chiang Kai-shek as much as Shidehara had, and Chiang wanted Japanese cooperation and support. In the fall of 1927 Chiang Kai-shek, who had temporarily resigned his offices, visited Japan to talk with Premier Tanaka. They spoke together at some length; Tanaka pledged Japanese friendship if Chiang would provide an effective counter to communism, which he felt required Chiang's concentration on the south, and Chiang stressed the importance of continuing to move north lest the revolutionary forces become more discontented and radical. He implied that cooperation was possible as long as the Japanese avoided the impression that they favored Chang Tso-lin. Each participant in the talks finished with an optimistic view of his persuasive powers.

In the summer of 1927 Tanaka had convened a conference of Foreign Office, War, Navy, Finance Ministry and General Staff officials to work out Japanese policies toward north China and Manchuria. The spurious Tanaka Memorial was supposedly a product of these deliberations. The conferees advocated a wide spectrum of opinions, and their final, although general, conclusion was that of Consul General Yada at Shanghai who argued that the Kuomintang government met Japan's criteria for a stable and noncommunist government that could protect Japanese interests in China, that it should therefore receive at least de facto recognition, and that the Chinese should be given no reason to suspect that Japan was aiding the Peking regime of Chang Tso-lin. All these positions had clear precedents in the postulates of Shidehara China policy. But

CHANG TSO-LIN. Manchurian warlord, whose murder by Kwantung Army elements in 1928 was followed by plans for Japanese military takeover.

there was one exception: from this time on Tanaka seems to have committed himself to the support of Chang Tso-lin *in Manchuria.* He interpreted the decisions against support to the "Northern regime" as not only ruling out Japanese defense of Peking but also as ruling out the Nationalist entry into Manchuria.

Thus when Chiang Kai-shek returned to power and the Northern Expedition resumed its course toward Peking, Tanaka's problems multiplied. Chang Tso-lin could not stand against the Nationalists. Upon his defeat, should he receive, and should the Nationalists be denied, entrance into Manchuria? How should Japanese exercise their responsibility for the "security" of the South Manchuria Railway zone? Throughout 1927 and 1928, the Japanese had been trying to get additional railway and economic concessions in Manchuria. Some of these had been promised in principle, and in an effort to make these promises mean something Tanaka opened negotiations through Foreign Office and South Manchuria Railway officials. When this failed, he tried private emissaries as well. There seems to have been a Japanese assumption that their special place in Manchuria could be secured before revolutionary nationalism reached that area.

The second Shantung intervention came shortly after the return of Chiang Kai-shek to China in December 1927. In January Chiang was once again in charge of the Nanking armies, and on 7 April the second stage of the Northern Expedition began. This time the Chinese Communists were no longer connected with the effort, and popular demonstrations and strikes did not threaten foreign interests. In addition the Kuomintang armies enjoyed the support of warlords like Feng Yü-hsiang and Yen Hsi-shan who had "joined" the Kuomintang. There was no basis for Japanese fears of Communist influence and every reason to expect cooperation. Despite this, as the Nationalist forces seemed about to seize Tsinan in Shantung, Tanaka and his war minister, over the misgivings of the General Staff, decided that it would be prudent to transfer troops to Shantung to protect the two thousand Japanese residents there. The troops were to stay in Tsingtao in the event that the Nationalists decided against marching through Tsinan.

But once Japanese troops were on the scene, a clash became likely. As Peking forces withdrew from Tsinan, Nationalist troops entered and made the city a local headquarters. The Japanese commander decided the prestige of his division would be better served by moving his men to Tsinan from Tsingtao. Even then, the transition was proceeding smoothly and the Japanese were at the point of withdrawing once more when a fight broke out between Japanese and Chinese Nationalist troops early in May. After unsuccessful efforts at local settlement and an armistice, the Japanese commander posed demands for satisfaction that were so harsh that no Nationalist commander could accept them; he then forced a military engagement. In some stiff fighting the Japanese seized Tsinan and its environs and held it under martial law until a settlement was reached in early 1929.

Tanaka's attempts to live up to his campaign propaganda thus "introduced new elements in Sino-Japanese relations not in the field of policy but of policy execution." The army units ended by diverting his diplomacy, and once they were involved, a predictable escalation of language and prestige brought the army commanders the backing of their fellows in the General Staff and War Ministry. Next, Manchuria was drawn into the maelstrom of party and power politics in both Nanking and Tokyo. This time the agents of change were found in the Japanese military establishment in Manchuria.

4. Manchurian Beginnings

MANCHURIA HELD a special place in Japanese imagination. It had been the site of bloody battles in which Japan had won its place at international conference tables, and the "blood of our fathers," as patriotic orators put it, had bought its soil. It was essential to the strategic concerns of Korea and itself the border for a Russian influence made the more dangerous by presumed motives of revenge and subversion. It was Japan's only frontier. Its resources in coal and iron constituted Japan's only hope of making its way in the world without being dependent upon the goodwill of the Western countries and their colonies. The Three Eastern Provinces, as the Chinese referred to them, had filled rapidly in the late nineteenth and early twentieth century with Chinese immigrants, but they were still capable of absorbing additional inhabitants. All of these hopes were incorporated in the pattern of rights the Japanese took over from the Russians at the Treaty of Portsmouth in 1905 and extended in Group II of the Twenty-one Demands in 1915.

These holdings, consisting of the leased Kwantung Territory, including Port Arthur and Dairen, were administered by a governor appointed by the Japanese cabinet. The area was served and knit together by the South Manchuria Railway, which ran to Changchun (where its extension became the Russian-controlled Chinese Eastern Railway) and which had been established in 1906 as a government-controlled corporation. The company controlled coal mines at Fushun and Yentai in addition to other mining, electrical and warehousing enterprises. Its zone of operation was protected by railway guards. The railway areas included several towns and large parts of important cities like Mukden and Changchun. In such areas Japan controlled police, taxation, education and public utilities. The area was protected by the Kwantung Army, the most important of Japan's overseas units. The Kwantung Army was directly responsible to the General Staff; the leased area was administered by civilians responsible to the cabinet; and in addition there were consular police who were responsible to the Foreign Office. The maintenance of these rights in a period of revolutionary nationalist agitation involved Japan in constant difficulties. The disorder in China suggested to many Japanese the desirability of consolidating the Manchurian holdings in order to stabilize a complex situation.

The administrative overlap that prevailed in 1931 had resulted from a series of compromises among the principal contenders for power. These began with the military, which sought to perpetuate the relative autonomy the expedition-ary forces had enjoyed during the Russo-Japanese War. Yet civilian administra-tors did not want the leased territory to be under army rule, nor did the Foreign Office, which was anxious to avoid the damage that military arrogance could do to Japanese relations with China and with the powers. From the beginning, Prince Itō had emphasized that Manchuria remained subject to Chinese sovereignty. The Foreign Office, army, and the South Manchuria Railway Com-pany were all strongly rooted in the Tokyo political and economic establish-ment, and none was able to score a clear victory over the other. The civilian governor of the leased territory was probably a poor fourth in influence.

Nevertheless there was no disagreement about the importance of Man-churia and Inner Mongolia to Japan, and many private, semiofficial and official efforts were undertaken to safeguard Japanese interests there. Some of these cen-tered on Chang Tso-lin. A shrewd, courageous, ambitious and illiterate young bandit leader, Chang had been captured by the Japanese during the Russo-Japanese War and spared at the insistence of Tanaka Giichi, who thought that Japanese armies might have use for Chang's horsemen. Other efforts centered on Manchu and Mongol princes. After the Ch'ing collapse in 1913, Japanese China adventurers twice tried to set up separatist governments in Manchuria and Mongolia with the help of low-ranking officers. The second of these attempts had the quiet support of Tanaka Giichi, who was now in the General Staff, but the fall of Yüan Shih-k'ai reduced its urgency, lessened Tokyo's support, and made it possible for Chang to rout the separatist forces and establish himself firmly.

Official Japanese government efforts had to be directed to Peking in efforts to secure formal recognition and extension of Japanese interests. In 1915 Group II of the Twenty-one Demands extended the duration and extent of Japanese rights in Manchuria but at cost of alarming the powers and alienating Chinese nationalists. In 1918 Prime Minister Terauchi tried to buy support against bolshevism from the Anfu warlords headed by Tuan Ch'i-jui. The Nishihara loans combined with Japanese successes at Paris to outrage young Chinese na-tionalists and spark the May Fourth demonstrations. Worse still, the Anfu forces that had been prepared with Japanese money and advice were defeated by Chang Tso-lin with his Chihli allies in 1920.

Now new decisions were needed. In 1921 Prime Minister Hara called a meeting of all major officials with responsibility for continental policy. In con-junction with the decision to withdraw Japanese forces from Siberia, it was agreed to support Chang Tso-lin in the defense of Manchuria and Korea against Bolshevik infiltration. "Indeed," John Young has observed, "the more these questions were discussed, the more indispensable the Manchurian warlord seemed to become." It was never an easy relationship. "Development" assistance was given for the construction of the Mukden Arsenal, which was described as the largest in the Orient. A later Tokyo cabinet, in 1924, resolved that "Chang should be consistently given proper guidance, so that he may be led to realize that the actual control he now holds is based on the backing of Japan's power ... and receive Japan consistently with a friendly attitude." The Kwantung Army saved Chang Tso-lin by preventing his enemies from pursuing him through the South Manchuria Railway zone and thereafter it was desirable to keep him in Manchuria. Once he set his sights on Peking, Japan would seem to be meddling in Chinese politics and Chang himself would get ideas about independence. On the other hand, a move to Peking offered Chang his best chance of escape from his protectors, so when the opportunity came to move south he seized it. In 1926 Chang drove Feng Yü-hsiang out of Peking and renamed his army the National Pacification Army (Ankuochün). The bandit chief was now technically head of state. It was in Peking that Chang received Sun Yat-sen shortly before the latter's death.

All this complicated the China policy of Foreign Minister Shidehara. In Mukden, Consul General (and postwar Premier) Yoshida Shigeru developed a lively dislike of Chang Tso-lin. South Manchuria Railway officials were eager for negotiations to consolidate privileges that had never been implemented since Yüan Shih-kai had granted them in the Twenty-one Demands. But Japan did not have the leverage on Chang Tso-lin in Peking that it did when he was in Mukden, and in the spring of 1927 the split between Chiang Kai-shek and the left wing of the Kuomintang seemed to offer hope of a new lease on life for Chang in Peking.

This was the state of affairs when Tanaka Giichi came to hold the positions of prime minister and foreign minister in April 1927. He had talked a great deal about the need of a "positive" policy and avoiding insult and injury from "antiforeign" Chinese. But he had also come to see the errors of Siberian intervention, and he had sufficiently won Prince Saionji's trust for him to seem an opponent of military extremism. He was also a popular figure.

The first problem to which Tanaka directed his attention was Japan's course in the event of the defeat of Chang Tso-lin in Peking. Should he be permitted to return to Manchuria with his forces, or were there alternate possibilities for Japanese support? Could Japan countenance the involvement of Manchuria in the civil war that was engulfing China? Tanaka never fully answered these questions. Instead of the tough policy he announced, he alternated between forceful gestures and hesitation. Initial caution about intervention brought a decision to evacuate Japanese residents from Tsinan, only to have him reverse it by providing protection in Tsinan—hence the first Shantung intervention. Next, during the summer of 1927 Tanaka convened the Far Eastern Conference. This brought into the open disagreement between the Foreign Office position, represented at one extreme by Yoshida Shigeru, that Japan should not tie herself down to the support of any particular warlord, and Tanaka's personal conclusion that "the stabilization of Manchuria's political conditions should best be left to the efforts of the Manchurian people. If an influential Manchurian should respect our special position ... and sincerely devise means to stabilize political conditions there, the Japanese government would support him as it considers proper." This position was not made public, but it represented a statement of Manchurian separatism, and there is little doubt that Tanaka's "Manchurian" was Chang Tso-lin. The trouble was that the "Manchurian" was in Peking and intended to stay there.

Negotiations for confirmation of Japanese railway and tariff rights in Manchuria now took a confusing course. In Mukden, Consul General Yoshida was permitted to proceed with a forceful program which included threats to cut traffic on the Peking-Mukden line. Yoshida, the Foreign Office noninterventionist, went ahead with his personal brand of positive diplomacy with great enthusiasm until he was brought to a halt by a protest from an army figure named Honjō Shigeru, who had been a military adviser to Chang Tso-lin, was serving as military attaché in Peking and would shortly become commander of the Kwantung Army. There were also efforts by the newly appointed head of the South Manchuria Railway Company to negotiate informally with Chang Tso-lin in Peking. These talks were going well when they were canceled by the forceful opposition of Japanese Minister Yoshizawa in Peking, who insisted that his office was the proper channel for such efforts. The Tanaka "positive" policy had thus threatened force only to pull back, and by the Shantung intervention it had strengthened Chang Tso-lin's determination to remain in Peking. The policy was designed not so much to extend as to consolidate rights to which the Japanese felt they were clearly entitled. What was new about Tanaka's policy, however, was its trend toward full support for Chang Tso-lin as Japan's instrument in Manchuria. This coincided with Chang's conclusion that Japan could be his instrument for control of China.

The early months of 1928 saw Chang Tso-lin's alternatives diminish. After his visit to Tanaka in Tokyo in November of 1927, Chiang Kai-shek returned to China to resume command of the Kuomintang armies. He was head of the Nationalist regime by March, and in April his armies resumed their advance to the north. By May Japanese Minister Yoshizawa was warning Chang Tso-lin that his defeat was certain and that he should return to Manchuria while his armies were still intact. Chang delayed as long as possible; the second Shantung intervention in April 1928 encouraged his delay and diverted Japanese efforts to work out a peaceful transition between Chang and his Nationalist successors. But by the end of May he had no choice but to withdraw, and on the night of 2 June his decision was reached.

This, however, required Tanaka to answer the question he had posed when he took office: What should Japan do if Nationalist armies drove Chang Tso-lin back to Manchuria? For a time it was decided to disarm all of Chang's soldiers at the Shanhaikuan barrier. Then, hopeful of an understanding with the Nationalists that they would not attempt to extend their sway into Manchuria by force, Tanaka countermanded this. Now it was the turn of the Kwantung Army, which had approved highly of the demobilization scheme, to object. Chief Staff Officer Colonel Kōmoto Daisaku decided to take things into his own hands and create a situation in which it would be necessary for the Kwantung

Army to keep the peace. On the morning of 4 June he had Chang Tso-lin's train bombed as it passed the point where the Peking-Mukden line ran underneath the South Manchuria line. Military insubordination thus brought the collapse of Tanaka's policy.

But Colonel Kōmoto's hopes were also dashed. His planning and preparation had been inadequate. Too few of his colleagues were ready to support the military takeover of Manchuria he had hoped for. Nor did Manchuria fall into chaos. Chang Tso-lin's son, Chang Hsüeh-liang, did not adopt the anti-Japanese posture that might have brought intervention; he could not afford to. His father's chief of staff and his father's brother-in-law, the leading alternative choices for rule in Manchuria, were closer to the Kuomintang than he was himself. Therefore, although he knew the facts about his father's murder, he temporized with the Japanese. In December 1928, after he felt he had things under control, he accepted the Kuomintang Nationalist flag and declared his allegiance to Nanking, which in turn recognized him as commander of the Northeastern Frontier Army and confirmed him as administrator of Manchuria. To this was added the border province of Jehol. There were few concrete changes in actual power and administration, but Manchuria was now open to Kuomintang organization. Party branches were established everywhere, and party publications that insisted on the abolition of special treaty rights had particular importance in an area where those rights were most sweeping.

In June 1929 Japan formally recognized the Kuomintang government. But within Japan the aftermath of the murder of Chang Tso-lin brought down the Tanaka government. When a gendarmerie report on the incident reached Tanaka, his first instinct was that punishment would be necessary to restore discipline. But the army division chiefs, with their strong lateral ties and anti-Chōshū bias, reacted strongly against this and argued that Colonel Kōmoto should under no circumstances be disgraced. To do so would hurt the army in public opinion and support, and publication of the facts would hurt Japan in international esteem. Opposition to the Saionji-Tanaka establishment was sufficiently strong to make it impolitic for the prime minister to propose punishment. On the other hand, Tanaka soon was under vigorous criticism in the Diet, where there were sharp demands for a public statement on the matter. The young emperor was among those who wanted to see justice done, and when he pressed Tanaka for the truth, the premier tried to reassure him and cover himself by denying the facts. In the process he lost his emperor's trust and his own position, which he gave up in July 1929. A new Minseitō cabinet headed by Hamaguchi came to power, and Shidehara returned to the Foreign Office.

Few governments have had more difficult problems than now developed. Japan's return to the gold standard came a few months after the world depression had taken most of Japan's trading partners off the gold standard. Hard money policies helped to worsen the shock of the depression in Japan. The government's participation in the London Naval Conference, which sought to extend to cruisers the ratios that had been worked out for capital ships at the Washington Conference, brought it into conflict with the navy, which had strong support in Japanese public opinion and in the Privy Council. Premier Hamaguchi won his fight, but in November 1930 he was mortally wounded by an assassin. During the same period negotiations with the Nanking government had been entrusted to Saburi Sadao, who was trusted by the Chinese. In November 1929 Saburi died under mysterious circumstances. As his successor Shidehara nominated Obata Yūkichi, but Nanking refused to accept him because of his earlier connection with the Twenty-one Demands. Shigemitsu Mamoru, later foreign and prime minister, succeeded instead.

Despite these government-level agreements, tensions were rising between Japanese and Chinese on the continent. Anti-Japanese propaganda drives and boycotts left few Japanese in doubt where they stood. Within Manchuria frustrations took the form of Chinese agitation against Korean agricultural settlers in areas close to the Korean border. The Japanese held that the Koreans, as "Japanese," enjoyed extraterritoriality and therefore insisted on their right to send consular police across the border. Many of the Koreans were in fact refugees from Japanese police measures, and Japanese "thought-control" police were especially eager to "protect" them. Anti-Korean riots in Manchuria were followed by anti-Chinese riots in Korean cities, and these in turn by anti-Japanese demonstrations in Tientsin and other Chinese cities. Agents provocateurs could find materials for political arson everywhere. To complete the picture, in the summer of 1931 a Japanese army captain disappeared while on a topographical reconnaissance in western Manchuria and eastern Mongolia. In August it was learned that he had been apprehended and shot by a detail of Manchurian army soldiers. Captain Nakamura was traveling as a civilian. Nonetheless, his murder aroused the Japanese military and public. Negotiations over the incident were still in progress when the Kwantung Army took matters into its own hands in September 1931.

Colonel Kōmoto's murder of Chang Tso-lin had crystallized the opposition of young anti-Chōshū staff officers to their military seniors. Under Colonel Itagaki Seishirō, Kōmoto's successor as senior staff officer, this generational and ideological division became more focused. Currents of change had long clustered around a group of young staff men who had begun to come together for weekly discussion sessions during the days when much was expected of Tanaka diplomacy. Their names included Itagaki, Nagata Tetsuzan, a brilliant planner, Tōjō Hideki, the future wartime premier, and Ishiwara Kanji, the mastermind of the Manchurian war. The Issekikai, formed in May 1929, drew others into this group: Kōmoto Daisaku, Chang's murderer; and Doihara Kenji, a Manchurian plotter. Later a "second Isseki Society" added younger men including the brilliant field commander Yamashita Hōbun (Tomoyuki) to the fellowship. Most of these men were from the fifteenth to the seventeenth classes of the Officers Academy; they were aware of the meaning of World War I for the "total war" of the future, acutely conscious of the unpreparedness of the imperial army and Imperial Japan for such challenges and intent upon the danger of a resurgent Russia.

Ishiwara Kanji, who came to the Kwantung Army as staff officer just before the reassignment of Colonel Kōmoto, illustrates the strengths and limitations of this group to a unique degree. Ishiwara graduated in the twenty-first class of the Officers Academy. In 1918 he graduated second from the top in the War College, where he was awarded the cherished "Imperial Sword." After a period of service in China, where he served with Itagaki, he lectured at the War College. In 1923 he was sent to study in Germany, at a time when the Reichswehr was going through a process of reevaluation under the influence of von Seeckt and Guderian. Its determination to avoid the errors of fixed positional warfare and its focus on mobility and maneuver made a deep impression on him. As von Seeckt instituted the Staff trip, during which commanders were to lecture on the possibilities of the terrain, so Ishiwara and Itagaki in Manchuria conducted reconnaissance trips by rail during which they lectured their colleagues. In Germany Ishiwara had also indulged his interest in the history of warfare, and upon his return to Japan he was assigned to the faculty of the War College as instructor in the history of war.

Ishiwara was also a follower of Nichiren Buddhism, and he combined its apocalyptic view of a final struggle with a personal theory of warfare in which the world was destined to know a final cataclysmic struggle in which Japan, as leader of Asia, must triumph over the United States. Ishiwara saw this struggle as one requiring long preparation. The first stages would be concentrated on the control of Manchuria and Mongolia, for their resource base was essential to Japan. Ultimately China too would have to make its contribution in the construction of an economically and militarily impregnable Japanese empire that would be ready for the final struggle with the United States. These views were not entirely unique. Kōmoto too had assumed that, as he put it, a "rational and thorough" plan for settling Manchurian problems would require the subjugation of Nanking, "for which war against China must be expected and war against the United States must be considered." The Kita-Ōkawa *Yūzonsha* publication also had foreseen the "fate of the Japanese nation as the great apostle in the war of emancipation of the human race." But in Ishiwara these views received a more structured and superficially scientific treatment, while they were also dependent upon his mystical faith in the emperor and his conviction in the holocaust predicted by Nichiren.

In Manchuria Ishiwara and Itagaki set their subordinates to work drawing up plans for the military seizure and occupation of the area. Kōmoto's failure had shown the need for careful preparation of public and headquarters support. Public support was now at hand in the development of vocal discontent among Japanese settlers in Manchuria. This focused on their lack of representation despite the newly instituted universal manhood suffrage within Japan. A Manchurian Youth League, established shortly after Ishiwara and Itagaki took up their assignments in the Kwantung Army staff, received the subsidization of newspapers and business organizations, of expatriate Japanese and, ultimately, that of the South Manchuria Railway. It complained of discrimination from Chinese, the misgovernment of the Manchurian militarists and indifference of Japanese colonial administrators and politicians. In speaking tours throughout Manchuria and, by the summer of 1931, to the principal cities of Japan, its leaders brought this message of distress and crisis wide publicity.

Headquarters support for the plotters was powerfully affected by a series of personnel shifts that War Minister Ugaki made in the summer of 1930. The principal posts in the Ministry and the General Staff—posts having to do with operations, intelligence and mobilization—now came to be held by Nagata, Tatekawa, Koiso, Okamura and, on lower levels, Hashimoto and Shigetō—men intimately involved in discussion of mainland problems and domestic reform. A series of position papers and intelligence estimates began to pose alternate courses of action that specified, if changes in Chinese accommodation were not forthcoming, the preparation of direct action by the Kwantung Army. To higher-ups like General Ugaki this last alternative probably seemed a remote and unlikely eventuality, but they endorsed the documents to keep the confidence of their subordinates and strengthen their leverage with their civilian colleagues. To the young planners it meant that time was on their side. To Ishiwara and Itagaki it meant that a timetable had been set which they might be able to advance.

Questions of priority between continental and domestic advances remained unresolved among the officers. The March incident of 1931 represented an attempt by Hashimoto Kingorō, head of the Russian section in the General Staff, to mastermind a coup d'état within Japan that would bring War Minister Ugaki to power as head of a reform government. Most of the plan's early backers became convinced that the plan could only hurt the army's popular image and, hence, its mission in Manchuria. Hashimoto and the most extreme of his Sakurakai contemporaries now drew gloomy conclusions about the trustworthiness of their superiors and considered killing the lot of them. After the establishment, including Saionji, became aware of the plot, Hashimoto was forced to disband his Sakurakai.

The March incident left the priority on Manchuria. The summer months of 1931 found the tide of activism running strong. Threatened budget cuts alarmed the army high command into taking stronger positions and issuing more belligerent statements. War Minister Minami, who suceeded Ugaki (who became governor general of Korea), took a particularly strong line in early August. By then the disclosure of the murder of Captain Nakamura in Inner Mongolia had provided the Kwantung Army planners with a better opportunity than they had expected. All that was required was a provocation to justify the tactical measures Ishiwara had prepared. August found Kōmoto ferrying proposals between his friends in Manchuria and Tokyo. Former gendarmerie Captain Amakasu, whose murder of Ōsugi Sakae had shocked the nation

GENERAL HONJŌ. The commander of Kwantung Army, acknowledging the cheers of Japanese residents in Mukden after the establishment of puppet state of Manchoukuo.

in 1923, was doing his best to stir up new Chinese riots against Koreans in Manchuria. Colonel Doihara of Special Intelligence had hopes of provoking anti-Japanese outbreaks in north China. Tokyo confederates in the General Staff knew of these activities. The General Staff intelligence estimate that had been officially adopted, in any case, specified action for 1932 unless diplomatic solutions were worked out. It did not seem unreasonable to think that the schedule might be advanced.

Still, in September, pressure from the prime minister, the foreign minister and Prince Saionji, powerfully underscored by some pointed questions the emperor was permitted to address to the war and navy ministers, made Tokyo headquarters decide it was premature to act. It decided to send Tatekawa, who was almost certainly fully informed of the Manchurian plans, to Manchuria to restrain Itagaki and Ishiwara. Hashimoto, upon learning of this from Tatekawa, quickly cabled Itagaki that there was no time to be lost.

A "tired" Tatekawa reached Mukden in the early evening of 18 September 1931. He was met by Itagaki, who left him in the company of a staff officer who helped him relax over warm sake. A few hours later a small contingent of Japanese troops arranged an explosion that dislodged just one length of rail on the South Manchuria Railway tracks just north of Mukden. The southbound express, which was due soon, managed to bump along over the break and arrive in Mukden on schedule. Yet this sufficed to trigger the plans Ishiwara had drawn up for seizure of the Mukden army barracks and arsenal. By dawn on 19 September, Mukden was in Japanese hands. Itagaki had used his authority as senior staff officer to order the troops into action. General Honjō, who had just taken command of the Kwantung Army, first hesitated to authorize the followthrough and then resigned himself with a soldierly, "Let us do our duty."

The success of the Ishiwara-Itagaki plans depended upon their ability to escalate the opening round into moves to occupy the rest of Manchuria and Inner Mongolia. The initial moves were completely successful. Careful tactical planning paid good dividends, and the assumption that negotiations would solve the issues made the Chinese commanders hesitant to risk their troops and arms. The discrepancy between the slender Kwantung Army forces, which totaled some ten thousand, and the Chinese armies in Manchuria, which outnumbered them almost twenty to one, made it essential for the Kwantung Army to create a real crisis in which it would be reinforced from Korea.

Tokyo did what it could to restrict the Kwantung Army. It forbade extending the scope of the occupation and ruled out a northward advance. When, despite this, the Kwantung Army justified a move against the Kirin army on 20 September on grounds of security needs, it was able to get the Korean army to cross the border in its support. Subsequently this required cabinet approval, which was granted reluctantly by Prime Minister Wakatsuki under the greatest pressure from the army. On this occasion the emperor's disapproval was so clear and army leaders so resentful that the court entourage concluded that it would be unwise to allow the emperor to interfere directly in such matters. Even so, Tokyo continued to show that it did not accept the army's account of what was happening in Manchuria. Under the circumstances the Kwantung Army leaders decided to follow the advice of their guest, Tatekawa, who had come to stop the whole scheme, to set up a puppet state under Japanese control instead of trying for open seizure of Manchuria. In some areas, civil administration was already going smoothly; Colonel Doihara, for instance, was functioning as mayor of Mukden. But it gradually seemed prudent to scale down the program to one that was realizable. Manchuria was to become a "paradise" of the five races (Mongol, Manchu, Chinese, Korean, Japanese), free of the racial strife that had taken place so recently. Japan would act as protector of the new order, with responsibility for foreign affairs, defense, communications and transportation. In the implementation of these, the Kwantung Army was clearly to be all powerful, and its commander served as ambassador and governor. The regional Manchurian army leaders were instructed to issue "independence declarations." Some did so willingly, but at least one did it with a Japanese pistol held to his temple. Meanwhile negotiations were begun with the last Manchu emperor, Pu-yi, to arrange his return from Tientsin, where he had taken refuge in the Japanese settlement. The Tokyo Foreign Office again interfered, and it required anti-Japanese riots in Tientsin engineered by Doihara to create the disorder in which Pu-yi could make his way to Port Arthur and Kwantung Army protection.

The top decision structure in Tokyo remained uncooperative for a long time. Those closest to responsibility, like War Minister Minami and Chief of Staff Kanaya, were anxious to end their compromising position; those a step below them, like Vice-Chief of Staff Ninomiya, were encouraging, while the bureau, division and section chiefs were enthusiastic about what was going on in Manchuria. Through most of October, the Kwantung Army leaders felt themselves unsupported, and Tokyo's efforts to force General Honjō to look to Chief of Staff Kanaya for even tactical supervision came close to precipitating resignations.

The final result required compromises on both sides. The Kwantung Army gave in on full Japanese occupation of Manchuria, and Tokyo gave way on its original desire for a return to 18 September. Tokyo was influenced by domestic approval for what was going on, for it was conscious of a groundswell of support for the forceful measures that had been taken. Tokyo was also influenced by fears of even greater radicalism and disorder. The "October incident," in which Hashimoto and his Sakurakai associates planned to annihilate the entire civilian leadership during a cabinet meeting, surround the War Ministry and General Staff and request the formation of an emergency cabinet, was exposed, but its leaders were treated with extraordinary leniency. Hashimoto, the most severely disciplined, received a knucklerap of twenty days' confinement.

In this kind of setting one can understand Saionji's hesitation to put forth his maximum strength in opposition. He had only one total weapon, the emperor, and this had to be saved for the ultimate crisis lest it lose its efficacy. Moreover, as Saionji told his secretary, it was apparent that there was a new sort of radicalism abroad in the army; unflattering stories were being told about the emperor. There seemed a possibility to some that the army might even be going communist. Even the Foreign Office found it prudent to shift its line; events in Manchuria were "the internal problem of the Three Eastern Provinces, which should be decided primarily by the people," and Chang Hsüeh-liang could no longer be regarded as a legitimate power.

And so the blueprints for the new structure the Kwantung Army had been working on were unrolled. Manchoukuo was independent of China. Japanese control would be exerted through the army, the transportation system and advisers. Each province would have a supreme adviser, and departments and boards would have advisers "to supervise and direct operations." The military radicals also saw to it that social policy would meet their objectives, for, as Itagaki put it, if soldiers "should discover upon return to their native places that the economic conditions have worsened from the time of their departure, or feel that the various enterprises in Manchuria have been monopolized by capitalists, concession hunters or party politicians, they might complain of their struggles

FIRST DIVISION MARCHING THROUGH TOKYO. On its way to assignment in Manchuria in spring of 1936, word of the division's impending transfer to the continent helped spark the February 26 insurrection.

and think that they suffered in vain." Manchurian problems had to be solved in connection with "the reform and progress of our social policy."

In moments of tension, Ishiwara and his fellows were even prepared to cast their lot with Manchuria as the harbinger of a new social order. "Let the government and central army headquarters do what they will," he said in October 1931, "the Kwantung Army is going to carry out its sacred mission. We must reach a basic solution to the Manchurian problem, even if it temporarily means giving up Japanese nationality." Ishiwara and others would have preferred a republican order. But advocates of tradition had their way, and with the return of Henry Pu-yi, the slogans changed from *minshu*, popular sovereignty, to *minpon*, popular base, the term Yoshino Sakuzo had popularized as a compromise for democratic and monarchist traditions earlier in the Taishō period. Pu-yi was installed as regent in March 1932.

The Manchurian incident marked the point at which Japan entered the road that led to World War II. Its results were far-reaching in all respects. Five at least deserve particular notice.

International opprobrium united Japanese public opinion. From the first, there was a good deal of public enthusiasm for the idea that after so much talk somebody was finally doing something about Manchuria. The social and economic crises of depression Japan also increased the readiness to seek relief in external adventures. But the hesitation of the civilians at the decision center was partly due to their sensitivity to the popular reaction. In this sense the melancholy events of the 1930s, while antidemocratic, also related to greater democratization and public participation. Many Japanese were unprepared for this new expression of popular chauvinism. Matsuoka Yōsuke, who returned to Japan apprehensive after the speech in which he had announced Japan's withdrawal from the League of Nations after that body had adopted the Lytton Report in 1933, returned to find himself a popular hero, and he never fully recovered from it. Thereafter he confused intemperance with courage and won himself a place among the practitioners of Axis diplomacy. The Western powers may also have contributed to these developments. They first held themselves studiously aloof, anxious to help Shidehara and the moderates who were, as Secretary of State Stimson phrased it, on the right side, and turned to criticism and abuse after the die had been cast. Thus they seemed to encourage the original miscalculations of foreign weakness and then confirm foreign prejudice. Instant denunciation, and subsequent moderation, might have had a different effect.

Within the Japanese military, insubordination had succeeded. The insubordination was less total than it seemed; occasionally it was no more than a loose construction of statements formally agreed upon, and sometimes it did not go beyond matters of timing and execution. Nevertheless the creation of a Manchurian enclave of autonomy left the military in a far stronger and more independent position for future opportunities. It vastly increased the proconsular potential.

Manchuria also involved interrelationships between reform at home and advance abroad. It provided an overseas adaptation and implementation of a much-expressed need for reform and change, and its institutions expressed, however imperfectly, the desire for more egalitarian and less capitalistic standards.

The tug-of-war between generations, ideologies and priorities within the armed services also contributed to Manchuria. To Hashimoto's disappointment, the affair did not lead to a basic restructuring of power and authority within the imperial army. Those who remained in control were less impetuous and less single-minded than the Sakurakai anarchists, the Ishiwara visionaries, or the agrarian enthusiasts. Nagata Tetsuzan and the others, however, were "moderate" not in that they were against internal reform but in their views of timing and method. They expected to dominate Japan through the use of a well-disciplined army. And so Nagata, Tōjō and the others did their best to control the Hashimoto radicals and established themselves as believers in "control." These tactics were to cost Nagata his life, but they brought Tōjō to the prime minister's office and Japan to Pearl Harbor.

Finally, the loss of Manchuria was critical to the future of Nationalist China. The immediate loss of Manchurian customs and tariffs reduced by 15 percent the customs revenue of the Kuomintang government. Worse, the long border with north China became a poorly patroled line through which Japanese goods flowed without customs checks. The expatriate armies of Chang Hsüeh-liang, in their impatience with Chiang Kai-shek's anticommunist drives, forced the second united front with the Chinese Communists that followed the Sian incident in 1936. Japan's seizure of the provinces to the north thus prevented the Kuomintang from achieving the internal unity which it had assumed was prerequisite to all national planning and reform.

5. The China Quagmire

IF THE JAPANESE had stopped with the Manchurian incident, it might have been possible to resume some sort of relationship with the government in Nanking. Chiang Kai-shek's hold on China was still too tenuous, and his outside support was still too uncertain, to permit him the luxury of all-out resistance to Japan. Foreign Minister Shigemitsu expressed this view years later in his memoirs: "If the Manchurian affair had ended with Manchoukuo it should not have been impossible to settle it internationally." But it did not end with Manchuria. The revision of strategic and security requirements that followed this extension of Japanese control guaranteed the involvement of north China. Japanese security interests as interpreted by military authorities produced the desire for buffer zones under cooperative Chinese forces with which the danger of confrontation was less. The Nationalist government, initially preoccupied with its campaigns against its Communist enemies, found it increasingly difficult to ward off calls for a united effort against Japan and its puppets. In 1936 the kidnapping of Chiang Kai-shek by Chang Hsüeh-liang led to a new united front between the Kuomintang and the Communists, and thereafter the Japanese could claim that they were fighting communism.

Japan helped make the Kuomintang a symbol of nationalism, and then destroyed it, leaving the field for the Chinese Communists. This disastrous course did not follow from a single massive miscalculation. Rather, it followed from a series of plans in which the tactical needs of the military were consistently allowed to outweigh the larger strategic interests of national policy. Precipitate action of field commanders and sporadic instances of insubordination played their part in drawing Japan into the quagmire of its China war. But the principal milestones along that path were policy decisions reached through normal channels and adopted after regularly instituted procedures. While the record of China decisions has to be considered together with the unstable course of Japanese politics, the process was sufficiently systematic and consistent to make for a disastrous whole.

The failure of the civilian cabinet to work out a satisfactory solution on Manchuria combined with domestic political maneuvering to force a general resignation of the cabinet in December 1931. Prince Saionji, consistent with the explicit instructions he received from the emperor to select someone who would avoid intemperate error and could control military insubordination, now selected Inukai Ki, the head of the Seiyūkai. Inukai had been a member of every Diet since 1890. He had been, with Ozaki Yukio, one of the "gods of constitutional government" the crowds had acclaimed during the Taishō political crisis of 1913. A long-time "China-firster," he had befriended Sun Yat-sen as well as Korean reformers in Meiji times, and he headed the Japanese delegation that went to Nanking in 1929 for the ceremonies that marked the formal interment of the Kuomintang founder on Purple Mountain. He had been critical of Shidehara diplomacy, but he was also an articulate defender of the Meiji constitutional order. He would be no friend of a new military fascism.

Inukai was preeminently a realist, and he showed it by withdrawing the cabinet opposition that had stood in the way of the completion of the occupation of Manchuria. In January 1932 the occupation of Chinchow brought Secretary of State Stimson's affirmation of an American policy of nonrecognition. Inukai saw no merit in further repudiation of independence movements in Manchuria, and he had little expectation of constructive moves by the League of Nations. He authorized the emergence of Pu-yi as head of an interim regime in March, and the next month the decision to go ahead with an independent state to be called Manchoukuo was made.

The Shanghai incident, which took place in January 1932, grew out of efforts to suppress disorders that accompanied an anti-Japanese boycott that was in turn a response to the Manchurian incident. The Japanese naval commandant, as senior commander on the scene, called in marines to maintain order, only to find himself confronted with unexpectedly strong Chinese resistance from forces loyal to a (recently established) dissident regime loyal to Wang Ching-wei. The Japanese had to commit a force of three divisions before an armistice was established on 5 May. Japanese authorities were dismayed by this violence, for it brought them into immediate international difficulties and cost them much-needed diplomatic capital in the League of Nations. Manchuria was relatively remote, but the fighting at Shanghai took place in the full glare of international publicity. Consequently the matter was settled quickly; neither side had any desire to escalate.

Within Japan the inauguration of Inukai's government failed to bring the stabilization that had been anticipated. Extremists were suspicious of the premier's intentions toward China in view of his repeated sentiments of friendship and understanding with the nationalist movement. He now selected Kayano Chōchi, a member of the group of adventurers who had worked with Sun Yat-sen, as messenger to Chiang Kai-shek, only to have this blocked by army opposition. Meanwhile Inukai's war minister, General Araki Sadao, reassigned virtually all the leaders of the Chōshū clique and replaced them with his own men. Araki's actions heightened tension and encouraged extremism. So did his rhetoric. The first prerequisite for any understanding of the international situation in which Japan found itself, Araki wrote, was self-realization: "We must firmly realize: 'I am—a Japanese'.... The fundamental essence of the Japanese system of government is the unity of high and low, of the Monarch and his people. This points clearly to the aim of the Japanese, which amounts to the glorification of the Emperor, for which purpose public welfare must take precedence over private, personal welfare." But, he went on, the Japanese had forgotten this and had forgotten who they were: "the Japanese themselves had forgotten their national pride, forgotten their convictions and lost their self-realization." Indeed the present "Manchurian incident arose not on the basis of such trivial questions as the ignoring of treaty obligations or the infringement of the rights and interest of Japan. The fundamental reason for the incident is the insult of Japan by China [and as a result] the Manchurian incident is for Japan a sign of the Gods."

There were other "signs of the Gods." A group of civilian assassins led by Inoue Nisshō, a Nichiren priest, organized the Blood Brotherhood League (Ketsumeidan) and assigned each member the assassination of a prominent symbol of the establishment. Two such, former Finance Minister Inoue Junnosuke and Mitsui executive Dan Takuma, were killed in February 1932. [Shortly before his suicide Mishima Yukio glorified the assassins' purity of motives in *Runaway Horses* (New York, Knopf, 1973).] On 15 May naval officers who were committed to an anarchist-tinged philosophy of reconstruction invaded the precincts of Prime Minister Inukai's residence and murdered the old man while he was trying to explain to them the nature of the crisis Japan faced.

Inukai's assassins thought of the murder as part of a larger plan to remove much of the established authority and forcibly bring about the appointment of a military government. Their ideology emphasized Japan's uniqueness, which made it inherently superior to any other country. They thought, as one of them explained to the court, "about destruction first. We never considered taking on the duty of construction. We foresaw, however, that, once the destruction was accomplished someone would take charge of the construction...." That someone, they hoped, was General Araki. He, in turn, noted that the assassins were selfless and pure; they had not been motivated by "Fame, or personal gain, nor are they traitorous. Their acts were performed in the sincere belief that they were for the benefit of Japan." Thus the Inukai era ended in a startling combination of purity and insurrection. And the China policy remained unsolved.

Saionji now felt it prudent to replace the martyred Inukai with a non-controversial figure around whom national unity could be restored. After some hesitation he turned to a retired admiral who had earlier been governor general in Korea. Under Saitō Makoto, who took office in May 1932 and held the premiership until July 1934, General Araki continued as war minister. During this period he showed his most dismaying tendencies of favoritism. He rode roughshod over opposition and insisted on a priority for "Japanese spirit" over technological modernization. When his measures were questioned by some of his subordinates, the star performers of the last few years, Nagata, Tōjō, Tatekawa and Koiso found themselves abruptly shifted to less important posts. Nagata, who was shifted to command an infantry regiment, was in virtual exile.

The Saitō cabinet represented a return to totally bureaucratic cabinets. The inner structure of the central government at Tokyo changed with remarkable flexibility to meet the new situation. More and more the five ministers— premier, foreign, finance, war and navy—functioned as an inner cabinet. They were less members of a centrally directed team than spokesmen for their bureaucratic interests and subordinates, and the prime minister was more chairman than leader. The right of supreme command meant that the war minister reported to the Ministry and General Staff, that he was recommended by (and often retired into) the Supreme War Council, and that he had the right of independent access to the throne. It was so also with the navy minister. Nothing could be done without the skills of the Finance Ministry, but as Japan's ties with international and especially Western society weakened, the Foreign Ministry lost status. In time a separate Asia Ministry deprived it of authority over key relationships. All of this meant an accelerated decentralization of power and policy. Decentralization had as consequence an increased irresponsibility, and it contributed to a willingness to accept high risks to achieve short-run gains.

It fell to Saitō to implement the policies Inukai had accepted with respect to Manchuria. The League of Nations had appointed an investigative commission headed by Lord Lytton in January 1932. The Tokyo government had little expectation of its approval and chose to accept the penalties of international nonrecognition of the new state. On 15 September 1932 the Saitō government recognized the state of Manchoukuo; by fall the Lytton Report was in, and the following spring Matsuoka took Japan's delegation out of the League of Nations.

Meanwhile the government had been under heavy pressure from the military to permit the extension of the Manchurian borders to the mountain barrier that separated Manchuria from north China. Jehol had already been added to the Manchurian realm of Chang Hsüeh-liang by the Kuomintang, and it was inevitable that the Kwantung Army would try to incorporate it in the new state of Manchoukuo. After the Lytton Commission Report was in, there seemed little reason to withhold approval of this extension, and in December 1932 the cabinet permitted the Kwantung Army to advance to Shanhaikuan. Next came the "Tangku Truce" in May 1933 between Kwantung Army and local north Chinese officials. Manchoukuo now extended to the Great Wall. Most important for future misunderstandings, the zone north and east of the Tientsin-Peking area was demilitarized, and the army had a direct interest in seeing to it that Nationalist influence was kept out of the Peking-North Hopei area. Dealings with local authorities were much more to its liking than compromise with Nanking. North China, more than Manchoukuo, proved to be the irreconcilable bone of contention with Chiang Kai-shek.

In October of 1933 the Saitō cabinet drew up a general set of guidelines for Japan's foreign policy in the immediate future. The document argued in favor of reliance on diplomacy in relations with Western countries while simultaneously advocating the construction of an impregnable basis for national defense. This would mean a period of peace with the Western countries while Japan developed its new holdings. The navy argued for greater naval strength as soon as possible to permit rivalry with the United States which, the document noted, did "not understand the historical context of Far Eastern problems." The army, on the other hand, argued for continued cooperation with the West in naval construction in order to permit stronger emphasis on the development of Manchuria. Both army and navy agreed that Japan "must make every Chinese political faction follow the policy of the Japanese government." Or, as the war minister put it more specifically, "we must, unless the present national government offers some concrete proposal to strengthen friendly relations with Japan, prevent the Nationalist government, by the application of appropriate means, from advancing into North China." Thus the aims of Tanaka for Manchuria had now been extended to north China. As James Crowley sums this up, "The Japanese government was by December 1933 committed to a policy which proposed to neutralize the influence of the Soviet Union, the Nationalist government of China, and the Anglo-American nations by a diplomacy rooted in the efficacy of Japan's military forces."

Japan was going it alone. In April 1934 a Foreign Office spokesman named Amau Eiji startled the Western world by emphasizing that it was, after all, Japan that was responsible for maintaining peace in Asia. Shortly afterward, the Japanese ambassador in Washington proposed a Japanese-American agreement that would, he thought, contribute to East Asian stability by putting an end to Chinese habits of playing one country off against another. When this received the frosty reception that might have been expected for it, Tokyo decided to abrogate both the Washington and the London naval treaties. The entire network of Washington agreements was now given up, for the Nine-Power pact had no allowance for Japan's new insistence on the "protection" of China.

In July of 1934 Admiral Saitō gave way to Admiral Okada as prime minister. Earlier that year General Araki was forced out of his post as war minister. His insistence on the "crisis of 1936," when the Soviets could be "ready," had become increasingly burdensome for planners who were anxious to build strength for a longer struggle, and when Araki by implication denounced them as procommunist, his colleagues were convinced of the need to remove him. Under his successor the rancor that Araki had aroused convulsed the army and the country.

Nagata Tetsuzan, whom Araki had exiled to an infantry regiment, returned as major general to head the Bureau of Military Affairs in the War Ministry. Nagata assembled an imposing roster of experts and indicated the directions of his leadership in a pamphlet that the War Ministry published in October 1934. "War," it began, "is the father of creation and the mother of culture." It went on to emphasize the importance of a total national defense state for economic planning and mobilization for the great war that might lie ahead. A new Cabinet Consultative Council and Cabinet Research Bureau coordinated efforts. Leadership was passing from the big business–party politics mode of the 1920s into a highly decentralized and very Japanese form of state planning.

Shortly afterward, the Nanking government gave Tokyo the opportunity to resume relations and discuss an overall settlement. Some form of recognition for Manchoukuo seemed obtainable in return for Japan's recognition of Nanking's authority in north China. Chiang Kai-shek was close to victory over the Communists; he needed time for his unification drives, and he was willing to compromise. But the preference of the imperial army for dealing with client Chinese governments along the northern border and its determination to keep Nationalist propaganda out of that area made it impossible for Foreign Minister Hirota to do more than express a polite interest in the Nanking offer. The staffs of the Kwantung Army and the Tientsin garrison warned of the importance of maintaining the Tangku Truce of 1933, under which the Japanese had secured a Chinese withdrawal, in all its details. "If we were to reveal carelessly a cordial feeling toward China, this would inevitably encourage the Chinese to become more presumptuous.... We should not, therefore, render any financial aid or express a friendly attitude towards the Nationalist government." When the Foreign Office nevertheless raised the status of its Shanghai consulate to embassy and experimented with exploratory talks with the Chinese, the field commands felt it necessary to guarantee their own position. In local agreements, Generals Umezu (the Ho-Umezu Agreement, 10 June) and Doihara (the Ching-Doihara Agreement, 23 June) guaranteed that the Kuomintang would not be allowed in the north China provinces of Hopei and Chahar.

Although Nanking persevered and pressed its efforts for understanding, by February 1936 the Okada government had defined a new China policy that was far closer to the drafts provided by the army than before. Military moves in north China were to be avoided, but a vigorous program of economic penetration was designed to strengthen Japanese ties and control. The Foreign Ministry would seek limited agreements with the Nanking government that would try to secure confirmation of the "special relationship" between north China and Manchoukuo.

While this was being formulated, a wave of violence brought new men to power in Tokyo. In August 1935 General Nagata was murdered by a Lieutenant Colonel Aizawa, who was taking vengeance for Nagata's efficiency in dealing with an incipient plot in which some young officers had been discovered. The shocking murder of a man who was by general agreement one of the most brilliant staff officers of his generation meant the resignation of War Minister Hayashi. It also led to a decision for a public trial for Nagata's murderer. The trial became a circus of ultranationalist hysteria and appreciably raised the temperature in the climate of extremism. It also, less dramatically, led to the decision to make a public example and scapegoat of Professor Minobe, whose interpretation of the emperor as an "organ of the state" had come under attack by exponents of Japanese *kokutai*. It further led to the new war minister's decision to approve the insistence of the China field commanders for an autonomous north China. Tokyo was now unable to take advantage of Nanking's proposals for compromise.

Within a few weeks, the hysteria generated by the Aizawa trial helped bring on the greatest insurrection in modern Japan. On the morning of 26 February 1936 elements of the First Division occupied the main army buildings overlooking the imperial palace. Special assassination squads murdered the Inspector General of Military Education, General Watanabe, the former Prime Minister and present Lord Keeper of the Privy Seal, Admiral Saitō, and Finance Minister Takahashi. Premier Okada narrowly escaped through an error of identification. Grand Chamberlain Admiral Suzuki, who would emerge as prime minister at the end of the war, was badly wounded. Prince Saionji and Count Makino escaped their assassins. The "Righteous Army of Restoration" expressed its anger with manifestos charging that the establishment against which it had struck had "trespassed on the prerogatives of the emperor's rights of supreme command ... in the London Naval Treaty and in the removal of the

FEBRUARY 1936 IN JAPAN. Columns of rebel troops march from police station on second day of insurrection in Tokyo, February 27.

Inspector General of Military Education ... and they united with disloyal professors in rebellious places.... May the spirit of our Imperial Ancestors assist us
in our endeavors to save the nation."

Although trials and quick punishment disposed of the leaders of the insurrection, the result was a stronger position for the General Staff that had suppressed it. In the months after the incident of 26 February, nationalism in Japan
resonated with nationalism in China. The Tokyo leadership was increasingly
military in origin and orientation and obsessed with the need to take a firm line
in negotiations with the Chinese. In China the fervor of the anti-Japanese sentiments that this produced forced Chiang Kai-shek to take a stronger line too.

Tokyo's position toward China remained arrogant and strong. Since September 1933 the foreign minister had been Hirota Kōki, a man who held that
office continuously until the February revolt, when he became prime minister.
Thus from 1933 to 1937, when he gave way to a cabinet headed by General
Hayashi, Hirota provided unusual continuity. After the four months of Hayashi
rule, he returned as foreign minister under Prince Konoe.

By the summer of 1936 Hirota saw that he had failed to win Nanking's
agreement to Japanese desires and adopted a more peremptory tone with the
Chinese. The Soviet threat was now uppermost in his mind. It seemed essential
to force Chiang Kai-shek, who could be assumed to be anti-Soviet, to cooperate
in anticommunist measures. In August a set of resolutions which fused, in
general terms, the desires of several Tokyo ministries, laid down the path
whereby Asia was to be restructured in a "spirit of co-prosperity and co-exis-
tence based upon the Imperial Way." The field armies, however, were to be
restrained. Steps were taken to promote a Mongol separatist movement, which
the Kwantung Army carried on under the nominal leadership of a Prince Teh,
and in September Japan signed the Anti-Comintern Pact with Nazi Germany.
This vaguely worded agreement for cooperation and consultation would, it was
hoped, restrain the Russians, sober the Chinese and please the British.

Meanwhile Communist moves in Shensi brought Chiang Kai-shek into the
field for his sixth and, he hoped, final extermination campaign against the "communist bandits." In view of the greater visibility of the Japanese threat, and the
vigorous Communist calls for a united front against that threat, Chiang's decision was unpopular. Students and workers struck and demonstrated. A month
later, in December, Chiang flew to Sian to inspect the army of Chang Hsüeh-
liang, who, instead, took him captive. This dramatic act transformed the China
scene, for the price of Chiang's freedom was his agreement to a new united front
with the Communists against the Japanese. By the time Chiang returned to
Nanking on Christmas day in 1936, this time with Chang Hsüeh-liang in his
custody, new policy decisions were required in Tokyo.

The decisions that resulted reflected a more sober view for the immediate
future. The Russians now seemed the main problem; "1936" was at hand, and
nothing was allowed to distract Japanese energies elsewhere. A halt was called to
efforts to promote further separatist movements in China. Regional interests
could still suggest different answers; General Tōjō Hideki, who was now chief

of staff of the Kwantung Army, argued that Manchuria and Hopei Province would suffice as supply points for war materials and thought that it would be wise to knock out the Nanking government prior to taking on the Russians. The General Staff thought otherwise. Ishiwara Kanji, now head of the Operations Section, had been drawing up ambitious five-year plans for the integration of the economies of Japan, Manchuria and north China to permit the building of a base for "autonomous defense." Ishiwara thought it would require two plans, or ten years, to bring Japan to a point of preparedness, and he wanted no chances taken in China or elsewhere until Japan was ready.

Given this agreement on the Russian menace, the need for time to develop the resources of the new territories, and the realization of the need for moderation with Nanking, the course of events that saw Japan's descent into the quagmire of the China war serves as a reminder of the difficulties of acting on intentions. In June 1937, General Hayashi's difficulties in dealing with the Diet suggested the desirability of a cabinet change. Saionji was running out of moderate military candidates. He turned instead to the popular young nobleman Konoe Fumimaro. And under this civilian's auspices there began the war that neither Chiang Kai-shek nor Japanese army central headquarters wanted, a war that ended by destroying both.

Konoe's own verdict of his efforts was that they represented sophisticated moves to checkmate the military. This "check" often took the form of appointment to office for hardliners in the hope of instilling a sense of responsibility in them. Konoe dignified his policies with lofty rhetoric calling for a "New Order in East Asia" and raised enthusiastic hopes that the age of Western imperialism was at an end. Historians have regarded him as an aristocratic and indecisive figure who was fatally disposed to compromise and surrender in moments of stress. His gambles on personalities turned out poorly, and when events careened out of control, he resigned rather than accept responsibility for the execution of policies he had set in motion. During his stay in office, the legislation of economic control for a "total defense effort" was installed, and he later presided over the construction of a single-party substitute for politics in the form of the Imperial Rule Assistance Association.

Konoe's initial choices as service ministers were General Itagaki, who, with Ishiwara, engineered the Manchurian incident, and Admiral Suetsugu, who had led opposition to the London Naval Conference. Cautious members of the Supreme War Council blocked both of these appointments at first, but Admiral Suetsugu later reappeared as head of the powerful Interior Ministry and General Itagaki came to be minister of war. In 1938 Konoe appointed General Araki as education minister, a post in which his vague and pious invocation of Japanese spirit combined with his authoritarian instincts to do incalculable harm. Thus Konoe, as a civilian "last hope," helped deliver his country over to extremist groups of the military.

The China Incident grew out of a skirmish between Japanese troops and units of the "Autonomous Political Council" of General Sung Che-yuan on the night of 7 July 1937 near the Marco Polo Bridge, about ten kilometers west of

Peking. The Japanese reported a man missing and requested permission to search the area. The Chinese proposed a joint search. The man in question soon rejoined his unit, but shots were fired, and by the morning of 8 July both sides had more men at the scene. The Japanese units in the area were poorly deployed for action, and the local Chinese units were too few for a confrontation. The Tokyo General Staff wanted no part of a larger incident and urgently promoted an on-the-spot solution by the local commanders. General Sung similarly sought to anticipate trouble. He attended the funeral of General Tashiro, the Japanese commander who died unexpectedly, and he extended his personal apologies for the outbreak of shooting.

During the ten days the field commanders were on the verge of settlement, higher headquarters on both sides, subject to political and nationalist pressures and inadequately informed of developments on the spot, combined to raise the state of preparedness and escalate the level of verbal violence. Preparedness was the responsibility of Ishiwara Kanji's office in the General Staff in Tokyo. In response to staff recommendations, Ishiwara twice forwarded requests for reinforcements to his superiors and then canceled them upon the receipt of encouraging information from north China. He remained convinced that Japan's danger came from Russia and that a China struggle would be the wrong war in the wrong place. In Nanking Chiang Kai-shek, under pressure to show that the new united front had some meaning, issued orders to General Sung to reject a settlement and began the movement of his best German-trained divisions toward the Peking area. While General Sung was apologizing to the Japanese, the Nanking government called for help from signatories of the Nine-Power pact. On 17 July, the day before General Sung apologized, Chiang Kai-shek made a public declaration of a policy of no retreat. He stated that the aggressor had now reached Peking and that if it were surrendered, Nanking would be next. This strong statement, accompanied by the dispatch of Nanking troops into the area the Tangku Truce had preserved as "off-limits," brought responses from Tokyo that doomed the original preference for quick agreement. Prince Konoe had announced that "since security in North China is a matter of urgent necessity for peace in East Asia, the Chinese authorities must apologize to us for illegal anti-Japanese actions and properly guarantee to refrain from repeating such action in the future."

By 22 July both armies were in strong positions and their field commanders were preparing for assault as they were trained to do. The drift was irreversible. The Japanese commander issued a deadline for withdrawal of Chinese troops, and before this expired those troops launched an attack. Konoe now abandoned local solutions to call for a "fundamental solution of Sino-Japanese relations." Proposals designed to speed these "fundamental" solutions, when forwarded to Nanking, proved to contain the same three points that Hirota had been offering the Chinese for several years; recognition of Manchoukuo, an anti-Comintern pact (and hence abandonment of the united front), and suppression of "anti-Japanese activity" within China. Foreign Minister Hirota fondly imagined that

these proposals would win "the respect of the whole world for the fair and disinterested attitude of our empire" and thought they would "probably be beyond
the expectations of the Chinese themselves." When the Chinese, instead of accepting them gratefully, bombed the Japanese naval installations at Shanghai on
14 August, the Konoe cabinet announced that "the Chinese, overconfident of
their national strength, contemptuous of our own power, and also in league with
the Communists, have assumed toward Japan an increasingly arrogant and in-
sulting attitude. . . ." Japan, it concluded, was "now forced to resort to resolute
action to bring sense to the Nanking government by punishing the atrocious
Chinese army."

The Konoe government's statement could better have been applied to
Japan, for surely the major factor in the series of miscalculations that led to
Japan's long involvement in the China war was Japan's confidence in its ability
to smash an enemy it had come to despise. In weakening that enemy and driving
it from its centers of power, Japanese militarism set up the expansion of Communist guerrilla strength, and in its behavior the Japanese army was frequently,
in the most literal meaning of the term it used of its enemy, atrocious.

In this sense the China war might best be credited to the whole complex of
attitudes, values and beliefs that had developed in Japan during six years of military escalation. Few were for it, but there were also few who were unreservedly
against it. General Ishiwara felt it a violation of wiser priorities and opposed its
inception and its extension, yet his subordinates could point to his own role in
getting the whole process started in 1931. Ishiwara's star soon went into eclipse.
He was transferred back to the Kwantung Army, where Tōjō kept him under
close control, and he ended his military service in unimportant posts in regimental commands in Japan. Others, notably Generals Itagaki and Tōjō, were confident of Japan's ability to smash Kuomintang strength and thus establish a
sounder base for the coming push against the Russians. Instead 1938 saw twenty-four, and 1939 thirty-four, divisions tied down in the China quagmire.

There were also miscalculations on the Chinese side. Although the tactical
situation seemed favorable in 1937 and 1938, thanks to Chiang's long husband-
ing of his resources, the modernization of his armies and German assistance, the
vigor of the Chinese response now had as an early product the loss of many of
the best divisions and much irreplaceable equipment. Distrust of Japanese intentions led to Chiang Kai-shek's initial rejection of attempts for local settlement,
and by the time revelation of Japan's offensive capacities brought him second
thoughts, it was too late to take up the earlier possibilities. The China war thus
illustrates the inner dynamics of events and miscalculations that result in major
conflicts whose substantive importance is out of all proportion to the possible
gains and losses involved. (In this sense there is some basis for the later tendency
of Japanese observers to compare the China war with America's involvement in
Vietnam in the 1960s.)

Even after the spread of hostilities to the Yangtze Valley, the China Incident did not immediately become the China war. During the fall of 1937

Japanese armies launched operations in Inner Mongolia, in which they tried to create a base for their puppet, Prince Teh. At Shanghai and the Yangtze Valley a Japanese drive culminated in the fall of Nanking in December. Attempts to secure that unhappy city led to orders for house-to-house searches for soldiers and weapons in the course of which the armies of General Matsui ran amok in an orgy of death and rapine. Yet even during these same fall months, the doors to negotiation were not entirely shut. Chiang Kai-shek might still have accepted the demands of the summer, and conditions the Japanese forwarded in early November through the Germans, who tried to mediate, could have served for discussion in December. On each occasion the Chinese had hesitated, only to find that the Japanese had raised their sights in the interim. Japanese demands for recognition for Manchoukuo were supplemented with requirements for recognition of regimes in Inner Mongolia and in north China, special rights for Japanese were phrased in ever more sweeping form, and indemnities for Japan were added to drive home the admission of defeat and humiliation.

At first it was the field armies that provided the pressure for a hard line. But in Tokyo decision-making circles, it was soon the civilian cabinet of Prince Konoe and Foreign Minister Hirota that outmaneuvered doubting members of the General Staff to have its will. Strong positions came increasingly to be formulated and defended by the new home minister, Admiral Suetsugu, a firebrand who was added to inner cabinet meetings and who, ranking the navy minister in seniority, added authority as well as venom to the discussions. Suetsugu's resentment of the London Naval Conference lived on in his explanation of "Colored Power" to a press conference after his appointment: "From the standpoint of world peace, unless the colored races are liberated so that they can receive the benefits of heaven's equality with the white peoples, and unless white domination of the world is reconstructed, the so-called justice and humanity so often voiced by the white peoples will remain but empty invocations." In his logic, support for China had become an aspect of a waning white imperialism, while Japan's drive for superiority became a push of the oppressed for equality. By January 1938 the cabinet had forced the General Staff into line, and Konoe announced that his government would no longer recognize the Kuomintang regime. Instead it looked "forward to the establishment and growth of a new Chinese regime" with which it could cooperate for the "adjustment of Sino-Japanese relations and the building of a rejuvenated China." With total goals and a total war at hand, the Diet quickly passed legislation giving the government control over Japanese society and economy. Soon the Education Ministry came under the control of General Araki, and aggression abroad was paralleled by intolerance and indoctrination at home.

Military victories gave Japan control of China's major coastal cities and the rail lines between them. The Kuomintang regime retreated to Chungking. By October 1938 Japanese armies were in Canton, which they entered by sea, and in Hankow. Connections between them, however, were not secured until 1944. Hainan and the coastal cities of Swatow and Amoy also fell.

6. *Decision for Disaster*

OM THE INCEPTION of the Manchurian incident, Japan's defense planners had
ked in terms of a national defense structure. Manchuria provided some of the
sources for a heavy industry complex, and talk of the economic integration of
rth China, Manchoukuo and Japan held out hope for an "autonomous" and
lf-sufficient Japanese empire. But it was some time before developments
would permit confidence in the ability to contain the Russians and longer still
before the Japanese-controlled sphere could provide materials for which Japan
was dependent on the United States. Throughout the 1930s almost one-third of
Japanese imports came from the United States. The cotton, scrap iron and oil
that dominated those imports provided the sinews of peacetime trade as well as
wartime strength. The problem was one of avoiding alienation of the United
States while working for freedom from dependence upon it. Every factor of
geography and politics combined to make the United States Japan's chief
maritime adversary. As the expiration of the United States–Japan treaty of commerce neared in January 1940, and when the apparent German successes in
Europe seemed to hold out hope of supplanting North American sources of supply with those of European colonies in Southeast Asia, the path seemed open to
liberation from American constraints.

The imperial navy was most dependent upon American goodwill through
its needs for oil, and it was most determined to maintain an adequate defense
capacity against American naval power. Navy spokesmen had the greater interest in seeing to it that their country avoided excessive involvement in continental adventures, not because they were pacifically inclined but because, as
they saw it, America posed the greater problem to Japanese independence. In
terms of military planning the 1930s thus saw the pendulum swings of military
indignation begin with naval opposition to the London Naval Limitations
Treaty in 1930 and end with naval insistence on the strike against Pearl Harbor
in 1941.

Japanese and American navies had considered each other natural rivals for
Pacific supremacy since the Russo-Japanese War. With the end of the Anglo-
Japanese alliance the Washington Conference had provided the first occasion to
try for security through agreement instead of competition. The Japanese entered
the conference with the determination to maintain 70 percent of American
strength, for the Battle of Jutland had shown that an attacker needed at least a
40 percent superiority to be sure of victory. In the end Japan settled for 60 percent, but the nonfortification clauses gave it security from the possibility of
American attack in the western Pacific. The Washington agreements were to be
extended to smaller ships at London in 1930, and the Japanese again began with
a firm determination for a 70 percent ratio; indeed, Premier Hamaguchi announced to the country that this was essential to the safety of the empire. An
unexpectedly strong American stand supported by Great Britain, which was in-

fluenced by Australian uneasiness about Japanese strength, carried the day
threatening the Japanese with an Anglo-American naval treaty that wo
hopelessly outclass them. The best the Japanese were able to do was to sec
American agreement to postpone construction of three cruisers for several ye
so that Japan would have its 70 percent ratio during the life of the treaty, or ur
1936.

The willingness of the Tokyo government to go back on conditions it h.
itself announced as essential and its ability to defy the will of its naval specialis
led to disputes over the "right of supreme command" and contributed to th
tensions which led to the murder of Hamaguchi, to Kwantung Army action ir
Manchuria and to right-wing extremism within Japan. It also led to the isolation
of naval leaders who had supported the treaty and to the prominence of fire-
brands like Admiral Suetsugu. Significantly, it was the naval leaders who were
determined to secure revision of these agreements in 1936, while army staff
planners like Nagata and Ishiwara, intent upon building industrial strength
against the Soviets, assumed the agreements should be renewed. It was the
government of Admiral Okada that decided to abrogate both the Washington
and London naval treaties in 1934.

The decade that opened with this intensity of dissatisfaction contained very
little to reassure either side. The Lytton Report, which was adopted in February 1933, provided a basis for judgment of the Manchurian incident, but it contained little to provide a satisfactory solution. American suspicions of Japanese
intentions, articulated by Secretary of State Stimson in "nonrecognition" and
through his famous letter to Senator Borah, led to moralistic statements of disapproval, but depression conditions, plus President Hoover's insistence that the
United States had no business taking on a police role in Asia, ruled out the
possibility of sanctions. Japanese action did, however, bring the United States to
cooperate with the League more closely than it ever had; it may have influenced
the American decision to recognize the Soviet Union in 1933, and it was important in Russian acceptance of League membership in 1934. But by then the
Japanese had already withdrawn from that body. The League reemerged in discussions after the China Incident flared in 1937, and at a Brussels Conference
subscribers to the Nine-Power pact of 1922 aired their misgivings. Yet condemnation of Japan was never combined with discussions of help for China, and
Tokyo opinion concluded that condemnation could be ignored and resisted.

Japan's relations with the Soviet Union during the decade were of particular importance. The Soviets began as the focus of the army's plans and fears and
provided the subject for General Araki's invocation of the "crisis of 1936" during his tenure in the Ministry of War between 1932 and 1934. Some of his "Imperial Way" faction advocated a preventative war. But as Araki's star began to
wane, pressure for such a stroke declined. Within a few years it was clear that
Soviet preparations had advanced to the point where a quick stroke was no
longer possible. What was needed now was a plan for the intensive exploitation
of Manchoukuo and measures that would prepare the army for a larger war.

The Russians, while associating themselves with Western disapproval, were also prepared to live with the Japanese as close neighbors with a minimum of moralistic disapproval. The Chinese Eastern Railway, the principal symbol of Russia's Manchurian hopes, became an untenable outpost after the Japanese seizure of northern Manchuria. The Japanese disclosed interest in purchasing the railway in 1932. Negotiations were opened in the summer of 1933 and ended with transfer of the railway in 1935. The Russians in effect recognized Manchoukuo and made every effort to allay Japanese fears while rushing their own defenses. Despite this, the Japanese military continued to focus on communism as the principal danger to the *kokutai*. The Anti-Comintern Pact seemed to offer European assistance. An unpublished clause of this agreement directed it specifically against the Soviet Union, with the promise that neither Japan nor Germany would do anything to aid Russia in the event of an attack or threat of attack. The pact also represented a growth of military over civilian power in Japan, for it was negotiated by the army high command, which insisted that its military significance made it a subject for specialist responsibilities rather than civilian generalities. Italy joined the pact a year later in 1937. In August 1937 the Russians negotiated a nonaggression treaty with the Nationalist government of China.

Russian-Japanese relations next passed through a period of stress that culminated in small wars on the Manchoukuo-Siberian border. These proved that the Russian forces there were formidable. A border clash took place at Changkufeng, at the juncture of the Manchoukuo, Korea and Russian borders, in July 1938. The issue was over a hill on the frontier which the Japanese saw Russians occupy and fortify. Skirmish led to engagement, until the Japanese committed a full division from the Korea army and supporting units from the Kwantung Army. The Russians proved unexpectedly strong and well equipped, and the Japanese fared badly. Stung by this setback in its "territory," the Kwantung Army demanded permission for a full-scale attack. This was denied. In August of 1938 the General Staff and War Ministry secured a diplomatic settlement of the affair whereby the Russians remained in control of their hill. The Kwantung Army decided that the Russian strength had been committed chiefly to embarrass Japan's campaign against Hankow in the China incident and managed to draw comfort from what it described as the "endurance and prudence" with which it had been "able to crush the mighty material power of the Soviet Union."

With nothing learned, the way was open to larger lessons the following year at Nomonhan. The setting was also more complicated. The army was anxious for arguments to use in its campaign for extending the Anti-Comintern Pact into a full-scale military alliance with the Germans. The outbreak of hostilities with the Soviets was sufficiently useful for Tokyo military politicians to make them equivocate on measures to halt it, while for the Kwantung Army it provided new opportunities for glory and arguments for reinforcement. The fighting began in May over a border dispute. It grew steadily in violence and led to air strikes and cavalry attacks. The Kwantung Army sustained crushing defeats and learned that its equipment, tactics and organization were seriously inadequate for any war with the Russians. But it lost none of its belligerence and confidence. Before the border war was stopped in September, the army was preparing the full commitment of all its strength to a battle that had already cost over eleven thousand casualties. International considerations combined to make the Tokyo leaders put a stop to it and dismiss the chief Kwantung Army commanders. On 23 August 1939 the Soviet-German Non-Aggression Pact was signed. It now seemed prudent to coordinate a Russian truce with Japan's new ambitions elsewhere. On 3 September World War II broke out in Europe. It was no longer a time for wasting military strength on obscure border issues.

The encounters with the Russians, so long desired by the Imperial Way partisans of General Araki, had the effect of guaranteeing the victory of the "control faction" with its insistence on the need for modern equipment. As War Ministry authorities put it in a statement of October 1939, the incident showed that in modern warfare the material aspect of equipment was of equal, if not superior, importance to the spiritual or mental aspect of military preparation. Thereafter the army devoted intense effort to improving its technological equipment and training, and there was respect for Russian strength. In April 1941 Foreign Minister Matsuoka's negotiation of a nonaggression pact with the Soviet Union put an end to frontier and boundary squabbles.

Not that either side trusted the other. The Kwantung Army continued to call for reinforcements in men and equipment. The Russians, for their part, were enormously helped in their planning by the most successful spy ring of the period. It was a group headed by Richard Sorge, a German World War I veteran who became a communist and was assigned to Japan in 1933. He operated as a correspondent, won for himself a place in the trust of the German embassy and went so far as to accept a post as counselor to its information services. Through Japanese members of his ring he secured entry into intellectual circles close to Prince Konoe. He transmitted, by radio and courier, thousands of rolls of documents from Japanese and German embassy sources and supplemented them with his own highly competent analysis of Japanese policies.

Sorge became an actor on as well as a reporter of the official scene. In 1938 he helped discredit the revelations a defecting Soviet general made about the demoralization of the Soviet Siberian armies; the Changkufeng border incident, which followed shortly thereafter, bore out his judgments for those who had doubted him. Sorge secured accurate information, which Stalin chose to ignore, about the nature and date of the German decision to attack the Soviet Union. He provided for Moscow a complete chart of Japanese military preparedness in the north and by October of 1941 radioed assurances that the Japanese would not attack in that direction. He also passed along information about the plans for the attack to the south. His mission accomplished, he was requesting recall when Japanese police closed in on his ring.

Despite Japan's adherence to the Anti-Comintern Pact in 1936, it would be easy to exaggerate the importance of the cooperation between the Axis powers and their Pacific ally. The German alliance was greatly prized by members of the military but distrusted by the elderly conservatives and moderates, as well as large segments of the business community, who had grown up in a world dominated by Anglo-American ideals and had seen their country rise to greatness under the shadow of the Anglo-Japanese alliance. The German tie became an issue in the internal power struggle in Japan. The military saw in it support for their position, while civilian forces saw in it reinforcement for the most erratic, arrogant and dangerous tendencies of their army men.

Konoe's foreign minister in 1940, Matsuoka Yōsuke, seemed to bridge these positions. He was Oregon educated and Western oriented. As an official and later head of the South Manchuria Railway Company, he had built close ties with the Kwantung Army, and as a diplomat he had led his delegation out of the League in Geneva and returned to find himself a national hero. Matsuoka was by turns arrogant and cordial, mercurial in his changes from intemperate abuse to reasonableness. And as an individual he was obsessed by an ambition, understandable in an "outsider," to make it to the top on his own through displays of oratorical and manipulative virtuosity.

Konoe himself was by no means free from pride of personal leadership. By the time of his return to politics in 1940, he had worked out the idea of a New Order or "New Structure" that would convert twentieth-century political theory into a distinctly Japanese form of strength and loyalty. Parties should go and be subsumed into a new party; national reconstruction and international achievement should combine to create a New Order in East Asia, one of coprosperity, peace and stability.

Matsuoka considered the German alliance his particular pride. The original Anti-Comintern Pact had been negotiated in 1936 through army channels so quietly that the German ambassador in Tokyo had asked Sorge to find out about it. By 1940 Matsuoka was sure that a stronger German tie would bring protection from interference by Britain and America as well as from the Soviet Union. He saw that Japan was weakened by the China incident, threatened by the economic pressures the United States was beginning to apply, and forced to strengthen its policies. Under the circumstances this could only be done by reliance on Germany, and Matsuoka confided to a colleague that he intended to ride on German coattails. The Tripartite Pact of September 1940 recognized Japan's leadership in Greater East Asia. This, Matsuoka thought, was a coup in view of German control of the colonial powers of France and Holland; what he overlooked was the lack of a German navy. The pact envisaged a world in which the West European powers would all but disappear, leaving Japan to contend with Germany, Russia and the United States.

Most marked in all this was Matsuoka's misjudgment of the United States. He thought his German pact might have some influence in the American elections of 1940 and felt confident that his tie with a conquering Germany would make the United States think twice before it sought to block Japan's needs or ambitions. But by the time of Pearl Harbor, Matsuoka, out of power, saw that "the Tripartite Alliance was my worst mistake. I hoped to prevent the United States from entering the war.... Instead we see the present calamity which indirectly resulted from the Alliance."

In the fall of 1940 things still seemed hopeful. The United States, to be sure, responded to the alliance by placing an embargo on exports of steel scrap to Japan. It now became important to get access to the raw materials of Southeast Asia. In order to free Japan's hands there, an agreement with the Russians seemed in order, and in the spring of 1941 Matsuoka embarked upon the whirlwind diplomatic tour that took him to Germany and Moscow, where he negotiated a nonaggression pact with the Soviet Union in April of 1941. He had no permanent expectations of goodwill from this but explained to the Privy Council upon his return that a three-year peace would be the most that could be expected. Moreover, if Germany should enter war with the USSR before that date, he would advocate Japan's coming to Germany's aid.

When the Germans unleashed their attack against the Russians in June 1941, Matsuoka was as good as his word and vigorously urged joint efforts with the Germans. Many Japanese army men shared his views, and the details of this controversy provided absorbing material for the Sorge ring to transmit to Moscow. The verdict went against Matsuoka. His intemperate advocacy of his ideas cost him his job. In at least one meeting, a colleague questioned his sanity, and the emperor himself discussed ways of removing him with Prince Konoe. In July the cabinet was restructured to leave out Matsuoka, and planning for moves to the south went into high gear. It is not difficult to see why the move on Southeast Asia had greater attraction than the proposals for war with Russia. If the Germans won their war, as seemed likely, Russia's holdings in Northeast Asia would be ripe for the picking anyway. Changkufeng and Nomonham had shown that they were strongly defended. Japan's great needs now were for raw materials, especially oil, and the European colonies in Southeast Asia looked like easy marks and rewarding targets.

The main problem there lay with the United States, which had moved much of its fleet to Pacific bases in Hawaii and was denying Japan access to oil and steel scrap. Most of Matsuoka's flamboyant diplomacy had been designed to checkmate the country he knew so well and understood so little. American disapproval of the Manchurian events that had brought Matsuoka to prominence had been clear though ineffective. When Japanese policymakers went on to the China imbroglio in 1937, American disapproval took more explicit forms. In October President Roosevelt's suggestion of a "quarantine" in which the community could protect the health of the many against the disease of the few, and his view of war as a contagion whose carriers ought to be identified, was meant to warn the Japanese, although it may have warned Americans more. Japanese field commanders were unimpressed. Later that fall, the American gunboat

Panay was bombed and sunk, and the British *Ladybird* was shelled by an artillery unit under the command of Hashimoto Kingorō, the founder of the extremist Cherry Society of 1930. As irritation rose, retaliation neared. The American public was stirred by its knowledge of the Nanking incident of 1937, and in July 1939 Japan was informed of the abrogation of its trade treaty with the United States, which was due to expire 26 January 1940.

This suggested to the Tokyo government the need for stronger steps to offset retaliation and lessen Japan's reliance upon American favors. With the German victories in Western Europe in 1940, the way seemed open to capitalizing on the German tie for seizure of raw materials held by countries the Nazis had defeated. "A drop of oil is a drop of blood," as the Tokyo slogan of those days had it, and the islands of Indonesia seemed to offer the most of the one with the expenditure of the least of the other. Unfortunately the Netherlands East Indies regime was loyal to the Dutch government in exile in London and not disposed to cooperate with Tokyo. By the summer of 1941 it was clear that the Japanese could not achieve their aims without violence.

The Tokyo leaders still saw some hope of combining a solution of the China war with an extension of their influence into Southeast Asia. They felt sure that it was foreign aid that made the endurance of the government of Chiang Kai-shek possible. In 1940 they pressed their negotiations with the former Kuomintang leader Wang Ching-wei for a puppet government at Nanking. In the fall, Britain was pressured into closing the Burma Road. Discussions were underway about cutting the supply routes through North Vietnam, which were presumed to be the lifeline for infiltration of war material into China. The Indochina government was responsive to German-dominated Vichy, and in September of 1940 the Japanese forced approval for occupation of the north and their use of air bases there. This was also the month Matsuoka negotiated the Tripartite Pact with the Germans and Italians, with its swift reprisals in the form of an American embargo on scrap.

The focus was now on reaching an understanding with the United States. Matsuoka thought his agreement with the Axis, followed by the treaty he had signed with the Russians, placed Japan in a much better position for negotiating. Konoe's penchant for nonprofessional and personal representatives found outlet in the appointment as ambassador to Washington of Admiral Nomura, who had been on good personal terms with President Roosevelt during his stay in Washington as naval attaché during World War I. Nomura's knowledge of Roosevelt was better than his mastery of diplomacy. His eagerness for the agreement he sought led him to grasp at straws, delay action on instructions he received and temper the wording of messages he thought would discourage his negotiations. As a result communications between the two governments were far more accurately and reliably maintained through Ambassador Grew in Tokyo.

Nomura's mission was also handicapped by the impetuous Foreign Minister Matsuoka, until he was replaced in July 1941. Matsuoka had already failed in his efforts to delay or halt a further move into Southeast Asia. Tokyo had determined upon the need to occupy southern Indochina in order to prepare the basis for whatever further moves might seem advisable. The decision for the move to the south rather than to the north led to the occupation of South Indochina early in July. This was responded to by the United States, which froze all Japanese assets in the United States on 25 July and blocked further shipments of oil to Japan.

In Tokyo the power of decision now passed to a series of liaison conferences, which were held every few days. Representatives of the cabinet and supreme command appeared at these. The cabinet endorsed, but never reversed, decisions reached in this manner. The transcripts of these meetings illustrate the way in which service representatives dominated the discussions with their plans and proposals. At times finance or planning board representatives were called upon, but always in a setting of action proposed by the army and navy, whose bureau chiefs also arranged the conference agenda. Imperial conferences endorsed the weightiest decisions in the presence of the emperor, but his sentiments were expressed through the form of questions directed by the president of the Privy Council.

By July the conferees had agreed that Japan should prepare for war and negotiate for peace. Success in the former required proper timing of the efforts for peace, with the result that a deadline for success, originally set for October, was extended several times thereafter until the services gave notice that they could defer no longer. The basic "either-or" decision could have come only from a group deeply united in basic postulates about Japan's problem and opportunity. These were that the American position on China, which called for Japanese withdrawal, would leave that country open to a Communist take-over. Consequently the Japanese would at no time countenance total withdrawal from north China. Furthermore the United States seemed to be forcing Japan to its will through economic sanctions and naval coercion; the shift of the fleet to Pearl Harbor, designed to restrain Japan, had the contrary result of requiring a prior strike against Hawaii before action could be contemplated elsewhere.

There were other features of these discussions. Policymakers appeared ever more as representatives of their services, with a duty to service that seemed almost to outweigh duty to country and, certainly, to the government. Thus Admiral Nagano on 5 November, could report in an imperial conference that "we would like to maintain even closer relations with the Government and attain our desired goal." In this extreme form of divided responsibility, Professor Hosoya has suggested, risk-taking was high. Foreign Minister Matsuoka had put it jauntily shortly before his dismissal in July: "Nothing ventured, nothing gained. We should take decisive action."

For the navy, the crisis was that of oil. The clock was running out. "There is a chance of achieving victory now," Admiral Nagano said on 24 July; "it will diminish as time goes on." On 6 September he warned that "by the latter half of next year America's military preparedness will have made great progress, and it will be difficult to cope with her." On 25 October he warned that "the Navy is consuming 400 tons of oil an hour. The situation is urgent. We want it decided one way or the other quickly." And on 1 November Admiral Nagano was firmer still: "Now! The time for war will not come later!" At best, Japan's supply of oil would have lasted a bare eighteen months by then. What she now demanded as her right she would soon have to beg as supplicant.

The immediate crisis was so great that it blunted long-range strategic planning. The alternative was sure disaster and retreat to a third-class power; should Japan not strike while she was still a first-class power? Admiral Nagano again put it most clearly: "The government has decided that if there were no war the fate of the nation was sealed. Even if there is war, the country may be ruined. Nevertheless, a nation which does not fight in this plight has already lost its spirit and is doomed." Or, as the president of the Privy Council summed it up for the emperor on 5 November, "It is impossible, from the standpoint of our domestic political situation and of our self-preservation, to accept all of the American demands.... On the other hand we cannot let the present situation continue. If we miss the present opportunity to go to war, we will have to submit to American dictation. Therefore, I recognize that it is inevitable that we must decide to start a war against the United States. I will put my trust in what I have been told: namely, that things will go well in the early part of the war; and that although we will experience increasing difficulties as the war progresses, there is some prospect of success."

By this time, mutual distrust had corroded both approaches too much to permit compromise. Distrust had in fact poisoned the negotiations from the first through the unfortunate interference of well-meaning nonprofessionals who had prepared a slate of proposals fully acceptable to neither Tokyo nor Washington and which each side understood to be of the other's composition. The counterproposals that followed this opening misunderstanding seemed, on both sides, to narrow alternatives rather than to broaden them. They certainly contributed to Secretary of State Hull's increasing disillusion with his adversaries.

The final manner of the severance of relations and outbreak of hostilities served to discredit Japanese honor. In 1904 Japan's surprise strike against the Russian fleet had been acclaimed in the Western world, but Pearl Harbor evoked a very different reaction. For success in the opening strikes, surprise was considered essential. Admiral Nagano had warned in June that "unless the declaration of war can be tied in with instantaneous military action, I don't think we will make a declaration." On 5 November Foreign Minister Tōgō reported to his colleagues that "as to whether we should declare war, or whether we should begin the war without declaring it, the majority opinion is that the problem needs to be studied." It was finally decided to allow notice, but not enough to imperil the strike.

Yet in the end the notice came after the strike for a ludicrous reason. By the time the last part of the final message came in to the Washington embassy, the only person with a security clearance high enough to work on it lacked technical typing skill. By the time young Mr. Okumura finished a clean copy by the "hunt and peck" system, the bombs had fallen at Pearl Harbor. Ambassador Nomura, who had had to telephone to delay his final meeting with Secretary Hull, now stood quietly while he was told that "In all my fifty years of public service I have never seen a document that was more crowded with infamous falsehoods and distortions — infamous falsehoods and distortions on a scale so huge that I never imagined until today that any government on this planet was capable of uttering them."

The story of the outbreak of the Pacific war provides few scoundrels or heroes. The International Military Tribunal for the Far East, which sat in Tokyo after the Japanese surrender to take up the responsibility for the war, found itself working in an unfamiliar area, one uncongenial to its search for a consistent purpose and plot in Japan's twentieth-century policies. Among those it sentenced to be hung were General Doihara, the Manchurian and Mongolian plotter; Foreign Minister Hirota; General Itagaki Seishirō, of the Kwantung Army and General Staff; and General Tōjō, prime minister when the final decisions were made for the Pacific war. Generals Araki, Baron Hiranuma, Hashimoto Kingorō and others prominent in the wartime scene received life sentences. On the whole, however, the court found that it was a good deal more difficult to pin down responsibility in a bureaucratic system like twentieth-century Japan's than in a monolithic, demonic structure like Hitler's Germany.

More recent verdicts of historians tend to modify the insistence of earlier writers on theories of recalcitrant army men and moderate naval officers, of insubordinate junior officers and powerless seniors, and proconsular field commanders. In Manchuria the General Staff approved, although the ministry did not, in China the ministry and cabinet supported, while the General Staff deplored, the escalation. There were few cases of truly successful insubordination, and most of the plans finally implemented were developed and forwarded through regular bureaucratic channels. The outstanding efforts of ultranationalist agitation, the March, October, May and February incidents, were uniformly failures. Nor was there a single master plan that unfolded as the months and years went along. Japan's problem, rather, was precisely a lack of such long-range strategic thinking (except on the part of a few apocalyptic extremists like Ishiwara) and a tendency to move from short-range decision to short-range decision, hopeful that maneuverability for larger shifts would always remain.

The events of the decade offer much reflection for the student of intelligence, war and crisis. The Japanese, long accustomed to praise for their achievements in the surprise strike against the Russians in 1904, never appreciated the response that Pearl Harbor would arouse. Because of the divided counsels and the essential nature of surprise, the details of plans for the attack were known to very few. As Roberta Wohlstetter summarizes, "It is doubtful that Army officials other than the Chief of Staff and his deputy heard more than rumors until October, or that the Army and Navy cabinet ministers heard about it much before December 1. The Minister of Finance, the Minister of Agriculture, the Minister of Communications, and the Foreign Minister were never apprised of the plan. Members of the crews participating in the attack were unaware of their destination and were briefed for the first time only after the port of departure had been cleared."

In actual fact, however, American authorities had at their disposal a large body of information drawn from many sources, most importantly the decode of the principal Japanese messages. Secretary Hull had on his desk the full text of the document Admiral Nomura had struggled to bring in clean typescript before the Pearl Harbor raids began. In the Philippines, which were bombed hours later long after word of Pearl Harbor was in, the tactical surprise achieved was no less disastrous for the defenders. Some American historians have tried to see in Washington's hard line a plot whereby the Japanese were tricked into attack in order to get the United States involved in Europe's war. This theory is not without its attractions for some defenders of the prewar cause in postwar Japan, but such oversimplification helps little. It overlooks the variety of indications, true and false, that surround all defense planners, and their reluctance to commit themselves to the acceptance of any one assumption. Stalin was fully informed by Sorge, and warned by Washington and London, before the Nazi attack in 1941, and yet his surprise and hurt were no different from that of the commanders at Pearl Harbor.

There were sound reasons for discounting predictions of a Japanese attack at Pearl Harbor and Manila. It seemed likely that the Japanese would strike directly at the Indies and Singapore in an attempt to get the supplies they needed without taking on the Americans. There was the knowledge of the difficulty of achieving surprise at such distances, and the problems of carrying out a torpedo attack in waters as shallow as those in the Hawaiian base. And there was the knowledge of the range limitation of fighter aircraft from Taiwan for any assault against the Philippines. We now know that these technical difficulties were overcome by the Japanese planners barely in time to make the operations possible.

Perhaps most important of all, there was an understandable but disastrous tendency to attribute to the Japanese thought processes and rationality of the order seen by officials who worked within a different value and decision structure. A country already bogged down in China, it was assumed, and committed through its actions in Indochina, would think twice before taking on the rest of the nonfascist world at once. It could best be restrained by forceful warnings, disarmed by cutting off its fuel and blocked by placing a massive deterrent like the Pacific Fleet in Pearl Harbor. Instead, the warnings served to feed a fierce determination to withstand such power. The shutoff of oil provided the need to seize it at its source, and the deterrent provided a target that made it possible to begin the war with an ocean cleared of enemy naval strength. It would restore, and indeed improve, at one stroke the ratios of naval security that had been demanded at the London Conference of 1930.

What brought the Japanese to Pearl Harbor was not so much an atavistic desire for conquest as a process of thought and action that led to the conclusion that any other course would mean failure for the century-long effort to achieve full independence and equality with the great powers of the West. Japanese leaders could not imagine a status between dependence and independence and had not yet accepted the possibility of interdependence. In Roberta Wohlstetter's words, "The decision for war was rather forced by the desire to avoid the more terrible alternative of losing status or abandoning the national objectives.... Step-by-step pursuit of a program of expansion in China, Korea, and Indochina had committed the Japanese to further steps in the same direction; so that stopping at any point always became equivalent to 'accepting national humiliation' or 'accepting the road to a second-rate power.'"

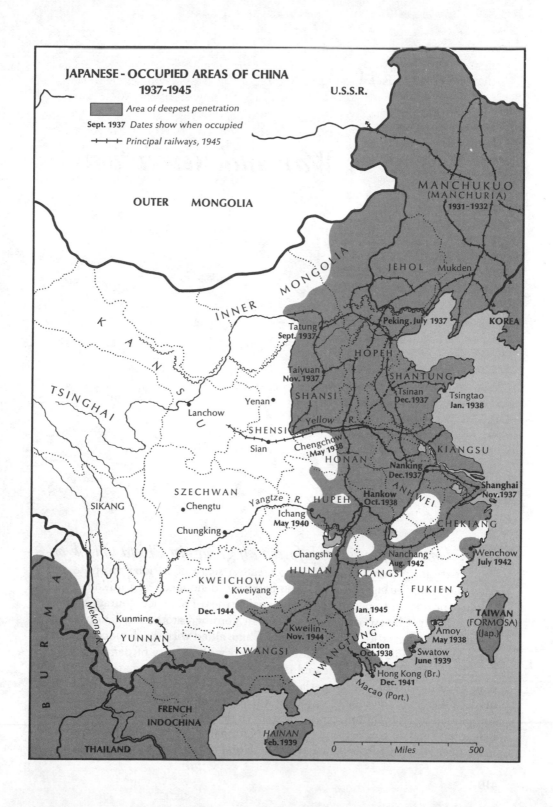

JAPANESE - OCCUPIED AREAS OF CHINA
1937-1945

Area of deepest penetration

Sept. 1937 *Dates show when occupied*

+—+—+ *Principal railways, 1945*

U.S.S.R.

OUTER   MONGOLIA

MANCHUKUO
(MANCHURIA)
1931-1932

INNER   MONGOLIA

JEHOL   Mukden

K A N S U

Tatung
Sept. 1937

Peking, July 1937

KOREA

HOPEH

TSINGHAI

Lanchow

Yenan

Taiyuan
Nov. 1937

SHANSI

SHANTUNG

Tsinan
Dec.1937

Tsingtao
Jan. 1938

Sian

SHENSI

Yellow   R.

Chengchow
May 1938

HONAN

KIANGSU

Nanking
Dec.1937

Shanghai
Nov.1937

SZECHWAN

Chengtu

Yangtze   R.

HUPEH

Hankow
Oct.1938

ANHWEI

CHEKIANG

SIKANG

Chungking

Ichang
May 1940

Changsha

HUNAN

Nanchang
Aug. 1942

KIANGSI

Wenchow
July 1942

KWEICHOW

Kweiyang

Dec. 1944

Jan.1945

FUKIEN

TAIWAN
(FORMOSA)
(Jap.)

B U R M A

Mekong   R.

Kunming

YUNNAN

Kweilin
Nov. 1944

KWANGSI

KWANGTUNG

Canton
Oct.1938

Amoy
May 1938

Swatow
June 1939

Hong Kong (Br.)
Dec. 1941

Macao (Port.)

FRENCH
INDOCHINA

THAILAND

HAINAN
Feb. 1939

0   Miles   500

CHAPTER 11

China in War and Revolution

*The relentless Japanese push forced all groups in China to look be-*yond partisan interests and helped to create a sense of national purpose and determination. Chiang Kai-shek, who had been denounced as a militarist and dictator, now came to personify the national virtues of patience, courage and integrity. Many Chinese and most American commentators hailed him as his country's savior. As the Pacific war found China allied with the democracies, the government and its leader became surrounded with an aura of democracy.

But the Japanese also defeated the Nationalist armies, drove the Kuomintang government into the hinterlands of Szechwan, and separated it from the modern sectors of the society in which it had developed. Military crisis was accompanied by an economic crisis, and as both deepened through weary years of defeat, an internal competition between Nationalists and Communists proved more decisive for China's future than the larger struggle with Japan.

410

1. Some Comparisons

NATIONALIST CHINA in the 1930s offered some interesting comparisons to militarist Japan. Both countries experienced severe economic dislocation. Japan's economy, which was related to international markets much more directly, was more affected by the depression in the West. China largely escaped the world depression until 1933, but from then on American silver policies helped to precipitate a severe internal depression and deflation. Japan's distress came earlier, and her recovery, thanks to orderly governmental procedures and spending, came much sooner. But China was also forced to endure the enormous physical damage of war. In both countries recovery was distorted by concentration on military goals. While these helped to focus government spending for a time, in the long run they produced an inflation fed by uneconomic spending and wasteful competition for scarce materials and foodstuffs. In both countries military planners were convinced of the need to accompany arms buildup with overall planning of the sort needed for modern war. In both countries they justified the sacrifices that were required by renewed emphasis on traditional and group ethics and by emphasis on the priority of society and nation over individual and family. Japanese moralists were working with a modern economy at their disposal, however, while China's propagandists too often stopped with words. Government controls lightened tenants' burdens in Japan, but government propaganda sanctified those burdens in China.

In both countries students were exhorted to surrender their personal liberties and give absolute loyalty to political authority. At times the same models— Hitler's Germany, Mussolini's Italy and even Stalin's Russia—were held up as examples in both countries. The military models of Germany served both countries. Ishiwara Kanji had learned from the teachings of General von Seeckt during his years in Germany, and the success of the Kwantung Army had been a product of his acceptance of the need for surprise and speed. The same von Seeckt came to China in 1933 at the request of Chiang Kai-shek to advise in the reorganization of the Chinese armies. The following year he returned as head of a military mission. After a year he was succeeded by General von Falkenhausen. A German mission of some seventy officers trained Chinese in the use of German military matériel and stressed the importance of the rapid development of an industrial base for a modern army. Under their guidance there was developed a core army, which began at eighty thousand and grew to more than three hundred thousand and which furnished the bulk of the best Nationalist units. The Yangtze delta area was fortified quietly in response to German advice. As was also true in the 1940s, when Stilwell was advising him, however, Chiang chose to dilute the Germans' emphasis on the necessity for a professional officer corps with his own insistence on the political importance of his Whampoa Academy favorites and political allies. Nevertheless the Nationalist armies improved steadily. Unfortunately many of the best and most modern divisions were lost in the fighting in the Yangtze delta that followed the outbreak of the China war in 1937.

Just as Ishiwara Kanji and Nagata Tetsuzan accepted the Germans' emphasis on the industrial base for modern war, Chiang Kai-shek tried to implement von Seeckt's advice through the establishment of a National Resources Planning Commission. But in the retarded stage of Chinese industrial progress, it required time to develop this. Chiang's reluctance to commit his modern forces to battle with the Japanese before he had effected full national unification and large-scale economic development should be compared with the refusal of the Meiji oligarchy to flex its muscles in international politics before the maturation of plans for industrial and institutional reforms. A good deal of the unity that Chiang came to command was the product of the Japanese outrage, and it is impossible to say what his progress would have been without it. But he would certainly have needed a minimum of several more years before he could have hoped to engage the Japanese successfully. Neither Tokyo nor Yenan allowed him that time.

The Nationalist revolution, like the Meiji Restoration, had been motivated by the determination to win international equality. The antiforeign demonstrations that broke out in Shanghai in 1925 and in Nanking in 1927, unlike the antiforeign incidents in Japan at the time of the Restoration, were large-scale and drew upon several decades of discontent and humiliation. As a result they required a clear response on the part of the national government, and the pace of its advance in rights recovery was rapid. The foreign concessions in Hankow, Kiukiang, Amoy and Weihaiwei were reclaimed, and antiimperialist propaganda was effectively used to marshal popular support. The Washington Conference had provided some scheduled steps toward diplomatic equality, and the tariff conferences that followed reached agreement on approval of a higher level of customs charges. Negotiations for tariff autonomy began in 1928 and were concluded successfully in 1930. Efforts to abolish extraterritoriality were less successful. The Nanking government attempted to announce its abolition unilaterally in 1929, but it succeeded chiefly in alarming the Japanese. The goal was not gained until 1943, in a wartime act of encouragement on the part of China's allies. As this gesture illustrates, a good deal of the Chinese government's achievement in gaining international equality was reform "from above," granted by the powers out of conscience.

Success in internal renovations depended on the control of the countryside. For reasons that have been discussed earlier, the Nationalist government found itself forced to abandon the land tax to the provinces. In contrast, the first acts of the Meiji government had been motivated by a desire to secure control over the traditional economy, and the land tax measures of 1873 provided the wherewithal for modernization. By the 1930s the bewildering disparity of taxation systems in China made it doubly difficult to prescribe remedies for rural distress. The nature of that distress differed sharply from place to place. Although there is an impressive literature focusing on land reform and tenantry in Nationalist China, statistical surveys permit little confidence in descriptions of the situation. At one extreme were the charges of Communist leaders like Liu Shao-ch'i, who claimed in 1950 that "less than 10 per cent of the rural population possess approximately from 70 to 80 per cent of the land and brutally exploit the peasants." On the other hand, one careful observer of conditions in rural China concluded that "well under 10 per cent of China's total farm production is used to pay rent, and even much of this rental crop goes to landlords who are themselves farmers and would be classified as poor by American standards." There may be no contradiction here; landlords "poor" by American standards could be "brutal" by tenant standards, and the Communist rule-of-thumb definition of "rich peasant" as one who could more or less make ends meet probably serves better than anything else to indicate the pervasive nature of the agricultural crisis in China.

Japan in the 1930s was also in the grip of an agricultural crisis, and rightist theorists and militarist activists were quick to cite the plight of the countryside as evidence of the injustice of the capitalist and political-party order. The government took hesitant steps toward equalizing rents by sponsoring agricultural associations and preparing for future land reform. But it is probable that equally important improvement came from the blush of prosperity that began to accompany Japan's military expansion in the 1930s. Labor shortages improved tenants' bargaining positions, and the army pay sent home by their sons increased farm income. Even more basic was the fact that an increasing number of farmers supplemented agricultural with part- or full-time industrial work.

Areas of culture and education provide further similarities and contrasts between China and Japan. The decade of the 1930s was one in which Chinese student nationalism grew steadily. There was increasing restlessness with the policy of political leaders and an increasing readiness to place country above self. The trend had begun with the May Fourth movement, but there were now more students. And there was more country, for the Kuomintang government roused much more hope than the warlord regime of Tuan Ch'i-jui. There was more urgency, for the imminence of the Japanese threat roused the most indifferent to the need for a Chinese response. National humiliation and crisis, the political foci of Chinese students, were problems Japanese students had not known since the Meiji period. But at that time they had been few, and they trained for service in a modern state that led and channeled their nationalist expectations. Chinese student nationalism came from below, and because it had been repressed and disappointed for so long it became almost inevitably a critical and revolutionary force.

On the other hand, the propaganda of the Japanese and Chinese governments had many points in common. In China student involvement was welcomed but also feared. Conservative reminders of the need for students to study and prepare themselves for national service were frequent. The New Life movement of 1934, in which Chiang Kai-shek tried to channel student enthusiasm and shape student values, had startling similarities to the Confucian tone of indoctrination in militarist Japan. Chiang thought of the New Life movement as a way of building national unity on a platform of Confucian puritanism. Public morality and social behavior needed reform and guidance. Exhortations for cleanliness and hygiene were constants in modern Chinese reformism from warlords like Feng Yü-hsiang to the great public campaigns of Communist China. In Chiang's case they focused on propriety and a sense of shame. The movement was inaugurated in 1934 in connection with efforts for reconstruction in the former communist zone of Kiangsi. "Chinese of today," as Chiang's wife explained, "seem to have forgotten the old source of China's greatness in their urge to acquire material gain, but, obviously, if the national spirit is to be revived, there must be recourse to stable foundations. In the four principles of ancient times, we have those foundations...." Rural reconstruction and reform, traditional morality operating as substitute for the selfish material-ism of communism, and Confucian propriety were designed to remold China. Throughout the country great banners and slogans bore down on homely and useful virtues. A missionary educator helped to coordinate the movement. Simi-lar sentiments could easily be produced from Japanese primers on morality in the 1930s.

Yet language of this sort meant little to students in either country. In both Japan and China the predominant current of social science analysis was that of Marxism, which seemed to provide an overarching explanation of national and international developments. Though official propaganda and censorship obscured Marxist phraseology, in most cases the Marxist tone came through easily. This was particularly true in literature, for the predominant tone in both countries was that of left-wing proletarian criticism. Both literatures empha-sized the themes of conflicts between generations, between modern and tradi-tional, urban and rural. In both societies the repression of left-wing organiza-tions added the appeal of danger to logic and provided the test of sincerity and conviction. In Japan a vigorous right wing attracted some of the same emotions that rewarded the left, but its repression and persecution were never as sharp as that which greeted the believers of the left. In China the chaotic state of society and the more casual forms of repression and brutality made it even more dan-gerous to be denounced as communist.

All this had meaning for students and intellectuals. In China, where a top-heavy educational structure had many universities and an inadequate public school system, frustrations were more numerous than in the orderly world of militarist Japan. China's student movement was, like Japan's, restricted to the modern cities. In 1931 college students in China numbered 44,176, about .01 percent of the population; 30 percent of these were in Peking and 24 percent in Shanghai, which, with its proximity to foreign culture and foreign freedom, was the center of the publishing industry and also of the modern proletariat. Pe-king's concerns focused on political frustration, and they were most im-mediately subject to Japanese humiliation and threat.

The Chinese educational scene was more structured and elitist than Japan's. Because China's institutions were inadequately developed, many educational and scientific leaders were foreign trained—not, as in the case of Japanese, garnished with a year or two of foreign residence after completion of their studies, but substantially educated in the West as had been common in Meiji Japan. Thus much of the Chinese scene was superficially more Western while actually less modern, but most of that scene was intensely nationalist, impatient, frustrated and volatile. Because of the predominance of Christian influence in higher education, one of the principal notes of the cultural movement of the 1920s was a vigorously anti-Christian persuasion. In the 1930s this began to pass. Christian influence had changed to emphasize more social work and liberal reform. Rural reconstruction, literacy and social campaigns were less doctrinally oriented than had been the case before. Moreover, the Japanese advance found American missionaries vigorous in protest, close to their students and able to affiliate with rising Chinese nationalism. Some of the great student demonstrations of the 1930s developed at missionary colleges like Yenching.

Chinese student anger had sparked the May Fourth demonstrations in 1919. The Japanese intervention in Shantung in 1928 found the new government eager to focus student discontent against Japan. This was understandable, for government officials had been beaten up by student mobs in 1919, the foreign minister's residence was sacked, and he himself thrashed, in 1925 and 1931. In 1930 Chiang Kai-shek took over the Ministry of Education to try to channel some of the students' antigovernment emotion, but the Kuomintang's problem was not a simple one, for the central government had only limited control over the content of local education. In many areas provinces and cities made a deliberate effort to increase anti-Japanese bias in history, geography and even arithmetic lessons after 1928, and these changes were in the forefront of the Japanese insistence that China put an end to anti-Japanese campaigns. After the Manchurian incident some school authorities were again directed to intensify anti-Japanese indoctrination, and students led in organizing boycotts and disseminating anti-Japanese propaganda in many ways. These activities could often get out of hand, and the Nanking Ministry of Education then had to do its best to get students back to their studies. In one sense the whole of the New Life movement could be seen as an attempt to get students back to their books. Whatever the justice of Japanese complaints about Chinese educational indoctrination, there was also little in Japanese press or primers in the 1930s to build respect or affection for the Chinese regime.

Chinese student protests against the Manchurian incident were particularly striking. They included the Shanghai boycotts that helped bring on the fighting there in 1932. Most remarkable of all was the wave of patriotic indignation that brought trainload after trainload of students to Nanking to demand action against the Japanese in the fall of 1931. Student groups commandeered trains in a pattern not unlike the activities of the Red Guards in the late 1960s. In Nanking a regular routine was adopted to deal with the only partly welcome guests.

Groups of several thousand students would be addressed by Chiang Kai-shek himself (as the Red Guards later hoped to parade before Mao Tse-tung). In his remarks Chiang would compare himself to leaders who had resisted outside invasion in earlier times. He would warn the students against traitors (i.e., communists) who might try to distract them and assure them that if they would return to their books their government would take care of the enemy in time. The next day the students received a sightseeing tour and a meal before they boarded a homeward-bound train.

Unfortunately Manchuria was followed by Shanghai, Shanghai by Jehol, and Jehol by the Tangku Truce. By 1934 the New Life movement had its work cut out for it in attempting to dam the tide of student indignation. When danger loomed again in 1935, the students took over. At the end of that year the maneuvering that followed the Ho-Umezu agreement seemed to threaten another Manchuria in north China. On 9 December students of universities in the Peking area organized to form massive demonstrations that moved through a rain of police blows and frigid streams from fire hoses. The march was repeated on 16 December. Hundreds were hurt. But the new Hopei-Chahar Council under General Sung Che-yuan proved to be a good deal less of a puppet than it might have been. Sung was able to tell the Japanese he could not be responsible for order in Peking if the talks continued, and the Japanese gave up attempts at formal autonomy for north China.

From Yenan the Communist Youth Corps praised the students and called on them to join a new "Resist Japan National Salvation Youth Corps." The student movements had been carefully organized and superbly orchestrated, and political leadership was evident. In later years official Communist historiography credited the major role to Liu Shao-ch'i. But at the start a good deal of the suggestion seems to have come from noncommunist journalists (including Edgar Snow) and teachers, and thereafter the surge of student opinion and anger would have been harder to dam than to stimulate.

Student nationalism, at times channeled and at times unwelcome, thus played an important role in putting pressure on Chiang Kai-shek to take a stronger stand against Japan. It also helped to push the Japanese into stronger indignation over "anti-Japanese" movements. It made for unity in China, for it knew no ideology except an unstructured radicalism and no loyalty except a national commitment to oppose the Japanese. After 1936, Sian and the second united front, the Chinese student movement was substantially suppressed as a political entity. Its nationalist goals had been achieved, and national unity ruled out political dissent. But by then the better part of a student generation had been radicalized. The students had also done their best, through rural recruiting and propaganda drives, to stimulate popular nationalism. It is probable, as John Israel concludes, that they rendered north China "more susceptible to wartime guerrilla activities; the strongest impact had undoubtedly been not on the peasants, but on the students, who gained firsthand knowledge of the life and thought of China's masses and became aware of the enormous problems of communication. This was a unique preparation for war and revolution."

During the same period, left-wing student movements in Japan also went into steep decline. The emphasis on national unity in time of danger and international criticism helped to dampen student spirits. Massive roundups of suspected leftists suppressed organized subversion. Most remarkably, under a combination of suppression and reeducation somewhat comparable to the "remolding" of personality in contemporary China, many leaders of the Left recanted and resumed their place in the larger family circle of imperial unity. As a result the political confrontation between China and Japan ended the shared experience of radicalism and liberalism that had seemed to relate their student generations in the years that followed World War I.

2. The Survival of the Chinese Communists

THE COMPARISONS between Kuomintang China and militarist Japan that have been suggested fade into insignificance when measured against the enormous contrast posed by the growth of a competing power center in China. The survival of the Chinese Communists in the years after their break with Chiang Kai-shek stands as evidence of the tenacity of their purpose and the endemic economic and political crisis of the Chinese countryside.

After Chiang struck down Communist power in Shanghai in 1927, they had lost their chief centers of student and labor support. Chiang and other military leaders dealt with suspected communists with brutal efficiency, and summary executions were taken for granted. The left-wing Kuomintang of Wuhan and, later, Canton also turned its back on former Communist allies. The Communists themselves, after massive losses and desertions that resulted from disastrous tactical orders Stalin sent from Moscow, gradually found themselves restricted to isolated and remote mountain redoubts in southeast China. Here they developed the tactics and independence that made possible their survival and growth during the years of the war with Japan. Survival would not have been possible if rural China had not remained in a state of crisis. The Communists had sacrificed their urban supporters, and their future depended on their ability to understand and organize agrarian discontent. This was preeminently the contribution of Mao Tse-tung.

Mao-Tse-tung had been assigned to study the revolutionary potential of his native province of Hunan in 1927. His famous report to the Central Committee of the Communist party of China stressed the importance of radicalism and the potential of peasant rage, and it suggested some of the lines of future Communist policy. Yet he was constrained to follow Kremlin orders for quick action, and his premature efforts to organize "Autumn Harvest" insurrections failed in the atmosphere of discouragement that followed Chiang's turn against the Communists. From Shanghai the Central Committee sent instructions calling for permanent insurrection; émeutes, selective murder and terrorism, robberies and small-scale attacks were to keep the authorities off-balance until the urban workers could come back with their support. Mao's experience in Hunan provided little support for this policy, though he did not challenge it in words. After his setbacks in Hunan he retreated to the Chingkang mountains on the border of Kiangsi and Hunan. Here Chu Teh, who had led an equally unsuccessful attack on the Kiangsi city of Nanchang, brought his troops in 1928.

Mao's words of this period found him less doctrinaire in his assumptions about class determinism and more optimistic about the interplay of will and revolution; he seemed more Leninist than Marxist. The same emphasis on the reform of personality and character that would characterize Communist reform programs until the Proletarian Cultural Revolution was visible in Mao's discussion of revolutionary potential. Soldiers, bandits, robbers, beggars, prostitutes could all serve the revolution, he wrote, and even old secret societies could help the modern struggle. Like the bandit-statesmen heroes of China's classic novels, Mao and his associates did their best to mold the human material available to them into purposeful fighters. At a 1928 "conference" of Communist leaders in the hills Mao came to the not very surprising conclusions that the Chinese revolution was distinguished by the fact that the revolutionary forces were weak and existed chiefly in poor and backward areas, while their enemies were strong and greatly exceeded them in military potential. On the other hand, China was still a semicolonial country, with a great variety of stages of social and technological development, and its huge size gave it numerous resources for revolution. Peasants in particular seemed ready to revolt and seize their land if they were given the opportunity. This chance should be given to them by a Communist army, which could survive its powerful enemies only if it enjoyed peasant support.

Mao and Chu Teh reached into the Chinese tradition of guerrilla war to formulate some simple aphorisms for the survival of their army:

> If the enemy advances, we retreat.
> If the enemy halts and encamps, we harass.
> If the enemy seeks to avoid battle, we attack.
> If the enemy retreats, we pursue.

But even this assumed local control over choice of military tactics, and it was some time before the orders from the Shanghai Central Committee (which could operate from the sanctuary of the International Settlement) and the Moscow Comintern could be sidestepped. Mao's conclusions about peasant support and the conditions of revolutionary survival had to go through much experimentation and experience before the right balance between radicalism and reformism in rural strategy was worked out. Radicalism could alienate small landholders, while reformism could fail to light the fuse of peasant anger for "revolutionary justice."

In 1929 Mao Tse-tung and Chu Teh moved from their mountain retreat to an area in south Kiangsi that centered on the town of Juichin. This they made the base of a Chinese Soviet Republic. After difficult fighting for several months, their forces probably numbered less than three thousand. While they were still in desperate straits, they received orders from Shanghai telling them that it would be better to divide their forces into small guerrilla bands that could do more harm to the enemy. Chu and Mao were both advised to leave the armies and asked to come to Shanghai to consult with Li Li-san, who had returned from Moscow to take over leadership of the Communist cause. Mao refused. While managing to seem to maintain discipline, he wrote to argue the need for a concentration of forces and the construction of a secure base. A rural setting, which had been the implicit target of the Shanghai directive, was, Mao argued, capable of revolutionary action so long as it was under proletarian (i.e., Communist) leadership.

In 1929 Mao's argument received further support. The Communist line shifted to one of optimism and insurrection. The American depression seemed to weaken world capitalism; Stalin's fiftieth birthday brought a chorus of adulation, and his personal enemies were removed and his political solutions pursued with single-minded fury. In north China, Chiang Kai-shek's trials with Yen Hsi-shan, Feng Yü-hsiang and Wang Ching-wei seemed to show the Kuomintang regime was falling apart. And so Li Li-san ordered a series of attacks to capture Kiangsi and Hunan. Mao, Chu, and their men went over to the attack. In the summer of 1930 they managed to take and hold the city of Changsha for a few days, but their forces proved inadequate to the task. Mao's first wife and his brother were among those sacrificed to the Kuomintang counterattack. Li Li-san was recalled to Moscow to face examination of the correctness of his instructions, and he did not return to China until 1945.

It was still four years before Mao would be in full control of Communist forces in China, but his rivals' errors increased the importance of his Kiangsi base. His immediate adversaries were a group of twenty-eight returned students from the Soviet Union who were accompanied by a Comintern agent, Mif, and who dominated the Shanghai Central Committee, where they worked closely with Chou En-lai. Mao decided that his most dangerous enemies were a group of Red Army officers who seemed to be betraying him. He charged them with cooperation with a Kuomintang undercover organization. In December 1930 a battalion revolted after he had ordered some arrests. In crushing this disaffection Mao probably took the lives of between two and three thousand officers and men. He now began to develop a personal machine of formidable dimensions. Outside his zone, politics continued to be volatile. In Shanghai enemies could fight by quiet denunciations to the Kuomintang, which struck with deadly strength. Suspected Communists were routinely killed. On at least one occasion the Communists struck back against such a defector by killing all the members of his extended family.

Throughout the countryside political and economic hardship made it possible for many forms of political banditry and opposition to survive. The Communists, with their organization and motivation, grew in power. Kuomintang defections were common. In November 1931 twenty thousand officers and men of the Twenty-eighth Route Army came over to the Communists. In November 1933 the Nineteenth Route Army, the same troops that had fought so well a year earlier against the Japanese at Shanghai, revolted against the Nanking government. On this occasion, Moscow's injunctions against cooperation with "bourgeois" reactionaries worked to discourage exploitation of the opportunity. Cautious agreements for military cooperation without political ties had no effect, for Nanking crushed the revolt in January.

The invasion of Hunan in which Mao Tse-tung's forces had taken part in 1930 failed, but it succeeded in arousing the alarm of Chiang Kai-shek. He now launched a series of "encirclement and extermination" campaigns against the Juichin Soviet. The first, conducted in the winter months of 1930–31, was aided by the revolt against Mao in December 1930. The Kuomintang sent about one hundred thousand men, and not its best, against the forty thousand men of the Red Army. Mao and Chu were able to pick off isolated units of the attacking force and capture a good deal of equipment. A few months later Chiang launched his second campaign, this time with close to two hundred thousand men who moved in seven columns by as many routes against the Juichin base. The Communists attacked these columns by turns, routed some, and captured large amounts of supplies. Chiang Kai-shek came to take charge of the third campaign in person. This time he brought his best troops, and his units were well on their way to Juichin when news came of the Japanese attack on Manchuria. The Kwantung Army's drive to save China from communism thus saved the Chinese Communists.

About this time the Central Committee of the Chinese Communist party decided to give up its uncertain existence under the eyes of Chinese and International Settlement police and join the other Communists at Juichin. Mao retained his position as chairman of the Central Executive Committee of the soviet, but for a time his initiative was sharply restricted by his new associates. Some of them deplored his peasant tactics as "guerrillaism" and advocated a sharper class line, with warfare from fixed positions in the conventional manner. During this period it becomes difficult to distinguish Mao's personal views. A new land law of November 1931 permitted "middle peasants" to retain their land, although it continued to emphasize the importance of mobilizing the countryside in order to increase agricultural production. Since Kuomintang armies blockaded the Kiangsi redoubt (and no foreigners penetrated that blockade), the importance of agricultural productivity was apparent to all. Where the Shanghai Communists had earlier viewed the Juichin base as secondary to the larger task of promoting revolution in the cities, they now, with nothing else left, attached extreme importance to maintaining its integrity. Mao seems to have lost much influence. A recent study by John Rue goes so far as to state that "as the summer of 1934 approached.... Mao was put on probation: he was excluded from party meetings and either imprisoned or kept under house arrest."

Meanwhile Chiang Kai-shek had returned to the attack with his fourth extermination campaign. It began with preliminary maneuvers in June 1932, and

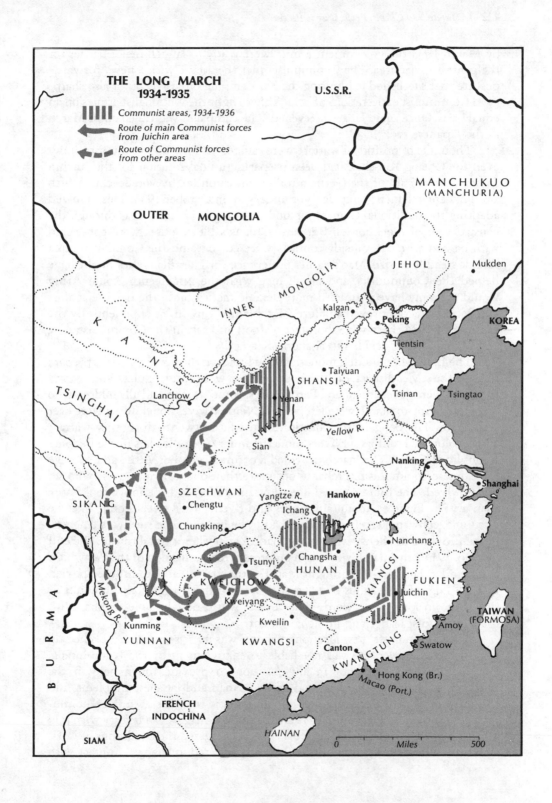

THE LONG MARCH
1934-1935

Communist areas, 1934-1936

Route of main Communist forces
from Juichin area

Route of Communist forces
from other areas

U.S.S.R.

MANCHUKUO
(MANCHURIA)

OUTER   MONGOLIA

Mukden

INNER   MONGOLIA   JEHOL

Kalgan

KANSU   Peking   KOREA

Tientsin

SHANSI

Taiyuan   Tsinan   Tsingtao

TSINGHAI   Lanchow   Yenan

SHENSI   Yellow R.

Sian   Nanking   Shanghai

SZECHWAN   Yangtze R.   Hankow

SIKANG   Chengtu   Ichang

Chungking   Nanchang

Changsha   HUNAN

Tsunyi   KIANGSI   FUKIEN

KWEICHOW   Juichin

Kweiyang   TAIWAN
(FORMOSA)

Mekong R.   Kweilin

Kunming   Amoy

YUNNAN   KWANGSI   Canton   Swatow

KWANGTUNG

BURMA   Hong Kong (Br.)
Macao (Port.)

FRENCH
INDOCHINA

SIAM   HAINAN   0   Miles   500

by March 1933 the government armies were ready to launch major battles for the central soviet area. The Communists met the attack with a new "forward" posture that succeeded in blunting the Kuomintang offensive, but it also sharpened Communist expectations of being able to fight the Nationalist armies on an equal basis. Once again Japan intervened. The campaign was called off in March as the Japanese took Jehol.

Thoughts of positional warfare were dangerous for the Communists, however, for Chiang Kai-shek had been preparing a final solution for the Juichin Soviet with the aid of the German military mission led by von Seeckt. A fifth and final encirclement campaign got underway in October 1933. This involved adapting the traditional Chinese method of strangling bandit areas through the construction of blockhouses. But now Chiang's blockhouses were connected with barbed wire. All outside contacts were cut off, and the Communist area shrank steadily in size. Mao's earlier preference for guerrilla tactics might have helped the Communists, and an alliance with the Nineteenth Route Army would certainly have permitted more flexible tactics. Since the defense against von Seeckt's tactics proved a failure, Mao blamed this on his opponents. By the summer of 1934 there were shortages of food and salt in the Communist area, and Mao and Chu decided to abandon Kiangsi.

The Long March found more than one hundred thousand partisans prepare to leave the soviet district. Eighty thousand men were army regulars, and twenty thousand were government and Party cadres. Some women and all children who were too young to march were left behind. Neither wives nor children were ever seen again. The Long March constitutes an epic in twentieth-century warfare and revolution. From its survivors came the inner core of leaders in the People's Republic of China. The march provided a cosmic legend of virtue and courage for Chinese communism. Probably not more than one in five of those who set out survived. The route covered five thousand miles, and the move took more than a year. Eighteen mountain ranges and twenty-four rivers, some, like the Tatu in Szechwan, fiercely defended, had to be crossed. The survivors emerged in the province of Shensi, where they made Yenan their capital toward the end of 1936. While the march was still in progress, a reorganization of the Party high command in January 1935 brought Mao Tse-tung to full and undisputed power. In 1936 Edgar Snow, in his *Red Star over China*, provided the classic account of the march in Mao's own words. The outside world now became familiar with the Communist leader and his achievement.

The Communists' new location in Shensi was more secure, for it backed up against Soviet power and was not liable to encirclement by the Kuomintang. But the Russians were not in any position to provide much help in the mid-1930s. They were hard-pressed with German and Japanese problems, and this influenced their decision to resume diplomatic relations with the Kuomintang government in December 1932 and to sign a nonaggression treaty with it in 1937. Thus, to a considerable degree Yenan perpetuated the conditions of isolation from which the Communists had already suffered in Kiangsi. Contact with the Chinese soviet had to be made through Kuomintang lines as before. Until the second united front of 1936 made entry through Kuomintang lines possible, Snow's was virtually the only account to reach the Western world. Dorothy Borg's survey of State Department reports of the Long March shows the tremendous range of confusion and the paucity of hard information that was available despite the extensive diplomatic service the United States then maintained in China.

The Communists had lost their Kiangsi base, their investment in land reform and in primitive industrial plants for the manufacture of war weapons. In Shensi they found themselves in a region less fertile and more forbidding. They had lost some fifty thousand soldiers in the course of their incredible year-long march. The fighting had been to Chiang Kai-shek's advantage in other ways as well. Much of it had been between the Communists and provincial warlord troops who fared poorly against the modern propaganda tactics of the Communists. The Nationalist armies which moved in pursuit of the Communists fastened Kuomintang rule on to large sectors of China that had been "centralized" only in the most tenuous sense. Thus while the Communists had escaped from one disaster, they still faced annihilation from Nationalist generals who now felt victory within their grasp. They were saved from that annihilation by their ability to marshal support for a national crusade against the Japanese aggressors.

COMMUNIST ARMY UNITS during the move to Yenan.

The united front followed by a decade the Communists' effort to work with the Kuomintang in the 1920s. But on that occasion they had joined the Kuomintang as individuals, to form a "bloc within." After their exclusion from the Kuomintang in 1927, they talked of their efforts to revolutionize the country against the Kuomintang as a "united front from below," but they got nowhere. Japanese aggression now provided the perfect opportunity to call for national unity.

The Manchurian incident of 1931 resulted in anti-Japanese boycotts in Shanghai. The Japanese undeclared war there in the spring of 1932 found them hard-pressed to overcome the Chinese Nineteenth Route Army. This was recognized as an opportunity in distant Juichin. The Chinese Soviet Republic, far from any Japanese, declared war against Japan in April 1932. At the time the Communists still considered the overthrow of the Kuomintang prerequisite to effective resistance against Japan. The next year, as the Japanese continued into Jehol, the Communists changed their line to indicate a willingness to cooperate with all forces against the Japanese provided the masses received arms "against Japan," attacks against soviet areas came to a halt, and "democratic rights" were granted by the Nationalist government.

Moscow was still not sure about this, as its own relations with Japan were involved. But communications were poor, and the details of the story continue to stir debate. At any rate the line was to change as the war came closer to home. The emergence of the Chinese Communists at Yenan now coincided with the Soviet Union's decision that all possible allies should be recruited for the protection of the Soviet Union against its fascist neighbors. In the summer of 1935 the Seventh Comintern Congress heard an important speech by Dimitrov, who called for all communist parties to "wipe fascism off the face of the earth" and asked them to cooperate in united fronts and even enter coalition governments if necessary to do this. No party needed the recognition and legalization that a united front could bring more than the Chinese Communist party. While still in Szechwan, on its way to Yenan, the Chinese Party indicated the need for all Chinese to unite to fight "Japanese imperialism and Chiang Kai-shek." By degrees they shifted to indicate a willingness to work with, and even under, Chiang Kai-shek in order to reach their goal. By the end of 1935 the Party had committed itself to a willingness to join in a government of national defense, and by March 1936 Mao Tse-tung made specific mention of willingness to extend "the hand of friendship" to Chiang Kai-shek if he "really means to take up the struggle against Japan."

The coincidence of this stand with Comintern directives was not immediately apparent, for it was squarely in line with the desires of most Chinese. As the Fukien revolt of the Nineteenth Route Army had shown, and as massive student demonstrations in December 1935 made clear, millions of Chinese were beginning to demand that internal bickering and civil war give way to a united resistance to Japan. Under the circumstances it was more difficult for Chiang Kai-shek to marshal support for a final effort against the Communist base at

Yenan. The Yenan leaders' nationalist propaganda was particularly effective with the troops of the Manchurian refugee Chang Hsüeh-liang which made up the front line units with which Chiang Kai-shek intended to crush the Communists.

So it was that in December 1936, when Chiang Kai-shek flew to Sian to take personal charge of what he hoped would be a final drive to crush Communist strength, he was instead kidnapped by Chang Hsüeh-liang. From Yenan came representatives of Mao Tse-tung, who persuaded Chang Hsüeh-liang not to harm Chiang and worked for his release. Any other course, they felt, would guarantee the full fury of Kuomintang military strength against the northwest, and it might even eventuate in a formidable coalition between Nanking and Japan to crush Chinese Communist strength.

The release of Chiang Kai-shek meant an end to the civil war that had continued without interruption since the break with the Communists. The Communists remained in secure control of the territory they held and promised to end armed uprisings and forcible land confiscations. Discussions got underway for a new political coalition. The Shensi Soviet would be a regional government, and the Red Army would be part of a Nanking-directed revolutionary army. This "political settlement" was to provide the lines of future competition, and all civil distrust was to be submerged in the coming crusade against the Japanese. Before these agreements were complete or mature, the Japanese military precipitated the Marco Polo Bridge incident in 1937. Shortly thereafter the Konoe government announced its refusal to deal with Chiang Kai-shek on grounds that the Kuomintang was communist tainted.

Nationalist political unification had thus been indirectly aided by the Communists, who provided the occasion for the Kuomintang to consolidate control in south and west China, and it was consummated by the Japanese, who drove the Communists into the Nationalist fold. In doing so, the Japanese saved the Communists from military destruction and provided them with the setting in which they could compete with the Kuomintang on favorable terms.

3. China at War

THE WAR with Japan that followed the Marco Polo Bridge incident of 7 July 1937 brought China the greatest national unity it had known since the fall of the dynasty in 1911. All groups united behind Chiang Kai-shek. A number of political groupings that contained respected national figures was organized to create the appearance of multiparty unity. The "National Salvation League," an amalgam of these groups, suggested through its name the enthusiasm of the time. But power, as Mao Tse-tung phrased it, came out of the barrel of a rifle in China, and the Kuomintang and the Communists were the only members of the multiparty coalition that had armies.

There was no doubt about Chiang's leadership of the whole country. His emergence from near-death at Sian to popularity after the outbreak of war gave him a larger-than-life appearance, and a new cult of the leader gave him national adulation. It was as though the national emergency had also proved his historic greatness. Chiang's puritanical devotion to his task, his Christian faith, his elegant and articulate wife, and their links to Sun Yat-sen made them perfect candidates for popularity in the West as well. International and national stature made it necessary to describe Chiang as a democrat. But he was neither democrat nor modern dictator. Chiang was a militarist. And there were still substantial limitations on his control over the armies of his allies.

The war opened with a determined defense of the Yangtze area by the Nationalist armies. Chiang committed his best units to the fighting around Shanghai and Nanking. Those cities cost the Japanese far more effort than they had expected, but Chiang's early successes tended to encourage him to modify his original plans to sacrifice space for time. As a result the attempt to defend China's principal cities cost the Chinese their best units and much of their modern equipment. But the Chinese armies were not destroyed, despite superior Japanese equipment and mobility. Atrocities, especially the horror in Nanking, unified Chinese determination to resist at the same time that they delayed and disorganized the Japanese advance. Nevertheless the retreats were disheartening for the Chinese. The mining of the Yellow River dikes in 1938 inundated a vast area and caused incalculable hardship and loss of life. Japanese armies advanced along communication routes. Hankow, and also Canton, which was taken from the sea, fell in 1938, and at the end of that year the national government moved its capital to Chungking in Szechwan. There it spent the balance of the war years.

The Nationalists' withdrawal to the west meant a new Long March. This time it was the flight of coastal, noncommunist, modern China, to a distant western province. Students, workers and entire families as well as soldiers marched west. Laden with books, machines and possessions, hundreds of thousands of refugees made their way to Szechwan to resume life in unfamiliar surroundings. Even more than the Long March of the Communists, this movement had the effect of unifying China. It made a national cause out of local disaster and further extended Kuomintang control to distant inland areas.

The national government's move left the Japanese in control of coastal China and the communication routes. They could move along them almost at will, but because of the distances involved and because of the misgivings of the Tokyo General Staff about excessive involvement in China, they never committed enough men to occupy and pacify the vast Chinese countryside adequately. Even so, there were over a million men on garrison duty in China. In the main, however, the Japanese thought that by cutting lines of communication and supply to Chungking they could bring the Kuomintang to surrender. A later Japanese advance to the south, occupation of Hanoi, then of Saigon, and finally of Burma, was expected to cut off the supply of essential materials to the

JAPANESE OCCUPATION OF CANTON, 1938.

Chinese. To paraphrase American concerns in Vietnam, the Japanese were preoccupied with cutting a "Chiang Kai-shek trail." One trail they never cut was a costly supply of Chungking by plane from India after the United States entered the war. This was a supply line run over the Himalayan-Tibetan "Hump." After the fall of Burma, Chinese units were moved to India for training and equipping, so that by 1945 Chiang Kai-shek had the makings of a modern army that had been trained and equipped in India, part of which retook the Burma route under the direction of General Joseph Stilwell. But the main Japanese armies in China were never defeated. When American air bases in south China seemed near completion for strikes on Japan in 1944 and 1945, the Japanese proved their ability to move and occupy whatever was essential to them.

In Szechwan the national government was cut off from its supporters in China's business, industrial and intellectual centers. Instead, it held a rich agricultural area that was little touched by the currents of modernization that had begun to alter China along the major communication routes. Fertile rice land, virtually the only form of wealth in the valley, became the basis of finance for a government that was now denied access to all customs and modern taxes. Landlord influence and rule had luxuriated in Szechwan. Peasants were taxed heavily, sometimes years in advance. This now became the base of Kuomintang power and had to support a swollen military establishment. It was assumed that all efforts at economic and political reform as specified in the Constitution would have to wait for a return to normal conditions. And since a beleaguered China lacked the wealth and strength to bring about a return to normality, it could only wait for the Japanese to tire or for allies to appear with help.

Thus the élan of 1937 and 1938 was not long sustained. Deprived of its income, the government relied upon the local land and excise taxes and meanwhile printed the money it needed. Industry was a hope of the future; what little there was was narrowly devoted to war purposes, necessarily directed by government and not accompanied by the kind of "middle class" or "liberal" influence that had obtained in the larger industrial centers of the coastal cities. The Japanese frontier was also destructive. Illicit trade with occupied and semioccupied areas could not be controlled during a half-decade and more of war. The Japanese looted where they would, and marauding expeditions were a constant danger. Bombing runs over Chungking itself were a regular and scheduled form of contempt.

The long military trial, seldom punctuated by decisive actions and almost never by victories, produced a gradual loss of mission and a sense of demoralization in western China. This was helped little by the steadily growing cult of Chiang Kai-shek as the savior of the nation as the effectiveness of his government was visibly diminished in all the ways his people could measure it. Rural injustice, arbitrary conscription practices and inadequate training and equipment oppressed the countryside. Intellectuals were harassed by secret police suspicious of subversion. All this combined to create a distaste for a government that had become more dictatorial and less efficient. Overhanging everything else was economic insecurity. Military expenditures grew constantly, but sources of income were fixed. A spiraling inflation destroyed confidence in the day-to-day management of affairs.

Within a short time a new competition with the Chinese Communist party became serious. For a brief period the united front produced cooperation. In September 1937 the Communists announced the abolition of their soviet government and of the Red Army. Everything was now part of the new national organization and all ideology subsumed under Sun Yat-sen's Three Principles. In the areas the Communists controlled (as in the Hopei-Chahar-Shansi "Border Government"), "democratic regimes" were set up in which the Communists limited themselves to one-third of the government posts. Programs of land confiscation were abandoned, and instead the Communists announced that they would enforce the rent limitation of 37.5 percent which the Kuomintang had legislated but never enforced. In the "democratic regimes" the noncommunist two-thirds of council members were chosen from "small peasants" and "patriotic landlords"; only the holdings of "pro-Japanese" and "die-hard" landlords were to be confiscated. Looking back, it is easy to see in this Mao Tsetung's later distinction between the "people" and "enemies of the people"; then, as later, the Communists provided the definitions for these terms. Nevertheless the Communist program and performance were skillfully oriented toward agrarian problems. Visitors to Communist areas came back persuaded of popular support and enthusiasm.

After Chiang's best units were damaged and destroyed in the Yangtze plain, the Chinese resistance behind the Japanese lines was limited to guerrilla activities. The Communists, with their experience of resistance to Nanking, were better prepared for this new competition. Their influence grew steadily in north China, and when they extended this to the Yangtze plain, which had always been the Kuomintang heartland, Chungking ordered the new communist Fourth Route Army to get out of the area. It did so reluctantly in 1941. As it moved north, open clashes between the Kuomintang and Communist units brought the hatred and distrust of the past decades to the surface again. There-after, the united front, though never repudiated in theory, lost most of its mean-ing. Nationalist armies expended much manpower and effort on blockading the Communist areas in north China

The Nationalist-Communist competition was not played out in a vacuum, for it was importantly affected by the policies of the Japanese during the war years. Japanese policies were often inconsistent, affected by the particular field armies involved and the importance central headquarters in Tokyo attached to the sector. In Manchuria the last Manchu emperor, Pu-yi, ruled as the Emperor Kang Te, representative of the "Kingly Way." He was surrounded by Chinese bureau heads who were directed by Japanese assistants and advisers. The head of the Kwantung Army was accredited as Japanese ambassador to the new state, and he also served as governor of the Kwantung leased territory. Manchuria was to become a "paradise of the five races." Japanese were encouraged to immigrate, but despite subsidies, relatively few Japanese farmers were willing to leave their familiar countryside for the more inhospitable climate of Manchuria. In-dustrialization was pushed by a series of five-year plans that were designed to make Manchuria a center of heavy industry for the New Order in East Asia. Communications, finance and the great dams over the Yalu represented a tre-mendous investment of Japanese capital to make Manchuria an industrial base. The Kwantung Army also sponsored a Mongolia Federal Autonomous Govern-ment, which was set up at Kalgan in 1937.

The North China Area Army, which had been set up partly to moderate the proconsular attitudes of the Kwantung Army, developed its own ambitions by sponsoring the Provisional Government of the Chinese Republic in Peking in December 1937. Most of its officials were well along in years. Many had been bureaucrats in Manchu days, and some had served in warlord governments friendly to Japan. Few were Western trained, and most were out of sympathy with the Nationalist republic. In Peking the Japanese emphasis was on Asian unity against communism. Mao Tse-tung's communist guerrillas were the chief focus of this propaganda, but at the same time the Kuomintang was excoriated for its cooperation with communism. Chiang Kai-shek and his government were also denounced as tools of Western imperialism. Propaganda emphasized the glories of traditional Chinese civilization and denounced the materialistic civilization of the West at the same time that it talked about the modernization of north China. A mass organization called the New People's Association tried to compete with Kuomintang influence. In areas under full Japanese control, impressive efforts for rural cooperatives, agricultural development, and education were launched; out of research efforts carried on in connection with these came some of the fullest and most detailed studies of the north Chinese countryside. Propaganda for modernization was limited to the benefits of agricultural reform. Contradictions were everywhere, perhaps nowhere more obviously than in the two principal slogans, "Build up the New Order!" and "Do not change the old family customs!" Since Peking's area of influence was limited to the zone of full Japanese control, it could not hope to dominate north China. In Hopei in 1939, for instance, Japanese garrisons could be found in only about 80 of 120 *hsien.*

The Peking government offered no solution for the pacification of China. Japan could not hope to garrison that vast country, and as preparations for the attack to the south developed and the Japanese army wanted itself free for this action, Tokyo sought some way of providing a true alternative to Chiang Kai-shek that would be able to compete with the growing Communist influence. The Japanese Central China Army tried to solve this with the establishment of the Restoration Government of Wang Ching-wei.

Wang had served with Chiang Kai-shek from 1932 to 1936 and had been close to Sun Yat-sen during the latter's closest cooperation with Japanese. In 1938 he was again named vice-president of the Kuomintang, but he found this

MANCHURIAN SHRINE. Shinto priests delivering the "spirit" for a new shrine in Harbin after the establishment of Manchoukuo. The combination of high-ranking army officers, modern transportation, and archaic ideology symbolizes some of the contradictions of the puppet state.

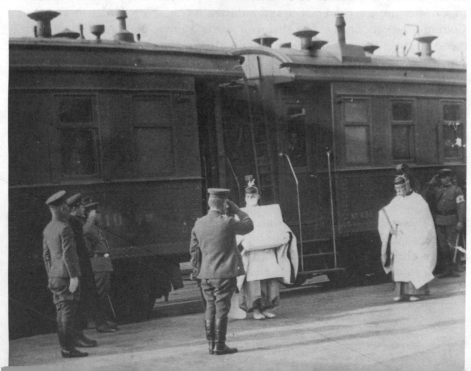

an empty honor. When the Japanese took Canton, which was Wang's chief center of influence, his apparent willingness to discuss "reasonable terms" with Tokyo seemed to commit him to a more conciliatory position than that of Chiang Kai-shek. Late in 1938 he flew to Hanoi with his family and several aides. Already before this, his representatives had been meeting with Japanese military representatives who were working zealously for a way out of the China quagmire. Japanese recognition was to be accompanied by Wang's break with Chiang; the military leaders of south China were to compromise with Japan without seeming to violate Chinese nationalism. But provisional arrangements were not finalized, and Prince Konoe's government did not keep its word. Tokyo was afraid of an embarrassing doublecross and was suspicious that someone as distinguished as Wang was merely using it for propaganda purposes. In Chungking, Chiang Kai-shek was doing his best to get Wang to come back. Tokyo retained its doubts about Wang's willingness to work with Japan and cherished some hope of bringing Chiang himself to terms. Chiang declared that Wang was a patriot "whose devotion and dedication to the cause of the party, the nation, and the war have been unexceptionable." As for Wang, his advisers were not united, and he wavered between trusting his Japanese contacts and doubting their ability to deliver on their promises. In Japan things were no clearer. Konoe gave way to Hiranuma, and Tokyo held off with a commitment.

In March 1939 a Chinese assassin narrowly missed killing Wang Ching-wei. The Japanese now became convinced that their man was approachable, and secret agreements brought Wang to Shanghai. Step by step he compromised his position. Tired and discouraged, he found the Japanese negotiators unable to deliver the promises from the military they had held out to him. Gradually he surrendered more and more of the points that were essential to his being able to provide an effective alternative to the Kuomintang. Wang did not become the candidate of the army headquarters until the alternatives to him were removed. After the death of the north Chinese warlord Wu P'ei-fu, who was the North China Army's preference, and after it was clear that Chungking would not surrender, Wang was installed as president of a new National Government of China at Nanking on 30 March 1940.

The Nanking government was managed by a group of Kuomintang members who were opposed to Chiang Kai-shek. Like Wang, they saw no possibility of defeating the Japanese and feared the revival of the Chinese Communists. Japanese propaganda of Asian solidarity against imperialism and communism was attractive and reasonable to them, and the prospects of peace that it brought gave some hope for a Chinese future. It was a prospect that could combine much of modern Chinese nationalism, itself anti-Western imperialist, with the legacy of Sun Yat-sen who had often, in a phrase selected by Wang Ching-wei as title for a volume of Sun's lectures, described Japan and China as "Natural Friends, Unnatural Enemies."

Despite this, the Nanking government of Wang Ching-wei had little appeal for Chinese nationalism. Wang had sacrificed too many points to the Japanese, and the Japanese military was too insensitive to Chinese pride for them to work effectively with Nanking. It was not a national government, as it styled itself, for the North China Army never trusted it in its area. Wang reluctantly agreed to virtual autonomy for north China, and he himself did not even make an official visit to Peking until October 1942. His realm was thus that of the Yangtze Valley and south China. Throughout this area the Japanese military was omnipresent and so were Japanese carpetbaggers. A civilian army of adventurers, peddlers, underworld profiteers and corporate concessionaires seized every opportunity for profit. According to Japanese estimates, there were ten times as many Japanese in China in 1944 as there had been in 1937. Furthermore, Japanese conscription of laborers (in "Self-Sacrifice Corps") and Japan's interpretation of its unrestricted rights to station troops and exploit resources "to effect joint anti-Communist defense" (in the language of the basic document outlining relations with Nanking) combined to make it clear that Wang Ching-wei's attempted solution to the Japanese advance was no solution at all.

As the Pacific war advanced and the Japanese found themselves having to adjust to the problem of Asian nationalism in other countries they had occupied, Nanking was treated with a little more dignity. Japan stationed a civilian ambassador there, and when the Western allies demonstratively gave up their extraterritorial rights in China, the Japanese did so too. The Japanese price for their declaration was a Nanking declaration of war on Great Britain and America. By then it was too late to raise the prestige of Nanking sufficiently to provide a political alternative to Chungking, however, for the Kuomintang now had powerful allies.

Japan's policies encouraged cynicism and distrust. It had sponsored a rival Kuomintang in Nanking with appeals for Chinese nationalism. In Peking it worked out a vague combination of republicanism with cultural obscurantism. In Manchoukuo progressive economic policies were combined with monarchy and talk of the "Kingly Way." Meanwhile, under the guise of communist suppression, it created intolerable conditions of life in north China.

The most important result of the Japanese presence in China was probably the way it strengthened and extended the influence of the Chinese Communists. Japanese control was relatively superficial and limited to the main population and communication centers. Between these, strings of small blockhouses, often equipped with primitive communication methods (a pile of burning straw often alerted the next blockhouse to a guerrilla attack) defined the Japanese presence throughout the countryside. Nights belonged to the Chinese local corps. The Communists had the best training and experience for operating under such conditions. Chungking authorities consequently were alarmed by their spread and inclined to leave the Japanese to the Americans while they prepared for a future struggle with the Communists. Communists drilled their soldiers carefully in tactics of cooperation with peasants, and Japanese reports agreed that the Communists treated villagers well. When (later foreign minister) Ch'en Yi's Fourth Route Army moved into Kiangsu in 1940, a Japanese report had it that "because of their strict observance of military discipline, the masses welcomed them fully. They did not requisition coolies and showed kindness to the masses." The Red

Army was indoctrinated in the need to avoid brutality, expropriation and theft. Its behavior was usually in decided contrast to what the commoners had come to expect of their own, not to speak of the Japanese, armies.

The Japanese advance served the Communists in many ways. From the first, the Communists had led in the demands for an all-out stand against the Japanese, a position giving the Kuomintang a choice between sacrificing its frontline units or sacrificing its standing with patriotic groups. In 1940, when peace sentiment seemed strong, the Communists exerted a powerful influence to keep the war going. Communist military strength was estimated at five hundred thousand at the end of the Pacific war. This was no ordinary guerrilla band. When the occasion seemed to require it, as in a great offensive in 1940, the Communists were capable of frontal attacks. But, on the whole, they preferred to conserve scarce material and to incite, rather than to attack, the Japanese, for they recognized in Japanese fury the best way to keep the war going.

Japanese efforts to crush the elusive Communist guerrilla organizations resulted in tactics of organized terrorism that drove the natural elite from the countryside and guaranteed the loyalties of those who remained to leaders of local resistance. As far as the Japanese army was concerned, Communists were "bandits," and the army took few prisoners. In futile efforts to cleanse the countryside of communist influence, the Japanese mounted great "pacification drives" that brought the war—and nationalism—home to the most unpolitical of peasants. Under General Okamura Yasuji, one of the charter members of the "reform" group of military in Japan in the 1920s, a scorched-earth policy that the Chinese Communists charged was designed to "kill everything, burn everything, destroy everything" resulted in massive, murderous and destructive *schrecklichkeit* in the manner advocated by German military leaders. An area so "purged" became a desert without houses or animals, and its able-bodied males were removed or killed. Such tactics drove large areas of the Chinese countryside into war and revolution. Japanese terror had a thoroughness quite different from the more haphazard atrocities of warlord armies. And since it was perpetrated by foreigners, the activation of a strong nationalist response was an inevitable result.

Chinese nationalism was thus stimulated by the Japanese. Popular outrage had been encouraged, though not always effectively, by earlier years of student protest and warning. As early as 1936, Peking students toured the countryside with simple antiforeign exhortations:

> Men, women, children! Listen to what we say: we have seen those things flying overhead every day. Those things are called "airplanes." Sitting in them are the devils of the East Sea, the Japanese devils. They speak a foreign tongue, live in the Eastern Sea, and fly their airplanes over here! Do you know what they are coming to do? ... They are coming to kill every single man and woman with their guns and knives, and to ravish our daughters and wives....[1]

---

[1] John Israel, *Student Nationalism in China, 1927–1937* (Stanford: Stanford University Press, 1966), p. 135.

For many Chinese the direct experience of Japanese occupation gave substance to these warnings during the years that followed. "As a general rule," Chalmers Johnson concludes, "the Communists were not able to establish guerrilla bases in regions that had had no direct experience with the Japanese Army." Where the Japanese "pacified," traditional elites fled. Thereafter Japanese propaganda attacked the Nationalists as corrupt opportunists and the Communists as Russian agents. But the Japanese failed to create a government or a movement with a genuine nationalist appeal. They overextended themselves and tended to drive out the Kuomintang and leave the area open for the Communists. A Communist victory was not necessarily assured by this. Kuomintang guerrillas could also have moved in, and in some areas, notably Shantung, they did so. But the fierceness of the Japanese focus upon Communist "bandits" had disturbing reminders of the Kuomintang "annihilation campaigns" of an earlier day. Thus the Nationalist-Communist clashes of 1938–40 in north and central China were, as the same author suggests, "the first skirmishes of the 1947–49 civil war."

4. The Communist Victory

IN THE THREE SHORT years between 1945 and 1948, Chiang Kai-shek and the Kuomintang experienced total victory and total defeat. The Japanese invader was driven from China, but the toasts of that celebration had scarcely been put down before the glasses were packed for flight to Taiwan. Historians have been able to argue that the victory had not been Chiang's as much as it had been America's and that the Kuomintang's position was far from secure at the war's end. Yet the change came with shattering suddenness for Moscow and Washington as well as Nanking. The involvement of the Allied powers, and especially of the United States, in those events provided the material for accusation and recrimination at home and abroad. The replacement of the Chinese ally of World War II with the Chinese enemy of the Korean War of 1950 produced a climate of doubt and distrust that distorted American life and politics for more than a decade.

The removal of Japan from China brought the Kuomintang-Communist competition to the forefront. The united front had fared poorly during the increasing acrimony that characterized Chinese politics after the new Fourth Route Army clash of 1941. Even before that Chiang Kai-shek had devoted a significant part of his strength in efforts to isolate the Communist areas, and by 1943 American representatives estimated that as many as four hundred thousand Kuomintang troops were involved in the blockade of the principal areas of Communist power. The Communist armed strength in the areas under blockade was variously estimated, but it constituted at least a half million men. In addition to serving as targets of the Nationalist blockade, these forces were also a principal focus of the Japanese North China Army's tactics, and they were the chief target of the ferocious tactics of General Okamura. These pressures combined to rule out military adventurism on the part of the Communists. Instead, they tended to combine political with military moderation. Every effort was made to develop tactics that would appeal to the peasantry. Twin issues of nationalism and well-being, with an anti-Japanese and agrarian emphasis, served as the core of the "mass line" which, Mao Tse-tung insisted, was essential to survival for a party and army dependent upon popular approval. Peasants provided intelligence and recruits that made it possible to compensate for the numerical and technological disadvantages under which the Communists fought. "By arousing the mass of the population and organizing them into a common united front," Professor Johnson argues, "the party obtained decisive advantages over its opponent in intelligence, recruitment, mobility, morale, and capacity for superior concentration in any pitched battle. Without the mass line, there could be no 'people's war.' ..."

The political expression of the "mass line" was Mao Tse-tung's important booklet, *On the New Democracy.* Issued in 1940, this analyzed Chinese society as containing colonial, semicolonial and semifeudal elements. A communist revolution therefore had to begin with a bourgeois-democratic stage, and only after that would it be possible to go on to a socialist revolution. And since

CAPTURE OF PU-YI. The Emperor of Manchoukuo, escorted by Soviet officers after Russia entered the Pacific War in August 1945.

wartime China was still in the first stage, democratic reforms and moderate measures were in order. Communist economic policies in the areas they controlled were not revolutionary. At that stage of China's development, the (Yenan) *Liberation Daily* explained in 1942, it was improper "to wipe out once and for all the system of feudal exploitation.... If it did, the support of the enlightened gentry might be alienated. Radical land confiscation without compensation is to be used only in dealing with Chinese traitors to the war of resistance.... Moreover, the capitalistic mode of production is still an advanced form of production for China at this stage of development." Support of the middle classes was essential to the war, and nothing was to be done to alienate it.

As a result, as Johnson puts it, "The peasants [in Communist areas] supported an agrarian policy designed to further the war effort and, with the exception of landlords and rich peasants, they profited from it." The "mass line" combined nationalism and economic improvement. And it worked. By 1945, as the same author shows, the Communists controlled six guerrilla bases in north China, ten in central, and two in south China, and thus controlled a vast area with a population of 160 million. A number of observers who were aware of the hostility that persisted between Communists and Nationalists were impressed by the evidence of popular support for the Communist government in the areas it controlled and thought that the future belonged to Yenan. By the end of 1944 State Department representatives reported that "the Chinese Communists are so strong between the Great Wall and Yangtze that they can now look forward to the postwar control of at least North China" and predicted that "power in China is on the verge of shifting from Chiang to the Communists."

These reports proved accurate. But they did not produce the alarm they might have because there was a good deal of disagreement about the nature of the Communist program. Surface examination of the Communist areas, with their "mixed program" and "mass line," convinced some that the Chinese Communists were not communist at all. As Ambassador Patrick Hurley put it, "Now when I go up into the Communist area of China ... I find the stores open, the stock market open, the highest bidder getting the property, money being exchanged, the profit motive in operation. Now, when anybody tells me that this is communism, I know that they are mistaken." A number of journalists were quite prepared to accept the dismissal of the Yenan system by Stalin, who told Ambassador Harriman that the Chinese Communists were "margarine communists," colored on the outside only. Ambassador Hurley thought them "democratic" but also weak. Others thought them strong and popular. There seemed reason to consider ways of getting the Communists to work with their Nationalist competitors. In view of the growing Soviet involvement in the Far East, it was important to avoid involvement in ideological disputes that could disrupt the larger pattern of Allied unity. It was assumed that the Chinese people were tired of ideology and war and anxious to work toward a peaceful settlement of political differences.

These expectations failed for a number of reasons. The first was that neither leadership group in China was tired of ideology or war; each was confident of its ability to gain a clear military decision. The Communists had grown through an advocacy of democracy and moderation, but their leaders were aware that these were tactical measures and not ultimate goals. In 1942 Mao Tse-tung had taken steps to tighten his personal and intellectual control over a party whose rapid growth was beginning to furnish cause for concern about its direction. His "rectification," or *cheng-feng* campaign, built Mao up as a major authority in ideology. It strengthened unity and discipline and stressed the importance of adapting Marxism to Chinese conditions. Mao charged that his enemies in the hierarchy were ignorant of the Party's development and experience and that they parroted Marxist phrases like rote learning. "A Communist is a Marxist internationalist," he wrote, "but Marxism must take on a national form before it can be applied. . . . We must discard our dogmatism and replace it by a new and vital Chinese style and manner, pleasing to the eye and to the ear of the Chinese common people." Mao warned about the errors of Confucianism, which ignored practice, and of empiricism, which he claimed hindered unity, and he called for criticism and self-criticism to eliminate all tendencies to deviate from a central line. Equipped with a political instrument responsive to his will, he was then prepared for the larger struggle. United front and political moderation were never, in his eyes, more than steps in a long-range revolutionary war that was to transform Chinese society.

The war years also brought a new ideological emphasis to the leadership of the Kuomintang. In 1943 Chiang Kai-shek, in *China's Destiny,* produced his own textbook for officials and people. He proposed Confucian universal harmony as an antidote to the class struggle. By invoking traditional virtues, as he had in the earlier New Life movement, he tried to counter both communism and liberalism. The two were equally foreign to Chinese tradition and needs, he wrote; one was drawn from Russian and the other from Anglo-American theories. Foreign aggression, greed, materialism and ideology had been responsible for most of China's ills, and it would be necessary to return to the native tradition.

In this clumsy rejection of outside influence, Chiang left much leeway for his Communist enemies, who were thereafter able to drape themselves in liberal colors. "The work which we Communists are carrying on today," *Liberation Daily* proclaimed in 1944, "is the very same work which was carried on earlier in America by Washington, Jefferson, and Lincoln; it will certainly obtain, and indeed has already obtained, the sympathy of democratic America." Yet the Communists never sought to deny or obscure their socialist goals, and most of the roseate colors in which their "democratic aspirations" were drawn were the work of superficial journalists who believed with Henry Wallace on his trip to China in 1944, that since Communists and Nationalists were all Chinese they must be basically friends and that "nothing should be final between friends." The trouble, was, of course, that these "friends" had been shooting at each other intermittently since 1927. The differences between them were personal, principled and deep.

American efforts to mediate and integrate in China began well before the Japanese surrender. They were based on a narrow view of the overriding importance of defeating the Japanese armies at the earliest possible moment and had little tolerance for the political considerations the Chinese brought to that struggle. Chiang Kai-shek, on the other hand, attached prior importance to his own retention of control. His view of control and loyalty was old-fashioned and parochial, but he proved himself a skillful and stubborn negotiator.

It began with the mission of General Joseph Stilwell to China. Stilwell proposed discharging inefficient Nationalist military commanders and training and equipping a core of thirty divisions for a campaign for the recovery of Burma in order to reopen an overland communications and supply route. Chiang needed no persuasion as to the desirability of a modern army, but one that was built upon impersonal criteria of efficiency would pose a threat to the pattern of Whampoa loyalties and personal relations that guaranteed his survival. He felt that he had better use for his own troops in China than in Burma, and he would not agree to the Burma campaign without assurance of greater American support than Stilwell could deliver. Chiang preferred that the American assistance be funneled into a greater tonnage of supplies over the Hump to support an air effort, and he enthusiastically supported General Chennault's proposals for air support and bombing bases against Japan.

Because the success of the Pacific campaigns against Japan was rapidly giving the China theater a lower priority in the war effort, President Roosevelt compensated by giving the China theater air support through Chennault. Out of this came security for Chungking and other Nationalist cities from Japanese bombers. In addition, a number of bases for American B-29's were built. These proved poorly suited to their purpose because of their dependence on supplies airlifted from India. They stung the Japanese into a series of land campaigns that proved the vulnerability of the Nationalist armies. The "East China campaigns" of 1943 were disastrous setbacks for China. As the evidence of failure mounted and when the Japanese drive was at its height, the United States government made a determined attempt to implement its program by demanding that Stilwell be named full field commander of Chinese forces. Stilwell demanded guarantees of autonomy that had grown out of his experience of obstruction by Chiang Kai-shek. "The Generalissimo," he insisted, "must refrain from any interference in operations." Instead of agreeing, Chiang demanded the recall of Stilwell. His gamble succeeded. Washington agreed and replaced him by General Wedemeyer without insisting on any of the demands raised by Stilwell.

Debate still surrounds this issue. No doubt the prickly personality of Stilwell, who referred to Chiang in his diary as "Peanut," made it unlikely that he could work effectively with the Chinese leader. Chiang must frequently have contrasted the earthy American infantryman to the austere General Staff products von Seeckt and von Falkenhausen with whom he had worked earlier.

No doubt also the American inability to come through with promises of support given in euphoric moments contributed to a guilt complex skillfully played upon by the Chinese Nationalists. The growing ties of the Kuomintang leaders with elements on the American political scene may also have been a consideration for the sensitive political radar of Franklin Roosevelt.

Still, it is difficult to avoid the impression that the American willingness to give up on the maximum program for an effective mainland force derived from a military decision, cemented by the loss of China's B-29 bases to Japanese armies, that China was after all less useful than the islands that had been taken from the Japanese. The war could be won by bypassing the China area altogether, and this altered the urgency of building a strong Chinese military force. Thereafter the main problem was to keep China from being the occasion of a rift in larger plans.

This became more urgent with the return of Russian power to East Asia. The Russians had been content to rebuff Kwantung Army border forays and keep to their part of the 1941 Non-Aggression Treaty with Japan. In March 1944 a supplemental agreement with Japan resolved questions of mining rights in north Sakhalin and fishing in Siberian waters. As the Nationalist armies tightened their blockade of Communist areas and retreated before the Japanese assaults on Chennault's air bases, however, the Russians hardened their line toward Chiang Kai-shek and refused American requests for a land route through Turkestan to supply the China theater. From the American point of view it now seemed urgent to improve Nationalist-Communist cooperation. One of the items in the showdown between Chiang Kai-shek and Stilwell was the latter's desire to provide American equipment for Communist forces so that they could make a more useful contribution to the war effort. Similarly, the Wallace mission of 1944 had as parallel aims the encouragement of a larger military effort by China and the improvement of Sino-Soviet relations.

As the Nazi defeat neared, American planners grew eager to increase and define the Russian contribution to the war against Japan. The Yalta Conference of February 1945 succeeded in eliciting a Russian pledge to enter the war. American authorities felt that a return of Russian power to Northeast Asia was in any case inevitable upon the collapse of Japan. They also credited Japan with great strength in the Kwantung Army and were anxious that Russia define her purposes in advance. If such purposes were then ratified by the Chungking government, there would be less likelihood of an open-ended expectation of Soviet help on the part of Yenan. Out of this came Stalin's assurance that the Soviet Union would enter into the war against Japan in two or three months after the German surrender, on condition that: Outer Mongolia would retain its autonomy (from China) and maintain its status quo (as Russian satellite) and that the "former rights of Russia violated by the treacherous attack of Japan in 1904" should be restored (south Sakhalin returned, Dairen internationalized under agreement of preeminent Russian interest, Port Arthur made a Russian naval base, joint Sino-Soviet administration established for the Chinese Eastern

MAO TSE-TUNG AND CHU TEH reviewing troops at Yenan in October 1944.

and South Manchuria Railroads, with recognition of the "preeminent interests" of the Russians, and surrender of the Kurile Islands to the Soviet Union). Since the arrangements for Mongolia and Manchuria would require Chinese concurrence, President Roosevelt was to "take measures in order to obtain this concurrence, on advice from Marshal Stalin." The USSR expressed its readiness to enter into a treaty of alliance and friendship with Kuomintang China, but its interests were in any case protected by agreement that "these claims of the Soviet Union shall be unquestionably fulfilled after Japan has been defeated."

Yalta does not represent a proud page in American statecraft. The agreement was kept secret, even from the Chinese, until such time as Stalin should "advise" the president to inform them. The same secrecy permitted the Russians to encourage the Japanese in their hope for Russian mediation for surrender, unaware that the latter had already agreed to attack them, presumably in retaliation for a "treacherous attack" in 1904. If more irony was needed, it was provided by the consideration with which American representatives worked out for their conscientious Russian allies an excuse for violating their Non-Aggression Treaty with Japan, which had until April 1946 to run. The device suggested was the invocation of the United Nations Charter (which had not yet been ratified) and the Moscow Declaration of 1943. And for those tolerant of further irony, Count 17 of the indictment of Japanese War Criminals at the International Military Tribunal for the Far East charged that the accused "between the

1st January 1928 and the 2nd September 1945, planned and prepared a war of aggression and a war in violation of international law, treaties, agreements, and assurances, against the Union of Soviet Socialist Republics."

The Yalta Agreement can be defended only as an attempt to define and contain Soviet gains which the United States was in no position to resist or restrain by force. As a quiet handover of Chinese rights so soon after ostentatious renunciation of imperialist grants in 1943, it deserves little respect, and in the secrecy with which it was kept from the Chinese it emphatically repudiated Washington's oft-repeated insistence that China was a "great power." As a recognition of political and military realities, it has been compared by Professor Tang Tsou to the Root-Takahira and Lansing-Ishii agreements of earlier days. As at those times, the American insistence on the Open Door and territorial integrity of China did not prevent the recognition of preeminent interests derived from contiguity. It is also true that the Russian failure to abide by even the Yalta agreements and products, notably the treaty that was signed with Chiang Kai-shek in 1945, and the advantages of the Japanese arms which the Russians provided Communist forces in Manchuria, made it easy to blame on "Yalta" evils that were not included in that mixed bag of errors. But most basic were the two shortcomings which Professor Tsou discerns in Yalta: it was intended to support the policy of peaceful unification, "which had no basis in Chinese politics," and the United States was unable and unwilling to use its ground forces to establish a "structure of power within which the Yalta Agreement might have found its place. As a result of errors of omission and commission, communist power gradually became dominant on the continent, leaving the United States in control of the island perimeter and the skies above."

Efforts for political unification began in 1944 when Ambassador Hurley proposed the integration of the Communist and Nationalist armies. A Coalition National Government would then preside over a National Military Council. This was unacceptable to the Nationalist government, however, which felt that coalition government would lead to certain defeat. Since the Hurley program seemed to tie coalition to democratic governmental reforms, no progress was made despite an energetic courtship of Chiang Kai-shek by Hurley and Chou En-lai, who came to Chungking to represent the Communists in the negotiations.

Matters were stalled on this point when the Japanese surrender forced a rapid acceleration. To anticipate Communist acceptance of Japanese surrender in north China and consequent access to Japanese arms, the United States transported half a million Nationalist soldiers by sea and air to north and central China. In the Tientsin-Peking area, American marines landed with the same purpose. The Russians had already occupied Manchuria, and in line with the treaty they had signed with Chungking in August they promised to time their departure with Nationalist arrival.

Contradictions were numerous. In some areas Japanese troops were asked to hold their positions pending Nationalist arrival. In Manchuria the Russians accepted a Nationalist request that they stay on and then ended by turning over to the Chinese Communists the stores of Japanese equipment which had fallen into their hands. Communist strength in Manchuria then grew rapidly and combined with Russian resistance to rule out for a time the entry of Nationalist troops. The fighting that led to full-scale civil war was to begin in Manchuria, and this violation of the Russian obligations to Chiang Kai-shek can be considered a more important advantage to the Communist cause than the formal arrangements worked out at Yalta.

As the situation deteriorated, President Truman asked America's most prestigious officer, General George C. Marshall, to go to China in December 1945 to work toward a political settlement of Chinese problems. His aim was to work out a coalition government under which Chinese armies would be merged and reduced in size. After this a viable economy could be worked out with American aid. American planners were aware of the dangers inherent in a coalition government but foresaw a Nationalist defeat in the civil war that loomed ahead. Armies that were retrained and reequipped would, they hoped, no longer "belong" to either party to the Chinese dispute. A situation in which military competition was replaced by political competition would stimulate the Kuomintang to make the reforms necessary for popular support. Out of this, it was hoped, would come a "strong, democratic, and united China."

In January 1946 Marshall got both parties to agree to a cease-fire. Planning was begun for a coalition government. A month later, agreement was reached on a military merger. A Political Consultative Conference worked out agreements under which both sides would hold the areas they had occupied. Three-man truce teams (one an American officer) would supervise and prevent infractions of the peace. A time chart was worked out for the development of the third stage that had been anticipated for Kuomintang government, from "tutelage" to "democracy" through an elected parliament. Marshall returned to Washington for consultation in March. By the time he returned to China in April, fighting had broken out.

Manchuria proved the touchstone. It was not included within the truce arrangements, and although ratios of Nationalist and Communist troops to be stationed there had been worked out, the Nationalist units had not yet arrived. Nationalist units had to fight their way in. Marshall and other American advisers did their best to dissuade the Nationalist high command from trying to force its way into Manchuria, but the Kuomintang leaders were insistent on regaining the areas whose loss had led to fifteen years of fighting with Japan. Important sectors of the Nationalist leadership were in any case very distrustful of agreements with the Communists. Hardliners were also to be found on the Yenan side. A policy of peaceful unification proved to have no practical basis in Chinese politics.

The Nationalists began the civil war far better armed and equipped than their rivals. They had about three million men, and the Communists had perhaps one-third as many. The Nationalists were also confident that their

American allies would back them if things went badly, and they greatly over-estimated the commitment of the American government to their cause. Marshall was determined to prevent any addition of arms to the Chinese arsenal that might encourage a commitment to a military solution. Early Nationalist successes in taking cities led to overextended lines of communications in which the Nationalist units fell heir to the role of the Japanese garrison troops, maintaining themselves against a countryside controlled by the Communists. Beginning with the arms seized in Manchuria, and augmented by stores captured from Nationalist units, the Communists grew in power as the Nationalists declined. By the middle of 1947, after a year of civil war, the Nationalists outnumbered the Communists by only two to one. Mao announced that if destruction of enemy forces continued the Communists would have the advantage within a year. In October 1948 the Nationalist armies in Manchuria, cut off from supplies, were forced to surrender. Now Chiang's best troops, the bulk of the thirty-nine divisions that were in the process of being retrained and equipped by American advisers at the time of the Japanese surrender, were lost. By the last half of 1948 the Communists were the stronger.

The civil war was no guerrilla victory but centered on three great confrontations. At Tsinan, in September 1948, the defection of an entire division helped the Communists enter a strongly fortified city. The Manchurian units, which gave up the following month, had held doggedly to a defense of fixed points, permitting the Communists to attack them one by one. The greatest battle and defeat of all came at the river Huai in November and December. Chiang Kai-shek committed one-quarter of the two hundred divisions he had left to form a strong point. By mid-November 340,000 Nationalists had been cut off and encircled, and before the battle ended the Nationalists had lost 550,000 men, of whom the Communists claimed 327,000 had surrendered. In each case, Chiang acted against the advice of his staff. In each case he trusted his old Whampoa associates by placing personal loyalty above efficiency and ability. By late 1948 the war had been lost militarily, and Chiang Kai-shek was diverting such supplies as came in to Taiwan, leaving his associates to struggle on without supplies or hope.

In this setting China's American ally saw little prospect of helping. Economic and medical supplies were made available in a short-range emergency program. Marshall, who left China permanently in January 1947, became secretary of state. He now instituted an embargo of combat equipment, one that was soon modified to permit transfer to China of "noncombat" military supplies. By 1948 American experience with the Soviet Union had altered the context of thinking to some degree. Political criticism grew. The China picture was more dismal than ever before. The coalition program was officially buried, and the Communists were held in "open rebellion" against the government. President Truman wanted it known that "we did not want any Communists in the Government of China or anywhere else if we could help it." The administration was willing to make an additional investment in the Chinese cause if only because it was necessary to bargain for congressional support for Marshall Plan outlays in Western Europe. The China Aid Act of April 1948 provided a fund of $125 million for the purchase of military materials and $275 million for economic aid. But bureaucratic delays on both sides meant that only a fraction of this was spent during the Nationalist campaigns on the mainland. Most of it was diverted to Taiwan.

To many Chinese, American aid, coming as it did at the eleventh hour, seemed to prolong the civil war without giving any promise of affecting its outcome. Increasing popular, especially urban and student, dissatisfaction with the Kuomintang extended to its American allies, and in 1948 China was swept by anti-American demonstrations. There was every reason for popular discontent. The economic collapse produced by the Communist ability to prevent operation of communications and industry and the inflation spawned by Nationalist military spending had bankrupted the middle classes. At one extreme, says John Fairbank, prices "doubled 67 times between January 1946 and August 1948 and then rose 85,000 times in six months." Much industry reclaimed from Japanese management ended under the control of the semigovernmental agencies that had been established in wartime Chungking. As a result that private enterprise, formerly the Kuomintang's chief support, now found itself stifled by bureaucratic controls and competition.

The Communists took Tientsin and Peking in January 1949. By fall they were in control of Canton and Chungking. The remnants of the Nationalist armies and leaders moved to Taiwan. In October the Communists proclaimed the establishment of the People's Republic of China and changed the ancient capital's name from the city of "Northern Peace" (Peiping) back to "Northern Capital" (Peking).

There were few who were prepared to predict a very long life for the regime that had been set up on Taiwan. Upon its reclamation from the Japanese, the island had been brutally mistreated and exploited by the Nationalist armies. When a protest was organized by leading Taiwanese, the armies of General Chen Yi reacted so savagely that estimates of people killed ran as high as ten thousand. But when, in December of 1949, Taiwan became the main, in fact only, base of the Nationalist government, the quality of leadership improved. About a million civilians and more than a half million troops, relatively well supplied and financed thanks to the China Aid Act, arrived. Chiang Kai-shek, who had resigned in January, resumed the office of president in the spring of 1950. Within months the Korean War gave his regime a new lease on life.

The collapse of American hopes for a friendly China produced a setting of recrimination in which sober consideration of the causes of the Nationalist collapse on the mainland was set back for many years. The United States's growing confrontation with the Soviet Union had now been compounded by the hostility of the new regime in China. American diplomats who remained at their posts to experiment with the attitudes of China's new leaders were treated with harsh disrespect. At home political opportunists rallied behind the leadership of

Senator Joseph McCarthy to charge that subversives within the American government had operated to prevent the extension of timely help that could have swung the civil war against the Communists. They gradually succeeded in securing the exodus from positions of influence and, often, employment of leading China specialists in the Department of State.

After the cold war began to thaw two decades later, some observers reacted to the unfairness of these charges by reversing the judgments of history on which they were based. It was now possible to argue that ideological rigidity and political timidity had cost the United States the opportunity to make friends of the leaders of the new China. In 1972 documentation came to light showing that Mao Tse-tung and Chou En-lai had offered to come to Washington to discuss matters with President Roosevelt in January 1945. Historians speculated on what might have been the course of events if these giants of the postwar world had established direct relations with Washington well before the Japanese defeat. Conceivably, one wrote, this form of American recognition might have speeded the Communist success and the Kuomintang decline, the United States would not have seemed guilty of helping to prolong the Chinese civil war, and Mao and Chou might have come to power without the animus that their initial treatment of American diplomats revealed. Washington would have recognized Peking, and East Asia might have been spared Korea, confrontation and Vietnam.

In fact the overture of the Chinese leaders in 1945 brought no response from the United States. It had been motivated by their distrust of General Hurley and their desire for more direct and reliable channels. It was thwarted by Hurley's interpretation of his mission as one to "sustain Chiang Kai-shek." Recognition of the Communist party at that point, he thought, would bring "destruction of the National Government . . . chaos and civil war, and a defeat of America's policy in China." Hurley, learning of an offer the Chinese had hoped to keep from him, responded by denouncing the military and diplomatic officials through whom it had been made and pledged his total devotion to the government to which he was accredited as ambassador. His charges provided the first fuel for the distrust that fed the flames of McCarthyism. It is, of course, just as possible that if the contacts with Yenan had been followed up—if Chiang had fallen sooner and if confrontation had nevertheless come in spite of this—the denunciations of the McCarthy years would have been even more vehement. It is improbable that a visit would have solved matters. The cold war was in origin a reaction to the American-Soviet confrontation in Europe, and Europe long maintained in postwar planning the priority that it had held in wartime strategy. It was more than a decade before either American or Chinese leaders were able to see beyond a simple polarity of the two superpowers.

Nevertheless in retrospect it is clear that American leaders would have been well advised to experiment with the opportunities that were open to them for direct initiatives with Mao Tse-tung and Ho Chi Minh. Such experiments would have given all concerned a certain amount of leverage with the Soviet

Union as well, even though the towering prestige of Stalin within the communist world limited such opportunities until his death. Instead American assumptions of a communist monolith helped to bring it into being and sustained its life. Strategic uncertainties combined with domestic political pitfalls to persuade American leaders to dismiss what opportunities there were as superficial and deceptive. It seemed safer to assume the worst of China's new leaders. Any other course would have required forthright decision and innovation. Instead a series of nondecisions deferred conclusions. Halfhearted measures of assistance to Chiang Kai-shek, to France and later to successor governments in Vietnam constituted a "safe" course that led to danger, when accepting dangers might have worked for safety. Mao never came to Washington, but two decades later President Nixon offered to come to Peking.

American attitudes hardened after the forces of North Korea crossed the 38th parallel in June of 1950. President Truman declared that the attack on Korea made it plain "beyond all doubts that Communism has passed beyond the use of subversion to conquer independent nations and will now use armed invasion and war.... In these circumstances the occupation of Formosa by Communist forces would be a direct threat to the security of the Pacific area." The Seventh Fleet was ordered to protect Taiwan and make it clear that a Communist attack on the Nationalist redoubt would bring a response from the United States. The Peking leaders chose not to challenge this position, although they bitterly denounced the American intervention. After the United Nations forces commanded by General Douglas MacArthur drove the North Koreans back across the 38th parallel, the Chinese decided to intervene in the Korean conflict. Their early successes in a winter counteroffensive transferred to China the principal onus of the Korean War and consolidated the American assumption of protection and assistance for the Nationalist regime on Taiwan. War and two decades of highly structured invective sealed a hostility between the United States and the People's Republic of China.

CHAPTER 12

The Postwar Era

In the century between the 1870s and 1970s the tone of interna-
tional affairs in East Asia had been dominated by the relationship between Japan
and China. Their search for outside assistance and the pressures of their rival
programs of modernization confused internal and external affairs inextricably.
The Sino-Japanese War of 1894–95 gave Japan a commanding lead in external
support and bilateral relationships. Japan's success made it a model for Chinese
reformers, and its academies and arsenals exercised magnetic attraction for
Chinese students and revolutionaries. In turn, the growing power and appeal of
Chinese nationalism accelerated sentiments for an increased Japanese presence
on the continent among Japanese expansionists in the 1920s and 1930s. The impact of Chinese nationalism was a primary source of political instability in twentieth-century Japan. Throughout the twentieth century tactics, ideology and
issues reverberated across the China Sea. Japanese radicalism spread through students and publications to influence the new generation in twentieth-century
China, and it returned from China, where it had greater freedom to develop, to
alarm Japanese conservatives. Right-wing radicals in Japan, impressed by the
way revolutionary doctrines infiltrated the new army of late Imperial China,

thought it possible to advance radicalism through the young officers in the army of Shōwa Japan. In the end the Shōwa army became an instrument of imperialist oppression abroad instead of revolutionary change at home as the Japanese invasions of China in the 1930s destroyed the Nationalist government of China and isolated Japan from its mainland neighbor.

After the Japanese surrender in 1945 there were no political relations between Japan and mainland China for a quarter century. Each country turned its back on the other. With the exception of modest cultural and economic relationships established through informal channels, these two countries, whose mutual relations had dominated East Asian politics for so long, were almost totally isolated from each other. After 1952 Japan's diplomatic and economic ties with the Republic of China on Taiwan emphasized its separation from the People's Republic in Peking. China looked to the Soviet Union for political security and economic assistance, and Japan turned to the United States. The sweeping political, educational and social reforms on both sides of the China Sea produced a growing chasm between the two societies. Changes in ideology and society created generations far removed from the close contacts that had existed between prewar groups through study, trade and travel.

In each country distance and isolation brought serious misapprehensions. In China the wartime image of an aggressive, militarist Japan lived on, bolstered by the new Japan's alliance with the United States and its ties with the rival regime on Taiwan. In Japan the separation from China brought uneasiness and the feeling that the chasm was unnatural. Neutralist and pacifist intellectuals and political groups dissatisfied with their cautious government's adherence to the Western camp were fearful of a commitment that might permanently separate Japan from its neighbor; they projected a new role for Japan as mediator and bridge between East and West. Guilt and nostalgia frequently combined to create a romantic view of Chinese reform that cut across political persuasion and belief.

However, the quarter century of separation produced the longest period of peace and quiet in the relations between the two since the opening of diplomatic relations between them in the 1870s. It was ironic that as the period of separation came to an end in 1972 the process was accompanied by charges of Japanese militarism from Peking and punctuated by a dispute over off-shore oil deposits near the Senkaku Islands, an appendage of the Ryukyu chain whose disposition had been the first issue between Imperial China and Meiji Japan.

1. Japan in Isolation

JAPAN'S POSTWAR ISOLATION was anticipated by wartime developments that separated its people from the outside world. The first of these was intellectual. The ideology of emperor and family-state was insistent on the distinction be-

tween the perfect moral order of Japan and the flawed polities of other countries. During the 1930s Japanese intellectuals struggled with the problem of accommodating these parochial standards to the requirements of world mission
and leadership. Their work is full of interest, for it marked the intellectual corollary of a century's political and economic struggle for leadership. Government
policy was articulated and rationalized by intellectuals who were informed by
German idealist philosophy and adapted it to the requirements of an indigenous
cult. Among their number were leading philosophers of Kyoto University, who
had numbered Prince Konoe among their students.

After it became clear that victory in the China incident would not be quick
or easy, a group of Konoe's advisers bent their efforts to making sense of the,
tragedy in long-range terms of historical development. The philosopher Miki
Kiyoshi, in an important lecture entitled "The World Historical Significance of
the China Incident," maintained that the incident marked the true beginning of
the twentieth century, a period in which the fulcrum would slowly but surely
swing from Europe-centered to Asia-centered dominance. European ideologies,
he stated, had proved empty and self-defeating. He linked the China incident to
"the unification of Asia" by discerning a world mission for Japan. Japan was to
construct a sphere in which the materialist exploitation that had marked European imperialism would come to an end and be replaced by programs of mutual
advancement and development.

Konoe's announcement of a New Order in East Asia in 1938 translated
these speculative affirmations into government policy. Japan was now committed to the construction of an Asian community capable of standing against
Western capitalism and Soviet communism. The men who raised these hopes
were aware of the imperfections that marked Japanese expansionism and
society, but they envisaged a domestic reform that would lead to success in
Japan's international mission, which was to struggle with the entrenched powers
of Western imperialism. They convinced themselves and their fellows that the
China incident and the struggle to which it led had an antiimperialist significance which endowed it with moral and ethical values.

The full flowering of this view came as Japan enlarged its efforts to insulate
Nationalist China from Western imperialism by moving against China's
Western allies. When these efforts brought reprisals from Western colonial outposts in Southeast Asia, Imperial Japan began to threaten those outposts. The
fact that Southeast Asia was also rich in raw materials for the Japanese war
machine gave added support to this strategy. The final rationale came with the
elaboration of a vision of the Greater East Asia Coprosperity Sphere in 1940–41.
The area of shared ideals was now to include Southeast Asia and, at times of
euphoria, Australia and New Zealand. Japan would construct a self-sufficient
zone that would throw off European influence. Its members would enjoy independence under Japanese protection. The sphere would constitute a new moral
order, free of the materialism of the capitalist imperialism that had hitherto
ruled the area.

Unfortunately the imperial army was the agent of this idealist construct. Its leaders, deeply involved in the elite structure of Japan's unreformed polity, proved to be poor representatives of the new and higher moral order. Ordinary Japanese soldiers and officers, who were trained in the arrogance of national superiority, served these goals more poorly still. Japanese bureaucrats and entrepreneurs, anxious to utilize the new conquests for domestic needs and profit, did little to translate the denunciations of materialist exploitation into actuality. Nevertheless many thoughtful Japanese, bemused by the overarching synthesis and historical sweep of the vision of national mission, struggled against the evidence that was at hand to persuade themselves of the validity of their nation's struggle.

Intellectual isolation was compounded by political separation. As Japan gradually withdrew from contact with its traditional Western trading partners, it moved into the circle of Axis diplomacy. Yet, with the exception of hostility to the West, the area of shared interest with Nazi Germany and Fascist Italy was very slight, and those relations were never close or meaningful. Foreign Minister Matsuoka, in fact, had hoped that the Tripartite Pact would give him leverage against the United States and help to bring it to heel. Instead it convinced Secretary of State Hull that Japanese and Nazi were two of a kind. Nor did Japan's nonaggression pact with the Soviet Union bring meaningful international contact. It served to stabilize the borders for the convenience of both parties, but it did not deter the Russians from joining the battle after Japan's energies were spent.

The overwhelming victories that followed Pearl Harbor seemed to augur a new age of East Asian community, but because of Japan's inability to maintain communications with its new domains these successes were only the prelude to a new Japanese isolation. The success of Japan's initial strike against Pearl Harbor was lessened by the absence from that base of American aircraft carriers, and these succeeded in turning the tide of battle in major engagements in the Coral Sea and Midway in 1942. The American counterdrive was slowed by the necessity to tool for war and by the decision to give first priority to the European theater of operations. Japanese leaders had realized the enormous technological and economic superiority the United States could bring to bear, but they had gambled on a German victory and American discouragement to prevent the full deployment of that power. They themselves were hampered by service rivalries, difficulty of access to their new raw materials and technological backwardness that prevented them from matching American sea and air power and radar. These differences were critical for the victory at Midway. During 1943 and 1944 American submarines made major contributions in cutting Japan off from its new empire. By the end of the war the Japanese merchant marine, which had included a total of ten million tons of steel-bottom shipping, had been reduced to less than one-half million tons. Submarines accomplished more than half of this destruction.

The China theater of operations, however central to Japanese imagination of Asian leadership, proved a backwater to the main American offensive through the Pacific islands, and it was important chiefly for the way the Japanese armies of occupation that were tied down in China alienated their hosts. After American efforts to modernize and train the Nationalist armies for a counterattack ran afoul of the maladroit diplomacy of General Joseph Stilwell and the suspicions and inefficiency of Chiang Kai-shek, greater emphasis was put on the Pacific route as the most direct path to Tokyo. Chiang's inability to defend the bomber bases built in south China from massive Japanese drives in 1944 sealed a decision for the alternative strategy that was already in the making. As General Douglas MacArthur and Admiral Chester Nimitz refined their strategies of island conquest, Japan lost its air and naval strength and saw the Pacific lanes upon which it depended increasingly dominated by American power. Saipan fell in 1944, and its loss resulted in the fall of the cabinet of General Tōjō. Later that fall the battle of the Philippines, preceded by the largest naval engagement ever fought in modern military history, ended the war for some of Japan's finest navy and army units. In the spring of 1945 the fall of Okinawa brought down the cabinet of General Koiso Kuniaki. Japan was now substantially cut off from Manchuria and the Chinese mainland. Its shipping largely was limited to small wooden vessels and its air force diminished to specially selected and highly motivated suicide units. In the spring of 1945 American B-29 bombers, operating from Pacific bases, turned all major Japanese cities except Kyoto into raging infernos of death for the Japanese civilian population.

By July it was clear to Japanese leaders that their isolation was complete. The only question was how much honor, territory and autonomy they could salvage in defeat. A cabinet headed by the aged Suzuki Kantarō, seventy-eight-year-old hero of the Russo-Japanese War, struggled with the determination of the army to force a final land confrontation in hopes of improving the terms of capitulation through a final bloodbath. The Soviet Union seemed the last remaining opening in the circle of Japan's isolation, and in July 1945 Tokyo requested the Russians to receive a special mission headed by Prince Konoe. That hope was doomed when Foreign Minister Molotov, after the Potsdam Conference, summoned the Japanese ambassador on 8 August and handed him a declaration of war. As Secretary of State Byrnes later wrote, "It is doubtful whether ever before in history a government delivered a message indicating willingness to surrender and simultaneously was handed a declaration of war."

The final horror came with the atom bombs of 6 and 9 August at Hiroshima and Nagasaki. These provided the final urgency and speeded the emperor's decision to intervene with a message phrased in terms of compassion and peace. "The enemy," he told his people in his surrender broadcast of 15 August, "has begun to employ a new and most cruel bomb, the power of which to do damage is, indeed, incalculable, taking the toll of many innocent lives. Should we continue to fight, not only would it result in an ultimate collapse and obliteration of the Japanese nation, but also it would lead to the total extinction of human civilization." As a result, he went on, choosing his words from the language of the Buddha in the *Sutra of 42 Sections,* "We have resolved to pave the way for a grand peace for all the generations to come by enduring the unendurable and suffering what is unsufferable."

The surrender message had been preceded by efforts to discover the dimensions of "the unendurable" and the "unsufferable." The Potsdam Declaration of 26 July, to which the Japanese now submitted, had shielded its demands in language that suggested conditions ("the following are our terms") rather than unqualified submission and held out hope for the survival and reconstruction of the Japanese nation in a peaceful future. Japanese leaders looked in vain for some guarantee for the imperial institution and asked that it should be understood that the declaration did not "comprise any demand which prejudices the prerogatives of His Majesty as a Sovereign Ruler." To this Secretary of State Byrnes returned a masterly obfuscation to the effect that the "Emperor and the Japanese Government" would be "subject to the Supreme Commander of the Allied powers" and that "the ultimate form of government of Japan" would be established "by the freely expressed will of the Japanese people." As the debate over this reply unfolded in Tokyo, the optimistic view, that a "subject emperor" was still an emperor, and that the "ultimate form of government" could have nothing to do with the existence of an imperial institution that had survived so many alterations in government since the beginning of Japanese history, gradually won out.

Even so, it required the direct and personal insistence of the emperor to win the day. Not until 1971 did the emperor make further comment on the nature of his role on this occasion. When he did, it was to deny that his intervention had been in any sense unusual or unconstitutional: "That decision was taken on the responsibility of Prime Minister Kantarō Suzuki," he said; "That was my interpretation." Yet the fact remains that nothing short of a "sacred decision" unique in Japanese history would have sufficed to persuade the military to lay down its arms peacefully. Without this sanction surrender would have seemed disloyal. As it was, and despite the traditional injunctions to prefer death to surrender, the vast war machine of Imperial Japan submitted almost at once. Imperial princes traveled to the farthest reaches of the battle lines to bring the message to the troops. In all, slightly over 500 persons, 376 of them in the army, chose suicide over surrender. Since there were at surrender 3,000,000 troops in Japan prepared to give their lives in combat and some 7,000 planes available for suicide squadrons, the power of the imperial pronouncement is evident.

Japan waited for the occupying armies with its cities destroyed, its stockpiles exhausted, industrial production at a halt and with dangerous shortages of food. The government whose boasts and guarantees had proved hollow was without respect, and its leaders were about to be charged with responsibility for the disastrous course that they had set. Spiraling inflation threatened what remained of national strength. Hoarding marred the long-praised community spirit of the populace, and black market transactions found city dwellers required to make daily trips on decrepit transportation through burned-out landscapes in search of food. The New Order had proven bankrupt in morality, and it had brought Japan isolation instead of leadership.

But a final isolation remained for the Occupation years. The structure that was set up under General Douglas MacArthur as Supreme Commander for the Allied Powers (SCAP) had as its goal the disarming and democratization of Japan. Through its headquarters staff, occupying armies and the constant flow of visiting consultants and experts, it opened Japan to outside influence. Yet in another sense it totally isolated Japan. As in the early Tokugawa period the Japanese, who had so recently been scattered throughout Asia, were suddenly restricted to their home islands. Those crowded islands now had to absorb another six or seven million returnees from Manchuria, China and Southeast Asia. Japan had no representation or diplomatic protection abroad. The Japanese embassy in Washington became the headquarters of the Far Eastern Commission that oversaw the occupation of Japan, and all Japanese embassies and consulates were closed. Information and contact with the outside world filtered into Japan only through American channels. Communication, press and mail were censored. For a half decade or more Japan was in total isolation from the rest of Asia and much of the West. This isolation was the more striking and total after a decade of Japan's Asian orientation and its dreams of international leadership.

Even closer parallels can be suggested with the early Meiji period. For a second time the condition of Japan's resumption of sovereignty and achievement of equality was the satisfaction of requirements set by the outside world, mediated through SCAP as the agent of the United States. Not until Japan's institutional structure had been revised to secure guarantees of democratic procedure and responsible participation would the constraints be removed. The scorn of Meiji leaders for the shortcomings of their feudal background was more than matched by the derogation Occupation-period Japanese had for the wartime leaders whose errors had brought them to this pass. Since Occupation policy and war-crimes trials were to a large degree based upon the belief that specific men and influences had been responsible for the errors of Shōwa Japan, it was easy for many Japanese to join in the denunciations and dissociate themselves from their leaders. Of all scapegoats none compared with the military as a target of abuse. After the soldiers, in quick succession came the financial interests and expansionist leaders who had gathered at the feast. Japan's modernization, impressive as its results had been, had still been partial in that it had been based upon inadequate popular participation. Because they had taken such slight part in the decision process, it proved easy for millions of Japanese to stand aside while their leaders were punished. The prospect of a new order in which effective responsibility would be extended farther throughout society, on the other hand, stirred them to genuine enthusiasm. An additional and important parallel with the

Meiji period is that the Occupation reforms built on trends long underway in Japanese society, though artificially suppressed by the conservative regimes of the 1930s.

The first tasks of the Occupation found the Japanese masses preoccupied with a desperate struggle for economic survival and scarcely able to concern themselves with matters of national policy. SCAP moved first to remove the supports of the militarist state. The armed forces were demobilized, nationalist organizations were dissolved and purges removed all individuals prominent in wartime activities from positions of responsibility. Some two hundred thousand individuals were affected by this program, and their temporary departure from leadership roles opened the way to an influx of new leaders. In Tokyo the International Military Tribunal for the Far East, though operating on legal and historical bases that were often dubious, tried General Tōjō and other war leaders on charges of conspiracy to commit aggression. Seven men were sentenced to death by hanging, and sixteen were given life imprisonment. Two received shorter terms; one of these men, Shigemitsu, later became foreign minister. Kishi Nobusuke, a member of Tōjō's cabinet who was never brought to trial despite his initial listing as a war criminal, later returned as prime minister in 1957.

Other measures dealt with the future. State Shinto was disestablished, and the emperor renounced his claims to divinity. The Home Ministry, which had controled Japan through its appointive governors and the national police, was abolished, and efforts were made to decentralize and vary the education system. The Occupation's role was often contradictory, for it strove to promote decentralization by directives issued to a central government. MacArthur worked through the Japanese government and directed its moves through directives or more discreet suggestions and thus functioned somewhat like the genro of earlier days. Yet his commitment to his mission and his personal example of samurai austerity made him an appropriate agent of change in a society accustomed to military virtues and authority, while his confident and soaring rhetoric helped provide purpose in a vacuum of belief so profound that it excluded even resentment. Traditional hierarchic views also made it easier for Japanese to accept direction from the most modernized of Western countries. For the Occupation, despite its authorization by the Allied Powers and the inclusion of small numbers of British Commonwealth units, was basically carried out by the Supreme Commander and his American subordinates. The Japanese were vastly relieved that it included no Chinese or Russian units.

Slogans of strength, achievement and leadership played an important part in activating Japanese drives toward modernization after the Meiji Restoration. In postwar days, the values most honored were those of peace and democracy. The new Constitution of 1947, prepared under the close supervision of SCAP, was the principal expression of this. Article IX, a product of Japanese war-weariness and Japanese and American idealism, contains the renunciation of war as a "sovereign right of the nation" and affirms that "land, sea, and air forces, as well as other war potential, will never be maintained." Although the 1950s saw the development of a Self-defense Agency with limited but well-armed land, air and sea forces, the rationale for this was that Japan had an inherent right of defense and that none of these forces could under any circumstances be used outside the home islands. Nor could any of their armaments or equipment be offensive in nature. Even this form of defense establishment was quickly contested by pacifist and neutralist leaders. Sharply limited in size and under firm civilian leadership in the Prime Minister's Office, the defense forces have shown none of the capacity for institutional aggrandizement that characterized the prewar military. They have also been relatively inexpensive, and postwar Japan's ability to limit defense expenditures to approximately 1 percent of its Gross National Product has been an important element in its economic resurgence. Pacifist emphases have been particularly important in the maintenance of a strict ban on atomic and nuclear weapons, which Japan has repeatedly vowed never to manufacture, admit or store.

The key to the institutional strength of the prewar military was its access to the throne in a setting of diffuse executive authority. The 1947 Constitution altered that setting radically. Opening with echoes of the Gettysburg Address, it defined the emperor as "symbol" of the state (he had been "head of the Empire" and "sacred and inviolable" under the Meiji Constitution) and declared that he derived his position from "the will of the people with whom resides sovereign power." The new constitution included a thirty-article Bill of Rights which extended to "minimum standards of wholesome and cultural living," collective bargaining and academic freedom, and it ruled out discrimination because of "race, creed, sex, social status, or family origin." The Constitution did away with Privy Council, peerage and palace authority and allocated power clearly to an elected Diet which was to select the executive from its ranks. For the first time in modern Japan the executive process was clearly defined and prescribed. Other changes made prefectural governors and local officials elective to make local government responsive to popular will. Despite the unfamiliar concepts and foreign inspiration of its language, the Constitution proved capable of flexible interpretation and worked well. It immediately received and retained enthusiastic popular support, and the inclination of conservative governments to seek its revision in later decades never made significant headway. Japan's experience with the Meiji electoral system had clearly prepared the way for the striking changes embodied in its new constitution.

Education also felt the American influence. SCAP advisers presided over the abolition of the multitrack system of prewar Japan which prepared some for technical education and admitted only a small elite to higher university training. Instead a standardized system, American in inspiration, admitted all students to liberal arts training. It also sought to lessen the dominance of the prestigious imperial universities by establishing prefectural universities modeled on state colleges in the United States. Compulsory education was extended from six to nine years. Within a decade, high school and college education were increasingly standard for students who could satisfy entrance examination requirements. College students numbered 268,000 in 1940; by 1971 their number had increased to 1,700,000. They were enrolled in 389 four-year colleges and universities and 486 junior colleges. This inflation of institutions did not, however, lower the prestige of the great state universities, for their resources contrasted strikingly with those of the new institutions. Since, furthermore, the vast majority of new institutions were private schools dependent on tuition charges, the public institutions, almost tuition free, became increasingly preferable for abler students who managed to pass the hurdle of their entrance examinations.

Economic democratization began with a land-reform program that converted tenants into owner-farmers. Japan's wartime government had made some changes in land relationships by interposing agricultural associations between owners and their tenants. In addition, as farmers' sons had often been able to send home part of their service pay while their relatives had had access to additional income through outside employment in war plants, the extreme rural hardships of the depression years had long been improved. The postsurrender black market further buttressed farm incomes. By a SCAP plan that became law in 1946, land commissions with representation for owners, tenants and landlords selected land for purchase and resale to eligible tenant purchasers. The land was bought and sold at preinflation prices under conditions so favorable to tenants that within four years the majority of new owners had liquidated their debts.

The land reform was highly successful. It limited farm size and virtually eliminated tenancy, and at one stroke it removed the rural injustice and hardship that had been the stock complaint of military radicals in the 1930s. Conservative postwar governments, initially lukewarm about reforms that struck at their principal supporters in the countryside, were gratified to find that the land reform created a stable base for prosperous owner-farmers and thus encouraged conservative politics in the new electoral system. Technological advances in agronomy combined with governmental subsidies for rice and protectionist policies against agricultural imports to make for a level of rural prosperity previously unknown.

By the late 1960s Japan had a large rice surplus, and consumer goods and household conveniences had changed the character of rural life. Burgeoning industry in the factory towns siphoned off more and more agricultural labor into the cities until less than 20 percent of the population worked in agriculture. By the 1970s, however, it was becoming clear that government favoritism could no longer discriminate against the urban masses, and programs were instituted to reduce the excessive production of rice. Farmers' net income, which had kept pace with national gains by growing more than 10 percent per year throughout most of the 1960s, began to slow, and as industrial productivity pulled away from rural productivity it became clear that new problems required new plans. More and more farmers near population centers were transforming their land into highly profitable residential developments.

Economic democratization was further advanced by measures encouraging the growth of labor unions. The release of political prisoners produced a vigorous group of socialist and communist leaders, but even without this political direction unionization would have proceeded rapidly because of the enthusiasm with which it was taken up. By 1950 56 percent of industrial workers were organized, with over six million workers in unions. The figure grew rapidly and numbered ten million in the 1960s, although the labor force grew even more rapidly, with the result that unionized workers constituted about 35 percent of the industrial labor force. Occupation-sponsored laws modeled on New Deal legislation guaranteed the right to organize, to bargain collectively and to strike, and a Labor Standards Law established minimum working conditions for factories.

Legislation similar to that of the United States did not by any means lead to comparable patterns of union organization and activities. The new Japanese unions were affiliated with national organizations, but they were organized along enterprise rather than craft lines. Negotiations for working conditions and pay were conducted within the enterprise format. The national organizations carried the responsibility for larger political and ideological issues. The principal nationwide unions were to be found in the area of government employment, with the result that railway workers and especially teachers came to play leading roles in the national associations. These in turn provided powerful support for the Japan Socialist party, but in the absence of the responsibility brought by political power and practicality brought by economic bargaining that organization's theoretical and doctrinaire position hurt its political effectiveness.

At the same time that it encouraged the organization of labor, the Occupation moved to limit the size and power of the great industrial combines. Occupation pronouncements described the *zaibatsu* firms as Japan's chief war potential and quickly targeted them for dissolution. The holding companies that constituted the core units of *zaibatsu* empires were liquidated, and their securities were made available for public purchase. Legislation to enforce fair trading and to guard against cartels and monopolies followed. The most successful and thorough of these measures were those that took control of the great firms like Mitsui and Mitsubishi away from *zaibatsu* families. The breakup of the conglomerates, however, presented more difficult problems. At one time plans were made to break up 1,200 operating companies into their constituent parts, but subsequently this target was revised downward to 325. In the end only 28 were broken up, and over one-third of these were electric power companies and not trading or manufacturing combines.

There were several reasons for this shift. One was to be found in differing degrees of conservatism and radicalism within the SCAP bureaus responsible for policy. Labor specialists were prounion, while banking specialists were more concerned with stability and order. Another reason was the great difficulty in persuading Japanese officials and managers of the benefits of full and, in their eyes, wasteful and destructive competition. An economy the size of America's, many Japanese maintained, might have room for this; Japan, with its postwar problems, did not. A third factor was the disruptive effect of the program of de-concentration on economic recovery. Economic planners, conscious that it was necessary to get Japan's plants producing again in order to establish economic health and remove the burden on American aid, were anxious to terminate the uncertainty that was costing Japanese consumers goods and Japanese workers jobs.

The growth of communist power in China lent additional urgency to recovery in Japan. Despite all of these inhibiting factors, the program left a per-manent residue of change. The *zaibatsu* family members never recovered the authority they had had. Breathing space was provided for new entrepreneurs and management groups. By the time the program of dissolution had run its course and prewar *zaibatsu* executives combined again in loose alliances (usually around the great banks), they found themselves confronting vigorous new groups prepared to contest economic leadership with them in market after market. It was significant that such giants of the postwar Japanese export world as Sony and Matsushita were new and independent firms. The great trading firms of Mitsubishi, Mitsui and a few others, however, grew in size. By 1974 the top ten handled 50 percent of exports, 60 percent of imports and 20 percent of domestic wholesale transactions. A final, ironically relevant note to the enthusiasm SCAP planners had for dissolution of Japanese combines is that dur-ing the 1960s the pattern of corporate mergers into massive conglomerates in the United States showed that belief in the blessings of across-the-board com-petition was not a great deal stronger in the United States than in Japan. As in-dustries became global and international in their thrust, arguments for size and against duplication reproduced in all countries some of the conditions previously found chiefly in Japan.

Social legislation of the postwar era saw energies and hopes long repressed by a conservative Japanese government spring to life. The civil code, which had buttressed the power of the male family head with legal support, was com-pletely rewritten to allow for equality between the sexes and joint inheritance rights. Women were given the vote and soon made their voices heard in all areas of civic life. Social legislation created strong interest groups, and the prospects of substantial reversal of postwar changes seemed slight. Massive redistribution of wealth resulted from measures like land reform, special war-profits taxes and the inflation that wiped out the holdings of the propertied classes. New, progressive income taxes were devised to prevent a recurrence of the worst of prewar tax in-justice. Throughout Japanese society the adjustments, in the words of Hugh Patrick, "represented transfers from a small minority to a large majority of the Japanese, who quite naturally responded favorably. The previous holders of power and wealth were under attack politically, economically, and socially, so they were not able to sustain their vested interests. Finally, because Japan was utterly defeated and close to chaos, tremendous sacrifices could be demanded of everyone simply to get the country back on its feet."

Most Japanese, then, had reason to approve of Occupation policy. The elite, whose interests were most seriously threatened, had little alternative to cooperation. Cooperation was the condition of the eventual return of sovereignty. Japanese cooperation was also rewarded by American efforts to ward off economic collapse and generate industrial recovery. By 1949 the United States had provided approximately $2 billion in aid to Japan, initially in foodstuffs and later in imports of industrial raw materials. On a per capita basis, this was about one-third of the American aid to West Germany, one-half of the aid to Italy and one-fifth of the aid to Great Britain. But it was of critical importance in a period when Japan's foreign earnings were negligible. In addition there was nonmonetary help in the form of sponsorship of Japanese exports overseas and technical missions like a 1948 delegation of the American Cotton Manufacturers' Association to advise SCAP on the problems facing Japanese textile sales abroad. It is small wonder that many Japanese were secure in their isolation, confident that their needs would be foreseen and disinclined to take difficult and unpopular decisions.

They were prevailed upon to take this course by a series of decisions made in Washington and communicated to the supreme commander. The growing strains of the cold war influenced Washington to take decisions to limit American expenses and increase Japanese contributions. Reconstruction now took precedence over further reform. SCAP's abrogation of the program of business deconcentration was part of this move, even though it was explained by an announcement from General MacArthur that *zaibatsu* dissolution had been successfully accomplished. George F. Kennan traveled to Tokyo for the State Department to discuss the urgency of Japanese reconstruction and recovery with General MacArthur. Shortly afterward SCAP policy on labor organization underwent significant changes, with new rules worked out against strikes by public employees and new moves against communist-dominated labor unions. The purge of industrial magnates was also brought to an end, with a statement by Secretary of the Army Kenneth Royall that the men who had led in building up Japan's war machine "were often the ablest and most successful leaders of that country, and their services would in many instances contribute to the economic recovery of Japan."

Most vexing was the problem of Japanese inflation, which was compounded by the uncertainties of the securities market during a period of deconcentration, the reluctance of the Japanese government to take unpopular steps of deflation and the assumptions of many Japanese that American assistance would in any case be forthcoming. In 1949 Joseph M. Dodge, a Detroit banker, was sent to Tokyo to oversee the rehabilitation of the Japanese economy. With a virtually free hand in devising policy, he set a stern line of fiscal retrenchment, economic and industrial rationalization and deflation. The changes that followed his measures initially led to widespread unemployment, but they left the economy on as firm a footing as did the deflationary reforms of Matsukata Masayoshi in the 1880s. The boom of Korean War expansion that followed Mr. Dodge's reforms more than righted the hardships that had resulted from his recommendations.

Japan's long isolation from the international setting of political and security problems was also coming to an end. Conservative leaders had placed their hopes on continuing American security assistance since at least 1947, but the nature of Japan's own commitment and interest had never been spelled out. Then, as would be the case in 1969, talk of an American withdrawal from East Asia brought a new realization of the need for the Japanese to consider their role in regional affairs. In 1949 Secretary of the Army Royall discussed in an informal news conference in Tokyo the likelihood of an American withdrawal and concentration on the security of Western Europe. He expressed the view that Japan would have to be written off in the event of a struggle with the Soviet Union. Such talk was calculated to increase the Japanese government's willingness to reconsider its pacifist position. A year later North Korean armies invaded the Republic of Korea and brought international rivalries to Japan's door. Premier Yoshida resisted the urgings of the Americans, who had earlier forced Article IX on Japan, for rearmament but he did agree to establish a "police reserve" that was gradually expanded into the Self-defense Forces. The international situation also seemed to increase the urgency of a peace treaty. There seemed little likelihood of securing Soviet agreement to a continued American presence in Japan, and treaty arrangements were worked out privately between the principal noncommunist allies before and during the command of General Matthew B. Ridgway, who succeeded General MacArthur as supreme commander in April 1951.

In September 1951 the peace conference convened at San Francisco. Under terms of a treaty that had been worked out in advance, Japan recognized the independence of Korea and renounced all rights to Taiwan and the Pescadores, the Kuriles and southern Sakhalin and gave up the rights to the Pacific islands to which it had held mandate since World War I. The Soviet Union attended the San Francisco Conference but failed to make its objections to the treaty heard and refused to sign. This made it possible for Japan to retain hopes of regaining at least the southernmost Kuriles through subsequent diplomatic efforts. The San Francisco agreements also recognized Japan's right to enter into collective security arrangements and noted the United Nations' recognition of an "inherent right of individual and collective self-defense," and this was exercised through the enactment of a security pact with the United States. Under its terms American forces would remain in Japan until Japan could "assume responsibility for its own defense." Japan agreed not to grant similar rights to a third power without American approval. American assistance in weapons, training and technology was to be extended to the Japanese defense forces. Major United States units, with the exception of air detachments and naval bases, were gradually removed to Okinawa, which was left in limbo under American rule. In subsequent years the United States recognized Japan's "residual sovereignty" over the Ryukyus, but the islands did not formally return to Japanese rule until 1972, at which time American bases there were placed on the same terms as those that remained in Japan.

The San Francisco Treaty went into effect in April 1952. India and Burma did not attend the San Francisco Conference, but India signed a similar document in 1952, and Burma did likewise in 1954. Subsequently agreements for treaties and reparations for the nations invaded by Japan during World War II were worked out. In 1956 Japan restored diplomatic relations with the Soviet Union without, however, working out a formal treaty of peace. In December of that same year, with the Russians no longer invoking their veto, Japan became a member of the United Nations. Japanese public opinion had eagerly awaited this as the symbol of the country's return to international society. Japan soon became a contributing member to the Colombo Plan group of nations for economic development in South and Southeast Asia, the General Agreement on Tariffs and Trade and the Organization for Economic Cooperation and Development. For many Japanese their country's return to international status and eminence was symbolized by Japan's hosting the Olympic games in 1964, sponsoring the development of the Asian Development Bank in 1966 and staging the International Expo '70 in 1970.

The key problem of relations with China, however, remained unresolved. After the People's Republic intervened in the Korean War, pressures mounted to side with Washington on the issue of Taiwan, and Prime Minister Yoshida finally capitulated to a warning from John Foster Dulles that Senate approval of the San Francisco Treaty would be in doubt unless Japan committed itself to the Republic of China on Taiwan. Yoshida, who had hoped for relations with both Chinas, accordingly wrote Dulles to assure him of this intent. In 1952 Japan negotiated a treaty with the Republic of China that did not, however, prejudice subsequent negotiations with Peking if Japan so desired and Peking agreed. Japanese relations with Taiwan subsequently led to lively trade and important economic ties with that regime.

Japan's treaty and security arrangements of 1952 saw it remain under American domination but able at last to design its internal policies. A process of accommodating postwar institutional ideals to Japanese reality now began. The most dramatic changes, however, were economic. Starting from the base line of Dodge reforms with a relatively balanced budget and stable currency, the Japanese were in a position to react instantly to the opportunities the Korean War offered for foreign exchange earnings and economic growth. Symbolic of the Japanese response was the experience of Mr. Kamiya Masatarō, head of Toyota Motors. Kamiya landed at Los Angeles on 24 June 1950 on his way to Detroit, where he hoped to be able to work out a financing arrangement that would rescue his struggling company. As soon as he heard about the Korean invasion the following day, he thought the better of his plans and returned to Japan, where he was able to secure vital contracts for repair and construction of motorized equipment for the American forces. From this narrow escape from dominance by Detroit, Toyota returned in the 1960s to compete successfully with American manufacturers. Full independence still lay in the future, but for the Japanese political and economic establishment the Korean War marked the first step in the turn from dependent isolation to full independence.

2. Divided Korea

JUST AS the Korean peninsula had been the object of Sino-Japanese and Russo-Japanese rivalry at the turn of the century it was the first object of postwar rivalries in East Asia. In the late 1940s two competing ideologies and strategies of modernization focused on Korea. In 1950 the Soviet-sponsored state, emboldened by an apparent American withdrawal, struck first and was saved from disaster only by the massive intervention of the People's Republic of China. In the south an American-sponsored state narrowly escaped extinction thanks to the intervention of United Nations, principally American, forces. The peninsula, which had escaped military damage during World War II, now found itself devastated by three years of inconclusive fighting. The war determined political positions for the next two decades. It renewed the United States's commitment to the Republic of China on Taiwan and confirmed the hostility between the United States and the Chinese government on the mainland. It left the Korean peninsula divided between two garrison states, each dedicated to hostility toward the other. It left the People's Republic and Japan committed to opposing systems of alliances.

The Korea that awaited liberating armies at the end of World War II was different from the backward land that Japan had annexed in 1910, for it had been changed by measures for material modernization forced upon it by the Japanese. This was particularly true with respect to communications; a rail system united the country. In the north the Japanese had developed an industrial plant on the basis of coal, iron and the power provided by the great Yalu dams. As the industrial development of Manchuria proceeded in the 1930s, the Japanese made every effort to tie it in with a complex of light-metal industries in northern Korea. Improvements in agronomy and progress in reforestation paralleled similar efforts in Japan. Most of this was done by Japanese and for Japanese advantage, and in 1945 three-quarters of the Korean labor force was still engaged in agriculture. Agriculture had grown in productivity, but much of the increase had been siphoned off for export to Japan and per capita consumption of rice by Koreans had actually declined. Japanese purchase and exploitation of land, huge parcels of which were in the hands of the Oriental Development Company, provided ever-present reminders of foreign control.

Similar patterns of blunted development could be found in education. The Japanese built lower schools that educated almost half the age group, but opportunities for middle and advanced schooling were severely limited. The imperial university that was established in Seoul was filled largely with Japanese students. Korean literacy in *han'gŭl*, the Korean phonetic script, probably exceeded 50 percent, but the rewards were for students trained in Japanese.

The intensity of Japanese occupation, residence and direction was best shown by the pervasiveness of the police structure. Korea was one of the most intensively policed parts of the world, with one civilian policeman for each 1,150 Koreans; if military police are added, the figure becomes a startling 400 persons per policeman. Police retained sweeping powers of summary settlement and punishment, and suspected troublemakers were dealt with swiftly and harshly. Probably no other colony was subjected to such omnipresent direction.

Most humiliating and damaging of all was the effort to blot out Korean nationality altogether in a program of total cultural assimilation that was launched in the late 1930s. In 1937 Korean-language instruction was abolished in all lower schools. The study of Korean history, and even linguistics, was forbidden, and many academic leaders were jailed. Koreans were pressured into changing their personal names to Japanese names. State Shinto was forced on the Koreans, most effectively in the schools and most objectionably on Korean Christians, who did not have the nationalistic tolerance for its ceremonies that their Japanese counterparts did. In 1942 Korea was declared an integral part of Japan, and theoretically ceased to be a colony, its administrators advised by the Home Ministry. All officials were appointed, although advisory councils (which advised only on request) were appointed and, on lower levels, elected by a very restricted electorate of the propertied classes. Japanese administrative personnel made up over half of the total administrative force, and they constituted more than 80 percent of higher level officials.

Material benefits dwindled with the exigencies of wartime shortages and military priorities, and they were more than canceled out by the psychological cost of Japanese rule. Measures of exploitation and modernization were inextricably mixed. Koreans experienced a thirty-five–year hiatus in political responsibility and experience, and except for expatriates and the several million workers who lived as second-class citizens in Japan, they were almost totally isolated from the outside world. The pervasive Japanese presence made it extraordinarily difficult to avoid involvement in the Japanese structure. Korean city crowds were manipulated by Japanese operatives in anti-Chinese demonstrations, and Korean youths were conscripted to serve as support troops in the Japanese armed forces. Under these circumstances Korean political life, or what was left of it, continued to manifest the extreme factionalism that had weakened the peninsula before the advent of the Japanese and made it easier for the Japanese to rule by dividing. The divisions were symbolized by absentee governments that clustered around liberation fighters such as Syngman Rhee in Hawaii and Kim Koo in Chungking and partisan leaders like Kim Il-sung in Manchuria. Within Korea itself moral and social leadership continued to lie with the Christian and Ch'ŏndogyo religious communities. But because they were subject to the suspicious observation of the Japanese police, the more covert organization of the Communist party, which recruited with particular effect among Koreans who had moved across the Manchurian border, grew steadily.

During World War II the Allied governments made promises of freedom for Korea but failed to follow them up with practical planning for peacetime. At Cairo in 1943 it was announced that Korea would "in due course" be free and independent, but little was done to prepare for such a future. Plans gradually developed for a trusteeship to be directed by the United Kingdom, the United States, the Soviet Union and China during a period of tutelage. But the postwar world held little prospect for the successful operation of such a scheme.

Russian troops entered Korea on 12 August, before the Japanese surrender, and a hasty arrangement was worked out with the United States to divide the peninsula at the 38th parallel for purposes of accepting the Japanese surrender. As in Indochina, where Chinese and British forces accepted the Japanese surrender and moved on to leave subsequent problems for others, the dividing line was intended as a temporary convenience without political significance. But by the time American troops entered Korea on 8 September the Russians were already entrenched along the 38th parallel. It proved an unlikely and unsatisfactory, but firm, dividing line for the country.

The Russians came equipped with a leader to back in the person of a former partisan commander and Moscow-trained Communist, Kim Il-sung. They also lost little time in beginning the preparation of a military force built around veterans who had experienced combat with units in Manchuria. Rapid organization brought the election of People's Committees and the preparation of a provisional government.

To the south, however, actions were less purposeful. The United States government had made little planning for the political future of Korea in the belief that Allied efforts could be coordinated after the Japanese surrender. Japan presented the major challenge to American security and leadership in Northeast Asia, and it was there that the best effort was made. American commanders dispatched to Korea refused to recognize political organizations that had taken shape before their arrival because they suspected that they represented Japanese or communist inspiration, and instead they awaited unification moves that were to be coordinated with the Russians. These went poorly. An initial agreement to cooperate under the aegis of a joint commission that would supervise a five-year period of trusteeship with transition to independence drew the fire of Korean nationalists who wanted immediate independence. Among these were the veterans Syngman Rhee and Kim Koo, who had led wartime refugee governments. The Soviet Union held that organizations and individuals out of sympathy with the trusteeship plans could not qualify for participation in the electoral campaigns that were scheduled, but American military government officials resisted this stance on grounds that it would restrict participation to pro-Soviet political groupings and rule out all the principal conservative leaders. American army officials also delayed action on economic measures such as land reform as premature, despite the fact that the hasty exit of the Japanese managers made them urgent.

Meanwhile the growing confrontation between American and Soviet power in the postwar world—in Iran, in 1946, in Greece in 1947–48 and in Berlin in 1948–49—combined with the Communist victory in China to polarize the Korean situation. Although American policymakers were reluctant to undertake commitments on the mainland of Asia, they were convinced that a firm stand to block Soviet action was essential. In 1947 the United States placed its Korean problem before the United Nations, which agreed to supervise elections for the creation of a national government for Korea. Because the Russians refused to allow the United Nations Commission to operate north of the border, the elections were restricted to South Korea, where they were won by Syngman Rhee's supporters. In August 1948 Rhee was inaugurated as president of the Republic of Korea, and American military government came to an end. A month later a similar process to the north of the parallel resulted in the establishment of the Democratic People's Republic of Korea. The Russians announced the withdrawal of their military forces that same December and called on the United States to follow suit. This was done in June 1949. In the meantime, however, the Russians had prepared and armed a highly efficient Korean force with artillery, tanks and air support. To the south preparations for building a defense force had begun with the help of a small American Military Assistance Group, but in June 1950 this Korean force was still poorly prepared. It had little artillery and no tanks, planes or reserves. Worse still, it had little knowledge of its northern neighbor's preparations or plans.

Despite statements of support from Washington, there were few reasons to expect America to assist in the defense of the Republic of Korea. The secretary of state had omitted Korea and Taiwan from what he described as an American defense perimeter in an address in January 1950, although the same statement included affirmations of support for the Republic of Korea. The Congress, in the course of bitter quarrels over the wisdom of American disengagement from the civil war in China, had voted against an aid bill for Korea in January before reversing itself a month later. The chairman of the Senate Foreign Relations Committee had been quoted in May as feeling that Russia, "whenever she takes a notion . . . can overrun Korea just like she will probably overrun Formosa when she gets ready to do it." A mainland invasion of Taiwan was expected shortly. The tendency to see all conflict in American-Russian dimensions made officials reluctant to involve American prestige in peripheral or exposed areas. Further dissatisfaction within South Korea had provided good opportunity for guerrilla activities, and border and coastal areas were in a state of intermittent disorder as conflict with the North sputtered and flared. Korea seemed a poor place to commit American prestige and power in a struggle that might lead to larger scale violence in theaters more important to American security. American authorities also doubted the likelihood of a formal invasion from the north. The Pyongyang government seemed to be having enough success with its guerrilla activities and political intimidation to keep the Seoul regime off balance. North Korea was seen as a Soviet puppet state, and it was assumed that the Russians were not prepared or willing to precipitate a general war.

These estimates proved wrong. No one can be certain why they did, but several possibilities have been brought forward. Power shifts within the Soviet leadership may have given a new importance to Asian affairs, and the emergence of a strong and confident Chinese ally certainly put new urgency on forceful leadership in East Asian matters. The well-armed and well-prepared North Korean army probably presented an instrument that offered tempting prospects for a smashing blow against America's client state on the Korean peninsula. By 1950 discussions of the Japanese peace treaty had been underway in Washington for some time, and it is also possible that the near-certainty of a continued American military presence in Japan in the future made the denial of continental bases to the United States more important to the Soviet leaders.

On 25 June 1950 North Korean tank-led units crossed the border. Within hours it was clear that an invasion in overwhelming strength had the capability of crushing the Republic of Korea. United States leaders saw the North Korean attack as a threat to the entire postwar structure of peace and security. Committed to the view that earlier resistance to Japanese, German and Italian aggression would have saved millions of lives that were lost in World War II, President Truman referred the issue to the United Nations Security Council. The Russians were then boycotting the council and made no move to block its condemnation of the North Korean attack. American units under General Douglas MacArthur in Japan were quickly sent to bolster the disintegrating South Korean forces, and in future months contingents from the United Kingdom, Turkey and other U.N. members joined the defense. At the same time that the decision to intervene in Korea was made, the United States changed its "hands-off" policy on the Chinese civil war. The Seventh Fleet moved to checkmate a possible invasion of Taiwan from the mainland. This was done to localize conflict in the event that the Korean fighting should prove to be part of a larger pattern. Nevertheless it represented a fateful decision that reversed previous American positions and helped lead to Chinese intervention in Korea. Chiang Kai-shek himself offered Nationalist troops for the defense of South Korea, but this offer was declined on the grounds that they might be required on Taiwan itself.

The Korean War consisted of two great campaigns of movement and a third of attrition. In the first North Korean forces swept south to the Pusan beachhead while American troops were committed piecemeal in attempts to slow and stop the drive. General MacArthur reversed this tide of disaster by a surprise September landing at Inchon that cut the North Korean army off from its supplies and virtually destroyed it as an effective unit. Within months South Korean units, rearmed and buoyed by victory, and their American allies had crossed the 38th parallel, taken Pyongyang and advanced upon the Yalu with the intention of unifying all of Korea under the Republic. A defensive war suddenly became a crusade, but it was one that had disastrous consequences.

The People's Republic of China, already alarmed by the new American commitment to Taiwan, saw the advance to the Yalu as a threat to its borders and perhaps to its internal security. It now prepared a massive intervention to counterattack. As American and South Korean units moved north through the passes of North Korea in the snow of December, Chinese units struck their flanks and nearly turned the United Nations victory into a smashing defeat. The Eighth Army succeeded in extricating itself, but it was unable to maintain its lines until Seoul had fallen a second time. General MacArthur now called for a wider war and full authority to attack the Chinese bases in Manchuria. This was denied him by Washington, and when MacArthur made his dissatisfaction public he was recalled by President Truman and replaced by General Matthew Ridgway. General MacArthur, as Ridgway later wrote, envisaged nothing less than "the global defeat of Communism.... His 'program' included not merely driving to the Yalu, but destroying the air bases and industrial complex in Manchuria; blockading Communist China's seacoast; demolishing its industrial centers; providing all necessary support to Chiang's invasion of the mainland; and the transportation of the Nationalist troops to Korea to beef up our ground forces there...." Instead of supporting MacArthur's plan President Truman dismissed him, and this reminder of the supremacy of civilian over military control was perhaps the last lesson of the Occupation for the startled Japanese.

In the meantime Eighth Army and South Korean forces had consolidated their lines again and had taken strong positions in preparation for an anticipated Chinese offensive. When this came in April and May of 1951, the superior fire and air power of the U. N. forces took an enormous toll, and the Eighth Army's ability to mount an immediate counterattack produced heavy setbacks for the Chinese. Over eleven thousand Chinese prisoners were taken, and General Van Fleet, now field commander in Korea, was again confident of victory in a drive to the north. The United States was determined not to commit additional forces for the conquest of North Korea, however, and the line gradually stabilized slightly to the north of the 38th parallel. In July 1951, after inconclusive but costly fighting, truce talks between the United Nations command and the North Koreans began. An armistice was signed in July 1953, after the death of Stalin and the replacement of President Truman by Dwight D. Eisenhower. In 1974 it still remained in effect; two divisions of American troops remained as symbols of the United States commitment to the Republic of Korea.

With the benefit of hindsight it is easy to see that the decision to advance to the Yalu was an error and that the United States and the United Nations leaders were carried away by the success of their military operations to the point of changing their initial limited objectives. The Chinese had given signals through neutral countries of their intention to intervene, but American military authorities assumed that they lacked the capability and intent. Well before the initiation of the final drive to the Yalu, there was clear indication that Chinese units were present in the north, but General MacArthur had refused to let them influence his plans. Thus it was essentially the failure to take the facts of Chinese power and prestige seriously that extended the war and the casualties. These were high, and the Korean War was a major conflict. Communist forces suffered over 1,500,000 casualties, perhaps two-thirds of them Chinese, while the United Nations forces counted approximately 500,000 casualties, 140,000 of them American. The number of Americans killed was 33,729, making Korea the fourth largest war in American history until Vietnam surpassed it in cost.

Having begun by underestimating the Chinese, the United States then overreacted by overestimating them. For the next two decades China was credited with responsibility for almost every form of instability, subversion and discontent that showed itself in Asia. United States representatives led the maneuvering that excluded the People's Republic from the United Nations until 1971 and visited upon the Chinese much of the fear previously reserved for the Japanese. The cost of the Korean War went far beyond its casualty lists, for it led the United States into vastly more costly errors in Vietnam in the 1960s. Korea not only had the dubious distinction of opening the postwar confrontation in east Asia. In 1960 its students also inaugurated a decade of worldwide youth protest. Throughout the 1950s the government of the Republic of Korea in Seoul continued to be dominated by the autocratic and irascible octogenarian Syngman Rhee. Increasingly out of touch with popular aspirations, blindly nationalistic and committed to bitter hatred of past and recent scourges, the Japanese and the Communists, Rhee confused his own tenure with the maintenance of independence for his country. In the years after the signing of the armistice at Panmunjom, the political development of his country fell far behind its economic progress. Buoyed by almost $2 billion in American aid, South Korea began to undergo dramatic change as an infrastructure of highways, bridges and dams provided a setting in which light industry began to provide jobs for the population, now swollen by refugees from the North. Unfortunately Rhee's one-party dictatorship made the state an embarrassment to its allies. Increasingly Korean students educated abroad avoided returning to their homeland. Within Korea police spies infiltrated all levels of activity. The presumed danger of a renewed outbreak of war with the North was used to justify the imposition of severe and highly unpopular controls. Although the constitution contained provisions against a self-perpetuating executive, Rhee altered it to run again in 1956 and 1960. In 1956 he received only slightly more than 50 percent of the vote, although his opponent died before the election. The opposition's leader four years later also died; Rhee advanced the election date and won a landslide with strong-arm methods. When students demonstrated at Masan, police fired on them. In April student demonstrations spread to Seoul, the principal university center, and the courage of the students in the face of police brutality convinced political and military leaders that popular opinion would not tolerate the scale of repression that would be required to cow the demonstrators. The April revolution ousted Rhee, who was permitted to retire to Hawaii, and replaced him with a new and more democratic government. Within weeks student movements in Turkey brought down an unpopular government, and shortly afterward the great demonstrations of May and June occasioned by renewal of the security pact with the United States brought down the Kishi cabinet in Japan.

Korea remained a garrison state in which a strong and disciplined army was the most cohesive body. When the post-Rhee government failed to work the economic and political miracles that had been expected of it, a military coup replaced its head with an army junta headed by General Park Chung-hee in 1961. Two years later a constitution and elections were declared. General Park gave up his uniform for civilian clothes and became president. During the early years of his leadership, he called for efficiency, probity and alertness as the best defense against the enemy to the north. In 1965 he negotiated a treaty of recognition and reparations with Japan, and as Japanese investment and commercial capital entered South Korea its economy began a marked upturn. Syngman Rhee's legacy of unremitting hostility to Japan gradually gave way to a close and increasing dependence upon Japanese capital and goods. By 1972 almost half of South Korea's imports were from Japan, much of South Korea's light industry was allied with Japanese parent plants, and many of its goods were marketed through Japanese trading companies. The treaty negotiations with Japan were fiercely but unsuccessfully opposed by student groups who saw the Japanese tie providing support for a militarist government, much as Japanese students in 1960 saw the security pact and Eisenhower visit as support for an unpopular Kishi government. The Korean government's subsequent close relations with Japan contained an explosive potential for youthful radicalism in the years that followed.

The People's Democratic Republic of Korea to the north provided fewer turning points for political history and analysis. The garrison state of Kim Il-sung developed a personality cult that eclipsed even those of Mao Tse-tung and Joseph Stalin, and its instruments of party and military kept all criticism to the minimum. Although Chinese influence was dominant for a time after the end of the Korean War, it was not long before the North Korean government found it possible to cultivate an independent path between Peking and Moscow in its search for economic aid and military matériel. Kim Il-sung regularly announced his intention of conquering the South, but in fact his first attention was given to a competing strategy of modernization.

North Korea remained virtually unknown to outsiders until the thaw in Chinese, Japanese and American relations in the 1970s. At that time journalists returned from carefully guided tours with accounts of a police state that had produced impressive economic gains. They described particularly a self-confident nationalism fueled by official praise of the dictator and by hatred for the United States and the government in the South. The thaw in international relations had been accompanied by hopes for a relaxation of tension between North and South Korea, but the intensity of that confrontation seemed undiminished.

3. *China Under the People's Republic*

THE FIRST ENTHUSIASMS of a united nationalist impulse in Meiji Japan turned toward events in Korea. The People's Republic of China was similarly drawn to concerns in Korea within a year of its establishment. The Meiji leadership, however, was afraid that external adventures would benefit outside powers and destroy unity at home and consequently decided against intervention in 1873. Mao Tse-tung and his associates, on the other hand, were reasonably confident in promises of help from their Soviet allies and were convinced that failure to intervene would threaten their borders and their base of power. The Korean War came after a long buildup of nationalist agitation in China. There had been a century's irritation with Western imperialism and a half century of military threat from Japan. The Communist leaders had fought for a quarter century against Chiang Kai-shek, and they had seen the Nationalists benefit from United States support. Then, just when it seemed that backing was finally being withdrawn from Taiwan, the Korean War had brought fresh assurances of American protection. It closed the door on an invasion of Taiwan that had seemed imminent and instead brought new American threats to China's borders in Manchuria. So the intervention of Lin Piao's "volunteers" in Korea was accompanied by slogans of "Resist America!" and "Aid Korea!" and a drumfire of charges of American germ warfare, carefully orchestrated by the propaganda machine of the new government, served to focus nationalist enthusiasm and unity on themes of resistance and outrage.

All this served to emphasize the importance of China's new ties with the Soviet Union. Immediately after the announcement of the establishment of the People's Republic in 1949, Mao Tse-tung journeyed to Moscow, and in nine weeks of bargaining between December 1949 and February 1950 committed his government to a thirty-year alliance against aggressive action by Japan or any Japanese ally, that is, the United States. In these negotiations the Russians claimed what they had been promised at Yalta: operation of the former Chinese Eastern Railway, their rights in the port of Dairen and the naval base at Port Arthur. In addition joint stock companies, similar to organizations that already functioned in Eastern Europe, were formed for the exploitation of the mineral resources of north China. Russia offered loans for the economic development of China. In the course of the next half decade, thousands of Chinese trainees traveled to the Soviet Union to study the Soviet model of modernization, and the traditional patterns of foreign trade and exchange between China and Japan and the West gave way to a flow across central Asia to the Soviet Union and its Eastern European satellites. "During the years from 1949–1956," in Benjamin Schwartz's words, "there can be little doubt that the goal of modernization *on the Soviet model* was assiduously pursued by the Chinese Communist leadership in many sectors. After the Korean War we have a gradual implementation of the Soviet model of economic development."

The immediate benefit of the Soviet tie and of China's Korean intervention was the modernization of the People's Liberation Army. As Allen Whiting pointed out, "Soviet military assistance to China after the latter's entry into the war completely re-equipped the PLA and provided Peking with a first-line jet air force second to none in Asia, except that of the United States. This tangible benefit, added to the deterrent effect of the alliance upon U.S. strategy during the war, justified Mao's policy of 'leaning to one side.' " Soviet models, organizational methods and equipment soon gave Peking a well-armed and highly indoctrinated two-million–man force that had no match in Asia. The strength of this military establishment made it an important factor in the political changes that were to follow. More immediately, however, China's new equipment and confidence also showed its effect in an increased assertiveness on other borders where Chinese power had traditionally been exerted. Chinese troops entered Tibet in October 1950 and set in motion social and political changes that gradually integrated that theocratic state with its mighty communist neighbor.

The death of Stalin in 1953, and the shake-ups of Soviet leadership that brought Nikita Khrushchev to the fore altered Chinese willingness to accept Russian leadership. The joint stock companies were liquidated, joint control of the northern railways came to an end in 1953 and the Russians gave up their Port Arthur rights in 1955. Economic development on the Russian model with the assistance of Russian technicians began with full confidence and enthusiasm in the early part of the decade but probably came to grief because of the disparity between the state of economic development in postrevolutionary China and postrevolutionary Russia. China was far behind the economic network of industry, accessible raw materials and transportation which the Bolsheviks had inherited in Russia. Moreover the vast population of China, now freed from the attrition of pestilence and war, grew at a rate that placed increasing pressure on the country's food production and made it far more difficult to extract an agricultural surplus for industrial investment than had been the case in postrevolutionary Russia or post-Meiji Japan.

The early early 1950s were, nevertheless, years of progress. The benefits that derived from unification and an end to internal disruption and disorder made it seem that rapid strides could be made. A Five-Year Plan was announced for the years 1953–57, and its agricultural and industrial goals seemed to have been substantially met. Rail communications to remote border areas in north and central Asia solidified the Chinese grip on areas that had always been lightly held and made it possible to move in Chinese settlers. During the same period Peking's prestige increased as a result of its apparent ability to challenge and stop the world's strongest power in the Korean War. Chinese leaders became confident that their country's liberation would become a model for the rest of the imperialist-dominated and underdeveloped world. After the French effort to reestablish colonial control in Vietnam collapsed with the disastrous defeat at Dien Bien Phu, China took part in the Geneva conference of the summer of 1954 as one of the great powers. Chou En-lai, sure that communist victories

RAILWAY CEREMONY (1958) hailing the inauguration of express rail service to Chengtu, Szechwan, from Peking. The People's Republic placed great emphasis on communications improvement.

would come in the national elections that were promised for Vietnam, took a prominent part in those discussions and gave the impression of a masterly negotiator, although he later expressed chagrin at having committed Hanoi to agreements that were never implemented. In April 1955 China also took a leading role at a conference of nonallied Asian and African states in Indonesia. The five "Bandung" principles then announced (mutual respect for each others' territory and sovereignty, mutual nonaggression, mutual noninterference in domestic affairs, equality of relationships and mutual benefit and peaceful coexistence) became a staple of Chinese foreign policy pronouncements in the decades that followed.

Chinese political, diplomatic and military confidence seemed to reach new heights after 1957. Mao journeyed to Moscow for additional agreements with the Russians in that year. The international setting seemed revolutionized by Russian successes in launching an intercontinental missile and in lofting the first "sputnik" artificial satellite. The Russians then promised their allies assistance in developing nuclear technology. Mao announced that the "East wind" had begun to prevail over the "West wind," and China began to demonstrate a new and tougher line on its borders. In 1958 a crisis involving the island of Quemoy seemed to carry dangers of war. In response American defense commitments were increased as the State Department under Secretary of State John Foster

Dulles became convinced of the necessity for intensified security measures to "contain" China. In 1959 an anti-Chinese rising in Tibet brought the flight of the Dalai Lama to India and the ruthless imposition of Chinese settlers and power. Waves of Chinese settlers were sent into other border areas as well. During the same period the Chinese, noting that the Geneva promises had not been kept, provided equipment for guerrilla activities in South Vietnam. In 1962 Chinese troops scored striking successes all along the Indian border in seizing communications routes between Sinkiang and Tibet.

   This same confidence extended to China's relations with the Soviet Union. Khrushchev's program of de-Stalinization offended the Chinese leadership, and the Russians' refusal to grant that Mao Tse-tung was now the senior communist theorist and leader laid the groundwork for vigorous hostility. Chinese confidence in a successful "transition to socialism" after the successes of the first Five-Year Plan seemed presumptuous to the Russians, while Russian reluctance to follow the Chinese lead in confrontation with the United States seemed cowardly and ideologically suspect to the Chinese. In 1960 Russian technicians were withdrawn from China, and within a few years violent argument replaced the slogans of socialist fraternity of the 1950s. As the 1960s unfolded, China and Russia confronted each other along one of the world's longest borders, the distrust between great powers sharpened by the ideological antagonism of rival claimants to world leadership of the socialist revolution. By 1972 it was reported that forty-nine divisions, almost one-third of the entire Soviet army, were stationed along the Chinese border, and Chinese fear of a Soviet preventive war led to major changes in Chinese foreign policy.

   Russian leadership in China's foreign affairs was thus only a few years in duration. John Fairbank has rightly compared this to earlier periods of British, Japanese and American dominance in China's foreign orientation, though unlike the others it had a united and resurgent China to build upon. Nevertheless it is true, as he writes, that "many outside peoples have had their day in aiding the transformation of the Middle Kingdom, but none permanently. All have been cast off."

   By the mid-1960s China was prepared with sweeping claims of leadership for the underdeveloped world. As the struggle between North and South Vietnam led to American intervention in 1964 and United States bombing of North Vietnam in 1965, Defense Minister Lin Piao elaborated a scheme of "wars of liberation" in which China's experience would provide the model for all underdeveloped countries, which were expected to fight as a world proletariat against the world's industrialized, bourgeois powers. Ultimately the industrialized "cities" were to be surrounded from "the countryside." But in fact the Chinese left the Vietnamese to work this out for themselves, as they turned inward to deal with pressing problems of revolutionary direction and priorities. As China slowly emerged from the Great Proletarian Cultural Revolution of 1966–68, Chou En-lai, still at the helm of state and foreign policy, kept up criticism of the Soviet Union with expressions of support for nearby wars of liberation while he rebuilt bridges to the Western world and Japan. Affirmation of world revolution had never been renounced, but it was clear that domestic and security priorities loomed larger for the Chinese leadership. Foreign constraints, which were dominated by a supposed threat from the United States in the 1950s, had gradually given way to the political and ideological danger posed by the Soviet Union in the 1960s. The facile optimism in socialist solidarity of the regime's early years would not be held a second time.

Whatever the twists of Peking's foreign policy, major goals and values remained constant. These related to strategies of modernization and nationalism as they were understood through the thought of Mao Tse-tung. On one level these goals of modernization were the same as those of every other late-developing country. The regime worked for the assertion of effective control of an activated and participating population. It worked for the breakdown of the local and familial particularities that had made reformers and revolutionaries despair of change in Chinese society. Sun Yat-sen had characterized that society as a "sheet of loose sand" with reference to the individual and atomized goals and loyalties of its members, and any program of reconstruction for China required greater cohesion than that sand had had in the past. The task of preparing the Chinese masses for participation involved a program of educating and reaching them through a new system of communications and education. The message of national needs had to be dramatized in basic terms. A simplified script, a better network of schools and a massive effort of indoctrination were required to build popular willingness to struggle and sacrifice. The economic and material product of this would be an industrial plant that would enable China to take its place with other modernized nations. Only through industrialization could goals of national strength be combined with goals of a better life for the Chinese masses. National strength had been the purpose of every proposal for change in China since the mid-nineteenth century, and the nationalist thrust of China's modernization programs had been characteristic of all latecomers to international society. China's drive for equality, so long delayed and frustrated, had inevitably become more urgent as the years passed.

By the time Peking implemented its strategies toward these goals, its leaders had developed a deep faith in the correctness of the Marxist-Leninist vision of strong state control exercised by a communist vanguard. In the nineteenth century the Meiji leaders accepted the vision of the industrialized, free-enterprise West as the most recent and modern of which they had knowledge, but by the mid-twentieth century the Soviet model seemed more appropriate to crash programs of national reconstruction. This view was reinforced by China's optimistic view of Soviet aid during the first decade of the regime's efforts. But the faith of the Peking leaders also had deeper roots, for it had developed immediacy and individuality through a quarter century of experience. Out of this experience came an abiding trust in the infallibility of the leadership and thought of Mao Tse-tung.

Mao's vision, as analyzed by Benjamin Schwartz, Alexander Eckstein and other scholars, was built upon a number of fundamental views that showed little real change despite a great flexibility in application. Mao had shared with Sun Yat-sen the view that latecomers to modernization, through observation of appropriate models, could cut corners and achieve remarkable speed; it was not necessary to replay for a second time the tedious process of trial and error that earlier modernizers had had to experience. Also, he accepted the traditional philosophic views of the unity of knowledge and action. Correct knowledge, based upon sound apprehension of Marxist-Leninist theory and practice, was basic to correct tactics and strategy. Endless meetings devoted to ideology and to the thought of Mao Tse-tung were necessary to keep the revolution on a correct course. The Meiji elite were constantly hortatory in their pronouncements, but they were also self-consciously elitist. In retrospect their critics have noted that they underestimated their people and never or seldom fully believed them capable of the acts of heroic self-denial and commitment that were required. On the other hand, Mao, while no less hortatory, often seemed to overestimate his people, with the result that he was frequently shocked to find residues of selfishness and privatism despite the enormous effort that had gone into ideological remolding. Mao's strain of populism, as Professor Schwartz describes it, centered on an emphasis on man as the "decisive force in history." Minds and wills could and must be transformed. Once these collective energies were mobilized, unlimited results were possible. No doubt the miracles of the Yenan years were basic to the elaboration of this optimistic and romantic voluntarism. As Mao phrased it, "Of all the things in the world, *people are the most precious.* As long as there are people, every kind of miracle can be performed under the leadership of the Communist Party." Moreover, this view had a direct economic and material carry-over for Mao. As he put it, "The more it is possible for men to carry out a conscious revolution in their own social relationships, the more they increase their power in the combat with nature, the more they can really command as by magic the latent productive forces, making them appear everywhere and develop rapidly." A "spiritual transformation," to use Schwartz's term, could bring about a new society of "collective man."

The obverse of this was the self-evident fact that not all could or would be saved. The "people" were contrasted with the "enemies of the people," those incapable of redemption. The morality of the former could be brought into productive interplay only through constant confrontation with the evil of the latter. It was the task of the Communist party to define, identify and in the end to vilify the "enemies of the people," and the morality play of the "rectification drive" was constantly required to maintain the "people" in their readiness for service and sacrifice, hence the uniqueness of the modernization strategy of the People's Republic. The Meiji drive was led from above and depended upon efforts to indoctrinate and educate. The Chinese drive was for total transformation, with the result that the ultimate drive for reconstruction, the Great

Proletarian Cultural Revolution of 1966, was aimed at the very agent of the transformation, the cadre of the Communist party. The philosopher-educator Hu Shih phrased it succinctly in the 1950s. It was well known, he observed, that the new China had no real freedom of speech. What was new was the realization that China also lacked freedom of silence. Affirmation had to be universal and total, for anything short of this would mean that "the people" were not properly supporting the transformation of society.

The rhythm of drive and counterdrive that characterized politics and society in the People's Republic during its first two decades has to be considered within this framework of values and belief. The revolution in its totality probably constituted the greatest upheaval in recorded history. Never before have so many people been led to alter their ways and beliefs with such incredible speed. Despite this, or perhaps because of it, the record of those changes and of the purpose and pace of change is sadly imperfect. As Fairbank and others have pointed out, China's society has been closed to Americans, and the evidence upon which analysis is based has had to be pieced together from fragmentary reports, statistics and interpretations of the official statements and exhortations of a leadership whose internal workings and relationships remain obscure. The tempo of change also meant a heavy overlap. One risks distortion in the effort to separate, for no change took place in isolation from the others. Consequently the sequence of drives is more often a requirement imposed by the limits of comprehension than an accurate indication of successive priorities.

After the proclamation of the People's Republic in October 1949, the first job was to develop the apparatus of government. The Communists came into power with a quarter century's experience in ruling, but their administrative staffs were far from adequate to control the vast areas of China. They began by stressing the coalition aspects of their strategy, and only gradually tightened the reins against non-Communist elements. At Yenan in 1940, Mao's *On the New Democracy* had stressed coalition with democratic groups as a justified tactic during the move through a democratic to a socialist revolution. At that stage, he argued, China was not yet ready for a dictatorship of the proletariat; its subjection to imperialism and its backward institutions required an intervening stage in which cooperation with democratic elements in Chinese society would be necessary.

The year 1949, however, brought "liberation" and was a definitive watershed in the three-thousand–year history of China. Mao's new statement was entitled *On the People's Democratic Dictatorship*. He announced that a democratic coalition under party leadership would also act as a dictatorship against the people's enemies. Mao defined "the people" as made up of proletariat, peasantry, petty bourgeoisie and national (or patriotic) bourgeoisie. All other groups stood against the course of historical progress and had to be reformed or eliminated. The key to power and survival now lay in the ability to identify and define "the people" over against "the enemies of the people," and a desperate urgency to be on the right side of history characterized the successive waves of self-examination and denunciation that swept China.

In 1949 a People's Political Consultative Conference convened at Peking to adopt a Common Program and an Organic Law. This announced that the working class was the center of the Republic, and since the Communist party was by definition representative of the workers, it naturally received full administrative powers. In the early years minor parties (even a reconstructed version of the Kuomintang) continued in existence in China, and posts of honor often went to non-Communists, among them many Western-trained intellectuals. Successive moves saw the power of non-Communist elements shrink. In 1954 a new government constitution was proclaimed, and two years later a new party constitution was adopted. Throughout this process the power of the Chinese Communist party grew steadily. It rapidly became the world's largest Communist party and numbered seventeen million in 1961. The Party, the People's Liberation Army and the government apparatus constituted the three fulcrums of power, but at all levels it was Party control that was central. Mass organizations orchestrated popular participation and support. For the first time in Chinese history an effective network of vertically controlled organizations recruited millions of Chinese of all walks of life for participation or resonance with state policy. Central, regional, provincial and local party committees directed and coordinated policy at all levels, but effective enrollment of the masses came through gargantuan structures of trade unions, Democratic Women, Democratic Youth, Communist Youth League, Young Pioneers, and the like. Party members held the key controls, but individuals were reached in every aspect of their technical or social roles. Thus the application of a "mass line" set by the party could be arranged at every point throughout society. For the first time the Chinese masses were successfully involved in the workings of their government and society, not, as in earlier days, in social units and through authority relationships congruent with the elitist values of the authorities, but in active and often strident conformity with a line that might involve them in denunciation of relatives and superiors. The possibilities in the new system for propaganda and demonstration were enormous, and within a short time the world saw evidence of mighty convulsions that swept a land long considered immune to radical change.

At the center a State Council headed by the durable Chou En-lai set the overall tone and policy. Until the upheavals of the 1960s there was remarkable continuity in high places, and into the 1970s China was ruled by survivors of the Long March. Like the Meiji leaders, the high command of the Chinese Communist party had a quarter century of shared experience of weakness and danger, and like them many were all-purpose generalists who had combined military command with civilian authority. Unlike the Meiji leaders, however, the Chinese had a single charismatic leader who ruled as well as reigned, and his authority in ideology grew steadily. Mao seemed to recede from the center of the stage for several years after 1958, when the leadership cult was deemphasized, but in the turbulence of the 1960s his stature became greater than ever as the booklet of his aphorisms became the companion of every citizen and the justification for every act and method.

In the early stages of this government building, the regime faced the urgent task of asserting control over the economy and the cities. The People's Republic had inherited a galloping inflation. The long years of warfare had left the communications network badly damaged. All public services had declined, and confidence in promises or currency had been eroded through the successive disasters of invasion and civil war. The Party that announced itself as the vanguard of the proletariat had to give first attention to the cities, where that proletariat was to be found. Its first need was for more revenue to put an end to the self-defeating process of printing worthless notes. More efficient methods and the ubiquitous nature of the Party's organizational initiative made it possible to collect taxes much more effectively than had been the case. Since the currency was all but worthless, initial efforts focused on in-kind taxes in agricultural goods and on sales, commodity, and business taxes that were set by "democratic" methods but at central inspiration. A system of commodity units temporarily bypassed the inflation-ridden currency by establishing values expressed in a combination of food and materials that were daily necessities. Workers paid in such units were less harassed by the inflation that had become their curse.

These efforts also benefited from the fact that the disorder of war had come to an end. Since guerrillas were no longer tearing up railroad tracks at night and the disruption of military movements had stopped, communications speedily improved. Trackage and highway mileage were expanded as rapidly as possible. These quick improvements were reminiscent of the achievements that the Nationalist regime had been able to score on a regional basis after the success of the Northern Expedition in 1927. The Communists, of course, had a far larger area under their effective control, and their ability to devise a truly centralized system for the circulation of goods, people and funds set them apart from any government China had previously known.

Although the regime permitted private enterprise to continue for a time, its real interest was in establishing government control throughout the economy. Its ability to accelerate this schedule was enormously increased by the wave of nationalism that accompanied the mobilization of support for the Chinese intervention in Korea. The urban business class capitulated in the political and economic climate that developed in the early 1950s. Since these great drives constituted one of the first and best-recorded orchestrations of popular sentiment, their implementation was full of interest for the future. Observers like A. Doak Barnett, who wrote from Hong Kong, were able to provide vivid pictures of the Three-Anti and Five-Anti campaigns of those years. The first of these concentrated on officialdom (much of which was still noncommunist), and its targets were corruption, waste and bureaucratism. Denunciations, "people's trials" and a steadily increasing volume of publicity and exposure raised the level of insecurity as the movement swept from Manchuria to Canton. The Five-Anti campaign focused on businessmen and called for an end to bribery, tax evasion, theft of state secrets, cheating in labor or materials and stealing state economic intelligence. It is apparent that the definition of these crimes could be stretched to include activities virtually essential to the maintenance of business in an era of corruption, inflation and revolutionary change.

As with all campaigns, the Five-Anti included important elements of self-examination. Everywhere Five-Anti committees were set up with teams of political workers under their control; activists, mobilized from among workers, sought out tension points, organized denunciations and provided guidance. "Tiger hunts" were staged to discover corruption that affected officialdom as well as business concerns; confession and denunciation by employees were encouraged, and both the Party and the bureaucracy struggled to eradicate deviationist and bourgeois thought. The political and economic drive, staged through the numerous organizations which the Party could manipulate, took on the character of an immense morality play. The drive included provisions for leniency for the contrite, but it dealt more harshly with merchants and speculators than with "productive" manufacturers and industrialists.

The campaign strengthened the regime through the inflow of currency in penalty payments and confiscations that it produced. From the point of view of the revolution, however, its demonstration of the importance of cooperation with the authorities may have been even more important. Initially, one suspects, businessmen disillusioned with Nationalist incompetence may have been quite willing to cooperate with the new regime. But for the regime itself it was important to establish a clear mastery over them and, in time, to undermine their influence. By the time the drive was over, Barnett concluded: "Many private enterprises are now private in name only, and all private enterprises are subject to innumerable controls." Thus while the Meiji reformers had bent their efforts to encourage the development of a vigorous and innovative middle class, and the MacArthur reformers tried to promote a new and individualistic bourgeoisie by penalizing the old *zaibatsu* firms, the Chinese had the opposite goal of asserting state leadership.

The regime's problems in rural China eclipsed its difficulties in the area of urban control. China remained overwhelmingly agricultural; its farms provided the only possible source of a surplus that could subsidize industrial development. It was in the countryside that the most astounding changes of all took place. In dealing with this the new government was hampered by some of the world's most intractable sets of problems. On its side was the initial enthusiasm of the postliberation setting and an extraordinarily industrious and able population. Working against its goals, however, were the facts of agrarian China: a countryside badly damaged during a civil war that hurt communications and riparian works and a burgeoning population that resulted in low per capita productivity. Stern efforts would be needed to prevent the agricultural gains from being used up through a much-needed rise in consumption.

These problems were much more difficult than those the Japanese modernizers had faced. The Meiji leaders, a century earlier, had inherited a much lower level of population density. Their need for an agricultural surplus led them to regularize landholding by granting title to occupants and ending all samurai claims to ownership. By confirming actual patterns of landholdings they had encouraged agricultural stability, and by regularizing the land tax they had provided incentives for increased production. The growth that resulted, estimated at about 2 percent per annum, provided the modest margin for the investment in the infrastructure of the modern economy that made possible Japan's economic growth at the century's end. After World War II the MacArthur land reform had also been designed to increase stability and ward off revolution in the countryside. It provided for representative land commissions that selected purchasers for land and mollified landlords and reassured purchasers through a pattern of modest and, in view of the inflation, quite nominal compensation. By that time Japan's population problem was also acute, but high rates of literacy and rising expectations of consumption and education made it possible to work for population control while continued industrial expansion provided urban employment for the larger labor force.

The Chinese leaders operated in a setting radically different, and their strategy was equally different. Their goal was also the production and allocation of an agricultural surplus for rapid industrialization, but they were committed to doing this by pressing rural revolution and destabilizing the countryside. It was not enough, in their eyes, to satisfy the peasants by giving them title to land and providing incentives for greater production. The peasants were too numerous, and their unmet needs were too great. The peasants had to become full participants in the revolution, and they had to be taught to contribute to its goals as a new breed of communist man. Unless the countryside was restructured and involved in social change, there could be no revolution in China. Mao Tse-tung had held a consistently high evaluation of the revolutionary potential of the peasants since the 1920s. His famous report on Hunan in 1927 pointed out that "Only one group in the countryside has fought hard and relentlessly from the very start: the poor peasants.... it was they who fought, who organized, and who did the revolutionary work.... They alone were capable of doing the destructive work.... To reject them is to reject the revolution; a blow at them is a blow at the revolution. Their revolutionary course is faultless from beginning to end." Mao's "poor peasants" were the landless and the exploited, groups that had been derided as rural drifters by some of his colleagues. But they were more numerous by far than the local gentry and landlords, and Mao exhorted his associates to encourage and utilize their revolutionary potential. His optimistic vision of the new personality structure possible under socialism was based on this human material.

The final steps of the civil war and liberation of the late 1940s provided evidence of the explosive potential of this social class. As had been the case with rural rebellions that exploded during periods of disorder in China's past, the villages through which the Communist armies moved were full of hatred and resentment that could be fanned by Party workers sensitive to their possibilities. Social revolution was endemic in numerous districts, and journalists like Jack Belden have left gripping accounts of the way a pattern of denunciation and judgment could be carried out. A village revolutionized through mass involvement in the cosmic social drama of its time was "liberated" and ready to make its commitment in human effort and recruitment for Party, mass organizations and army.

After its establishment in 1949 the new regime extended nationwide tactics that had been developed in the north China countryside. The liberation of the villages set the style and model for drives that later affected the cities, private enterprises and universities. Skilled Party activists arrived to identify the most promising targets of local hate and resentment. Poor peasants would be recruited and encouraged to express their discontent in "speak bitterness" meetings. Struggle meetings operated around the clock to raise the level of emotion and intensity. "Class warfare was essential," A. Doak Barnett wrote at the time, "even though it disrupted agricultural production for long periods of time, because the landlord class had to be discredited thoroughly as well as 'economically eliminated.'" "Bitterness" could quickly cross the line of "violence" as "people's courts" made summary disposition of "enemies of the people." A community that had once crossed the line of participation could be assumed to have committed itself to the revolution. Peasant organizations were formed to assess the class status of villagers and upon these definitions depended the determination of parcels of land that were to be redistributed to appropriate elements of "the people."

This first stage of land reform was not yet socialist, but part of the "new democracy." Land titles were given to those who would work the land. The gentry and landlords were eliminated, sometimes physically through summary punishment, sometimes removed to work camps and at times tolerated during periods of reconstruction and self-reform. By 1952 the regime announced that land reform had been virtually carried out. The two contemporaneous land reforms, in Japan and China, thus provided extraordinarily striking contrasts in methods, goals and results.

The Peking regime was now able to demand high taxes from peasants who were no longer subject to landlord exploitation, but its needs for income were not met; agricultural production rose too slowly. The new units of land were often smaller and less economic than the old ones; the new multiplicity of owners created dangers of higher consumption instead of greater contributions to the revolution. Now began a gradual move toward collectivization. The first step was the organization of mutual-aid teams. By pooling scarce equipment efficiency could be improved, and by pooling labor the worst effects of fragmentized holdings could be overcome. Mutual-aid teams in turn led to producers' cooperatives; by 1955 the regime claimed that 15 percent of all agricultural acreage was included in these. According to the government explanation, in the cooperatives "members invest their land in the common enterprise, being credited with the corresponding number of shares." It was to be an "economic organization of unified management and collective labor, based on private ownership of land." The cooperatives were formed by the merger of several mutual-aid teams, and although the peasants theoretically retained ownership of their plots, in actuality they lost control over them.

By the mid-1950s there were enthusiastic reports of increased production. Mao Tse-tung now made a startling proposal to bring all forms of capitalistic enterprise in the countryside to an end. The entire nation was to be organized in producers' cooperatives of fifty families each. This plan was energetically pushed by local Party cadres, and by late spring of 1956 the government was reporting that nine-tenths of the peasants had complied. Next they were urged to give up their shares in the cooperatives and become wage laborers on collective farms. The Soviet experience was to be telescoped into a much shorter time period.

In each village the cooperatives, now transformed into collective farms, were charged with all the functions of leadership and organization that intensive agriculture on the Chinese model required. Communal work projects for roads, irrigation ditches and field work that had always been directed by local gentry and rural leaders were now the responsibility of the cadre of the Communist party. Ambitious plans set targets for agricultural output and improved programs of rewards in terms of health and recreation opportunities. The mobilization of labor that was anticipated was to make it possible to remake the face of the Chinese earth through gigantic efforts in reforestation, irrigation and electric power production.

No sooner was this vision outlined when in 1958 the most drastic experiment of all was called for. Under the "Great Leap Forward" of that year, a program of total organization of the agriculturalists was announced. "Communes" were to be the agricultural accompaniment of small-scale but instant industrialization plans. China's greatest economic problem, her overpopulation, was to be converted into her greatest asset through the organizational and manipulative skills that the Communist party had developed.

The communes were to vary in size from a single village to the area formerly served by a market town. Each would perform all government functions and coordinate all economic activities under Party control. The Chinese commune was far from the utopia of free-form, free-association relationships that the word "commune" acquired in the United States during the 1960s. Labor brigades marched off at dawn to work the fields, build roads, move earth, or plant trees. As a Party magazine proudly described it,

> At daybreak, bells ring and whistles blow to assemble.... In about a quarter of an hour the peasants line up. At the command of company and squad commanders, the teams march to the fields, holding flags. Here one no longer sees peasants in groups of two or three, smoking and going slowly and leisurely to the fields. What one hears are the sounds of measured steps and marching songs. The desultory living habits which have been with the peasants for thousands of years are gone forever....

All private plots of land were taken over. The new socialist man was to live for the state in barrack conditions, deposit his children in communal nurseries, eat in mess halls and visit his elderly parents in the "Happiness Homes" to which they had been assigned. The authoritarian strains in the Chinese tradition had not been invoked to such extremes since the Taiping rebels had organized their theocratic state a century before.

Although it was never fully renounced and although model communes survived for demonstration to foreigners in the 1970s, this effort for total regimentation could never be implemented. It had been conceived without the aid of expert agronomists or economists, who were under the ban together with other intellectuals as doubters. Government leaders were furthermore deceived by grossly inaccurate reports from overenthusiastic and unscientific local leaders who reported astounding gains in production that seemed to justify and reward ever greater exertion and effort. The farmers, however, found themselves without incentives or rewards, and their exhaustion and disillusion showed that Mao's populist emphasis had seriously overestimated the transformation of the new socialist man. There were also objective difficulties that would have created problems for any program. The existing physical makeup of village and countryside worked against the perfection of organization. Also the withdrawal of the Soviet aid as the Sino-Soviet split came into the open made the ambitious schedule of industrial targets more difficult to attain. Another element more difficult to appraise was that of climatic reverses on which the regime blamed agricultural setbacks. Whatever the balance between these factors and the exhaustion of an overregimented populace, it is clear that the boasts of the late 1950s turned into the disasters of the early 1960s. The years 1960–62 brought an acute economic crisis.

Since agricultural success was central to the hopes of the regime and to the livelihood of its people, it is worth examining in greater detail a rhythm of cycles that Alexander Eckstein has described. The problem, as he saw it, was inherent in the discrepancies between Mao Tse-tung's vision of Chinese possibilities and the facts of China's economic backwardness—"a high degree of population pressure, rapid population growth, a technically backward agriculture, and a low per capita food supply." These intractable conditions presented the leadership with obstacles so great that it sought for "ideological commitment, mass mobilization and organization" to overcome them in the absence of resources in expertise and equipment. Years of high agricultural productivity required a combination of favorable climatic circumstances and policy moderation to provide incentives for the agriculturalist. Because of the primacy of agriculture in China's national income and all developmental programs, however, a poor harvest would "necessarily lead to a decline in the output of manufactured consumer goods, ... depress exports, and the capacity to finance imports."

The policy cycle Eckstein discerned was one in which favorable harvests promoted confidence and optimism (never entirely absent from Mao's belief in the possibilities of socialist transformation) which led to decisions for greater mobilization of manpower and greater allocation of funds for modernization. This mobilization and allocation, however, resulted in lessening the incentives for farmers to produce, with the result that the expectations of dramatic increases in output, frequently fed by overenthusiastic reporting, proved seriously wide of the mark. If this condition was worsened by climatic setbacks, disaster could result; but in any case, the anticipated growth was not forthcoming. The regime then found it necessary to backtrack, admit its error, castigate its cadres and then replace some of the incentives that had recently been removed. There was a "general easing of the pressure on the peasantry, that is, more favorable prices, more favorable terms of trade, easing of the collection pressures, greater scope for the private plots, greater scope for the free rural markets, and less control over labor allocation and degree of labor mobilization." The most visible evidence of this was seen in the striking fluctuation of freedom allowed private plots, rural fairs and free markets. These were closed in 1955–56 and reopened in September 1956, closed again in August 1957 and reopened in September 1959. In the case of the communes, the terminology outlived the fact. The "production team" became ownership units in 1961; some of the nomenclature survived but the attempt at total mobilization had retreated. Relaxation of effort, however, carried with it the danger of a rebirth of "capitalist" tendencies. During the first two decades of the People's Republic, this "danger" was promptly countered by a new "drive," and this alternation of drive and danger provided the rhythm of moves toward collectivization.

The ability of the leadership to admit its errors and retreat from them was an important element in its endurance. At the same time the backward step was never a full one. Each time much of the terminology and some of the reality of the previous upward spiral survived. When United States reporters were allowed to visit rural China again in 1971, they found a countryside that seemed to them better kept, and a populace better off, than the one they had last been able to visit two decades before. A *New York Times* reporter who visited the "Chinese-Vietnamese Friendship People's Commune" near Peking found it a small world of thirty-eight thousand people, its thirty-five original villages organized into six production brigades and further subdivided into ninety-five production teams. The team, with five or six hundred people (dimensions that suggest, and perhaps perpetuate, the lines of village marketing systems of the traditional countryside), was the basic economic unit. Its people owned their homes, and family life went on as before, although elderly members without families to help them were housed in separate quarters. The commune had been created out of six cooperatives with the specific purpose of making large-scale reclamation projects possible. New dams and reservoirs and several hundred miles of irrigation ditches had transformed the landscape and provided a setting in which fruit trees, rice, wheat, soybeans and corn could be maintained. Private plots made it possible for people to grow their own vegetables. Larger enterprises for animal husbandry were conducted by the commune, and their products were reserved for sale through state channels. Production teams paid peasants in work points based upon a classification of skill, ability and "cultural and ideological development," a rating that was multiplied by the number of days worked. Earnings of the production team from sales to the state were distributed proportionately after the state was paid a fee for use of the land and after the leaders decided how much to reserve for reinvestment. Medical services, though rudimentary, were cheap and schooling was free. Clothing was rationed and of poor quality but available at standardized prices.

By 1971 agricultural policy had thus settled into a compromise between traditional village and compulsive mobilization organization. *Times* reporters said that peasants "chuckled and dismissed as 'inventions' stories that peasants in communes had been regimented in dormitories." Thus the gap between the claims of the regime's propagandists and the quiet drag of the agricultural situation with its limitations of resources and incentives made it difficult to judge Chinese reality. Increasingly, however, observers agreed in their descriptions of a setting in which pervasive but small-scale technological improvement had been accompanied by modest but egalitarian gains in livelihood.

Nothing made it more difficult for Western specialists to study China than their isolation from their friends and contacts among Chinese intellectuals. The intellectuals were early objects of Peking policy, and control over them was naturally as important as control over the urban and rural economies. Given the importance of doctrine and ideology in communist movements, intellectual leaders were both necessary and suspect. In the Maoist tradition orthodoxy had received a high priority long before the liberation. During the Yenan years a process of "rectification" directed particularly against the intellectuals focused on thought correction with emphases on personal confession and reeducation. Mao Tse-tung and Liu Shao-ch'i set the line in all matters of philosophy and action. It was the Chinese Communist party's advocacy of a "mass line" that made its acceptance by intellectuals particularly vital. As for the intellectuals themselves, their upper class origin and their long association with the Western and imperialist world that was the source of modern knowledge made them particularly inviting targets for examination and reproof. During the first years of the Peking regime, many who went over to the new regime received posts of honor and importance, but it was not very long before the same efforts that were bringing about change in rural and urban society focused upon them.

In 1951 and 1952 the Three-Anti and Five-Anti movements were conducted on university campuses as well as in business establishments. But it was the larger scale and longer lasting process of "thought study," often called "brain washing," that held Western observers in shocked fascination. The drive was directed against foreigners who had remained in China as well as against American prisoners taken in the Korean War, and it fed on the fervid and xenophobic nationalism that the war helped produce. Its most startling manifestations were in the centers of Chinese student and intellectual life. The movement combined, in Robert Lifton's words, "external force or coercion with an appeal to inner enthusiasm through evangelistic exhortation." Subjects were approached as patients in need of help and salvation and treated with techniques related to those of group therapy. In a controlled environment they were brought face to face with basic questions about their identity and morality. Their need for approval of their interlocutors, and the psychological dependence upon the group that resulted, produced confessions that made possible a grateful return to the organization of peers from which they had been ostracized. For many of those who recanted and confessed, compliance was no doubt surface and partial, but it is probable that the majority came through the experience deeply disturbed and shaken and unable to throw off the entire experience as meaningless.

By the mid-1950s the leaders seem to have thought that they had succeeded in remolding Chinese intellectuals into an appropriate instrument for the transformation of Chinese society and thought. There was fear of growing bureaucratization in the ever-growing army of Party cadres and government officials. They needed criticism to keep them up to the mark, and in 1956 the Hungarian rebellion provided graphic illustration of the dangers that could face a regime insensitive to long-smoldering discontent. A new campaign for self-criticism was launched under the slogan "Let The Hundred Flowers Bloom," with reference to the free play of schools of thought in classical times. As a government directive phrased it, thought reform was to continue, but there was to be "freedom of independent thinking, freedom of debate, freedom of creative work, freedom to criticize, to express one's own views." Most intellectuals, not certain of the new rules, chose to keep their peace. But after repeated encouragement by political authorities, sparked by a statement from Mao himself "On the Correct Handling of Contradictions among the People," they concluded that they were within their rights as "people" to offer "nonantagonistic" criticism of the Party in what had become a national campaign for "Rectification of Party Members." To the government's astonishment the "Hundred Flowers" that bloomed soon grew in number far beyond those appropriate for nonantagonistic criticism and speedily included nonsocialist weeds. Some even sprouted among nonintellectuals and semiintellectuals who joined in the criticism. Every aspect of Party leadership, dogma and practice came under searching criticism. When it was apparent that the intellectuals were far from cowed or contrite for past errors, the Party machinery swung into attack with calls for correction of "rightist" and even "bourgeois" elements. Before long the Party was back at its earlier task of correcting those who had presumed to correct it. The intensity of the new drive against the "rightists" carried over into the ideological paroxysm that accompanied the Great Leap Forward and the drive for communes. New study groups and new rectification schools and centers were the order of the day. Socialist man proved to have propensities for backsliding that tried even the confidence of Maoist populism.

Another, and perhaps even greater, drive was yet to come. After the economic disasters of the Great Leap Forward in the early 1960s, an interlude of calm prevailed as the cycle of socialist reconstruction gave way to tolerance for human frailty and the need for material incentives. But basic problems remained unresolved. To some it seemed that the reversal of the policies of the Great Leap had left Mao Tse-tung compromised in his position of infallibility. Rumors of his increasing incapacity and ill health were frequent. Further, the growing intensity of the struggle with the Soviets was troublesome for those who were committed to modernization of the armed forces through armament and machinery. As the Viet Cong began to threaten the government of South Vietnam and American intervention slowly increased, issues of foreign policy and foreign danger resonated with internal politics and leadership. Was the American imperialist at the southern gate more dangerous than the former ally along the northern border? If so, was it not a first priority to strengthen the armed forces with weapons where they were available and to refrain from upsetting peasant morale with further leaps to socialist collectivism? Did China's recent difficulties in modernization strategy dictate an increasing emphasis on technical competence, or was the ideological purity of the revolutionary spirit more important? Was continuing revolution and upheaval compatible with China's security needs?

The Proletarian Cultural Revolution of 1966–69 was Mao Tse-tung's response to these questions. Mao had retired from active leadership in 1958, but in 1962 he called for another campaign of "socialist education." When this failed to receive the response he desired, he turned to youth and to the army in order to correct the Party and the bureaucracy. The army had become bureaucratized on the Soviet model, with a pattern of ranks and privileges that set it apart from the informal comradeship that had characterized the guerrilla fighters in Yenan years. Defense Minister P'eng Te-huai, who seems to have favored maintaining the ties with the Russians, had been ousted in 1959 and replaced by Lin Piao, who had led the Chinese forces in Korea. The army was swiftly repoliticized with a massive new infusion of political leaders. Youth was encouraged to organize into Red Guard units that proliferated on every campus throughout the land. They first reformed or reviled their professors for bourgeois thinking and rightist tendencies and then sallied forth as agents of reform to war on the Party and government bureaucracies. Giant posters appeared everywhere on walls to denounce the evils of bureaucratism and opportunism. In many centers violence followed as local groups competed for power and influence. When disorder became excessive, army units stepped in to reestablish discipline.

Before the turbulence came to an end, the People's Republic had experienced its first real shake-up of leadership. Liu Shao-ch'i, chief of state and announced successor to Mao, was denounced, humiliated and dismissed as a "revisionist." Teng Hsiao-p'ing, secretary general of the Party who had, like Liu, cooperated in the first stages of the Cultural Revolution, was similarly dismissed. Into the limelight came Marshal Lin Piao, now Mao's "closest comrade in arms," and his introduction to the booklet of the aging leader's thoughts became the standard commentary to that philosophy for millions of readers. Gradually order returned as revolutionary committees containing "revolutionized" Party cadres, People's Liberation Army and "revolutionary masses" were set up in all major administrative units. In 1969 a new Party Congress selected a new Central Committee. A new party constitution named Lin Piao as Mao's successor. Throughout the land the political position of army leaders and representatives was far stronger than it had been. One of the few leaders to survive the shifts was the moderate and durable Chou En-lai, who remained as premier.

The events of the Proletarian Cultural Revolution were particularly traumatic for the intellectuals. The Red Guards, who were supposed to learn revolution by practicing it, quite naturally began with their schools and their professors. In one sense they were a Chinese refraction of the worldwide student movement of the 1960s; in a deeper sense, however, they were the chosen instruments of an aging revolutionary who set out to purify and consolidate his revolution while there was still time. During the 1960s virtually all higher education came to a halt in the People's Republic. As order returned students were expected to do manual work among "the people" at least half the year. Schools became instruments of revolution. Entrance examinations in colleges were denounced as "tools for the restoration of capitalism," and new enrollment systems specified that no student who had not completed two or three years of

THE GREAT PROLETARIAN CULTURAL REVOLUTION, 1966. Lin Piao greets a vast throng of Red Guards on behalf of Mao Tse-tung. Chou En-lai and Chiang Ch'ing, Mao's wife, are on Lin's right.

productive labor and who had not satisfied his workmates and local authorities of his ideological preparedness was to be admitted. All courses in higher education were stripped to a minimum considered essential for productive purposes; six-year engineering programs were shortened to three, and much of the time saved was to be devoted to politics, farming and military training. Gradually this extreme also passed. By 1972 the new thaw had made it possible to criticize the excesses of egalitarianism again, and in September of that year it was announced that entrance examinations would once again be used for admission to schools and colleges.

The revolution carried out in the People's Republic has been the largest in human history. Tumultuous change continued for over two decades, and whenever people, government or Party seemed to be relaxing a new and titanic drive would provide fresh energy and intensity to the process. The change was conditioned by aspects of China's philosophical, social and political traditions. Mao's optimistic view of man, the pattern of rule by a dedicated elite schooled in the official ideology and the extraordinary ability of the regime to marshal the lives of millions all owed something to the Chinese past. The recent past played an even larger part in providing targets and goals. The pervasive hatred of imperialism, the determination to build a strong state that could hold its own with all possible competitors and the constant exhortations to cleanliness, industriousness and civic consciousness echoed themes that distinguished every reform effort from the time of the late Ch'ing self-strengtheners. Denigration of individualism and assertion of state control over industrial production also continued themes that earlier governments had emphasized, though far less successfully.

But it is also apparent that those who had preached a changeless China and had predicted a short and turbulent life for the new regime were most mistaken of all. The "changeless" nature of that China was a misapprehension more in the eye of the beholder than in the facts of the land, and the perpetuation of the myth was only another aspect of the world's ignorance of its most populous country. By the 1970s no one could doubt that sweeping and permanent change had taken place in Chinese society. The cost had been high, but the new regime had also made important strides toward its modernization goals within the priorities it had set. To a remarkable degree the goals of nationalism had been achieved.

Modern technology had been devoted first of all to national security. A growing nuclear scientific potential existed side by side with traditional agricultural technology. Throughout the country local and small-scale industrial development was devoted to support and modernization of agrarian pursuits. Organizational innovations made it possible to involve the world's largest population in a national effort of revolutionary reconstruction. The threshold of national endurance, participation and consumption had been raised and the lintel lowered, to bring about a vast homogenization of existence and experience. Rudimentary literacy, simple moralisms and propagandistic art diffused the story of renewal and participation among the masses. Perhaps most important of all, however, national pride had been recovered. China stood alone among the powers, beholden to none.

4. The Japanese Recovery

AFTER THE CONCLUSION of the San Francisco Treaty of Peace, the Japanese government moved rapidly to resume its international contacts. The two decades that followed witnessed striking changes in Japan's position and power. Japan began as an American protégé, its economy still weak and its external and internal security guaranteed by American forces that could, as the American-Japanese Security Pact put it, "be utilized to contribute to the maintenance of international peace and security in the Far East and to the security of Japan against armed attack from without, including assistance given at the express request of the Japanese Government to put down large-scale internal riots and disturbances in Japan, caused through instigation or intervention by an outside power or powers." The Japanese economy had profited from services the United States had received during the Korean War, but Japan's standard of living and of production were still low. The economy had grown steadily at an average of slightly over 10 percent annually since the surrender, but the base line of 1945 had found things at such a low ebb that such growth, given Japanese industry and American assistance, was not startling. It was usual to speak of Japan's "economic dilemma" and to ruminate gloomily on the discrepancy between large resource needs and food deficiencies and limited export capabilities.

Two decades later Japan's ability to continue its economic growth at approximately the same rate had created a radically different picture. In 1960 the security pact had been renewed, its more unequal features softened or eliminated to Japanese advantage. Its language no longer envisaged the use of American troops to maintain order in Japan itself. The Japanese economy had provided the most striking example of sustained growth that the postwar world had seen. In 1954 Japan's Gross National Product was slightly over $21 billion, by 1967 it was three and a half times that figure, and it was to double again between 1966 and 1970, when it stood at $200 billion. It continued to grow until the oil crisis of 1973, but by then inflation made the dollar figures less meaningful. Throughout the period the Japanese pursued a cautious line in foreign affairs, shunning the limelight and concentrating on their own affairs. Yet by 1972 their astounding achievements in economic growth had resulted in a pattern of interrelationships that had stabilized and changed the Pacific world, and in 1974 former Prime Minister Satō was awarded the Nobel Prize for Peace in recognition of Japan's continued abstention from the nuclear race.

Japan's economic achievement in the 1950s and 1960s was made possible by a combination of factors. Japan had come out of World War II with its in-

TOKYO DESTROYED (above). In spring 1945, only large and modern buildings, many of them gutted, survived destruction after fire raids.
TOKYO REBUILT (below). Expressways, high-speed rail communications and modern office buildings symbolize the changes economic growth has brought.

dustrial plant substantially destroyed, but its productive skills had been sharpened during the long struggle with the world's most advanced industrial powers. The plant had to be rebuilt, and it was naturally reconstructed along lines more advanced and functional than those that characterized countries that had experienced less devastation in war.

The skill and the discipline of the Japanese labor force had been proved during the lean years of depression, war and surrender. Postwar labor legislation brought improved working conditions and labor unions to modern industry, but the unions remained organized on enterprise lines that permitted a high degree of loyalty to individual firms. On the enterprise level patterns of job security, permanent commitment, seniority pay and company paternalism that had developed in prewar days brought a close sense of community between enterprise and employees. Job security and seniority pay minimized worker resistance to technological change, and enterprise loyalty combined with a steadily rising standard of living to work against serious strikes in all but a few declining areas such as the coal industry. Throughout the decades of the 1950s and 1960s worker productivity rose more rapidly than wages in modern industrial firms, due partly to the low level of wages at the beginning of the period and partly to the steady technological advance. The area of shared interest between management and labor was symbolized by the increasingly generous twice-yearly bonus and the growing range of worker benefits for housing, medical and recreational needs. Since public welfare measures lagged behind the rise of prices and since job transfers in large firms were few, workers had every reason to feel loyalty to enterprises. The relationship was symbolized and sometimes satirized by the company song, worker excursions and morning calisthenics.

The new industries were managed by a new generation of business leaders. Occupation purges had removed the top levels of the old business establishment, and the confusing scene of postwar competition facilitated the emergence of new and imaginative captains of industry. They were less parts of the old elite, less bound to patterns of government approval and favoritism, more international in contacts and outlook and more able to respond quickly to opportunity and innovation. By the time the old executives reemerged in the 1950s, the rules of the game had changed against them. New patterns of trade, labor and fiscal arrangements had altered the Japanese economy beyond their ability, power or even desire to restore the oligopoly of prewar days.

The discipline of the labor force was a reflection of the discipline of the Japanese masses. Japan's recovery as an industrial power depended upon its ability to earn the foreign exchange required for raw material imports, and this required restraints upon consumer demand. Into the 1960s opportunities for consumer spending were limited in numerous respects. Housing was in particularly short supply in the crowded cities, and most Japanese lived poorly but also inexpensively. Government welfare measures lagged behind what was needed, and most social security depended upon personal planning and saving. Rapid changes in society and economy put a premium on modern education for the young, and it was the private schools and colleges that absorbed the majority of Japan's student masses. In 1971 the six largest national universities enrolled a total of approximately 77,000 students, but the ten largest private universities claimed 344,300 students. Private universities enrolled 80 percent of all college students. There was a premium on saving, and Japanese savings were extraordinarily high, running at 20 percent of disposable income. These savings, along with a large percentage of enterprise profits, were transformed into investment and reinvestment to fuel the continuing cycle of productive expansion.

Throughout the decade the Japanese government was in the hands of moderate conservatives of the Liberal Democratic party. Leadership was provided by factions that dated from the days of Yoshida Shigeru (1878–1967), who had set Japan's postwar course during Occupation days. After Yoshida's retirement the Finance Ministry constituted the principal career path for political leadership. Not only did the prime ministers of the 1960s come up through the Finance Ministry, but in the Satō cabinet of 1971 ministers of Justice, Foreign Affairs, Finance, Economic Planning, Health, and International Trade and Industry all had had previous Finance Ministry service. Under these leaders the Japanese government taxed moderately, pursued a consistent policy of trade expansion through its allocation of foreign exchange credits, depreciation allowances and tax credits and a continuation of the vigilant watch on foreign imports and capital that had begun in Occupation days to protect the Japanese economy from powerful competitors. By the end of the 1960s the danger of foreign takeover was past, and steps for import and capital liberalization were far advanced. By then a drumfire of foreign and especially American criticism of Japanese exclusion was beginning to produce protectionist sentiment among some of Japan's overseas customers.

Japan's leaders staked their country's political and economic future on the maintenance of close ties with the United States. This decision had important consequences for Japan's economic growth. The security pact that maintained American troops on Japanese soil freed Japan from any necessity to undertake large-scale rearmament, and Japan's Self-defense Forces were maintained at a modest level of 1 percent of Japan's Gross National Product. Japan particularly profited from the existence of the American "nuclear umbrella," which spared it the burden of the massive investment in nuclear development that received high priority in China during these same years. These savings also coincided with Japanese inclinations, for Japan was not conscious of any outside threat. It regarded the Soviet Union as a satisfied power, it recognized no danger from a traditionally nonexpansive China and it felt the most profound repugnance for any form of nuclear development in the aftermath of Hiroshima and Nagasaki. Moreover it was important for Japan to project a pacifist image in Asian markets. When rash suggestions for the use of Japanese troops in South Korea were made in the American Congress, President Syngman Rhee had observed that the South Korean forces would feel impelled to drive such forces into the sea before returning to deal with the North Korean invaders. American security guarantees thus coincided with Japanese pacifist inclinations and diplomatic needs as well as economic priorities.

The American tie was also vital to Japanese economic recovery through the importance the American market came to assume for Japanese industry. Denied access to the mainland markets that had taken a large share of its prewar exports of low-cost goods, Japan now prepared to enter the high-quality markets of the industrialized West. This need coincided with an "American era" of free trade and export surpluses in which Japanese goods posed no threat or problem. Since, in addition, American sponsorship introduced the new Japan to all of the important international organizations and encouraged Japanese to enter friendly markets, Japan's ability to work against the rancor that remained from wartime occupation and destruction in Southeast Asia was materially advanced. This had important consequences for Japan's access to raw materials, in which there were further benefits that resulted from a decline in world prices in the 1950s. Japan's exports grew at a rapid rate. During the 1960s they grew approximately 15 percent per year, a figure more than double the world rate. During the decade Japan's trade with the United States made up approximately one-third of its total balance, and Japan emerged (after Canada) as America's second largest market.

None of this would have sufficed if Japanese goods had not met the test of quality and cost, and for this Japan's access to imported technology, most of it American, may have been most important of all. Between 1950 and 1968 approximately ten thousand separate arrangements were made for puchase, contract or cooperation in the import of industrial technology into Japan at a total cost of close to $1.5 billion. Japanese industry, when destroyed in World War II, had been far inferior technologically to its principal competitors overseas. It was now rebuilt and expanded on the most advanced levels available at a fraction of the cost and, especially, time that would have been required for developing it without outside assistance. In case after case Japanese engineers went on to devise techniques and procedures that increased the productivity of the technology that had been brought in. Japanese technological innovation was directed particularly toward production processes rather than toward basic research, and it was only in the early 1970s that substantial costs in research and development signaled a waning of Japanese reliance upon imported technology. There was less to be had, and Japan's competitors were no longer so willing to share.

While the American tie was important to Japan, Japan's performance was equally beneficial to the United States, for Japanese economic growth did more to stabilize the western Pacific than the Seventh Fleet. It provided powerful arguments for the vitality of democratic institutions. It made Japan an inviting market for producers all over the world and resulted in Japanese ability to supply manufactures to Asian countries and to contribute to Asian economic development. Most of all, however, it transformed Japan itself.

A number of structural changes in the Japanese economy marked Japan's emergence into the ranks of highly modernized nations. The first of these was the drastic change in the relative proportions of industrial to agricultural output. Agriculture was by no means stagnant in postwar Japan. Advances in agronomy, increased application of fertilizer, improved incentives resulting from the land reform and government willingness to subsidize the price of rice resulted in dramatic increases of agricultural productivity and a rice surplus. At the same time, however, the rising productivity and well-being in the industrial sector made agriculture less desirable for young Japanese. As the percentage of agricultural workers dwindled steadily—during 1971 alone it fell by 6 percent—the political reasons for artificial supports for agricultural products declined in importance. This coincided with foreign pressure for liberalization of agricultural imports. As a result Prime Minister Tanaka disclosed a "new vision" which projected increased agricultural efficiency through the rationalization of small plots into larger units, increased mechanization and improved communications to diffuse industry further throughout the Japanese countryside.

Changes in the Japanese economy also produced one of the world's largest consumer markets. In the 1930s the conventional Marxist explanation for Japanese imperialism was that the lack of a domestic market among Japan's exploited workers had forced Japanese industrialists to seize overseas markets and raw materials by imperialist expansion. But postwar Japan, without the help or burden of empire, proved able to buy raw materials at world prices and sell in world markets at the same time that its consumers demanded and received an increasing share of their products. The range and quality of Japanese household appliances, which began modestly with improvements like electric rice cookers in the 1950s, grew steadily. By the 1970s there was jocular reference to the fact that the householder's "three treasures" (as opposed to the old imperial regalia of sword, mirror and curved jewel) were the "three c's" of color television, car and air conditioner. The potential of the Japanese market was reflected in growing American insistence that access to it be liberalized.

Growing standards of expectation and affluence operated to keep the Japanese population in check. Japanese married later, had fewer children and wanted more education for them. Population restrictions, initially encouraged through the legalization of abortion in the 1950s, made Japan the first Asian country to slow its growth to the rate common in other highly industrialized societies. By 1972 the distribution of age groups within the population was beginning to resemble that in other modernized countries. Japanese were living longer; in 1971 life expectancy was seventy for males and seventy-five for females, and there were increasingly vocal demands for additional welfare provisions for the aged. Economic growth had produced a labor shortage.

Within Japanese manufactures there was a sharp increase in the proportion of value added through labor and a decline in the proportion of import cost. Manufactures were more sophisticated and high quality, and the relatively simple processing that imports had received in prewar textiles gave way to complex production for highly developed markets. In textiles cotton gave way to synthetics. In the area of raw materials Japan had become a principal beneficiary of bulk transport. Giant ore carriers and supertankers, most of them fabricated in Japanese shipyards, lowered the unit cost of raw materials to even out the discrepancy between Japanese manufacturers and their American competitors in Chicago or Pittsburgh, whose ores had to come in smaller containers from increasingly distant points. Japanese coastal plants provided economical access to world shipping lanes. With economic growth Japan's import needs, especially of sources of energy, rose at extraordinary speed. In item after item Japan became the world's largest importer. In 1970 the number of oil tankers (thirty-five thousand tons or over) that entered Tokyo Bay each day numbered 123; in 1971 the figure rose to 214. Some projected for 1980 a line of two hundred thousand ton tankers, spaced forty nautical miles apart, all the way from Tokyo Bay to the Persian Gulf.

Economic growth of this order brought with it many problems of social and environmental maladjustment. The environment was the first to suffer. In the early 1970s Japan stood third in Gross National Product, after the United States and the Soviet Union; on a per capita basis, it stood about fifteenth, approximately with Italy. But if national product was measured on an area basis, Japan's economic activity was five times as intensive as that of the United States and if the unit measurement was changed to that of arable land, Japan's ratio was ten times that of America. In terms of environmental well-being the Japanese suffered more pollution, more crowding, more carbon monoxide and other noxious chemicals than any other nation, and the appeal of slogans of growth and limitless economic expansion had begun to run their course. But they had left Japan a strikingly productive society, one better able to deal with the problems that faced it than it had ever been. Japan had become a power whose economic strength easily balanced out its military diffidence in speculations affecting the future world balance of power.

During the 1950s and 1960s political developments remained largely within the channels set in Occupation days. The Liberal Democratic party, which represented a merger of the two major parties of prewar days, was dominant for the entire two decades, although its election pluralities and percentages dwindled slowly throughout the period. Liberal Democratic rule seemed most nearly shaken in 1960. The cabinet, which had taken power in 1957, was headed by Kishi Nobusuke, a member of the Tōjō cabinet of 1941; his autocratic manner affronted Japanese notions of political leadership. Kishi's rigid anticommunism resulted in closer ties with Taiwan and a total break in trade with the People's Republic on the mainland. In the same period renewal of the security pact with the United States for ten years alarmed many Japanese who had felt only slightly involved by the original agreement, which had been negotiated at a time when Japan was only partly sovereign. These issues were further complicated by the state visit planned by President Eisenhower. His trip was first planned as a follow-up to a visit to Moscow, but its import seemed to change when the Moscow visit was canceled after the Soviet Union shot down an American U-2 observation plane. What had begun as a symbol of coexistence now became a tour of U. S. Pacific bases, one designed, it was charged, to bolster the falling popularity of the Kishi government. The Kishi government next used its majority to ram the security pact extension through the Diet. Opposition to the Eisenhower visit now became opposition to Kishi. Great student demonstrations shook Tokyo day after day. The treaty survived, but Eisenhower's visit had to be canceled, and Kishi resigned in July of 1960. It was in this setting that Prime Minister Ikeda, Kishi's successor, announced goals of doubling the national income in ten years (an objective that was far surpassed) and that Japan settled down to a decade of economic development.

The ruling party itself was subdivided into seven or eight factions, each of which was headed by a potential candidate for national leadership and each of which received support from elements of the business establishment. Elections to the House of Representatives tended to be waged on local issues, and Liberal Democrats, as members of the party in power, could point to practical benefits and achievements. The balance of factions within the ranks of successful candidates determined the outcome of party convention contests for party leadership. The party leader in turn was sure of election to the prime ministership by a House of Representatives in which Liberal Democrats held the majority of seats. Factional alternation or shifts of factional strength within cabinets served to allow a measure of shifts of policy or emphasis behind the unbroken continuity of conservative cabinets. With the exception of a brief period in the mid-1950s, however, party leadership was securely in the hands of Yoshida Shigeru and his chosen successors Kishi Nobusuke (1957–60), Ikeda Hayato (1960–64) and Satō Eisaku (1964–72). These men were able bureaucrats and cautious moderates. They were not broadly popular or in any sense charismatic figures, but they were durable administrators and operated well within the Japanese tradition of consensus and convergence of opinion.

The Japan Socialist party, the Liberal Democrats' principal opponent, relied principally upon the support of the major labor federations. Its leaders, themselves divided into factions of personal and ideological preferences, were veterans of the battles over theory during prewar days when government repression restricted radicals to bookish struggles, and their calls for class revolution received only sectional support in a society in which the standards of well-being of most groups were advancing rapidly. The Japan Communist party, which was able to reform and operate freely for the first time, had at one time seemed a likely beneficiary of the postsurrender confusion. Elections held in the aftermath of the Dodge deflation of 1949 saw it receive 10 percent of the votes cast. Its appeal dwindled rapidly thereafter, however, and for a time the party received only a negligible share of the vote. During the 1960s the party's leadership managed to work out a strongly nationalist position independent of both Peking and Moscow, however, and as the pressures of metropolitan congestion and environmental pollution began to dim the glamor of economic growth, the Communists' electoral appeal improved again. By the late 1960s the party was receiving 5 percent of the popular vote; in 1969 the figure had climbed to 6.8 percent, and in 1972 this rose to close to 11 percent, with forty seats in the lower house of the Diet. By 1969 an additional element in the political picture was the Clean Government party (Kōmeitō), an arm of the postwar Sōka Gakkai religious movement. This vigorous revival of Nichiren Buddhism had developed remarkable strength through organizational skill in proselytizing new recruits to the urban and labor population, and it provided a focus of identity and activity in the impersonality of the new mass culture.

With the exception of 1947–48, Japan's conservative politicians won every election, formed every cabinet and named every prime minister. They could not have done this, however, if they had not been operating under an electoral system that allotted 62 percent of Diet seats to rural and semiurban districts. In these areas the conservatives predominated, and they took 63 percent of the vote as late as 1969. But in the metropolitan districts, where most Japanese now lived, the conservatives took only 39 percent of the vote in 1969. The conservatives' share of the total vote in fact declined steadily over the decades from a high of 66 percent in 1952 to a low of 46.5 percent in 1972. Because the opposition was divided and ineffective, this did not cost the Liberal Democratic party its power. But the prospect for the future was that mass politics in metropolitan areas would force a revision of tactics and produce centrist coalition governments. Such governments seemed likely to be committed to nondivisive tactics, among which a low level of military activity seemed probable. The international and economic climate, however, could at any time bring changes in this, and a political system that had benefited from an annual 10 percent growth for two decades had not, as yet, met a serious test.

The 1960s brought with their economic growth many indications of Japan's increasing international stature. In 1966 Japan played a leading role in the establishment of the Asian Development Bank. The tumultuous disorder of the Proletarian Cultural Revolution in China discountenanced the extreme Left in Japanese public opinion for a time, and the Japanese Communist party began a careful and successful campaign to separate itself from the charge of subservience to China. The government, in turn, pressed its claims for Japanese territory still under foreign rule. In 1967 Prime Minister Satō secured the return of the Bonin Islands to Japanese rule. Okinawa and the Ryukyu chain proved more difficult. The San Francisco Treaty had provided that, pending United Nations agreement to a trusteeship administered by the United States (one that was never requested), the United States would have all administrative rights. By the late 1960s American colonial control over the million inhabitants of Okinawa was becoming a serious liability to American-Japanese relations and a handicap to the conservative Japanese government. In the fall of 1969 Prime Minister Satō and President Richard Nixon agreed on the return of Okinawa and the Ryukyus to Japanese rule, with American bases there subject to the same restrictions that applied to those on the Japanese home islands. Early in 1972 it was arranged for Okinawa to revert to Japanese rule in May of that year. With this move, in Prime Minister Satō's words, the postwar era had come to an end. Japan now turned to press the Soviet Union for the return of the southernmost islands of the Kurile chain. Far less populous and more distant from the Japanese imagination than Okinawa, however, these bleak outposts had never excited the concern in Japanese opinion that Okinawa had. Japanese felt their sovereignty restored and territory regained. Within weeks a new independence in policy toward China reflected the change in climate.

5. The End of the Postwar Era

THE YEAR 1972 can properly be considered to mark the end of the postwar era. In February President Richard Nixon, for two decades the symbol of unyielding hostility to accommodation with communism, traveled to China and at Shanghai worked out a joint statement with Premier Chou En-lai defining and diminishing the distance between American and Chinese positions. In May the United States returned Okinawa to Japan, ending the last vestige of the Occupation. In July the governments of the two Koreas hesitantly reached agreement on a series of steps designed to lower the level of invective. In September Prime Minister Tanaka of Japan traveled to China and, in a communiqué with Premier Chou En-lai at Peking, opened the way to regularization of relations between Japan and the People's Republic. Late in 1971 the People's Republic was admitted to the United Nations, and early in 1973 the long agony of American intervention in Vietnam drew to a close.

With these steps direct relations between the two great powers of East Asia which had begun so unfortunately at Shimonoseki in 1895 were resumed after a quarter century hiatus. The half century that followed Shimonoseki had been one of steady and uninterrupted Japanese advance. It was an advance made possible by Japan's speedy modernization as a nation-state, but at the same time the military, economic and psychological gains of that advance helped fuel and channel the character of Japanese modernization. For China the challenge from Japan had been only one of many outside pressures it had known. The initial shock of Shimonoseki, as Liang Ch'i-ch'ao later recalled, had awakened China as though from a dream of four thousand years. The image of Meiji Japan had attracted the attention of tens of thousands in their desperate search for applicable models of modernization. The collapse of empires around the world and the departure of the first generation of modernizers left twentieth-century Japanese leaders without sure bearings in a world full of new opportunities. Most of these originated in the weakness of Japan's giant neighbor on the continent, and the discrepancy between its traditions and its dismal prospects was so great that a generation of Japanese thought they saw a mission to lead and to direct. Ques-

Administrative Divisions, People's Republic of China

SINKIANG UIGHUR
AUTONOMOUS REGION

• Urumchi

TSINGHAI

TIBETAN
AUTONOMOUS REGION

• Lhasa

Y

0   100   200   300   400   500 Miles
0   100   200   300   400   500 Kilometers

© R. McN. & CO.

tions about the nature of the opportunity and the mission helped to destabilize twentieth-century Japanese politics. By their interference and final intervention on the continent the Japanese helped to channel China's response to the twentieth century politically and economically, and that intervention provided a particularly powerful spur to the emotional and psychological dimensions of China's change. Not recognizing the fervent nationalism they had helped inspire, the Japanese ended by standing directly athwart those currents and thus doomed the efforts of twentieth-century Chinese to work out a moderate, individualist and nationalist model of development.

The China war led to the shattering of Imperial Japan in the Pacific war; 1945, in turn, was followed by a quarter century of almost total separation for Japan and China while Pacific affairs were dominated by larger struggles and confrontations. While Japan and China struggled to rebuild, each found itself committed to an alliance hostile to the other. China's experiment with, and rejection of, the Russian tie has already been described. The Japanese experience with China policy can be briefly told.

Japan's groping toward Pacific participation was complicated by its long association with its former colony of Taiwan, its gratitude for Nationalist moderation at the time of the surrender and its obligations to its American ally. At the time of the San Francisco Peace Treaty, Prime Minister Yoshida wanted to delay a commitment to either Chinese government, and the absence of both of those governments from San Francisco seemed to make this possible. Yoshida thought in terms of representation with both governments, and he hoped for a trade office in Shanghai as well as one in Taipei. Secretary of State Dulles, however, convinced Yoshida that the United States Senate would not approve the Japanese peace treaty without assurance that Japan would recognize the Republic of China on Taiwan. Yoshida's hand was now forced, and shortly afterward Tokyo negotiated a peace treaty with that regime. Throughout the 1950s and 1960s this policy served Japan well. While mainland policies and economic shifts were frequently in turmoil, Japan's relations with the Republic of China led to the development of a flourishing trade, and Japan made important contributions to the economy of Taiwan. Within Japan's Liberal Democratic party a so-called "Taiwan lobby" for economic and political interests grew in importance. As Japan's relations with the mainland remained tenuous, Chiang Kai-shek was able to hold the Japanese government to its commitments. By the end of his career Prime Minister Yoshida himself seemed a strong proponent of the Taiwanese connection.

Relations with the mainland also developed, although without formal diplomatic or political ties. During the next two decades the Japanese tried to maximize their mainland connections within the limits of their relationship with the Republic of China on Taiwan. In 1953 an unofficial trade pact was signed between private Japanese groups, or "friendly firms" as they were called (often fronts for established firms), and mainland authorities. Together with the industrial countries of Western Europe, Japan worked to relax the list of embargoed goods that had been enforced against China during the Korean War. The 1960s saw additional, semiofficial, developments in trade through "Memorandum" channels worked out between Tokyo and Peking. As China turned away from its Soviet and East European ties, Japan gradually became the People's Republic's most important trading partner. By 1971 trade with the mainland stood slightly over $900 million, while trade with Taiwan was more than $1 billion. Each of these constituted only about 3 percent of Japan's total foreign trade and less than one-tenth of Japan–United States figures, but the Japan trade constituted nearly one-third (27 percent) of foreign imports for the People's Republic and about 40 percent of foreign imports for Taiwan. Although Japanese trade balances with Taiwan were somewhat larger than those with the mainland, the potential of trade with the latter was obviously far larger. Furthermore, while support for closer Taiwan relations tended to be concentrated within certain factions of the Liberal-Democratic party, pressure for normalization of relations with the People's Republic mounted steadily within many sectors of Japanese society and, especially, the mass media.

The alacrity with which Japan moved to normalize its relationships with the People's Republic after American intentions became known left little doubt of its basic inclination. When the Nixon plan to visit China was announced in July 1971, it caught the Japanese by surprise and led them to expect still more sweeping changes. In actuality the Nixon trip offered no solutions to the problems that were outstanding between Washington and Peking, though it did greatly lessen the tensions. A joint communiqué that was worked out stated the dimensions of the conflicting viewpoints. The United States, while acknowledging its intention to withdraw its forces from Vietnam in due course, reiterated its proposals for settlement there, its support for the Republic of Korea and its high estimation of the importance of its friendly relations with Japan. China reaffirmed its support for the positions of North Vietnam and the Viet Cong and North Korea, and it warned against the revival of Japanese militarism. Peking emphasized its claims to Taiwan, and the United States, while not challenging the fact that "all Chinese on either side of the Taiwan Strait maintain there is but one China and that Taiwan is a part of China," emphasized its interest in a peaceful settlement of that question by the Chinese themselves and indicated its intention to "progressively reduce its forces and military installations on Taiwan as the tension in the area diminishes." It was agreed that there would be further discussions for the development of trade and exchanges in science, technology, culture, sports and journalism.

The significance of the Shanghai communiqué lay in the fact that China and the United States had come to realize that neither threatened the security of the other. The Chinese seemed to put aside thoughts of a military solution to the Taiwan problem, while the Americans agreed that it was ultimately a Chinese problem. Taiwan remained, as the Chinese put it, "the crucial question obstructing the normalization of relations between China and the United States," but it no longer represented an American challenge to China's territorial integrity.

Washington, in turn, after years of viewing Peking as the source of all evil in Asia, now agreed that "normalization of relations between the two countries is not only in the interest of the American and Chinese peoples but also contributes to the relaxation of tensions in Asia and the world."

China policy now became the most urgent issue in Japan. It was capable of uniting conservative businessmen and left-wing journalists. The press kept up a drumfire criticism of government caution on the issue by raising questions of national interest and Japan's moral responsibility for aggression in the 1930s. Increasing numbers of Japanese businessmen attended Chinese trade fairs; in 1971 several thousand were at the Canton fair. In the fall of 1971 the People's Republic of China was admitted to the United Nations and occupied the seats on the Security Council and specialized agencies previously held by representatives of the government on Taiwan. China was now one of the principal members of the organization against whose flag its armies had fought in Korea.

As pressures for change in Japan's China policy became overwhelming, Peking also indicated a lively interest in formal relations with Japan. One price was Japan's revocation of its treaty with the Republic of China. Another was a change of government. China would not deal with Prime Minister Satō, whom it regarded as an architect of the policies to which it objected. Prime Minister Satō's dilemma was heightened by the manner of the Nixon visit to China. Although his government had staked its future on close ties with the United States, Washington had failed to consult its principal Pacific ally in advance of its plans for rapprochement with the mainland regime against which it had so long warned Japan. Satō was subjected to a torrent of criticism for having "missed the bus" in China relations and having misread American intentions. His decision to join Washington in a lastditch and unsuccessful opposition to the United Nations defeat for Taiwan completed his discomfiture. In the summer of 1972 he was succeeded in office by Tanaka Kakuei.

Prime Minister Tanaka made normalization of relations with China his first order of business, and he was in Peking within months of assuming office. At Peking he and Premier Chou speedily worked out arrangements for the establishment of diplomatic ties with the People's Republic. Japan indicated its full understanding of China's position on Taiwan and broke off diplomatic relations with the Republic of China. Work on formal treaties of peace, trade, navigation and commercial air routes was undertaken shortly afterward, and air connections with Peking were inaugurated in 1974. "The abnormal state of affairs" that had existed between the People's Republic and its Japanese neighbor was terminated on the date (29 September 1972) of the publication of this statement. Thus forty years of hostility between Japan and the mainland regimes of China came to an end.

Relations with Taiwan remained problematical. In 1969 Prime Minister Satō had agreed with President Nixon that the security of the "Taiwan area," along with that of the Republic of Korea, was important to Japan and by inference part of the justification for the security pact between America and Japan.

THE END OF 75 YEARS OF HOSTILITY. Prime Minister Tanaka and Mao Tse-tung and Chou En-lai in Peking in 1972. Mao has just given Tanaka a volume of Chinese poetry.

After the Nixon China trip, however, both Satō and his successor argued that the situation had changed so basically that the statements of 1969 were no longer relevant. On the other hand, although many Japanese had come to question the entire basis of the security pact, the Chinese, who had been most alarmed by visions of Japanese militarism in league with American imperialism, now gave evidence of beginning to see it as much less dangerous.

The early months of 1973 saw the process of accommodation quicken. In January the long agony of the Vietnam War ended in a cease-fire agreement that made it possible for the United States to withdraw its command in the hope that a political competition would replace the military confrontation in Indochina. In Taiwan the Japanese embassy was renamed the Interchange Organization; its officials went on "leave" from the Foreign Office and continued to lubricate the economic relations between Japan and Taiwan. Japan had fully reversed its stand, and now "friendly" firms tried to deal with Taiwan in such a way as to minimize antagonism in Peking. Meanwhile Tokyo and Peking opened formal diplomatic relations. Washington, with firmer political ties to Taiwan, was unable to do this but instead selected a senior diplomat to head a "liaison office" in

Peking, while the People's Republic made similar arrangements for representation in Washington.

It seemed probable that Chinese fears of their former Soviet allies had played a primary role in making this accommodation possible. In addition to deterring the imposing Russian force on their border, the Chinese had an interest in discouraging Americans and Japanese from cooperating with the Russians in plans for the development of Siberian resources. A second goal was an increased capability to complete the isolation of Taiwan. A third was to encourage the Japanese to loosen their ties with the United States. In any case, the result was that East Asian diplomatic relations began anew.

The Chinese were helped in these moves by the world détente and the desire everywhere to normalize relationships and curb long-standing hostilities. They were stronger also because of the priority they had given military strength; their developing missile force provided useful arguments for statesmen to use in explaining moves toward Peking. They remained, however, hampered by other factors. One was economic weakness. In 1971 China's Gross National Product was only 60 percent of Japan's, and on a per capita basis the discrepancy was startling. A second weakness was the aftermath of the political instability of the 1960s, which increased the need for urgency in normalizing foreign relations. Mao Tse-tung and Chou En-lai, their confidence in succession plans repeatedly proved wrong, were clearly eager to stabilize their country's external relations while they still had time.

Within the Peking leadership Prime Minister Chou En-lai, with Mao Tse-tung and Chiang Kai-shek one of the most durable statesmen of the postwar era, survived attacks by Red Guard extremists in the late 1960s to emerge as unquestioned leader of the Chinese regime. Chou, who was seventy-six in 1974, spoke to foreigners of his desire to see China fully represented at international conference tables again before power slipped from his hands. In September 1971 his principal rival for power, Defense Minister Lin Piao, disappeared under mysterious circumstances amid charges that he had wanted to restore relations with the Soviet Union instead of risking the détente with the United States and Japan. Months later Peking sources let it be understood that Lin Piao had planned a coup in which the venerable Mao Tse-tung himself would have been murdered. With the stage temporarily cleared of major rivals, Chou En-lai thus found it possible to work rapidly toward his goal of maneuvering between China's industrialized neighbors. In 1974 it was disclosed that Liu Shao-ch'i, a casualty of the Proletarian Cultural Revolution, had died. Teng Hsiao-p'ing, however, had reemerged from obscurity and denunciation to play an important role. Solutions to problems of succession remained obscure.

Leadership changes in Japan were less dramatic. Prime Minister Tanaka Kakuei had held cabinet office under Satō Eisaku and was a member of the same "mainstream" faction of the Liberal Democratic party. Yet upon closer examination Tanaka, a self-made businessman who had entered the finance bureaucracy without following the normal path of Tokyo University and peer group, also marked a break from the succession of conservative bureaucrats who had ruled Japan during the 1950s and 1960s. Once in office he sought to establish for himself the image of a "nonpolitical" manager who would bring fresh and practical ideas to bear on the pressing problems of environment, trade and foreign policies. In this he was unsuccessful. Problems of inflation and charges of financial impropriety brought about Tanaka's resignation in 1974, when he was succeeded by Miki Takeo.

The problems were real enough. Some were inherited, others were world-wide and still others were due to Japan's unprecedented growth. The trade problems were in this category. Japan's spectacular surge in exports in the late 1960s had changed the United States' willingness to look tolerantly on continuation of restraints on imports and investments in Japan, many of which had been initiated during the Occupation. Throughout the 1950s and 1960s Japan had struggled with unfavorable trade balances that resulted from rapid economic growth and increased imports, leading to what was called an "overheated economy." In the late 1960s, however, Japan suddenly overcame this pattern and began to accumulate impressive dollar reserves. In 1971 the Japanese-American trade balance stood at close to $3 billion in Japan's favor and made up the largest item in a steadily worsening balance-of-payments crisis for the United States. In 1972 it rose to $4 billion.

The sudden Japanese prosperity coincided with a world monetary crisis precipitated by the weakness of the dollar. The United States was overcommitted around the world, inflation-troubled and saddled with an expensive and futile war in Vietnam. This put new strains on the Japanese-American alliance, which had already been shaken by the China issue. In 1971 the Nixon administration added economic "shocks," as the Japanese called them, to its "China shock." In complex maneuverings that included import surcharges, "voluntary" quotas enforced under threat of a 1916 "Trade with the Enemy" act and currency revaluation, Washington forced the Tokyo government to increase its commitment to free international trade by accelerating programs of trade and capital liberalization.

The inflation was not restricted to the United States, however, but spread through all industrialized nations. Soon it was particularly virulent in Japan, where productivity increases no longer kept ahead of price increases. Once in office Prime Minister Tanaka released a new plan for the improvement of communications and diffusion of industry throughout the Japanese islands. His critics soon charged that this expansive vision had helped bring on startling price rises, especially in land value, throughout the country. As Japanese products increased in cost and imports increased in volume, the favorable trade balances were soon a thing of the past.

Japan's export surge had been based upon availability of low-cost supplies of energy, and the Arab-Israeli war and oil crisis of 1973 changed this situation also. Japan's staggering requirements of oil were virtually all imported from abroad, and as these rose rapidly in cost they produced a new round of inflationary pressures. An "energy shock" had now been added to earlier setbacks.

The environmental strains brought on by rapid industrialization had already brought into question many of the major assumptions of postwar Japan. Unlimited growth and economic primacy were beginning to lose some of their appeal, and a new sensitivity to the dimensions of the national image abroad was beginning to develop. Everywhere the heroic expectations that had been held of Japanese continued growth were moderated by these reminders of the ways in which that economy was vulnerable to external constraints.

As the twentieth century entered its final quarter, Japan's new role and national goals remained unclear. No twentieth-century society had known more rapid change. The suicide of the writer Mishima Yukio in 1970 and the 1974 surrender of a lone lieutenant in the Philippines who had continued a one-man war in blind obedience to his orders came as jarring reminders of the distance Japan had moved from the warrior ethos of an earlier day. Clearly the country's development would depend upon the international environment in which it found itself, as had been true throughout Japan's modern history. Slights from friends or threats from rivals could exacerbate a reviving confidence to produce decisions for greater political and military strength. Japan's long-standing tendency to see international society as a hierarchy of developed countries also had little precedent for the experience of emerging at the head of the line without appropriate models for emulation or attachment.

Yet the recent past also had only limited relevance to Japan's new situation. In the East Asia of the 1970s there were no prizes to win by force nor could there be force adequate to meet the presence of Japan's newly powerful neighbor. Self-sufficiency was no longer within the realm of possibility for a country so dependent upon world resources and trade, and the country that went to war under the sanctions of an oil embargo in 1941 now found itself helpless to ward off a need grown far more critical to its national life. On the other hand, while China could no longer be cowed, it did not seem a threat. Under whatever regime, it was certain to be occupied for years to come with its enormous problems of internal development and modernization. Despite formidable resources of manpower and ideology for a revolutionary world, it did not command the resources and the productivity, nor did it demonstrate the intent, to dominate East Asia. The epoch of the United States, in turn, was drawing to a close, and the Vietnam experience seemed certain to temper American enthusiasm for undertaking future commitments.

East Asia was now dominated by powers whose resources were curiously disparate and even complementary. The United States had overwhelming economic strength and the military force that equipped it for struggle with a competing superpower, but its success in limited conflict was less impressive. The Soviet Union had towering military strength, but it was supported by a troubled economy and preoccupied with an imagined threat from China. The People's Republic, fearful of its mighty neighbor to the north, had an exportable ideology and unlimited human resources but a very poorly developed economy. Japan's strength, in turn, was principally economic, and neither arms nor ideology equipped it to influence its neighbors. History offered few guides for such a situation. The Japanese had never accepted second-class status in international society, but neither had they ever known a time when the rewards for self-assertion seemed so few.

Yet of all these powers it seemed probable that it was Japan, however its potential might be limited or its ambitions chastened, that was most likely to increase its role in international affairs. Its basic interests in the future clearly lay with those of the trading countries of the industrialized world, and its relationships with the United States had become particularly complex. Even the most euphoric predictions for Japanese trade expansion with China failed to suggest an interdependence comparable to that which existed with the United States in 1974. What still had to be worked out, however, was Japan's relations with its less-developed neighbors. The way these were defined would determine the economic health and political stability of East Asia in the last quarter of the century.

Sources

There are now many bibliographies available, and this section is designed solely to identify sources and take the reader one step further into the growing literature that is available on the history of modern Japan and China, though it is not intended to be comprehensive.

Standard and reliable texts that provide well-rounded treatment of twentieth-century East Asia are John K. Fairbank, Edwin O. Reischauer, and Albert M. Craig, *East Asia: The Modern Transformation* (Boston: Houghton Mifflin, 1965), and more concisely in *East Asia: Tradition and Transformation* (Boston: Houghton Mifflin, 1973). Franz H. Michael and George E. Taylor, *The Far East in the Modern World*, rev. ed. (New York: Holt, Rinehart and Winston, 1965), and later editions have particular detail for China; George Beckmann, *The Modernization of China and Japan* (New York: Harper & Row, 1962), provides a detailed discussion of modernization, and Paul Hibbert Clyde, *The Far East: A History of the Impact of the West on Eastern Asia* (Englewood Cliffs, N.J.: Prentice-Hall, 1948), and later editions are focused on international relations. James B. Crowley, ed., *Modern East Asia: Essays in Interpretation* (New York: Harcourt

Brace & World, 1970), provides essays by twelve scholars. Immanuel C. Y. Hsü, *The Rise of Modern China* (New York: Oxford University Press, 1970); O. Edmund Clubb, *Twentieth Century China* (New York: Columbia University Press, 1964); and Hugh Borton, *Japan's Modern Century: From Perry to 1970* (New York: Ronald Press, 1970), provide national surveys.

Essential collections of source materials are brought together in Ssu-yü Teng and John K. Fairbank, *China's Response to the West* (Cambridge, Mass.: Harvard University Press, 1954); William Theodore de Bary, Wing-tsit Chan, and Burton Watson, *Sources of Chinese Tradition* (New York: Columbia University Press, 1960); Ryusaku Tsunoda, William Theodore de Bary, and Donald Keene, *Sources of Japanese Tradition* (New York: Columbia University Press, 1958); Theodore McNelly, *Sources in Modern East Asian History and Politics* (New York: Appleton-Century-Crofts, 1967); and David J. Lu, *Sources of Japanese History*, 2 vols. (New York: McGraw-Hill, 1974).

Chapter 1

THE PROBLEM OF modernization is discussed in C. E. Black, *The Dynamics of Modernization: A Study in Comparative History* (New York: Harper & Row, 1966). Mrs. Isabella Bird Bishop was an indefatigable and formidable traveler. Her comments on Korea are from *Korea and Her Neighbors: A Narrative of Travel* (London: J. Murray, 1898). President McKinley's education in the geography of Southeast Asia is taken from Margaret Leech, *In the Days of McKinley* (New York: Harper & Row, 1959), who takes it from the Foraker papers. William Elliot Griffis's comments on the scenery are from his *The Mikado's Empire* (New York: Harper & Brothers, 1876), p. 545. Kenneth B. Pyle, *The New Generation in Meiji Japan: Problems of Cultural Identity, 1885–1895* (Stanford, Calif.: Stanford University Press, 1969), discusses problems of modernization and cultural identity in nineteenth-century Japan. The Fujita Tōko anecdote can be found in Richard T. Chang, *From Prejudice to Tolerance: A Study of the Japanese Image of the West, 1826–1864* (Tokyo: Sophia University Press, 1970), p. 46. Ch'ien-lung's celebrated edict can be found in Teng and Fairbank, *China's Response to the West*, pp. 19–21. Bertrand Russell's comment is quoted by Immanuel C. Y. Hsü, *The Rise of Modern China*, p. 207, from J. L. Cranmer-Byng, "Lord Macartney's Embassy to Peking in 1793," *Journal of Oriental Studies* (Hong Kong) 4 (1957–58): 182. The Taiping edict is taken from Thomas Taylor Meadows, *The Chinese and Their Rebellions* (1856; reprinted Stanford, n.d.), p. 262. The Reverend Issachar Roberts's dilemma is described in "Reverend Issachar Jacob Roberts and the Taiping Rebellion" by Yuan Cheng Teng, *Journal of Asian Studies* 23 (November 1963): 55–67. The early Meiji edict urging respect for Westerners is quoted in Osatake Takeki, *Kokusai hō yori mitaru Bakumatsu gaikō monogatari* (Tokyo, 1926), p. 73

Chapter 2

THE EXCHANGE between Admiral Itō and Admiral Ting is taken from Vice-Admiral Viscount Nagayo Ogasawara, translated by Jukichi Inouye, *Life of Admiral Togo* (Tokyo: Seito Shorin, 1934), p. 135. Further details of the war can be found in Vladimir (pseudonym for Z. Volpicelli), *The China-Japan War* (London: Low and Marston, 1896); and J. C. Perry, "The Battle off the Tayang, 17 September 1894," *Mariner's Mirror* 50, no. 4 (1964). Local government under the Ch'ing is described in T'ung-tsu Ch'ü, *Local Government in China Under the Ch'ing* (Cambridge, Mass.: Harvard University Press, 1962); Kung-chuan Hsiao, *Rural China: Imperial Control in the Nineteenth Century* (Seattle: University of Washington Press, 1960); and Chung-li Chang, *The Chinese Gentry: Studies on Their Role in Nineteenth-Century Chinese Society* (Seattle: University of Washington Press, 1955). General Yamagata's comments on China and the Chinese armies are from his essay on the Japanese army in Alfred Stead, ed., *Japan by the Japanese: A Survey by Its Highest Authorities* (London: William Heinemann, 1904), pp. 107–9. The treaty-port system has received its definitive treatment in John K. Fairbank, *Trade and Diplomacy on the China Coast: The Opening of the Treaty Ports, 1842–1854,* 2 vols. (Cambridge, Mass.: Harvard University Press, 1953); the Opium War has received its most authoritative treatment in Hsin-pao Chang, *Commissioner Lin and the Opium War* (Cambridge, Mass.: Harvard University Press, 1964). Early reform efforts are analyzed in Mary C. Wright, *The Last Stand of Chinese Conservatism: The T'ung-Chih Restoration, 1862–1874* (Stanford, Calif.: Stanford University Press, 1957). Chiang Kai-shek's ruminations on the evils of foreign concessions are in *China's Destiny* (New York: Macmillan, 1947). All earlier studies of the Taiping Rebellion have been dated by Franz Michael in collaboration with Chung-li Chang, *The Taiping Rebellion: History and Documents,* 3 vols. (Seattle: University of Washington Press, 1966, 1971). China's relations with its tributaries, of which Korea was the most important, can be studied in John K. Fairbank, ed., *The Chinese World Order* (Cambridge, Mass.: Harvard University Press, 1968). The war with France is the subject of Lloyd E. Eastman, *Throne and Mandarins: China's Search for a Policy During the Sino-French Controversy, 1880–1885* (Cambridge, Mass.: Harvard University Press, 1967). Li Hung-chang is the subject of a biographical study by Stanley Spector, *Li Hung-chang and the Huai Army* (Seattle: University of Washington Press, 1964), and a series of studies by Kwang-ching Liu, of which the first, "Li Hung-chang in Chihli: The Emergence of a Policy, 1870–1875," in Albert Feuerwerker, Rhoads Murphey, and Mary C. Wright, eds., *Approaches to Modern Chinese History* (Berkeley: University of California Press, 1967), has been particularly useful. Li's views of relations with Japan can be found quoted in Teng and Fairbank, *China's Response,* p. 71 and (after the Taiwan incident) p. 119, and his exchange with Itō at Shimonoseki, p. 126. The most recent and carefully documented account of Japan's early Korea policy is by Marlene J. Mayo, "The Korean Crisis of 1873 and Early Meiji Foreign Policy," *Journal of Asian Studies* 31, no. 4 (August 1972). The Japanese-Chinese rivalry that culminated in the outbreak of the Sino-Japanese War can be followed in Hilary Conroy, *The Japanese Seizure of Korea: 1868–1910* (Philadelphia: University of Pennsylvania Press, 1960), a standard source. Fukuzawa's jubilant response to the war is from page 255. Other accounts include C. I. Eugene Kim and Han-kyo Kim, *Korea and the Politics of Imperialism: 1876–1910* (Berkeley: University of California Press, 1967). Kozaki Hiromichi's *Reminiscences of Seventy Years* (Tokyo, 1933) contains his conversation with Stead. The response of popular culture in Japan to the war is treated by Donald Keene, "The Sino-Japanese War of 1894–95 and Its Cultural Effects in Japan," in Donald H. Shively, ed., *Tradition and Modernization in Japanese Culture* (Princeton: Princeton University Press, 1971).

Missionary problems and policies in late Ch'ing China are the subject of a number of contributions to the Harvard University Regional Studies Seminars, *Papers on China,* including Irwin Hyatt, "The Chengtu Riots (1895): Myths and Politics," vol. 18, pp. 26–54, who provides the "recent judgment" which is quoted. Recent valuable contributions are those of Paul A. Cohen, *China and Christianity: The Missionary Movement and the Growth of Chinese Antiforeignism* (Cambridge, Mass.: Harvard University Press, 1963); and Edmund S. Wehrle, *Britain, China and the Antimissionary Riots, 1891–1900* (Minneapolis: University of Minnesota Press, 1966). German advances in Shantung and Chinese tactics of resistance are the subject of John E. Schrecker's important *Imperialism and Chinese Nationalism: Germany in Shantung* (Cambridge, Mass.: Harvard University Press, 1971), which clarifies the means Chinese officials used to restrict and combat German imperalist advances. Organizations of examination candidates are described in John E. Schrecker, "The Pao-kuo hui: A Reform Society of 1898," *Papers on China,* vol. 13 (1960), p. 50. For K'ang Yu-wei's memorial in its setting, see Ichiko Chūzō, "Ni-Shi senji Chūgoku no shusenron," in *Kindai Chūgoku no seiji to shakai* (Tokyo, 1971), p. 207. Yen Fu receives masterly treatment in Benjamin Schwartz, *In Search of Wealth and Power: Yen Fu and the West; Western Thought in Chinese Perspective* (Cambridge, Mass.: Harvard University Press, 1964). K'ang Yu-wei has been discussed in a series of authoritative monographs by Kung-chuan Hsiao, "Weng T'ung-ho and the Reform Movement of 1898," *Tsing Hua Journal of Chinese Studies* (April 1957); "The Philosophical Thought of K'ang Yu-wei," *Monumenta Serica* 21 (1962); "The Case for Constitutional Monarchy: K'ang Yu-wei's Plan for the Democratization of China," *Monumenta Serica* 24 (1965); "In and Out of Utopia: K'ang Yu-wei's Social Thought," *Chung Chi Journal,* 7, 8 (1967–68); "Economic Modernization: K'ang Yu-wei's Ideas in Historical Perspective," *Monumenta Serica* 27 (1968); and "Administrative Modernization: K'ang Yu-wei's Proposals and their Historical Meaning," *Tsing Hua Journal of Chinese Studies* 8 (1970). J. P. Lo has translated K'ang's autobiography and edited a series of essays about him in *K'ang Yu-wei: A Biography and a Symposium* (Tucson: University of Arizona Press, 1967). Liang Ch'i-ch'ao has been studied by Joseph R. Levenson, *Liang Ch'i-ch'ao and the Mind of*

Modern China (Cambridge, Mass.: Harvard University Press, 1953): some of his conclusions are modified by Hao Chang, *Liang Ch'i-ch'ao and Intellectual Transition in China, 1890–1907* (Cambridge, Mass.: Harvard University Press, 1971); and Philip C. Huang, *Liang Ch'i-ch'ao and Modern Chinese Liberalism* (Seattle: University of Washington Press, 1972). The quotations for K'ang's talks with his emperor can be found in Teng and Fairbank, *China's Response*, p. 178. Chang's "Exhortation to Learn" is available in the same source, pp. 166–74. The court edict on page 38 is from Hsiao, "Weng T'ung-ho," p. 190. Pu-yi's autobiography appeared in English in Peking in two volumes entitled *From Emperor to Citizen: The Autobiography of Asin-Gioro Pu Yi* (Foreign Languages Press, 1965). The quotation on page 39 is from volume 1, page 41; that on page 40 from page 49.

Contrasts of practice and belief between China's Great Tradition and the world of popular belief are the subject of E. Zürcher, *Dialoog der Misverstanden* (Leiden: Brill, 1962). The imperial grant of political privileges for missionaries is quoted from Wehrle, *Britain, China and the Antimissionary Riots* p. 128. On the Boxers, Chester C. Tan, *The Boxer Catastrophe* (New York: Columbia University Press, 1955), remains standard. The decree quoted on page 41 is from pages 31–32, but the account on the palace meeting on page 43 is taken from Li Chien-nung, *The Political History of China, 1840–1928*, translated and edited by Ssu-Yü Teng and Jeremy Ingalls (Princeton: Van Nostrand, 1956), pp. 174–75. Fang Chiao-ying's biographical account of Jung-lu is in Arthur W. Hummel, ed., *Eminent Chinese of the Ch'ing Period*, vol. 1 (Washington, D.C.: U.S. Government Printing Office, 1943), pp. 405–9.

Chapter 3

SCHOLARSHIP ON THE Tokugawa period has increased greatly in amount and depth in recent years. Among the works drawn on here are Gilbert F. Rozman, *Urban Networks in Ch'ing China and Tokugawa Japan* (Princeton: Princeton University Press, 1973), which breaks new ground in analysis of urban developments in pre-Perry Japan; John W. Hall and Marius B. Jansen, eds., *Studies in the Institutional History of Early Modern Japan* (Princeton: Princeton University Press, 1969); John W. Hall, *Government and Local Power in Japan, 500 to 1700: A Study Based on Bizen Province* (Princeton: Princeton, University Press, 1966); Thomas C. Smith, *The Agrarian Origins of Modern Japan* (Stanford, Calif.: Stanford University Press, 1959); R. P. Dore, *Education in Tokugawa Japan* (Berkeley, University of California Press, 1965); Herschel Webb, *The Japanese Imperial Institution in the Tokugawa Period* (New York: Columbia University Press, 1968); Robert N. Bellah, *Tokugawa Religion: The Values of Pre-Industrial Japan* (Glencoe, Ill.: The Free Press, 1957); Donald Keene, *The Japanese Discovery of Europe, 1720–1830*, 2d ed. (Stanford, Calif.: Stanford University Press, 1969). For the events of the opening of Japan and the Tokugawa overthrow, reference should be to W. G. Beasley, *Select Documents on Japanese Foreign Policy, 1853–1868* (New York: Oxford University Press, 1955). The Meiji Restoration receives its most rounded treatment in the same author's *The Meiji Restoration* (Stanford, Calif.: Stanford University Press, 1972); more specialized studies include David M. Earl, *Emperor and Nation in Japan* (Seattle: University of Washington Press, 1964); H. D. Harootunian, *Toward Restoration: The Growth of Political Consciousness in Tokugawa Japan* (Berkeley: University of California Press, 1970); Albert M. Craig, *Chōshū in the Meiji Restoration* (Cambridge, Mass.: Harvard University Press, 1961); and Marius B. Jansen, *Sakōmoto Ryōma and the Meiji Restoration* (Stanford, Calif.: Stanford University Press, 1971). Economic development can be followed in Thomas C. Smith, *Political Change and Industrial Development in Japan: Government Enterprise, 1868–1880* (Stanford, Calif.: Stanford University Press, 1955); and W. W. Lockwood, *The Economic Development of Japan: Growth and Structural Change, 1868–1938* (Princeton: Princeton University Press, 1954). Meiji modernization is treated in five volumes published by Princeton University Press for the Conference on Modern Japan of the Association for Asian Studies: Marius B. Jansen, ed., *Changing Japanese Attitudes Toward Modernization* (1965); W. W. Lockwood, ed., *The State and Economic Enterprise in Japan* (1965); R. P. Dore, ed., *Aspects of Social Change in Modern Japan* (1967); Robert E. Ward, ed., *Political Development in Modern Japan* (1968); and Donald H. Shively, ed., *Tradition and Modernization in Japanese Culture* (1971). George B. Sansom, *The Western World and Japan* (New York: Knopf, 1950), remains an essential and stimulating work. The discussion of the Meiji Constitution owes much to Joseph Pittau, S.J., *Political Thought in Early Meiji Japan, 1869–1889* (Cambridge, Mass.: Harvard University Press, 1967), and the emperor's oath upon promulgation of the Constitution is taken from page 188 of this work. The development of the Imperial Rescript on Education is the subject of Donald H. Shively, "Motoda Eifu: Confucian Lecturer to the Meiji Emperor," in D. S. Nivison and A. F. Wright, eds., *Confucianism in Action* (Stanford, Calif.: Stanford University Press, 1959). Prince Itō's relief that his constitution won respect is taken from George Akita, *Foundations of Constitutional Government in Modern Japan, 1868–1900* (Cambridge, Mass.: Harvard University Press, 1967), p. 13, as are Itō's comments on party politicians. British Minister Satow's observations are taken from George A. Lensen, ed., *Korea and Manchuria Between Russia and Japan, 1895–1904: The Observations of Sir Ernest Satow* (Tallahassee, Fla.: The Diplomatic Press, 1966). Foreign Minister Mutsu is the subject of Marius B. Jansen, "Mutsu Munemitsu," in Albert M. Craig and Donald H. Shively, eds., *Personality in Japanese History* (Berkeley: University of California Press, 1970). Fukuzawa's disillusionment with international law can be traced in Carmen Blacker, *The Japanese Enlightenment: A Study of the Writings of Fukuzawa Yukichi* (Cambridge: At the University Press, 1964), p. 129; and Albert M. Craig, "Fukuzawa Yukichi: The Philosophical Foundations of Meiji Nationalism," in R. E. Ward, ed., *Political Development in Modern Japan*, p. 128. The quotation used is the translation of Craig in Fairbank, Reischauer, Craig, *East Asia: The Modern Transformation*, p. 566. For the Shimonoseki indemnity and the Hanyehp'ing

Company, see Marius B. Jansen, "Yawata, Hanyehping, and the Twenty-one Demands," *Pacific Historical Review* 23 (February 1954). Russian developments in Manchuria are described in John A. White, *The Diplomacy of the Russo-Japanese War* (Princeton: Princeton University Press, 1964), chap. 2. The quotation from Hara Kei's diary is taken from an unpublished doctoral dissertation by Lawrence A. Olson, Jr., "Hara Kei: A Political Biography" (Harvard University, 1955), but the finest discussion of the decision process is that of Shumpei Okamoto, *The Japanese Oligarchy and the Russo-Japanese War* (New York: Columbia University Press, 1970), who also quotes Hara on page 93. General Kodama's prediction of third-power intervention is from Hosoya Chihiro, "Japan's Policies Toward Russia," in James W. Morley, ed., *Japan's Foreign Policy 1868–1941* (New York: Columbia University Press, 1974), p. 365. The *London Times's* praise of the surprise attack on Port Arthur is taken from Richard Storry, *A Short History of Modern Japan* (Baltimore: Penguin Books, 1960), p. 139. The Hoshi Tōru expression of impatience with "old men" like Itō is taken from Akita, p. 142; the statement by Hoshi's assassin can be found in the form it originally appeared in *Jiji shimpō* in Nakamura Kikuo, *Meijiteki ningenzō; Hoshi Tōru to kindai Nihon seiji* (Tokyo, 1957), pp. 270–71. It is translated in Robert A. Scalapino, *Democracy and the Party Movement in Prewar Japan* (Berkeley: University of California Press, 1953), p. 264. Namier's comment about the military is taken from Robert F. Hackett's admirable summary of the Japanese army, "The Military," in Robert E. Ward and Dankwart A. Rustow, eds., *Political Modernization in Japan and Turkey* (Princeton: Princeton University Press, 1964), p. 328. Itō's language about mercenaries is from Akita, *Foundations,* p. 129. The military language of Yamagata's lieutenant is taken from Roger F. Hackett, *Yamagata Aritomo in the Rise of Modern Japan,* 1838–1922 (Cambridge, Mass.: Harvard University Press, 1971), p. 196, and Yamagata's career and views can be followed in the same source.

I have followed the analysis of Meiji economic growth by Kazushi Ohkawa and Henry Rosovsky, "A Century of Japanese Economic Growth," in W. W. Lockwood, ed., *The State and Economic Enterprise in Japan,* particularly in its emphasis on the qualitative changes of the early twentieth century; and W. W. Lockwood, *The Economic Development of Japan.* Discussion of the new business class can be found in Johannes Hirschmeier, S.V.D., *The Origins of Entrepreneurship in Meiji Japan* (Cambridge, Mass.: Harvard University Press, 1964); Byron K. Marshall, *Capitalism and Nationalism in Prewar Japan* (Stanford, Calif.: Stanford University Press, 1967); and Scalapino, *Democracy and the Party Movement;* the excerpt from *Taiyō* is from Scalapino, p. 267, and the discussion of the growing electoral weight of the cities from p. 255. Herbert Passin, in *Society and Education in Japan* (New York: Columbia University Press, 1965), treats the development of public education. The lower school's teachings of a family-centered state polity are illustrated in Robert King Hall, *Shūshin: The Ethics of a Defeated Nation* (New York: Columbia Teachers College, 1949). The quotation from the teacher's manual of 1914 is taken from John Caiger, "The Aims and Content of

School Courses in Japanese History, 1872–1945," in Edmund Skrzypcak, ed., *Japan's Modern Century: A Special Issue of Monumenta Nipponica* (Tokyo: Sophia University Press, 1968), p. 67. Uchimura Kanzō is treated by John F. Howes in "Uchimura Kanzō: Japanese Prophet," in Dankwart A. Rustow, ed., *Philosophers and Kings: Studies in Leadership* (New York: George Braziller, 1970); the quotations, however, are taken from Kimitada Miwa, "Crossroads of Patriotism in Meiji Japan," Princeton University Ph.D. dissertation, 1967. The relationship between the Education Rescript, the Uchimura case and official patriotism is discussed in Kōsaka Masaaki, ed., *Japanese Thought in the Meiji Era*, translated by David Abosch (Tokyo, 1958). Bureaucratic efforts to channel patriotism in late Meiji years can be followed in Kenneth B. Pyle, "The Technology of Japanese Nationalism: The Local Improvement Movement, 1900–1918," *Journal of Asian Studies* 33, no. 1 (November 1973); Richard J. Smethurst, "The Creation of the Imperial Military Reserve Association in Japan," *Journal of Asian Studies* 30, no. 4 (August 1971); and W. M. Fridell, *Japanese Shrine Mergers, 1906–12: State Shinto Moves to the Grassroots* (Tokyo: Sophia University Press, 1973).

Chapter 4

THE *Report of the International Conference on the Problems of Modernization in Asia, June 28–July 7, 1965* (Seoul: Korea University, 1966), contains a large number of reports and papers which have been extremely useful for consideration of historical and social developments in modern Korea. I have profited also from the recent history by William E. Henthorn, *A History of Korea* (New York: The Free Press, 1971), and from the long standard work by Takashi Hatada, now available in English as *A History of Korea* (Santa Barbara, Calif.: American Bibliographical Center, 1969). For early Korean contacts with the West, there is a fascinating study by Gari Ledyard, *The Dutch Come to Korea* (Seoul: Royal Asiatic Society, Korea Branch, 1971). Korea's political tradition receives thoughtful treatment in Gregory Henderson, *Korea: The Politics of the Vortex* (Cambridge, Mass.: Harvard University Press, 1968); chapter 10 of Reischauer and Fairbank, *East Asia: The Great Tradition;* and a recent revision of the usual view that examinations were closed to nonelite by Yong-ho Ch'oe, "Commoners in Early Yi Dynasty Civil Examinations: An Aspect of Korean Social Structure, 1392–1600," *Journal of Asian Studies* 33, no. 4 (August 1974). The account of the Tonghak movement is principally based on Benjamin B. Weems, *Reform, Rebellion, and the Heavenly Way* (Tucson: University of Arizona Press, 1964).

The political narrative of Korea's fortunes in the late nineteenth and early twentieth centuries is taken up by Chong-sik Lee, *The Politics of Korean Nationalism* (Berkeley: University of California Press, 1963); and E. I. Eugene Kim and Han-kyo Kim, *Korea and the Politics of Imperialism, 1876–1910* (Berkeley:

University of California Press, 1967). Hilary Conroy's *The Japanese Seizure of Korea* is an essential source which covers the entire terrain of this chapter, and I have drawn upon it for the the account of Inoue's work (from chapter 6), Williams's views (p. 325) and the *Mainichi* statement (p. 390). On the Japanese side, the official *Kokuryukai* account, Kuzū Yoshihisa, *Nik-Kan gappō hisshi (The Secret History of the Merger of Japan and Korea)*, 2 vols. (Tokyo, 1930), adds much detail. A recent, careful and stimulating account of Uchida Ryōhei's goals and tactics in Korean annexation is that of Nishio Yotarō, "Kyūshū ni okeru kindai no shisō jōkyō," in *Nihon kindaika to Kyūshū* (Tokyo, 1972). Sugiyama's role can be followed in Ichimata Masao, "Yamaza Enjirō: Meiji jidai ni okeru tairiku seisaku no jikkōsha," in *Kokusai hō gaikō zasshi* vol. 72, no. 3 (October 1973). Contemporary appraisals of Japanese efforts include George Trumbull Ladd, *In Korea with Marquis Ito* (New York, 1908); and F. A. McKenzie, *The Tragedy of Korea* (New York, 1908). George Kennan's articles appeared in *Outlook* (1905), and their titles suggest their contents: "Korea: A Degenerate State"; "The Korean People: The Product of a Decayed Civilization"; "The Japanese in Korea"; "What Japan Has Done in Korea." Minister Satow's comment is found in *Korea and Manchuria Between Russia and Japan*, p. 246.

Chapter 5

THE TERRAIN OF this chapter is covered in close detail with full documentation in Marius B. Jansen, *The Japanese and Sun Yat-sen* (Cambridge, Mass.: Harvard University Press, 1967; reprinted, Stanford, Calif.: Stanford University Press, 1970), and "Japanese Views of China During the Meiji Period," in Albert Feuerwerker, Rhoads Murphey, and Mary C. Wright, eds., *Approaches to Modern Chinese History* (Berkeley: University of California Press, 1967), and I have used some of the same language in "Japan and the Chinese Revolution of 1911," to appear in John K. Fairbank, ed., *Cambridge History of China*, vol. 8 (Cambridge: At the University Press, © forthcoming).

Li Hung-chang's proposal of 1863 is taken from Teng and Fairbank, *China's Response*, p. 71. Japanese attitudes toward China are discussed by Eto Shinkichi in numerous works, among them "Nihonjin no Chūgoku kan: Takasugi Shinsaku ra no bawai," in *Commemorative Essays Dedicated to Dr. Niida Noboru*, vol. 3 (Tokyo, 1970), pp. 53–71. The impact of war experiences on those views is the subject of Irokawa Daikichi, "Nichi-Ro sensō shita no aru nōmin heishi no kiroku: Ōsawa jōtōhei senchū nikki," no. 24 (Tokyo Keizai Daigaku: *Jimbun shizen kagaku ronshū*, 1970).

My understanding of K'ang Yu-wei's thought and action owes a great deal to the studies by Kung-chuan Hsiao cited for Chapter 2, but space makes it impossible to do justice to the richness of his material and the subtlety of his argument. I have also profited from the study of K'ang edited by J. P. Lo, *K'ang Yu-*

wei: A Biography and a Symposium (Tucson: University of Arizona Press, 1967), especially Richard C. Howard, "Japan's Role in the Reform Program," pp. 280–312. For more detailed discussion of the reformers' knowledge about Japan I have learned from the studies of Hō Taku-shū, "Kō I-wei no henhō undō to Meiji Ishin," *Jimbun gakuhō,* no. 30 (Kyoto, 1970), and "Ryō Kei-chō no Meiji Ishin kan to Chūgoku henkakuron," in Sakata Yoshio and Yoshida Mitsuo, eds., *Sekaishi no naka no Meiji Ishin* (Kyoto, 1973): Liang's letter to Ōkuma is discussed on page 104–5. Wang T'ao is the subject of Paul A. Cohen, "Wang T'ao's Perspective on a Changing World," in Feuerwerker, Murphey, and Wright, eds., *Approaches to Modern Chinese History*; Cheng Kuan-ying is discussed in Ichiko Chūzō, *Kindai Chūgoku no seiji to shakai* (Tokyo, 1971); and Huang Tsun-hsien is discussed by Sanetō Keishū in *Meiji Ni-Shi bunka kōshō* (Tokyo, 1943), and especially by Noriko Komachi, "Huang Tsun-hsien (1848–1905): His Response to Meiji Japan and the West" (Harvard University Ph.D. dissertation, 1972). Liang Ch'i-ch'ao is discussed by Joseph R. Levenson, *Liang Ch'i-ch'ao and the Mind of Modern China* (see under Chapter 2), and also by George M. Wilson, "Politics and the People: Liang Ch'i-ch'ao's View of Constitutional Developments in Meiji Japan Before 1890," *Papers on Japan,* vol. 1 (1961). Two more recent works, Hao Chang, *Liang Ch'i-ch'ao and Intellectual Transition in China, 1890–1907* (Cambridge, Mass.: Harvard University Press, 1971), and Philip C. Huang, *Liang Ch'i-ch'ao and Modern Chinese Liberalism* (Seattle: University of Washington Press, 1972), have not been incorporated into my text; the former warns against exaggeration of Japanese influence on Liang, and the latter contests the sharpness of the stages Levenson discerned. My reference to Liang's shipboard poem is from an unpublished paper presented by Yue-him Tam at a Princeton University seminar. The exchange between Itō and the Kuang-hsü emperor is taken from Teng and Fairbank, *China's Response,* p. 180.

The discussion of late Manchu reforms owes much to John K. Fairbank, in Fairbank, Reischauer, and Craig, *East Asia: The Modern Transformation,* chap. 8. Chang Chih-tung's views on Japan policy are taken from Chester C. Tan, *The Boxer Catastrophe,* p. 87. The reform proposals quoted can be found in Teng and Fairbank, *China's Response,* pp. 197–210. Yüan's army reforms are traced by Ralph L. Powell, *The Rise of Chinese Military Power, 1895–1912* (Princeton: Princeton University Press, 1955); and his career is the subject of Jerome Ch'en's *Yuan Shih-k'ai (1895–1916)* (Stanford, Calif.: Stanford University Press, 1961). The count of future leaders in Yüan's units is that of Powell, p. 80, as corrected by Y. C. Wang, *Chinese Intellectuals and the West,* p. 298. The abolition of the examination system is treated by Wolfgang Franke, *The Reform and Abolition of the Traditional Chinese Examination System* (Cambridge, Mass.: Harvard University Press, 1960), and the edict quoted is from John C. Ferguson, "The Abolition of the Competitive Examinations in China," *Journal of the American Oriental Society* 27(1906): 79–87. Wang, *Chinese Intellectuals,* offers some thoughtful observations on the significance of changes in education. Yen Fu is the subject of the outstanding study by Benjamin Schwartz noted under Chapter 2, and Ma Chien-chung is studied by Banno Masataka, "Furansu ryūgaku jidai no Ba Ken-chū," *Kokka Gakkai Zasshi* 84, no. 5 (1971).

Chang Chien's observations to Yüan Shih-k'ai about constitutionalism can be found on page 199 of S. Y. Teng's translation of Li Chien-nung, *The Political History of China,* and he is the subject of a recent study by Samuel C. Chu, *Reformer in Modern China: Chang Chien (1853–1926)* (New York: Columbia University Press, 1965). Sheng Hsüan-huai's career furnishes the focus of Albert Feuerwerker's *China's Early Industrialization: Sheng Hsüan-huai (1844–1916) and Mandarin Enterprise* (Cambridge, Mass.: Harvard University Press, 1958). The Kailan mines are treated by Ellsworth C. Carlson, *The Kaiping Mines (1877–1912)* (Cambridge, Mass.: Harvard University Press, 1957). The effect of the constitutional reforms is discussed in P'eng-yüan Chang, "The Constitutionalists," and John Fincher, "Political Provincialism and the National Revolution," in Mary C. Wright, ed., *China in Revolution: The First Phase, 1900–1913* (New Haven: Yale University Press, 1968).

For the student movement to Japan the basic source is Sanetō Keishū, *Chūgokujin Nihon ryūgakushi* (Tokyo, 1960); all tables and statistical details can be found there. Ching Mei-chiu's autobiography appeared in Japanese translation as *Ryūnichi kaiko: Chūgoku anakisuto no hansei* (Tokyo, 1966). Student journalism is discussed by Robert A. Scalapino in "Prelude to Marxism: The Chinese Student Movement in Japan, 1900–1910," in Feuerwerker, Murphey, and Wright, *Approaches.* The foreign orientation of Chinese intellectuals is discussed by Y. C. Wang, and the illustration of the publishing company is his. Tsou Jung's *The Revolutionary Army* is available in an English translation by John Lust (The Hague and Paris, 1968), and Ch'en T'ien-hua is the subject of studies by Shimada Kenji, *Chūgoku kakumei no senkusha tachi* (Tokyo, 1965), and Ernest P. Young, *Papers on China,* vol. 13 (1959).

The revolutionary movement receives its most rounded treatment in the papers edited by Mary C. Wright, *China in Revolution.* The short but masterful *Origins of the Chinese Revolution, 1915–1949* by Lucien Bianco (Stanford, Calif.: Stanford University Press, 1971) presents a personal and eloquent synthesis. Harold Z. Schiffrin's authoritative *Sun Yat-sen and the Origins of the Chinese Revolution* (Berkeley: University of California Press, 1970) takes Sun to 1905. The statement about "selective modernization" is from page 344; that from Bianco which follows will be found in Bianco, p. 18. Y. C. Wang's reversal of the traditional slogan is from his *Chinese Intellectuals and the West,* p. 357. For Yamagata's views of a racial struggle, see Hackett, *Yamagata Aritomo,* p. 270. The patriotic societies are discussed in Jansen, *The Japanese and Sun Yat-sen.* Konoe's diary has recently been published in six volumes: *Konoe Atsumaro nikki* (Tokyo, 1968–69). Sun Yat-sen's conversation with Miyazaki Tōten is from the latter's autobiographical account, *Sanjū-sannen no yume.* For the various views of Sun Yat-sen's learning or lack of it, see Yen-p'ing Hao, "The Abortive Cooperation Between Reformers and Revolutionaries (1895–1900)," *Papers on China,* vol. 15 (1961), p. 96. For Chang Ping-lin and Wu Chih-hui, see pp. 35–36 of

Chün-tu Hsüeh, *Huang Hsing and the Chinese Revolution* (Stanford, Calif.: Stanford University Press, 1961). For the influence of Liang Ch'i-ch'ao in Tokyo, see Y. C. Wang, *Chinese Intellectuals,* p. 227. The analysis of T'ung-meng hui membership and organization is from the unpublished dissertation by Shelley Hsien Cheng, "The T'ung-meng-hui: Its Organization, Leadership and Finances, 1905–1912" (Seattle: University of Washington Press, 1962). Revolutionary publications and rhetoric are analyzed by Michael Gasster in *Chinese Intellectuals and the Revolution of 1911: The Birth of Modern Chinese Radicalism* (Seattle: University of Washington Press, 1969). The reference to "freedom of the group" is from page 116. The quotations from *The Revolutionary Army* are from the translation by John Lust, cited earlier. An important disciple of Huang Hsing is treated in a recent study by K. S. Liew, *Struggle for Democracy: Sung Chiao-jen and the 1911 Chinese Revolution* (Berkeley: University of California Press, 1971). The quotation by Lord Curzon is from Schiffrin, p. 132. For Sung and Japan, see Noriko Tamada, "Sung Chiao-jen and the 1911 Revolution," *Papers on China,* vol. 21 (1968), p. 191. Kita Ikki, who was with Sung during the events of 1911, is the subject of George M. Wilson, *Radical Nationalist in Japan: Kita Ikki, 1883–1937* (Cambridge, Mass.: Harvard University Press, 1969). Kita's telegrams and letters to Uchida Ryōhei reporting on the revolution have now been published as an appendix to a Fukuoka UNESCO publication, Takahashi Masao, ed., *Nihon kindaika to Kyūshū* (Tokyo, 1972), pp. 409–80. Mrs. Wright's reference to revolutionary tradition is from *China in Revolution,* p. 57.

Chapter 6

THE DISCUSSION OF the ends of empires owes much to Akira Iriye, *After Imperialism: The Search for a New Order in the Far East, 1921–1931* (Cambridge, Mass.: Harvard University Press, 1965). John Schrecker, in *Imperialism and Chinese Nationalism,* discusses the way Chinese officials maneuvered against imperialism. For the events of the Revolution of 1911 I am indebted to articles by Ichiko Chūzō in *Kindai Chūgoku no seiji to shakai* which emphasize the traditional nature of the Szechwan gentry opposition and in Mary C. Wright, ed., *China in Revolution: The First Phase, 1900–1913.* The quotation by Li Yüan-hung is from Li Chien-nung, *The Political History of China,* p. 248. Events from the revolutionaries' perspectives are described in K. S. Liew, *Struggle for Democracy* (quotation on page 180) and in Chün-tu Hsüeh, *Huang Hsing and the Chinese Revolution.* Yüan Shih-k'ai is discussed by Ernest P. Young in Mary C. Wright, ed., *China in Revolution,* and by Jerome Ch'en, *Yuan Shih-k'ai;* for descriptions of his ceremonies, see pages 180 and 200. The abortive attempt to take the throne is described by Ch'en in chapter 10 and analyzed by J. R. Levenson, "The Suggestiveness of Vestiges: Confucianism and Monarchy at the Last," in D. S. Nivison and A. F. Wright, eds., *Confucianism in Action* (Stanford, Calif.: Stanford

University Press, 1959). Pu-yi's recollections of the restoration attempt are taken from his *From Emperor to Citizen*, vol. 1, p. 92. Pu-yi's English tutor was R. F Johnston, whose *Twilight in the Forbidden City* (New York: Appleton-Century, 1934) provides an interesting period piece.

The best discussion of the genro in the late Meiji period is that of R. F. Hackett in Robert E. Ward, ed., *Political Development in Modern Japan*. The background of the trip that took Itō Hirobumi to Harbin is discussed by Tsurumi Yusuke in "Itsukushima yawa" in *Chūgoku*, no. 18 (Tokyo, 1965). Etō Jun discusses the Nogi suicide and Natsume Sōseki's response in "Natsume Sōseki: A Japanese Meiji Intellectual," *American Scholar* 34 (Autumn 1965) 603–19, and Mark R. Peattie, "The Last Samurai: The Military Career of Nogi Maresuke," in *Princeton Papers in East Asian Studies: Japan* 1 (1972). *Kokoro* can be read in a translation by Edwin McClellan (Chicago: Henry Regnery, 1957). Takayoshi Matsuo, however, warns that Natsume's fiction did not necessarily reflect in politics in "A Note on the Political Thought of Natsume Sōseki in His Later Years," in B. S. Silberman and H. D. Harootunian, eds., *Japan in Crisis: Essays on Taishō Democracy* (Princeton: Princeton University Press, 1974). In the same volume Harootunian's "A Sense of Ending and the Problem of Taishō" provides a thoughtful introduction. The Taishō political change can be followed from different perspectives in Hackett, *Yamagata Aritomo*, and Tetsuo Najita, *Hara Kei in the Politics of Compromise, 1905–1915* (Cambridge, Mass.: Harvard University Press, 1967). China's border difficulties to the north after the fall of the dynasty can be followed most conveniently in Fairbank, Reischauer and Craig, *East Asia: The Modern Transformation*. For Japanese-Russian relations I am indebted to Chihiro Hosoya, "Japan's Policies Toward Russia," in James W. Morley, ed., *Japan's Foreign Policy, 1868–1941: A Research Guide* (New York: Columbia University Press, 1974). The background of Japanese intervention in Siberia is taken up by James W. Morley, *The Japanese Thrust into Siberia, 1918* (New York: Columbia University Press, 1957). Yamagata's views on foreign policy are conveniently available in a document translated on pages 714–16 in Tsunoda, Keene and de Bary, eds., *Sources of Japanese Tradition*. Japanese policy toward the Chinese revolution is discussed in Jansen, *The Japanese and Sun Yat-sen*; by Masaru Ikei, "Japan's Response to the Chinese Revolution of 1911" *Journal of Asian Studies* 25, no. 2 (February 1966); and by Kwanha Yim, "Yüan Shih-k'ai and the Japanese," *Journal of Asian Studies* 25, no. 1, (November 1964). Concerning Yüan's comment about Katō, I have also profited from an unpublished paper, "Katō Takaaki and the Politics of the Twenty-one Demands," read by Kwanha Yim at the 1969 meeting of the Association for Asian Studies. Detail on Sun Yat-sen and Dietrick is provided in Jansen, *The Japanese and Sun Yat-sen*, and the discussion of additional Japanese loans is from Albert A. Altman and Harold Z. Schiffrin, "Sun Yat-sen and the Japanese: 1914–1916, *Modern Asian Studies* 6, no. 4 (1972): 387–400.

Ambassador Paul S. Reinsch's account of his part in the Twenty-one Demands can be found in his *An American Diplomat in China* (New York: Doubleday, 1922); the quotations are from pages ix, x, 310, 317 and 321. Arthur S. Link, *Wilson: The Struggle for Neutrality, 1914–1915* (Princeton: Princeton University Press, 1960), provides an authoritative account of the handling of the demands in Washington; quotations are from pages 272, 276, 277, 284 and 294. For the Nishihara loans I have relied on the unpublished dissertation by Frank C. Langdon, "The Japanese Policy of Expansion in China, 1917–1928" (Berkeley: University of California Press, 1953).

Chapter 7

YEN FU'S CHANGING viewpoint on the West is quoted from Benjamin Schwartz, *In Search of Wealth and Power,* pp. 234–35. Liang Ch'i-ch'ao's conclusions from his consideration of World War I are quoted in Joseph R. Levenson, *Liang Ch'i-ch'ao and the Mind of Modern China,* p. 203, but Levenson's views are modified by Huang, *Liang Ch'i-ch'ao,* p. 144. A discussion of the different relations between nationalism and the state in China and Japan can be found in Masao Maruyama, *Thought and Behaviour in Modern Japanese Politics,* edited by Ivan Morris (New York: Oxford University Press, 1963), p. 137. For Korean hopes of help from Woodrow Wilson, see Chong-sik Lee, *The Politics of Korean Nationalism* (Berkeley: University of California Press, 1963), p. 122. Documentation for the introduction of baseball, bargain sales and a host of other cultural phenomena into twentieth-century Japan can be found in *Meiji sesō hennen jiten* (Tokyo, 1965). Useful treatment of the transmission of radicalism from Japan to China can be found in Martin Bernal, "Chinese Socialism Before 1913," in Jack Gray, ed., *Modern China's Search for a Political Form* (New York: Oxford University Press, 1969), and "The Triumph of Anarchism Over Marxism, 1906–1970," in Mary C. Wright, ed., *China in Revolution: The First Phase,* pp. 97–142; and Kawakami is discussed by Gail Berstein in Silberman and Harootunian, eds., *Japan in Crisis.* The reference to the confused ideological setting of young radicals in Japan is taken from Rodger Swearingen and Paul Langer, *Red Flag in Japan* (Cambridge, Mass.: Harvard University Press, 1952), p. 197; Mao Tsetung's recollections of a comparable setting are from Edgar Snow, *Red Star Over China* (New York: Random House, 1938), pp. 147–48. Li Ta-chao's elation at the Bolshevik victory can be found in W. T. de Bary, W. Chan and B. Watson, eds., *Sources of Chinese Tradition,* pp. 862–63. There is also a recent study by Maurice Meisner, *Li Ta-chao and the Origins of Chinese Marxism* (Cambridge, Mass.: Harvard University Press, 1967).

The discussion of Taishō intellectual life owes much to Tatsuo Arima, *The Failure of Freedom: A Portrait of Modern Japanese Intellectuals* (Cambridge, Mass.: Harvard University Press, 1969). The patriotic Church statement, which is on page 51 of the 1961 Harvard University dissertation on which the book is based, did not survive into the printed version. The Mushakōji quotation can be found on page 113 and "urban pastoral melancholy," Arima's phrase, on page 98. Nishida's *Study of Good* is available in a translation by Valdo H. Viglielmo (Tokyo, 1960), and his early life is discussed by the same author in "Nishida Kitarō: The Early Years" in Donald H. Shively, ed., *Tradition and Modernization in Japanese Culture* (Princeton: Princeton University Press, 1971). Watsuji Tetsurō is discussed by Arima and also by Robert N. Bellah, "Japan's Cultural Identity: Some Reflections on the Work of Watsuji Tetsurō," *Journal of Asian Studies* 24, no. 4, (August 1965). Discussions of constitutional law and teaching can be followed in Frank O. Miller, *Minobe Tatsukichi: Interpreter of Constitutionalism in Japan* (Berkeley: University of California Press, 1965), and Richard H. Minear, *Japanese Tradition and Western Law: Emperor, State, and Law in the Thought of Hozumi Yatsuka* (Cambridge, Mass.: Harvard University Press, 1970). Itō's views on the position of the monarch are quoted from Akita, *Foundations of Constitutional Government in Modern Japan,* p. 276. Yoshino Sakuzō is the subject of an unpublished doctoral dissertation by Walter S. Perry, "Yoshino Sakuzō, 1878–1933: Exponent of Democratic Ideals in Japan," (Stanford University, 1956), and he is also analyzed by Bernard Silberman, "The Political Theory and Program of Yoshino Sakuzō," *Journal of Modern History* 31 (1959). T. Najita's perceptive "Idealism in Yoshino's Political Thought," in Silberman and Harootunian, eds., *Japan in Crisis,* appeared after this work was already in proofs. Yoshino can be found in translation in *Sources of Japanese Tradition,* pp. 724–46. Excerpts from Minobe follow on pages 746–53. The *Reimeikai* and *Shinjinkai* were first discussed by Henry D. Smith II in "The Shinjinkai (1918–1921): The Making of an Intelligentsia," *Papers on Japan,* vol. 3 (1965), and more fully in *Japan's First Student Radicals* (Cambridge, Mass.: Harvard University Press, 1972), which adds important coverage of Taishō left-wing thought and activities. The quotations are drawn from pages 58 and 71 of the book and page 179 of the 1965 article, and the passage from Yoshino about China is from Nomura Kōichi. "The 'Japan-China Problem' in Modern Thought," *Japan Interpreter* 7 (Autumn 1972), p. 271.

The discussion of the Korean independence movement is taken from the works cited above for Chapter 4, and Frank A. Baldwin, "The March First Movement: Korean Challenge and Japanese Response" (Columbia University dissertation, 1969), and "Missionaries and the March First Movement," in A. C. Nahm, ed., *Korea Under Japanese Colonial Rule* (Western Michigan University, 1973).

For the May Fourth movement the basic work to which all scholars are indebted is that of Chow Tse-tsung, *The May Fourth Movement: Intellectual Revolution in Modern China* (Cambridge, Mass.: Harvard University Press, 1960). Y. C. Wang, *Chinese Intellectuals and the West,* adds important data and reflection. Ch'en Tu-hsiu's writings are taken from Chow, p. 45, and Benjamin Schwartz, "Ch'en Tu-hsiu and the Acceptance of the Modern West," *Journal of the History of Ideas* 12, no. 1 (January 1951). The quotations from Hu Shih are from Wen-han

Kiang, *The Chinese Student Movement* (New York: King's Crown Press, 1948), pp. 45 and 72, and Liang Ch'i-ch'ao's derogation of "Mr. Science" is from the same work, p. 41. Franz Michael and George Taylor, *The Far East in the Modern World,* provide a thought-provoking analysis of May Fourth themes and their effects in a section entitled, "Pragmatism, Materialsm, and the Question of Metaphysics," pp. 231–35. Tagore's trip is the organizational focus for the important discussion by Stephan N. Hay, *Asian Ideas of East and West: Tagore and His Critics in Japan, China, and India* (Cambridge, Mass.: Harvard University Press, 1970).

The discussion of Lenin owes much to Louis Fischer, *The Life of Lenin* (New York: Harper & Row, 1964). Chow Tse-tsung provides useful cautions about the pace of Leninist and communist influence on the new youth in *The May Fourth Movement,* p. 354. A classic treatment of Leninist influence on early communist thought in China is that of Benjamin Schwartz, *Chinese Communism and the Rise of Mao* (Cambridge, Mass.: Harvard University Press, 1951).

Bianco's summary of the role of Marxism among Chinese intellectuals is from his *Origins of the Chinese Revolution,* p. 48. Mark R. Peattie's comments on the Japanese military are from a doctoral dissertation, "Ishiwara Kanji (1889–1949) and the Japanese Army" (Princeton University, 1972), now in press.

The May Fourth influence on modern men of letters is the subject of Leo Ou-fan Lee's sensitive dissertation, "The Romantic Generation: A Study of Modern Chinese Men of Letters" (Cambridge, Mass.: Harvard University Press, 1970).

Chapter 8

THE REFERENCE TO "poverty, abuse, and early death" for the inhabitants of the Chinese countryside is from Lucien Bianco, *Origins of the Chinese Revolution,* p. 87. The figures for communications mileage in China are taken from the valuable work by Arthur N. Young, *China's Nation-Building Effort, 1927–1937: The Financial and Economic Record* (Stanford, Calif.: The Hoover Institution Press, 1971), p. 29. The discussion of rural China draws on T'ung-tsu Ch'ü, *Local Government in China Under the Ch'ing,* and Kung-chuan Hsiao, *Rural China: Imperial Control in the Nineteenth Century.* Professor G. William Skinner's discussions of market systems in rural China, "Marketing and Social Structure in Rural China," appeared in three successive issues of the *Journal of Asian Studies* 24, nos. 1, 2 and 3 (1964): 3–43, 195–228, and 363–99. Further discussions by him of the bureaucratic and nonofficial elite came in the course of the research conference in August 1965 that resulted in Mary C. Wright, ed., *China in Revolution: The First Phase, 1900–1913.* The discussion of provincial assemblies owes much to John Fincher, "Political Provincialism and the National Revolution," and P'eng-yüan Chang, "The Constitutionalists," Chapters 4 and 3, respectively, in the Wright volume, *China in Revolution,* and the reflections on the gentry have been stimulated by Chūzō Ichiko, "The Role of the Gentry: An Hypothesis," in the same volume, as well as by Professor Ichiko's articles in *Kindai Chūgoku no seiji to shakai,* cited previously.

The warlords have been described by the studies of James E. Sheridan, *Chinese Warlord: The Career of Feng Yü-hsiang* (Stanford, Calif.: Stanford University Press, 1966) a particularly fine book, and Donald G. Gillin, *Warlord: Yen Hsi-shan in Shansi Province, 1911–1949* (Princeton: Princeton University Press, 1967). The material on Feng and Yen derives from these studies, and the Pearl Buck quotation is from Sheridan. Feng is also the subject of a short study by Herbert Weisshart, "Feng Yü-hsiang: His Rise as a Militarist and His Training Programs," *Papers on China,* vol. 6 (1954); and warlords are discussed in the recent volume of Lucian W. Pye, *Warlord Politics: Conflict and Coalition in the Modernization of Republican China* (New York: Praeger, 1971). Warlord politics and fighting can be followed in Harley Farnsworth MacNair, *China in Revolution* (Chicago: University of Chicago Press, 1931). The anecdotes about Chang Hsüeh-liang and Yang Yü-t'ing are taken from the account by Seki Hiroharu, "Manshū jihen zenshi," *Taiheiyō sensō e no michi* (Tokyo 1966), pp. 287–440. Yüan Shih-k'ai's military structure and the system that followed it are discussed in Ralph Powell, *The Rise of Chinese Military Power,* introduced previously. Ch'en Chiung-ming is treated by Winston Hsieh, "The Ideas of a Warlord: Ch'en Chiung-ming, 1878–1933," *Papers on China,* vol. 16 (1962). Lucien Bianco's statement about the role of the peasantry in the revolution is from his *Origins of the Chinese Revolution,* pp. 98–99. The May Thirtieth movement in Shanghai is the subject of William Ayers, "Shanghai Labor and the May Thirtieth Movement," *Papers on China,* vol. 2 (1948).

For the period under review Sun Yat-sen is chronicled in Lyon Sharman, *Sun Yat-sen: His Life and Its Meaning* (New York: Day, 1934). Professor C. Martin Wilbur, in "Military Separatism and the Process of Reunification Under the Nationalist Regime, 1922–1937," in Ping-ti Ho and Tang Tsou, eds., *China in Crisis,* vol. 1, book 1, *China's Heritage and the Communist Political System* (Chicago: University of Chicago Press, 1968), pp. 203–63, provides a richly documented discussion of the reunification period. The Borodin mission is discussed by Louis Fischer, *The Soviets in World Affairs* (New York: Vintage Russian Library, n.d.), chap. 22; Jonathan Spence, *To Change China* (Boston: Little, Brown, 1969), chap. 7; and Benjamin Schwartz, *Chinese Communism and the Rise of Mao,* cited previously.

The *San Min Chu I* lectures are readily available in the translation by Frank Price, *San Min Chu I: The Three Principles of the People, by Dr. Sun Yat-sen* (Chungking, 1943, and later printings). Chiang's ruminations about the Soviet Union can be followed in his *Soviet Russia in China: A Summing-up at Seventy,* by Chiang Chung-cheng (Chiang Kai-shek), abridged (New York, Farrar, Straus, 1965). The Whampoa Academy and its military role are discussed by F. F. Liu, *A Military History of Modern China, 1924–1949* (Princeton: Princeton University Press,

1956). The catechism Feng Yü-hsiang worked out for his troops is taken from Sheridan, pp. 212–13. Kuomintang-Communist politics is treated by Conrad Brandt, *Stalin's Failure in China, 1924–1927* (Cambridge, Mass.: Harvard University Press, 1958), and Conrad Brandt, Benjamin Schwartz, and John K. Fairbank, eds., *A Documentary History of Chinese Communism* (Cambridge, Mass.: Harvard University Press, 1952), in which Mao Tse-tung's 1927 report on Hunan can be found. International aspects of the period of the Northern Expedition can best be followed in the important work by Akira Iriye, *After Imperialism: The Search for a New Order in the Far East, 1921–1931,* introduced previously.

The Nationalist decade is still inadequately studied. In addition to the Wilbur chapter in *China in Crisis,* mention must be made again of Arthur N. Young's *China's Nation-Building Effort,* which is a rich source of figures for central government and especially financial concerns.

Chapter 9

THE OPENING PHRASE about "Economic problems, social unrest," is from Edwin O. Reischauer, "What Went Wrong?" pp. 504–5 in James W. Morley, ed., *Dilemmas of Growth in Prewar Japan* (Princeton: Princeton University Press, 1971), the concluding volume of the Conference on Modern Japan's "Studies in the Modernization of Japan." The reference to historical conspiracy is to David Bergamini's *Japan's Imperial Conspiracy* (New York: Morrow, 1971).

Seiyūkai tactics under Hara Kei are the subject of Tetsuo Najita's *Hara Kei in the Politics of Compromise, 1905–1915* (Cambridge, Mass.: Harvard University Press, 1967). The figures for the bureaucracy are from Masamichi Inoki, "The Civil Bureaucracy: Japan," in Robert E. Ward and Dankwart A. Rustow, eds., *Political Modernization in Japan and Turkey* (Princeton: Princeton University Press, 1964). Katō Komei and his policies are treated by Peter Duus, *Party Rivalry and Political Change in Taishō Japan,* and the discussion of election frauds on page 326 is also indebted to the same work. Land problems in prewar Japan receive careful analysis in R. P. Dore, *Land Reform in Japan* (New York: Oxford University Press, 1959). Tanaka's China policy is discussed in Akira Iriye, *After Imperialism.* A basic source for the politics and contention that swirled around the London Naval Treaty is the diary of Prince Saionji's confidential secretary, which has been translated by Thomas Francis Mayer-Oakes as *Fragile Victory: Prince Saionji and the 1930 London Treaty Issue, from the Memoirs of Baron Harada Kumao* (Detroit: Wayne State University Press, 1968). Significant examples of textbook political moralism are analyzed in an unpublished dissertation by John Caiger, "Education, Values, and Japan's National Identity: A Study of the Aims and Content of Courses in Japanese History, 1872–1963" (Canberra: Australian National University, 1966), and the essay by the same author cited in Chapter 3.

The discussion of Taishō economic developments is based principally on Kazushi Ohkawa and Henry Rosovsky, "A Century of Japanese Economic Growth," in W. W. Lockwood, ed., *The State and Economic Enterprise in Japan,* and also W. W. Lockwood, *The Economic Development of Japan,* cited previously, and G. C. Allen, *A Short Economic History of Modern Japan* (London: George Allen & Unwin, 1946). The slogans about frugality in the 1920s can be found in Duus. The quotation on page 330 about the government's handling of its monetary policies in the 1920s is taken from Hugh Patrick, "The Economic Muddle of the 1920's," in J. W. Morley, ed., *Dilemmas of Growth in Prewar Japan,* p. 213. The discussion of traditional aspects of early modern labor recruitment in Japan draws on Solomon B. Levine, "Labor Markets and Collective Bargaining in Japan," in W. W. Lockwood, ed., *The State and Economic Enterprise in Japan*; the quotation on page 333 is from page 646. A brilliant account of Japanese labor practices can be found in Ronald Dore, *British Factory—Japanese Factory: The Origins of National Diversity in Industrial Relations* (London: George Allen & Unwin, 1973). The figure for 1934 tenantry on page 333 is from page 223 of Thomas C. Smith, *The Agrarian Origins of Modern Japan* (Stanford, Calif.: Stanford University Press, 1959). Police controls on tenants are described in Shinobu Seisaburō, *Taishō seiji shi,* vol. 3 (Tokyo, 1952), pp. 754–94. The 1915 election law violation study is referred to in Duus, p. 11.

The phrase quoted from Nakano Shigeharu is taken from Tatsuo Arima, *The Failure of Freedom,* p. 253. Leftist currents in Chinese literature of the same period are treated in Leo Lee and in summary by Lucien Bianco, both cited previously. Shinto nationalism is treated in D. C. Holtom, *Modern Japan and Shinto Nationalism* (Chicago: University of Chicago Press, 1943). An annotated translation of the Education Ministry's pamphlet on *kokutai* is available; John Owen Gauntlett, trans., and Robet King Hall, ed., *Kokutai no Hongi: Cardinal Principles of the National Entity of Japan* (Cambridge, Mass.: Harvard University Press, 1949). *Nōhonshugi* is discussed by Dore, *Land Reform in Japan,* p. 91, and has now received full-scale treatment in Thomas R. H. Havens, *Farm and Nation in Modern Japan: Agrarian Nationalism, 1870–1940* (Princeton: Princeton University Press, 1974). Communist origins and vicissitudes are described in George B. Beckmann and Okubo Genji, *The Japanese Communist Party 1922–1945* (Stanford, Calif.: Stanford University Press, 1969). *Gondō* is translated in part in Tsunoda, de Bary, and Keene, *Sources of Japanese Tradition,* pp. 770–73. E. O. Reischauer, in "What Went Wrong?" in Morley, *Dilemmas,* summarizes the sources of military discontent. Asahi Heigo's testament after his murder of Yasuda can be found in *Sources of Japanese Tradition,* pp. 767–68. Kita Ikki is translated in part in *Sources,* pp. 773–84, and analyzed by George M. Wilson, *Radical Nationalist in Japan: Kita Ikki, 1883–1937.* Recollections of the assassins of the 1930s are taken from the Tokyo monthly *Bungei Shunjū* (February 1967), pp. 321 and 322, and pp. 30–34, "The Mystery of Assassination," by Hashikawa Bunzō, ed., *Chōkokka shugi: Gendai Nihon shisō taikei,* vol. 31 (Tokyo, 1966). The 26 February insurrection is the subject of Ben-Ami Shillony's *Revolt in Japan: The Young Officers and the February 26, 1936, Incident* (Princeton: Princeton University Press, 1973). The Ishiwara Kanji quotation is provided by Hashikawa Bunzō on page 35 of *Chōkokka shugi*, and Ishiwara himself is the subject of Mark Peattie's *Ishiwara Kanji and Japan's Confrontation with the West* (Princeton: Princeton University Press, 1975). The discussion of army factionalism draws on Seki Hiroharu, "Manshū jihen zenshi," in *Taiheiyō sensō e no michi* (Tokyo, 1966), and James B. Crowley, "Japanese Army Factionalism in the Early 1930's," *Journal of Asian Studies* 21, no. 3 (May 1962): 309–26. The course of asassinations and plots is followed by Richard Storry in *The Double Patriots: A Study of Japanese Nationalism* (Boston: Houghton Mifflin, 1957). Prince Konoe is the subject of Oka Yoshitake's recent *Konoe Fumimaro* (Tokyo, 1972), and the currents of thought of the time can be followed in the study of his political associate, "Nagai Ryūtarō: The Tactical Dilemmas of Reform," by Peter Duus, in Albert M. Craig and Donald H. Shively, eds., *Personality in Japanese History* (Berkeley: University of California Press, 1970). The discussion of divided responsibility and resultant irresponsibility owes much to the work of Professor Chihiro Hosoya, who has also published widely in Japan on this theme. The quotation from Prince Saionji on keeping one's head is taken from Takashi Oka, "Saionji and the Manchurian Crisis," *Papers on China*, vol. 8 (1954). Reischauer's summation is from his essay in Morley, *Dilemmas*, p. 505.

Chapter 10

JAPAN'S SECURITY CONCERNS are ably detailed by James B. Crowley, *Japan's Quest for Autonomy: National Security and Foreign Policy, 1930–1938* (Princeton: Princeton University Press, 1966), and "Japan's Military Foreign Policies," in James W. Morley, ed., *Japan's Foreign Policy,* cited previously to which the discussion of the Washington and London conferences is much indebted. Shidehara's posture on Chinese nationalism is drawn from Akira Iriye, *After Imperialism,* cited earlier. Lenin's 1920 statements can be found in David J. Dallin, *The Rise of Russia in Asia* (New Haven: Yale University Press, 1949), pp. 164 and 203. Japanese-Russian relations have been discussed in great detail by Chihiro Hosoya in many publications and in English in "Japan's Policies Toward Russia," in Morley, ed., *Japan's Foreign Policy.* Katsu H. Young, "The Nomonhan Incident: Imperial Japan and the Soviet Union," *Monumenta Nipponica* 22, nos. 1–2 (1967), has a good account of that undeclared border war. The Japanese-Chinese trade figures on page 367 and the summary quotation on Japanese policy on pages 368 and 371 are taken from Akira Iriye, *After Imperialism,* pp. 58, 68 and 183. The 1924 Tokyo policy statement on the aims of dealing with Chang Tso-lin on pages 373–74 is drawn from Shinkichi Etō, "The Policy Making Process of the Proposed Interception of the Peking-Mukden Railway — Tanaka Diplomacy and Its Background," *Acta Asiatica* 14 (Tokyo: Tōhō Gakkai, 1968), p. 30. Iriye, *After Imperialism,* p. 167, has an able summary and persuasive reflection on the dilemmas Tanaka faced with Chang Tso-lin which I have followed. The first stages of Japanese policy toward Chang Tso-lin are the subject of John W. Young, "The Hara Cabinet and Chang Tso-lin, 1920–21," *Monumenta Nipponica* 27, no. 2 (1972).

Early developments in Manchuria are summarized by Shimada Toshihiko, *Kantōgun* (Tokyo, 1965). The background of Kwantung Army planning is brilliantly summarized by Seki Hiroharu in his section of *Taiheiyō sensō e no michi*, which has been cited earlier. In English the best treatment is by Sadako N. Ogata, *Defiance in Manchuria: The Making of Japanese Foreign Policy, 1931–1932* (Berkeley: University of California Press, 1964). For Ishiwara I have drawn on the study by Mark R. Peattie. Japanese ultranationalism and extremism in the 1930s can be studied in chapter 27, "The Rise of Revolutionary Nationalism," in R. Tsunoda, W. T. de Bary and D. Keene, eds., *Sources of the Japanese Tradition*; Richard Storry, *The Double Patriots: A Study of Japanese Nationalism* (Boston: Houghton Mifflin, 1957); and the still useful Hugh Byas, *Government by Assassination* (New York: Knopf, 1942). For the successive permutations of security and military plans, I have drawn heavily upon Crowley, *Japan's Quest for Autonomy*; quotations on pages 389, 390, 394–95 and 396 are from his pages 193, 195, 213, 332, 343 and 362. The Sorge case is unraveled in Chalmers Johnson, *An Instance of Treason: Ozaki Hotsumi and the Sorge Spy Ring* (Stanford: Stanford University Press, 1964), and F. W. Deakin and R. Storry, *The Case of Richard Sorge* (London: Chatto and Windus, 1966). Matsuoka's tactics and statements figure importantly in David J. Lu, *From the Marco Polo Bridge to Pearl Harbor* (Washington, D.C.: Public Affairs Press, 1961) (his quote on page 402 is from page 119), and he is treated in greater detail in the recent biography by Miwa Kimitada, *Matsuoka Yōsuke: sono mingen to gaikō* (Tokyo, 1971). The road to war is the subject of Herbert Feis, *The Road to Pearl Harbor: The Coming of the War Between the United States and Japan* (Princeton: Princeton University Press, 1950), based principally on American documents, and Robert J. C. Butow, *Tōjō and the Coming of the War* (Princeton: Princeton University Press, 1961). Invaluable detail is added in Dorothy Borg and Shimpei Okamoto, eds., *Pearl Harbor and History: Japanese-American Relations 1931–1941* (New York: Columbia University Press, 1973). Professor Butow has cleared up confusion surrounding early "proposals" in "The Hull-Nomura Conversations: A Fundamental Misconception," in *American Historical Review* 65, no. 4 (1960), and in "Backdoor Diplomacy in the Pacific: The Proposal for a Konoye-Roosevelt Meeting, 1941," *Journal of American History* 59 (June 1972). Nobutaka Ike has translated the documentary section of *Taiheiyō sensō e no michi* in *Japan's Decision for War: Records of the 1941 Policy Conferences* (Stanford, Calif.: Stanford University Press, 1967), and I have drawn on his pages 66, 106, 139, 186, 202 and 224 for quotes used in following the decision process. Admiral Nagano's summation of the case for war is cited by Crowley in Morley, *Japan's Foreign Policy*, p. 98. Professor Butow tells the story of the slow-moving typist in the Washington Japanese embassy on the day of Pearl Harbor in *Tōjō and the Coming of the War*, p. 381. The wisdom and equity of the war crimes charges are challenged by the recent and persuasive book by Richard H. Minear, *Victor's Justice: The Tokyo War Crimes Trial* (Princeton: Princeton University Press, 1971). The details of the Pearl Harbor planning and its significance for deterrents and incentives are superbly discussed in Roberta Wohlstetter, *Pearl Harbor: Warning and Decision* (Stanford, Calif.: Stanford University Press, 1962). Quoted material on pages 406–7 is from pages 353 and 380.

Chapter 11

CHINESE STUDENTS DURING the period are the subject of John Israel's *Student Nationalism in China, 1927–1937* (Stanford, Calif.: Stanford University Press, 1966), and student protests against the Japanese aggression are described on pages 21, 49 and 61. The development of Nationalist military strength is described by F. F. Liu, *A Military History of Modern China, 1924–1949,* cited previously. Problems of estimating rural conditions remain formidable. One view is the work of Richard Walker, *China Under Communism: The First Five Years* (New Haven: Yale University Press, 1955), but many disagree sharply. The development of the New Life movement and the role of American participants is described by James C. Thomson, *While China Faced West: American Reformers in Nationalist China, 1925–1937* (Cambridge, Mass.: Harvard University Press, 1969). The quotation from John Israel is from his *Student Nationalism,* p. 137. The early years of Mao's career as communist leader are treated in Benjamin Schwartz, *Chinese Communism and the Rise of Mao,* and John E. Rue, *Mao Tse-tung in Opposition, 1927–1935* (Stanford, Calif.: Stanford University Press, 1966); the quotation about Mao's loss of influence is from page 263. The classic account of the Long March was given by Mao himself to Edgar Snow, who reported it in *Red Star Over China.* American diplomats' knowledge of what was going on is discussed in valuable works by Dorothy Borg, *American Policy and the Chinese Revolution, 1925–1928* (New York: Institute of Pacific Relations, 1947), and *The United States and the Far Eastern Crisis of 1933–1938* (Cambridge, Mass.: Harvard University Press, 1964). United States involvement in the China theater of fighting is the subject of the highly readable account by Barbara W. Tuchman, *Stilwell and the American Experience in China* (New York: Macmillan, 1970). Tang Tsou, *America's Failure in China, 1941–50* (Chicago: University of Chicago Press, 1963), provides an invaluable summary of political and military developments. Graham Peck's *Two Kinds of Time* (Boston: Houghton Mifflin, 1950), a superb book that has had too little attention, provides a Brueghel-like canvas of rural China during the war years that makes it possible to put the political and military maneuverings into perspective. Chalmers A. Johnson, *Peasant Nationalism and Communist Power: The Emergence of Revolutionary China, 1937–1945* (Stanford, Calif.: Stanford University Press, 1962), is the standard study of communist growth in areas occupied and despoiled by the Japanese armies. Japanese policy in north China was observed and analyzed by George E. Taylor, *The Struggle for North China* (New York: Institute of Pacific Relations, 1940).

The Wang Ching-wei episode is treated by David Lu, whose *Marco Polo Bridge to Pearl Harbor* has been mentioned; Gerald E. Bunker, *The Peace Conspiracy: Wang Ching-wei and the China War, 1937–1941* (Cambridge, Mass.: Harvard University Press, 1972); and John H. Boyle, *China and Japan at War, 1937–1945: The Politics of Collaboration* (Stanford, Calif.: Stanford University Press, 1972). The Japanese praise of communist discipline is taken from Johnson, p. 145, and his concluding estimate is quoted from page 146. The student propaganda pamphlet quoted on page 433 is from Israel, *Student Nationalism*, p. 135.

The reference to "mass line" on page 435 draws on Chalmers Johnson, "Chinese Communist Leadership and Mass Response: The Yenan Period and the Socialist Education Campaign Period," p. 406, and the first *Liberation Daily* quotation is from page 42; the article appears in *China in Crisis*, vol. 1, *China's Heritage and the Communist Political System,* edited by Ping-ti Ho and Tang Tsou, (Chicago: University of Chicago Press, 1968), p. 421. Professor Tsou's discussion of the Yalta Agreement, *America's Failure*, p. 237, and his thoughtful analysis have been extremely useful. There is, of course, a vast amount of literature, much of it polemical in nature, on this issue. The Nationalist-Communist civil war is the subject of several recent books, one by John F. Melby, *The Mandate of Heaven: Record of a Civil War, China, 1945–49* (Toronto: University of Toronto Press, 1968), and its highlights are skillfully summarized by John K. Fairbank in *East Asia: The Modern Transformation*, p. 859. The quotation about postwar inflation is taken from the same work. Barbara W. Tuchman, "If Mao Had Come to Washington: An Essay in Alternatives," *Foreign Affairs* 51, no. 1 (October 1972): 44–64, discusses the 1945 possibility and explains why it did not take place.

Chapter 12

THE SENSE OF isolation and search for meaning of Japanese intellectuals and writers during the war years have been little studied. I have profited from James B. Crowley's "Intellectuals as Visionaries of the New Asian Order," in James W. Morley, ed., *Dilemmas of Growth in Prewar Japan* (Princeton: Princeton University Press, 1971), and Donald Keene, "Japanese Writers and the Greater East Asia War," in *Landscapes and Portraits: Appreciations of Japanese Culture* (Tokyo and Palo Alto: Kodansha, 1971). Discussions of Japanese psychological responses to defeat are found in Kazuko Tsurumi, *Social Change and the Individual: Japan Before and After Defeat in World War II* (Princeton: Princeton University Press, 1970). The wartime attrition of the Japanese economy is treated by Jerome B. Cohen, *Japan's Economy in War and Reconstruction* (Minneapolis:

University of Minnesota Press, 1949). The Japanese surrender received its classic treatment in Robert J. C. Butow's *Japan's Decision to Surrender* (Stanford, Calif.: Stanford University Press, 1954); and a vivid recreation is provided by the Pacific War Research Society, *Japan's Longest Day* (Tokyo and Palo Alto: Kodansha, 1965). The emperor's 1971 comments were reported in *The Japan Times* of 17 November 1971. The figures for suicides were taken from David Bergamini's *Japan's Imperial Conspiracy*, p. 112. The comparison of Occupation and Tokugawa isolation is drawn from Sabata Toyoyuki, *Sekai no naka no Nihon* (Tokyo, 1971). The Occupation of Japan is treated in Kazuo Kawai, *Japan's American Interlude* (Chicago: University of Chicago Press, 1960), and Edwin O. Reischauer, *The United States and Japan* (Cambridge, Mass.: Harvard University Press, 1950), but it still awaits a satisfactory account. The war crimes tribunal is sharply attacked by Richard H. Minear, *Victors' Justice: The Tokyo War Crimes Trial* (Princeton: Princeton University Press, 1971). The land reform program is best described in R. P. Dore, *Land Reform in Japan* (London, Oxford University Press, 1959), and the changes in labor organization are most conveniently treated by Solomon Levine, "Labor Markets and Collective Bargaining in Japan," in W. W. Lockwood, ed., *The State and Economic Enterprise in Japan,* and "Postwar Trade Unionism, Collective Bargaining, and Japanese Social Structure," in R. P. Dore, ed., *Aspects of Social Change in Modern Japan,* both cited previously.

The description of Japanese responses to Occupation reforms and the figures for American aid are from Hugh Patrick, "The Phoenix Risen from the Ashes: Postwar Japan," in James B. Crowley, ed., *Modern East Asia.* A good discussion of Japanese responses to the possibility of a United States "withdrawal" in the late Occupation years is to be found in Baron E. J. Lewe van Aduard, *Japan from Surrender to Peace* (The Hague, 1953), and the development of Japanese defense policy is followed by Martin E. Weinstein, *Japan's Postwar Defense Policy, 1947–1968* (New York: Columbia University Press, 1971). The story about Mr. Kamiya of the Toyota company derives from Asahi Shimbunsha, ed., *Nihon to Amerika* (Tokyo, 1971), p. 177. This volume was subsequently translated as *The Pacific Rivals* (New York, 1972).

Postwar Korea was discussed by George M. McCune, *Korea Today* (Cambridge, Mass.: Harvard University Press, 1950). The Japanese legacy was described caustically by Andrew J. Grajdanzev, *Modern Korea* (New York: Day, 1944), and less negatively by David Brudnoy, "Japan's Experiment in Korea," *Monumenta Nipponica* 25, nos. 1–2 (Tokyo, 1970). Education receives treatment in an unpublished work by Harry K. Bang, "Japanese Educational Policy in Korea during the Colonial Period, 1905–1945." Andrew C. Nahm, ed., *Korea Under Japanese Colonial Rule* (Kalamazoo: Western Michigan University Press, 1973), appeared while this work was being printed. Discussions of the reasons for and thinking behind the invasion from the north are offered by Dean Acheson, *Present at the Creation* (New York: Norton, 1969), and, more plausibly for me, by George F. Kennan, *Memoirs,* vol. 2 (Boston: Atlantic—Little, Brown,

1972). The American intervention is discussed by Glenn D. Paige, *The Korean Decision* (New York: The Free Press, 1968); Allen Whiting, in *China Crosses the Yalu: The Decision to Enter the Korean War* (Stanford, Calif.: Stanford University Press, 1968), analyzes the Chinese response. General Ridgway's recollections are taken from Matthew B. Ridgway, *The Korean War* (New York: Doubleday, 1967), p. 148. Korean politics are treated by Gregory Henderson, *Korea: The Politics of the Vortex* (Cambridge, Mass.: Harvard University Press, 1968).

The best summary of scholarly study and informed opinion I have drawn on about the People's Republic of China since its establishment in 1949 is to be found in the third edition of John K. Fairbank, *The United States and China* (Cambridge, Mass.: Harvard University Press, 1972). Its bibliography, pp. 454–76, is also particularly good. The quotation with reference to the failure of Russian leadership in China is from page 387. Like everyone else, I have profited over the years from the thoughtful and dispassionate analyses of Benjamin Schwartz, the best of which have been brought together in *Communism and China: Ideology in Flux* (Cambridge, Mass.: Harvard University Press, 1968). I have drawn here on the introduction and the stimulating essay, "Modernization and the Maoist Vision: Some Reflections on Chinese Communist Goals" (1965), and the passages quoted appear on his pages 170 and 175. Allen Whiting's observation on the profits of the Korean War for China are from his *China Crosses the Yalu: The Decision to Enter the Korean War* (Stanford, Calif.: Stanford University Press, 1968), pp. 166–67. Mass organizations in China have been analyzed by Franz Schurmann, *Ideology and Organization in Communist China* (Berkeley: University of California Press, 1966); I have profited from his "The Attack of the Cultural Revolution on Ideology and Organization," Chap. 9, in *China in Crisis,* vol. 1, book 2, *China's Heritage and the Communist Political System,* ed. Ping-ti Ho and Tang Tsou (Chicago: University of Chicago Press, 1968). Chapter 12 of the same volume, Alexander Eckstein's "Economic Fluctuations in Communist China's Domestic Development," provides the discussion of agricultural cycles which is summarized, albeit inadequately, in the text. The quotations are from his pages 697, 718 and 709. A. Doak Barnett's reports of the early 1950s are brought together in *Communist China: The Early Years, 1949–55* (New York: Praeger, 1966); the Five-Anti drive quotations are from pages 135, 137, 143 and the quotation on pages 481–82 is from his page 292. Mao Tse-tung's 1927 discussion of peasant revolutionary potential is from the famous report translated in Brandt, Schwartz, and Fairbank, *A Documentary History of Chinese Communism,* p. 87. Revolutionary violence in the countryside is summarized in Lucien Bianco's *Origins of the Chinese Revolution,* p. 188, and graphically described by Jack Belden in *China Shakes the World* (New York: Harper, 1949). The quotation on page 482 describing commune organization is from Stanley Rich, "The Communes—Mao's 'Big Family,' " *Problems of Communism,* 8, no. 1 (1959). The 1971 discussion of life in the Chinese-Vietnamese Friendship People's Commune is from articles by Audrey Topping and Tilman Durdin reprinted in *The New York Times Report from Red China* (New York: Quadrangle, 1971). Wartime thought reform in China can be followed in Boyd Compton, trans., *Mao's China: Party Reform Documents, 1942– 44* (Seattle: University of Washington Press, 1952), while the standard work for the 1950s is Robert Jay Lifton, *Thought Reform and the Psychology of Totalism: A Study of "Brainwashing" in China* (New York: Norton, 1963). My quotation is from page 13. All attempts to summarize ideological thrust and change in China fall short of the mark when compared with the subtlety with which Professor Schwartz treats these issues in *Communism and China: Ideology in Flux.*

Brief discussions of the Japanese recovery can be found in Edwin O. Reischauer, *Japan: The Story of a Nation* (New York: Knopf, 1970). Perceptive reportorial essays by Lawrence Olson were brought together in *Dimensions of Japan* (New York: American Universities Field Staff, 1963). I have also summarized principal trends in recent editions of the *Encyclopaedia Britannica.* Japan's economic recovery is ably analyzed by Hugh T. Patrick in "The Phoenix Risen from the Ashes: Postwar Japan," in Crowley, ed., *Modern East Asia,* cited previously; by William W. Lockwood, "Japan's New Capitalism," in Lockwood, ed., *The State and Economic Enterprise in Japan* (Princeton: Princeton University Press, 1965); and by Henry Rosovsky, "The Economic Position of Japan: Past, Present, and Future," in *United States International Economic Policy in an Interdependent World,* vol. 2, (Washington, D.C.: U.S. Government Printing Office, 1971), pp. 111–28. I have also benefited from other essays, some still unpublished, and many discussions with Professor Rosovsky. Studies by Dr. Saburo Okita of the Japan Economic Research Center and the International Development Center have placed me deeply in his debt.

Some extremely perceptive, though quite unstructured, commentary and coverage can be found in the Asahi volume, *Nihon to Amerika,* translated as *The Pacific Rivals,* introduced earlier. Postwar politics is analyzed by Nathaniel B. Thayer, *How the Conservatives Rule Japan* (Princeton: Princeton University Press, 1969), and illuminated by Gerald Curtis, *Electioneering Japanese Style* (New York: Columbia University Press, 1971). Sōkagakkai and Kōmeitō are studied by James W. White, *The Sōkagakkai and Mass Society* (Stanford, Calif.: Stanford University Press, 1970). The events of 1960 are the subject of George R. Packard's *Protest in Tokyo: The Security Treaty Crisis of 1960* (Princeton: Princeton University Press, 1966). Defense planning is traced by Martin E. Weinstein, *Japan's Postwar Defense Policy, 1947– 1968* (New York: Columbia University Press, 1971). This only begins to indicate what is available for the last quarter-century's developments in China, Korea and Japan.

Index